Nahmanides

Nahmanides

LAW AND MYSTICISM

Moshe Halbertal

Translated from the Hebrew by Daniel Tabak

Yale UNIVERSITY PRESS

New Haven & London

Published with assistance from the Mary Cady Tew Memorial Fund.

Yale University Press books may be purchased in quantity for educational,
business, or promotional use. For information, please e-mail sales.press@yale.edu
(U.S. office) or sales@yaleup.co.uk (U.K. office).

Set in Adobe Garamond type by IDS Infotech Ltd., Chandigarh, India.
Printed in the United States of America.

Library of Congress Control Number: 2019957743
ISBN 978-0-300-14091-0 (hardcover : alk. paper)

A catalogue record for this book is available from the British Library.

This paper meets the requirements of ANSI/NISO Z39.48-1992 (Permanence
of Paper).

10 9 8 7 6 5 4 3 2 1

To the memory of Sidney Morgenbesser

Contents

Translator's Preface

Moshe Halbertal has a gift for making complex ideas readily understandable in his lucid and logically compelling Hebrew prose. It has been a pleasure to translate his work and thereby introduce more of his ideas to an English readership.

This translation, however, has required that I translate the words of R. Moses Nahman almost as much as those of Moshe Halbertal. This great responsibility was not easily discharged. Nahmanides's style could not be more different from that of the other famous medieval R. Moses—Maimonides—who wrote in a highly organized, systematic manner. Nahmanides was not nearly as systematic. His arguments do not advance with the same kind of ineluctability. He often preferred to intimate rather than expressly state, making the reader work harder. Moreover, he typically qualified and revised by keeping pen to parchment and writing on, leaving the old and the new in tension. This signature style cuts across all genres of Nahmanides's writing and probably contributed to the unfortunate state of his works at the beginning of the age of print, by which time they already were riddled with errors. Scribal or other errors more often than not have corrupted not only his words but his ideas and arguments, too. The translator's duty is to translate a text as precisely as possible, but with the printed texts as they are, I had to consult manuscripts of his works, which thankfully can be accessed conveniently through Ketiv, at http://web.nli.org.il/sites/NLIS/en/ManuScript/.

Despite my reliance on manuscripts for many of Nahmanides's works, I have not noted those instances in which I translated based on manuscript readings rather than the standard printed editions, because doing so would have needlessly encumbered, visually and otherwise, the present book. A corollary of this is that I was unable to use existing translations of Nahmanides's works, especially those produced by R. Charles Ber Chavel. While Chavel mostly did a fine job in his translation given the state of the printed texts, he was not always precise in translating even those texts. Moreover, his Hebrew editions, on which his translations were based, have additional serious drawbacks that others have pointed out elsewhere.

As such, all translations here are original, unless otherwise noted. I have tended toward a more literal translation of Nahmanides's words, especially in kabbalistic contexts, where rigor is of cosmic significance. Wherever Nahmanides, or other medieval authors, launched into rhymed prose, I have tried to convey this shift in register in the translation. In order to declutter the text, however, I have omitted all instances of "may his memory be a blessing" and the like. For similar reasons, I have not given full references to the rabbinic sources on which Nahmanides drew unless they are relevant to Nahmanides's argument or Halbertal's analysis. The interested reader will refer to Chavel's editions, where all these sources are provided.

A word about translating kabbalistic sources is in order here. Often the meaning of Nahmanides's kabbalistic allusions remains obscure (as he would have wanted), and I had to strike a tricky balance between what his words can evidently bear, and the full exposition given by the supercommentaries, which I mostly combed through in manuscript. The same holds true for translating biblical verses: Nahmanides often does not say how he reads a given verse kabbalistically, so I had to reconstruct the most likely reading while trying to achieve the same balance.

Translating kabbalah is a thorny, complicated, messy business. In order to signal to the reader that certain words are cognomens of sefirotic entities, or are associated with particular *sefirot*, I have employed capitalization. The supercommentaries occasionally also understood certain other words in this way, but I have chosen not to capitalize them if they are not crucial to Halbertal's argument and may represent a later imposition on Nahmanides's original intent. In order to minimize potential confusion, I did not capitalize non-kabbalistic phrases that are often capitalized in English; therefore, I render it "the land of Israel" rather than "the Land of Israel."

I must now turn to the much more challenging task of translating emotions and states of mind into words. I must thank Moshe Halbertal for this opportunity, and for the trust he has displayed throughout the long process of translation; Menachem Butler, my dear friend, for his friendship and academic life support; Shaul Seidler-Feller, a man after my own heart, for our many discussions and his helpful suggestions; Jonathan Dauber, for giving unstintingly of his time and understanding in all matters kabbalistic; my Doktorväter Ephraim Kanarfogel and David Berger; and, of course, my parents, Peggy and Brian Tabak, and my in-laws, Michele and Leonard Fuld, for their ongoing encouragement and support in all ways. Ever deserving of my boundless gratitude are my wife, Jessie, and my daughters, Shoshana and Aliza, who have given me everything and more. As I have devoted much of my finite time and energy to this worthy project, I dedicate the fruit of my labors to them.

Daniel Tabak

Acknowledgments

While writing the book I was fortunate to receive comments and suggestions from friends, colleagues, and teachers. Adam Afterman, Menachem Fisch, Jonathan Garb, Moshe Idel, Ruth Kara, Menachem Lorberbaum, Biti Roi, Haim Soloveitchik, Israel Ta-Shma (may his memory be blessed), and Sandra Valabregue-Perry commented on different chapters of the book. I am grateful for all that I have learned from them. The two anonymous readers of the manuscript for Yale University Press have given me important comments and suggestions; I thank them for their effort and wisdom. My deepest gratitude is to Toby Freilich, for her support and advice.

Special thanks I owe to Daniel Tabak, the translator of the book from Hebrew, for his remarkable translation and for the exquisite care that he invested in the project. I was blessed to have Jessie Dolch as the copyeditor of the book; her thorough and attentive reading of the text was most valuable. The publication of the book was made possible by the consistent support of Jennifer Banks, executive editor for religion, and Heather Gold, associate editor for classics and ancient world, at Yale University Press. I thank them for their encouragement and trust.

Nahmanides

Introduction

R. Moses b. Nahman (1194–1270), known in English as Nahmanides, was the greatest halakhist of the thirteenth century and remains one of the most original and creative expositors of the Bible that the Jewish tradition has ever produced. In his Talmudic novellae, Nahmanides consummated the interpretive and analytical achievements of his twelfth-century predecessors; the conceptual distinctions he minted have become tools of the trade in halakhic analysis, faithfully serving generation after generation of Torah scholars. He left his mark on each and every Talmudic sugya that he engaged with his analytical brilliance, linguistic aptitude, and meticulous reading of the sugya's progression in all its thick detail. His novellae provided the nourishment for the subsequent flowering of Talmudic creativity in Catalonia, inspiring as they did the novellae of R. Solomon Ibn Adret (Rashba, 1235–1310), R. Yom Tov Assevilli (Ritva, 1260–1320), and R. Nissim Gerondi (Ran, 1315–1376). Nahmanides's prodigious creativity and exegetical prowess are readily apparent on every page of his Commentary on the Torah. The commentary's novelty lies in the combination of his psychological insight into the biblical personae and their struggles, his astute grasp of the sociopolitical conditions in which they lived, and his literary sensitivity, which is partly expressed in his treatment of broad textual units as the building blocks of the exegete.

In addition to his stature as a biblical commentator and as the greatest Talmudic scholar of his century, Nahmanides was one of the most important mystics and kabbalists of medieval Jewish tradition. Between the lines of his rich Torah commentary, he interspersed kabbalistic allusions that he crowned "the way of truth." In so doing, he crafted an exceptional work that addresses two different audiences. The vast majority of those studying his commentary are incapable of penetrating the veil of secrecy created by Nahmanides's allusions and so view the formulaic expression "by way of truth" as a green light to pass over what follows until the commentary returns to its exoteric stratum. Moreover, some scholars from Nahmanides's own school apparently held his exoteric commentary in the highest esteem while expressing misgivings about the esoteric allusions. According to R. Isaac b. Sheshet Perfet (Rivash), his teacher Ran, who was one of Nahmanides's greatest grand-disciples, had this to say: "I likewise have informed you that my teacher, our master R. Nissim, told me privately that Nahmanides clung excessively to the belief in kabbalistic doctrine."[1] At the same time, the minority of kabbalistically informed readers have viewed the esoteric stratum as the center of their interest, as evidenced by the various works written solely to explain Nahmanides's allusive comments. The kabbalistic allusions in his Commentary on the Torah and his fragmentary commentary on Sefer Yetzirah constitute a relatively small, and mostly inaccessible, body of material when compared with the rest of his oeuvre. Nahmanides was very sparing in his disclosure of kabbalistic traditions, dropping mere morsels here and there, so the reader can hope to grasp them only by putting them all together and interpreting them through oral traditions that were recorded by his grand-disciples long after his passing. Such students of his disciples Rashba and R. Isaac b. Todros included, among others, R. Shem Tov Ibn Gaon and R. Meir b. Solomon Abusahulah, who respectively wrote Keter Shem Tov and Peirush Sodot ha-Ramban.[2] One would be mistaken, however, to infer from the limited written material that kabbalah was a peripheral interest of Nahmanides that had negligible influence on his thought. For Nahmanides, kabbalah was the deepest bedrock of truth on which his whole worldview rested.[3] He considered it to be an oral tradition transmitted from one generation to the next ever since Moses received it at Sinai, imparting to a restricted elite the deepest meaning of the Godhead, the Torah, and all existence. Aside from Nahmanides's formative influence on a very important school of kabbalistic thought, his authority as a master halakhist and exegete was of serious weight in getting kabbalah recognized as the authentic esoteric truth of Judaism.

  Besides his monumental achievements in the fields of halakhah, kabbalah, and biblical interpretation, each of which alone would have provided him with a fulfilling and full life, Nahmanides was also deeply involved as a communal leader in the realms of social, political, and religious matters. He effected a change in the Jewish leadership of Barcelona and the character of its community,[4] played a decisive role in the Maimonidean controversy of the 1230s,[5] and stood tall as the stalwart defender of Judaism during the public disputation with the Dominicans in the court of the Aragonese count-king.[6]

The present book attempts to provide a broad, systematic account of Nahmanides's thought: his conception of halakhah and his approach to the central concerns of medieval Jewish thought, including his conception of God, history, revelation, and the reasons for the commandments.[7] My discussion of Nahmanides's ideas and positions on a range of matters emerges out of conversation with the work of other scholars on particular aspects of his thought, including Chayim Henoch's book *Nachmanides: Philosopher and Mystic*, which focuses on his reasons for the commandments, and Haviva Pedaya's book *Nahmanides: Cyclical Time and Holy Text*, which explores Nahmanides's conception of time and the Torah.[8] The first two chapters of the present book take as their topic Nahmanides's approach to halakhah: Chapter 1 examines his philosophy of halakhah, and Chapter 2, his conception of halakhic history and his theory of custom. Subsequent chapters are devoted to Nahmanides's thought, deciphering his kabbalah, and the relationship between the exoteric and esoteric aspects of his writings.

Aside from its own inherent qualities, Nahmanides's thought was particularly weighty and influential because of his stature as a halakhist. If one were to compile a comprehensive list of the various halakhists and Talmudists of the thirteenth century, one would be hard put to point to someone whose output is more critical, systematic, and consistently insightful than that of Nahmanides. In his Talmudic novellae and glosses, one can readily see his dissatisfaction with local, forced solutions to the intricate problems that arise in the explication of the Talmudic sugya, and his inexhaustible drive to develop fundamental and systematic distinctions as a way of neatly resolving contradictions and untangling knotty problems of interpretation. This feature of his thought process forces the scholar to presume that under all of his thought—even his kabbalistic thought—there lies a well-developed, systematic worldview, even if only the tip of the iceberg is visible in any one place. The attempt to complete this picture and position it on a theosophical, metaphysical foundation guides the chapters on Nahmanides's understanding of sin, death, and redemption; his conception of the chain of being and hidden miracles; his theory of prophecy; his conception of history; and his reasons

for the commandments. These threads of his thought are all intertwined and
wrapped around a central religious posture rooted in his theology.

Nahmanides was a systematic thinker in the extreme. Unfortunately, he
did not leave us a systematic opus akin to R. Judah Halevi's *Kuzari* or Moses
Maimonides's *The Guide of the Perplexed*. To systematically reconstruct his
thought requires painstaking attention to the snippets dispersed throughout
his Commentary on the Torah, Commentary on Job, fragmentary commentary on Sefer Yetzirah, Sefer ha-Ge'ulah, Torat ha-Adam, Torat Ha-Shem
Temimah, and his discourses on Ecclesiastes and the New Year.[9] The exploration of Nahmanides's Torah commentary focuses, therefore, on the aspects
that express his thinking on the issues central to his conception of Judaism.
The commentary is treated here as the key to Nahmanides's thought because
aside from his main exegetical undertaking in it, he used it as a framework in
which to present his ideas on the great questions of Jewish tradition. This
characteristic of the commentary is evident from his inclusion of relatively
lengthy disquisitions on core topics of his thought, digressions from the
straightforward objective of a Torah commentary. These sections cover miracles, prophecy, the uniqueness of the land of Israel, the problem of anthropomorphism in the Targum Onkelos, the magical-demonological worldview,
the chain of being, and the reasons for the commandments. Taking all these
together, one can generate a quite coherent picture of his thought; in fact,
Nahmanides himself must have thought so, for in his discourses, which contain the most systematic presentation of his thought, we can find almost verbatim and at considerable length parallels to these excursive passages.[10]

As we excavate the esoteric layer of Nahmanides's thought on each issue,
we repeatedly encounter a fascinating phenomenon. The components that
together make up the idea of a personal God fade away and are replaced by
patently causal and structural ones. The Judaism of the Bible and midrash is
founded upon a deity in a living, complicated, interpersonal relationship with
humans, which can be portrayed by way of analogy or contrast with the relationships between father and son, king and subject, master and slave, judge
and accused, husband and wife. Within the framework of the anthropomorphic imagination, religious creativity is expressed by coining new analogies
for understanding the religious posture, analogies that go on to reverberate in
the construction of religious ritual and in the historical self-understanding
of the community. A paradigmatic example of such religious creativity can be
seen in Talmudic literature, which produced the teacher-pupil and land-
owner–hired hand analogies, as well as the very influential image of God

reflected through the prism of the midrashic king parables, which both compare to and contrast with the Roman emperor. Furthermore, the complexity and density of religious life derive from the simultaneous application of all these analogies to a single divine personality—to take but one example, God is simultaneously both judge and father. Creation, history, revelation, the commandments, and other elements of Judaism were shaped within the biblical and midrashic literature that contains this anthropomorphic perspective on human-divine relations. As I try to demonstrate in the various chapters of this book, the anthropomorphic conception of God increasingly gives way to a kabbalistic one in which a multidimensional entity replaces this many-hatted personality. As with every other major change to tradition that occurs through processes of interpretation, here too emphasis is placed on those earlier voices within the tradition that were drowned out by the mainstream, on those ideas abandoned by the wayside of the royal road that connects and runs through biblical and midrashic literature.

This sea change, which forms one of the central axes of this book, to a certain extent situates Nahmanides's kabbalah and medieval Jewish philosophy within the same broader context. The Jewish intellectual elite of the Middle Ages experienced a crisis as they felt ill at ease with the traditional, anthropomorphic depiction of God. The esoteric stratum of R. Abraham Ibn Ezra's commentaries on the Torah and the secrets of Maimonides's *Guide* attest to a sidelining of the idea of God as a personality; as with Nahmanides's writings, the more their esoteric ideas are exposed, the more one can see how the foundation of a personal God has been replaced by something else. There are, to be sure, stark differences between these esotericists, but they stem primarily from the different causal and cosmological schema each one chose as the foundation for his reinterpretation of tradition.

Unlike the Zohar, Nahmanidean kabbalah contains no mythical personae, intricate midrashic tapestries, or exciting frame stories. The distilled form of the kabbalah Nahmanides transmits, and the role of his towering stature in solidifying kabbalah's position as the authentic secret corpus of Jewish teachings, allows us to examine his thought in the wider context of medieval Jewish culture. If it is indeed correct that the esoteric stratum of medieval Jewish thought replaces the anthropomorphic conception of God with a causal-systemic one, then the question of the relationship between kabbalah and philosophy, and the place of kabbalah in Jewish tradition, is ripe for reassessment. The divide between kabbalah and philosophy is typically understood through the categories of myth versus reason, or as the result of a gap between the kabbalist's internal, authentic

voice that bursts forth from the depths of his primordial religious consciousness
and the philosopher's carefully reasoned, discursive voice he adopts from non-
Jewish sources. But these contrasts prove unsuitable for explaining kabbalah
and philosophy because their hostility and disparity notwithstanding, on a profound level the two both reflect the triumph of the Greek category of nature. It
catalyzed Jewish philosophers and kabbalists alike to provide causal explanations of major concepts of the Jewish tradition, and under the esoteric veil they
reinterpreted tradition until it no longer looked quite the same. The conclusion
of this book situates the picture that emerges from the preceding chapters
within the wider panorama of medieval Jewish thought.

Nahmanides's Talmudic novellae and Bible commentary share one remarkable feature, which is a direct result of his extraordinary cultural positioning. In these two immense undertakings, Nahmanides developed his
unique views and groundbreaking ideas in dialogue with the diverse array of
halakhic and cultural approaches of the Jewish world he inherited. In his
Commentary on the Torah, he consolidated his thought in conversation with
the central Jewish thinkers of the eleventh and twelfth centuries: R. Solomon
b. Isaac (Rashi), Ibn Ezra, and Maimonides, each of whom represented a
distinct strand of medieval Jewish thought. Nahmanides characteristically invited all of them to participate in a discourse of his hosting, as he was, conveniently, in the right place at the right time: thirteenth-century Catalonia was
a unique cultural basin toward which all of these opposing and divergent
streams of the Jewish world made their way.[11] The same is true of Nahmanides's Talmudic novellae, in which we find the systematic breakdown of geocultural barriers, an unparalleled phenomenon in medieval Jewish works. His
frame of reference in Talmudic and halakhic study was not limited to the
discourse of his own native cultural region; he formulated his positions from
a synoptic vantage point that extended beyond the range of Talmudic literature to the various halakhic traditions of the twelfth century—northern
French, Provençal, Andalusian, and North African. His broad horizons also
owed much to the diverse backgrounds of his own halakhic teachers R. Judah
b. Yakar and R. Meir b. Nathan of Trinquetaille, who introduced Nahmanides to the traditions of the northern French scholars the Tosafists and the
halakhists of southern France and Catalonia.[12] Nahmanides's predecessors did
not have access to such an all-encompassing view, and even in his own writings the discourse only widened over time, until in his novellae he consistently established his position over against those of Rashi, R. Jacob b. Meir
(Rabbeinu Tam), R. Abraham b. David (Ra'avad), R. Zerahiah ha-Levi

(Razah), R. Isaac Alfasi (Rif), Rabbeinu Ephraim, R. Joseph Ibn Migash, Maimonides, and others.[13]

The twelfth-century halakhists who preceded Nahmanides had had very limited discussion of nonlocal halakhic traditions. It is astounding but true, for example, that Maimonides did not relate to any of Rashi's commentaries. His halakhic discourse was limited mainly to the traditions of Andalusia and North Africa upon which he was reared, beyond which it was as if nothing else existed. The state of affairs in Germany and northern France was similar, although perhaps less so. The number of times Rabbeinu Tam related to Rif is quite meager; his halakhic discourse focused upon establishing his own creative interpretations in the face of Rashi's positions and Rhenish traditions and included extensive discussions with his northern French contemporaries. In Provence, circumstances were different, owing to its nature as a crossroads between Christian Spain and Ashkenaz (Franco-Germany), and so the discursive scope of Ra'avad, R. Isaac b. Abba Mari (author of 'Ittur Soferim), and especially Razah was broader. Each of the twelfth-century halakhists, who so comprehensively transformed the nature and character of halakhah, worked in his own world, a world in which geocultural borders oftentimes defined the boundaries of discourse and debate. Nahmanides's Talmudic novellae are the supraregional halakhic texts par excellence in terms of range—all the distinct creative streams of the long twelfth century drain into them. This development, which began in Provence and culminated in Nahmanides's Catalonian novellae, parallels a similar, albeit slightly earlier, revolution that made medieval law supraregional, too.[14]

Nahmanides's uniqueness as the first halakhist and thinker to draw upon the totality of Jewish culture is apparent in his stance and standing in the Maimonidean controversy of the 1230s. He was the only participant amid the harsh strife to address both sides: on one hand, the sages of northern France, who banned Maimonides's writings, and on the other, Maimonides's supporters, the so-called Maimunists, of southern France and Christian Spain. Like his magnificent compositions on the Torah and Talmud, Nahmanides's letters to rabbinic personalities in northern France and communal leaders in Catalonia, Aragon, and Provence reflect his intimate familiarity with and absolute command over the internal codes of the vastly differing cultural languages of medieval Jewry. Again, his unique cultural position afforded him the ability to adopt an original position that would put out fires in the greatest culture war of the thirteenth century.

The complicated interrelationship between Franco-German and Andalusian sources of influence has preoccupied various scholars who have tried to situate Nahmanides along the axis between Ashkenaz and Sepharad. The conclusion of the book returns to this question, and that of Nahmanides's position in the controversy over Maimonides's writings. What is important to stress at this introductory stage is that in contrast to the many voices in the exoteric layer of Nahmanides's commentaries and novellae, the esoteric layer of his kabbalah has a lone, authoritative voice that cannot be described by geocultural terms like "Ashkenaz" or "Sepharad." Kabbalah is just as Nahmanides makes it sound—"the way of truth," which he considered a received tradition that must be preserved from additions or subtractions. Unlike his novellae and commentaries, in his kabbalah he does not mention anyone else, be they kabbalist predecessors or contemporaries. He does not mention R. Isaac the Blind, usually referred to in the writings of the Gerona kabbalists as "the pious one" (*he-hasid*), and he cites R. Ezra of Gerona's writings only twice—anonymously and indirectly. Nahmanides viewed himself as a tradent of kabbalistic traditions that were not open to speculation or reasoning and should not be examined in light of the parallel kabbalistic positions maintained by the Geronese and Provençal kabbalists. The source of his kabbalistic traditions, however, remains mysterious and obscure, as evidenced by the enigmatic, and possibly ironic, name of his kabbalistic teacher, whom Nahmanides's grand-disciples referred to as Ben Belimah.[15] In any case, the absence of the Geronese kabbalists and R. Isaac the Blind from Nahmanides's writings teaches us that his kabbalistic traditions were independent of them and that despite his presence in Gerona he should not be associated with the circle of kabbalists there.[16]

The nature of the kabbalistic stratum within Nahmanides's thought and its relationship to the exoteric reveals a deep tension within his personality and approach, between the innovation and creativity that mark his Talmudic novellae and Bible commentary, on one hand, and the conservatism and strict adherence to tradition that characterize his kabbalistic doctrines, on the other. In addition to this tension, there is an observable gap between the contents of the esoteric stratum, which forms the innermost core of Nahmanides's thought, and his exoteric positions. Through the medium of secrecy and esotericism, Nahmanides introduced a radical dimension into his thought that he anchored in kabbalah and tradition. Chapter 8, "Esotericism and Tradition," does not analyze specific esoteric doctrines of Nahmanides but his approach to esotericism itself. The chapter focuses on how he understood the need for esotericism and its limits, and what motivated the particular path he adopted in transmitting the esoteric tradition. Beyond the multifaceted creativity evidenced in Nahmanides's exoteric writings lies this uniform esoteric layer that further complicates his personality and thought.

Of all the extraordinary figures to come out of medieval Jewry, the only one worthy of comparison to Nahmanides in terms of breadth, complexity, stature, and influence is Maimonides. These two halakhic giants, who were also both physicians and had close ties to the royal court,[17] played decisive roles in shaping the sweeping change wrought by medieval Jewish thought: Maimonides by bringing philosophical motifs into the heart of Judaism, and Nahmanides by claiming that kabbalah constitutes the innermost, profoundest teachings of Jewish tradition. Each believed he alone was privy to the deepest and secret meaning of the Torah, and both anchored this tremendous revolution within medieval Jewry in the esoteric stratum of Judaism. Their imposing halakhic authority to a large extent lent legitimacy and protection to these opposing worldviews that changed the face of Judaism. Nahmanides, who was born almost certainly in 1194, was approximately ten years old at Maimonides's passing, and from the day he became a Torah scholar, exegete, and kabbalist, he maintained a complicated relationship with Maimonides's views, by turns adopting them, dismissing them, praising them, polemicizing against them, and defending them.[18] Despite the vast daylight between their worldviews, the two men share the same deep tension between halakhah and thought, between the exoteric and the esoteric.

Nahmanides's achievements as the supreme halakhist of the thirteenth century and as one of the most creative commentators of the Torah make him a medieval luminary of the revealed aspects of the Jewish tradition. By comparison, his kabbalistic colleagues in Gerona, namely Rabbis Ezra, Azriel, and Jacob b. Sheshet, are known only for their kabbalah. Were we to take their esoteric teachings away from them, there would be no trace of their contribution to medieval Jewish creativity. Nahmanides could not be more different. The fecundity reflected in his Talmudic novellae and Torah commentary is plain for all to see, and those works are more than enough to entitle him entry into the pantheon of the greatest medieval halakhists and thinkers. Yet studying carefully the esoteric layer of his thought exposes the deep gap between the revealed dimensions of the Jewish tradition and the dynamic processes that were hiding beneath its surface level. Understanding Nahmanides's conception of halakhah and clarifying the nature of his esoteric thought, along with the basic religious drive to maintain it alongside his halakhic, manifest work, serve as the axis of discussion in this book.

CHAPTER I

Nahmanides's Philosophy of Halakhah

Were Nahmanides left to his own devices, he would not have taken the trouble to formulate a systematic philosophy of halakhah. R. Solomon b. Isaac (Rashi, 1040–1105), R. Jacob Tam (Rabbeinu Tam, 1100–1171), and R. Abraham b. David (Ra'avad, 1120–1198), those halakhic titans who deeply influenced Nahmanides's approach and to whose positions he gave serious consideration, did not concern themselves with a theory of halakhah. Freestanding statements about the theory of interpretation in halakhah or the phenomenon of controversy in halakhah are nowhere to be found in their writings, nor do we find systematic expositions of their notions of halakhic authority. Two obstacles stood in the way of their formulating such a theory. First, the total immersion demanded by their meticulous interpretive undertaking made it difficult to achieve the distance necessary for constructing a theory of halakhah. Second, the lack of systematicity in Talmudic discourse itself concerning such issues disinclined them from such theorizing, along the lines of the Talmudic assertion that "generalizations are not instructive." Anyone interested in bringing to light their implicit positions on these issues must therefore wade through the minutiae and pan out those rarely encountered nuggets about halakhic discourse itself.

In contrast to the leading twelfth-century halakhists of northern France and Provence, Maimonides considered the formulation of a philosophy of halakhah crucial to his enterprise. In the introduction to his Commentary on

the Mishnah, which he authored in his twenties at the very outset of his halakhic career, he methodically dealt with questions such as how to account for
controversy, how interpretation relates to innovation and tradition, and where
to properly situate prophecy in the hierarchy of halakhic authority. He continued to revisit these issues in the prefatory Principles to Sefer ha-Mitzvot, in
the introduction to the Mishneh Torah, in the Mishneh Torah itself, and in
The Guide of the Perplexed. Maimonides's preoccupation with these questions
grew out of his all-embracing philosophical interest and his Islamic cultural
milieu, in which legal philosophy was a well-developed field. Beyond that,
however, his need for a theory of halakhah derived from his monumental attempt to impose on the Talmudic chaos the order necessary for producing an
exhaustive and systematic code. Such an endeavor required him to construct
a theoretical framework that would serve as a crucible into which he could
pour Talmudic discourse, purify it, and then recast it with an eye toward systematicity.

The twelfth-century halakhists of northern France and Provence, who
paved the way for the entire genre of Talmudic novellae, considered the goal
of Talmud study to be the expansion of Talmudic discourse. Tosafot, Ra'avad's
Talmud commentaries, and the novellae of Nahmanides and his school represent the fecundity of Torah study, in the same way that the Talmud, until it
was sealed, was a self-propagating organism. Those engaged in broadening
the discourse do not typically concern themselves with the theory of it, which
would require them to look at it from the outside, and they usually do not
produce comprehensive codes, which would put a stop to the continuous,
ever-expanding, unlimited dynamism of the discourse. Therefore, extensive
codifying activities were not only in direct opposition to the local and plural-
istic character of Franco-German halakhah, but were inimical to the very
purpose of study—to aggrandize the Torah and glorify it.

In Maimonides's wake, Nahmanides was forced—at the end of his days
and against his will—to take a position on the fundamental questions concerning revelation, interpretation, and controversy. Had Maimonides not defined his approach to these questions against those of the Geonim who
preceded him, perhaps Nahmanides would not have taken notice. His devotion to defending the Earlier Authorities required him to craft his own systematic perspective that could hold its own against the one Maimonides set
forth in the prefatory Principles to his Sefer ha-Mitzvot.[1] With Nahmanides
joining the fray, the most important medieval debate about the philosophy
of halakhah took literary form in Maimonides's Sefer ha-Mitzvot (Book of

Commandments) and Nahmanides's glosses on it. A proper analysis of Nahmanides's positions, then, requires an understanding of Maimonides's, which itself necessitates an adequate grasp of the Geonic ones that Maimonides impugned. It is therefore worthwhile to proceed by presenting the prevalent Geonic approach and Maimonides's response to it, and only then to analyze Nahmanides's approach as formulated in his polemical glosses on Sefer ha-Mitzvot. In the end, this inquiry will yield three philosophical approaches to halakhah—the Geonic, the Maimonidean, and the Nahmanidean. The three put forward different, incompatible theories of the fundamental concepts of the halakhic system: controversy, truth, interpretation, and authority.[2]

I

The mainstream approach of the Geonim to controversy was summarized in an accurate, if simplistic, manner by R. Abraham Ibn Daud in the introduction to his Sefer ha-Kabbalah:

> The purpose of this *Sefer ha-Kabbalah* (Book of Tradition) is to provide students with the evidence that all the teachings of our Rabbis, namely, the Sages of the Mishnah and the Talmud, have been transmitted: each great sage and righteous man having received them from a great sage and righteous man, each head of an academy and his school having received them from the head of an academy and his school, as far back as the men of the Great Assembly, who received them from the prophets. Never did the Sages of the Talmud, and certainly not the Sages of the Mishnah, teach anything, however trivial, of their own invention, except for the enactments which were made by universal agreement in order to make a hedge around the Torah.
>
> Now, should anyone infected with heresy attempt to mislead you, saying, "it is because the rabbis differed on a number of issues that I doubt their words," you should retort bluntly and inform him that he is "a rebel against the decision of the court," and that our Rabbis never differed with respect to a commandment in principle, but only with respect to its details; for they had heard the principle from their teachers, but had not inquired as to its details, since they had not waited upon their masters sufficiently. As a case in point, they did not differ as to whether or not it is obligatory to light the Sabbath lamp; what

they did dispute was "with what it may be lighted and with what it may not be lighted." Similarly, they did not differ as to whether we are required to recite the *Shema*ʿ evenings and mornings; what they differed on was "from when may the *Shema*ʿ be recited in the evenings" and "from when may the *Shema*ʿ be recited in the mornings." This holds true for all of their discussions.[3]

According to this approach, which could be termed "the restorative approach," the revelation at Sinai included all necessary halakhic knowledge. The Sages did not invent anything of their own accord; the authority of the Oral Torah is anchored in Mount Sinai, from which the all-inclusive content of revelation has been transmitted as a tradition from one generation to the next. In consonance with this approach, the self-avowed purpose of Sefer ha-Kabbalah (and any other work of halakhic history) is to trace the unbroken, reliable chain of tradents who have ensured halakhic continuity from Moses, through the rabbinic period and until the very composition of the book.[4] This approach, which coalesced partially out of anti-Karaite polemic, had to grapple with the phenomenon of controversy.[5] (The Karaite movement developed from the eighth century onward and denied the authority of the Mishnah and the Talmud, relying solely on biblical authority.) If the law had been given at Sinai as a finished product, why did the Sages dispute what should have been evident to them through tradition? Proponents sidestepped this obstacle by claiming that controversy had resulted from errors in the transmission process. At Sinai, the question of when to recite the Shemaʿ at night was answered, but because of careless students who were unwilling to wait upon their teachers sufficiently, the answer was forgotten and became unrecoverable. Because of the error in transmission and loss of information, the Sages had to use their powers of reasoning to reconstruct the lost knowledge, and so they debated and crossed swords, for example, about the meaning of "when you lie down" (Deut 6:7), which is supposed to demarcate the period for the nighttime Shemaʿ in the Written Torah.

This approach of Ibn Daud and the Geonim bases the authority of the entire halakhah in the revelation at Sinai. The explanation given for controversy, however, undermines the reliability of the transmitted tradition. In order to minimize the resulting damage to tradition, Ibn Daud tried to restrict the incidence of controversy to the margins of halakhah. The Sages did not dispute the existence of an obligation to recite the Shemaʿ at night, but the appropriate time for its recital. The Sages did not dispute the existence of an obligation to light the Sabbath lamp, but what fuels can be used. The important kernel of tradition remains intact, and even if controversy reflects a kink in the chain of tradition, according to this approach, corruption within the transmission process has only a marginal impact on halakhah.

The restorative approach constitutes a coherent theory of halakhah in which all of the important components hang together: interpretation, controversy, truth, revelation, and authority. Interpretation, according to this approach, does not generate new knowledge to augment the normative halakhic corpus. There is ab initio no place for human creativity in halakhah, as it is rooted in toto in the detailed revelation at Sinai.[6] Interpretation is the last resort of those desperate to reconstruct and rediscover their lost Sinaitic tradition. Flowing from this conception of revelation and interpretation is the restorative approach's conception of halakhic truth: whenever a dispute arises, one side must perforce be mistaken, and the yardstick of truth is the conformity of an opinion with what was transmitted at Sinai. We may never know which of the disputants is wrong, for the dispute itself arises from the forgetting of tradition, but it is crystal clear that there can be but one correct answer, an answer given long ago. This conception of halakhic truth can be called "truth by correspondence," along the lines of the philosophical theory that defines truth in terms of its correspondence to reality—the correspondence theory of truth. Under this theory, a claim about the world is true if it corresponds to a fact. In the restorative approach, a halakhic claim is true or false to the degree that it lines up with the particulars of the Sinaitic revelation. In addition, the Geonic approach posits a chronological conception of halakhic authority. Since halakhic knowledge can be lost or corrupted in transmission, the greater the antecedence of any particular halakhist in the chain of transmission, the greater his authority. Greater historical proximity to the source of revelation confers reliability upon a tradent because it implies familiarity with halakhic material prior to data loss, so earlier authorities take precedence over later ones.

Maimonides was born and educated in Cordoba in a world that had developed its own independent intellectual resources far away from the influence of the Geonim in Baghdad. Throughout his legal work Maimonides challenged the authority of the Geonim, and it is not surprising that when his great code Mishneh Torah reached Baghdad it got a hostile reception among the heirs of the Geonim. One major source of contention revolved around the foundations of legal philosophy, and Maimonides offered a critique of every element of the Geonic restorative approach in the introduction to his

Commentary on the Mishnah. In its stead, he proposes his own systematic approach, which could not be more different and which could be termed "the cumulative approach." In his introduction, he divides the norms of halakhah into three basic components. The first component includes laws given to Moses at Sinai that were then passed on through tradition. In opposition to the Geonic approach, Maimonides asserts that this component has never been subject to dispute: "The first group: the interpretations received from Moses [. . .] There is no debate about them whatsoever. Whenever someone says 'I have received such and such [a tradition]' any debate disappears."[7] The second component of the halakhic corpus includes commandments innovated by the Sages through their interpretation of the Written Torah. This area of halakhah attracts controversy because it is traditionless: "The third group: these are the laws derived through *qiyās* (broadly: syllogism),[8] and they are subject to debate, as we have said, and the law concerning them is decided in accordance with the majority."[9] Controversy thus entered halakhah on issues with no tradition when the Sages attempted, by their own reasoning, to provide an answer for problems they faced:

> But the applications (lit. branches[10]) not heard from the prophet [Moses] concerning matters that are inferred from them, the laws being extrapolated through *qiyās,* with the thirteen rules given to him at Sinai, which are "the thirteen *middot* by which the Torah is interpreted." And among those extrapolated [laws were] matters that disagreement did not occur in them, but rather there was consensus about them; but in some of them there was disagreement between the two syllogisms [. . .] for this typically occurs with the dialectic syllogisms.[11]

The third component of halakhah includes various rabbinic decrees and enactments that are neither part of tradition nor a product of exegesis.

Maimonides therefore opines, in opposition to the Geonim, that the Sinaitic revelation did not include all the normative contents of halakhah.[12] Significant portions of halakhah have been generated by human interpretive activity, and controversy emerges when the human factor enters into the production of halakhah through reasoning. Controversy cannot be a consequence of a breakdown in the process of transmission, because the kernel given to Moses at Sinai has been fully preserved without any objections. Controversy came on the scene when the Sages tried to create new laws through the medium of interpretation. Maimonides sharply attacks the Geonic account of controversy's origins as follows:

But the notion of those who believe that even disputed laws were received from Moses yet came under dispute due to transmission errors or forgetfulness, such that one received the truth and the other erred in his reception, forgot, or did not hear from his teacher everything he needed to hear, and bring proof from their [the Sages'] statement: "when the students of Shammai and Hillel who did not sufficiently wait upon [their teachers] proliferated, controversy proliferated within Israel and the Torah became like two Torahs" (*Sotah* 47b)—this, God knows, is extremely repugnant and disgraceful. They are the words of those who do not comprehend and do not have a solid grasp of the principles (lit. roots[13]) yet cast aspersions on those who transmitted the Torah. This is void and null. What led them to this ruinous belief is deficient comprehension of the words of our Sages found in the Talmud.[14]

The Geonic position receives such harsh treatment because its claim regarding the origins of controversy undermines the reliability of tradition. Maimonides preserves tradition in its pristine state by claiming that no controversy had occurred concerning the laws received at Sinai. At the same time, he maintains that the bulk of halakhah in its fine detail has human fingerprints all over it. The times for the morning and evening recitations of the Shema' were not transmitted at Sinai, because if they had been, then no rabbinic controversy ever could have ensued. The sole revelatory sources pertaining to the appropriate time for the recitation of the Shema' are the two expressions in the Written Torah, "when you arise" and "when you lie down," and the rabbinic dispute surrounding them is a direct result of the attempt to wring precise temporal parameters from these legally vague expressions.

The disagreement between Maimonides and the Geonim about the etiology of controversy manifests an inherent tension between the two options, a tension generated by the complex interaction of revelation, tradition, and controversy. Choosing either of the options is a theologically and normatively problematic compromise. On one hand, the Geonic attempt to anchor the source and authority of halakhah with its myriad details in revelation undercuts the reliability of the tradition. On the other hand, the Maimonidean assertion that the tradition has been preserved and remains uncorrupted prevents grounding the entirety of halakhah in revelation. This approach must allow for human creativity within halakhah, which is in evidence wherever controversy rears its head. The theological and normative price that

Maimonides must pay for the preservation of tradition was astutely formulated in the seventeenth century by R. Yair Bacharach: "The Master [Maimonides] has constructed a reinforced wall around the Oral Torah by writing that it is not subject to forgetfulness. Would only that we could strengthen and support it, which to my mind we cannot, not to mention the fact that he loses any gains by writing that all other rabbinic disputes, which comprise the vast majority of the Oral Torah and practically all the Orders of the Mishnah, are not from Sinai at all."[15] Maimonides's contention with the restorative approach leads him to offer a drastically different theory of halakhah's conceptual foundations. The Geonim opined that halakhic knowledge had started out perfect and complete, only to be worn down over time because of imperfections in the transmission process, whereas Maimonides believes the opposite to be true—not only does halakhic knowledge not deteriorate, it in fact accumulates over time. Revelation, in his account, furnished the compact kernel, which had been transmitted from one generation to the next without deteriorating and to which additional normative content was added through interpretation. The two approaches view the human contribution to halakhah in completely different ways, because for Maimonides interpretation does not merely rediscover laws already revealed at Sinai, it is a creative medium through which new norms are deduced from the divinely revealed ones. Relying on their power of reasoning, scholars, in Maimonides's opinion, are capable of generating religiously meaningful obligations through creative interpretation.

The cumulative approach of Maimonides also has a different conception of truth. To begin with the commonalities, it agrees with the restorative approach of the Geonim that there is only one right side in a dispute, and even makes use of the same Talmudic account of controversy as arising from altercations between the insufficiently motivated and, consequently, inadequately learned disciples of Shammai and Hillel.[16] Controversy indicates a decline in the capacity for legal reasoning and disagreement over hermeneutics. Where this approach differs, however, is that it turns the Geonic idea of halakhic truth on its head. The Geonim measured the truthfulness of any opinion by the extent to which it corresponds to the original content of the Sinaitic revelation, but Maimonides cannot agree, because the very existence of controversy means the disputed law could not possibly have been stated explicitly at Sinai. Truthfulness for Maimonides is established by the extent to which a new norm is consistent with the earlier norms given at Sinai. He replaces "truth by correspondence" with something akin to what philosophers call the coherence theory of truth. Under this theory, the truthfulness of any proposition is tested by asking whether it flows consistently and coherently from prior propositions from which it is derived. Since interpretation derives new norms from preexisting ones, it can be tested, like any other kind of inference, by the extent to which the conclusion coheres with the premises from which it was derived.[17]

Maimonides's approach also has implications for halakhic authority. Since he maintains that the transmitted material has been pristinely preserved, antecedence does not entail precedence. At every point in halakhic history the same revealed knowledge is present, so no point in time can be privileged solely on the basis of chronological considerations.[18]

These two approaches, the restorative and the cumulative, differ essentially in their basic accounts of the history of halakhah and the role of revelation. These, in turn, generate essential differences in how they understand those concepts fundamental to the philosophy of halakhah—interpretation, truth, authority, and controversy. Nahmanides and his disciples offer a third position on controversy and these other fundamental concepts, but in order to understand it properly we must first sharpen our understanding of Maimonides's notion of interpretation, which was the main point of Nahmanides's disagreement. Their dispute plays out mainly in Nahmanides's glosses on the prefatory Principles of Maimonides's Sefer ha-Mitzvot, where Nahmanides concentrates his argument on the question of what should be enumerated in the count of commandments, and what "given to Moses at Sinai" means when said about the 613 commandments.

II

Maimonides articulated his views on legal interpretation in his composition Sefer ha-Mitzvot (the Book of Commandments). This composition is dedicated to the enumeration of the biblical commandments, following a Talmudic tradition that 613 such commandments were given to Moses in the revelation at Sinai. Maimonides's approach to the concept of the "commandment" in Sefer ha-Mitzvot is intrinsically linked to what he considered to be the very point of enumerating them. He criticized previous enumerators, scholars and poets alike, because he considered the entire genre to be plagued by haphazardness and a lack of systematicity. Their failure, however, does not sufficiently explain why Maimonides took it upon himself to write his own enumeration of the commandments. Trying to arrive at exactly

613 commandments because the Talmudic tradition gives that number appears to be, on the face of it, like trying to solve a tricky puzzle; and writing a guide to solve it—even one that surpasses all previous guides—would be undertaking an intellectual challenge for its own sake, which does not characterize Maimonides's modus operandi. He composed monumental, groundbreaking works, like his commentary on the entire Mishnah and the Mishneh Torah, and the kind of literary task required here would not have been consonant with his self-image as a halakhist.

The answer to this question is bound up in the purpose of the enumeration, namely, to serve as the organizing principle for the Mishneh Torah.[19] If the enumeration is viewed within this context, the concept of the "commandment" takes on a new definition that is fundamentally at variance with the one used by previous enumerators.[20] According to Maimonides, the "commandment" is a category for organizing a particular commandment's halakhic details. We can see this in his use of the commandments as secondary subtitles for the various books in his Mishneh Torah, and from his statement that the books are arranged "such that there will be no commandment whose full complement of laws will not be discussed."[21] In each book, the enumeration of the pertinent commandments in the subtitle, followed by the detailed presentation of laws flowing from them, constitutes a full halakhic treatment of a given subject. For this reason, Maimonides does not enumerate in his count every admonitory "do not" or hortative "do" that appears as a command in the Torah. For him, an explicit command does not count as a commandment unless it also constitutes a category that organizes a cluster of laws. A full exposition of this principle can be found in Principle Seven of his Sefer ha-Mitzvot, which posits that one does not count halakhic details in the enumeration of the commandments: "Know that a single commandment is a complete, discrete unit, and that premise [the introductory commandment] entails the many commands and injunctions about the laws of the commandments."[22] Maimonides tries to lay the foundations of halakhah and his theory of it in his Sefer ha-Mitzvot. The enumeration provides the hardy, uncontested kernel of the law that can be traced directly to the exclusive authority of Moses. What is more, embedded within this kernel are organizational categories from which halakhah can grow and expand.

Owing to the long tradition of enumeration from which he was consciously deviating, Maimonides decided to write his Sefer ha-Mitzvot as a detailed defense for his unexplained enumeration of the commandments in his Mishneh Torah. Sefer ha-Mitzvot, then, is the only planned commentary penned by Maimonides on his Mishneh Torah, and its scope is limited—it covers only the enumeration of the commandments at the beginning of each book. This in itself points to the centrality of the enumeration for the organization of the Mishneh Torah.[23]

Maimonides devoted most of the prefatory Principles to setting up a distinction between commandments that serve as organizing principles and those that are merely commands. In other Principles he similarly set out to identify biblical laws that appear normative but in truth are not.[24] In these Principles, he added a second condition for a command to qualify as a countable commandment: not only must it be organizational, but it must have been given to Moses at Sinai. Maimonides provided the basis for this in the first two Principles, which inquire into the meaning of being "given to Moses at Sinai." This is where Maimonides's theory of halakhic interpretation comes into sharper focus, and it is also here that Nahmanides's serious disagreement with him over the nature of interpretation occurred.

In Principle One, Maimonides declares that he will not include rabbinic commandments in the enumeration. He would have thought this obvious had the author of Halakhot Gedolot, R. Simeon Kayyara, not included rabbinic obligations in his count, such as the recitation of Hallel, the kindling of the Hanukkah lamp, and the reading of the Megillah: "Know that this matter need not have been raised on account of its obviousness, because once the Talmud said '613 commandments were said to Moses at Sinai,' how could we say that something Rabbinic (de-rabbanan) is included in that number?"[25] The claim appears simple enough, but Maimonides's justification of the claim entails a complex and radical argument. He claims that we should not count rabbinic commandments since they have not been given at Sinai, as he says further on regarding the obligation to light the Hanukkah lamp: "I do not believe that anyone could imagine or entertain the notion that it was said to Moses at Sinai that he should command us [as follows]: if, at the end of our sovereignty, such and such should happen with the Greeks, we will be obligated to light the Hanukkah lamp."[26] According to Maimonides, the distinction between Biblical (de-oraita) and Rabbinic (de-rabbanan) commandments is not only legal; it marks the ontology of revelation, its limits.[27] The distinction between Biblical and Rabbinic determines that the entire complex of halakhic norms that do not appear in the Torah were also not given at Sinai.

Maimonides strengthens this argument by asserting that nobody in the world could possibly believe that the Jewish people were commanded at Sinai about some holiday to be celebrated in the times of the Greeks and Hasmoneans. Despite his confident tone that presumes no disagreement, Maimonides is in fact trying to still a deep current in rabbinic literature and in the history of halakhah that seeks to subsume the entire normative halakhic corpus in the Sinaitic revelation.[28] After all, the vast majority of everyday halakhic observance consists of Rabbinic obligations, so one can readily appreciate the persistent drive to tie them directly to the divine word. Observance of halakhah is supposed to constitute service of God through the fulfillment of his will, but if hundreds of anthropogenic directives, with no direct link to revelation, are interposed between what God wants and what gets done, how have the Sages improved observance? Those who believe that whatever a bright student thinks up today was already said to Moses at Sinai do not view the Biblical-Rabbinic distinction as delimiting revelation but as a legal distinction internal to halakhah. Revelation did include the entire system of halakhic norms, they argue, from the Decalogue all the way down to the finest legal points and enactments of Torah scholars. The expression "613 commandments were given to Moses at Sinai" does not mandate that a halakhist like Kayyara distinguish Biblical obligation from Rabbinic enactment. One could even argue the contrary—that a halakhist should strive to eradicate the division between Rabbinic directives and Biblical obligations so as to incorporate the full set of norms into revelation itself.

The Maimonidean approach, which identifies the content of the revelation at Sinai with the halakhic category of Biblical, distances from revelation the thick stratum of norms termed Rabbinic. In order to isolate Moses's authority from the Sages', Maimonides knows that he must wrestle with the long-standing rabbinic tradition bent on incorporating within revelation all normative strata of halakhah, rabbinic enactments included. He brilliantly neutralizes this tradition in the continuation of Principle One. According to Maimonides, rabbinic directives are anchored in revelation at Sinai through the mediation of the prohibition "do not deviate from what they tell you" (Deut 17:11). This biblical warning, which commands one to obey the courts' decisions, establishes according to Maimonides the narrow bridge connecting the massive Talmudic corpus to revelation: "everything the Sages ordered be done and enjoined from doing Moses had already been ordered to command us to observe, which is His statement [that] 'You should act in accordance with the law that they will teach you and the judgment that they will tell you' (Deut 17:11). And He cautioned us against violating their instruction about anything they have enacted or derived [through the middot] by saying, 'do not deviate from what they tell you' (ibid.)."[29] According to Maimonides, the specific content of rabbinic enactments was not mentioned at Sinai, and so the connection between the enactments and the word of God is mediated by a second-order obligation that anchors them in revelation. Through "do not deviate," one can say that Maimonides considers everything commanded by the Sages to have been "given at Sinai."

In the continuation of Principle One, Maimonides cites only one source which implies that the entire halakhah was given at Sinai. With "do not deviate" as a second-order norm, he interprets this source in a novel manner: "The text of the Talmud in *Shevu'ot* (39a): 'I only know the commandments commanded on Mount Sinai, whence [do I know] those that will be invented, such as the Megillah reading [i.e., reading the book of Esther during the holiday of Purim]? The verse teaches, "They received and accepted" (Esth 9:27)—they accepted what they had already received.' That is, they will accept upon themselves any commandment that the prophets or sages institute in the future."[30] This Talmudic statement cited by Maimonides can be taken to mean that the institution of the reading of the Book of Esther during the holiday of Purim was related at Sinai, and after a long passage of time it became an obligation. As an opponent of the idea that a revealed norm can predate its historical relevance and applicability, Maimonides adds his own explanation of the Talmudic dictum: "That is, they will accept upon themselves any commandment that the prophets or sages institute in the future." At Sinai, the Jewish people accepted the obligation to read the biblical Book of Esther only as part of their general commitment to obey the future enactments of prophets and sages, like someone who signs a contract with details to be filled in at a later date. "Do not deviate" as a mediating norm thus anchors the authority of the Sages' halakhic activity in Sinai, and it also enables Maimonides to reinterpret Talmudic sources which claim that the halakhic revelation at Sinai went down to the very last detail.

The belief that the revelation at Sinai was all-encompassing, which Maimonides rejects, is only one expression of the tendency to bring all of normative life under the umbrella of revelation. Another expression of the same tendency, which is just as important in the history of halakhah and Jewish thought, is the assertion that revelation is an ongoing process initiated at Sinai.[31] After Moses, revelation continued through the prophets and thenceforth to the Sages, who, if they did not quite have prophecy, were privy to a heavenly voice that imbued halakhah with a touch of the divine. This, too, is implicit in Kayyara's enumeration, because he counts clothing the naked as an independent commandment based upon the verse from the prophet Isaiah "when you see the naked, clothe him" (Isa 58:7). Maimonides, who does not give Kayyara a free pass here, restricts the authority of prophets just as he did with the Sages. In his view, only Moses was granted the authority to legislate through prophecy. Prophets who succeeded Moses were to preserve the Mosaic Torah, they were not to create a new Torah or add to the existing one.

In the introduction to his Commentary on the Mishnah, Maimonides establishes that a prophet who has the audacity to legislate, or even to decide in favor of one side in a rabbinic dispute, in the name of prophecy proves himself to be a false prophet and is liable for death by strangulation.[32] Not only that, but as with the Sages, so with the prophets—prophetic status is established through a mediating, second-order norm that is part of the Mosaic revelation. In the Mishneh Torah, Maimonides claims that a prophet does not obligate his intended audience through the direct force of his revelation, even if it is determined to be truthful on the basis of the process outlined in the Torah (Deut 18:18–22). The obligation to obey the words of a prophet flows from the Biblical command to heed prophetic proclamations. Given that this is so, a prophet who wants to change or subvert the Mosaic Torah undercuts his own authority, which itself derives from the Torah of Moses.[33] Maimonides makes the line dividing law from prophecy especially sharp by arguing that there is no other source of revelation aside from the Mosaic Torah, to which all legitimate obligations must be traceable. Revelation is not an ongoing source of halakhic obligation; it began and ended at Sinai.

The assertion that rabbinic enactments have absolutely nothing to do with revelation and the giving of the Torah proves rather easier to substantiate than this assertion about the status of post-Mosaic prophecy. After all is said and done, for the former Maimonides relies on a sugya in the Babylonian Talmud (Shabbat 23a), which claims that the clause "and [God] commanded us" recited in the blessing over a ritual activity, such as kindling the Hanukkah lamp, can be sourced to "do not deviate." Maimonides also considers the obligation to read the Megillah as halakhically Rabbinic and so attacks Kayyara for including it in his enumeration of the commandments, yet it presents somewhat of a unique problem. The Megillah was composed through divine inspiration, so one could say that the holiday of Purim was established through revelation. Purim does not fit neatly into the absolute overlap Maimonides sets up between Biblical laws and revelation. He skillfully handles this challenge in Principle One:

It has already been explained that everything the prophets who came after Moses enacted is also Rabbinic. They explicitly said (*'Eruvin* 21b): "When Solomon instituted *'eruvin* and [washing the] hands, a heavenly voice went forth saying, 'My son, if your heart is wise my heart shall rejoice etc.' (Prov 23:15)." Elsewhere they explained that *'eruvin* are called Rabbinic and [washing the] hands are from the words of the Sages (*mi-divrei soferim*). It is therefore clear to you that every-thing enacted after Moses is called Rabbinic. I have explained this to you so that you do not think that since the Megillah reading is a pro-phetic enactment it is considered Biblical, because *'eruvin* are Rab-binic even though they are the enactment of Solomon b. David and his court.[34]

Maimonides exemplifies his sweeping statement that everything mentioned in the Prophets is Rabbinic through 'eruvin and hand-washing, which are at-tributed to King Solomon in the Talmud yet are considered halakhically Rab-binic. He thereby precludes any potential distinction between what tradition identifies as prophetic enactments, which are considered Rabbinic, and what is written in the Prophets, which was said through divine inspiration. Mai-monides wants the reader to conclude from these clear cases that whenever prophets legislate and make enactments, they do so in their capacity as Torah scholars. New normative content present in the Prophets—including Pu-rim—does not come from revelations of prophetic trances but from sober scholarly activity. Purim was instituted by Mordecai and his rabbinic court, the same way 'eruvin and hand-washing were instituted by Solomon and his rabbinic court.

In Principle One, Maimonides isolates Mosaic revelation from the rest of the halakhic system in two ways. First, he redefines "given at Sinai" narrowly, pushing rabbinic enactments out of the general revelation at Sinai. Second, he endows the revelation of Moses with exclusive legislative authority, a move that rejects the possibility of ongoing revelation about halakhah and makes the division between Moses and all other prophets absolute. The two foci of authority—scholars and prophets—ultimately derive their power from a second-order obligation found in the Mosaic Torah. The authority of scholars flows from the prohibition of "do not deviate," and the obligation to obey prophets is located in Deuteronomy 18. The normative content in the books of the Prophets and the enactments of the Sages are not part of the revelation at Sinai, but their binding force is absolutely rooted in that revelation. These two

NAHMANIDES'S PHILOSOPHY OF HALAKHAH   25

moves that Maimonides makes are part of his endeavor to unseat and reinterpret those rabbinic traditions that envision revelation as an all-encompassing normative event. But what Maimonides discarded decisively Nahmanides brought back to the fore with his impressive gloss on Principle One.

III

Nahmanides's gloss on Principle One exemplifies, to a tee, the general manner in which he handles the criticism that later authorities leveled at earlier ones.[35] Here, he elevates what Maimonides construed as Kayyara's negligence into a deliberate and sophisticated methodology. Reading through the gloss, one is persuaded that Maimonides treated Kayyara unjustifiably harshly and imperiously, even if one is not persuaded that Kayyara is correct in all things (Nahmanides himself does not agree with Kayyara on every point). As Nahmanides writes at the end of the gloss: "We have hereby vindicated the author of the Halakhot [Kayyara] from having made the gross errors which the Master [Maimonides][36] imputed to him."[37] One is also persuaded that Nahmanides, who knew the Talmudic tradition like the back of his hand, has provided us with an impressive and complex alternative set of answers to the fundamental questions Maimonides raised about the philosophy of halakhah.

To discern Nahmanides's main move in this long gloss, it is helpful to consider the way he arranges and responds to Maimonides's arguments. Nahmanides identifies four arguments Maimonides made against Kayyara. The first, which serves as the focal point for the important disagreement on the fundamental issues of the philosophy of halakhah, is tied to the meaning of the phrase "given to Moses at Sinai." The second and fourth arguments Maimonides arrayed fall under the category of the slippery slope argument. In the second argument, Maimonides challenges Kayyara as follows: If he includes Hanukkah and Purim in the count of 613 because on those days we recite a blessing that includes the expression "and [God] commanded us," then why does he not count 'eruvin and hand-washing, which also receive such a blessing? Maimonides's fourth argument is similar: If Kayyara does not distinguish Biblical from Rabbinic, why does he not enumerate all Rabbinic prohibitions, such as all those on the expanded list of rabbinically forbidden relations, which would raise the number of commandments into the thousands? (The third argument against Kayyara constitutes Maimonides's critique of counting the obligation to clothe the naked as an independent commandment, because it is so mentioned in the Prophets.)

Nahmanides deftly parries the slippery slope attacks. He claims that Kayyara did not count 'eruvin and washing the hands, which are Rabbinic enactments over which one recites a blessing, because they are not absolute obligations. If one wants to eat bread, one must wash one's hands; if one wants to move items from one's house to one's courtyard on the Sabbath, one must prepare an 'eruv. No independent obligation to wash one's hands or to prepare an 'eruv exists here, which is not the case with the obligation to kindle the Hanukkah lamp or read the Megillah. Kayyara did not omit 'eruvin and hand-washing because his approach was amateurish and unsystematic, but because he was making a learned distinction between various types of Rabbinic obligations.[38] As to why Kayyara did not count all Rabbinically prohibited sexual liaisons, Nahmanides resolves this by recruiting one of Maimonides's very own principles: aspects of a single commandment are not to be counted as their own separate commandment. The Rabbinically prohibited relations were prohibited by the Sages as a safeguard around the Biblically prohibited sexual liaisons. They therefore cannot be considered independent prohibitions since they are merely extensions of the forbidden relationships they are intended to prevent. Kayyara did not enumerate these prohibitions for the same reason that Maimonides did not count the white tzitzith and blue ones as independent commandments.[39] Nahmanides's solutions to the second and fourth arguments, which seemed poised to reduce Kayyara's enumeration to rubble, restore Kayyara's credibility in the face of the Maimonidean onslaught. But the chief difficulty—both theological and halakhic—is to be found in the first argument about the meaning of the phrase "given to Moses at Sinai."

Nahmanides's first responses to Kayyara's enumeration of commandments that do not appear to have been "given to Moses at Sinai" are local. Their rhetorical purpose is to weaken the gravity of Maimonides's charge, to soften the blows. First of all, says Nahmanides, the very phrase "given to Moses at Sinai" does not appear in the Talmudic manuscripts used by the Geonim.[40] Therefore, the Biblical category did not constrain the early enumerators of the commandments. Nahmanides supplements this with another argument: the Sages often claim that various commandments were stated in the Torah, even when the link to the Torah can be construed only as an *asmakhta* (an artificial retrojection onto the biblical text). The expression "given to Moses at Sinai" must be a flexible descriptor, one capable of encompassing Rabbinic enactments as well. In his third response, which is as local as the first two, Nahmanides argues that rabbinic formulations sometimes concern the majority rather than the entirety of something. Most of the 613 commandments were "given to Moses at Sinai," not all. If Kayyara added commandments that were not given at Sinai, he stayed within the usual bounds of generality that marked the phraseology of the Sages.[41]

So far we have seen Nahmanides's narrower responses. As the gloss continues, he takes a fundamental position against Maimonides, although it is interrupted by a lengthy digression that begins as follows: "Since we are on this matter, we are led to speak about how the Master has perplexed us." This excursus, which comprises most of the gloss,[42] criticizes Maimonides's understanding of the prohibition of "do not deviate." It plays a central role in the debate between Maimonides and Nahmanides, and I will return to it shortly. At the end of the excursus Nahmanides sets out his central argument, which gainsays Maimonides's main assertion that the distinction between Biblical and Rabbinic delimits revelation:

> The incredulity displayed by the Master that "Moses charged us with the *Torah* [numerologically 611]" (Deut 33:4) could allude to the Megillah and Hanukkah lamp is not significant. For they [the Sages] have already expounded (*Megillah* 7a): " 'write this as a remembrance in the book' (Exod 17:14): 'write this'—what is written here and in Deuteronomy; 'as a remembrance'—what is written in the Prophets; 'in the book'—what is written in the Megillah." Because the Torah explains, commands, informs, and alludes. It has already alluded to our exile through numerology, as they have said (*Gittin* 88a) that the Holy One did a kindness with the Jewish people by moving up [the exile] two years before *ve-noshantem* (Deut 4:25) [numerologically 852]. They likewise said in the first chapter of *Berakhot* (5a): "What is [the meaning of] the verse, 'and I shall give you the tablets of stone, and the Torah, and the commandment, which I have written to instruct them' (Exod 24:12)? 'tablets of stone'—this is Scripture; 'the Torah'—this is the *Mishnah;* 'the commandment'—as it sounds; 'which I have written'—these are the Prophets and Writings; 'to instruct them'—this is the Talmud. This teaches that all of them were given to Moses at Sinai." In the Jerusalem Talmud in tractate *Megillah* (1.5, 70d): "Rav, R. Hanina, R. Natan b. Kappara, and R. Yehoshua b. Levi were sitting and saying that this Megillah was said to Moses at Sinai, only there is no chronological order to the Torah."[43]

The stratum of the Torah that bears normative import is not exhaustively expressed through the Torah's explicit directives. As Nahmanides says, the

Torah "explains, commands, informs, and alludes," which includes whatever a bright student might come up with at some future date.

Maimonides's firm determination that only commandments considered halakhically Biblical were given at Sinai collapses under the weight of Nahmanides's collection of Talmudic sources, which all seek to subsume the entire normative, sacred, and epoch-spanning content of Judaism under the revelation at Sinai. Nahmanides goes to the trouble of including at least one source that demonstrates specifically how revelation is not shackled by time. According to this midrash, the numerological import of the word *ve-noshantem* indicates when the final exile began. This shows that Maimonides was overconfident when he said, "I do not believe anyone could imagine or entertain the notion . . ."[44] The infinite revelation shows no regard for the constraints of time; outdoing even Janus, it simultaneously faces the past, the future, and the present.[45]

In line with his conception of revelation as an event that encompasses all the sacred elements of Jewish tradition, in the final portion of the gloss Nahmanides criticizes Maimonides's position, which excluded prophetic enactments from the list of things transmitted to Moses at Sinai. Nahmanides agrees that Solomon's institutions of 'eruvin and hand-washing are indeed Rabbinic, and with his exceptional erudition he even cites additional enactments traditionally ascribed to various prophets. He parts ways with Maimonides in arguing that anything written explicitly in the Prophets is considered Biblical:

> But what is written through prophecy imperatively, such as exhortation about a positive commandment or caution regarding a negative one, is Biblical (*devar Torah*). The reason is that since we have been warned in the Torah "These are the commandments" (Lev 27:34), which teaches that "henceforth a prophet may not innovate anything" (*Megillah* 2b), we know that the product of prophecy is Biblical or is the explanation of a biblical verse, which they possessed as a law given to Moses at Sinai.[46]

Moreover, Nahmanides brings various proofs from the Talmud that verses in the Prophets are entitled to the same exegetical treatment as those in the Pentateuch. He unequivocally argues that Rabbinic enactments were given at Sinai and at the same time grants Biblical standing to the words of the Prophets, which flies in the face of Maimonides's rule that anything written in the Prophets is Rabbinic, the product of scholars who also happened to be prophets.[47]

IV

Maimonides and Nahmanides present two different perspectives on the relationship between halakhah and revelation. The first posits that there is a unique, immutable kernel of halakhah that was expressly revealed to Moses at Sinai, which must be distinguished from the rest of the ramified corpus of halakhah. The second subsumes everything with halakhic valence under revelation. This difference between Maimonides and Nahmanides arises repeatedly throughout the latter's glosses on the Principles, and it seems to have far-reaching consequences for their notions of revelation and interpretation.

Maimonides, who severs any direct connection between revelation and the Rabbinic stratum of halakhah, justifies rabbinic authority through the explicit Torah obligation to listen to the Sages. This view forces Maimonides to cram into "do not deviate" all of the halakhic output of Torah scholars— exegesis, enactments, legislation, all of it. Without such an inclusionary definition, all things Rabbinic could lay no claim to the authority of revelation. In his lengthy excursus in the very first gloss, Nahmanides lays siege to this quite broad definition of "do not deviate": "See how the Master builds a high wall around the words of the Sages, but it is 'as if reduced to rubble, a breach in a towering wall whose crash comes suddenly, in a flash' (Isa 30:13)."[48] According to Nahmanides, if Rabbinic enactments were to draw their authority from "do not deviate," then anyone failing to comply with a Rabbinic obligation would, in fact, be in violation of a Biblical one: "It would be appropriate, according to this opinion, to be very stringent about the words of the Sages (*divrei soferim*), for they are all Torah; there is no distinction between them."[49] Since Maimonides ensures that the connection between enactments of Torah scholars and revelation can occur only through a second-order biblical prohibition, he closes the legal gap between Biblical and Rabbinic. Similarly, his expansive rendering of "do not deviate" means that the law of the "rebellious elder" and member of the court who refuses to follow the court's decision should apply to Rabbinic enactments and decrees as well,[50] and Nahmanides tries to prove that this is not so, that it applies only to disagreement with the Sages' interpretations of the Torah and not with their enactments. This contrary position of Nahmanides anchors the authority of the Sages in the prohibition of "do not deviate" only with respect to how they exegete the biblical verses, and not to the enactments they make:

> In any case, the Master's Principles are erroneous. But what is clear and free from any error is that this prohibition of "do not deviate" only

applies to what they said in their interpretations of the Torah, such as those matters derived from the Torah through a *gezeirah shavah* (verbal congruity), *binyan av* (general rule), or any of the rest of the thirteen *middot* by which the Torah is expounded, or through the contextual meaning of the verse itself, and also what they received as a law to Moses from Sinai, the Oral Torah. That is, if they deem something prohibited or permitted according to the Torah based on exegesis of Scripture, its interpretation, or an oral law transmitted from our master Moses, and he [the rebellious elder] deems it contrariwise, he must nullify his own opinion and believe in what they have said.[51]

When the Talmud sources a Rabbinic enactment to "do not deviate," Nahmanides construes it as an *asmakhta*: "But their words about this prohibition are merely a [scriptural] support to strengthen [it]; it should not be [inferred] from them that this prohibition has any Biblical weight."[52]

Nahmanides's disagreement with Maimonides about the extent of "do not deviate" is not disconnected from their more basic disagreement about the nature of revelation and its relationship to Rabbinic enactments. Maimonides puts "do not deviate" to work as a second-order rule mediating between the entire corpus of Rabbinic laws and revelation. Nahmanides reads "do not deviate" narrowly and so in effect burns the bridge Maimonides erected between Rabbinic enactments and the revelation at Sinai. According to Nahmanides, the revealed norm of "do not deviate" lends its authority to the Sages only so that they may interpret the Torah as they understand it. If Nahmanides is correct, and in fact "do not deviate" in Talmudic literature has no connection to the legislation of the Sages, then Maimonides would be left with a host of Rabbinic norms that have no link to revelation. Nahmanides does not find this troubling because he believes the content of Rabbinic enactments to be latent within revelation itself. He sees no need for a second-order rule to mediate between Rabbinic laws and revelation. The link between the scope of "do not deviate" and the relationship between Rabbinic laws and revelation is described by Nahmanides as follows:

> I am perplexed by the Master. He has made up his mind, unshakably glued to the idea that one who transgresses the words of the Sages, whether they are enactments or innovated commandments, transgresses a positive and negative Biblical commandment, for we have been commanded by Moses, from the mouth of the Almighty, to accept every commandment that they establish and perform it because

of "do not deviate." Why, then, does he find it oppressive that the author of the *Halakhot* [Kayyara] included the commandments of Hanukkah and the Megillah in what was "said to Moses at Sinai"? Although we opine that they have nothing to do with this prohibition, still it is the custom of the Sages to use this kind of language, because they were authorized by God, based on tradition, to enact and establish, and they expound many allusions and numerologies for this purpose [. . .] Because the Torah explains, commands, informs and alludes.[53]

This broad and all-inclusive conception of revelation allows Nahmanides to tie the Sages' enactments to Sinai, even as he construes "do not deviate" narrowly.

Nahmanides, as we have seen, reads "do not deviate" as applying only to the Sages' exegesis of the Torah. Consequently, he explains in a unique and striking manner that "do not deviate" is what grants the Sages exclusive authority to interpret the Torah:

> For the Torah was given to us by Moses in writing, and it is obvious that not everyone will be of one mind about unforeseen matters. God ruled that we should listen to whatever the high court says, whether they have received an interpretation about it or say it based on the contextual meaning of the Torah and what they believe to be its intent, because it is in accordance with their understanding that God commands and gives us the Torah. This is [the meaning of] their saying that even if they say that left is right and right is left, for that is the command enjoined upon us by the Lord of the Torah, so that no disputant will say: "How can I permit this to myself when I know with certainty that they are wrong?" In fact, he has been told, "so are you commanded."[54]

The Sages do not expose the meaning of revelation, they constitute it: "because it is in accordance with their understanding that God commands and gives us the Torah." Later, Nahmanides repeats this constitutive notion of interpretation: "because it ['do not deviate'] obligates us to believe in the Torah according to the interpretation that they impart to it."[55] The Torah, in this imagining, has no meaning independent of that which the Sages impart to it. The rabbinical high court is thereby protected from any possibility of error, for the claim that the court has erroneously interpreted the Torah is

predicated upon the Torah having an independent meaning beyond the alleg-
edly erroneous one the Sages have given it. But in Nahmanides's line of thinking, "do not deviate" places the meaning of the revealed Torah in the hands
of future Torah scholars, so one cannot possibly attribute any error to them.
One must obey the court even if it declares right to be left and left to be
right, because the normative aspect of these categories depends upon the determination of the court. Nahmanides's approach to interpretation should be
termed "the constitutive approach."

The constitutive approach, which seems to disallow the attribution of
error to the rabbinical high court, stands in contradiction to the first mishnah
in Horayot. The mishnah rules that a member of the court or a disciple worthy of giving public instruction who holds the court to be in error on a ruling,
yet obeys and follows the court's ruling, must bring a sin-offering. In other
words, the court member and erudite disciple must follow their own judgment if they believe the court to be in error. Nahmanides deals with the
difficulty posed by the mishnah by qualifying it:

> There is a qualification about this, as anyone who carefully considers
> the first [mishnah] in *Horayot* will comprehend. Namely, if in the time
> of the Sanhedrin the high court rules permissively about a matter, and
> a scholar worthy of giving instruction believes that they have erred in
> their ruling, then he has no obligation to listen to the words of the
> Sages, and he may not allow himself what is prohibited. Rather, he
> should act stringently for himself [. . .] He has an obligation to appear
> before them and make his arguments so that they may discuss it with
> him, and if the majority agree to reject the opinion he has voiced and
> dismantle his arguments, he should act in accord with their opinion
> after they dismiss him and come to a consensus about his argument.
> That is what emerges from those laws. In any case, he must accept
> their opinion after they come to a consensus no matter what.[56]

In Nahmanides's eyes, as long as the Torah scholar has not made his case in
front of the court, the court's ruling is no ruling, and at that stage he can indeed attribute error to the court. Once the court has heard him out and ruled
against him, however, he is obligated to obey their ruling.

Nahmanides suppresses the potential of this mishnah in Horayot. The
mishnah on its simple reading does not distinguish between the various stages
of adjudication and requires the scholar to follow his own opinion always. An
unencumbered reading of the mishnah dictates that the court does not have

exclusive rights over the interpretation of Scripture; the Torah does have an independent meaning that a Torah scholar must follow when he finds himself at odds with the court's interpretation. Nahmanides, however, restricts the mishnah, taking the edge off of it, because his constitutive conception of exegesis does not allow a scholar to attribute meaning to the text other than the meaning of the court.[57]

This locution of Nahmanides, "because it is in accordance with their understanding that God commands and gives us the Torah," became the subject of various interpretations by his successors, as we will see below.[58] In his Commentary on the Torah, Nahmanides himself offered another reason for the infallibility of the rabbinical court, which will also shortly be addressed. In any event, the constitutive approach Nahmanides developed in the context of his explanation of "do not deviate" conflicts with Maimonides's approach to interpretation, which he developed in Principle Two, and which Nahmanides criticized in his accompanying gloss.

V

In Principle Two, Maimonides states: "not everything extrapolated through one of the thirteen middot (rules of interpretation) by which the Torah is expounded or through ribbui (amplification) ought to be counted."[59] This Principle continues the project begun in Principle One of isolating that exclusive and immutable kernel of Mosaic revelation from the rest of the halakhic system. In Principle Two, though, Maimonides takes it to the next level, in terms of both conceptual boldness and attitude toward Talmudic literature. Here, he attempts not only to distance rabbinic enactments and prophetic utterances from the Mosaic revelation, but to drive a wedge between the Torah per se and the Sages' interpretation of it. Maimonides claims that anything derived from the Torah through the thirteen middot (the thirteen rules of interpretation) should not be counted as part of the 613, because, in his view, laws so arrived at do not have the status of a commandment "said to Moses at Sinai," and laws without such status are not to be included in the enumeration. The halakhic status of such a law—notwithstanding its derivation via the interpretation of the Torah—can only be Rabbinic.[60] Biblical status belongs only to those interpretations received by Moses, not those laws produced by the Sages, even by way of the thirteen middot. For Maimonides, the division between the interpretations transmitted by Moses from Sinai and those produced by the Sages originates with the Sages themselves. When the Sages stated explicitly that an interpretation is "explicitly stated in the Torah"[61] or is Biblical, they, as tradents, were attesting to the law's standing, which is a sign that they had received it from Moses. Wherever they did not make an explicit attestation, therefore, the law's standing can be only Rabbinic:

> Since this is the case, not everything that we find that the Sages extrapolated by one of the thirteen *middot* can be said to have been "said to Moses at Sinai," nor can we call Rabbinic everything in the Talmud for which they brought a prooftext through one of the thirteen *middot,* because it may be a received interpretation. The rule is this: Anything which you do not find explicitly in the Torah, and you find that the Talmud derives it through one of the thirteen *middot,* if they themselves explained and said that it is a principle of the Torah or that it is Biblical, it is proper to count it, for the tradents of the Oral Torah said it is Biblical. But if they do not clarify this and say so explicitly, it is Rabbinic.[62]

The presumption is that everything derived by means of the thirteen middot is Rabbinic, unless the Sages clarified that it is "a principle of the Torah" or Biblical. A reference of this sort, according to Maimonides, can be taken as an attestation that the interpretation at hand was received by Moses at Sinai.

Beyond the legal distinction between these two types of laws, those received and those generated through interpretation, Maimonides distinguishes them in another manner in the introduction to his Mishnah commentary, as discussed above.[63] The received interpretations have never been subject to debate; controversy has surrounded only those laws derived through the thirteen middot. But the fact that there is no controversy on record about a particular exegesis does not transmute it from Rabbinic to Biblical, because such a change requires an accompanying certification of pedigree. The absence of controversy may not be a sufficient condition for an interpretation to be considered a tradition transmitted by Moses, but it is a necessary condition. One can conclude from Principle Two that in order for a commandment to be counted in the enumeration and to be considered a Biblical obligation, it must be a tradition "said to Moses at Sinai" and must not have become the subject of debate. Any interpretation that has no attestation in the tradition is Rabbinic.

A closer look at the halakhic structure carefully engineered by Maimonides reveals that he attempts to excavate a vein of undisputed, received laws that runs through the mother lode of Talmudic exegesis and interpretation. His line of reasoning dictates that only these laws have Biblical standing and only they were given to Moses at Sinai. Maimonides's efforts to piece together this kernel of halakhah imposes a new division upon the Talmudic corpus—received interpretations on one side and unreceived ones on the other. The distinction between genuine interpretations and *asmakhta'ot* does exist already in the Talmud. In various Talmudic passages, exegesis of a scriptural verse is offered as support and a source of authority for a rabbinic enactment or decree, although the interpretation of the verse is not taken to mean that the law is Biblical. But the distinction between received and unreceived, and the accompanying claim that this distinction determines Biblical standing, is not to be found in the Talmud. The Talmud classifies a law derived from the thirteen *middot* as Biblical even if it was not received at Sinai, and if it is not classified as Biblical, it must be an *asmakhta* and not a genuine interpretation.[64]

On top of the misalignment between Maimonides's bifurcation of laws into received and unreceived and the Talmud's own manner of distinguishing the Rabbinic from the Biblical, another difficulty arises. Maimonides's second criterion requires received interpretations to be free from debate, but is it true that there have never been debates about interpretations that Maimonides considers received? Talmudic disputes do surround, for example, the pecuniary interpretation of "an eye for an eye" and the betrothed maiden who fornicated while still in her father's household.[65] These problems attracted Nahmanides's critical eye to Principle Two, and his condemnation is particularly unforgiving. At the end of his long gloss on this Principle he writes: "I know of many statements in the Talmud that contradict the words of the Master. This work of the Master [Sefer ha-Mitzvot] is sweet and delightful aside from this Principle which uproots great mountains of Talmud and fells Talmudic ramparts. / For those who learn the Talmud it is vile and bitter, / let the matter sink into oblivion and never be uttered."[66] In contrast to Maimonides, Nahmanides thinks laws derived from the Torah through the thirteen *middot* have Biblical standing in Talmudic literature, a point he returns to over and over again: "But we have not found this to be the opinion of the Sages, for they consider all of the *middot* as something explicit in the Torah, and they expound them as they see fit."[67] And again: "These *middot* are like an explicit statement of the Torah."[68] Nahmanides buttresses this equation with many Talmudic proofs, and he also points out the internal contradictions in which Maimonides becomes entangled as a result of the gulf separating the rule set forth in Principle Two and his various rulings based upon rabbinic sources. The stream of proofs marshaled by Nahmanides leads him to reverse Maimonides's presumption: "According to this, we should say the opposite, that everything expounded in the Talmud through one of the thirteen *middot* is Biblical, unless we hear them say that it is an *asmakhta*."[69]

In addition to the lack of correspondence between Maimonides's position and the Talmudic sources, Nahmanides raises an additional conceptual problem within Maimonides's conception of interpretation:

> "It is beyond my ken, so lofty that I cannot grasp it" (Ps 139:6), for if we say that the expository *middot* were not received at Sinai, we would not be commanded to expound and explicate the Torah through them. If so, they are not veracious and the truth is the simple meaning of the verse (*peshateih di-kera*) and not the exposition, like the saying of theirs that he [Maimonides] mentioned: "A verse does not leave the realm of its *peshat* [philological-contextual meaning]" (*Shabbat* 63a). We would be uprooting the root of our tradition—the thirteen *middot* by which the Torah is expounded, and the majority of the Talmud that is predicated upon them. Then, the Master concedes that the reason is not that they lack veracity. But if they are veracious, then what difference does it make when they mention this [i.e., that the law is Biblical] explicitly and when they don't? For if we say that since the matter is not written in the Torah it is not included in the commandments, [then] even those [matters] said to be Biblical in the Talmud are [derived] from a *gezeirah shavah* (verbal congruity) or *ribbui* (amplification), which also are not written [in the Torah]![70]

Nahmanides formulates in this passage a deep conceptual problem. On one hand, if Maimonides considers the Sages' interpretations as having no real substance, making them not Biblical but Rabbinic, he risks undermining the entire authority of halakhah. On the other hand, if the interpretations are genuine and veracious, why deny them Biblical status? Maimonides himself claims, as Nahmanides duly notes, that he does not base his position on the fact that Rabbinic exegeses are unfounded and merely *asmakhta'ot*: "Perhaps you will think that we refrain from counting them because they are not clear[ly true], such that the law derived from a *middah* is perhaps correct or incorrect—this is not the reason."[71] If this is Maimonides's position, from a conceptual standpoint one must ask the following: How can an interpretation of a text be considered correct but not have the legal status of the text itself? Similarly, the glosses of Nahmanides floodlight the great chasm dividing the Maimonidean position from the Talmudic corpus. Maimonides is well aware of these problems and the internal contradictions formed by the pressure of Principle Two. Why, then, does he regard it as crucial to his approach? Put differently, why does he construct a theory of halakhah in which a sizable part of halakhah does not fit into its categories? Moreover, what hermeneutical theory does Maimonides propose in order to extricate himself from the conceptual conundrum raised by Nahmanides?

VI

The metaphor Maimonides chose to describe the interpretations via the middot, and which serves as the key to his hermeneutics, appears in Principle Two. The derivations are "branches from the roots that were said explicitly to Moses at Sinai, which are the 613 commandments."[72] An analysis of this metaphor will show how it relieves Maimonides of the conceptual difficulty noted above. In order to clarify the aptness of the arborescent metaphor for describing the relationship between text and interpretation, it is helpful to distinguish between two kinds of interpretation. The first aims to clarify or decode the meaning of words in the text, and its guiding principles concern definition and decoding. The second does not clarify the text but draws additional conclusions from it, and its guiding principles are closer to rules of inference (not in the strict logical sense).

Let us consider the following known example. Suppose a statute states that "vehicles may not enter a public park." Someone trying to interpret the statute faces the following problem: What is the scope of "vehicle"? Does it include even bicycles, or perhaps scooters, or only motorcycles, and so on and so forth? Someone trying to argue that the statute forbids entry to scooters is engaged in clarifying the terminology of the law, that is, "vehicle." A different kind of legal interpretation occurs when the interpreter infers another law from the first: "vehicles may not enter a schoolyard." In this instance, it is obvious that "public park" cannot include a schoolyard, so the interpreter is not engaged in determining the scope of "public park"; rather, she or he is trying to derive an additional prohibition from the statute through analogical reasoning or an a fortiori argument—if the legislator prohibited vehicles from entering the public park out of concern for the safety of children, then surely their entry into a schoolyard should be prohibited. This interpreter employs specific rules for inferring additional prohibitions from existing ones. She or he does not try to clarify the statute's terminology and its semantic scope, only whether additional prohibitions can be inferred from the statute.

Returning to our topic, rules of interpretation can have two different purposes, similar to the two kinds of interpretation observed in the example above. There are rules of decoding or definition and rules of inference. Maimonides maintains that the thirteen middot are rules for inferring additional laws from those said to Moses at Sinai. The laws given to Moses are unambiguous, whether on a regular reading or through explanations transmitted through tradition. Using the thirteen middot does not clarify these revealed laws or explain their terminology; instead, it derives new laws from these "premises." A good example of this kind of interpretation is the prohibition on sexual intercourse with one's daughter. As Maimonides writes, the Torah never says, "You shall not uncover the nakedness of your daughter." An a fortiori argument or *gezeirah shavah* teaches us this prohibition. In his Sefer ha-Mitzvot, Maimonides explains the derivation:

> It [Scripture] said about your son's daughter and your daughter's daughter "they are your nakedness" (Lev 18:10), and it said regarding the prohibition of a woman and her daughter, her son's daughter, and her daughter's daughter "they are kindred, it is depravity" (Lev 18:17). In the same way that in the prohibition of a woman and her son's daughter or her daughter's daughter her [own] daughter is prohibited, so too in the prohibition of his son's daughter or daughter's daughter his [own] daughter is also prohibited.[73]

Maimonides cites a *gezeirah shavah* between the two laws ("they are" [*hennah*]): in the same way that a man may not have sexual relations with a woman and her daughter, or with a woman and her granddaughter (her son or daughter's daughter), so too the Torah's prohibition against relations between a man and his own granddaughter (his son or daughter's daughter) includes a prohibition on his own daughter. Such a prohibition, Maimonides continues, should be Rabbinic since it is derived via the thirteen middot, and it is considered Biblical only because it has been transmitted as such.[74] This example demonstrates how the thirteen middot function as rules for inferring new laws from the one revealed to Moses at Sinai. These interpretations do not clarify the premises that yield the conclusion, for these "roots" are plain as day and uncontested. Interpretation consists of making inferences from these "roots," using the received rules of inference—the thirteen middot—to produce "branches."

The conception of interpretation as a kind of inference appears as a leitmotif whenever Maimonides speaks of an exegesis derived through the thirteen middot. When he describes what the thirteen middot do, he always uses the Arabic verb that denotes extrapolation (*istikhrāj*) instead of verbs that denote exegesis, interpretation, or clarification. In the introduction to his Commentary on the Mishnah, for example, Maimonides refers to "the laws extrapolated (*al-mustakhrajah*) by means of *qiyās*"[75] and "the matters which you see us extrapolate (*nastakhrijuhā*) through a generalization followed by a specification and likewise through the rest of the thirteen *middot*,"[76] and he does the same in many other places.[77] Furthermore, throughout the introduction to his Commentary on the Mishnah he likens the commandments given to Moses, the uncontested Biblical kernel, to "roots" (Arabic *al-'uṣūl*) and the extrapolations made by an interpreter to "branches" (Arabic *al-furū'*).[78] The botanical imagery of roots and branches, combined with the verb denoting extrapolation, furnishes us with a picture of interpretation through the thirteen middot as a process of deriving new laws from existing ones through rules of inference, which in this case are the thirteen middot.

Maimonides characterizes the thirteen middot as rules of inference in his Mishneh Torah when he details the obligation to spend a third of one's day studying Talmud, which he explains as follows: "a third [of the day] one should spend in thought, deducing conclusions from premises, extrapolating one thing from another, comparing one thing to another, contemplating the *middot* by which the Torah is expounded until one knows the essence of the *middot* and how to extrapolate what is prohibited, permitted, etc. from those matters learned through tradition. This is called *talmud*."[79] The thirteen middot constitute the means by which one can extrapolate what is forbidden and permitted from the preexisting revealed material that is transmitted orally. Maimonides has a *terminus technicus* for these thirteen middot, which appears in the introduction to his Commentary on the Mishnah:

> But the branches not heard from the prophet [Moses] were subject to discussion, the laws being extrapolated (*tustakhraju*) through *qiyās*, with the thirteen rules given to him at Sinai, which are "the thirteen *middot* by which the Torah is interpreted." And among those extrapolated (*al-mustakhrajāt*) [laws were] matters that disagreement did not occur in them, but rather there was consensus about them; but in some of them there was disagreement between the two syllogisms [. . .] for this typically occurs with the dialectic syllogisms (*al-maqāyīs al-jadaliyya*).[80]

In Maimonides's brief outline of the role of the thirteen middot, he uses his usual imagery and the triliteral Arabic root *kh-r-j* to denote "extrapolation." The novelty here is his use of the Arabic technical term *al-qiyās al-jadalī*, "the dialectic syllogism," to describe the thirteen middot.[81] A syllogism is deductive, and the thirteen middot are rules of deduction. Thus, Maimonides not only uses the same imagery of interpretation, but even employs the technical term of *qiyās* to define the thirteen middot as rules of inference.

It is also noteworthy that the term *qiyās* has a long history in Islamic jurisprudence. In that field, *qiyās* refers to an analogy that allows someone to extend the existing corpus of tradition in order to find solutions to new questions. In this role, it does not reveal the meaning of the received tradition, but extends it. Maimonides refers to the thirteen middot as "dialectic syllogisms," a clearly technical term for an extension of a corpus with the aid of analogy in Islamic legal tradition.[82] By employing this concept with its special meaning Maimonides reinforces the impression that the thirteen middot are rules of inference and not rules of decoding.

The notion of interpretation as inference rather than decoding facilitates surmounting the conceptual hurdle raised above: How can a correct interpretation, arrived at through proper interpretive methods, be considered correct yet not part of the text? The imagery of branches and roots quite effectively puts distance between text and interpretation. If interpretation were to define the roots, and rules of interpretation were to establish how to discover their meaning, it would indeed be difficult to argue that this interpretation is somehow distinct from the text itself. If interpretation explains the terminology of the text, what would the text be without the interpretation?[83] Returning to the statute example, it would prove difficult to argue that the interpretation of "vehicle" as "scooter" is correct yet is not part of the text. In contrast, with an additional prohibition like "vehicles may not enter a schoolyard," which we have argued is not a clarification of "public park" but the deduction of an additional rule, this prohibition is correct but not part of the text. Maimonides's conception of interpretation as inference preserves the distance between text and interpretation without undermining the reliability of the interpretation.

This account of interpretation reveals Maimonides's conception of halakhah, which could not be more in conflict with Nahmanides's hermeneutic theory. Maimonides believes in an uncontested kernel of meaning that has exclusive status, a status that flows from its direct connection to Moses. From this kernel, halakhah is extended by scholarly interpretation, but the interpretation is distinct from the kernel since it does not define it. Interpreters do not alter the terms of the premises in any way; they use these preexisting building blocks to derive new laws. Disagreement emerges while scholars are engaged in such interpretative inferences, and it is at this juncture that controversy enters halakhah. The kernel, however, stays above the fray and is unaffected by these disagreements.[84] Because these interpretations do not define the premises, they do not constitute part of the text; rather, they grow out of it like branches from roots. This preserves the nonpareil status of Moses within the theory: only Moses's words possess unique Biblical standing in the eyes of the law, and it is on those uncontroversial words that the entire sprawling edifice of halakhah is built. What makes Maimonides's hermeneutical theory particularly interesting is that interpretation usually involves the interpreter's attempt to acquire some of the text's authoritativeness—he or she dares to speak on behalf of the text, investing himself or herself with its authority.[85] According to Maimonides, however, no one partakes of Moses's authority, even in the process of interpreting the Mosaic text. The comparison of interpretation to outgrowth distances the authority of an interpreter's extrapolations from that of the roots themselves. The words of Moses are Biblical; the additional laws derived from them are Rabbinic.

VII

Nahmanides, in diametric opposition to Maimonides, describes the act of interpretation as affecting the kernel itself. In the citation above, "it is in accordance with their understanding that God commands and gives us the Torah,"[86] Nahmanides expresses his belief that the interpreter not only clarifies the words of the text but also retroactively constitutes their meaning. Rules of interpretation are not only rules of clarification, but rules that establish meaning. As Nahmanides puts it, interpretations are "the Torah itself," because the text is understood only through the interpreter. These opposing perspectives on midrashic interpretation of Scripture—interpretation as deduction versus interpretation as creation of meaning—arise from the conflict between Maimonides and Nahmanides about the meaning of the rabbinic statement that "a verse does not leave the realm of its *peshat* (its plain straightforward meaning)" (henceforth the "peshat rule"). Maimonides brings it as proof that those laws derived via the thirteen middot or *ribbui* should not be counted in the enumeration of commandments. Such laws were not given to Moses at Sinai and are exegetical additions to the Sinaitic tradition:

Ignorance has already led them [previous authors] into even graver [error], namely, if they found a *derash* [midrashic derivation] of some verse that requires doing or refraining from certain things, all of which are undoubtedly Rabbinic, they enumerate them in the total [number of] commandments, even though the *peshat* of the verse (*peshateih di-kera*) does not indicate any of those things. This is despite the principle that they [the Sages] taught us when they said, "a verse does not leave the realm of its *peshat*," and whenever we find a verse from which many matters have been derived through clarification and inference, the Talmud inquires, "of what does the verse itself (*gufeih di-kera*) speak?"[87]

Maimonides understands the peshat rule to mean that the peshat layer of the text exhausts what is written in the text. Interpretational inferences that go beyond the straightforward sense of the text are additions to the text and therefore Rabbinic. Nahmanides has a sharp retort to this reading of the peshat rule, in which he accuses Maimonides of taking this rule out of the realm of its peshat:

The Master has suspended this fallen mountain on a strand of hair. He said: ". . . the principle that they imparted to us when they said, 'a verse does not leave the realm of its *peshat*,' and since the text of the Talmud inquires everywhere and says, 'of what does the verse itself speak?' " God forbid! None of the *midrashim* about the commandments take a verse out of the realm of its [Scripture's] *peshat*. Rather, all of them are included in the text (*lashon*) of Scripture, even though they may be included through amplifications. The *midrash* about honoring Torah scholars from the phraseology "The Lord your God shall you fear" (Deut 10:20) does not remove the verse from its *peshat*. Similarly, if we say that "When a man takes a wife" (Deut 24:1) [it] is through money it does not remove it from its sense and *peshat*, nor does any *et, gam*, amplification, limitation, *akh, rak*, and all the rest of the midrashic cues. Indeed, Scripture encompasses everything; *peshat* is neither what those unschooled in grammar nor what the Sadducees say, because the book of the Lord's Torah is perfect, it has no superfluous or missing letter—they [the letters] were all written with wisdom.[88]

In the first part of the paragraph, Nahmanides does not use "peshat" in the sense of the immediate, conventional meaning of the text but in the broader sense of the written text itself and everything that it contains. Extrapolations and amplifications are not additions to the text but part of its essence. It is in this sense, he argues, that the midrashim do not remove the verse from its peshat. The text of the Torah contains many layers of meaning that go far beyond the straightforward sense of Scripture. The Torah has semantic plenitude such that every so-called defective or plene spelling is intended, every crown coronating a letter was tied on by God to convey meaning.

Moreover, the peshat rule does not establish that peshat exhausts what is written in Scripture. In fact, the contrary is true. According to Nahmanides, the rule should be understood as follows: although Scripture includes midrash in its text, it is worthwhile to preserve the peshat as something distinct from midrash.[89] In the continuation of the gloss, Nahmanides accuses Maimonides of mangling the straightforward sense of the Talmudic peshat rule. In Shabbat 63a, for example, the Talmud considers weapons to be adornments, making it permissible to traverse public and private domains on the Sabbath while bearing arms. The sugya advances the following verse as proof: "Gird your sword upon your thigh, hero, your glory and your splendor" (Ps 45:4). Since the verse makes it sound as if the sword is the glory and splendor, it is considered an adornment. R. Kahana questions the probative value of this verse by arguing that notwithstanding its simple meaning, the verse has nothing to do with weaponry, since the midrash, in typical fashion, allegorizes words of Torah and the Torah scholar as a sword and hero. Mar b. Ravina responds to R. Kahana: "a verse does not leave the realm of its peshat." Nahmanides explains this exchange:

> They wish to convey here that if arms were a disgrace to the hero, it would not have used them as a parable for words of Torah. Instead, they are an adornment for him, so the verse used them for its parable, saying that he should have words of Torah and wisdom in hand, like the sword on the hero's thigh, girded and accessible to him whenever he wishes to unsheathe it and use it to overpower his fellow—this is his glory and splendor. This is the idea wherever they expound a midrashic parable or allegory; they believe that both the internal and external are true.[90]

According to Nahmanides, Mar b. Ravina does not reject the allegorical reading of the verse; he simply argues that one also should preserve its simple sense. Interpreting the peshat rule in this way suits an allegorical reading quite nicely, so Nahmanides makes sophisticated use of it. A parable must retain its peshat level of meaning, for without basic agreement on the contents of the parable, one cannot properly convey its moral. The existence of the moral does not empty the parable of its content, for the very ability of the parable to signify the moral depends upon preservation of the parable's contents. In the example before us from tractate Shabbat, the straightforward sense of the text that considers a weapon an adornment must be preserved; otherwise, the verse cannot be applied to words of Torah. Nahmanides expands this idea of preserving the internal and external meanings—the parable and its moral—to all midrashic expositions of Scripture. In Nahmanides's view, the peshat rule does not, as Maimonides would have it, demote midrash and promote peshat. It asserts that midrash has the standing of Scripture itself, while simultaneously cautioning that it does not have exclusive rights to Scripture; the expositor must preserve the peshat. Nahmanides sums up his position in the following way: "That is their dictum, 'a verse does not leave the realm of its *peshat*,' but it has *midrash* alongside its *peshat*, and does not leave either one of them. The written text bears all of it, such that both are true."[91]

VIII

Maimonides and Nahmanides each offers his own epistemological account of controversy, even as they both agree that in a dispute there can be no error about what is Biblical. To explain this, we should avail ourselves of another model of interpretation. In this model, authorial intent defines the meaning, and the interpreter either discovers the meaning or proves to be unequal to the task.[92] Should a dispute arise about a text's interpretation, one party must be mistaken. A text has a strict meaning fixed by its author's intent, and it is against that original meaning that we assess the correctness of a proposed interpretation.

As we saw above, Nahmanides's hermeneutical theory stands out in sharp relief against this model. For Nahmanides, instances of controversy do not entail error on anyone's part, and neither does interpretation writ large. In his theory, prior to interpretation there exists no single, fixed meaning by which we can determine the correctness of an interpretation. The Torah was given "in accordance with their [the Sages'] understanding," and there is an obligation to obey them even when they seem wrong because they define the text's meaning.

Like Nahmanides, Maimonides also is of the opinion that error cannot be ascribed to anything considered Biblical, but for his own reasons. According to him, by definition there is complete agreement and no controversy about any aspects of the Biblical kernel. When Maimonides discusses the phenomenon of halakhic controversy, he repeatedly emphasizes that the principles are not subject to dispute; controversy enters the picture only when additional laws are inferred from the accepted principles. According to the model of inference described above,[93] two interpreters starting with the same two premises can end up with contradictory conclusions, and one need not claim that they understand the premises differently or that one of them misunderstands them completely. Perhaps one of them makes a mistake in his or her inference, as in fact Maimonides believed that there are correct and incorrect inferences. Certainly they do not dispute the premises, only the conclusions to be drawn from them.[94] With a logically sound deduction, disagreement about the conclusion indicates a lack of understanding or agreement concerning the premises, but with the less ironclad kinds of deduction Maimonides is discussing, full comprehension and agreement is possible even when debate surrounds the conclusions. Debate arises from the fact that the semantics of these deductive rules is, by its very nature, imprecise.[95]

It would be appropriate now to try to pin down the kind of interpretational inference Maimonides describes and its relationship to logical deduction. Recall the example of the law against vehicles in the public park. Let us say that someone makes an a fortiori argument and on that basis prohibits vehicles in the schoolyard. Let us also posit that someone disagrees and invalidates the a fortiori argument, because schools and public parks are different. That person explains that we want parents to drive their cars into the schoolyard to drop off their kids, which has no parallel in the public park. No one here disputes the premise, the prohibition from which another prohibition was derived; all parties agree that one may not drive a vehicle into a public park. What they do dispute is whether an analogy can be appropriately drawn between the two cases, that is, whether the schoolyard resembles the public park in every respect relevant to denying vehicles entry. The semantics of inferential rules like a fortiori and verbal congruity do not lend themselves to absolute formalization, as they are forever open to questions such as "congruous to what?" or "is this truly the stronger?" These kinds of inferences generate debate even when all interpreters accept the premises. Maimonides can therefore argue that interpretation is inference without disagreement about the premises, only about the conclusions drawn.

Let us return to Maimonides's structure of halakhah. The reader will recall that the central, undisputed kernel is directly linked to Moses, and this kernel alone has Biblical status because it was said to Moses explicitly. The thirteen middot are rules of inference for generating debatable new laws that have Rabbinic status, even though they are not *asmakhta'ot* but genuine interpretations. The idea of this kernel is the main innovation in Maimonides's structuring of halakhah, and as a consequence of this idea the thirteen middot must be rules of inference and not of definition. By conceptualizing the thirteen middot as rules of inference, Maimonides is able to distinguish the interpretation from the text in Principle Two. He keeps the ambition of the interpretive process in check by arguing that an interpretation is merely an addition to the text that cannot acquire the status of the text itself. Unsurprisingly, of all the elements of Maimonides's theory of halakhah, this one meets the most obstacles from the Talmud. Like it or not, interpretation is, at the end of the day, partially an attempt to partake of a text's authority as interpreters try to confer the text's authority on their own words through the act of interpretation.

Maimonides's motives for constructing his halakhic theory as he did emerge more clearly when examined alongside Nahmanides's own theory. Nahmanides tries to include, to the greatest extent possible, all strata of interpretation within the text of the Torah itself. He purposes to infuse the entire halakhic corpus with the substance of the divine word. He elevates the status of rabbinic exegesis to that of the Torah. He anchors the long historical chain of halakhic interpretation Mariana-Trench deep within Holy Writ. At the same time, he diminishes the uniqueness of Moses and of his direct revelation from God. Nahmanides's view is that the Mosaic Torah is not a perfect divine diamond impervious to interpretation; it is a corpus that can be worked and reworked by successive generations of scholars who reconstitute its meaning as they go, adding laws and removing them as they see fit. Now, Maimonides did believe that unreceived interpretations derived through the thirteen middot are ever-ripe for change by a later court that has a different view of matters.[96] But to say the same for the received kernel would undermine Maimonides's conception of the political conditions that enable us to believe in the Torah as a divine work.

Maimonides lays out the conditions vital for the Torah to lay claim to divine authority in *The Guide of the Perplexed*, and they inform his theory of halakhah. The divine Torah must be immutable and uniform; otherwise, it loses its credibility. In the *Guide*, Maimonides uses this to explain the prohibition of adding to or taking away from the Torah and the punishment of the rebellious elder:

Inasmuch as God, may He be exalted, knew that the commandments of this Torah will need in every time and place—as far as some of them are concerned—to be added to or subtracted from according to the diversity of places, happenings, and conjunctures of circumstances, He forbade adding to them or subtracting from them, saying: "you shall not add anything to or take away anything from it" (Deut 4:2). For this might have led to the corruption of the rules of the Torah and to the belief that the latter did not come from God.[97]

To admit controversy about the Biblical kernel is not to erroneously portray tradition but to undermine one of its fundamental principles. As quoted above, he writes in the introduction to his Commentary on the Mishnah: "But the notion of those who believe that even disputed laws were received from Moses yet came under dispute due to transmission errors or forgetfulness [. . .] this, God knows, is extremely repugnant and disgraceful. They are the words of those who do not comprehend and do not have a solid grasp of the principles."[98] This harsh language indicates that this is not just any mistake but dangerous heresy. Granting Biblical status, the status of the Torah itself, to the unreceived interpretations of the Sages drags the precious kernel into the "war of Torah" where the dust never settles, which Maimonides considered intolerable for a supposedly divinely revealed system of law: "it might have led to the corruption of the rules of the Law and to the belief that the latter did not come from God." Revelation must be protected from being deconstructed by multiple interpretations that shape its meaning retroactively. In Maimonides's idea of authority, the foundational kernel of the divine Torah must be kept apart because it does not change and cannot be enlarged, although extensions can be derived from it.[99] In addition, the isolation of this kernel emphasizes Moses's exclusive standing, which is of utmost importance for Maimonides's theories of prophecy and law.[100] According to Maimonides, Moses was always in a league of his own: prophets could never attain his level of prophecy, and scholars could never speak with his authority in their interpretations.

IX

Maimonides may preserve the exclusiveness of revelation and the purity of tradition, but the price of that isolation is the severance of the direct link between the halakhic system and God's word. Aside from the relatively small kernel transmitted to Moses, the rest of the enormous normative system—rabbinic exegesis and legislation—retains its connection to God only through the narrow bridge of the second-order command of "do not deviate." Nahmanides, by way of contrast, brings the entire halakhic corpus into the warm embrace of the revelation, but by bringing them into direct contact he jeopardizes revelation by foregoing immutability and a fixed meaning. At the beginning of the chapter, we noted the tension between Maimonides and the Geonim about anchoring halakhah in a tradition from Sinai versus preserving the reliability of the tradition, and this same tension exists between Maimonides and Nahmanides about revelation. If one claims that whatever a bright student thinks up today was already included in the Sinaitic theophany, then revelation loses its solid shape and sharp edges. If every *et, gam,* and letter *vav* in the Torah carries normative meaning, Scripture becomes a kind of Atlas, bearing worlds of meaning.

Nahmanides is able to envision the entirety of halakhah within the divine word because he has a more expansive understanding of revelation. In his gloss on Principle Two, he alludes to the infinite quality of the divine word: "Indeed, Scripture encompasses everything [. . .] because the book of the Lord's Torah is perfect, it has no superfluous or missing letter—they [the letters] were all written with wisdom."[101] In typical fashion, Nahmanides conceals his kabbalistic perspectives in his halakhic writing here. A closer look at his concept of the Torah, as he articulates it in the introduction to his Commentary on the Torah, reveals the profundity of the idea that divine revelation is all-inclusive. Nahmanides thinks that the Torah is, in essence, an extremely long sequence of divine names.[102] The version we have in front of us, which divides the sequence into readily intelligible words, presents but one way of reading the Torah. In principle, one could divide this divine *scripta continua* into a different set of semantic units, which would expose a completely different meaning of the text:

> We further possess a true tradition that the entire Torah consists of names of the Holy One, such that the words can be divided into names with another meaning. Consider, for example, how the verse of *Be-Re'SHYT* [*BaRa' 'eLoHYM*] can be divided into different words, such as: *BR'SH YTB R' 'L HYM* [. . .] It appears that the Torah was written through Black Fire on White Fire, in the manner that we have mentioned, namely, continuous writing without any break between words. It could be read according to the names or according to our

reading about the Torah and the Law (lit. commandment). It was given to our master Moses according to the division [that yields] the reading of the commandments, and the reading of the names was orally transmitted to him.[103]

The most basic unit of Scripture that is not subject to change is not the word but the letter and its location within the long string of letters. This idea deeply undermines the text's stability and is fraught with antinomian potential, because the biblical text becomes dynamic, showing a different face each time the sequence is parsed in a different manner.[104]

The approach to the Torah as a sequence of divine names implies that revelation is not a moment of linguistic communication between God and humans; it is rather the self-disclosure of God's essence, which is his name. God does not transmit his divine word through revelation but reveals himself, his name. This conception of revelation is epitomized by Nahmanides's understanding of the divine voice in Scripture as a kabbalistic symbol for God himself rather than a reference to the word of God. The sefirot themselves are called "voices" because divine "speech" is not God addressing humans but a symbol for God emanating himself outward from his innermost recesses. The sefirot become increasingly differentiated as the emanatory process continues, so they are comparable to a sound emerging from the vocal cords that gradually makes itself understood in clear syllables and crisply enunciated words. Unlike regular speech, the divine "speech" of revelation does not use language to communicate content from divine speaker to human audience; it exposes God himself with his many "voices," his sefirot, at different levels of apprehension.[105] It should not come as a surprise, then, that the "Torah" in Nahmanides's kabbalistic symbolism does not refer to God's revelation but to God himself.[106] One could say that the present division of words in the biblical text is only one aspect of God's infinite essence.[107] If the Torah reveals God's essence, then the current division of letters resulting in our Torah is merely one of the innumerable kaleidoscopic manifestations of the divine essence. The Torah as identical with God must be infinite and all-encompassing, and the Godhead as a living being appears within it through the infinite permutations of dividing the text. As such, revelation encompasses the wisdom of the entire universe, reaching light-years beyond the normative components of halakhah that Nahmanides discusses in his gloss to Principle Two. Solomon, the wisest of all men, learned from the Torah the secrets of the entire universe, from the structure of matter to birdsong: "everything can be learned from the Torah.

King Solomon, to whom God gave wisdom and understanding, acquired it all from the Torah, and he learned from it until he knew the secret of the entire natural world, even the powers of the grasses and their unique properties."[108]

The pains taken in writing a Torah scroll with absolute precision, requiring careful attention to instances of full and incomplete spelling and the letterforms, confirms the text's semantic plenitude, according to Nahmanides. On the face of it, the presence or absence of these features should not matter semantically, as a full or incomplete spelling of a word does not affect its meaning. Insisting on precision in these matters makes sense if the letter—not the word—is the basic unit of the text. If the letters were to be divided into some other arrangement, a full or incomplete spelling would have disastrous consequences: "On account of this, a Torah scroll in which one letter is mistakenly full or incomplete is invalid, because this matter requires us to invalidate a Torah scroll that is missing a single *vav* [. . .] even though it does not seem to make a difference."[109] The connection Nahmanides makes between the form and semantic fullness of the text generates an interpretive paradox. The more we insist that each and every crownlet has meaning, the more numerous the interpretive possibilities become. To put it differently, the more restrictions we place upon the possible ways to write the text (through exacting laws about the letterforms), the more ways there are to read the text. A text with this degree of semantic potential supports every possible interpretation, and it increasingly ceases to function as a stable generator of norms. There is dissonance between the view of revelation as an expression of God's infinite and dynamic essence and its status as the solid bedrock of a system of religious law. This tension is the basis for the debate between Maimonides and Nahmanides about revelation and interpretation, a debate that continues unabatedly throughout the length of Nahmanides's glosses and that concerns the semantic fullness of the Torah's imperative language.

X

In the prefatory Principles to Sefer ha-Mitzvot, Maimonides formulates criteria for identifying a commandment. For him, the precise definition is an organizing command given to Moses at Sinai. As we have seen above, Maimonides dedicates the first group of Principles, namely Principle One and Principle Two, to clarifying the requirement of "given to Moses at Sinai." In the second group of Principles, which includes most of the remaining ones, he focuses on distinguishing an organizing command from a local command.

He devotes the third group of Principles to setting up distinctions between a true command and other linguistic constructions in the Torah that appear to be imperatives and were taken as such, mistakenly he believes, by previous enumerators. An example of this sort of Principle is Principle Five: "It is not proper to enumerate the reason for a commandment as an independent commandment."[110] According to Maimonides, his predecessors erroneously considered the rationale for a commandment as a countable commandment. The verse states, "Do not degrade your daughter and make her a harlot, and do not (*lo*) let the land fall into harlotry" (Lev 19:29). These are not two separately countable commandments, because the second half does not carry normative content; it states the reason for the immediately preceding imperative.

Principle Eight also engages in distinguishing imperative verses from ones that have the semblance of an imperative. This principle asserts: "It is not proper to enumerate negation like we do prohibition."[111] Maimonides profoundly encapsulates an important, general problem with normative language. In Hebrew, the word *lo* is not used only to prohibit a certain action; it has a broader function of negation. In the verse, "There has not (*lo*) arisen in Israel a prophet like Moses in Israel since" (Deut 34:10), *lo* obviously negates and does not prohibit. The language Maimonides spoke, Judeo-Arabic, has two clearly separate words for these uses, which prevents confusion: *lā* for prohibition, and *lam* for negation. While Hebrew does have words reserved solely for the imperative, such as *hishamer* and *al*, it more frequently uses *lo*, which can be construed as a prohibition or a negation. Maimonides argues that his predecessors could not discern one from the other clearly: "He (lit. our other) [Kayyara] was ignorant of this, to the extent that he counted 'she shall not (*lo*) go out like the male slaves do' (Exod 21:7). He did not know that this was a negation and not a prohibition."[112] Maimonides asserts that this clause is not a prohibition but a negation. It negates the application of a particular law to the Israelite maidservant, in the same way that the clause "you shall do nothing to the girl" (Deut 22:26) is not a prohibition but states that the raped maiden does not face the death penalty. Because no formal linguistic cue indicates the intended meaning of *lo*, Maimonides uses context to disambiguate: "There is nothing which enables us to differentiate between negation and prohibition except context; the word itself does not [enable us to differentiate] since the word for negation and prohibition in Hebrew is the same word, which is *lo*."[113]

The rules Maimonides formulates to distinguish between imperative verses and those that only seem imperative, and the repeated accusation that Kayyara was unable to differentiate between these different meanings, restricts the normative semantic potential of the text. According to Maimonides, not every clause in the Torah's legal discourse relates new normative content. Sometimes, even legitimate imperatives are not included in the enumeration of the commandments because they do not add anything to existing prohibitions; they serve only to reinforce and emphasize them. In Principle Four he establishes, "It is not proper to enumerate commands that include all of the commandments."[114] By this rule, he excludes commands of a general nature because they do not carry specific normative content and are only intended to strengthen and stoke the flame of vigilance about existing commandments. Likewise, in Principle Nine he says, "It is not proper to enumerate the negative and positive commandment, only those matters concerning which we are prohibited to do or commanded to do."[115] A multiplicity of thou-shalt-nots does not reflect an equivalent number of prohibitions, because some commands are repeated for emphasis alone. In sum, Maimonides's attempt to define those commands that have specific and additional normative content constricts the normative capacity of Scripture.

In his glosses on this set of Principles, Nahmanides goes in the opposite direction, because his goal is to fill verses to their semantic capacity: every statement is brimming with fresh normative data. In his gloss on Principle Five, which distinguishes a prohibition from its rationale, he says: "we have not seen our rabbis in the Talmud consider prohibitions of the Torah to be redundant because they are a reason for a preceding prohibition unless they come to add or take away, in other words, so that we may learn a new law from that reason."[116] Reasons for the commandments, even if they appear to be nothing more than reasons, are to all intents commandments. When the Torah prohibits the substitution of a murderer's ransom for the death penalty, it adds, "and you shall not bring sin upon the land" (Deut 24:4). In Nahmanides's reading, this is indeed a reason for the prohibition but also much more: it is a prohibition aimed at the court. In his signature style, Nahmanides flips Maimonides's presumption: "Everything stated in the language of prohibition is to enjoin."[117] Unless the reason adds normative content to the commandment itself, as long as it has the semblance of a commandment, it is in fact to be taken as its own commandment.

Nahmanides takes a similar tack toward Maimonides's distinction between negation and prohibition. In Nahmanides's view, the word *lo* can be read as a negation, rather than a prohibition, only when this negation conveys specific normative content. The word *lo* in the Torah's legal language is never neutral from a halakhic perspective; therefore, even when instances of *lo* are explained as negations, we must infer that some other norm should have applied if not for the Torah's negation. Alternatively, if the negation does not convey normative information of some kind, it should be interpreted as a bona fide independent prohibition. Nahmanides adduces proof to this idea from the way that the Babylonian Talmud handles disputes between Rabbis Akiva and Yishmael about whether certain verses should be read as optional or obligatory. One such example concerns the verse at the beginning of the pericope of the wayward wife, "the spirit of jealousy came over him and he warned his wife" (Num 5:14):

> A further example of this is their discussion in tractate *Sotah* (3a): " 'and he warned his wife'—an optional act, the words of R. Yishmael. R. Akiva says: an obligation. 'he becomes ritually impure for her' (Lev 21:3)—an optional act, the words of R. Yishmael. R. Akiva says: an obligation. 'of them you take bondmen forever' (Lev 25:46)—an optional act, the words of R. Yishmael. R. Akiva says: an obligation." About this they asked: "Shall we say they argue in this way throughout the entire Torah, one master saying 'an obligation' and one master saying 'an optional act'?" And they explained, "they disagree about the verses," meaning, the *midrashim* of the verses. "What is R. Yishmael's reason? Like it is learned in a *baraita:* 'Regarding that which the Torah said, "Do not hate your brother in your heart" (Lev 16:17), one might think [a case] such as this [the wayward wife], so the verse states, "the spirit of jealousy came over him and he warned." ' And R. Akiva['s reason]? Another warning is written." [. . .] You see that they all agree about negations wherever the verse needed that negation, that is to say, where it needed to permit us something or make it optional, and when it does not need to permit us anything they declare it a positive or negative commandment.[118]

R. Yishmael maintains that "the Torah speaks in the language of humans," and he represents the position that Scripture, like every text, sometimes employs rhetorical devices such as narrative, repetition, and emphasis. That is why the narrative framework of the law is not necessarily laden with normative meaning, and the expression "he warned his wife" is merely part of the unfolding of the story and does not carry normative meaning. R. Akiva takes the same expression as a command because he believes in the semantic plenitude of Scripture, and those same rhetorical flourishes ought to be expounded as if they add new normative information.

The dispute between Maimonides and Nahmanides is seemingly a medieval iteration of this same dispute of antiquity. However, Nahmanides shows how the Babylonian Talmud repositions R. Yishmael's approach to be conceptually quite close to R. Akiva's.[119] The Talmud rejects the possibility that they have a running dispute throughout the course of the entire Torah about how to read Scripture. Instead, it posits that in R. Yishmael's view the "optional act" is not legally neutral; it comes to allow and make legitimate an act that otherwise would have been prohibited under a different law. In the case of the wayward wife, the husband should not have been allowed to air his suspicions and put her on notice because there is a prohibition against hatred, so the verse permits him to caution his wife. If not for the prohibition governing this activity, R. Yishmael, like his counterpart R. Akiva, would have understood the verse as a command, as an obligation. Thus does the Talmud prove Nahmanides correct: negations are not normatively neutral, and if they do not allow something that would otherwise be prohibited, they are imperatives.

In the Principles where Maimonides distinguishes pseudo-commandments from real ones, he shrinks the normative capacity of the text. Reasons, negations, repetitions, general principles—none of these carries normative information, none is a command. Kayyara saw normativity everywhere in Scripture; Maimonides judged him careless and misinformed. He took Kayyara's confusing the imperative with the descriptive as evidence of his ignorance about the formal structure of legal language. Nahmanides goes to the opposite extreme and tries to inflate the text's normative capacity. Every single element of legal discourse has the capacity to convey normative information, and if it cannot be detected, then it is to be understood as its own independent command.[120] The utterly different perspectives of Maimonides and Nahmanides on how to conceive of interpretation and the status of rabbinic exegesis thus boils over into the issue of the semantic fullness of biblical legal language. The common denominator between the two disagreements is the hard question of how to understand revelation and its relationship to the entire halakhic system.

Maimonides expected that, once published, his Sefer ha-Mitzvot would assume its rightful place as the last word on the enumeration of the commandments: "When their enumeration is clarified in this work through unquestionable proof, the reader clearly will see the error made by those who compiled any other enumeration."[121] Indeed, with its systematicity and exemplary organization, Sefer ha-Mitzvot has utterly overshadowed the seemingly superficial and random enumerations of the Geonim. Maimonides's luck changed, however, with the rise of his arch-challenger. Nahmanides denied the Great Eagle his perch, contesting Maimonides's categorical Principles and their supporting arguments at every step by drawing on his own exceptional discernment and vast erudition. The perfect conceptual forms of the Maimonidean categories shattered when Nahmanides brought them in contact with the rugged terrain of the Talmud that he knew so well. Nahmanides's conceptual power, for which he partly had Maimonides to thank, enabled him to turn the apparently desultory enumeration of Kayyara into something principled and conceptually coherent. He defended earlier authorities like Kayyara with the very same tools their successors used to pillory them. Nahmanides's feelings about the independence, sharpness, and harshness of Maimonides and other twelfth-century all-stars appears toward the end of the polemic in his glosses. In reaction to a withering condemnation of Kayyara, Nahmanides responds:

> I am perplexed and bewildered by the Master. He condemns the author of *Halakhot Gedolot* and criticizes him, but why does not he scrutinize his words, why does he not even give them a glance? Had he been responding to one of the students, it would have befitted the Master, given his wisdom and the dignity of his bearing, to peruse the work of the student and give it consideration, which is all the more true when responding to one of the greatest Geonim and condemning him, regarding him as addled, God forbid![122]

XI

In Nahmanides's glosses on Sefer ha-Mitzvot, he contended with Maimonides's philosophy of halakhah, and in so doing he shaped the main components of his own halakhic philosophy, particularly his view on revelation and its relationship with interpretation, authority, and controversy. Turning to other areas of his oeuvre in which he discusses his conception of interpretation, we arrive at a fuller and richer picture of that view. In his Commentary on the Torah, Nahmanides repeats his constitutive theory of rabbinic interpretation:

> " 'right or left' (Deut 17:11)—even if they tell you that right is left and left is right"—the language of R. Solomon [Rashi]. This means: even if you believe they are mistaken, and the matter is as simple to you as

knowing left from right, do as they command. Don't say, how can I eat this completely forbidden fat or kill this innocent man? Say instead, thus has the Lord, Who commands the commandments, commanded me, that I should perform all of His commandments in accord with everything instructed by those who stand before Him in the chosen place, and in accordance with their construal of meaning He has given me the Torah, even if they err. This is like the incident of R. Yehoshua and Rabban Gamaliel on the Day of Atonement that fell out according to his calculation. The need for this commandment is very great because the Torah was given to us in writing, and it is well known that not everyone will be of one mind about unforeseen matters. Disputes will proliferate and the Torah will become many Torahs! Scripture ruled that we should listen to whatever the high court, which stands before the Lord in the chosen place, says about the interpretation of the Torah, whether they have received its interpretation [as a tradition] from the mouth of Moses from the mouth of the Almighty, or say it based on the contextual meaning of the Torah or its intent. Because it is in accordance with their opinion that God has given us the Torah, even if in our eyes it seems like right has been switched with left. Certainly you should believe that right is right, because the Spirit of the Lord is upon the ministers of His Temple and does not abandon His pious ones; they are forever preserved from error and blunder. The language of *Sifrei:* "even if they point to right as left and left as right, listen to them."[123]

The constitutive understanding of rabbinic interpretation, according to Nahmanides, can be read strongly or weakly, and his disciples have left us different versions of his statement that "it is in accordance with their opinion that God has given us the Torah." On the strong reading, rabbinic interpretation retroactively establishes the text's meaning. Scripture has no normative meaning prior to that given to it by the high court, no meaning by which one could judge the court mistaken. Since it has no meaning aside from the court's, whoever reasons that he cannot permit himself to eat forbidden fat since the court is mistaken is himself mistaken by attributing error to the court. The weaker reading of the constitutive approach, by comparison, argues that the court can err but we must heed it all the same. Scripture does have meaning independent of the court's interpretation, a prior meaning that can be used as a standard by which to judge the court's interpretation.

The prohibition of "do not deviate" entails that even when someone definitively knows that the court has erred, that person is still obligated to follow the court. No normative distinction arises from these two readings of Nahmanides's position, as the obligation to obey the court remains in full force according to each explanation. The sole difference pertains to his theory of meaning.

Nahmanides's own formulations can be read in these two ways. His novel formulation in his glosses tip the balance in favor of the stronger reading: "it is in accordance with their understanding that God commands and gives us the Torah"; "it ['do not deviate'] obligates us to believe in the Torah according to the interpretation that they impart to it."[124] In this reading, one who casts doubt on the court's interpretation must obey the court and also believe that the court's opinion is that of the Torah itself. While the same formulation appears in his Torah commentary, Nahmanides appends an additional clause: "in accordance with their construal of meaning He has given me the Torah, even if they err." The additional clause—"even if they err"—which appears only in his Commentary on the Torah, seems more in line with the weaker reading.[125] Moreover, Nahmanides justifies his idea out of concern for widespread controversy and factionalism, and the need for some ultimate authoritative body to be able to make binding decisions about the law. This reads better according to the weaker version. If the specter of controversy drives Nahmanides, then his constitutive approach derives not from a theory of interpretation and meaning, in which the text's meaning depends on what its authorized interpreters say it is, but from a political concern about unity and authority. One could still claim that Nahmanides employs a broader theory of meaning, driven by fundamental considerations, about the relationship between revelation and its expositors in order to solve a problem of authority. The example he brings from the mishnah in tractate Rosh ha-Shanah, in which R. Yehoshua submitted to Rabban Gamaliel's calculation of the new moon, can also be read in two ways. Either the court establishes the new moon, and so as a matter of tautology it cannot be mistaken, or the court can be mistaken but we listen to it anyway to avoid factionalism and disunity.[126]

Of Nahmanides's students, the author of Sefer ha-Hinnukh interpreted Nahmanides's words in line with the weaker reading:

> The reasons (lit. roots) behind this commandment: Since people have different opinions, and many minds will never be in accord on matters, the Lord of all things knows that if the intent of Scriptural verses

were to be entrusted to every individual, each according to his intellect, each of them would interpret the words of the Torah in accord
with his reasoning, and controversy would proliferate within Israel
about the meaning of the commandments, and the Torah would become like many Torahs [. . .] Therefore our God, Who is all-wise,
perfected our Torah, the true Torah of truth, with this commandment,
in which he commanded us to follow it [the Torah] according to the
true interpretation received by our early Sages [. . .] By way of truth
and great praise about this commandment, they said: " 'Do not deviate from it right or left' (Deut 17:11)—even if they tell you that right is
left and left is right, do not deviate from their command." That is to
say, even if they should err about some matter it is improper for us to
disagree with them; instead, we should act in accordance with their
error. It is better to endure one error and have everything entrusted to
their consistently good judgment rather than have everyone act according to their own opinion, for that would lead to religious ruin,
strife, and the total loss of the nation. On account of these issues the
intent of the Torah was entrusted to the Sages of Israel. For this reason,
too, we were commanded that the minority should always be subject
to the majority, as I have written there concerning the commandment
to follow the majority.[127]

The author of Sefer ha-Hinnukh undoubtedly fell under Nahmanides's
influence. In the continuation, he cites extensively from Nahmanides's second gloss, and above we see that his formulation is quite close to that of
Nahmanides—"On account of these issues the intent of the Torah was entrusted to the Sages of Israel." That said, he remains in the camp of the weak
reading because he accepts the possibility that the court can err and that we
must obey it nonetheless. The prohibition of "do not deviate" asserts that it is
better to follow the court's erroneous ruling than to expedite the disintegra-
tion of central authority. The Torah was not entrusted to the Sages so that
they could constitute its meaning but so that they could issue its binding,
normative law.

In contrast to the account given by the author of Sefer ha-Hinnukh, the
strong version of the constitutive approach to interpretation fits with Nahmanides's conception of revelation, which views divine language as multifaceted and all-encompassing. When the high court establishes the normative
meaning of a text, it decides the text's meaning, shutting down a range of

other, diverse possibilities. The connection between revelation as multifaceted and the text's meaning constituted by the court's decision is raised by Nahmanides's grand-disciple R. Yom Tov Assevilli (Ritva). Ritva (1250–1320) studied in Barcelona in the school formed by Nahmanides and eventually became a judge and a rabbi in Saragossa. His work serves as one of the main sources of expanding and interpreting Nahmanides's works. Ritva's approach to controversy and revelation appears in his commentary on an important Talmudic statement concerning the controversies between the house of Hillel and the house of Shammai. The Talmud states: "these and those [the words of the house of Hillel and the words of the house Shammai] are the words of the living God, and the law is according to the House of Hillel" (*Eruvin* 13b). On this Talmudic statement Ritva makes the following comment:

> The rabbis of northern France asked, how it possible for both of them to be the words of the living God when this one forbids and that one permits? They answered that when Moses ascended on high to receive the Torah, about every single matter they showed him forty-nine aspects to forbid and forty-nine aspects to permit. He asked the Holy One about this, and He said that it would be entrusted to the sages of Israel in every generation such that the decision would follow them. This is correct according to the *derash,* and by way of truth there is a secret reason for the matter.[128]

"The rabbis of northern France," namely the Tosafists, explained the dictum—"these and those are the words of the living God"—literally: both sides of the dispute were revealed to Moses at Sinai. The revelation at Sinai was not monolithic but multifaceted; Moses received forty-nine arguments to support each of the opposing opinions. Moses wondered what, then, the law should be, and he was answered that deciding the law is a matter given to the court of each generation. That Torah was given with its diverse possible interpretations, and the Sages decide and constitute the determinative meaning of the Torah by means of the majority.[129] This notion cited by Ritva is at variance with both the Geonic and Maimonidean account of controversy.

Maimonides and the Geonim considered controversy a symptom of decline and deterioration, which is why their accounts of controversy made reference to the rabbinic statement, which led them to support their position with the statement from Sotah 47b: "when the students of Shammai and Hillel who did not sufficiently wait upon [their teachers] proliferated, controversy proliferated within Israel and the Torah became like two Torahs." They differed on the nature of this decline as well as the character of controversy, though, as we saw above. The Geonim maintained that this decline was a direct result of the botched transmission of information given at Sinai, whereas Maimonides considered it a failure of inferential reasoning within the process of interpretation. Be that as it may, they both agreed that controversy arises from undesirable conditions. One is therefore not surprised to discover that neither the Geonim nor Maimonides cites the dictum "these and those are the words of the living God," which seems to reflect a different attitude toward controversy. Ritva, in interpreting this very dictum, demonstrates his belief that controversy reflects the multifaceted nature of revelation.

The position of Ritva, which he ascribes to the rabbis of France, is expressed even more strongly by R. Samson of Sens (1150–1230) in his commentary on a mishnah in 'Edduyot, which rules that we preserve the opinion of an overruled individual Sage together with the opinion of the majority so that we can rely on the individual in the future:

> "Why do we mention the view of an individual?" That is, whenever there is an individual opinion and an opinion of many the law follows the many, so why are the opinions of individuals mentioned together with the many? So that if a court, like the Amoraim who decided laws, deems the individual's opinion correct and agrees with his reason, they can rule in accordance with it. For if his words were lost, the Amoraim would not be able to expressly disagree with the Tannaim, who were wiser and more numerous than they. Using this support, they can rule according to his opinion, for the Torah already said "follow the majority." Although the opinion of the individual was not accepted the first time and the many did not agree with him, when a subsequent generation arises in which the many do agree with his reason, the law follows them, because the entire Torah was said to Moses with aspects to render impure and aspects to render pure. They said to him, how will it be clarified? He said to them, "follow the majority." Still, these and those are the words of the living God.[130]

Controversy does not reflect the deterioration of some ideal, or at least superior, state of affairs; it is rather the very starting point of the system, since revelation itself was presented with a plurality of meanings and options. It is for this reason that dissenting opinions are preserved and recorded for future possible application.

The Geonim, Maimonides, and Nahmanides all present us with completely different approaches to the fundamental questions of a philosophy of halakhah. The differences between them are more starkly illuminated when applied to a test case, such as the first mishnah in Berakhot, which contains a debate over the appropriate time for the nighttime Shemaʻ. According to the Geonim, God explicitly told Moses the precise time of night at Sinai, but it was subsequently lost over time, which led to this debate. According to Maimonides, the very existence of debate means that Moses could not have been told anything aside from the biblical expression of "when you lie down," and the debate emerges from the attempt to infer the proper time from that expression. According to Nahmanides and his school, the various mishnaic opinions of R. Eliezer, R. Gamaliel, and the Sages were given at Sinai, and the interpreters try to constitute the meaning of the expression "when you lie down" from this multiplicity. In the restorative approach of the Geonim, revelation covered everything and was perfect, so the only place to go from there was down. Interpretation is an attempt to reconstruct that perfect law lost over time. In Maimonides's cumulative approach, God revealed an unchanging kernel upon which further laws accumulated over time through interpretation. In Nahmanides's constitutive approach, revelation encompassed everything possible, including all halakhic disputes, and the interpreter constitutes the meaning of the text from the plurality of choices latent within it. The differences between these three approaches about the character of revelation and the meaning of the interpretive act entail respectively different attitudes toward the phenomenon of controversy and differing conceptions of halakhic truth.

At the end of Ritva's quotation of the Tosafists, he writes that their approach accords with the "way of truth," an expression used in Nahmanides's study hall to mark a kabbalistic tradition—"by way of truth there is a secret reason for the matter." Ritva seemingly connects halakhic pluralism, which exists in revelation, with the theosophical conception of the kabbalists in which the multifaceted dynamism of the Godhead is mirrored in revelation itself.[131] Interpretation, under this approach, does not discover a fixed meaning but decides between various interpretive possibilities that exist within the text, due to the multifaceted nature of the Godhead. The quotations from Sefer ha-Hinnukh and Ritva show that Nahmanides's school interpreted in different ways his coinage "it is in accordance with their understanding that God commands and gives us the Torah." It seems, therefore, that the Tosafist concept of controversy, and the connection to Nahmanides's esoteric tradition, tips the scales in favor of Ritva's reading of Nahmanides's constitutive approach.

Beyond the tension generated by Nahmanides's constitutive approach, in his Commentary on the Torah he adds an element that is not present in his glosses and that raises a much deeper question about his hermeneutics. After he introduces his constitutive approach as a rationale for adhering to the high court's ruling, he adds an additional reason to obey the court:

> Because it is in accordance with their opinion that God has given us the Torah, even in our eyes it seems like right has been switched with left. Certainly you should believe that right is right, because the Spirit of the Lord is upon the ministers of His Temple and does not abandon His pious ones; they are forever preserved from error and blunder. The language of *Sifrei:* "even if they point to right as left and left as right, listen to them."[132]

The Holy Spirit grants the court immunity from error, not because it constitutes Scripture's meaning, but because the Holy Spirit guides them to the truth. The case before the court has a correct answer, then, and the court receives divine assistance in reaching it. Nahmanides might have restricted this to the Sanhedrin that convened in the chamber of hewn stone in the Temple, because he explicitly mentions the phrase "the ministers of His Temple." Whatever the case may be, the question is how this squares with the preceding constitutive approach, whether on the stronger or weaker readings. A tentative answer lies in the kabbalistic theory underlying the concept of revelation and its connection between the activity of the court and the Sages.

In Nahmanides's interpretation of the verse "Gather for me seventy of Israel's elders" (Num 11:16), he describes a quasi-prophetic quality to the judgment of the Sanhedrin. He links the number of the gathered elders to the number of judges on the Sanhedrin and sets the prophetic character of the Sanhedrin's adjudication within a kabbalistic framework:

> "Gather for me seventy of Israel's elders." Our rabbis have already mentioned that the seventy nations speak seventy languages, and each one has a zodiacal sign in the firmament and a minister above [. . .] He commanded this number of judges of Israel, because this number includes all opinions since it comprises all the powers, and nothing is beyond them. Likewise, at the giving of the Torah [it says], "and seventy elders of Israel" (Exod 24:1), because with this complete number it was fitting for the glory of *Shekhinah* to rest upon them, as it is in

the supernal camp, for the Israelites are the hosts of the Lord on earth. Similarly, the Ark, cover, and Tabernacle were made in the figure of the ministers on high, and the tribes were organized in the likeness of the Chariot beheld by Ezekiel, in order to draw *Shekhinah* upon them on earth in the same way *Shekhinah* is in the heavens. Moses' presiding over the seventy elders is an allusion to Israel, which is a singular nation on earth. Our rabbis have a tradition that every great Sanhedrin that sits in the house of the Lord, in the place that He chooses to abide (*le-shikhno* = *Shekhinah*), should number seventy and the president presides over them like our master Moses, making them seventy-one. Similarly, the seventy-two letters of the Great Name correspond to the ministers and the Unique Name, which is the single Lord over them all. This is what the verse alludes to when it says, "God stands in the congregation of God, judging in the midst of judges (*elohim*)" (Ps 82:1), because *Shekhinah* is with them to give them approval. The verse says, "Until when will you judge perversely" (Ps 82:2), warning them: since the Glorious Name [*Shekhinah*] is with them during judgment, how can you not fear it and pervert judgment? [. . .] It further said: "I said you are supernal beings (*elohim*), all of you are sons of the Most High" (Ps 82:6), because your number is like the number of lofty ministers and the singular Ruler.[133]

The presence of Shekhinah in the court is based on the isomorphic principle of "attraction" that Nahmanides identifies in a number of different contexts. The idea is that the Godhead can be made present in the world by creating symbolic structures on earth that parallel supernal ones, and this parallelism is the secret to drawing down God's presence into the world. The seventy elders of the Sanhedrin parallel the supernal ministers of the nations, upon which Shekhinah rests. Shekhinah comes to rest upon the members of the Sanhedrin by way of the similarity created between the judges and the ministers. The Shekhinah is represented by the president of the court appointed over the elders, who symbolizes Israel, a singular nation on earth, and the singular Master, namely, Shekhinah. Nahmanides also repeats the importance of location, as he brings proof that the insistence upon seventy with a presiding personality—a central component in creating the isomorphic foundation—exists only in the Sanhedrin that convenes in the Temple: "Our rabbis have a tradition that every great Sanhedrin that sits in the house of the Lord, in the place that He chooses to abide (*le-shikhno* = *Shekhinah*), should number seventy." Shekhinah is not present in the court to render divine assistance to the judges; it is tied to the hermetic-talismanic principle that is manifestly causal.[134]

Nahmanides sees the same principle behind Shekhinah's presence in the Temple and its presence in the Sanhedrin. The Temple was also designed as an isomorphic structure of the supernal chariot, which caused Shekhinah to be drawn to it: "Similarly, the Ark, cover, and Tabernacle were made in the figure of the ministers on high, and the tribes were organized in the likeness of the Chariot beheld by Ezekiel, in order to draw *Shekhinah* upon them on earth in the same way *Shekhinah* is in the heavens."[135] Narrowing the gap between halakhah and prophecy not only has consequences for the composition of the court and its isomorphic character. Seemingly, Nahmanides even blurs the distinction for individual Torah scholars in their interpretation of the following Talmudic statement: "From the day the Temple was destroyed, prophecy was taken from the prophets but not from scholars" (Bava Batra 12a). Rashi in his Talmudic commentary understands this to mean that prophecy was taken away from those prophets who were not also scholars and remained in the hands of only scholar-prophets. Nahmanides challenges this reading on the basis of the Talmudic requirement that a prophet must be wise, strong, and rich (Nedarim 38a). Even before the destruction, prophets must have been scholars, too. He understands the dictum in a different light: "Rather, this is what it is saying: Although the prophecy of the prophets, which is through sight and vision, was taken away, the prophecy of the Sages, which is through wisdom, was not taken away, as they know the truth through the Holy Spirit in their midst."[136] Nahmanides does not give us more than a wink here. What is this Holy Spirit in the midst of Torah scholars? In the court, the Holy Spirit is present through its isomorphic structure and specific geographical location, so how can it be in the midst of individual Torah scholars? Along the same lines, what is the distinction between the prophecy of "sight and vision" and the scholarly prophecy that is "through wisdom"?

A complete answer to these questions can be given only after a thorough and comprehensive treatment of Nahmanides's theory of prophecy.[137] In the meantime, several points can be raised that should aid in understanding his intent here. An investigation of his theory of prophecy yields his belief that beholding God through the eye of the soul is greater than intellectual apprehension that is stripped of any visual component. Prophetic prophecy surpasses scholarly prophecy because an aspect of God is seen by the prophet, which is not the case with the intellectual prophecy of scholars. The prophecy of scholars may not reach the level of the prophecy of prophets, but it is prophecy nonetheless, a prophecy conducted through wisdom and the Holy Spirit in their midst.

Crucial here for our purposes is the fact that Nahmanides conceives of prophecy as a product of cleaving to the divine, and levels of prophecy are dictated by the height of a prophet's cleaving. Torah scholars also cleave to God, as Nahmanides describes in "Sha'ar ha-Gemul":

> They [the rabbis] mention the matter of their existence through the existence of the object of their intellection, and their becoming one entity—this is the interpretation of what the Torah says "and to cleave to Him" (Deut 11:22), and it says [further], "yet the soul of my master shall be bound up in the bundle of life with God your Lord (*et Ha-Shem Elokekha*)" (1 Sam 25:29). Hence R. Akiva came to teach that " 'The Lord your God (*et Ha-Shem Elokekha*) shall you fear' (Deut 6:13) includes [fear of] Torah scholars."[138]

The expression "their becoming one entity" is an extreme expression of the *unio mystica* that umbilically supplies the cleaving individual with the qualities of Shekhinah.[139] In Nahmanides's view, the identity between mystic and Shekhinah forms the basis for the rabbinic exposition, which teaches that the obligation to fear Torah scholars stems from the verse commanding the fear of God. Fear of God and fear of Torah scholars who cleave to God are one and the same.

In his description of scholarly prophecy, Nahmanides uses the expression "the Holy Spirit in their midst." Read carefully, Nahmanides is not saying that the Holy Spirit is not external to the scholars voluntarily revealed by God to them. Shekhinah is rather in their midst because the scholars are in a state of cleaving. Cleaving enables prophecy in which the intellectual activity of the scholar is in fact the activity of Shekhinah itself, which rests within the scholar. Perhaps this understanding of prophecy through cleaving bridges the gap between the different versions of the constitutive approach to rabbinic interpretation. The Sages constitute the meaning of the Torah because their interpretive activity, through their state of cleaving, actually continues revelation.

Nahmanides took exceptional care not to expose his kabbalistic views unless a specific context warranted their inclusion. By putting together his opinions on various matters, though, one can surmise that his philosophy of halakhah is shaped in large measure by these kabbalistic views. The great debate between Maimonides and Nahmanides that spans his glosses to Sefer ha-Mitzvot is the most important composition ever written about the philosophy of halakhah. This debate reflects profound disagreement on fundamental concepts: revelation, controversy, the interpretive act, truth, and authority. Maimonides strove to isolate the Mosaic revelation from the rest of the corpus as an immutable, undisputed, adamantine kernel of unmatched halakhic status. For that reason, in his account of interpretation he tries to protect the kernel from those who would presume to speak in its name through the interpretive act. Nahmanides displays the opposite tendency when he tries to include the entire halakhic system in the primary revelatory event. His idea of revelation as multifaceted and encompassing the entire body of halakhic norms, and of interpretation as an ongoing revelation that constitutes meaning by selecting the normative one from a plethora of other options, forms the basis of his halakhic philosophy in his glosses to Sefer ha-Mitzvot.

CHAPTER 2

Custom and the History of Halakhah

I

In the twelfth century, the greatest Talmudists developed rich, sophisticated conceptual systems that enabled them to shine new and eye-opening light on Talmudic sources. Beside the new analytic tools developed during this century, the Tosafists also approached the Talmud synoptically, examining each and every sugya in the light of other sources in the Talmudic literature that directly or indirectly related to the topic at hand.[1] In this synoptic view, any marginal or even indirect reference in the Talmudic literature to the subject of discussion can induce a completely fresh reading of the central sugya in which the topic is examined. In the twelfth century, then, halakhic creativity had two dimensions: the first, the ability to create sharp and fundamental legal distinctions, which could overcome conceptual roadblocks, resolve tensions, and reorganize and reevaluate the material under discussion; and the second, analogical reasoning, which enabled comparison between similar and dissimilar and made the entire Talmudic corpus available and accessible, facilitating the clarification of an issue through comparison of the complete set of its direct and indirect appearances. The conceptual breakthroughs made and the synoptic outlook formed in the study halls of the twelfth century made the achievements of the Geonim look crude and rudimentary by comparison. The great twelfth-century Tosafists looked back on the Geonic tradition with the gaze of scientists who, having developed advanced instrumentation for observation and analysis, look back on the benighted era before the telescope and microscope.

The foci of twelfth-century halakhic creativity were varied and diverse, and so were the points of friction between the halakhists and the Geonim. R. Jacob b. Meir (Rabbeinu Tam) and R. Abraham b. David (Ra'avad), depicted as having the virtuosity necessary to render a dead creeping animal ritually pure via 150 arguments, generated superlative, bold, and novel halakhic insights using their newly established methods.[2] Maimonides, by way of contrast, was rooted in the world of Andalusia and so was more attached to particular halakhic traditions of the Geonim. While the drive to innovate and the principle that reason trumps all—come what may—motivated Rabbeinu Tam and Ra'avad in their revolutionary decisions, Maimonides turned his intellectual might to an organizational overhaul of the totality of halakhah, and to arranging it systematically and sequentially. Maimonides's points of divergence from the Geonic world primarily occur in meta-halakhic contexts that relate to understanding the basic categories of halakhah, or conceiving of its frameworks of authority. Maimonides heaps scorn upon one of the greatest Geonim, R. Simeon Kayyara, author of Halakhot Gedolot, specifically in the Principles that preface Sefer ha-Mitzvot, which are dedicated to clarifying the basic category of the halakhic method and not to specific rulings. For example, in Principle One, which was analyzed at length in the previous chapter, Maimonides attacks Kayyara and his successors by distinguishing between commandments given at Sinai and those legislated at a later date: "for them it is as if the Talmud were composed in a foreign language that they did not understand."[3] Maimonides's intellectual freedom is expressed by his contempt for those who adhere to Geonic positions out of blind faithfulness to the past. He complains that "the truth of the matter is examined not on its merits, but by whether it accords with the statements of earlier authorities, and without examining said statements."[4]

Nahmanides, living in the thirteenth century, carried the same toolkit as the twelfth-century halakhists; the lenses of his microscope and telescope had no less a polish than those of his predecessors. His tools of conceptual analysis did not fall short of those of Rabbeinu Tam or Ra'avad, whose modes of analysis and thinking profoundly influenced him. Like them, he also had colossal command over the range of halakhic sources, which allowed him to adopt the synoptic approach that he inherited from his Tosafist predecessors.[5] He even sharpened those instruments, whetting them to perfection.

Nahmanides's Talmudic novellae constitute, therefore, a clear and impressive continuation of the great change that occurred in the twelfth century. The novellae discuss questions that the Geonim did not even think to ask, and they reflect a towering world of halakhah that overshadowed its predecessors and left the Geonic inheritance in the dust.

What set Nahmanides apart from his eleventh- and twelfth-century predecessors, however, was his decidedly different attitude toward the world of the Geonim. In the specific sections of his novellae that touch upon subjects previously dealt with by the Geonim, he took the tools he had inherited and enhanced and used them for purposes quite at odds with those of their inventors. He employed the very working methods that leading twelfth-century halakhists had used to undermine certain halakhic traditions in order to restore them.[6]

In the introduction to his glosses on Maimonides's Sefer ha-Mitzvot, Nahmanides sketched the basic history of halakhah as he understood it, as well as his unique role within that historical framework. This picture becomes clearer during a rare moment of self-reflection, in which he surveys his halakhic methodology from the bloom of youth to ripe old age: "From my youth it has raised me like a father, and out of my mother's womb I have held it with strong grip, / and unto senescence and old age I will not let it slip. / I have held this trait close and will not let my commitment dip / [. . .] to vindicate the Earlier Authorities (*Rishonim*),[7] / to explicate Geonic profundities, / for in our Talmudic study / they are the cornerstone and foundation."[8] The defense of Geonic tradition and R. Isaac Alfasi (Rif, 1013–1103) characterizes all stages of Nahmanides's halakhic writing, from his early composition Milhamot ha-Shem, in which he responded to the glosses of R. Zerahiah ha-Levi (Razah, the author of Sefer ha-Ma'or) on Rif's Halakhot, and through the composition of his twilight years, a set of glosses on Sefer ha-Mitzvot, in which he defended Kayyara and the other Geonic enumerators of the commandments from Maimonides's scathing onslaught. In his introduction to his glosses to Maimonides's Book of Commandments, Nahmanides describes his debut in halakhic literature, Milhamot ha-Shem, as follows:

> I, smallest of my tribe and lowliest of my banner, / when in years tender, / heard a holy man [Rif] speak words of gold, / stringing together pearls manifold. / But a prince of the first rank gathered all his might, / to rip out, tear down, smash, and smite. / I cloaked myself in zealousness [. . .] I consulted the books that they composed [. . .] Until I

returned the Torah to its owner of right, / erecting upon its tell its new homesite.⁹

In the continuation, he describes his glosses to Sefer ha-Mitzvot, written at the end of his journey through halakhic literature, as closing the circle of his life's work:

> Today, when my face gleams from the stars of my beard, / I have a vision from God and behold! right here, / is a treatise of sapphire [. . .] by the great Master [Maimonides] a composition, / a fortress and bastion / [. . .] The Master too rages against the Earlier Authorities (*Rishonim*) in his treatise, / with leonine vehemence / he produces evidence / [. . .] a spirit moved me to vindicate them.¹⁰

Wherever the Geonic past is concerned, Nahmanides viewed his halakhic activity as counteracting the previous century's halakhists, whose activity he compared, in a few brief but perceptive lines, to a terrifying tidal wave that nearly washed away the authority of the ancient tradition:

> In generations of Late (*dorot aharonim*) we have taken notice, / that those of intellectual prowess / have become multitudinous. / With the roar of a lion and the gnar of a lioness / they essay via question and argument / to demolish ramparts reinforced up to the battlement. / They wield a double-edged knife / to kill and grant life / —killing off words of the wise that should not die, / and sparing those things that should stay where they lie.¹¹

In Nahmanides's eyes, the twelfth-century halakhists had unjustifiably undermined the halakhic world of the Geonim and Rif by turning the fine-tuned trebuchets of their intellects against their predecessors.

In the introduction to his glosses on Sefer ha-Mitzvot, Nahmanides set his contra-Maimonidean project within the broader cultural context of his response to "generations of Late." This broader context informs us that he did not perceive Maimonides's combination of sweeping independence and self-assured, critical tone as the idiosyncratic product of genius wedded with a particular constitution. He regarded this stance to be an expression of the mentality of an entire stormy and critical period, which is why he also viewed his glosses as part of a comprehensive move to push back against this period. The ferocious felines who, as Nahmanides put it, "essay via question and argument to demolish ramparts reinforced up to the battlement" are not only those explicitly mentioned in his introduction, that is, Razah and Maimonides, because Nahmanides devoted specific works to polemicizing with them. To Maimonides and Razah one can add three more halakhists, giants of the eleventh and twelfth centuries who are featured in the discourse of Nahmanides's novellae: R. Solomon b. Isaac (Rashi), Rabbeinu Tam, and Ra'avad. These five halakhists, whose writings dictated the commentarial order of the day for Nahmanides, were active in the distinct cultural centers of Andalusia, Provence, and northern France. They differ fundamentally in the way they think through things, the way they organize their halakhic material, the various traditions that influenced them, and, needless to say, the particular content of their interpretive decisions. If one looks closely at Nahmanides's halakhic compositions, it becomes apparent fairly quickly that his relationship with and estimation of each of the five differs, too. Nahmanides's differences of opinion with Ra'avad in the shorter works he wrote to defend Rif from him, namely, Sefer ha-Zekhut and his glosses to Ra'avad's Hilkhot Lulav, do not even begin to compare to his trenchant rebuttals of Razah's ideas in Milhamot ha-Shem.

Nahmanides, as we have said, was a clear and brilliant successor to the conceptual and analytical breakthroughs of the eleventh- and twelfth-century Torah giants. Yet, from his point of view, one element united those scholars and placed them along the same front opposite him: their Talmudic and halakhic methodology demonstrates intellectual independence from ancient halakhic traditions, an independence responsible for, among other things, a level of creativity unprecedented in the history of Talmudic and halakhic interpretation. In addition to the works Nahmanides dedicated to debate with Maimonides, Razah, and Ra'avad, whose purpose was to defend the positions of the Geonim and Rif, his Talmudic novellae evidence the dozens of times in which he rejects the ideas of Rashi, Rabbeinu Tam, and Ra'avad in favor of the positions taken by Rif and the Geonim.[12] In Nahmanides's binoculars, the front line is homogenous—all are considered recruits from the "generations of Late," despite the fact that they all have essentially different lines of attack and criticism, which in turn necessitate wildly different defensive strategies and responses. This opposing front represents a singular element of Nahmanides's self-consciousness as a halakhist.

Nahmanides's loyalty to the halakhic traditions of Rif and the Geonim is not blind or absolute. In the introduction to his glosses on Sefer ha-Mitzvot, after describing his general approach of defending his forebears, Nahmanides has the following reservation:

Although my inclination and aspiration vis-à-vis the Earlier Authorities (*Rishonim*) is to be their pupil, / to preserve their words and keep them principal, / to fashion from them a choker for my neck and a bracelet for my carpal, / I shall not carry their tomes in perpetuity like a pack animal. / I may choose their path / and know their worth, / but when they say things I cannot wrap my head around, / I shall make my case before them from the ground, / and rule based on what I have found. / When the law is clear, / in matters of Torah I hold no one dear.[13]

The defense of Geonic traditions and Rif is no statute set in stone, and Nahmanides does, at times, disagree with their rulings on a practical level. Vindicating the Earlier Authorities serves as more of a broad tendency and policy, one that his twelfth-century predecessors did not follow.

We should also bear in mind that the traditions of the Geonim and Rif are not cut from one cloth, and Nahmanides is aware of the differences within this larger tradition. Rif merits pride of place in Nahmanides's scheme, and he consistently refers to Rif in his writings as Rabbeinu ha-Gadol, "our Great Master."[14] An anonymous designation of this kind, in which a halakhist is not referred to by name but is called Rabbeinu, "our master," is a classic sign of authoritativeness. The positions of a halakhist whose name is omitted no longer represent those of the halakhist but assume the authority of halakhah itself. For the same reason, R. Judah the Prince was called Rabbi, "Master," and hundreds of years later Rabbi Joseph Caro was referred to as Maran, "our Master." Nahmanides oftentimes disagrees with one of the Geonim, and whenever Rif disagrees with the Geonim Nahmanides generally takes Rif's side, unless otherwise forced because of particularly compelling reasons. In the majority of instances, Nahmanides does not disagree with the Geonim and Rif when they present a united front, and when he does disagree in the isolated case, he typically comes down on the side of stringency while voicing his reservations.[15] Nahmanides also distinguishes within the group of Geonim in his writings, conferring honor upon R. Sherira Gaon and R. Hayya Gaon by referring to each of them as Rabbeinu ha-Ga'on, "our master, the Gaon."[16]

Nahmanides's attitude toward preceding halakhists can be graded fairly accurately by the rhetoric he uses in relating to them, particularly when he disagrees with them. Nahmanides carefully considers his manner of expression toward his predecessors, resulting in consistent patterns. He mostly does not attribute error to Rif, and if he finds difficulty in Rif's words, he generally blames his own inadequate comprehension. In such cases, Nahmanides uses one of the following stock expressions: "his reason has not become clear to me," "it requires study," "the formulation he wrote is not clear," "Rabbeinu ha-Gadol's reason is not evident to us," "the words of Rabbeinu ha-Gadol have not become clear enough," and others.[17] These formulaic expressions set the following general condition: he who disagrees with Rif has the burden of proof, because Rif deserves the benefit of the doubt, excepting cases where his position is plainly untenable. By comparison, Nahmanides reserves a quite different set of statements for all the halakhists of the twelfth century, French and Andalusian alike. These include "this is incorrect," "wrong," and "he blundered here." The opinions of Rashi, R. Joseph Ibn Migash (Ri Migash),[18] Maimonides, Rabbeinu Tam,[19] Ra'avad,[20] and other Tosafists[21] are sometimes cast aside with such phrases, their interpretations portrayed as erroneous and mistaken. Nahmanides treats them as equals, and when one of them goes up against the traditions of Rif and the Geonim in Nahmanides's arena, they typically lose.

At the other end of the rhetorical scale we have the inversion of Rif with Razah, whose opinions are frequently invalidated by Nahmanides as "nonsensical words" or "a response of no substance." Such disparaging stock phrases are not directed at any other twelfth-century halakhist in Nahmanides's writings; he holds it in reserve for Razah alone.[22] Even so, Nahmanides's barbs do not begin to approach the rhetorical heights from which Ra'avad sent forth his volleys of stinging insults against Razah. Absent from Nahmanides's statements are the tone of personal rivalry, the sense of insult, and the open wounds that accompanied the exchange of verbal blows between Ra'avad and Razah. In his introduction to Milhamot ha-Shem, Nahmanides even apologizes for his sharp tone against Razah, a product, he claims, of his youthful passion and ardent outrage. He declares that he has changed his attitude toward Razah out of respect for him and his status in his glosses on Ha-Ma'or ha-Katon on the order of Mo'ed, which were written after his glosses on Ha-Ma'or ha-Gadol on the orders of Nashim and Nezikin.[23] In any case, the more rhetorical usages of "nonsensical words" or "windiness," instead of "wrong" or "incorrect," reflect his attempt, similar to Ra'avad's, to eject Razah from the circle of productive halakhic discourse. Razah's halakhic originality and eccentricity do not exceed those of Rabbeinu Tam or Ra'avad, but what is permitted them is forbidden to him. Ra'avad and Rabbeinu Tam support their originality with, one could say, a terrifying, analytical coup de grâce. Even when they seem to be mistaken, then, Nahmanides still considers them fruitful participants in the halakhic conversation. In his eyes, Razah lacks the mastery and hyperacuity that justify such originality; the only thing left for Nahmanides to do is to clear the halakhic path of an unproductive, unbudging nuisance.[24]

This analysis of Nahmanides's rhetorical politics places in sharp relief the difference between the status of Rif and Geonic tradition, on one hand, and the status of the leading halakhists of the twelfth century, on the other. It will be useful to exemplify Nahmanides's general approach through the prism of one interpretive, halakhic question, which will enable us to better see how deep and how far the limits of his loyalty go, as well as to clarify his methodology. This will yield insights into the nature of his halakhic activity, which puts the achievements of the twelfth-century halakhists to work in defending the Geonic tradition they themselves had undermined. The question that needs to be examined relates to one of the customs and rulings of the Geonim that came under intense criticism, which Nahmanides analyzes in his Milhamot ha-Shem and Discourse on the New Year. Since this discourse was among his later works and Milhamot ha-Shem was his first, the consistency between these two sources in his treatment of the question speaks volumes, attesting as it does to the constancy of his approach over his lifetime.

The ruling of the Geonim relates to the dispute between the Sages and Rabban Gamaliel discussed in the Babylonian Talmud (Rosh ha-Shanah 33b, 34b–35a) over the prayer leader's recitation of the 'amidah prayer: Does it discharge the congregation's obligation, or must the congregants do so by means of their own silent 'amidah? Rabban Gamaliel opined that the prayer leader does discharge their obligation, which means that the sole purpose of the silent 'amidah is to enable him to prepare his prayers. The Sages contended that the congregation fulfills its obligation individually with the silent 'amidah, which means that the prayer leader repeats the 'amidah aloud in order to discharge the obligation of only those who are unfamiliar with the prayers and so cannot say them silently. The Talmud cites a statement of R. Yohanan that the law follows Rabban Gamaliel with respect to the 'amidah blessings on the High Holidays, and medieval Talmud commentators disagreed about the halakhic implications of this statement.[25] During the High Holidays of Rosh ha-Shanah and Yom Kippur, three additions are made to the prayer of mussaf of other holidays: the blessing of "malkhuyot," which is related to God's kingship; the blessing of "zikhronot," which is related to the theme of remembrance; and the blessing of "shofarot," which touches upon the blowing of the shofar and its diverse scriptural appearances. Geonic tradition cited in various places had it that on the New Year the congregation would pray seven blessings silently and omit the additions of "malkhuyot," "zikhronot," and "shofarot," and then the prayer leader would recite the nine[26] blessings aloud.[27] This custom seems incomprehensible. If the law follows Rabban Gamaliel, then the congregation prays the silent 'amidah so that the prayer leader can prepare, so why would they not say the same prayer as the prayer leader? And if we say that the congregation discharges its obligation even without the silent 'amidah, what would be the purpose of the seven-blessing prayer that omits "malkhuyot," "zikhronot," and "shofarot"? The Andalusian rabbi Isaac Ibn Ghiyyat (1038–1089), one of the earliest medieval authorities to cite this Geonic custom, rejects it. What is more, he even testifies that the early Andalusian practice opposed the Geonic one: "We have a tradition from our greatest sages, decisors, and leaders (*anshei ma'aseh*), who themselves received the tradition from previous great sages, such as Rabbi Samuel ha-Levi, who [in turn] received it from R. Hanokh and the elders of his generation, that the law as practiced is that we never pray seven, only nine. Thus do we instruct and act."[28] Similarly, the difficulty with the Geonic position and the different customs in Andalusia and northern France led Razah to use this case as a parade example of halakhah's mutability, which provided legitimacy for the new halakhic creativity: "Do not be taken aback by our statement that from earlier to later generations practices have changed. I myself recall seeing in my youth the entire congregation praying seven for the *mussaf* prayer and the prayer leader alone praying nine. They attributed this practice to the customs of the Geonic academies, for they found as much written in their books. [. . .] Now everyone has returned to praying nine blessings."[29] Nahmanides is well aware of the difficulties raised by Ibn Ghiyyat, but he rushes to the defense of the Geonim:

> The master's [Ibn Ghiyyat's] arguments are without a doubt serious ones, but the Geonim have attested that it was never done this [Ibn Ghiyyat's] way in the academy. Rather, the practice was always for the individuals to pray seven and the prayer leader nine. Whether we like it or not, we must accept their testimony, for the Geonim received [their tradition] from and saw [the practices of] the Savoraic rabbis, and so the Savoraic rabbis from the Amoraic rabbis. They preside over and provide instruction from the academy of and upon the seat of Rav Ashi, and they pray in his synagogue. Moreover, their custom has spread throughout most of Israel, until R. Isaac Ibn Ghiyyat decided

to return the west [i.e., Andalusia] to its custom. I have therefore poured my heart into this, fulfilling the Rabbinic dictum that whenever a rabbinic court pours its heart into something, it will succeed.[30]

Despite the initial difficulties, Nahmanides accepts the Geonic custom. He raises a fundamental argument, which will be discussed soon at length, that the Geonim had a direct tradition leading back to the last generation of Babylonian Amora'im, which gives them precedence. The halakhist's duty is to use his interpretive skills not to effect halakhic change, but to vindicate Earlier Authorities.

After declaring the Geonic practice to be reliable, Nahmanides applies a distinction that allows him to solve the problem raised by it. According to Nahmanides, Rabban Gamaliel does not require the congregation to say the prayers, so there is no reason to require them to pray silently the same prayer that will be repeated aloud by the prayer leader. However, R. Yohanan's statement that the law follows Rabban Gamaliel with respect to the 'amidah blessings on the New Year has no bearing on the seven blessings that constitute the basic 'amidah format of all holidays; it pertains only to those blessings added for the occasion of the New Year: "Subsequently, it was ruled that the law follows Rabban Gamaliel about the New Year alone. They [the congregation] are therefore not obligated to say the nine blessings, by whose recitation the prayer leader exempts even those who know their prayers, but they are obligated in the seven just as they are on other holidays, for the obligation of the day is like that of the other holidays."[31] As Nahmanides would have it, the decision that the law follows Rabban Gamaliel for the prayer of the New Year does not pertain to the contents that the prayer shares with other regular holidays, but only to the New Year additions. That explains why members of the congregation must say seven blessings in the silent 'amidah of mussaf on the New Year, just as everyone agrees they must pray those seven during the 'amidah of the morning and afternoon. The prayer leader discharges the congregation's obligation of "zikhronot," "shofarot," and "malkhuyot," which are accompanied by shofar blowing. A distinction such as this is a characteristic product of the analytical methods given new life in the twelfth century. It generates what nineteenth-century Yiddish-speaking Talmudists would come to call *tzvei dinim*, "two aspects," in this case within the New Year's prayer. Nahmanides, in his way, uses this method to rethrone the Geonic and Babylonian halakhah.

In the continuation of the piece about prayer on the New Year, Nahmanides demonstrates the correctness of the Geonic position from an analysis of the Jerusalem Talmud. This broadening of the halakhah's horizons from the Babylonian and Geonic to the Palestinian is, again, a prominent achievement of some of the twelfth-century halakhists.[32] Nahmanides adopts this expansiveness from his predecessors and broadens it still more, but as with his study method, he uses this, too, to restore the Babylonian tradition to its rightful place.

This example showcases Nahmanides's unique approach in instances where the rulings of the Geonim and Rif met opposition, an approach whose essence combines novel analytical techniques in the service of the traditional halakhah. What is fascinating about this example is that Nahmanides's decision does not prefer the Andalusian custom over the Franco-German one. Ibn Ghiyyat shows that the repudiation of Geonic tradition began as Andalusian halakhah took its very first steps, and it continued until the teachers of R. Samuel ha-Nagid. Here, as elsewhere, Nahmanides aspired to turn back the clock to pre-Andalusian Geonia. A look at his writings reveals that those he refers to as "the greatest Andalusians," among them Rif's disciple Ri Migash and grand-disciple Maimonides, did not merit the special status reserved for the Geonim and Rif. In the renaissance Nahmanides tried to cultivate, he strived to return to the earliest source of Eastern halakhah.

As noted above, Nahmanides does not fall short of his inventive predecessors, and as a halakhist he most definitely does not use them as a crutch. In fact, he should be viewed as their exceptional successor with respect to making innovative, analytical breakthroughs. This begs the following question: What scheme of halakhic history did Nahmanides internalize, which compelled him to try to keep the standard of the Geonic halakhic tradition flying even in the face of what he perceived as overwhelming opposition from the twelfth century? The answer to this question lies in his unique and original way of dividing the history of halakhah through the categories of the "Earlier Authorities," Rishonim, and the "Later Authorities," Aharonim.

II

The division between Rishonim and Aharonim within the history of the halakhah is usually understood as a fifteenth-century development, and various scholars have unpacked its meaning as a sign of crisis and closure.[33] The uniqueness of the category of Aharonim, as it appears in the fifteenth century, lies in the fact that it does not reflect chronological relativity, according to which those considered Aharonim in one period would come to be

considered Rishonim in the next, but instead serves as a fixed boundary between eras. In the self-consciousness of fifteenth-century halakhists, in the
mid-fourteenth century a fault line formed within the history of halakhah,
widening the gap between Rishonim and Aharonim such that the latter could
no longer be said to match the former. It has escaped the notice of scholars
studying this topic that Nahmanides was the first halakhist to make this systematic and important division between Rishonim and Aharonim as a marker
of eras, a division that stands at the center of his conception of halakhic history. He might not have been as self-deprecating as the fifteenth-century halakhists in his use of this division, but he absolutely did see it as marking the
superiority and authoritativeness of the earlier period over the one succeeding
it. This distinction of Nahmanides's creation did not reflect the spirit of the
age; in fact, owing to his unique role within the history of halakhah and his
reaction to preceding halakhists, Nahmanides retroactively imposed this distinction upon twelfth-century halakhists who certainly did not share this self-
consciousness.

According to Nahmanides's chronological division, the period of the Rishonim includes the Geonim and ends with Rif. Nahmanides refers to the
combination of the Geonim and Rif as "the Rishonim and Rabbeinu [ha-
Gadol]," which appears throughout his variegated halakhic oeuvre. Since Rif
died at the very beginning of the twelfth century, a substantial line of division
is created by Nahmanides which marks that period between the halakhic authorities of the ninth, tenth, and eleventh centuries and what came after
them. The inclusion of the Geonim and Rif within the category of the Rishonim appears in numerous places. As he says in his Milhamot ha-Shem:
"Now the matter is decided in accordance with the words of the Rishonim
and Rabbeinu ha-Gadol."[34] Nahmanides uses "Geonim" and "Rishonim"
synonymously, even switching between them within the same paragraph:
"The author of the Ma'or [Razah] did not hear the words of the Rishonim
[. . .] We will not heed his words to breach the wall of the Rishonim [. . .] So
ruled all of the Geonim and Rabbeinu."[35] In another context, where he again
switches back and forth between the designations, he attributes the reason for
the superiority of the Rishonim to their trustworthy tradition: "Moreover, the
tradition of the Geonim is decisive, for even Rashi attested that his masters
would explain it this way, in line with the tradition of the Rishonim."[36] The
interconnection between the Torah taught by the Geonim and trustworthy
tradition, as well as the power of the descriptor "Rishonim" to represent the
authority of tradition, appears in his Torat ha-Adam in the context of an

argument between Maimonides and the Geonim: "And as for us—on whom should we rely? Let us rely on the words of the Rishonim, whose words constitute tradition and require no reinforcement."[37]

The descriptor "Rishonim" occasionally serves as a platform for nostalgic sentiment. In one of his glosses that deals with the laws of inheritance and gifting, Razah criticizes R. Hayya Gaon and Rif: "These words are far from our mind and too deep for our intellect, and we have not fathomed what he or Rabbeinu Hayya Gaon, in whose name these words were said, had in mind. The sages of the previous generation [R. Abraham b. Isaac Av Beit Din (Ravi Abad)] found difficulty with what is written in the *Halakhot*, but we have nothing other than the formulation of our Rabbis."[38] Nahmanides begins his retort to Razah as follows: "I will explain what the Geonim had in mind." At the end of the piece, after much discussion, he identifies these Geonim with the Rishonim: "Now the perplexity of Rav Av B" D [Ravi Abad] dissolves without leaving a trace behind. / While true that it would be nice to expound upon his words of another kind, / still one who learns the Torah of the *Rishonim* is like drinking wine that has been refined."[39] Aharonim, in Nahmanides's usage, describes the Talmudic commentators and halakhists who came after Rif, up to and including Nahmanides's own time. Sometimes, Nahmanides juxtaposes the explanations of Rif and the Geonim with an opposing position of later commentators whom he calls "the Later commentators (*ha-mefareshim ha-aharonim*)." As he puts it: "Such is the opinion of the Geonim and Rabbeinu ha-Gadol, but we have seen most of the Later commentators explain . . ."[40] Maimonides, for example, is included within the category of Aharonim in Nahmanides's Talmudic novellae: "I have seen some of the Later codifiers (*ha-mehabberim ha-aharonim*), including the great codifier R. Moses b. R. Maimon the Andalusian."[41] Likewise, in Nahmanides's novellae on tractate Shabbat he refers to Ra'avad as one of the "Later authors."[42] At times he uses "the Later rabbis of Andalusia (*rabbanei Sefarad ha-aharonim*)" as a way of referring to Rif's disciples broadly construed, inclusive of Ri Migash and Maimonides: "The Geonim and all Later rabbis of Andalusia agreed."[43]

An instructive case of Nahmanides's use of this basic distinction between Rishonim and Aharonim pertains to the explanation of the mishnah in Makkot (1.5) about chain disqualification of witnesses. The mishnah reads as follows: "If others came and disqualified them [the first set of witnesses], and others came and disqualified them, even a hundred—they all die. Rabbi Yehudah says this is a conspiracy, and only the first set is killed." Nahmanides

tests two possible interpretations that each fall on opposite sides of his peri-
odic distinction. The first interpretation understands the mishnah to mean
that the same single set of witnesses disqualifies all other sets that come to
testify about the same case. The Sages say all are killed because all have been
disqualified and thus shown to be lying in a capital case. R. Yehudah says that
since a single set is disqualifying each and every group that comes to testify,
there is suspicion of a plot afoot, so the later sets are not killed. The second
interpretation understands this to be a case where the first set disqualifies a
second set, then that second set disqualifies a third set, and so on. Nahmanides says about the first approach: "All of our Later masters (*rabboteinu ha-
aharonim*) agree that this is the interpretation of the *mishnah,* that the first set
disqualifies the rest, who all testify that the same murderer killed that person."[44] The second interpretation, according to Nahmanides, was adopted by
the Rishonim: "The Earlier Geonim explained that others came and disqualified these who had disqualified the first set [. . .] The *Rishonim* explained it
like this, and although they were not prophets, they were sons of prophets,
whose waters the *Aharonim* drink after them."[45] Nahmanides describes the
superiority of the Rishonim in very strong terms: they are sons of prophets
from whose Torah the Aharonim drink.[46] Aware though he is of the advan-
tages to the interpretation proposed by the Aharonim, he shows how the sugya can be explained according to the Rishonim, even bringing proof from
the Tosefta. Here is his final word: "This is what I have come up with to fix
up the words of the *Rishonim.* Although I know and recognize that the text of
the passage fits the words of the *Aharonim,* the support I found for them [the
Rishonim] in the books of the Tosefta required this of me."[47]

The way in which Nahmanides periodizes the history of halakhah teaches
us about the special position Rif held in this historical pecking order. Most of
the time Rif is mentioned independently, included in neither of the broad
categories of Rishonim and Aharonim. Nahmanides appends him to the Rishonim as an independent entity, describing them together as "the Rishonim
and Rabbeinu ha-Gadol" or "the Geonim and Rabbeinu ha-Gadol." He thus
paints a historical picture in which it is the Rishonim plus Rif versus the Aharonim. The singling out of Rif alongside the Rishonim implies that Rif stands
at the end of the era of the Rishonim, while simultaneously representing its
culmination. Rif is almost like the *batra'ei,* the last and thus most authoritative of the Rishonim, whom the law ought to follow. From Rif and onward,
that is, from the outset of the era of the Aharonim, the law no longer follows
the chronologically latest authority. Indeed, Nahmanides asserts that Rif is

superior to all who follow him, as he remarks about a dispute between Rabbeinu Ephraim and Rif: "The end of the matter is that the law does not follow the disciple in the presence of the master."[48] With this trifold division that makes Rif the pivot of halakhic history, Nahmanides in practice makes the following argument: Rif has the advantage over his predecessors because he is the apogee of the era of the Rishonim, and Rif is superior to his successors because next to him they are Aharonim.

In the introduction to his glosses on Sefer ha-Mitzvot, which was cited above, Nahmanides says that the transformation in the field of halakhah took place "in generations of Late (*dorot aharonim*)." This corresponds, then, to the watershed line of halakhic history, which in Nahmanides's eyes distinguishes the Rishonim from the Aharonim. This line, which separates Rif from his successors, signifies for Nahmanides the detachment of halakhah from the longstanding chain of tradition that lent the Rishonim precedence. The pinpointing of this moment as the one of transition and fracture in halakhic history is not artificial, for it coincided with the geographical transfer of the centers of Torah from Iraq and North Africa to Andalusia. Likewise, this moment heralded the creative and furious development of methods of study and analysis, accompanied by a sense of independence and boldness. Many of those whom Nahmanides calls Aharonim would have agreed that their own time was a transformative period in the history of halakhah. But the lion's share of them, those who did not deem the Geonim a special source of authority, would have viewed Nahmanides's take on things as upside down. Nahmanides ascribed to the Rishonim a trustworthy tradition with roots stretching back to the final generations of the Amora'im. Though he valued the transformative breakthroughs, he also could not help but see the gaping holes they had left. He therefore made use of the recent achievements to find footing for a teetering tradition.

III

This conception of the history of halakhah, with its division into the two determinative periods of Rishonim and Aharonim, is reflected in the favored status shown to Geonic custom in Nahmanides's theory of custom (*torat ha-minhag*). A thorough clarification of this requires an understanding of his general theory of custom, which he formulates in the context of the first systematic discussion of custom in the history of halakhah, a discussion broached by Razah and Ra'avad.

Razah constructs his systematic and all-encompassing position on this complex issue at the end of the first sugya in Makom she-Nahagu, the fourth chapter of tractate Pesahim. At the close of his discussion of the various rules governing custom, he gives his account an air of comprehensiveness and finality by employing a biblical formulation: *zot torat ha-minhagot*, "this is the teaching regarding customs."[49] Although he used this for rhetorical effect, his contemporaries and later authorities adopted torat ha-minhagot to refer to a halakhic theory of custom. Razah's attempt to formulate a comprehensive theory, and especially its pretension and rhetoric of being the final word, obviously met with strong criticism. Ra'avad, who tries to present a rival account of the evidence, mocks Razah in the opening line of his gloss: "Look at him! He thinks he has assembled a comprehensive theory of custom, but he hasn't got even the half of it."[50] Criticism notwithstanding, Razah's endeavor obligated subsequent halakhists to formulate their own systematic legal theories that would define custom's source of validity, its status within the hierarchy of other obligations, and the extent of its dependence upon the local conditions in which it arose. At the center of this effort stands a problem that the halakhists all face: How does one assimilate the realm of custom into a regulated, hierarchical halakhic system when that realm, by its very essence, springs up alongside halakhah, whose particular content and specific historical circumstances that organically give rise to it are exempt from the positive norms and structures of halakhic authority laid out in the Babylonian Talmud? Israel M. Ta-Shma noted that the consolidation of such consuetudinary theory was one of the hallmarks of custom being tamed and delivered into the hands of critical halakhists.[51]

The sugya at the beginning of Makom she-Nahagu, which served as the launching point for the formulation of consuetudinary theory, focuses on the local nature of customs and how people changing locations should act with respect to practices in their places of emigration and immigration. The sugya presents different and contradictory cases, and the attempt to integrate them into a comprehensive and coherent theory underlies any theory of custom. The basic tension, whose solution is the subject of a disagreement between Razah and Nahmanides, concerns the mishnah and a baraita that appears in the course of the sugya. The mishnah (4.1) makes the prohibition to work on Passover Eve until midday dependent upon local custom: "In a place where the custom is to work . . . we may work; in a place where the custom is not to work, we may not work." As for someone in transit: "Someone traveling from a place where they work to a place where they do not, or from a place where they do not to a place where they do, we impose upon him the stringencies of his place of departure and the stringencies of his destination. A person may not act differently, out of concern for quarrels (*mahloket*)." The baraita cited by the Talmud, however, formulates the following principle: "That which is permitted but others have the practice to prohibit, one may not permit in their presence" (Pesahim 51a). According to the baraita and its accompanying sugya, if the practice in the new place of residence is prohibitive, one may follow the permissive practice of one's hometown in private. Not only that, but the sugya's continuation asserts that the privacy requirement is necessary only where ignoramuses are present, because permitting it in their presence would lead them to permit other forbidden things on their own. In the presence of Torah scholars, on the other hand, one may follow one's permissive practice even in public. In summary, according to the mishnah one who leaves a permissive place for a restrictive one should be prohibited from working on Passover Eve—no exceptions. According to the baraita and the sugya that follows, however, the prohibition applies only in the public eye, and even then it is relaxed in the presence of Torah scholars.

Razah tries to solve the contradiction by interpreting the mishnah in light of the baraita, which results in the following complex structure. The mishnah's ruling applies only when one intends to return to one's place of departure, which explains why the stringencies of the place of departure are imposed. One is obligated in one's hometown customs because "it constitutes the tradition of the fathers (*kabbalat avot*), to which applies: 'Heed, my son, the discipline of your father' (Prov 1:8)."[52] That is why one cannot shake off the restriction of one's place of departure, and work on Passover Eve remains prohibited in the new, permissive place. In the other direction, if one intends to return to a permissive place and only temporarily relocated to a prohibitive one, then the mishnah's restriction is limited in accord with the baraita. That is, one cannot work in public view of ignoramuses, because it will spark quarrels, but wherever there are Torah scholars, or in private, one can act as if in one's hometown. The mishnah, according to Razah, is dealing only with a case of someone intending to return home, but someone with no such intent is completely exempt from hometown stringencies, and that person must adopt the custom of the new home, without any exception. This reading of the mishnah, which Nahmanides challenges, is difficult, for it drastically reduces the mishnah's scope to a quite specific and forced case, with the admitted benefit of aligning it with the sugya and baraita.

Razah's fundamental position, as analyzed by Israel Ta-Shma,[53] is that the community in which one resides establishes the consuetudinary obligation, and the validity of it flows from the obligation to observe "the tradition of the fathers." The fathers in this case are not one's biological father but the "fathers" of the community to which one belongs by virtue of the very decision to live there. In addition to this fundamental idea and the various distinctions that flow from it, Razah sets up an additional distinction within his consuetudinary theory that constitutes the critical turning point in the conceptualization of custom. He asserts that one is considered obligated to follow the prohibitive custom of a destination only if those observing it know that it is not, strictly speaking, prohibited by law, and that they have taken it upon themselves as a custom to act stringently. If, however, they mistakenly believe their custom to be prohibited by law, then one has no obligation to do as the Romans do when in Rome; rather, one may permit in their presence what had been customarily prohibited. Here is Razah: "All of this applies to things he knows are permitted but treats as forbidden. But if the custom developed out of error, we permit it in their presence in all instances, and one need not be concerned about that custom."[54] He produces proof from a statement in the Jerusalem Talmud: "Regarding something that he does not know is permitted and mistakenly treated as forbidden, he may consult [a scholar] and we release him" (Pesahim 4.1 [30d]). The Jerusalem Talmud's principle concerns a practice adopted by an individual, but Razah expands its purview to the totality of communal customs. According to this approach, if the communal custom is not supererogatory but reflects a particular understanding of halakhah, it must stand up under scrutiny of the relevant halakhic texts. If the custom is erroneous, it should be publicly repudiated. The strength of custom, therefore, lies in the realm of the supererogatory—it is of no weight when it comes to halakhah itself. This essential distinction, as we will see, is fundamentally accepted by Nahmanides, and it has far-reaching consequences for consuetudinary theory, which is discussed below.

Nahmanides disagrees with Razah's understanding of the mishnah and baraita, although he uses Razah's own distinction to resolve the contradiction between the two sources. In Nahmanides's view, even someone intending to return home must follow the custom of the destination—even in the presence of Torah scholars, and even in private. He reads the mishnah straightforwardly and therefore requires someone to follow the new location's stringencies in all circumstances. The mishnah's concern about quarrels is not, as Razah believed, that quarrels would serve to undermine the custom in the presence of ignoramuses. Quarrels mean factionalism and fragmentation, so one must accept the local custom even if one intends to return home; one should not march to one's own drum. Nahmanides understood "out of concern for quarrels" as a stronger and more forceful argument, by dint of which the newcomer must follow the local practice even in the presence of Torah scholars, and even in private.

This understanding of the mishnah necessitates accounting for the baraita and sugya, which prohibit acting permissively only in the presence of ignoramuses and permit following one's hometown custom privately or in the presence of Torah scholars. In order to distinguish the mishnah from the baraita, Nahmanides adopts Razah's distinction between knowing the true legal status of the custom and misconstruing it. In keeping with this distinction, Nahmanides limits the baraita to a case where the practitioners erroneously believed the custom to be forbidden by law. In such a case, Nahmanides says, the practice has no binding force. In contrast to Razah, who believed that in such circumstances the customary prohibition may be permitted even in the presence of ignoramuses, Nahmanides contends that such a permit would be allowed only in the presence of Torah scholars.[55] Nahmanides reads the baraita as follows: "That which is permitted but others have the practice to prohibit," because they mistakenly believe it is the law, "one may not permit in their presence."[56]

Nahmanides justifiably claims that his approach better fits the simple meaning of the mishnah and that Razah's attempt to read the baraita into the mishnah is forced. At the same time, Nahmanides is forced to limit the baraita to a case where the custom is mistakenly thought to be the law. The language of the baraita—"but others have the practice to prohibit"—does not justify such a reading; the baraita should have read "but others prohibit."[57] In addition, Nahmanides's interpretation of the mishnah does not distinguish someone planning to stay from someone intending to return—both are equally obligated to follow the practice of the new location. And yet, the Talmud makes such a distinction with respect to Rabbah b. Bar Hannah, who left the land of Israel for Babylonia and ate the fat on the lesser curvature of the abomasum, which Babylonian custom forbade. The custom of the land of Israel followed R. Akiva, who ruled such fat halakhically permitted; the custom of Babylonia followed R. Yishmael, who ruled it halakhically forbidden. The Talmud asks: Why did Rabbah b. Bar Hannah not act in accord with the stringencies of his destination, as the mishnah requires? Rav Ashi answers that he intended to return to the land of Israel. This question and answer should fit with only Razah's approach, in which intent to return requires one to comply with local custom only in public and when ignoramuses are present.

Nahmanides surmounts this difficulty by creating a new, additional category for his consuetudinary theory:

> If the practice is due to a biblical prohibition and is not necessarily erroneous, such as [prohibiting the consumption of] the fat on the lesser curvature, and he intends to return home, he has no consuetudinary obligation regarding this. Instead, he may treat it permissively in public. He may not, however, permit it for them, for it is impossible to do so since even according to the opinion of his own hometown, the custom of the town in which he is visiting now is not considered a blatant mistake in law, but rather they would only be considered to have erred in the weighing of opinion. His permissive treatment of it poses no problem of "quarrels" because they did not take up the practice originally as a custom but as a stringency in deciding that the law is thus. It is like a biblical prohibition for them, which requires no reinforcement, for they already know it to be a dispute between sages and that the practice of their city is not decisive. If there are ignoramuses among the city residents,[58] then he can act permissively in private, but not in their presence, for they will become habituated [to permitting what is prohibited], which is the case of Rabbah b. Bar Hannah.[59]

According to Nahmanides, a custom based upon siding with one rabbinic authority in a Talmudic dispute, like the Babylonian custom that followed R. Yishmael's opinion, is not at all the same thing as a regular custom the community takes upon itself as a stringency beyond the law. Nahmanides believes that a newcomer must follow the local custom even in private if it is a regular one, "out of concern for quarrels," whereas a custom rooted in taking one side of a dispute does not require the new arrival to observe it. He treats the latter type differently because the prohibition's source is not communal power or authority, but the halakhic position adopted by the community. Undermining the community's decision does not affect its authority. As Nahmanides says: "There is definitely no concern of 'quarrels,' because this is like the quarreling between the Schools of Shammai and Hillel, each of whom followed their own opinions, yet treated each other with love and brotherhood."[60] Nahmanides likewise identifies this case as one of error in the weighing of opinion, and distinguishes it from a case where the communal practice is mistaken for law. His distinction between a mistake about an explicit law that is on the books and a mistake in weighing opinions is borrowed from a discussion in tractate Sanhedrin about erroneous judicial rulings. Nahmanides believes that a decision to follow one Talmudic opinion, even if it is mistaken, can generate a legitimate, unimpeachable custom. Therefore, a newcomer may continue to follow the practice of the hometown but cannot release the local residents from their practice. In the case of a prohibitive custom based on an utterly mistaken construal of the law, a newcomer may even expressly annul the erroneous practice before Torah scholars. It emerges that not only is a custom derived from a mistaken interpretation of the law invalid, but so is a custom derived from taking the wrong side in a Talmudic dispute. Custom does not supply legally binding interpretations of halakhah; its entire validity derives from the fact that it adds some particular stringency to the preexisting law.

Nahmanides's consuetudinary theory thus comprises the following rules: (1) Individuals who intend to return home practice the stringencies of their temporary place of residence, even in the presence of Torah scholars and even in private, out of concern for sparking quarrels and because they have become denizens for a day. (2) If the stringent practice is mistakenly thought to be the law, newcomers may permit the practice in front of Torah scholars but not in front of ignoramuses. (3) If ignoramuses consult a scholar to be released from this mistakenly founded stringency, the scholar may absolve them because their observance of it is already weak. (4) If the stringent practice is the result of a decision to follow a particular authority in a Talmudic dispute, and a Torah scholar believes it to be an error in the weighing of opinions, he may not absolve them, but he may follow his own lenient practice in the presence of Torah scholars. (5) Individuals who do not intend to return home follow the local practice, even if it is the result of an error in the weighing of opinions.

The manner in which Nahmanides defines custom within the ramified halakhic system points to a profound change in the conceptualization of custom shared by Nahmanides, Ra'avad, and Razah. Custom can have two meanings, one broad and one narrow. In its broad sense, custom is the manner in which halakhah itself is implemented and practiced in the day-to-day life of a community faithful to halakhah. Halakhah is not, according to this view, a set of norms inscribed in canonical, binding texts but the way of life of the pious and God-fearing. Custom has binding force and cannot be invalidated even when it appears to contravene the authoritative sources of halakhah, because the community's way of doing things attests to an ancient, reliable halakhic tradition. Custom, therefore, assumes a status on par with, and even preferable to, the written, canonical sources of halakhah, particularly the Babylonian Talmud. "The custom of Israel is Torah," and in a case where custom seems to run counter to halakhah as it appears in texts, the sources should be interpreted to make them conform to this indubitable, living testimony. The broad definition of custom as a living, binding halakhic tradition prevailed in Ashkenaz, and, as Haim Soloveitchik portrays it, it was predicated upon the presumption of the unwavering, punctilious, and sacred devotion of the Franco-German community to the Torah.[61]

Beside its broad meaning, custom more narrowly defined is the store of stringencies, safeguards, and supplements that the community takes upon itself beyond the written, binding norms of the halakhah. Custom, in this sense, represents what is beyond the law; it is not some faithful witness to the contents of halakhic positive law, and it bears no interpretive validity that would force a halakhist to reexamine and reinterpret sugyot that appear to contradict it.

Nahmanides, in the footsteps of Razah, issues a rejection—sharper than Razah's—of custom's broader sense and instates the narrower one. In his opinion, a custom based on the premise that it is the law, or on a decision to rule like one side of a Talmudic dispute, has no binding validity, and its reliability should be vetted in the light of the written, authoritative sources of halakhah. Once custom is defined more narrowly as something the law permits but the people do not, a categorical distinction between halakhah and custom emerges that serves to vitiate custom's force as a binding, living testimony about halakhah itself.

In its broader sense, custom is witness and tradition, rendering superfluous and meaningless the question of its validity and authority. After all, as R. Hayya Gaon argues in his discussion of custom as tradition, even the authority of the canonical texts of the law—including the Written Torah—depends upon the trustworthiness of communal tradition regarding the source of those texts in revelation.[62] In contrast to this broader approach to custom, those halakhists who define custom narrowly must ground the source of custom's validity in a recognized and binding halakhic institution. For if custom is no witness to halakhah but an accretion upon it, what indeed makes it binding? The vow and oath offer themselves as central sources for this type of reduction, because, according to halakhah, individuals or communities can take oaths or make vows to obligate themselves in a legally valid obligation whose particular content does not derive from halakhah itself. Nahmanides, in the wake of Ra'avad, sees the validity of custom in the oath:

Rather, the rule applies specifically to the customs of a place which were practiced as customs per se, and which earlier authorities knew contained no prohibition and took them upon themselves to erect a safeguard around a commandment, like in our *mishnah*. That is when we do not permit [their customarily prohibited practice to] them, even though they may wish to repeal [the custom], as with the residents of Beit She'an. [. . .] Because we do not absolve someone who takes an oath to fulfill a mitzvah and consults [a scholar], as it is stated in tractates *Gittin* and *Bekhorot,* and R. Abraham [Ra'avad] says likewise.[63]

In the broad sense of custom, a custom is undermined when it becomes clear that it is of recent vintage. In the narrow sense described here, under which custom is a kind of vow or oath, the questions of late appearance on the scene and the supposed reflection of tradition are rendered superfluous, because the validity of custom does not flow from its antiquity or its unimpeachable testimony about ancient halakhic tradition. An oath becomes binding the second one utters it, and if done for mitzvah-related purposes, one cannot be released from it; therefore, its antiquity makes no difference one way or the other. If, however, one took an oath under the mistaken impression that it was the law, then it was a mistaken oath from which one can be absolved, just as one can be released from an erroneous vow. The shift in the halakhic legitimation of custom as a tradition to a kind of oath, which represents the shift from the broad to the narrow sense of custom and which also removes the force of custom as interpretive witness, turns on the polysemous characterization of custom as "the tradition of the fathers." Whereas in the first and broader sense of custom "the tradition of the fathers" (Kabalat Avot) means a tradition received and then transmitted by the fathers, in the second, narrower sense of custom the expression indicates an obligation that the "fathers" of the community took upon themselves, which then devolves upon the local residents. "Kabbalah" could mean either reception or obligation.

Ra'avad and Nahmanides both bridle custom with the reins of halakhah in two basic moves, although the latter does it with greater precision. First, they deny custom the standing of an authoritative interpretation of halakhah and reposition it in a field beyond the law. Then, as a corollary, they base custom's narrow sense and its validity upon the recognized halakhic institutions of vow- and oath-taking. Custom is thereby removed from the strict purview of halakhah while it is defined as binding via a recognized halakhic institution. This shift in the conceptualization of custom is based upon the interpretive widening of a statement in the Jerusalem Talmud, which calls to mind the procedures of vows and oaths. This was only partly cited above and is now produced in full: "R. Elazar b. Rabbi Bun says: Anything which one does not know is permitted, treats as forbidden, and then consults [a scholar], we permit him. Anything which one knows is permitted, treats as forbidden, and consults [a scholar], we do not permit him." Aside from the connection between custom and vow created by the halakhists, they also concluded from this statement that custom has no interpretive force, such that if it is performed on the faulty premise that it is the law, it is void. This unique statement, which is absent from the Babylonian Talmud, speaks only of the individual, and even then it is not clear that it is talking about a vow. From an interpretive point of view, turning this lone statement in the Jerusalem Talmud into a full-fledged conceptualization of custom is more than a little thin. This interpretive leap gives us a glimpse of the motivation behind the scenes: the submission of custom to the yoke of halakhah and its written authoritative sources. The narrow conception of custom considers the community an organic factor that can add stringencies to existing halakhah, but it lacks the power to testify about the nature of halakhah itself. Clarification of any binding norm is in the hands of Torah scholars, and it is they who sit in judgment over customs.

IV

Nahmanides puts his conceptualization of custom into practice in his Talmudic novellae and Milhamot ha-Shem. A close look at his various treatments of customs reveals that he does not consider prevalent communal practices as testimony of any gravity about the nature of halakhah. Nahmanides examines customs themselves in light of Talmudic sugyot and quite frequently rejects them, even as Franco-German halakhists defend them.

The first example of this approach appears in Nahmanides's discussion of the prohibition on wearing certain kinds of rings while moving from one domain to another on the Sabbath. A person is prohibited from moving objects from the private domain to the public domain during the Sabbath, but if the object is considered part of one's clothing or adornment, he or she is allowed to move such an object from one domain to the other. According to the Babylonian Talmud (Shabbat 59b–60a), since men typically wear signet rings during the week, only such rings can be considered an adornment with respect to the Sabbath and may be carried. If a man wears a ring that lacks a seal while changing domains, he has violated the Sabbath. Since women do not wear signet rings during the week, they may not change domains on the Sabbath while wearing a signet ring, for the very same reason. Nahmanides attests that the common contemporary practice was for men to violate this prohibition, in contravention of Talmudic law. Ashkenazic halakhists defended this communal custom,[64] and Rabbi Eliezer b. Nathan, one of the important halakhic figures in Ashkenaz during the twelfth century known as Ra'avan, did so as follows:

> Today, when people are unaccustomed to [wearing] signet rings, and both men and women place a ring on their finger during the week as an adornment and ornament, it is permitted. It seems to me that the earlier authorities who preceded us, who were wiser and more discerning than I am, relied on this [reality] and did not object to them, because if it is considered an adornment for the weekday, then the same is true for the Sabbath.[65]

Ra'avan refrains from forbidding this communal practice because its wide spread indicates the approval of past halakhists. To impeach the practice would have meant casting doubt upon the reliability and greatness of earlier authorities. He finds grounds to permit it in the fact that the men of his day wore non-signet rings during the week. Nahmanides, though, considers a ring sans signet to be a part of feminine costume and thus off limits to men: "A man may not adorn himself with feminine adornments." This led him to reject Ra'avan's permit: "Therefore, the times (lit. generations) do not change the law, and it is inappropriate to rule this way."[66]

An additional example of Nahmanides's disapproval of an accepted practice upheld by Franco-German halakhists concerns ritual immersion of the body in a river during the rainy season. The dispute first appears in the Babylonian Talmud (Shabbat 65b): Rav opines that rivers are disqualified because the spring water is mixed with rainwater, while Shmuel argues that even in the rainy season the majority of the river's water is still spring water, making it fit for immersion. The rule is that the law follows Rav in ritual matters, and because the sugya itself inclines toward his opinion as well, Nahmanides rules in accordance with Rav that one may not immerse in a river during the rainy season and the period following it. Nahmanides mentions the prevalent custom, which deviates from this ruling: "It is difficult for us, because they have the practice to immerse in rivers whether it is Nisan or Tishri." He is likewise aware of the Franco-German halakhists who rule like Shmuel and uphold the practice by relying, as is their wont, upon a marginal and indirect Talmudic reference, in this case one appearing in tractate Bekhorot.[67] He nevertheless rejects their position: "*Sefer Yere'im* also so ruled in the name of Rabbeinu Tam. The ruling is incorrect and should not be relied on."[68] He summarizes his own opinion at the end of the piece: "To our mind, we should be concerned about every river until the following is clear to you both for the sunny season and the rainy season: the extent of its spring, and the source of its headwaters and its majority [of waters]. The law certainly follows Rav."[69]

Nahmanides's clearest deviation from the Ashkenazic consuetudinary orbit appears in his rejection of the precentor's practice to insert liturgical poetry into the statutory prayers. The insertion of liturgical poetry was a central element in the Franco-German world of spirituality, even though, on the face of it, tractate Berakhot seems to prohibit any additions to the fixed form of the blessings: "Where they said to make a long [blessing] one may not shorten [it]; where they said to make a short [blessing], one may not lengthen [it]" (Berakhot 11a). Franco-German halakhists, Rabbeinu Tam among them, reinterpreted the Talmudic sources, thereby endorsing the poetic additions to the text of the blessing.[70] Nahmanides, who analyzed the meaning of these expressions, rejected the restrictive interpretation given by the Franco-German halakhists; instead, he believed that one may not play with the length of the text of the blessing: "According to our approach, we learn that those who add liturgical poems and hymns are not acting as they ought (*ke-shurah*). I have also found in *Midrash Kohelet:* ' "It is better to hear the reproof of a wise man"—these are the homilists, "than for a man to hear the song of fools"—these are the precentors,' for they add to the statutory prayer. The matter is obvious."[71] In Nahmanides's conceptualization, communal custom receives its stamp of approval only when the law is murky and unsettled. In his responsum on the knotty issue of reducing a debt via deduction, he writes, "At the end of the day, let the public act [as it does] with respect to this law, for it is a law that is not settled, it is shaky and our hold on it is loose."[72] In Torat ha-Adam he repeats this formulation: "It is a shaky law, about which one can respond by saying 'go out and see how the people act.' "[73] A fundamental formulation of custom's limited place within halakhah appears in his novellae, in a comment concerning the Talmudic assertion that the question of returning wedding presents depends upon local custom—"In a place where the custom is to return, we return." This leaves the decision up to the local custom, which, as Nahmanides reports, is interpreted in two ways:

Some interpret "a place where the custom is . . ." throughout the entire passage without qualification, as if to say "a place that has the
custom." Because if there is a custom, then obviously we would follow
the custom, even in a case where he [the person who received the pres-
ent] died, and no one disputes it. Others say that we consider a custom to be of substance when, for instance, the townspeople or seven
bon viri of the town (*shiv'ah tuvei ha-'ir*) in an assembly made a stipulation about it. Other customs, however, would not trump a law except when the law is shaky. The law follows the latter version.[74]

Nahmanides explains "In a place where the custom is to return, we return" as
applying only to a case of stipulation and explicit consent on the part of the
community to adopt the custom. In such a case, the custom's validity does not
derive from its being a witness to ancient law, but from the force of consent
in monetary matters, which allows one to make stipulations even contrary to
what is written in the Torah. An organic practice of the community cannot
decide the law—"Other customs, however, would not trump a law except
when the law is shaky." The rule that "custom trumps law," which obligates
halakhists to reinterpret written sources in light of custom, is here confined to
instances where the law is shaky.[75]

Nahmanides's conception of custom does an about-face when it comes to
customs of the Geonim. In his discussions of Geonic customs, he switches to
custom's broader sense of an unchallengeable witness to an ancient tradition
with which written halakhic sources should be aligned. He casts aside his own
opinion in the face of Geonic custom, even in cases where he believes the
straightforward meaning of a sugya contradicts their position. In his discussion of the order of the Torah reading on the new moon, Nahmanides cites
the Geonic position and adds: "This is the explanation of the *Rishonim,* and
such was their practice in these places for generations. I am perplexed about
the wisdom of the *Rishonim,* which was as wide as the Entrance Hall [of
the Temple], for what have they gained through this repetition [of the previous reader's verse]?"[76] After discussing the merits of the Geonic approach to
the sugya and to tractate Soferim, Nahmanides says: "But the custom practiced by the Geonim based on this explanation of theirs [. . .] no one here
agrees with it. Still, we should not meddle with a practice instituted by the
Geonim."[77] This complete bending of the knee in the face of Geonic custom
is anchored in the premise that the Geonim had a tradition reaching back to
the final years of the Amoraic period, as we saw above in his statement about

the Geonic custom of High Holiday prayer: "Whether we like it or not, we must accept their testimony, for the Geonim received [their tradition] from and saw [the practices of] the Savoraic rabbis, and so the Savoraic rabbis from the Amoraic rabbis. They preside over and provide instruction from the academy of and upon the seat of Rav Ashi, and they pray in his synagogue."[78]

A similar picture emerges from Nahmanides's treatment of the Geonic custom regarding prayer on public fast days, referring to public fast days that are ordered in response to a calamity that afflicts the community such as severe plague or drought. The Babylonian Talmud states that "there is no public fast in Babylonia" (Ta'anit 12b). Medieval Talmud commentators agreed that the statement concerns the additional afflictions of public fast days, such as the prohibitions on working and wearing shoes, which were not observed in Babylonia except on the ninth of Av and Yom Kippur. Some medieval halakhists, however, thought that it also applied to the special liturgy of the public fast— the twenty-four blessings, the ne'ilah prayer, and the soundings (blowing of the shofar or trumpets). In northern France, Nahmanides attests, the custom was not to pray ne'ilah or sound the shofar on a public fast day. He reports the same about his own place of residence: "But what can I do? Many tribulations have passed due to God's abundant mercies, and we have neither seen nor heard anyone pray ne'ilah."[79] The Geonim of Babylonia, on the other hand, did have the custom of reciting the entire special liturgy,[80] and Nahmanides tries to muster proofs that the statement "there is no public fast in Babylonia" does not apply to the special liturgy. Similarly, Nahmanides defends the Geonic opinion that the sounding on a public fast day is performed with a shofar and not, as Razah believed, with trumpets. In his Discourse on the New Year, Nahmanides sums up his opinion and his reliance upon Geonic custom:

> All of these are supports and proofs for the Geonic custom, and certainly that was the practice in the two academies—they had the custom of their forefathers from the days of Rav Ashi. We therefore have the practice in Spain to blow with a shofar on fast days of sounding the alarm, which they do not do in northern France at all, perhaps because they believe "there is no public fast in Babylonia" means even with respect to the liturgy, that is, the twenty-four [blessings], ne'ilah, and the soundings. We have already dealt with the crux of this issue using Talmudic proofs and Geonic practice [to show] that there are public fasts in Babylonia for all aspects of the liturgy—ne'ilah, the twenty-four blessings, and the soundings.[81]

One can see that Nahmanides identifies Geonic custom with trustworthy tradition. Elsewhere, the upshot of his discussion equates objecting to the customs of the Geonim, "who have the custom of their forefathers going back to the days of Rav Ashi," with undermining the very preservation of the oral tradition. Nahmanides makes this argument in response to Razah's creative position, mentioned earlier, that one should pray nine blessings in every 'amidah prayer of the High Holidays, and not only during the 'amidah of mussaf. Razah argues that the absence of any such practice makes no difference, because practice is not static but dynamic. As proof, he notes that even in his own lifetime he witnessed a shift from individuals praying seven blessings in the silent 'amidah, as was the Geonic custom, to praying nine blessings, which was not. About this Nahmanides says:

> If Israel were obligated to pray nine in every 'amidah prayer on the New Year—'arvit, shaharit, and minhah—how could everyone allow this to be so badly bungled? Why did the earlier Geonim, who received [their tradition] from the Savoraic rabbis, who constituted the end of instruction, not have this practice? How could there not remain in the two academies a single prayerbook from those of the later Talmudic sages? Truthfully, anyone who entertains doubts about this matter invalidates the chain of tradition, because this custom has been accepted by, assented to, and disseminated throughout the entire Jewish people, and no one has ever voiced any qualms about it. I have already demonstrated to you expressly from the Talmud that even in the days of our Rabbis, those sages of the Talmud, it was thus, and you have learned that deviating from the words of *Rishonim* is tantamount to separating from life [itself]. May God double the reward for the labors we have undertaken to judge them favorably, and may he judge us favorably.[82]

In his novellae, Nahmanides criticizes customs on the basis of novel Talmudic readings all the time, but when a custom received from the Geonim passes into his crosshairs, he deems criticism equivalent to calling into question the very concept of tradition.

The general statements in the Talmud and Ashkenazic halakhic literature about the preferred and leading position of custom in determining the law are translated by Nahmanides from prevalent contemporary customs to Geonic customs. In his discussion of the complex question about rendering a slaughtered animal ritually inedible on the basis of pulmonary adhesions, Nahmanides raises a doubt about a particular permissive ruling of the Geonim: "The words of the Geonim require study. Since they were permissive in practice, I do not possess interdictive power without proof, for in cases like this the custom of Israel is Torah."[83] The principle that "the custom of Israel is Torah" was often used by medieval Franco-German authors to glorify the living practices of their communities, and it gives expression to the idea that custom is normative even when it appears to contradict the law.[84] Nahmanides, in consonance with his broader approach, applies the rule to Geonic custom and tradition, but not to the prevalent customs of his day.[85]

One of the more interesting cases that has bearing on Nahmanides's relationship with the Geonim is his refusal to implement the Geonic enactment regarding "the rebellious wife," that is, a wife who refuses to fulfill her uxorial duties. His unique attitude toward the Geonim becomes evident when compared with the way other great medieval halakhists dealing with this problem rejected the Geonic enactment. The Geonic enactment states that when a woman who claims to want a divorce from her husband refuses to fulfill her marital obligations, the husband is forced to give her a writ of divorce and she is paid her ketubbah. This bold enactment, which fundamentally changed the wife's standing, was rejected by a large number of medieval halakhists, including Rabbeinu Tam and Maimonides.[86]

Rabbeinu Tam scathingly attacked the enactment out of tremendous apprehension about coercing divorce writs, and out of concern that it enabled Jewish women to set their sights on other men and rid themselves of their husbands without difficulty or penalty. In this connection, Rabbeinu Tam formulated a sweeping statement about the stature of the Geonim: "Granted that the Geonim can make an enactment that allows a woman's *ketubbah* [to be collected] from movable property, whether based on the law or their own reasoning, because it is a monetary matter, but no one since the days of Rav Ashi has ever had the power to permit an invalid writ of divorce, nor will they until the Days of the Messiah."[87] According to Rabbeinu Tam, the Geonim do not possess the authority to make such enactments, as they involve the removal of a prohibition. When it comes to making enactments, the status of the Geonim equals that of any other court, which may separate money from its owner through the principle of "what a court declares ownerless is ownerless (*hefker beit din hekfer*)." The Geonim do not, however, have the power to permit a married woman to seek potential suitors by compelling the husband to give a writ of divorce.

Maimonides, who also rejected the Geonic enactment, did not deprive the Geonim of the authority to make enactments. Instead, he attacked the validity of this particular enactment on the basis of his overarching account of Jewish legal history, which he outlined in the introduction to his Mishneh Torah. Geonic enactments are not binding owing to the shortfall in their geographical reach: "The Geonim said that they have other customs regarding the rebellious wife in Babylonia, but the customs have not spread throughout most of Israel, and many and great [scholars] disagree with them in most places. So it is proper to follow the Talmudic law."[88] The opposition of Maimonides and Rabbeinu Tam to the Geonic enactment concerning the rebellious wife forms part of each one's larger stance, which sees fit to limit the standing of the Geonim. Rabbeinu Tam objected to their very authority to make such enactments, and Maimonides voided the binding force of Geonic enactments beyond their original time and place.

Nahmanides, who discusses the rebellious wife enactment in his novellae to tractate Ketubbot, identifies with the harsh tone of Rabbeinu Tam's opposition to compelling a bill of divorce in such a case: "Anyone who heeds someone ruling this way and acts upon it is making a grave error, increasing bastards among Israel, and permitting a married woman [to seek other men]. They [those ruling this way] are worse for the world than the diluvial generation. Rather, the rebellious wife is divorced with her husband's consent."[89] Notwithstanding his basic sympathy for Rabbeinu Tam's position and his own anxiety about coercing a divorce writ, Nahmanides does not call into question, as Rabbeinu Tam did, the ability of the Geonim to make an enactment of this kind. Likewise, as someone who systematically relies on Geonic traditions, Nahmanides does not think that Geonic enactments are nonbinding, as Maimonides did. In the same piece he goes out of his way to underscore their authority:

> God forbid that I should disagree with a Geonic enactment. Who am I to disagree and change the time-honored practices of the Geonic academies? Moreover, I cry down those who say it is proper not to follow their enactment but the Talmudic law. It would be proper to heed them and implement their enactment, but one who acts stringently in a case like this does not lose out. With respect to the Talmudic law, however, I have said that we do not coerce [a bill of divorce]; the matter is clear and well-known. Nowadays it is proper to be very concerned not to put this enactment into practice at all, because it has been voided by generations of licentiousness.[90]

Nahmanides is, fundamentally, no less alarmed than Rabbeinu Tam by this enactment's ramifications. Given his loyalty to Geonic traditions, customs, and enactments, Nahmanides expends effort, not without some degree of contortion, to show that he does not question the right of the Geonim to make enactments and does not have the power to invalidate this particular enactment.[91] In his view, the Geonic enactment no longer applies because of the upsurge in licentious behavior, and not because Aharonim have the right to undermine Geonic authority on the basis of their own reasoning. By relying upon the change in historical circumstances that occurred, as it were, with the increase in wantonness, Nahmanides is able to square his localized aversion to the rebellious wife enactment with his absolute recognition of Geonic authority. Although he agrees with the great twelfth-century halakhists about the content of the enactment, the way he handles it underscores the great divide between them concerning all aspects of their relationship to the Geonic legacy.

The boundary Nahmanides creates in the history of halakhah between Rishonim and Aharonim marks, then, a signal change in his attitude toward custom. For everything pertaining to customs of the Rishonim, Nahmanides adopts the broader sense of custom, because he views Geonic customs as a reliable source of ancient, binding tradition with which the written halakhic sources must be brought into line. He co-opts the Franco-German attitude to custom writ large and restricts it to Geonic custom alone, thereby stripping the existing, living custom of its authoritativeness. The transition from Rishonim to Aharonim establishes a fault line in the continuity of halakhic tradition. From the Rishonim and onward, therefore, custom is no bearer of ancient, binding tradition but has the force of a vow or oath to make additions to the positive norms of halakhah. Living custom during the period of the Aharonim lost that reverenced patina of antiquity with which it had been encrusted. Once a chronological line divided Geonim from Aharonim, custom fell under the dominion of halakhists, who went on to define its validity and contents by means of their consuetudinary theories, and then vet and critically evaluate those contents in light of the written, authoritative canon of halakhah.[92]

V

Nahmanides's vision of halakhic history and of his role within it, coupled with his self-consciousness as a halakhist, as they have been explained in this chapter to this point, enable further consideration of the complex interrelationships between halakhah and kabbalah in Nahmanides's thought. His prodigious creativity in the field of halakhah[93] stood in a certain tension with his self-consciousness as a kabbalist. When it comes to the esoteric teachings of kabbalah, he believed that reason has no power to advance kabbalistic knowledge. Kabbalah, in his eyes, is a tradition to which nothing should be added and from which nothing should be subtracted; it should be transmitted carefully and esoterically as is.[94] This conception of kabbalah developed from, among other things, discord with contemporary kabbalists, such as R. Azriel of Gerona and R. Jacob b. Sheshet, who conceived of kabbalah as a corpus of open knowledge, the content of which could be expanded through creativity and innovation. R. Jacob was convinced that the development of kabbalah is given to the same processes of innovation and dissent that augment the halakhic corpus, and by means of reason one can add fresh knowledge to the existing kabbalistic corpus.[95] Nahmanides tried to stand in the breach against the creative kabbalah that had been waxing great in Provence and Gerona since the turn of the thirteenth century, and which Nahmanides viewed as overturning the traditional and esoteric nature of kabbalah. Similarly, the great flowering of kabbalistic literature at the end of the thirteenth century, culminating in the creative and innovative Zohar, stood in opposition to the traditional character of Nahmanides's kabbalah, and his disciples and successors tried—without success—to suppress this literature.[96] The consistent and uncompromising conservatism of Nahmanides as a kabbalist exists, it would seem, in some measure of tension with his innovation and creativity as a Talmudic commentator.

Understanding Nahmanides's composition of halakhic and commentarial works as the reaction of a conservative allows us to put together a clearer and more balanced picture of the relationships between tradition and innovation and between kabbalah and halakhah in his thought and writing. As the reader will recall, Nahmanides made use of the same new and sharp interpretive tools that effected the halakhic revolution of the twelfth century in order to restore the traditions of the Rishonim to their former glory. He ascribed to the Rishonim a halakhic tradition, a kabbalah, which needed securing against the tsunami of creativity that had flooded the halakhic field during the twelfth century. The conservatism of his halakhah, as with his esoteric teachings, finds expression in his use of the term *kabbalah* in both his halakhic and kabbalistic writing. Nahmanides does not reserve this term for esoteric knowledge about theosophical and theurgic matters, the kind entrusted by teachers to discerning disciples, but so designates all knowledge transferred by way of a reliable tradition, halakhic traditions included. The sheer number of times that he uses the term *kabbalah*—one of the most beloved in his halakhic oeuvre—to anchor Geonic positions as a source of halakhic authority reflects his sophisticated conservatism in matters both esoteric and exoteric: "Since it is a tradition (kabbalah) in the possession of our masters, the Geonim, we will accept it with good humor."[97] This "good-humoredness" toward Geonic traditions includes the recruitment of the interpretive and analytical resources of the twelfth-century revolution in order to defend the Rishonim.

There is, of course, a difference for Nahmanides between the status of tradition within halakhah and its status in the esoteric aspect of the Torah. In the latter, tradition exclusively establishes the limits of knowledge. Likewise, kabbalistic lore that has already been transmitted cannot be subjected to analysis even for purposes of aggrandizing the Torah; rather, one must transfer it in the same state as one received it to someone discerning who does not need things spelled out and can understand by his own lights. By contrast, in the field of halakhah it may be true that Nahmanides parts ways with his predecessors by investing Geonic tradition and Rif's words with significant—even if not decisive—weight, but he does not consider them exhaustive of all that may be thought and thought anew. Nahmanides's Talmudic novellae prove his bona fides as the foremost heir to the twelfth-century halakhists, because each and every folio includes conceptual and interpretive breakthroughs that travel far beyond the discursive horizons of Rif and the Geonim. And when it comes to anything relating to the defense of Geonic traditions and Rif, Nahmanides makes sophisticated use of the conceptual categories that he inherited and devised. Even halakhic traditions received, in effect, from the Geonim and Rif can be subjected to scrutiny, but usually for purposes of storm-proofing, plugging the holes, stemming the tide.

The complex conservatism that Nahmanides displays toward his twelfth-century predecessors can be explained by many factors. First and foremost, his own personality, as revealed through his writings, fuses furious creativity with a deep-seated conservative bent. This combination will come into sharp relief in the coming chapters that discuss Nahmanides's thought. His worldview, particularly as it relates to the esoteric, subverts and overturns the basic concepts of the exoteric tradition. His esoteric Torah is revolutionary and quite radical. Justification for the great gulf between the exoteric and esoteric can be found in his adherence to the idea of kabbalah, of a tradition received in unadulterated form, and his unbending restriction of the esoteric corpus to all but a handful of the best and brightest. Perhaps this complex combination of intellectual creativity and conservative leanings resulted in the reality that the more his powers of fresh insight into and original thinking about Talmudic sugyot grew, the more he tried to anchor the practical conclusions derived from them in a fixed Archimedean point—the Geonic tradition and Rif.

The second reason for Nahmanides's unique position vis-à-vis his predecessors can be traced to the community in which he found himself. Rabbeinu Tam and Ra'avad were active in an environment in which absolute fealty to halakhah was not called into question. In the communities of Provence and northern France of the eleventh and twelfth centuries, no one stepped out of line. In the immediate environs of Nahmanides's Catalonia, however, loyalty to halakhah was neither absolute nor presumed. The Jewish courtier elite, at least as Nahmanides saw them, were quite selective in their absolute adherence to halakhic minutiae, and the simple Jews struggling with everyday existence needed constant encouragement and support. In one of his bitter letters relating to the struggle for Jewish communal leadership in Barcelona, Nahmanides, in a rare moment of reflection, reveals how he viewed the leadership of the community in which he was active: "Why is our generation different from all other generations: / propping up perpetrators of transgressions, / even granting them positions, / and obsequiously dishing out contributions / to those suspected of illicit relations? / The community we freely consign / to people who neither pray for their lives nor bless when they dine, / and have no scruples about [gentile] bread and wine, / and in private do not observe their Sabbaths."[98] While it is possible that animosity and rivalry clouded Nahmanides's judgment, it still proves difficult to imagine Rabbeinu Tam portraying the communal leaders of Ramerupt or Troyes in such strong terms of disintegrating faithfulness to halakhah. In Nahmanides's circumstances, it was most prudent to avoid coming to earthshaking halakhic conclusions by way of Talmudic dialectics, as they would provide more grist for the mill of those predisposed to treat halakhic matters lightly from the get-go. The absolutely unquestionable fidelity of the God-fearing Jews in northern France and Provence granted Rabbeinu Tam and Ra'avad the necessary confidence for creative halakhic expansion, confidence that perhaps did not exist in Nahmanides's environment.

The third cause behind Nahmanides's reenvisioning of the history of halakhah and his own particular activity within it is connected to the singular junction in which he was situated as a halakhist. The halakhic revolutionaries of the eleventh and twelfth centuries each worked within their own geocultural spheres. Maimonides did not mention the positions of Rashi and Rabbeinu Tam even once. His halakhic discourse was limited mainly to the tradition of Andalusia and North Africa upon which he was reared, beyond which it was as if nothing else existed. The state of affairs in Germany and northern France was similar, although perhaps less so. The number of times Rabbeinu Tam related to Rif is quite meager; his halakhic discourse focused upon establishing his own creative interpretations in the face of Rashi's positions and Rhenish traditions and included extensive discussions with his northern French contemporaries. In Provence, circumstances were different, owing to its very nature as a crossroads between Christian Spain and Franco-Germany, and so the discursive scope of Ra'avad, R. Isaac b. Abba Mari (author of 'Ittur Soferim), and especially Razah was broader. Each of the twelfth-century halakhists, who comprehensively transformed the nature and character of halakhah, worked in his own little world, a world in which geo-cultural borders oftentimes defined the boundaries of discourse and debate. In Nahmanides's halakhic writings, these regional barriers are systematically broken down in a manner unprecedented for the Middle Ages.[99] His Talmudic novellae are the supraregional halakhic text par excellence in terms of range—the distinct creative streams of the long twelfth century all drain into his novellae from as far away as northern France and North Africa, Provence and Andalusia. The full gamut of that great burst of creativity, with all its diversity, was at Nahmanides's fingertips. This development, which began in Provence and culminated in his Catalonian novellae, parallels a similar, albeit slightly earlier, revolution that made medieval law supraregional, too.[100] Unlike Western canon law, however, halakhic tradition encompasses more diversity, because it includes an entire world of law developed by Islamicate Jewry. Nahmanides's resurrection of the myth of Geonic tradition and his newfound reliance on it represent the reaction of a halakhist who found himself in a unique position with respect to his predecessors, because he had access to the fruits of each region's creativity, to all the tesserae that together formed the mosaic of that great creative outburst. The borderline that Nahmanides placed between the Rishonim and Aharonim was a product of his attempt to anchor and stabilize halakhah in what was for the first time in the history of medieval halakhah a world without borders.

CHAPTER 3

Death, Sin, Law, and Redemption

Nahmanides is undeniably one of the most tightlipped authors in the history of kabbalah. He self-censors his kabbalistic allusions to maintain strict esotericism; he may show us an inch, but out of sight he keeps secrets that run miles deep.[1] His methods of writing prove challenging for any expositor attempting to piece together a complete picture from his fragmentary formulations. Expositors' efforts are further frustrated when they try to shine light through the veil of secrecy in the hopes of illuminating the deeply rooted, existential longings that move a mystic and halakhist of Nahmanides's proportions. Yet, the monumental impediment emplaced by Nahmanides's self-restraint also offers an interpretive advantage. His linguistic discipline is built upon a systematic and precise set of symbols, such that one can productively compare scattered allusions and carefully combine them to form a picture of real substance. The purpose of this chapter, which begins our exploration of Nahmanides's thought, is to lay bare the existential foundations of his worldview. These foundations will be illuminated by analyzing the primary elements of the human condition: death, sin, and redemption. Since it is Nahmanides's view that humanity's fate and existential condition reflect the divine drama itself, this analysis will serve as a basis for clarifying his conception of the Godhead, the chain of being, and the universe, all of which will be further clarified in the coming chapters.

Discussion of Nahmanides's thought demands constant reflection upon the nature of the relationship between his halakhah and his thought. His Talmudic novellae furnish us with a grand total of two references to his kabbalistic traditions. One concerns the difference between a vow and an oath,[2] and the other discusses the theory of prophecy in an aggadic context.[3] We can see that his kabbalistic ideas do not shape his particular halakhic determinations, even if kabbalah more broadly supplies the internal meaning of religious praxis. Various scholars who have researched Nahmanides's thought have considered his identity as a halakhist to be a formative principle in his kabbalah.[4] The state of affairs appears to me to be much more complicated—his writings contain considerable tension between halakhah and kabbalah. This tension does not concern the details of religious praxis but the very idea of the commandment and the law and their place in human life. The legal order is supposed to bridge the gap between "ought" and "is," but as will be demonstrated over the course of this chapter, liberation from the rule of law is an essential part of the redemptive process. The approach of the greatest thirteenth-century halakhist interconnects death, sin, and law, which are transcended during the period of redemption that lies beyond the Era of the Torah[5] and the law.

I

Torat ha-Adam, a work Nahmanides dedicated to the halakhic and philosophical question of death and retribution, begins with an opening salvo against the philosopher's attitude toward death. Freedom from the terror of death and the readiness to face it with equanimity are the hallmarks of philosophy as a way of life.[6] The philosopher overcomes the fear of death first and foremost by accepting it as inevitable. People do not experience something as a loss if it is necessarily beyond their reach; people who equate death with tragedy are living under the illusion that eternity is attainable. What sustains this illusion is the fact that people cannot imagine themselves as nonexistent, which in turn robs them of the ability to internalize the cold hard fact of their finitude. The philosopher, on the other hand, faces death with composure, for the philosopher has accepted it as an inevitable part of nature taking its course.

In keeping with this philosophical ethos, Maimonides places a limitation on the grief that one should feel upon the death of a loved one: "A person should not grieve excessively over his deceased, as it says: 'Do not weep for the dead, and do not lament over him' (Jer 22:10). In other words, excessively, for it is the way of the world, and one who pains himself over the way of the world is a fool."⁷ Foolishness is the inability to distinguish the possible from the impossible, a distinction that forms the basis for the equanimity possessed by those lovers of wisdom. In diametric opposition to the philosophical ethos, Nahmanides, in his preface to *Torat ha-Adam*, justifies mourning by seeing death as something that historically has not always been inevitable:

> Behold I shall apprise / what my heart thinks and my mind decides. / Since death is human's destiny, / from day one it would befit him to make his bed in death's-shadow valley. / Why tear ourselves up over someone's expiry / and agree to grieve and cry, / when the living know that they will die? / I am perplexed by those who know it, yet when it be / call upon the farmhand to mourn and moirologist to offer eulogy! / The answer in this is that man's constitution is for everlasting life, / but since the Original Sin⁸ all succumb to death's knife; / therefore, they tremble / for they and their nature are disassembled.⁹

Fear of death, according to Nahmanides, is rooted in the recognition that humans, by nature, should live forever. Death is experienced as loss because it marks humans' estrangement from their original, eternal nature, the wretched outcome of the Original Sin. If the philosophers were correct that death is the way of the world, there would be no room whatsoever for the halakhic institutions of lamentation, eulogy, and weeping.

Nahmanides is aware that the challenge of Greek philosophy does not stem only from its faith-shaking metaphysical claims about the world. The existential freedom that philosophy offers as a guide to personal redemption presents no less grave a threat: " 'My son, if sinners entice you, do not give in' (Prov 1:10), for you will find many statements of the Greek philosophers and philosophizers of their wisdom giving people encouragement / and psychological reinforcement / —the joy they bring is hollow, / their consolations are empty, they let go of the past and deny tomorrow."¹⁰ The great divide already separating the approaches of the philosopher and Nahmanides to the question of death's necessity deepens in the presence of this second, but no less important, philosophical attitude toward death. At the basis of the attractive consolation of philosophy stands the attempt to achieve equanimity, that is, the internal freedom from dependence upon the ever-changing and uncontrollable circumstances of our lives. The philosopher gives people "encouragement" by severing humans' connection to themselves and their surroundings, thereby redeeming them from the experience of loss.

Suffering, worry, and fear are the outcome of assigning value to the world around us and to our own lives. This value is intensified through love, which is the umbilical cord that ties us to ourselves and the world. Philosophers who identify one, and only one, object fit for love—Wisdom—condition themselves to the eventuality of death by emotionally distancing themselves from their concrete existence and from the brimming particulars of their lives. Nahmanides describes this Stoic mindset in the continuation of the same piece: "For Socrates, sage of the nations, dictated in writing: 'They asked me, "Why have we never seen you distraught?" I said [to them], "Because I have nothing that I would be distraught over were I to lose it." ' He said further, 'He who understands the world is neither glad when things are good nor worried when they are bad.' They [the philosophers] said that the wretched person is someone who worries even a bit."[11] The price of this equanimity is apathy, loss of interest. The happiness that philosophers achieve is hemmed in, then, by the possibility of chronic melancholy, a kind of nihilistic introversion. One can say that philosophers overcome fear of death by anticipating it, thereby making them the living dead.

Nahmanides describes this philosophic mindset and indifference to the world and attacks it: "He [Socrates] said further, 'How very foolish is he who knows that he is leaving this world and yet makes efforts to cultivate it!' He and his philosophical cohorts have many [sayings] like this."[12] Equanimity and nihilism go hand in hand, because whoever divests the world of value is not going to work at cultivating it. An ancient, canonical expression of this stance can be found in Ecclesiastes, and it is not for naught that Nahmanides turns to the book as a precedent for wrestling with a world without worth: "King Solomon through the Holy Spirit outdid them all—he considered everything a vanity / and next to beasts saw in man no superiority. / Still, auscultate and investigate he would / and discern evil from good, / in order to separate truth from falsehood. / On a good day he ordered man to be in good cheer / and on a day of misfortune to shed a tear, / as it is written, 'A time to cry,' and it says, 'a time to mourn' (Eccl 3:4)."[13] According to Nahmanides, therefore, mourning expresses the world's value, and its halakhic institutionalization counters the Stoic mindset. A fundamental formulation of this religious consciousness appears near the end of the introduction to *Torat ha-Adam*: "For part of one's service to God is to be involved in worldly matters, in preservation of the species, so that God's desire (*hefetz*) in creating us shall be everlasting. We should know and believe that in helping us thrive and by establishing through us the foundations of the world, God has shown us favor in His eyes."[14] In desiring the existence of the world, God endows it with value. This turns involvement in worldly matters into the service of God, because it carries on God's creative, formative activity.

The principled position that Nahmanides takes against the Stoic attitude is of special interest because disengagement from worldly matters and the concept of death as release have characterized many approaches in the history of mysticism, too. Nahmanides therefore places himself in opposition not only to the Stoic equanimity of the philosopher, but also to a particular conception of cleaving to the divine (*devekut*) maintained by some mystical thinkers, at the core of which lies the idea that the annihilation of the self liberates humans from all that is concrete and individualized. The question of death, which Nahmanides treats in *Torat ha-Adam*, therefore provides the key to understanding his kabbalah more generally.[15]

II

Nahmanides, as already mentioned, believes that prelapsarian Adam would have enjoyed life eternal. His idea that death is an unnatural state imposed upon Adam after his sin is laid out in his Commentary on the Torah:

> According to the natural philosophers, man had been destined for death from the moment of his creation, on account of his being composite. Now He decreed that if man should sin, he would die for the sin, as do those deserving death at the hands of Heaven [. . .] where the intent is that they die for their sins before their time. [. . .] According to our Rabbis, had he not sinned, he would have never died, because the supernal soul bestows everlasting life, and the divine desire (*hefetz*) in him [i.e., in humans] at the moment of creation cleaves to him in perpetuity, sustaining him forever [. . .] Know that composition does not entail corruption except to those of little faith [who believe] that the universe is necessary. But according to men of faith, who say that the world was created *de novo* by pure divine desire, its existence will last for the entire eon of desire. This is an evident truth.[16]

Nahmanides also takes this position in "Sha'ar ha-Gemul" ("The Gate of Retribution"), the chapter on retribution in *Torat ha-Adam*. There, he adds the claim that in the World to Come, which he considers to be the present world after the Resurrection of the Dead, humans' prelapsarian nature will be restored, and they will live in their bodies forever.[17]

On the face of it, Nahmanides's position on the eternality of the material body derives from a belief in God's power to create and to work miracles, which would explain why he sets up an opposition between natural philosophers and people of faith. Unlike the former, the latter maintain that the universe was created de novo and believe that everything hangs on the will of God and the miracle of creation, in which case God can also desire that the body be eternal. An examination of Nahmanides's theology, as it emerges from "Sha'ar ha-Gemul," shows that his position on the divine will and the relationship between sin and death is rather more complex. The relationship between sin and death is not merely one of transgression and punishment, but in order to understand the deeper, causal connection between the two we must recognize that for Nahmanides the two form part of a triad, whose third element is individuation. In order to better understand the relationship between sin and death, we must first examine the connection between death and individuation, and only then return to sin and death.

Death is an affair for individuals; genera and universals do not die. Humans as a genus are eternal, as are the generic, nonpersonal elements every human being has in common. The material from which humans are composed never completely ceases to exist. It may change its configuration, but it does not vanish. In the language of contemporary biology, one could say that one's genetic material can be preserved for many generations, because it is transmitted to one's progeny and the power of the erotic urge serves to preserve it. Death, therefore, eliminates only the individual elements of humans.

This connection between death and individuation has provided a broad swath of philosophical and mystical schools with the means to sidestep the problem of death by adopting a more universal perspective. Maimonides, for example, understood the immortality of the soul to be the eternality of the knowledge apprehended by individuals during their lifetimes. Because this knowledge never ceases to exist and becomes identical to the soul, it promises the soul eternity. The soul's immortality is not some reward bestowed upon humans for fulfilling the divine will, but a natural, causal outcome of humans' acquisition of truth during their lifetimes, and of humans' identification with a universal aspect of existence.[18] Maimonides's successors wrestled with the question of how this perspective could allow for any kind of individualized immortality. In what sense can one say, according to Maimonides, that a particular person lives on forever, if all that remains of that person are universal elements of eternal truths? Maimonides himself did not offer any answers; it is clear, however, that the loss of individuality did not bother him all that much, because his stance reflects the spiritualization of religion, which meant the establishment of the attainment of knowledge as the deeper telos of Judaism.

This approach to overcoming death, which adopts a universal perspective and blurs all individuality, has echoes not only in philosophy but in mysticism as well. As Bezalel Safran has shown, R. Azriel of Gerona exemplifies the mystic who sees the problem of death as inherent to individuation. According to Azriel, and in contrast to Nahmanides, prelapsarian Adam had no body; he was but a soul cleaving to the first three sefirot in a state of spiritual, incorporeal existence.[19] Adam was not an individuated being distinct from the Godhead.

The connection between death and individuation is also at the heart of Nahmanides's understanding of eternality, but the question of individuation does not appear in the context of his discussion about the concrete preservation of the body. Instead, the connection between death and individuation comes to the fore rather starkly in the way Nahmanides understands Adam's sin, which he considers the source and cause of mortality:

> The most elegant [explanation] to me is that Adam would have acted naturally, in accord with what befitted his natural constitution, in the same way that the heavens with all their hosts are reliable actors who move predictably—they never change their charge, they do not act out of love or hatred. The fruit of this Tree would give rise in its consumers to the will and the desire to choose one thing or its opposite for good or evil. It is therefore called the "Tree of *da'at* for good and evil," because in our language [Hebrew] *da'at* can mean the "will." In their language [Rabbinic Hebrew]: "they only taught this in a case where he is of a mind [*da'ato*] to return," and "he is of a mind [*da'ato*] to remove it," and in the language of Scripture [Biblical Hebrew]: "what is man *va-teda'ehu*" (Ps 144:3), that You should desire and will him?[20]

Adam in his natural, prelapsarian state was deprived of autonomy. He did what he should have by nature, like the astronomical bodies and other natural forces, and not by an act of choice. Upon eating the fruit, he came to will good and evil. In other words, humans became autonomous beings with free will. Adam's sin, then, was the very creation of the human will, and it is the archetype of all sins because every sin contains an expression of human will bucking divine command. Nahmanides's central insight is that what sets humans apart from the rest of creation is not their residing in a particular corporeal body but their having their own will. This insight is tied to the basic intuition that links autonomy and individuation. The formation of Adam as an autonomous being was in effect the emergence of the individuum, and upon gaining his own free will he lost his primordial connection to God. The price of this individuation was death, which became humanity's destiny from the moment humans became possessors of their own will.

Nahmanides's interpretation of Adam's fall raises a problem of circularity noted by many commentators: How could sin be possible without will? Put differently, and more sharply: How could autonomous will emerge from a state of no will?[21] I treat this question shortly, but relevant now is the particular connection between death and individuation that ties the existence of death to the appearance of the autonomous will. This connection emerges clearly from Nahmanides's description of the World to Come as a time in which the autonomous will will cease to exist and humans will return to their primordial, immortal nature. Nahmanides interprets the future "circumcision of the heart" as a negation of desire and will, as a return to humanity's prelapsarian state:

> "God, your Lord, shall circumcise your heart" (Deut 30:6) [. . .] What I am going to say is borne out by Scripture. From the time of Creation, man could do as he pleased, [he could be] righteous or wicked. And so it has been for the entire Era of the Torah, so they can be awarded merit for choosing good, and punishment for willing evil. In the Days of the Messiah, however, the choice for good will come to them naturally, their heart will not crave what is inappropriate and shall not desire it at all. This is the circumcision mentioned here— covetousness and cravings are a foreskin to the heart, and circumcision of the heart means that it shall neither covet nor crave. At that time, man will once again be how he was before the sin of Adam, when he naturally did what he ought to do, and his will was not conflicted [. . .] This is what our Rabbis said (cf. *Shabbat* 151b): " 'Years will come about which you will say I have no desire in them' (Eccl 12:1)—these are the Days of the Messiah, which have neither merits nor demerits." For in the Days of the Messiah man will have no desire; he will do what he ought to do naturally. That is why they have neither merit nor demerit, because merit and demerit depend upon desire.[22]

The abolition of human autonomy has a critical consequence for the standing of the law. Law, which enjoins upon humans how to behave, presumes the possibility of their free will, and its role is to bridge between "ought" and "is" through coercive force. The Torah as currently known applies only during the "era of desire," between the Original Sin and the advent of the Messiah. The Days of the Messiah constitute the period in history during which the activities prescribed and proscribed by the law go from being one possible course of action to the natural course of action. Without will, there can be no law.

The anomian character of this idea is accentuated by the startling phrase Nahmanides uses in this passage: "the Era of the Torah." The Torah is temporary, existing only for the length of time in which humans can do things their own way. Will, law, and death are bound up with one another in this scheme. Autonomy requires law and entails individuation, which eventuates in death. It would seem that the problematic standing of the will, and its connection to law and death, introduces a distinctly anomian dimension into Nahmanides's thinking. Particularly surprising is that this idea was propounded by the greatest halakhist of the thirteenth century.[23]

In order to clarify Nahmanides's position and its radical character, we should distinguish two different notions of sin: sin as misdirection of the will, and sin as flowing from the very existence of the will. Each, of course, has different relationships to law. If sin is misdirection of the will, then law is the answer to sin, for it purposes to redirect the will. If sin flows from the very existence of the will, then law is sin's partner in crime, because it presumes and affirms the existence of the autonomous will, which is the source of sin itself. The two notions of sin also offer different concepts of repentance. If sin is misdirection of the will, repentance allows for recalibration of the will. If sin flows from the very existence of the will, repentance means foregoing one's will, offering it up and delivering it into the hands of God, who in his abundant mercies will direct humans in the right way. The latter is the Pauline account of sin and grace as was understood by Augustine, and it forges an intimate connection between law and sin, such that redemption from sin requires offering up one's will to God's grace.

Nahmanides does not subscribe to this deeply antinomian Pauline position, in which law is sin's progenitor and the response to the problem of sin is to give up the struggle of one's will against sin and deliver oneself to God's grace. He does, however, express hostility toward the phenomenon of free will, which is why he views law as an ex post facto reality—the factum in this case being the primordial fall—a reality that he expects to disappear someday. Nahmanides is the first Jewish Bible commentator to claim that free will

played a role in Adam's sin,[24] and Shlomo Pines pointed to Christian influences upon Nahmanides's interpretation.[25] But these influences go beyond
the exegetical examples to which Pines points; they relate to fundamental
questions about Nahmanides's attitude toward law and his conception of redemption. His insistence upon the preservation of the body in the World to
Come and his positive attitude toward the corporeal dimensions of existence
do not spring, as some scholars have believed, from his identity as a halakhist.
His understanding of Adam's sin as part of the emergence of free will, and of
redemption as part of the end of the Era of the Torah, led him to view the
commandments as a suboptimal necessity that would pass at the end of this
"eon of desire."

III

Nahmanides articulates the connection between individuation and death
in mystical language that ties the Edenic sin—the formation of a separate,
autonomous will—to the fall from the state of primeval cleaving. One can re-
attain eternal life by returning to this state of cleaving not only in the World to
Come but even in the days preceding it, which is possible for spiritual adepts:

> It is possible that it [i.e., the verse, "and to cleave to Him" (Deut 11:22)]
> includes cleaving to say that you should remember God and His love
> always, [that] you should not separate your thoughts from Him as you
> take to the road, lie down, or wake up, to the point that conversation
> with other people is with the mouth and tongue but not the heart,
> which is in God's presence. It is possible for people at this level to have
> their souls bound up in [eternal] life even as they live, for they them-
> selves become an abode for the *Shekhinah*.[26]

Similarly:

> Those who withdraw from the affairs of this world and, as if disem-
> bodied, do not attend to it [this world], their every thought and undi-
> vided attention upon their Creator alone, as was the case with Elijah,
> will live forever in their body and soul through the cleaving of their
> soul to the Glorious Name [i.e., *Shekhinah*], as we can see from what
> is written about Elijah.[27]

These depictions of cleaving include a neglect of the body through the
concentration of one's consciousness—attention and thought—upon the

Creator. According to Nahmanides, someone who cleaves to the sefirah of Shekhinah, also known by its cognomen "the Glorious Name," will live forever in body and soul like Elijah. In contrast to Neoplatonism, Nahmanides does not view cleaving to the divine as entailing the separation of the soul from the body but as effecting a profound transformation in the state of the body and its longevity. Elijah underwent such a change in bodily state, and so lives in his body forever.[28]

A fuller account of keeping one's body in a sustained state of cleaving appears in "Sha'ar ha-Gemul," where Nahmanides describes the subsistence of Moses's body upon the radiance of the Shekhinah alone:

> They [the Sages] likewise said about Moses: "Whence did he eat? He was nourished by the radiance of the *Shekhinah.*" [. . .] For the soul subsists by uniting with the Supernal Intellect, just as the angels subsist through it. The transcendence of the soul over the body nullifies the faculties of the body, as we have mentioned another time, until the body, like the soul, can subsist without food or drink, as Moses subsisted for forty days on the mountain. If we attribute this to a miracle, Elijah disproves [it]—his body was neither cast off nor separated from the soul, yet he still lives and will continue to live forever. Such was also the case with Enoch, according to the *midrash* of our Rabbis.[29]

As Nahmanides tells it, the survival of Moses for forty days and forty nights without physical food was not a one-time miracle; it was produced by the state of cleaving that Moses had achieved, as proved by the eternal bodily subsistence of Elijah and Enoch. Nahmanides explains the natural mechanism underlying this phenomenon in the context of his argument for eternal corporeality after resurrection:

> If you challenge us from the fact that the body always subsists upon lowly things, we have already responded to you that the subsistence of the body will be like that of the soul. The soul subsists by uniting with the Supernal Intellect, and the sustained becomes like the sustainer by uniting with it [. . .] We likewise believe in, and all hold to be true, the visibility of the spiritual faculty upon the gloomy body as it cleaves to the Supernal Intellect, as with Moses's facial radiance being like the surface of the Sun and Joshua's like the surface of the Moon. Our Rabbis spoke similarly of Adam and anyone cleaving to his Creator and clothing himself in the Holy Spirit. They said about Phineas that

ापत

when the Holy Spirit rested upon him, his face was inflamed like a torch. They said about R. Eliezer the Great that when he would expound the Account of Creation, the rays shining forth from him were like Moses's, and no one could tell if it was day or night. They also said in *Sifrei* (*Devarim*, sec. 10): "In the future, the faces of the righteous will be comparable to the Sun, Moon, firmament, stars, lightning, lilies, and Temple lamps."[30]

The radical change effected in the state of the body through cleaving is explained here in a brief but arresting formulation: "the sustained becomes like the sustainer by uniting with it." That is, the cleaving subject acquires the properties of the object to which it cleaves. Mystics actually receive the properties of Shekhinah, rendering their bodies self-sufficient and without material needs, and if mystics can perpetuate this state of cleaving, their bodies become de facto eternal. Elsewhere in "Sha'ar ha-Gemul," Nahmanides writes a brief but sharp formulation of his understanding of cleaving in terms of *unio mystica,* that is, union with God:

> They [the rabbis] mention the matter of their existence through the existence of the object of their intellection, and their becoming one entity—this is the interpretation of what the Torah says "and to cleave to Him" (Deut 11:22), and it says [further], "yet the soul of my master shall be bound up in the bundle of life with God your Lord (*et Ha-Shem Elokekha*)" (1 Sam 25:29). Hence R. Akiva came to teach that " 'The Lord your God (*et Ha-Shem Elokekha*) shall you fear' (Deut 10:20) includes [fear of] Torah scholars" (*Pesahim* 22b).[31]

Just as Shekhinah is not subject to the accidents of Nature and is eternal, the same becomes true of the righteous person cleaving to and becoming identical to it—"their becoming one entity." According to Nahmanides, the identity between mystic and Shekhinah forms the basis for R. Akiva's bold exposition, which teaches that the obligation to fear Torah scholars stems from the verse commanding the fear of God. Fear of God and fear of Torah scholars who cleave to him are one and the same. Elijah and Enoch attained this state of identity while still living in this world, which is the same state experienced by denizens of the World to Come, and the same state enjoyed by prelapsarian humanity. As Nahmanides put it: "Our Rabbis spoke similarly of Adam and anyone cleaving to his Creator and clothing himself in the Holy Spirit."[32]

The cleaving described by Nahmanides is not of the ecstatic type, in which the mystic's soul leaves the body and the body is considered dead for a period of time. Instead, he describes a state in which the cleaving of the soul overflows into the body, thereby sustaining and nourishing it. Nahmanides does not think some unfathomable, mysterious phenomenon makes this happen. He labors to explain how exactly it is possible for the body to exist eternally, and he tries to make it reasonable through a series of psychophysical parallels:

> We have seen that those of pure soul sustain their bodies from subtle substances, and the purest among them from the subtlest of the subtle, because the people of the manna subsisted on the manna that was absorbed into their limbs, which partakes of the nature of the Supernal Light as made manifest by the will of its blessed Creator, and they merited it from the moment their souls became elevated through their apprehension of the miracles at the sea.[33]

And further on in "Sha'ar ha-Gemul":

> We also see that when the soul's desires are met to its satisfaction they give the body pleasure, and add luster, beauty, corpulence, and health, even if they are achieved through exertion and toil. This is all the truer regarding wisdom for the wise, like the import of the verse, "A man's wisdom illuminates his face" (Eccl 8:1).[34]

In the state of cleaving that nullifies the faculties of the body, the body continues to be nourished in one of two ways. Either the body is sustained by the Supernal Light, by the radiance of Shekhinah, in the same manner that angels are sustained; or, alternatively, it subsists upon a partly coarsened element that is desublimated from the radiance of Shekhinah. Nahmanides identifies this substance with the manna that kept the Jewish people alive in the wilderness. The refined and pure can subsist on rarefied matter, and as they approach asymptotic purity, they can be sustained by the most ethereal of substances and live forever.[35]

In this state, the body itself—nourished by the Light—becomes a kind of luminous being. That is how Nahmanides describes the resplendent radiance that occurs during cleaving and which was Adam's lot.[36] This entity of light, however, always has discernible, concrete dimensions. Adam's fall from his primordial state of cleaving, his separation and estrangement from God through the creation of his own autonomous will, led to the densification of his body.[37] His supply line to the Light, or the manna made manifest from the Light, was cut off, and he began to sustain his body on the ephemeral and variable, like the grass of the field and bread of the earth. Nahmanides makes reference to this in his comments about the Edenic fruit:

> It may be that the fruits of the Garden of Eden were absorbed into the limbs like the manna, thereby sustaining their consumers. But when He decreed upon him [Adam] "you shall eat the grass of the field, and by the sweat of your brow shall you eat the bread of the earth" (Gen 3:18–19), this caused the corruption [of Adam's composition], because he is [made of] earth, he eats earth, and he will return to the earth.[38]

Those nourished by the earth return to the earth; those nourished by the Supernal Light continue to exist for as long as it sustains them. Cleaving is refinement, the nullification of the body's cravings and faculties, and so it enables subsistence upon the most subtle substance, the very radiance of Shekhinah, which can sustain the body interminably.

IV

The connection Nahmanides makes between Adam's primordial cleaving and eternality, and his understanding of the fall from that state unto death, places him within the larger camp of those who identify death with individuation. Nahmanides, though, carves out his own niche within this school of thought. He maintains that individuation did not begin with the descent into a corporeal state, because Adam was embodied before the sin. Individuation came with the birth of the will, and the price of that autonomy is death. According to Nahmanides, undoing that individuation, and therefore the attainment of eternity, does not entail leaving the corporeal body behind; rather, it requires the achievement of complete self-mastery by nullifying the body and aligning one's will with the divine, which together bring one into a state of cleaving that nourishes the body. A return to the state enjoyed by humans before their disconnection from the divine undoes the lethal individuation, but for Nahmanides that state is still more differentiated and concrete than Maimonides or R. Azriel believed.

Even though Nahmanides pairs cleaving with eternality and individuation with death, he recognizes that his take on the state of cleaving entails more differentiation than other philosophers and mystics allow. As he says in "Sha'ar ha-Gemul":

Certainly the question raised above about the everlasting existence of the body does not apply to the philosophers nor to some of our sagacious commentators on the Torah, because the philosophers uphold the eternity of its universality [. . .] Just as they believe, based on their [philosophical] speculation, that universals exist forever, so too we can believe, based on our tradition, in the existence of the individual through the exalted Will. Just as there is a general will in the universal, so there is an individual will in the individual. Despite the fact that we see in the world that individuals perish and the universal persists, our belief is that this happened to the ensouled because of the Original Sin and its resulting punishment, but the eternal Will can fulfill His wish for all eternity.[39]

Nahmanides tries to co-opt the idea of eternal universals for eternal individuals, because, among other things, the distinctiveness of the individual becomes blurred in the state of cleaving. Nahmanides places Originary Adam into this tension between cleaving and distinct individuality, in which he experiences the unique state of eternal cleaving while retaining his distinctiveness.

Originary Adam lacked autonomy and his own will, so he did not fall under the Era of the Torah, and the commandments did not apply to him. Through his cleaving he became identical to Shekhinah, which turned him into a luminous being that was not subject to wasting away or death, and which sustained him through the radiance his limbs absorbed. This luminous being retained the human form but consisted of the most subtle substance, such that perhaps one could pass through it the same way one passes through a beam of light. The dimensions of this being, before postlapsarian densification and diminution, exceeded those of the present size of *Homo sapiens*. Originary Adam, before the fall, lived a singular, fraught existence.

Nahmanides's motivation in arguing for the corporeality of the body in the World to Come has been subject to scholarly speculation. Some have attributed it to his desire to preserve the status of halakhah, while others have suggested that it formed part of his struggle against the spiritualizing tendencies in medieval Jewish philosophy and mysticism.[40] And yet, we find deeply spiritualizing elements in Nahmanides's own depiction of the resurrected, who he believes will return to the prelapsarian state that existed before Adam became an autonomous individuum. According to Nahmanides, the World to Come—or, as he calls it, "the Era of the Resurrection"—constitutes the great reward and telos of a life lived according to the Torah's dictates, but the Era of the Torah will end in the world because free will will be absent from it. Similarly, the resurrected will find themselves in a continuous state of intellectual delight, their corporeality notwithstanding. Nahmanides's emphasis on the pleasure that accompanies contemplation puts him in agreement with Maimonides's approach and arouses his admiration for him. This is the only time in "Sha'ar ha-Gemul" that Nahmanides expresses sentiments of the kind that follow:

> How precious are the words of the great R. Moses, few in number yet speaking volumes, who wrote about this world [i.e., the World to Come] in his commentary on chapter *Helek*. He said that in the World to Come our souls will apprehend secrets of the Creator in the same way they apprehend, in this world, secrets of the stars and spheres, or even more. They [the Sages] similarly said that the World to Come has neither eating nor drinking, the righteous sit with crowns on their heads and bask in the radiance of the *Shekhinah*.[41]

This pleasurable state of consciousness enjoyed by the resurrected upon their return to the Garden of Eden is described in an important passage in "Sha'ar ha-Gemul":

> In truth, that place, the Garden of Eden, also will serve as a material reward in its most literal sense for the Era of the Resurrection. This is what our Rabbis said: "The Holy One will make a feast for the righteous in the Garden of Eden etc." (*Bava Batra* 75a). And they also said: "The Holy One will make a circle of the righteous in the Garden of Eden, and He will sit among them. Each and every one will point to Him as if with his finger, as it says: 'Behold, this is our God' (Isa 25:9)' " (*Ta'anit* 31a). This delight and reward will be during the Era of the Resurrection. The pointing to the *Shekhinah,* as if with a finger, from the circle is the attainment of such status and the delight of unity amidst corporeal joy. [This is] to convey that people of that world can reach the level of Moses, whose soul transcended his body to the point where his bodily faculties were nullified, and who was enveloped at every moment in the Holy Spirit. [It was] as if his sight and hearing were through the eye of the soul alone—unlike the rest of the prophets whose physical eye mediates—by means of the nullification of the body and the soul shedding its [the body's] faculties so that the Holy

Spirit could overflow onto it and thereby see through its own sight, as when Michael or Gabriel are seen. And this is the true sight and the proper hearing. For the philosophizers who negate the Torah at will have no ironclad argument against us which disproves this belief of ours that Gabriel has vision and hearing, and [which demonstrates that] the apprehension he [Daniel] acquired from Michael should be termed figurative.[42]

The rapturous state mentioned above can be better understood by means of a distinction between two pleasurable but incompatible states of consciousness. The first state is one of absolute tranquility, in which liberation from the agonizing pull of the will and desire brings about a pleasurable state of perpetual serenity. In the other state of consciousness, pleasure comes through an amplification of the senses—the threshold of stimulation increases and the heightened, attuned sensations are pleasurable. The two states are essentially different: the first is calm and lacks stimuli, and the second has abundant stimuli and is full of activity. Mystical pleasure is largely identified with striving for a state of ultimate tranquility, whereby the mystic, through cleaving, is supposedly freed of the tormenting pendulum of desire and arrives at perpetual serenity. Indeed, in his description of the future pleasure to be enjoyed in the World to Come, Nahmanides notes the nullification of the body's faculties, a characteristic usually attributed to the idea of pleasure as liberating and not heightening. Yet, he mentions the nullification of the faculties of the body specifically with respect to the amplification of the audiovisual. The shedding of the covering of the corporeal eye allows the eye of the soul to emerge, and by means of this inner eye the mystic can see things that the physical eye cannot.[43] This enhancement induces perpetual pleasure.[44]

This perpetual pleasure of the World to Come has manifestly spiritual features and does not relate to activity in or cultivation of this world. Denizens of the World to Come do not will or desire; they live a life beyond good and evil, and they have no halakhic or political existence. The World to Come, says Nahmanides, is Light,[45] and the resurrected, who are bathed in this Light, engage in perpetual intellection that supersedes anything attained by those inhabiting our world: "In this world, the Sages apprehend through the Holy Spirit seven *sefirot* [. . .] In the Days of the Messiah the eighth *sefirah* will be apprehended, and they [the Sages] hint to it. In the World to Come, the apprehension will be complete with all ten *sefirot,* and they allude to them."[46] As with the question of halakhah's status, here too we should disjoin

Nahmanides's position on the body's continued existence from the question of the centrality of the material and practical in his thought. The existence of the body does not stand in the way of the ideal of apprehension; in fact, it enhances it through the ocular medium.

The markedly spiritualized nature of the World to Come is also prominent in Nahmanides's understanding of the Days of the Messiah. Nahmanides, in contrast to Maimonides, believes the World to Come will not be a postmortem world but the end of history, that is to say, the historical period following the messianic era. The Days of the Messiah will last from the year 5118—calculated by Nahmanides to be the beginning of the End—until 6000.[47] Following on the heels of the Days of the Messiah will be the World to Come. The messianic age with its historical and political dimensions, which does not appear at all in "Sha'ar ha-Gemul," will be temporary. The World to Come, however, which will follow the messianic era, will have no law, no politics, and no history, because neither will nor desire will be present. The resurrected will be absorbed in their state of cleaving and reveling in the continuous, contemplative pleasure through the enhanced eye of the soul.

Nahmanides's position has much more of the antinomian in it than does Maimonides's. Maimonides emphasizes more than once that the Torah and law will still exist in the Days of the Messiah. According to him, the Days of the Messiah will not be a transitory period in human history to be followed by the World to Come; Torah, like human history, will never end. That said, during the Days of the Messiah halakhah will be nothing but a means, although an eternally effective one, for attaining a higher degree of apprehension.[48] Nahmanides, by contrast, depicts a corporeal existence unregulated by law, because the autonomous component of the human being will be out of the picture. Law is necessary only because of the decline from an eon in which "ought" and "is" were one and the same, which they will be once again in the World to Come.

On the basis of the foregoing, one can see that Nahmanides did not develop his ideas about the Resurrection of the Dead and the World to Come as an antidote to the antinomianism and spiritualization of contemporary philosophical and mystical thought. One could say that as far as the specter of antinomianism goes, Nahmanides made matters worse with his hostile outlook on human autonomy, which he deemed the harbinger of death and law. As for spiritualization, he himself believed that the resurrected will live an exceptionally spiritual existence, even if they will still be embodied. Nahmanides resolved the tension between the eschatology of the Talmud, which is quite physical and corporeal, and the spiritualism of the Middle Ages not through an innovative take on the concrete, but by distinguishing the ethereal from the coarse. Clarification of this point requires a full treatment of his doctrine of divine retribution and of Gehenna and the Garden of Eden. After this clarification, I will return to his approach to the question of sin and death.

V

In "Sha'ar ha-Gemul," Nahmanides formulates his doctrine of divine retribution and his eschatology out of a complex and animated dialogue with three traditions. One tradition includes midrashic literature with its mythic presentation of retribution and redemption.[49] Another tradition is that of Maimonides, against which Nahmanides crystallizes his own position, carefully selecting some aspects for reappropriation and others for rejection. The third tradition is kabbalistic, of which Nahmanides's kabbalah represents a particular strand. The entire "Sha'ar ha-Gemul" is a work of art in which Nahmanides spars with Maimonides, marries midrash with the kabbalah underlying his worldview, and emerges with an impressive, interpretive synthesis of midrashic sources that forms a coherent and overarching account.

Nahmanides undertakes to create an organized, systematic account of the basic landmarks on the midrashic eschatological map—Gehenna, the Garden of Eden, the Days of the Messiah, the Resurrection of the Dead, and the World to Come. He points out that of these elements, Gehenna, the Garden of Eden, and the Resurrection of the Dead have no real place in Maimonides's doctrine. In Maimonides's doctrine of retribution, immortality of the soul is the causal outcome of apprehending truths during one's lifetime. According to Maimonides, and in line with his naturalistic perspective, a sinner's ultimate punishment is the withholding of immortality from that sinner's soul, which undergoes excision and passes out of existence. In his writings, one catches no glimpse of the terrifying image of Gehenna as a multitiered dungeon populated by sinners undergoing condign punishments; Hell hath no fury at all. Hell and its torments serve as an allegory for what Maimonides views as the most terrible punishment of all—annihilation of the soul.[50] Maimonides also presses the concept of the Garden of Eden into this allegorical mold. The Garden of Eden is a continuous state of pleasurable intellection; in Maimonides's spiritualized approach, it is not a terrestrial place with spatial dimensions, nor do its fruits contain any pericarp. The Original Sin did not occur in any particular place or time; it is the allegorical expression of the change in humanity's existential state, precipitated by the plunge from cleaving to the pure knowledge of truth to wading through the mire of good and evil, struggling to prevail over desire.[51]

The Resurrection of the Dead also does not fit neatly into Maimonides's account, and not for nothing did a controversy surrounding it erupt during his lifetime. If death is freedom from the body's constraints for the delight of perpetual apprehension, why should the righteous be doomed to return to their bodies during resurrection? It is not surprising, then, that Maimonides does not mention the Resurrection of the Dead in his "Laws of Repentance," in which he presents his theory of divine retribution, as was discerned by many critical and perceptive readers of the Mishneh Torah. In other contexts, he describes Resurrection of the Dead as a temporary stage during which people will be given a second chance to merit the World to Come. That is, after resurrection they will die once more, and if they are worthy of it, they will gain the ultimate, all-important reward of the intellective soul's eternal life.

Apprehension as the pinnacle of human attainment is also expressed in Maimonides's subordination of the Days of the Messiah to this end. The messianic era, in its political sense of freedom from subjugation to foreign dominion and the return of rulership and the land to the Jewish people, is not the telos of a life of Torah. In his view, the importance of the Days of the Messiah lies in the opportunity they provide to more easily attain the World to Come. During their span, the sociopolitical conditions most conducive to the apprehension of knowledge and truth, which in turn promise life in the World to Come, will prevail. The Days of the Messiah, therefore, constitute a route for successfully reaching the World to Come.[52]

Naturalism and spiritualism are the two factors driving Maimonides's reinterpretation of the midrashic-biblical version of retribution and eschatology. He uses naturalism to explain the soul's immortality in causal terms, without having to resort to the anthropomorphic or miraculous, and also to negate the conception of Hell as an extensive penal system for dead sinners. Spiritualism drives Maimonides to view a life of the mind as the loftiest human achievement, and when achieved without a body, it promises eternal, transcendent bliss. That is why he describes the World to Come as a world of pure apprehension that comes after death. This same spiritualism also forces Maimonides to make the Resurrection of the Dead, which one can sense is an artificial graft onto his account, a short-term phenomenon, and to relegate the Days of the Messiah that occur within history to a supporting role for the eternal World to Come. The hermeneutic favored by spiritualism is allegory, which Maimonides uses to empty the Garden of Eden and Gehenna of their corporeality, taking them from being spatial-temporal places to abstract concepts.

Nahmanides disagrees with Maimonides's allegorical reading every step of the way. He asserts the following about the elaborate, vivid midrashic depictions of the Garden and Gehenna: "These and similar statements should not be construed as a parable or riddle, because they [the rabbis] mentioned its location, measured its length and breadth, and discussed it when deciding a ritual matter."[53] Later, he adds the following with respect to the Garden of Eden: "the words of our Rabbis and traditions of the forefathers on these matters are not 'words of wind,' trivial parable, [or] rhetoric; it is all true and reliable, exoteric and esoteric."[54] If Nahmanides were satisfied with the kind of midrashic fundamentalism espoused by R. Moses Taku, "Sha'ar ha-Gemul" would not be all that intricate or complex. He would sound the clarion call for believers to take Aggadah and midrash literally, and he would reject out of hand any attempt to reinterpret canonical midrashic sources, which philosophers often attempt to do in order to square their ideas of non-Jewish provenance with Jewish sources. While Nahmanides does view the Garden of Eden and Gehenna as spatiotemporal existents, like the simple reading of the Aggadah and midrash, a closer look at his approach reveals that he preserves, in his own way, the naturalist and spiritualist elements of retribution and redemption. He accomplishes this by rejecting the philosophical opposition between the abstract and the concrete in favor of a different opposition between subtle matter and gross matter.

In Nahmanides's account of creation, the process is the shift from an ethereal, indistinct existence to a coarse, distinct one. As the chain of being extends downwards, so its existents become more distinct and coarser. Every level in the chain maintains symbolic relations with the level above it, so, again, the farther down one goes, the less transparent everything becomes. This structure, which transitions from the ethereal to the coarse, allows for spiritualization without the need for abstraction or allegory, and one can see an excellent example of this in Nahmanides's treatment of Hell and hellfire.

Hellfire, according to a midrash cited by Nahmanides, was created on the second day of creation, a sure sign of its ethereality.[55] The earthly, concrete fire is nothing but a coarse manifestation of this ethereal fire. The earthly fire, to be sure, consumes the body, but it lacks the power to injure the soul. Only ethereal hellfire has the ability to burn a rarefied element such as the soul:

> Rather, that fire of Gehenna, which we believe consumes souls, is completely dissimilar to this-worldly fire—not the fire we make use of through coal or flame, nor the elemental Fire that is in the Sphere of Fire, even though it [the sphere] is a subtle body and it [the Fire] inheres in created bodies with the three [other] elements. It is still more subtle [. . .] I have already mentioned what our Rabbis said that one of the infernos of that place of torments is a flaming river that issues from under the Throne of Glory. See how they elevate its ethereality up to the Throne of Glory, which is the substrate of every created thing and innermost of them all.[56]

In the great chain of being, hellfire is directly below the Throne of Glory, which is Shekhinah itself. Earthly fire is nothing but a third-rate coarsening of this ethereal fire.

The soul, too, according to Nahmanides is not an abstract principle but a very subtle entity whose spirituality does not fall short of, and perhaps even surpasses, what the philosophers attribute to it:

> Why do they [the philosophers] think themselves superior to our tradition by making the soul subtle, by depicting it through angelical terms and stories? For we have yet to see from their writings any attribution other than to the Sphere of the Intellect, or [from] their speculators [other than] to the caste of angels. We, however, based on the truthful tradition of our holy fathers who did not dandle foreign darlings, elevate it and subtilize it far more than they do [. . .] In any case, one can see from here that the soul's subtilization by the gentile philosophers and their adherents does not exceed its subtilization by our Rabbis.[57]

Whereas the philosophers conceive of the soul as emerging from the Active Intellect, the kabbalists trace its source to the innermost aspects of the Godhead—from the sefirah of Binah on down. The soul's subtlety, like hellfire's, allows Nahmanides to walk the tightrope between the corporeality and spirituality of these existents.

In the same vein, even as Nahmanides speaks of hellfire's rarefied spiritual aspect, he also gives a clearly naturalistic, causal account of Hell's torment:

Man undergoes this punishment of Gehenna immediately after death. Right after a wicked person dies his soul is tied to the Sphere of Fire. From there it adheres to a flaming river that issues from under the Throne of Glory, which is one of the foundations of the Sphere and the potency of all that is fiery. [The river] descends unto Gehenna, and [the soul] is swept along with it, descending there. This matter is similar to the return of all creations to their [original] state of being, which is correct and accepted even by those engaged in philosophical speculation. This soul returns and adheres to the elemental Fire and sooner or later is drawn to transcend and cleave to supernal things, like all other things whose nature it is to return. But the density of the iniquities and coarseness of the sins which have separated it from its Creator obstruct it, so it is drawn and adheres to the fire of Gehenna. This withheld thought causes suffering and terrible, unfathomable pain that is not exceeded except by the torment of Gehenna.[58]

The fire that burns the soul of the wicked is not the physical, coarse kind but the ethereal fire that is the source of the primordial Fire, before its densification into a physical, coarse fire. After death, the soul yearns to return to its source in the upper folds of divine existence, but the sinner's soul became dense because of the grossness of its sins. It therefore cannot generate enough lift to rise to its source in the sefirotic structure and ends up in the Sphere of Fire at a lower plane of existence. Nahmanides considers this explanation to be naturalistic enough to satisfy philosophers, as noted at the end of his discussion on Gehenna: "Such is the belief of all who uphold the words of our Rabbis or believe in their tradition. Given our explanation, no philosopher should alienate what they say unless he be a philosophaster or godless."[59] Nahmanides's substitution of the in-between category of ethereality for abstraction and his naturalistic explanation of the soul's striving to return to its source also serve him well in his explanation of the Garden of Eden. The Garden is, in fact, a real place that one cannot access in one's normal state of corporeality, because it is on a plane of existence that is more rarefied than this earthly, coarse one:

The Garden of Eden, its four rivers, the Tree of Life, the Tree of Knowledge that God planted therein, and so the Cherubs and the fiery ever-turning sword, and also the fig leaf, belts, and skins—all are literal and just as they sound, that is the absolute truth of the matter. And it is a wondrous mystery, for they are like blueprints for understanding the secret of a profound matter. [. . .] Similarly, the holy work of the Tabernacle took place in three places: the courtyard, the tent, and behind the screen. In the Temple [they were] the courtyard, the holy, and the holy of holies. And everything in every single place—implements, forms of the cherubs—were all to understand the secrets of the activity of the supernal, intermediate, and lowly worlds, with allusions there to the dimensions of the entire Chariot. Similarly, the creatures themselves in their formation were created in the Image [. . .] Originary Adam, the handiwork of the Holy One, was the choicest man in wisdom and insight, and the Holy One settled him in the choicest of places to bring pleasure and benefit to the body, and He designed in the glorious place all the activity of the supernal world.[60]

The Garden of Eden exists concretely in space, but as with the Temple and other creatures formed in the divine image, it occupies a higher rung of symbolic transparency with respect to the sefirotic system. In this space, owing to its symbolic clarity, humans merit looking at the divine essence in a more meaningful form than is otherwise available to them when they are enveloped by symbolic opacity.[61] When the soul of the righteous leaves its body and is still subject to the effects of embodiment, it reaches the spatial Garden of Eden for twelve months and henceforth passes into a more rarefied existence in the Upper Garden and Upper Eden—the sefirot of Malkhut and Tif'eret.[62] The nature of the Garden of Eden as a concrete space of transparent symbolism transforms one's presence within it into the pleasure associated with apprehension:

> During those twelve months, it is the soul's lot in the Garden of Eden to take pleasure in the supernal world in a manner that tends toward the physical. Our Rabbis did not intend that the souls will luxuriate in the fruits of that Garden or bathe in the rivers. The intent is that it [the Garden] is the gate to Heaven through which one is illuminated by the Light of Life. [. . .] Due to the soul's apprehension in that place, it is elevated to the cleaving of the supernal world and attaining spiritual delight.[63]

VI

Nahmanides returns the soul to the body, but this return does not change the evidently spiritual quality of future existence. This luminous body

manages without food, drink, or sex, and especially without the commandments and law. What purpose does the spiritualized existence of the body
serve, appearing as it does to be a mere vestige adhering to the soul rather
than any kind of body in the regular sense of the word? Nahmanides antici-
pates this question:

> If you respond to us [that] the body is composed of executive faculties
> for the activities of the soul, the three parts mentioned by the philoso-
> phers, namely, the digestive organs, reproductive organs, and organs
> for the betterment of the body, and that the necessity of the body's
> existence more generally is for the sole purpose of eating food to sus-
> tain the body and reproduce in its likeness, then with the removal of
> said purpose in the World to Come, which has no eating or drinking,
> why should the body go to waste when there is nary a useless thing in
> God's handiwork? The answer to all this is that this creation [the hu-
> man body] was [intended] for the period of the Resurrection of the
> Dead to perform the aforementioned functions, and God does not
> desire that it be scrapped afterwards. Moreover, this form contains
> profound secrets, because the creation in this form was not random
> and without reason but for a great need and glorious purpose, and the
> exalted Maker wants it to exist.[64]

Nahmanides connects the Resurrection of the Dead to the profound secrets
inherent in the human form that is preserved after resurrection. The foregoing makes clear that the central and important aspect of the body's postresur-
rection preservation is not any bodily function, for those will have ceased,
but the body's iconicity, "because the creation in this form was not random."
Nahmanides takes care not to reveal the meaning of his reference, but
from other contexts identified by Yair Lorberbaum one can divine his intent,
which seems to be tied to his conception of the divine image in which humans were created.[65] The human form as a representation of the sefirotic
system, and the seven lower sefirot in particular, acts as a focal point for drawing down the divine emanation from within itself. The form of the human
body draws down Shekhinah in the same way that the Temple once did by
creating an isomorphic structure of the configuration of the Godhead and the
cosmos.[66] Humanity's iconicity sets the limit of the divine emanation from
within itself.

The reason behind the body's survival by means of resurrection connects,
then, to the more fundamental problem of the limit of the divine outflow

from within itself. The elimination of the body in the World to Come and Resurrection of the Dead means, to all intents, that the configuration of the Godhead retreats into itself in the World to Come. According to R. Azriel, the emanation extends only to the sefirah of Binah because the World to Come is essentially a restoration of that original and perfect state of existence before the fall, and he believes that the prelapsarian emanation of the Godhead extended to only the first three sefirot. One's position, then, on the body's existence does not reflect one's outlook on the status of law or one's attitude toward the body; instead, it depends on the level of particularity and distinctiveness of the divine emanation in the primordial universe that preceded Adam's sin, to which it will return in the World to Come. The removal of the body reflects the restriction of divine emanation to a higher limit, which is both more rarefied and less distinct.

R. Azriel and Nahmanides both comprehend Adam's sin as an act of individuation, "cutting down the saplings," whose source lies in the emergence of an autonomous will, and both believe that the sin had fateful consequences for the entire sefirotic configuration. According to R. Azriel, this act yanked down the divine emanation too far, which led to the emergence of the seven lower sefirot and the existence of the material body. Nahmanides maintains, however, that this act of individuation played out on a more distinct level of existence. Even without Adam's sin the seven lower sefirot would have been emanated, and Adam was already embodied before he "cut the saplings." Adam did not generate his body through sin, but he did create his will and death. In a much broader sense, Adam's sin led to the coarsening of Nature and rendered it an inert, independent entity with its own laws of functioning and without any direct line to the configuration of the Godhead.[67]

One could put it this way: The great inner tension of the divine drama, as presented in kabbalistic thought, is between the desire of the divine organism to retreat into the deepest recesses of Ein-Sof, and its internal aspiration to gush out and be emanated outward. The preservation of uninterrupted balance between the two poles of this movement is at the root of theurgic worship and mystical contemplation, and the fate of all existence depends upon this equilibrium. If the efflux does not emerge, nothing exists beyond the divine Naught, Ayin, itself; if it does not return to Ayin, the emanation is liable to lose the source of its being. The difference between R. Azriel and Nahmanides lies in their respective characterizations of this point of equilibrium, as expressed in their differing descriptions of the prelapsarian state of the sefirot and of Adam, and in positions that take on the body's existence in the World to Come. R. Azriel puts the point of equilibrium on a more rarefied and abstract plane than does Nahmanides. There is no doubt that what divides them is a product of Nahmanides's broad affirmation of concrete existence, which cannot be ascribed simply, as some would have it, to his view on the standing of halakhah, because Nahmanides says this inner-divine balance prevailed before the "eon of desire," which is identical to the Era of the Torah, and will obtain again after it.

The link between the existence of the body in the World to Come and the divine oscillation between the poles of Ayin and distinct existence complicates Nahmanides's account. He himself believes that this equilibrium, achieved at the end of creation and before Adam's fall, is not static but dynamic and variable. The fall of Adam reflects the overextension of the divine emanation, and the march of history toward the seventh millennium is a return to the prelapsarian state of the world. This state, though, is relatively fleeting in its own right because of the dynamism of the divine movement expressed in the doctrine of cosmic cycles (torat ha-shemittot) that Nahmanides espouses. According to this doctrine, after the seventh millennium, that is, after the World to Come, another cycle is inaugurated by new divine stirrings. Seven such cycles—fifty thousand years—culminate in a "jubilee year," during which the divine efflux returns to its source in Absolute Privation. Nahmanides conveys this tension between conjuncture and longue durée, to borrow historiographical terms, when he says that Adam "should have existed and lived forever if only he had not sinned that sin, and even though we believe in the destruction of the universe in the sabbatical year."[68]

I cannot answer how Nahmanides resolved the eternality of the body with the destruction of the world in the "sabbatical year."[69] It should not escape our attention, however, that through the doctrine of cosmic cycles he overtly identified with a nonlinear conception of history that understands everything concrete and emanated to be transient and subject to dynamic forces.[70]

The anomian foundations of this conception are exceptionally radical, because every cycle has a unique manifestation of the Torah, a dynamic expression of God's essence. While all these manifestations of the Torah do have one thing in common, namely, the same sequence of letters that constitute the revelation of God's names and essence, they differ in that each cycle appears to have its own unique division of that sequence into words.[71] This idea supplies additional grounds to undermine the conjecture that Nahmanides's halakhism led him to insist upon the persistence of the body and the concrete dimension of existence. As noted above, in the World to Come, the seventh millennium, the body exists without commandments; its purpose inheres in its iconic function of setting the limit for divine emanation, although this limit fluctuates according to the variability and dynamism of the intradivine movement of the divine organism, as conveyed through the secret of the cosmic cycles. Nahmanides's anomian eschatology and his view of history as cyclical and nonlinear are especially extreme when one considers their provenance—the study hall of the greatest thirteenth-century halakhist.

VII

The existence of the body in the World to Come reflects, as we have seen, the restoration of the original human condition. In the Garden of Eden before the fall, Adam was in a state of cleaving that promised him eternal life. The emergence of the autonomous human will disrupted this cleaving as it individuated humans from the Godhead, thereby leading ineluctably to their eventual death. During creation—before that will was around—the sefirotic configuration was in equilibrium; balance prevailed between the drive of the divine organism to retreat into the deepest recesses of Ein-Sof and its impulse to well up and be emanated outward. Adam's sin, which Nahmanides defines as "cutting down the saplings,"[72] crucially impacted the internal organization of the sefirot and their interrelationship.

Since humans are an icon that defines the outer limit of the emanatory diffusion, their detachment from the Godhead drew it down to a plane of particularity and distinction that disrupted the internal equilibrium of the divine organism. The question is how Adam, devoid of any autonomous will of his own, could commit a sin whose significance is individuation and the creation of an autonomous will. This question can be posed in terms of circularity: How could Adam sin if before that sin he lacked his own will to discriminate between good and evil? If the sin is that Adam became a creature with an autonomous will, how could a state in which will was absent give rise to will unless it caused itself? The key to solving this problem of circularity lies in the fact that humans are a symbolic representation of the configuration of the Godhead, and if the Original Sin was an event reflecting processes of differentiation and crisis within the Godhead itself, then Adam's sin was the symbolic expression of these intradivine processes of differentiation and crisis, and his will and individuation were not self-caused.

The sefirot emanate from Naught through the demarcation of limits, distinction, and separation of the sefirot from one another.[73] The individuating principle thus inheres in the configuration of the Godhead, because without interstices nothing could exist outside Absolute Privation. From Nahmanides's allusions and his disciples' partial elucidations of them, we see that this very principle, which is what enables the sefirotic emanation, is also what triggers the crisis within the Godhead itself,[74] whose earthly parallel is Adam's sin.

The idea of a crisis within the emanatory process arose from kabbalistic interpretation of certain midrashim, which depict the Primal Light reserved for the righteous in the future and the diminution of the Moon's original stature. Here is one such midrash:

> R. Shimon b. Pazzi posed a contradiction. It is written, "The Lord made the two greater luminaries" (Gen 1:16), and it is written, "the greater luminary and the lesser luminary" (ibid.). The Moon said before the Holy One: "Master of the world! Is it possible for two kings to use one crown?" He responded to her: "Go reduce yourself" [. . .] The Holy One said: "Bring an atonement [offering] on my behalf [on the New Moon], because I diminished the Moon" (Hullin 60b).[75]

Nahmanides views the diminution of the Moon as an earthly expression of crisis within the Godhead itself:

> They also said there [i.e., Bereshit Rabbah]: " 'And he separated' (Gen 1:4)—R. Yehudah b. R. Shimon says, 'He separated it for Himself'; the Rabbis say, 'He separated it for the righteous for the future.' " If you are able to understand their intent in saying "Coronet ('Ateret) of Splendor [i.e., Tif'eret] for the Womb-carried" in the blessing over the new Moon, you will know the secret of the First Light, [its] preservation, and the separation [about] which he [R. Shimon] said "He separated it for Himself," and the secret of the two Kings who use one Crown, when in the end the light of the Moon [i.e., Shekhinah] shall be like the light of the Sun [i.e., Tif'eret], which in turn will be sevenfold.[76]

The Sun and the Moon symbolize the sefirot of Tif'eret and 'Atarah (Shekhinah), respectively, which originally paralleled each other and constituted the perfect harmony between Mercy and Judgment. The diminution of the Moon is a physical manifestation of the fall of the sefirah known as

Shekhinah from its parallel and equal stature to Tif'eret down to the bottom of the configuration of the Godhead. When the divine emanation was in its original state, the sefirah of Yesod was the final sefirah of the Godhead. Subsequently, Shekhinah fell to an even lower rung in which it could only receive the efflux without being itself an independent source of emanation, an event given celestial expression in the diminution of the Moon. R. Shem Tov Ibn Gaon explains this slightly more explicitly:

> If you understand the emanation, and the secret of the two luminaries that is conveyed to you through the two Kings [i.e., *Tif'eret* and *Shekhinah*] who use [one Crown], you will understand it, because the secret is very esoteric, and I have no permission to allude to it. With respect to what is associated with the Seventh Day [*Yesod*], they [the Sages] said in an aggadah: "The Sabbath [*Yesod*] said before the Holy One: 'Master of the universe! You have given a consort to all of them [i.e., the Days], but you have not given Me a consort etc.' " [. . .] When you comprehend that he [*Yesod*] originally completed the [sefirotic] structure and had no recipient until the Moon was diminished—to which I will allude in the portion of *Bereshit*—and then He said to him [*Yesod*]: "The Congregation of Israel [i.e., *Shekhinah*] shall be your consort," you will understand it. This took place on Sabbath Eve—delve into this.[77]

In stating that this occurred on Sabbath Eve, which is when Adam sinned, Ibn Gaon alludes to the interconnection between the sin and the emanatory disruption, the diminution of Shekhinah, and the latter's isolation from Tif'eret.[78] Later, he makes the parallel clearer in the allusion mentioned above:

> *Tevunah* [*Binah*] separated it [*Tif'eret*] because of what the Moon [i.e., *Shekhinah*] said, and separated it for itself so that the King [i.e., *Binah*] flows into it. It [*Binah*] diminished the Moon such that it would receive power from the Median Line [i.e., *Tif'eret*]. And so every month it receives [power]. It is a great diminution when the Queen [i.e., *Shekhinah*] herself does not come to the King. [. . .] When you comprehend this, you will comprehend why man was created on the day he was and the service of the luminaries, and you will glimpse his sin and the Primordial Snake which is *Pahad* [i.e., *Gevurah*], and the sacrifice and its efficacy.[79]

In a different context he takes the parallel one step further:

> The secret of the Primordial Snake is the accusatory side and the evil
> inclination, from the side of the Attribute of Fear [i.e., *Gevurah*]. It
> seduced her with words, beguiled her into thinking that by taking his
> counsel she would win all the glory for herself, and into saying that she
> would rule with her attribute over the male attribute. In this, too, you
> will understand the parable of the Moon and its diminution, to which
> I have alluded, for here too it was overturned—"and He [*Tif'eret*] will
> dominate You [*Shekhinah*]" (Gen 3:16)—because the Moon too will
> shine through the power of the Sun. I cannot explain further, and this
> should be enough for anyone enlightened. He sinned, too, in intend-
> ing to seize the attribute of the Coronet after seeing that the lowly
> world was sustained by her hand, and this was his sin. This is what
> they [the Sages] said, that he ate because he separated the Fruit from
> the Tree in practice and also in thought.[80]

According to this supercommentary on Nahmanides's secrets, the duo Tif'eret
and Shekhinah, Sun and Moon, are isomorphs of man and woman. In the
same way that Tif'eret and Shekhinah were created equal and parallel to each
other, so were man and woman created *du partzufin*, as the midrash calls it;
they were double-faced, two halves that together make a complete whole. R.
Isaac of Acre explains the analogy: "Consider how Originary Adam was created double-faced, nape to nape, [both] equivalent *in potentia* and *in actu*,
truly one [. . .] From one they became two, but although they are two, they
are one. As it says, 'they shall become one flesh' (Gen 2:24), and he always
strives for her and she always strives for him."[81] According to this approach,
at the beginning of all things humanity was in tune with the original, natural
state of existence, meaning that the relationship between man and woman
was horizontal and reciprocal. Man's dominion over woman and the patriarchal structure of the family and society were produced by the fall and the
breakdown of the primordial sefirotic configuration. It follows that the eventual rectification of this fall will also lead to the destruction of the vertical
relationship between the sexes.[82]

Kabbalists tend to imbue social relationships with metaphysics, because
for them these relations symbolize the divine reality. They therefore lend the
rickety structures put up by humans throughout history—with crooked tim-
ber no less—an essential and fixed character. But with this idea of Nahmanides and his students, the metaphysical structure that symbolizes these gender

relations is itself flawed. It will be repaired in the World to Come, when the light of the Sun will be like the light of the Moon.[83]

The rise of the autonomous will and Adam's individuation reflect processes internal to the sefirotic configuration. Humanity's disconnection from the Godhead is an externalized expression of Shekhinah's break with Tif'eret and the diminution of the Moon. The circularity mentioned earlier as problematic is broken by the fact that in this isomorphic scheme Adam does not induce his own individuation or sin under the power of a self-generated will, because it comes from a higher, divine, plane of existence. Still, we can shift this question up one level: What precipitated the intradivine crisis? The midrash anthropomorphizes Heaven and its celestial residents—the Moon competes with the Sun for the Crown and is punished by the Holy One. Finding this and similar depictions unsatisfactory, Nahmanides and his disciples turned to a methodological approach that translated the anthropomorphized figures of midrashic literature into a causal structure. In the writings of Nahmanides, one finds not even a trace of what caused Shekhinah's "rebellion" and its fall from the harmonious state it shared with Tif'eret. Nahmanides views the whole matter as a closely guarded secret that cannot be revealed, only alluded to indirectly.

One can see the glimmerings of an answer emerge from the words of Ibn Gaon, who also conducts himself with exceptional care in this matter. The allusion in this case is not from the sefirot to earthly events, but vice versa. Since earthly events express loftier ones, one can glean information from them about the crisis within the Godhead. The first factor that leads woman to sin is the snake, and Ibn Gaon explains the snake's symbolism: "The secret of the Primordial Snake is the accusatory side and the evil inclination, from the side of the Attribute of Fear. It seduced her with words, beguiling her into thinking that by taking his counsel she would win all the glory for herself."[84] Based on the analogy, the Strong Attribute of Judgment caused the loss of Shekhinah's harmonious state with Tif'eret. One could say that the Strong Attribute of Judgment is the principle of separation and distinction within the Godhead itself, absent which, as noted earlier, there would be no room for individuation of any kind, not even within the emanating Godhead. This factor of emanation is the culprit responsible for the crisis within the emanatory process, because it allowed the differentiation to go too far.

The outspreading of the Godhead, then, generates so much momentum that it overshoots its bounds. This results, the reader will recall, in Shekhinah breaking away, in the creation of human individuation and the dominion of inert Nature. The Godhead repairs itself by retracing its movement, a never-ending cycle of rupture and repair. The time elapsing between rupture and repair, between the Original Sin and the World to Come, is the Era of the Torah, the "eon of desire." During this period, humans can either ameliorate the effects of the rupture or exacerbate them through the theurgic power of the performance of the positive commandments or violation of the negative ones. This catastrophic overextension, which ruins the balance between Hesed and Din, will in time equilibrate itself by reverting to its original state in the seventh millennium. In that eon, human beings' individuation as distinct creatures with free will will come to an end, and humanity will no longer be subject to the sentence of death. Nahmanides's negative attitude toward human autonomy is tied to his conception of cleaving and the inner structure of the Godhead, but it does not reduce the radical anomian aspect of his understanding of sin and redemption.

This chapter has dwelt upon the question of death and redemption, and so, naturally, it has touched upon the most existential aspects of Nahmanides's thought. The future return to the primordial state that preceded the great rupture of the Original Sin indicates the existential longing that animates Nahmanides's kabbalistic system. Humans before the sin and after the redemption overcome death through the loss of individuation, which entails the erasure of human autonomy. The emergence of an independent will is the problematic aspect of individuation; it is the source of crisis and death. The restored state of cleaving, however, will not completely ignore selfhood, because each person will still possess his or her own individual, if ethereal, body sustained by Shekhinah. The core of Nahmanides's anthropological and mystical thinking turns on the idea of the cardinal sin as the willful individuation of the self, and on the attempt to regain the lost state of cleaving without completely giving up the self. Caught in this tension between communion and individuation, mystics acquire eternity at the cost of freedom and preserve their identities as an extension of the Godhead itself. The isomorphic quality of Nahmanides's conceptualization transforms this existential human tension, which straddles the fence between individuation and cleaving, into a reflection of a much broader metaphysical and theological issue. The causal connection between the supernal and lower worlds turns the human existential crisis into a mirror image of the intradivine movement that is propelled by the very same tension between unity and distinction. In the same way that Adam, in the primordial crisis precipitated by the amplification of his will, was torn from his blissful state of harmony, so too the Godhead, via the processes of differentiation within itself, went one step too far and Shekhinah became cut off from the original unity to which it will ultimately return. For Nahmanides, the oscillation between these two poles, which perforce builds up a kind of destructive momentum for which the Godhead has an internal repair mechanism, dictates the religious drama in both of its dimensions— the human and the divine.

CHAPTER 4

Miracles and the Chain of Being

I

The overextension of the divine emanation, including its resultant fracture, was reflected in Adam's devolution into a distinct creature possessing his own will.[1] Moreover, as it will become apparent, this act of separation had broad cosmic consequences in creating a Nature that is separate from the divine plane of existence. If we imagine all that exists—divine, cosmic, and human—as a chain emanating from the divine Naught (*Ayin*), we can think of the chain's strength gradually growing slack, each link pulling away from the preceding one and thereby becoming overly distinct and differentiated from it. To use a different image, the transparency of the chain of *sefirot* became increasingly opaque. This chapter examines the following question: How does this conception of the chain of being and of the primordial rupture that occurred within it inform Nahmanides's conception of miracles, providence, and Nature? Before we enter into a detailed analysis to answer this question, we should take a moment to clarify his theory of creation and how he envisions, in consonance with Neoplatonic tradition, the chain of being.

In his commentary on the biblical creation narrative, Nahmanides claims that forms from the triliteral Hebrew root *b-r-'* ("create") uniquely designate *creatio ex nihilo*. Other roots that appear in the narrative, such as *'-s-h* ("make") and *b-d-l* ("separate"), indicate the act of creating something out of other preexisting matter, or *creatio ex materia*. Nahmanides, following R. Abraham b. Hiyya and R. Abraham Ibn Ezra, interprets the earth (*aretz*) and heaven (*shamayim*) mentioned in the first verse of the Torah to be speaking of two kinds of hylic matter. These two alone were created ex nihilo, and they are neither the earth nor the heaven we know. Instead, they are the hylic matter that forms the material substrate that receives the defined forms of heavenly and earthly bodies. In more technical language, one could say that the heavenly hyle and earthly hyle have the property of the privation of the forms of heaven and earth and all they contain, in the same sense that the matter of wood has the property of the privation of the table's form, that is, the wood has that same original property that enables it to become a table. Nahmanides describes this hyle as follows:

> In the Holy Tongue we cannot express *creatio ex nihilo* save through the language of *b-r-'*. Not everything under the Sun or above it had its first beginning in Naught (*Ayin*). He produced from Complete and Absolute Privation an extremely subtle element which has no substance but is a productive potency (*ko'ah mamtzi*) that is prepared to receive the form and to go from being *in potentia* to *in actu*. This is the primal matter, called "hyle" by the Greeks. Subsequent to this hyle, He created (*bara*) nothing else, but He formed (*yatzar*) and fashioned (*'asah*), for from it He produced (*himtzi*) everything, clothed them in forms, and perfected them.[2]

In other contexts Nahmanides compares this hyle to a geometric point:

> at first, God, Who is the omnipotent Creator, created (*bara*) heaven and earth, that is to say, from Absolute Privation and complete Naught He created (*bara*) an existent (*yesh*), a point smaller than a mustard seed which is heaven and everything in it, and another point which is the earth and everything on it, and they are the hylic heaven and hylic earth. Henceforth, He created (*bara*) nothing but produced (*himtzi*) one existent from another.[3]

Two hylic points were thus created from Naught for heaven and earth. At first they were *tohu*, meaning they were undefinable, but they were subsequently "clothed" with elemental forms called *bohu*.[4] The imagery of the universe beginning as a single point that emerged from Naught, from which everything was then created ex materia, is tied to the fact that in geometric space a point is the privation of all geometric shapes, from which one can then form a line, and from that line create a shape. If we have but a single point, we can construct an entire universe from it. This helps explain why the first hyle is depicted as a single, subtle point of no substance out of which the entire universe was made.

Nahmanides alludes to the fact that the creative process through which heaven and earth were made symbolizes the emanation of the sefirot themselves. As he writes at the end of his comment on the very first verse of the Torah:

> But if you merit understanding the secret of the word *be-Reshit,* and why it does not place [God] first to say "God created *be-Reshit,*" [then] you will know that by way of truth Scripture speaks of lower things and alludes to supernal ones—the word *be-Reshit* alludes to *Hokhmah,* which is the Beginning (*Reshit*) of beginnings as I have mentioned. Therefore, the *Targum Yerushalmi* translated *be-Hakhmeta* [i.e., through *Hokhmah*], and the word is crowned with the Crown [*Keter*] of [the letter] *bet.*[5]

The sefirah of Hokhmah is the source of the entire world of sefirot, and from it the supernal Heaven and Earth were emanated within the sefirotic configuration. In the same context, Nahmanides hints at the meaning of *tohu* and *bohu* in the configuration of the sefirot: "This is [the meaning of] the verse, 'and He shall stretch out upon it a line of *tohu* and stones of *bohu*' (Isa 34:11), for it is the Line by which the architect draws up his structural blueprint [. . .] and the Stones are the forms of the structure."[6] The sefirah of Binah is the hylic line that emerged from the sefirot of Keter and Hokhmah symbolized by the word *be-Reshit* (the Beginning),[7] from which and by means of which a blueprint could be made and the building blocks of the divine structure, the seven lower sefirot that are distinct and defined, could be emanated. Binah is akin to tohu in the sense that it lacks its own form and eludes definition, while the other sefirot are like bohu, as they represent a phase of definition and differentiation that derives from the primordial Line.

The parallelism between the creation of the universe and the emanation of the sefirot points to a deep transformation in the meaning Nahmanides, like the other Geronese kabbalists, gives to the expression *creatio ex nihilo.* The nihil, the naught, is not a vacuum or emptiness in which existence appears; it is the divine Naught, Ayin, that is, Ein-Sof (Infinity). One will not find any mention of Ein-Sof in Nahmanides's writings, because he refers to it as "Absolute Privation."[8] From Ayin sprang the entire sefirotic system, and the very first point is none other than the breakthrough of one hylic point

from the divine Ein-Sof. In light of the symbolic meaning of Absolute Privation as marking divine Ayin, Nahmanides's comment on Genesis takes on a
whole new meaning: "He produced from Complete and Absolute Privation
an extremely subtle element."[9] Hylic heaven and earth constitute this subtle
element that emerged from Absolute Privation, from Ein-Sof.

The parallelism in this account between the lower heaven and earth and
the supernal Heaven and Earth gives rise to the following problem. What
exactly is this hylic heaven and earth that emerged from Ein-Sof? Are we talking about the simultaneous creation of two pairs of points, the first pair being
the sefirot of Tif'eret (Heaven) and Shekhinah (Earth), or perhaps Hokhmah
and Binah, and the second pair being the hylic points of the lower heaven and
earth? Or, are we speaking of one act of *creatio ex nihilo* of the sefirotic world,
from which everything else is *creatio ex materia*? The crux of the problem is
whether there is an essential gap between the sefirot and the rest of the universe, or perhaps the universe was created ex materia out of the sefirot themselves that emerged from Ayin. We find a surprising answer to this question
in another comment of Nahmanides, in which he characterizes with utmost
clarity the nature of these primordial points of existence:

> The verses explain that the first creations (*nivra'im*) were from *Ayin*
> [*ex nihilo*], and the rest were produced from the primal matter that is
> created (*nivra*). Do not be troubled by what R. Eliezer the Great said,
> "Whence was heaven created (*nivra'im*)? From the Light of the Rai-
> ment of the Holy One," which also appears in *Bereshit Rabbah*, be-
> cause the Sages want to elevate the primal matter as much as possible
> and subtilize it to the greatest extent possible. They do not consider
> heaven, which is a body in motion possessing matter and form, to
> have been created from *Ayin*; instead, the Light of the Raiment was
> the first creation (*nivra*), from which issued forth the substantial mat-
> ter (*homer ha-mammash*) in heaven. He gave the earth a different mat-
> ter that is not as subtle as the first, namely, the "snow" beneath the
> Throne of Glory, because the Throne of Glory was created (*nivra*),
> and from it [issued forth] the "snow" beneath it, from which the ter-
> restrial matter was made. It is thus tertiary in creation.[10]

The hylic points created ex nihilo were the subtlest of existents, and they
seem to represent the sefirot themselves. The celestial hyle was made ex materia from a different subtle existent that R. Eliezer called the Light of the Rai-
ment, which may represent Hokhmah or Tif'eret, whereas the terrestrial hyle

was made from an even less rarefied hylic point known as the Throne of Glory, by which Nahmanides may intend Shekhinah.[11] The material substrate of the physical universe was not created, then, ex nihilo, but was a product of a prior, subtler existent—the very sefirot emanated from the divine Ayin. Therefore, an unbroken line of existents produced from one another extends from the Godhead down to the world, such that the world is none other than a gradual solidification of the divine Being itself. Unlike the universe, the Godhead has no physical existence, but it also is not an abstract entity. The Godhead transcends the world in the sense that it is the subtlest of subtle existents that encompasses a gradation of being.

Nahmanides refers to the terrestrial hyle as "tertiary in creation," because the process of creating the more physical hyle is a gradual transition from a subtle, indistinct state of being to a dense, distinct one. From the subtle point of the Throne of Glory, which alone was created from Ayin, the "snow" beneath the Throne was formed, from which the terrestrial hyle was made. As the chain of being extends downwards, so its existents become more distinct and coarser. Every level in the chain maintains symbolic relations with the level above it; the farther down one goes, the less transparent the symbolic quality of objects becomes. Nahmanides depicts the processes of emanation and creation—in keeping with the Neoplatonic and kabbalistic tradition—as transitioning from the indistinct to the distinct, from the subtle to the coarse, a depiction that characterizes the manner in which the sefirotic configuration itself draws away from Ayin. As Moshe Idel has demonstrated, in Nahmanides's thought the emanatory process begins with an act of divine contraction, in which the plenitudinous Ayin makes space for the efflux that will emanate from it.[12] In Nahmanides's terms:

> "*Hokhmah.*" This is the limit of what man can apprehend with his thought. The tradition on the matter is through allusion, because the plenitude of the exalted *Keter 'Elyon* comprises more than the heart can conceive of its Glory. It constricted the essence of the Glory as if to the measure of the front of the screen [*parokhet* (*sic*)] and between the two cherubs, which is one handbreadth. Darkness thus was over the All [i.e., *Ha-Kol*], because the privation of light is darkness. It drew out from the Source of Everything the Bright Light called "*Hokhmah.*"
>
> "Thirty-two paths." Each Path inscribes upon the darkness the letters in their forms and the *sefirot* in the measure of the Will of the blessed, exalted Ordainer, and they become differentiated from one

another. The inscription of the Light of the paths and their ensuing differentiation from one another is called "engraving."[13]

In the darkness, that is, the space emptied of Keter's plenitude by way of Keter's self-contraction to the span of a handbreadth, the sefirot and letters that emanated from the Source of Everything were engraved, becoming differentiated and separate. This empty space resulting from the contraction constituted the medium into which the Bright Light engraved the sefirot and letters in a measure and manner that rendered them separate from one another.[14] In his explanation of the term *peli'ot* in Sefer Yetzirah, Nahmanides describes the differentiation and separation via his oft-used image of subtlety (*dakut*): " '*Peli'ot*.' As in 'If [a matter] is baffling (*yippale*)' (Deut 17:8), which we render in Targum as 'is separate.' As if to say, they emerge separate and differentiated from one another. Due to the unfathomable subtlety, the name *pele* [wonder] befits them and not a name of differentiation and separation."[15] Aside from this differentiation and separation of Ayin's plenitude, the process of emanation also marks a transition from the subtle to the less subtle. At the end of his commentary on Sefer Yetzirah, Nahmanides figuratively portrays this process of densification as exhalation. The air a person expels from the mouth and that turns into a mist represents the emergence of the sefirah of Binah from Hokhmah: " 'Three: Water from Wind.' This is *Binah*, which is the subtleness of essence, like water which is the subtle[st] of the [sefirotic] structure. For you see that water comes from wind, like the wind of the mouth."[16] In a brief sentence in Torat ha-Adam, Nahmanides describes the order of creation as a process of an emanating chain that gradually moves toward distinction and densification: "the creations of the first [day] were more subtle and proximate to the first cause and to the primordial element than those created on the second day, and so [those on] the second [day] than those on the third, as you can see even from the plain sense of the verses."[17] This depicts all of existence as a continuous chain that begins with Ayin and maintains a direct link, it would appear, from the Godhead to the universe. Nahmanides complicates this Neoplatonic picture of existence by adding the aspect of fragility to the chain of being, which entails its dynamic and variable nature as well as humans' ability to affect its state through their activities. This chain of being suffered the primordial rupture that led to hyperdensification and hyperdifferentiation, a rupture that will be made whole again through the cyclical movement of emergence from Ayin and the return to it.[18] Through this rupture of hyperdifferentiation, through which humans broke away and became autonomous creatures, Nature as well became causally inert and independent from the structure of the Godhead. Divine providence became mediated and lost its direct transparent presence in the universe, which it had previously been at the first stages of creation. Each rung in the chain of divine and cosmic being has its own set of rules, its own regularity, order, and logic, which plays a decisive role in Nahmanides's understanding of the concepts of Nature, providence, and miracles, to which the rest of this chapter is devoted.

II

Nahmanides's theory of the hidden miracle is probably the most famous and familiar aspect of his thought. This unique and creative concept, with its sweeping theological implications, has drawn the attention of his readers. The various interpreters of Nahmanides have thought that his theory negates the concept of the existence of an independent causal natural order that is disconnected from the causation of the supernal realms and that acts according to its own causality. In their opinion, Nahmanides maintains that whatever looks like the regular, causally determined activity of a Nature indifferent to the actions and religious standing of humans is truly a directly willed act of God concealed from the observer. Seasonal rains or prolonged drought appear to be natural phenomena, but they do occur as divine reward or punishment. When that happens, they are "hidden" miracles because they can be construed causally.

This predominant understanding of Nahmanides's theory characterizes the difference between the manifest and hidden miracle in the following manner. The manifest miracle is a wonder, the whole point of which is to break, manifestly, the regular rhythm of natural activity, which explains why someone in the presence of such an event clearly recognizes God's deliberate involvement. The hidden miracle, on the other hand, is a volitional act of God masked by a natural process, as it were, such that an observer would be likely to chalk it up erroneously to some causal process. According to this, Nahmanides does not believe in any real metaphysical distinction between manifest and hidden miracles; the difference lies only in the eye of the beholder—both phenomena are equally miraculous, except that one is manifest and the other is hidden. This leads to the characterization of Nahmanides as either anticipating early-modern occasionalism or resuscitating philosophical notions of the Kalām, which viewed Nature as an illusion concealing the perpetual and ongoing volitional activity of God.

To take one example among many of this characterization of Nahmanides's position, let us consider Gershom Scholem's sharp words:

> This theory [of hidden miracles], as it appears in Nahmanides's writ-
> ings, is based upon standing Maimonides's theory in the *Guide of the
> Perplexed* on its head. It does not diminish or take away from miracles
> but on the contrary it radically expands the scope of the miraculous to
> the greatest extent possible. This includes the tendency to convert
> what we call laws of nature into some kind of illusion, because what we
> view as disclosing order is, in truth, nothing but a single sequence of
> miracles through which the hidden promise of the Torah is revealed.[19]

Several formulations of Nahmanides seem to substantiate this reading, as they
apparently imply that he rejects the very idea of Nature in toto:

> From the greatest public miracles, a person concedes the hidden mir-
> acles, which are the foundation of the entire Torah, because no one has
> a portion in the Torah of our master Moses until he [lit. we] believes
> that all our affairs and experiences are entirely miraculous. For both
> the public and the individual there is nothing natural about them nor
> [are they] the course of the world, only if someone performs the com-
> mandments will he receive his reward, and if he violates them his pun-
> ishment shall cut him off—everything by the decree of the Most High,
> as I have mentioned already.[20]

In a very important article on this topic, David Berger demonstrates that
this understanding of Nahmanides's doctrine of the hidden miracle is faulty,
and he sheds new light on the issue.[21] The key text that Berger analyzed in
order to sharpen our understanding of Nahmanides's position is found in his
Commentary on Job, on the verse "He does not withdraw His eyes from the
righteous" (Job 36:7):

> The reason [that God extends His providence to individual humans]
> is clearly known: since man recognizes his God, He watches over him
> and protects him [. . .] For this reason He protects the righteous, for
> just as their heart and eyes are always with Him, so the eyes of God are
> upon them from the beginning of the year until year's end, to the ex-
> tent that the completely pious person (*hasid*) who cleaves to his God
> always, such that no worldly matter severs the cleaving of his thoughts
> to Him, will be protected always from all accidents, even those which

occur through Nature. He will be protected from them by a miracle constantly performed on his behalf, as if he were one of the supernal beings that are not subject to generation and corruption by accidents. To the extent that he comes close to his God by cleaving to Him, he shall enjoy superior protection. But one who is far from God in his thoughts and deeds, even if he does not deserve death on account of some sin of his, shall be forsaken and left to accidents [. . .] Since most of the world belongs to this intermediate group, the Torah commanded the mobilization of the military, the matter of the priest anointed for war sending back the fearful so that they not sap the courage of their comrades, and every tactical maneuver in the Torah and the Prophets [. . .] Had they been meritorious, they would have sallied forth few in number and prevailed without arms, and had they deserved defeat, a multitude would have been of no avail. In this case, however, they deserved to be treated in the manner of Nature and accident. The Master [Maimonides] explained this matter well in the *Guide of the Perplexed.*[22]

According to the above, only the pious who continuously cleave to God are providentially protected from harmful accidents and Nature by constant miracles. The rest, which comprises the vast majority of people, are left in the hands of happenstance—as Nahmanides puts it, "most of the world belongs to this intermediate group." The Torah itself presumes that most people are subject to accidents, which is why it gives orders about how to go about prosecuting a war and why it permits the use of medicine, as Nahmanides notes elsewhere.[23] In opposition to the occasionalist position, one can see, then, that in Nahmanides's view there is an inert, blind Nature that acts upon most people, and God reserves his miraculous and continuous providence for the perfectly pious alone.[24] The hidden miracle does not replace Nature and accidents but operates at a level above natural causality exclusively on behalf of these perfect individuals.

Nahmanides's conception of providence structurally parallels Maimonides's position, as noted by Nahmanides: "The Master explained this matter well in the *Guide of the Perplexed.*" In the *Guide,* Maimonides puts forward the principle that the degree of providence afforded a person is proportional to that person's degree of perfection.[25] Berger, however, sees this solely as a parallel in structure, as the contents of each structure are utterly different. While Maimonides defined the perfection that induces providence as intellectual-philosophical perfection, Nahmanides, according to Berger, does not characterize the pious person's perfection in those terms. Moreover, Maimonides interpreted providence naturalistically, such that an enlightened individual cleaving to God would be ipso facto providentially protected through a causal feedback effect and not as a result of God's voluntary intercession on that person's behalf. Nahmanides, says Berger, preserves the element of God's continuous volitional involvement, as God changes the laws of Nature for the pious individual.[26] These distinctions will be treated at length in the pages that follow, but Berger undoubtedly has demonstrated quite clearly that Nahmanides's idea of the hidden miracle does not mean that natural laws are illusory. He recognizes that Nature has laws, especially astrological ones. As he reiterates many times, in astrology the nations of the world fall under the sovereignty of the zodiacal signs, and only the pious of Israel escape blind Nature and the clutches of accidents for the continuous providence of the hidden miracle.[27]

The rest of this chapter attempts to understand the esoteric aspect to Nahmanides's theory of the hidden miracle. Various scholars who have researched it have not considered it within the wider context of his kabbalah.[28] An analysis of the connection between the miraculous and the inner aspects of the Godhead, and a clarification of how these phenomena relate to Nahmanides's conception of cleaving, yields a completely different understanding of matters.

III

From Nahmanides's Commentary on the Torah one can see that the distinction between the hidden miracle and manifest miracle is not merely a conceptual one about the level of God's direct involvement in the miracle, but also a historical one. From the era of the Patriarchs until Moses, no manifest miracles occurred, but that changed once Moses was chosen to lead the Jewish people. While it may be true that God afflicted Pharaoh's household on Abraham's behalf, the temporal juxtaposition of Sarah's kidnapping and the afflictions could be explained causally. The same is true for Abraham's miraculous victory on the battlefield. Only in Exodus do we find manifest miracles, such as the splitting of the sea and the falling of the manna. Nahmanides identifies the following verse, which distinguishes Moses from the Patriarchs, as the interpretive, theological key to grasping this dramatic change in the manner of God's self-disclosure: "I appeared to Abraham, Isaac, and Jacob through El Shaddai, but I did not make Myself known to them through My name Y-HWH" (Exod 6:3). When the name El Shaddai appears earlier in Genesis, Nahmanides explains its meaning and its connection to the hidden miracle:

> Rabbi Abraham [Ibn Ezra], in the name of [Samuel] ha-Nagid, ex- plained it [i.e., the name El Shaddai] as deriving from *sh-d-d,* that is to say, He vanquishes and devastates (*meshadded*) the celestial configura- tion. This [explanation] is the correct one, because it is the [Weak] Attribute of Strength [i.e., *Gevurah*] that governs the world, which the Sages call the Lower Attribute of Judgment. The reason for mention- ing the name now is because through it hidden miracles are performed for the righteous—to rescue them from the jaws of death, sustain them in famine, and save them from slaughter in war, like all those miracles performed for Abraham and the Patriarchs, and all those enu- merated in the blessings and curses in the Torah readings of *Im be- Hukkotai* and *Ve-Hayah Ki Tavo.* These are all miracles because it is unnatural for rains to come at the right time when we serve God, or for the heavens to dam up when we plant in the seventh year, and likewise for all of Torah's promises. They are in fact all miracles, and in all of them the configuration of the zodiac is overruled. They do not entail, however, a change in how the world runs, as do those miracles performed by our master Moses: the ten plagues, the splitting of the sea, the manna, the well, and others, which were wonders that pub- licly changed Nature and were performed through the Unique Name that He told him.[29]

Following Ibn Ezra, Nahmanides explains the name El Shaddai to mean a force that devastates and overpowers the zodiac. He claims that hidden mira- cles are performed through this name: "The reason for mentioning the name now is because through it hidden miracles are performed for the righteous." The connection to Nahmanides's kabbalah is made through his identification of El Shaddai with a particular sefirah: "because it is the [Weak] Attribute of Strength that governs the world, which the Sages call the Lower Attribute of Judgment [i.e., *Shekhinah*]." The Lower or Weak Attribute of Judgment refers to Shekhinah in kabbalistic symbolism.[30] According to Nahmanides, the instantiation of hidden miracles in the world occurs by way of Shekhinah. The manifest miracles, in contrast, occur through the Unique Name, the Name of Being (*shem havayah*), the Tetragrammaton known to Moses, and Nahmanides does not single out its sefirotic correspondent in this passage:

"wonders that publicly changed Nature and were performed through the Unique Name that He told him." The Patriarchs were able to rise above their zodiacal fate by sustaining a special connection with Shekhinah, but because they could reach no higher than Shekhinah, their connection to the Godhead could not induce a manifest miracle. The limitations of this connection were permanent, which Nahmanides sees reflected by the fact that in Genesis the words "my Lord" (Adonai) or "God" (El or Elohim) are always appended to the Tetragrammaton: "see how our forefather Abraham never mentioned the Tetragrammaton (*shem yod hei*) except in conjunction with the name written with an *aleph dalet* or together with 'the Most High God' (*El 'Elyon*), and he usually refers to 'God' (*Elohim*)."[31] The Patriarchs' connection to the inner-most aspect of the living Godhead, represented by the Tetragrammaton, was always intermediated through names that represent the sefirah of Shekhinah.

Nahmanides explains the significance of the Tetragrammaton (*shem ha-vayah*) within the Godhead and its connection to the manifest miracle in his commentary on the second half of the verse "but I did not make Myself known to them through My name Y-HWH":

> God said to Moses: I appeared to the Patriarchs through the power of My Hand [i.e., *Shekhinah*],[32] by which I devastate the zodiacal signs and aid my chosen ones, but I did not make Myself known to them through My name *yod he* [the Tetragrammaton], by which every exis-tent was brought into being, in order to create (*livro*) new things for them by changing Nature (*ha-toladot*) [. . .] Everything R. Abraham [Ibn Ezra] said about this matter is correct, except it is as if he proph-esies unawares [. . .] The Patriarchs received a revelation of *Shekhinah* and divine speech through the Weak Attribute of Judgment, and He governed them through it. He made Himself known to Moses and governed him through the Attribute of Mercy, which is through His Great Name, as in the meaning of [the verse], "Who made His Arm of Splendor [i.e., *Tif'eret*] march at the right hand of Moses" (Isa 63:12), and it is written, "Thus did you lead your people, to make for yourself a Name of Splendor [*Tif'eret*]" (Isa 63:14). That is why hereafter Moses does not mention the name *El Shaddai*.[33]

Unlike the Patriarchs, Moses was sent to the Jewish people through the sefirah of Tif'eret, or as Nahmanides puts it elsewhere, "He [God] informed him [Moses] that he was sent to them through the Attribute of Judgment that is in the Attribute of Mercy."[34] Nahmanides hints in various places that this connection between Tif'eret and the manifest miracle is no coincidence. The world was created ex nihilo through the Tetragrammaton, so the manifest miracle, which is for all intents and purposes a new creation, is performed through the same creative potency of the Godhead. Nahmanides says in his Discourse on Ecclesiastes: "Through the Unique Name overt signs and wonders are newly created in the world, as you can see plainly in its letters, which are the language of being (*havayah*), for through His name He spoke and the world came into being."[35] And in his discourse Torat Ha-Shem Temimah: "He mentioned the Tetragrammaton, which is the Essential Name and the foundation of being, through which signs and wonders are performed that change the fabric (lit. being) of the world and its natural course. This is the name revealed to Moses when he was going to make new signs and wonders, not [the Name] known to the Patriarchs, which is *El Shaddai*."[36] The new creation of an existent ex nihilo is connected to the Name of Being through which the world was created, and this name is identified with the sefirah of Tif'eret.[37]

In addition to the opposition between the hidden miracle and Shekhinah versus the manifest miracle and Tif'eret, Nahmanides sets up another opposition that sheds light on the theosophic depths of the matter—the Weak Attribute of Judgment versus the Attribute of Mercy. The hidden miracle occurs through the Weak Attribute of Judgment because of Shekhinah's sefirotic connection to the Attribute of Judgment. Tif'eret, on the other hand, governs "through the Attribute of Mercy, which is through His Great Name." Consequently, the ontological difference between the hidden and manifest miracles parallels the difference between Rahamim (Mercy) and Hesed, which constitute existence through their efflux, and the Weak Attribute of Judgment, which can only alter astrological judgments but cannot create something new. One could say that as the inner emanatory processes of the Godhead descend, the creative potency is drained, and all existence takes on a permanently fixed form. Shekhinah is considered the Weak Attribute of Judgment because as the last sefirah it acts as a kind of funnel: it serves as the channel through which the efflux of the Godhead reaches the world while limiting that efflux enough to allow for the existence of an individuated world. As the Weak Attribute of Judgment, Shekhinah does not have the power to create the new existent necessary for a manifest miracle, but it can effect internal changes within the zodiac.

In order to appreciate fully how the two types of miracle relate to their respective aspects of the sefirotic structure, we must redefine the difference between them. As mentioned above, scholars have tended to attribute the difference merely to the observer's point of view, while positing that in essence both the hidden and manifest miracles demonstrate God's voluntary involvement. Since previous scholars did not differentiate the different layers involved in the hidden and manifest miracles within the Godhead, they used a simple criterion to distinguish one from the other: Can God's involvement be discerned or not? Hidden and manifest miracles are equally miraculous, but one is simply concealed and one is plain for all to see. Examining the miracles through a kabbalistic lens, however, has afforded us the additional insight that the two kinds of miracle are profoundly and metaphysically distinct, and not only observationally so. The manifest miracle, on one hand, is a kind of new creation, so its source lies in the creative Attribute of Mercy within the Godhead. The hidden miracle, on the other hand, derives from a lower rung of the Godhead that intermediates the potency of the divine efflux; therefore, it can rearrange the causal relationships of Nature but cannot introduce something new into the equation. According to this interpretation, the hidden miracle originating in Shekhinah can indeed be seen by all, and Nahmanides explicitly describes such a case. While one can rationalize the apparent protection of a righteous individual from harm as statistically plausible and perfectly natural, one cannot make the same argument for a large population. Even if protection of a large group does not involve some new creation, everyone can clearly see the miracle in it: "but that one land, in its entirety, and one people should always have rains that fall at the appropriate time, and [have] abundance, tranquility, peace, health, might, and the crumpling of its foes, the likes of which does not exist elsewhere in the entire world—everyone knows that this comes from God."[38] The fact that this hidden miracle is visible to all, because no reasonable causal alternative can be found, does not transform it into a manifest miracle, because the manifest miracle is rooted in the sefirah of Tif'eret and entails a new creation. When seen against the background of its kabbalistic roots, the distinction between manifest and hidden miracles reflects an unbridgeable metaphysical gap between their respective sources in the Godhead.

IV

An analysis of Nahmanides's statements points to the following chain of being organized in ascending order: Nature, the hidden miracle, and the manifest miracle. This reading of Nahmanides presents much more complexity than the simplistic characterization of him as a Nature denier, who believes that everything that happens is a direct manifestation of God's will, there being no essential difference between the hidden and manifest miracles. For Nahmanides, Nature does exist as an inert, independent entity, with the hidden miracle above it and the manifest miracle above them both. This chain of being is anchored to different cosmic rungs of existence. Nature, which sits at the lowest level and is farthest from the Godhead's plane of existence, reflects the rule of the astrological signs, which operate causally and are blind to humans' religious observance or lack of it. The hidden miracle is linked to Shekhinah, which is the lowest sefirah, and those who cleave to it, such as the Patriarchs, are liberated from the dominion of zodiacal accidents. This liberation does not occur through the creation of something new but by the reorganization of the forces of Nature for the protection and benefit of the cleaving. The manifest miracle is connected to the sefirah of Tif'eret, the source of all existence, and as such it has the power to create a new, supernatural creation, like the miracles that marked the Israelite exodus from Egypt.

If we combine all of our observations to this point—the correspondence between the chain of being comprising the zodiac, Shekhinah, and Tif'eret with blind Nature, the hidden miracle, and the manifest miracle—we realize that we must reevaluate the involvement of the divine will in miracles. Since the categories of the hidden and revealed miracle break down into two separate aspects of intradivine emanation, the following question arises: In what sense do these phenomena embody a voluntary act on the part of God? One could argue, of course, that God chooses volitionally to act sometimes through the sefirah of Shekhinah to work a hidden miracle and at other times through the sefirah of Tif'eret to work a manifest miracle. This exposition of Nahmanides's view treats the divine Attributes as instruments available to the divine will to carry out its desire. Aside from the difficulties inherent in such a view, Nahmanides's formulations incline us toward a different, more causal account of the hidden and manifest miracles. Any examination of this issue demands great care, because Nahmanides, in typical fashion, scatters the relevant pieces throughout his oeuvre and buries them in allusions. Any analysis therefore cannot yield an unequivocal answer to this issue, which is already complicated enough conceptually, but it might serve to illuminate a different path forward.

Our point of departure for examining this issue will be an attempt to understand why God governed the Patriarchs through the attribute of El Shaddai (Shekhinah) and the hidden miracle, while he governed Moses through the Tetragrammaton (Tif'eret) and the manifest miracle. What internal logic dictated the dramatic change in the way God manifested himself on the historical stage? One might think that Moses's unique personality caused God to grant him manifest miracles and remake creation for him, which God did not do for the Patriarchs. But Nahmanides goes a step farther. He aligns this disparity in wonderworking with the differing degrees of sefirotic apprehension attained by the Patriarchs and by Moses. Nahmanides articulates this in his comment on the aforementioned verse "but I did not make Myself known to them through My name Y-HWH":

> The way of truth follows the plain sense and meaning of the verse, saying: "I, the Lord [i.e., *Tif'eret*], have appeared to them through the Speculum of *El Shaddai* [i.e., *Shekhinah*]"—as in the meaning of [the verse], "I make myself known to him through the Appearance"[39] (Num 12:6)—"but I as the Lord did not make myself known to them, for they did not see through the Speculum That Shines such that they would know Me"—as in the meaning of [the verse], "The Lord spoke to Moses Countenance to Countenance" (Exod 33:11). The Patriarchs knew the Unique Name but not through prophecy, so when Abraham converses with God he mentions either the Unique Name together with *aleph dalet* or *aleph dalet* alone. The Patriarchs received a revelation of *Shekhinah* and divine speech through the Weak Attribute of Judgment, and He governed them through it. He made Himself known to Moses and governed him through the Attribute of Mercy, which is through His Great Name.[40]

The Godhead's governance of the Patriarchs through hidden miracles mirrors the extent of their apprehension of the Godhead. In Nahmanides's view, the Patriarchs apprehended the Tetragrammaton only through the intermediation of Shekhinah, the Speculum That Does Not Shine.[41] Moses uniquely enjoyed the unmediated apprehension of Tif'eret, referred to as "Countenance to Countenance."[42] Elsewhere, after distinguishing between the hidden and manifest miracles, Nahmanides makes this distinction again:

> Jacob always mentions *El Shaddai,* but our master Moses never mentions it. If you are worthy, you can understand this fully from what they [the Sages] said in tractate *Yevamot* (49b): "All of the prophets looked through the Speculum That Does Not Shine." Isaiah therefore said "I saw my Lord" (*Adonai*) (Isa 6:1). But Moses looked through a

Speculum That Shines. He therefore said "man cannot see Me and live" (Exod 33:20), because "I saw my Lord (*Adonai*)" is written with *aleph-dalet*.[43]

Nahmanides points out the inherent connection between the prophet's degree of apprehension or quality of prophecy and the sefirah that governs his life. The Patriarchs were governed by Shekhinah's hidden miracles because their direct apprehension reached only that high, whereas Moses apprehended Tif'eret and so was governed through the manifest miracles sourced to Tif'eret.

This connection between prophetic stature and degree of providence attests to the fact that this operates outside the normal bounds of divine recompense, in which a person's degree of righteousness dictates the kind of divine providence that person merits. We can understand the operative principle here if we clarify the connection between the hidden and manifest miracles and cleaving in Nahmanides's thought. In the preceding quotations from Nahmanides's commentary on verses from Genesis and Exodus, he does not mention cleaving anywhere, but he does mention it in other passages that deal with the hidden miracle. In his Discourse on Ecclesiastes, for example, he mentions cleaving when he argues that all of Ecclesiastes was said through the Weak Attribute of Judgment, which explains why the Tetragrammaton never appears in the book. According to him, this explains the centrality of the natural course of events in Ecclesiastes:

> The reason [that Solomon mentions only God (*Elohim*) and not the Tetragrammaton] is because this book speaks about the natural course of the world under the Sun—how it was created and how all people are governed through the Attribute of Judgment. The righteous in this book who follow Solomon's guidance are like Abraham, Isaac, and Jacob, to whom [God] appeared through *El Shaddai* [. . .] That is why the Patriarchs and the righteous of this book are, on rare occasion, subject to accidents, as this book says: "As it happens to the fool, so will it also happen to me" (Eccl 2:15), as if to say, sometimes it is an accident but not always [. . .] Through the Unique Name overt signs and wonders are newly created in the world, as you can see plainly in its letters, which are the language of being, for through His name He spoke and the world came into being.
>
> Those who cleave to it are not subject to accidents; instead, it splits the sea and Jordan for them, rains down manna for them, and does

other such things associated with our master Moses, when they need the natural course of the world to change.[44]

Those who cleave to the Tetragrammaton have manifest miracles performed for them: "Those who cleave to it are not subject to accidents."[45] In a passage already cited from his Commentary on Job, Nahmanides states even more sharply the relationship between cleaving and liberation from blind Nature: "the completely pious person (*hasid*) who cleaves to his God always, such that no worldly matter severs the cleaving of his thoughts to Him, will be protected always from all accidents, even those which occur through Nature. He will be protected from them by a miracle constantly performed on his behalf, as if he were one of the supernal beings that are not subject to generation and corruption by accidents."[46] The correspondence that Nahmanides sets up in his Commentary on the Torah between the respective prophetic attainments and divine apprehension of the Patriarchs and Moses, on one hand, and their providential governance through manifest and hidden miracles, on the other, acquires an additional, deeper dimension in these passages from his Commentary on Job and Discourse on Ecclesiastes. A prophet's ability to induce the performance of manifest miracles depends upon his cleaving to Tif'eret, and a person's deliverance from the rule of accidents to the providential realm of the hidden miracle is similarly attained through cleaving to Shekhinah.[47] The different levels of prophecy reflect, therefore, different levels of cleaving to the configuration of the Godhead itself: the Patriarchs cleaved to Shekhinah but Moses cleaved to Tif'eret, which is what drove the historical change in God's self-disclosure.[48] Moses's stature indeed did bring manifest miracles onto the stage of history, but in Nahmanides's thinking it was specifically his prophetic stature, which in turn indicated a higher-order cleaving. The connection between the manifest miracle and Moses's prophetic stature can be seen in how Nahmanides understands Moses's concern that "they will not believe me" (Exod 4:1): "Or they will say the Great Name has not appeared to you through the Attribute of Mercy to perform signs and wonders for us, as you have said, because you are no greater than the Patriarchs."[49] Nahmanides offers little about the whys and wherefores behind the difference in stature between Moses and the Patriarchs. What transformational event in Moses's life enabled him to surpass Shekhinah and cleave to Tif'eret? Nahmanides, unfortunately, leaves no detailed answer.

From a few scattered passages in Nahmanides's writings we learn about the extraordinary benefits of cleaving, which can liberate humanity from inert causality and even stave off death: "Those who withdraw from the affairs of this world and, as if disembodied, do not attend to it [this world], their every thought and undivided attention upon their Creator alone, as was the case with Elijah, will live forever in their body and soul through the cleaving of their soul to the Glorious Name [i.e., *Shekhinah*], as we can see from what is written about Elijah."[50] Descriptions like this of the cleaving state, which were discussed in detail in the previous chapter, include the nullification of the faculties of the body due to the continuous concentration of one's consciousness—attention and thought—upon the Creator. According to Nahmanides, someone who cleaves to the sefirah of Shekhinah, also known by its cognomen "the Glorious Name," will live forever in body and soul like Elijah. The eternally corporeal existence of Elijah and Enoch is not some special miracle but has its own natural mechanism, which Nahmanides explains quite clearly in "Sha'ar ha-Gemul" when he discusses the eternity of the body after the Resurrection of the Dead: "If you challenge us from the fact that the body always subsists upon lowly things, we have already responded to you that the subsistence of the body will be like that of the soul. The soul subsists by uniting with the Supernal Intellect, and the sustained becomes like the sustainer by uniting with it."[51] The radical change effected in the state of the body through cleaving is explained here in a brief but arresting formulation: "the sustained becomes like the sustainer by uniting with it." That is, the cleaving subject acquires the properties of the object to which it cleaves. Mystics actually receive the properties of Shekhinah, rendering their bodies self-sufficient and without material needs, and if mystics can perpetuate this state of cleaving, their bodies become de facto eternal. Elsewhere in "Sha'ar ha-Gemul," Nahmanides writes a brief but sharp formulation of his conception of cleaving in terms of *unio mystica,* that is, union with God:

> His mentioning the matter of their existence through the existence of the object of their intellection, and their becoming one entity—this is the interpretation of what the Torah says "and to cleave to Him" (Deut 11:22), and it says [further], "yet the soul of my master shall be bound up in the bundle of life with God your Lord (*et Ha-Shem Elokekha*)" (1 Sam 25:29). Hence R. Akiva came to teach that " 'The Lord your God (*et Ha-Shem Elokekha*) shall you fear' (Deut 10:20) includes [fear of] Torah scholars" (*Pesahim* 22b).[52]

Just as Shekhinah is eternal and not subject to the accidents of Nature, the same becomes true of the righteous person cleaving to and becoming identical to Shekhinah—"their becoming one entity."

Let us take stock of what we have said so far. First of all, Nahmanides posits a difference in the sefirotic origins of the hidden and manifest miracles. Then, he sets up a correspondence between these two kinds of divine providence and the stature and prophecy of Moses and the Patriarchs. In his Discourse on Ecclesiastes and Commentary on Job, he also connects prophecy to the act of cleaving, thereby assigning the hidden and manifest miracles to different states of cleaving. Last, in the Commentary on the Torah and "Sha'ar ha-Gemul" he depicts the state of cleaving as one in which the body of the pious individual is liberated from accidents by becoming identical to Shekhinah during the cleaving state.[53]

The composite picture we have developed enables us to return to the question posed at the beginning of this section about the role of God's will in the hidden miracle. The link Nahmanides makes between the hidden miracle and the state of cleaving, and his description of what resulted from the cleaving attained by Moses and Elijah, points to a mystical process with its own set of rules, a process in which God's voluntary involvement dissipates. Mystics do not divest themselves of their bodies but unshackle their bodies from Nature's laws by cleaving to Shekhinah. In Nahmanides's providential theory, the hidden and manifest miracles are traced to two different aspects within the intradivine emanation that are also involved in mystical cleaving, which serves to obscure the volitional basis of these miracles. The distinction between accidental Nature and the two kinds of miracle is not, therefore, between blind Nature and the perpetually direct, voluntary intervention of God, but between different rungs in the chain of divine being to which mystics are able to ascend. The intimate connection that mystics forge with aspects of the Godhead is what frees them from blind causality, to the point that some mystics could work manifest miracles involving new creations. R. Solomon b. Abraham Ibn Adret (Rashba) was Nahmanides's chief disciple in matters exoteric and esoteric, and he describes how the pious individual, by achieving a state of continuous cleaving, can cause a miracle to be performed through regular causality—no voluntary divine intervention necessary:

> through the cleaving of their soul to its source, the pious (*hasidim*) have the power to transcend the workings of the lower realms and change natural phenomena—even though they are acted upon and governed through the power of the Spheres—and remove them completely from the bounds of Nature, like splitting the sea, as Moses did to the Sea of Reeds, and certainly [they can change] what does not

deviate completely from the course of Nature, like halting the flow of rivers that occasionally dry up and cease flowing. All of this is because they rise above and the supernal acts on what is below.[54]

Rashba, who refers explicitly to cleaving—"through the cleaving of their soul to its source"—asserts that both hidden and manifest miracles are performed by the power of the pious to transcend Nature. The testimony of Nahmanides's greatest disciple and successor carries significant weight for our understanding of the relationship between the pious and miracles.

The tension between the account of miracles as involving direct divine intervention and the kabbalistic account that explains it through cleaving is expressed in Nahmanides's own dual language. In "Sha'ar ha-Gemul" and his Commentary on the Torah, Nahmanides describes the state of Originary Adam before Original Sin, an embodied state that would have continued in perpetuity had he not sinned. In the former, Nahmanides equates Adam's prelapsarian state with those of Moses, Elijah, and Enoch:

> For the soul subsists by uniting with the Supernal Intellect, just as the angels subsist through it. The transcendence of the soul over the body nullifies the faculties of the body, as we have mentioned another time, until the body, like the soul, can subsist without food or drink, as Moses subsisted for forty days on the mountain. If we attribute this to a miracle, Elijah disproves [it]—his body was neither cast off nor separated from the soul, yet he still lives and will continue to live forever. Such was also the case with Enoch, according to the *midrash* of our Rabbis. They similarly said: " 'whatever God does shall be forever' (Eccl 3:14)—R. Simon said: Based on this verse, man was fit to subsist and live forever. Why was he penalized with death? 'God does it so that men should fear Him' (ibid.). 'That which was still is' (Eccl 3:15)—R. Yudan and R. Nehemiah. One said: If someone should say to you, 'Is it possible that had Adam not sinned he would have lived and existed forever?' tell him that Elijah did not sin and he lives and exists forever." See how they explained that God's Will in his creations sustains them forever, and they brought proof to this from Elijah.[55]

Prelapsarian Adam enjoyed the same state of cleaving as did Elijah, which is why he was supposed to live in his body forever.[56] The state of cleaving that sustains the body eternally and liberates it from natural accidents is nothing but a return to the primordially natural state of humans. Nahmanides emphasizes in the passage above that liberation from death is not a one-time miracle: "If we attribute this to a miracle, Elijah disproves [it]." The original eternality of humankind is explained through the inherent workings of the cleaving state and the nature of the human body in that state. Yet, in the very same passage Nahmanides connects it to the divine will: "See how they explained that God's Will in his creations sustains them forever." This divine will cannot be completely incompatible, then, with a fixed, causal system. The application of God's will is not a continuously voluntaristic activity but an essence—the Will—that cleaves to humans.[57] One finds a similar tension in a passage from his Torah commentary that also discusses the eternality of prelapsarian humanity:

> According to our Rabbis, had he [Adam] not sinned, he would have never died, because the supernal soul bestows everlasting life, and the divine desire in him [that is, in humanity] at the moment of creation cleaves to him in perpetuity, sustaining him forever [. . .] Know that composition does not entail corruption except to those of little faith [who believe] that the universe is necessary. But according to men of faith, who say that the world was created *de novo* by pure divine desire, its existence will last for the entire eon of desire. This is an evident truth. Therefore, "on the day you eat from it you shall surely die" (Gen 2:17), because then you will be mortal, you will not be sustained forever through my desire.[58]

Careful attention to the use of the word "desire" in this passage reveals a complicated polysemy. When Nahmanides argues that the world is not eternal but "was created *de novo* by pure divine desire," this desire implies volition. God's perpetual desire that humans exist enables their composite, finite bodies to exist forever. Those who deny such a possibility and instead argue that corporeal death was part of Originary Man's essence are perforce "of little faith." Those who believe in *creatio de novo,* that is, the principle that everything exists because God wills it, also believe it possible that God's sheer will can make the body exist eternally, even if it appears to contravene Nature. At the very same time, Nahmanides gives a different meaning to "desire." At the beginning of the quotation, he asserts that the presence of the supernal soul within humans grants them everlasting life: "because the supernal soul bestows everlasting life." The human soul, according to Nahmanides, has its source in the sefirah of Binah;[59] therefore, the interface between humans and the divine essence within them bestows everlasting life upon them. As the sentence goes on, Nahmanides uses "desire" not in the sense of continuous divine volition but in the sense of this divine essence cleaving to humanity: "and the divine desire in him at the moment of creation cleaves to him in perpetuity, sustaining him forever." Purely on the basis of the language, one could have explained this desire that cleaves to humans as God's continuous desire for their existence, but the beginning of the sentence indicates that the desire is a divine essence to which humans are connected.[60] Humanity's detachment from this divine essence is a death sentence; by nature, humans are supposed to be immortal. From the "exoteric" perspective, the natural causality of the hidden miracle is a continuous voluntary act; from the "esoteric" perspective, the continuous voluntarism is part and parcel of the internal structure of the planes of existence.

In his Commentary on the Torah, Nahmanides admits his debt to Ibn Ezra: "Everything R. Abraham [Ibn Ezra] said about this matter is correct, except it is as if he prophesies unawares."[61] The causal account of the miraculous can be filled out by analyzing Ibn Ezra's position on this issue and paying attention to the way Nahmanides translates it into his kabbalistic terminology. It is therefore appropriate at this juncture to expand upon Ibn Ezra's theory of the miraculous and its relationship to his theonymic theory.

Ibn Ezra elaborates his theory of divine names in his long comment on Exod 3:15. The Tetragrammaton is the specific name of God that refers to God's essence, whereas the names Adonai and Elohim are substantives that describe the potencies dependent upon God, which is why they are grammatically plural. The latter names refer to the angels that constitute the astrological order of the universe. Since the source of the human soul is in the supernal realms, humans have the ability to transcend the astrological system and perform miracles through a connection to the Tetragrammaton:

> Man's soul is of their [the angels'] kind, and it receives a supernal power in accord with the configuration of the planets and each planet['s position] with respect to the great host at the time of its creation. If the soul is wise, it can stand in the midst of the angels and receive great power from a supernal power which it received by the light of the angels. Then it will cleave to the glorious Name.[62]

In the continuation of the same piece, Ibn Ezra describes two responses to death:

> Since Adam saw that he would die, he sired a son to preserve the species, who received the power of existence by way of the collective [. . .]

The prophetic initiates would seclude themselves on the chance that they each would receive according to his power. Through this name signs and wonders are created and called forth into the world, and when this glorious Name was said to him he sought signs and wonders.[63]

The natural system of astrology ensures the preservation of species in the world. But beyond that, some enlightened individuals of the human race are able to rise above astrological causality by cleaving to the divine name through which signs and wonders are performed in the world. In his commentary on the verse "I appeared to Abraham, Isaac, and Jacob through El Shaddai, but I did not make Myself known to them through My name Y-HWH" (Exod 6:3), Ibn Ezra lays out his theonymic theory and its relationship to wonderworking, about which he asserts, "This is the secret of the entire Torah."[64] Not all of the spiritual elite can extricate themselves from the astrological system and effect changes in Nature to the same extent, and the differences between them result from their different levels of cleaving: "The Patriarchs were not able to cleave to God like Moses, who knew God 'face to face' (Exod 33:11). Therefore, Moses could change the nature of the lowly world and summon forth new signs and wonders that the Patriarchs could not have."[65] The miracle here is not a free expression of God's will but the product of the very human ability to transcend the astral system and receive a wonderworking power from the Tetragrammaton itself.

Ibn Ezra's theory of the miracle, like Nahmanides's, is an esoteric one. As he writes about the sins of Moses and Aaron at the waters of Meribah:

The explanation that I consider correct I will reveal through allusion. Know that when the individual knows the All (*Ha-Kol*) he cleaves to the All and through the All summons forth new signs and wonders. Truthfully, God told Moses, "and you shall speak (*ve-dibbartem*)" (Num 20:8) and not "speak (*dabberu*)" because of the people's strife with Moses; the individual was thus [only] an individual. He hit the rock but water did not come out until he hit it a second time.[66]

A miracle depends upon the individual knowing the All and cleaving to it. The term "the All" (*Ha-Kol*) as used by Ibn Ezra refers to God and the Tetragrammaton: "and God is the One, He is the Creator of all and He is the All, but I cannot explain."[67] Moses in the passage above is the "individual" who should have been able to work miracles through his cleaving to the glorious

Name, but because of his discord with the people, he had to resort to hitting the rock. The secret of the Name that accompanies astrological-magical knowledge explains the miracle in the framework of a causal structure, and in this way it is similar to Ibn Ezra's esoteric understanding of law and ritual.[68]

Nahmanides, who acknowledges his indebtedness to Ibn Ezra for his own theory of divine names and its relationship to miracles, borrows the structure that Ibn Ezra constructed and raises it up one level in the chain of being. Whereas Ibn Ezra identified the Tetragrammaton with God himself and Elohim or Shaddai with the zodiac and other powers, Nahmanides sees all of these names as referring to the Godhead. The Tetragrammaton, which he consistently refers to as "the Great Name," represents the sefirah of Tif'eret, and Elohim or Shaddai represents the sefirah of Shekhinah, which he also calls "the Glorious Name."[69] Despite this important switch of theonymic referents and Nahmanides's very different conception of the divine as an organically stratified Godhead, Nahmanides accepts Ibn Ezra's basic causal account: cleaving enables spiritual aspirants to transcend one system of powers for a supernal one that confers upon them wonderworking powers. Similarly, Nahmanides borrows Ibn Ezra's idea that a change in the degree of cleaving, as represented by different divine names, can be used as a profound hermeneutic for understanding the change in divine providence from Genesis to Exodus.

V

The providential governance of the hidden miracle does not grace only those mystics liberated from zodiacal domination, but also the entire geographical expanse of the land of Israel. In his commentary on the blessings and curses in the Torah portion of Be-Hukkotai, Nahmanides claims that the land of Israel can exist in a perpetual state of hidden miracles. He does not mean only the pious, cleaving individuals but the corporate Jewish people:

> The reason for this [why the preceding blessings differ from these] is that those blessings may be miraculous but they are hidden miracles with which the entire Torah is filled, as I have explained. They are even for the individual worshipper, because when the pious person (hasid) keeps all of the commandments of the Lord his God, He keeps him from sickness, sterility, and his children predeceasing him, and He fills his life with goodness. But the blessings in this Torah portion are

universal for the nation when our entire nation, every single member, is righteous. It therefore constantly says "the land" here.[70]

Both the pious individual and the collective in the land of Israel are liberated from accidents by virtue of their connection to Shekhinah. The individual breaks free of the domain of blind, inert Nature by actively cleaving to Shekhinah. As for the collective in the land of Israel, the land itself, owing to its direct link to Shekhinah, is a geographic region whose borders mark where the sovereignty of natural causality ends. Nahmanides spells this out in his comment about the land of Israel ejecting those who engage in illicit sexual relations:

> "The land became defiled and I called it to account for its iniquity, and the land spewed out" (Lev 18:25). Scripture is very severe regarding illicit sexual relations for the land's sake, because it becomes sullied by them and spews out the transgressors. Yet illicit sexual relations are a personal obligation that does not depend upon [living in] the land! The secret of the matter is in the verse which says, "When the Most High gave nations their homes and set the divisions of man, He fixed the boundaries of peoples . . . For the Lord's portion is His people . . ." (Deut 32:8–9). The idea is that the Glorious Name created everything and put the power over lower beings into supernal ones, placing over each and every nation in its own land a particular planet or zodiacal sign, as is known in astrology. This is [the meaning of] the verse, "those which the Lord your God allotted to all peoples" (Deut 4:19), because He allotted signs in the heavens to all of them. Above them all are the supernal angels whom He appointed to be ministers over them [. . .] The Glorious Name is the supreme Power and highest Lord for the entire world, but the land of Israel—the center of the ecumene—is the Lord's domain, unique to His Name; He did not appoint over it an angelic sovereign, lord, or ruler.[71]

In contrast to all other lands, the land of Israel is under the sovereignty of neither zodiacal signs nor the ministers above them. In the continuation of the piece, Nahmanides hints at the connection between Shekhinah and the land of Israel:

> but if you merit understanding the first instance of "the Earth" (ha-Aretz) mentioned in the verse [beginning with the word] be-reshit and mentioned in the Torah reading of Im Be-Hukkotai, you will know an

exalted and esoteric secret, and you will comprehend the Rabbinic statement that the supernal Temple is set opposite to the earthly Temple, to which I have already alluded for you in the verse, "for the Earth (*ha-Aretz*), All (*Kol*), is Mine" (Exod 19:5).[72]

The first "Earth" mentioned is Shekhinah, as emerges from the comment on Exod 19:5 that he references. There, Nahmanides notes the connection between the Earth and the expression "All" (*Kol*), which typically represents the sefirah of Shekhinah: "for the Earth, which is called All (*Kol*), is Mine."[73] Elsewhere, Nahmanides sets up a parallel between Shekhinah as the life-giving force of the entire universe and the land of Israel as nourisher of all other lands: "There is a profound secret in it, because this Land is sought through the All, which is everything, and all lands are nourished from it in truth."[74]

The direct connection to Shekhinah, and the indirect one to the higher sefirot through Shekhinah, marks off the land of Israel as a literally supernatural space in which the zodiac holds no sway, where inert Nature ceases operating. Within the borders of the land of Israel Shekhinah acts through hidden miracles. Above, we raised the question of divine volition regarding the pious individual who escapes the astrological system and accidents, and the same question arises here too: To what degree does divine volition play a role in the hidden miracles occurring in the land of Israel? One can say, of course, that God volitionally punishes those sinners who inhabit his special domain more than those living elsewhere, and that God also chooses to reward those who do as he wishes in his land. But since the land of Israel, in Nahmanides's kabbalah, constitutes an axis mundi to Shekhinah given its location at the center of the ecumene, it seems more intuitive to view this geographically dependent reward and punishment as an outcome of the self-regulating interface between the two planes of existence. Punctiliousness in performance of commandments in the land of Israel is demanded by the very nature of the location, so it is not surprising that Nahmanides claims that centuries before the Torah's prohibitions were given at Sinai, the Patriarchs were careful to observe them in the land of Israel.[75] The center of gravity shifts from the fulfillment of God's will or lack thereof, with its consequent reward or punishment, to a matter of ontology bound up in the presence of Shekhinah—the land does not abide certain kinds of sinners. Once Nahmanides defines the land of Israel as an area with particular essential qualities that generate a state of hidden miracles, being and will collapse into a single entity and seemingly leave no room for the volitional aspect of the miraculous.

Nahmanides refrains from stating this outright, but he does quote Ibn Ezra on the land of Israel without adding any reservations:

> R. A[braham] wrote on the Torah portion of *Va-Yelekh* (Deut 31:16): "We know that God is one and that variability comes from the recipients. God does not vary His actions, as they are all through wisdom. Service of God includes preserving the capacity of reception in accordance with the location. It is therefore written, 'the law of the God of the land' (2 Kgs 17:26), and Jacob said, 'remove the foreign gods' (Gen 35:2). Cleaving to illicit relations is antithetical to the location. The enlightened will understand." These are his words.[76]

Ibn Ezra writes that the punishment of the wicked in the land does not flow from some intentional change in God's relationship to humans. God is one; he does not vary his actions. The punishment visited upon the sinner in the land of Israel is generated by the nature of the location and people's behavior there—"variability comes from the recipients." Nahmanides quotes this without qualifications, and it accentuates the unwilled character of the hidden miracles that occur in the land of Israel.

VI

When the pious achieve a state of cleaving, or when a person is simply present in the land of Israel, they are freed from zodiacal dominion through their connection to Shekhinah. This parallels the primordial state of paradisiacal Adam. In the citations from "Sha'ar ha-Gemul" above, prelapsarian humanity is depicted as enjoying a state of cleaving to Shekhinah that grants eternal existence, in the manner of Elijah, Enoch, and Moses. Adam existed on the plane of continuous hidden miracles, subsisting on the Edenic fruit that Nahmanides identifies with manna, that is, the nourishment desublimated from Shekhinah's radiance that his body absorbed completely. His fall from this state sealed his mortal fate. In Nahmanides's account, the Days of the Messiah and World to Come will be a return to this prelapsarian state of being. Nahmanides repeats this motif of redemption as a return to humanity's origins in a few places:

> What I am going to say is borne out by Scripture. From the time of Creation, man could do as he pleased, [he could be] righteous or wicked. And so it has been for the entire Era of the Torah, so they can

be awarded merit for choosing good and punishment for willing evil. In the Days of the Messiah, however, the choice for good will come to them naturally, their heart will not crave what is inappropriate and shall not desire it at all. [. . .] At that time, man will once again be how he was before the sin of Adam, when he naturally did what he ought to do, and his will was not conflicted.[77]

The scope of the eschatological restoration of this primordial state reaches beyond the human race to Nature more generally. This emerges quite clearly from Nahmanides's comment on the clause "I will grant the land respite from the viciousness of beasts" (Lev 26:6):

when the commandments are observed, the land of Israel will be like the world was at its beginning, prior to Adam's sin—no beast or creeping animal will kill man [. . .] [This is] because the predaceousness of vicious beasts is only due to Adam's sin, as it was decreed that he would be prey for their fangs, and it also became their nature to prey upon one another, as we all know [. . .] When the world was created it says that the beasts were given grass to eat, as it is written: "And to all the beasts on land, to all the birds of the sky, and to everything that creeps on earth, in which there is the breath of life, [I give] all the green plants for food" (Gen 1:30), and the verse continues: "and so it was," because that was the nature implanted in them forever [. . .] When the land of Israel reaches perfection, their ferocious behavior will cease and they will return to the primal nature implanted in them at the time of their creation, which I have already mentioned in the portion of *Toledot Noah.* Scripture therefore said about the days of the redeemer of Jesse's stock that he will return peace to the world, and the predaceousness and viciousness of every beast and creeping thing will cease, which was their original, natural state.[78]

This passage posits three corresponding states: the Garden of Eden, the land of Israel, and the Days of the Messiah, in each of which God carries out his promise that "I will grant the land respite from the viciousness of beasts." Within human history this occurs in the land of Israel, and at the end of it, in the Days of the Messiah, the entire world will experience this restorative utopia. Nahmanides follows one opinion in the midrash, R. Shimon's, which reads the verse as describing not the future absence of ferocious beasts in urban areas, but the elimination of ferociousness itself from animals. The pristine world had no carnivores, and in the land of Israel the original condition still obtains.[79] What in the here and now is limited to the geographic borders of the land of Israel will be true everywhere in the eschatological world, as Nahmanides writes in Torat Ha-Shem Temimah:

> He [R. Shimon] brought proof from the Days of the Messiah to the verses of blessing [concerning the land of Israel], because the two times are equivalent—this one in the land and that one in the entire world. This seems correct because predation arose due to the sin of Adam [. . .] the same is true of all other beasts, perhaps they did not prey upon one another until that sin, on account of which the earth was cursed, and which will be null in the Days of the Messiah.[80]

The primordial state of the world serves as a map for possible futures, a glimpse of what the world will look like during the Resurrection of the Dead and messianic era, and it reflects the elimination of predatory behavior from the world. The common denominator all three share—the original state of Nature, the land of Israel, and the Days of the Messiah—is the state of the sefirotic configuration and the presence of Shekhinah. From what Nahmanides writes about the land of Israel, one can make inferences about the Garden of Eden and the World to Come, too: " 'I shall bring Peace into the Land' (Lev 26:6) [. . .] By way of truth, He will bring Peace into conjunction with the Land, and this is the Peace of the All (*Ha-Kol*), which is equivalent to the All (*Ha-Kol*)."[81] A few verses later, he comments on the clause "I will walk among you" (Lev 26:12): "But by way of truth these blessings are also heavenly blessings in the supernal realms, as I explained, 'I shall bring Peace into the Land' (Lev 26:6) and 'My Soul will not repel you' (Lev 26:11). Similarly, 'and I will walk among you' is an allusion to the Attribute our Rabbis call '*Shekhinah*.' "[82] Based on the equation Nahmanides makes between the Garden of Eden and the land of Israel, one could characterize the state of the Garden and the prelapsarian world as one of hidden miracles and without the rule of natural causality. As Nahmanides tells it, the Original Sin led to carnivorousness, but behind the scenes stands something of far greater cosmic significance—inert, causal Nature was created as a state of being in the wake of Adam's sin. If not for his sin, the zodiac would have no dominion, in the same way that it currently has no power in the land of Israel and will have none in the World to Come. The rule of inert Nature over the human body is a product of the fall from humanity's state of cleaving to the divine. Moreover, the very existence of the blind natural causality of the zodiacal signs emerges from Adam's sin. Adam, then, did not have his umbilical cord to the Godhead severed and tumble into the hands of the zodiac and Nature's accidents, but in fact brought about their rule.

Adam's fall from his state of cleaving had fateful reverberations for all planes of existence in the universe. As noted in the previous chapter, Nahmanides interprets *da'at* to mean "will" and so understands the eating from the Tree of Will as the generation of a personal and autonomous will. As creatures possessing their own will, humans became individuated from the configuration of the sefirot, thus ending their state of cleaving. One can say that cleaving is achieved by aligning one's will with the divine, such that humans in their original state lacked free will and acted on the basis of their connection to the Godhead. The appearance of Adam's new autonomous will was the first and most meaningful step in differentiating humanity from the configuration of the Godhead, leading to the eventual fall from the state of cleaving. Human differentiation from the Godhead was simultaneously accompanied with the separation of Shekhinah from the sefirotic configuration, which is symbolized by the detachment of the Fruit from the Tree. Adam's fall coincided with and reflected a catastrophe of cosmic proportions. Inert Nature was therefore created as a product of the universe's estrangement from the sefirotic configuration, an estrangement brought on together with humans' transformation into creatures possessing their own will. The Nature we know as a rung in the great chain of being that is inert and frozen is, in fact, a result of the emanatory process gone awry, of the imbalance within the Godhead's own internal equilibrium.

In the messianic era, the original state of humanity will be restored. The biblical description of the Days of the Messiah, "Years will come about which you will say I have no desire in them" (Eccl 12:1), describes a period of no desire, no will. The eschatological restoration of the universe to its original condition will not only free humanity from the dominion of accidents so that human beings can live forever in their bodies, but will eliminate the dominion of accidents entirely by restoring balance to the emanatory process. In the eschatological era, zodiacal rule will come to an end and the entire world will come under the immediate, unmediated governance of Shekhinah, as Nahmanides describes in his comment on the distinction between the land of Israel and everything outside the land:

> Outside the land, although everything belongs to the Glorious Name, perfect purity is unattainable because of the planets that rule over it,

and the nations stray after their ministers to worship them as well. The verse therefore says, "He will be called God of the entire earth" (Isa 54:5), because He is the supreme Power Who rules over everything, and in the end He will call to account the lofty host on high in order to remove the dominion of the supernal beings and to lay waste to the configuration of the planets, after which he will call to account the earthly kings on the earth.[83]

Our analysis of the kabbalistic underpinnings of the theory of the hidden and manifest miracle reveals an interesting paradox. Nahmanides's theory of the hidden miracle has been characterized as the pinnacle of voluntaristic theology in medieval Jewish thought. Many have considered it a kind of late Jewish iteration of the radical Kalamist position that Nature is nothing but a willed act of God that is direct and nonstop. However, the kabbalistic distinction between different levels within the Godhead and the attribution of the two kinds of miracle to the different levels depending upon humanity's degree of cleaving yields a completely different account. In place of a personal God who voluntarily intercedes on behalf of the pious, we find a chain of emanation that responds, according to its own internal causality, to humanity's degree of conjunction with or estrangement from the different levels of the Godhead. This commensurate response is not willed by God; instead, it results from a kind of order observed by the various levels of being within the Godhead itself. This same involuntaristic feedback is behind the miracles and the elimination of the dominion of zodiacal signs in space and time—the land of Israel, the Garden of Eden, and the messianic age—because liberation from accidents in these dimensions of time and space also depends on a special existential connection to Shekhinah and the rest of the configuration of the Godhead.

At this point it is worth restating the difference between the natural and the miraculous in Nahmanides's thought, because it cannot be captured by the usual—and, it turns out, facile—distinction between inert causality and God's intentional intervention in breaking the causal process. The first distinction between the natural and the miraculous is that natural causality is blind to humanity's religious standing, or any other standing for that matter, whereas the causality of the miraculous system responds in kind to humanity's actions and standing. Second, the miraculous as a state and activity operates outside the bounds of Nature's perceptible causality, and the divine potencies involved act independent of this causality. This miraculous activity even if it has its own causality is directly linked to the Godhead, whether to

Tif'eret or Shekhinah. Nature, in contrast, is a rung in the chain of being directed by an independent chain of causality. Nahmanides does not object to Nature as an exclusive and exhaustive category because he believes causality to be in conflict with the divine will, but because above the perceptible causality of Nature he places the divine rungs of existence that realize radically other possibilities of existence.

Our discovery that the voluntaristic doctrine of a personal God turns out to be only skin-deep, that underneath it lies the divine organism, raises the broader question of the relationship between kabbalah and the biblical-midrashic depiction of a personal God.[84] The kabbalistic view of the Godhead as an ensemble of dynamic potencies displaces the biblical and rabbinic anthropomorphism. Kabbalists translate those human attributes predicated of God, such as will, mercy, anger, jealousy, and others, into different kinds of dynamic potencies that together sustain a quite mechanical system of mutual feedback. The kabbalistic view that humanity's theurgic mission, and the import of the commandments, is to affect the internal equilibrium of this system of dynamic aspects of the Godhead also is at odds with the idea of a personal God. Behind the allusive veil lies a theosophy that systematically undermines the foundation of a personal God and the interpersonal nature of humanity's encounter with God. This fact, as was mentioned, fundamentally alters one's perspective of the natural and the miraculous, but one can also detect its pervasive influence in Nahmanides's esoteric religious thought. This approach will continue to be traced in the coming chapters, which will serve to profoundly elucidate the broader implications of this approach for medieval Jewish philosophy and for understanding the relationship between kabbalah and philosophy, and halakhah and kabbalah.

The analysis of death and the will in the previous chapter concluded that in the period of redemption, free will will disappear, as will individuation and death. The messianic era with its absence of desire will also mark the end of the Era of the Torah, and so law as a system of commands will pass from the world. This chapter's analysis of Nature and the miraculous allows us to conclude that in the messianic era inert causality will also cease operation, and the universe will be restored to its original state of divine governance through the hidden miracle. The eschatological obsolescence of law observed in the previous chapter and the cessation of inert causality emerging from this chapter are deeply connected.

According to Nahmanides, messianic longing reflects the most basic grievance about the unjust state of the world as it exists between Original Sin and ultimate redemption. In the world such as it is, an immense gap exists between what ought to be and what actually is. Human beings do not perform the good out of their natural state, but the good is mediated through humans' autonomous will, a will that needs the law to direct it and command it. The commandment is supposed to bridge the gap between "ought" and "is." The law, as given during the Era of the Torah, addresses humanity's will and orders it to align itself with the "ought." The very existence of free will turns the good into something that cannot be taken for granted and requires striving for its realization. This gulf between "ought" and "is" is expressed as well in the realm of inert causality. This causality, which according to Nahmanides is astrological, is completely blind to humanity's religious standing; the causal gears continue to turn regardless of humans' behavior. This clearly demonstrates the estrangement of Nature from the good and from how the world ought to be. We live in the Era of the Torah, in an eon of inert causality, and so we feel the moral, and ontological, strain of the rift between the way things are and how they ought to be, the pain of estrangement from the immediate divine presence due to humanity's free will and Nature's causality. Nahmanides views redemption as the abrogation of law and blind causality because the rift will be healed, the gap between "ought" and "is" will be hermetically sealed. This gap resulted from the hyperdifferentiation and hyperdistinction within the chain of being, and in the messianic era the Godhead, and thus the universe, will move from a state of estrangement to one of alignment and transparency. This striving for transparency, for having the capacity to sense the immediate presence of the Godhead with all of its aspects, stands at the center of Nahmanides's theory of prophecy.

CHAPTER 5

Revelation and Prophecy

The catastrophe of Shekhinah's fall from its original state of harmony with Tif'eret and its new position as the lowliest sefirah turned Shekhinah into the weakest link of the divine structure. Nahmanides allusively reveals Shekhinah's complex status, the result of the overextended self-emergence of the Godhead from Absolute Privation, in two places.

The first context in which he refers to this duality of Shekhinah is in his kabbalistic reading of the festival of Shemini 'Atzeret (the Eighth Day that immediately follows the seven days of the festival of Sukkot): "By way of truth, 'because the Lord made Six Days, Heaven, and the Earth' (Exod 20:11), and the Seventh Day is the Sabbath which has no consort, so the Congregation of Israel is its consort, as it says, 'and the Earth,' which is the Eighth [Day]. 'It is *'Atzeret*' because the All (*Ha-Kol*) is retained (*ne'etzar*) therein."[1] "The Congregation of Israel," a cognomen for the sefirah of Shekhinah, is represented by and referred to as "the Eighth Day" because of its pairing to "the Seventh Day," the Sabbath. It is also called 'Atzeret because the emanatory process ends with it—it comprises the All. In the continuation of the piece, Nahmanides uses the unique halakhic status of Shemini 'Atzeret vis-à-vis the immediately preceding festival of Sukkot to characterize the complex relationship of Shekhinah with the other sefirot. Shemini 'Atzeret is a festival unto itself in many halakhic matters, for which the Talmud employs the Hebrew acrostic PZR QShV. Yet, in spite of Shemini 'Atzeret's independence from Sukkot, it is also its continuation, because on Shemini 'Atzeret people can redress the sacrifice they did not manage to bring on Sukkot. The Talmud refers to Shemini 'Atzeret both as a festival unto itself and as redress for the sacrificial obligation incurred on the prior festival of sukkot (*rishon*) of Sukkot (Hagigah 17a). This complex interplay between separation and continuity symbolizes Shekhinah's relationship with the other sefirot: "This is [the meaning of] their dictum that *Shemini* is a Festival unto itself with respect to *PZR QShV* and it is redress of the First (*rishon*)—it is an emanation of the Earlier Ones (*rishonim*) but does not partake of their unity."[2] While the other sefirot are unified and in harmonious balance with one another, Shekhinah's bond to them is somewhat attenuated. Although the bond is strong enough to partake in emanation, it is too weak for unity.

Nahmanides has another interesting formulation of Shekhinah's ambiguous standing in his discussion of the kabbalistic symbolism of the four species taken on Sukkot. The halakhah does not require that the citron and palm frond be bound together, but if the palm frond and other species are taken without the citron at all, the obligation of taking is not discharged.[3] This state of affairs symbolizes the complicated relationship of differentiated dependence between Shekhinah ("the Citron") and the other sefirot, especially Tif'eret ("the Palm Frond"): "From here you understand and comprehend that the Citron is not included in the [Palm] Bundle yet is a sine qua non for it, for it corresponds to [*Shemini*] '*Atzeret,* which is a Festival unto itself and redress of the First. Thus they are one *in potentia* but not *in actu.*"[4] Shekhinah's demotion to the final sefirah established its connection to the other sefirot as a potential, rather than actual, unity.[5]

As previous chapters have shown, the primordial crisis in the emanatory process resulted in humans' unique status as creatures with their own will, living in the Era of the Torah bookended by the Original Sin and the ultimate redemption. Beyond that, Shekhinah's instability within the configuration of the sefirot, united in potential but not in reality, is the focal point of Nahmanides's kabbalistic interpretation of the Torah in many other contexts. Shekhinah's alternating relationship with Tif'eret and the rest of the sefirotic structure has wide-ranging, cosmic ramifications: it determines the various ways in which God reveals himself; it gives rise to the vicissitudes of human history; and it serves as the esoteric, deeper telos of observance of the commandments, the purpose of which is to hold together the shaky structure of the Godhead until its ultimate restoration in the seventh millennium.

The religious drama of Nahmanides's esoteric commentary on the Torah revolves around the variable and dynamic relationship between Tif'eret and Shekhinah. The other components of the sefirotic structure—Keter, Hokhmah, and Binah—have brief cameos in the very first lines of his Torah commentary on Genesis and in his fragmentary commentary on Sefer Yetzirah. The sefirah of Binah receives attention in connection to the doctrine of cosmic cycles (*torat ha-shemittot*), as will be discussed in the next chapter. In the postlapsarian world where Shekhinah assumes its position at the lowest level of the Godhead, the relationship between Shekhinah and Tif'eret occupies center stage when it comes to revelation, prophecy, and mystical contemplation.[6] The historical drama of humanity becomes a reflection of Shekhinah's unstable state, and observance of the commandments is intended to stabilize its unity with Tif'eret, which is liable to be sundered if left unattended and unaided. This chapter and the two that follow clarify Nahmanides's theories of revelation and prophecy, his concept of history, and his reasons for the commandments.

I

Shekhinah is the first sefirah met in the encounter between humans and the Godhead. Sometimes it is called "the Back" (*Ahor*)[7] and sometimes "the Countenance" (*Panim*),[8] for it is both the end of the divine emanation and the "countenance" that the Godhead shows this world.[9] This duality is further evidenced by the vast number of Shekhinah's cognomens and its role in Nahmanides's kabbalistic hermeneutics and theory of prophecy.

One such cognomen, "the Beginning" (*Reshit*), signifies Shekhinah's special character. Shekhinah as the Beginning already appears in one of Nahmanides's very first comments on the Torah, in which he objects to R. Abraham Ibn Ezra's attitude toward midrashic literature. The debate concerns those rabbinic midrashim that connect the word *be-reshit*, which begins the Torah's account of creation, to other scriptural appearances of the word *reshit* and assert that the world was created for other things also designated as *reshit*—the Jewish people, the dough offering, tithes, the first fruits, and even Moses (Deut 33:21). Ibn Ezra viewed this midrashic medley as proof that sometimes midrashic literature has no interpretive significance, even if it has educational and edificatory value. In this Ibn Ezra was criticizing Rashi, who cited such midrashim as if they had exegetical value. He accused Rashi of failing to grasp the aggadic nature of midrashic literature because, among other things, Rashi's methodology of peshat, the philological-contextual sense of Scripture, was unsophisticated.[10] Nahmanides, at the outset of his interpretive enterprise, is at pains to situate himself in the middle ground between the two diametrically opposed poles of Rashi and Ibn Ezra, and he intends the position he stakes out to apply to the entire run of his commentary. He does not adopt Rashi's naiveté, which grants exegetical weight to the literal meaning of a midrash, nor is he prepared to accept Ibn Ezra's reduction of midrash to didacticism. His way out is to show that there is more to midrash than meets the eye by digging down deep and exposing its esoteric, symbolic layer, through which one can see his profound interpretive prowess at work.[11] Rashi did not have the kabbalistic key to unlock the profound interpretation of the midrash, and Ibn Ezra, one of those whom Nahmanides styles "those of little faith," erred in belittling the importance of midrash.

Nahmanides endows the series of midrashic exegeses on the word *be-reshit* with kabbalistic significance. This is predicated upon the fact that the word simultaneously refers to two sefirot, each of which constitutes the beginning of the universe in some sense. The sefirah of Hokhmah is the beginning of the divine emanation, and the sefirah of Shekhinah is the beginning of the extradivine universe:

> They [the Sages] intend by this that the word *be-Reshit* [through *Reshit*] hints that the world was created through the ten *sefirot* and is an allusion to the *sefirah* called *Hokhmah*, in which is the foundation of All (*Kol*) [. . .] It is the gift to the priest [*Terumah*], it is holy, and it has no measure in the minuscule comprehension of its creations. When someone counts ten measures and separates one from ten, it is an allusion to the ten *sefirot*, of which the Sages contemplate the tenth and speak about it. [. . .] The Israel that is called "the Beginning" (*Reshit*) (Jer 2:3) is the Congregation of Israel, which is parabolically spoken of as a Bride in Song of Songs, which Scripture calls "Daughter," "Sister," and "Mother."[12]

A structural parallel is created, then, between Hokhmah and Shekhinah, which exemplifies Nahmanides's understanding of the biblical account of creation as simultaneously relating to the process of divine emanation from Ayin and to the creation of the universe outside of this divine emanatory process, as discussed in the preceding chapter.[13] The two sefirot of Hokhmah and Shekhinah are both geneses—the one the emanation of the Godhead from within itself, and the other the creation ex nihilo of the universe—and both are symbolized by the word *reshit* (beginning) in various rabbinic midrashim. For Nahmanides, the depth of the multiple symbols that the midrash uses for *reshit* points to the different relationship humans have with each of the two sefirot. Hokhmah is symbolized by the gift to the priest because such a gift (*Terumah*) has no fixed measure, and this sefirah also has no measure, since it cannot be apprehended by the human mind and has no definition or delimitation. Shekhinah is symbolized by the well-defined levirate tithe because within the sefirotic configuration Shekhinah is sufficiently distinct and differentiated, making it the focus of mystical contemplation: "the Sages contemplate the tenth [sefirah] and speak about it."[14]

Nahmanides's theory of prophecy rests upon Shekhinah's role as the central object of the Sages' mystical contemplation and as the facet of the Godhead that faces the world. Shekhinah, in Nahmanides's conception, is the space in which the entire Godhead is pent up, and it is the primary means of relating to the Godhead. As Nahmanides says: "For it [*Shekhinah*] is the Sea which comprises the All (*Ha-Kol*) from the All (*Ha-Kol*), like the import of the verse, 'all the streams flow to the sea' (Eccl 1:7). It is the House of the King, as when those who desire to see the King ask, 'Whither is the House of the King?' and afterwards ask, 'Whither is the King?' "[15] In Nahmanides's theory of prophecy, seeing or speaking to an angel is not considered prophecy, because prophecy is initiated by a connection with Shekhinah. Nahmanides develops his theory against that of Maimonides, who asserted that Mosaic prophecy was sui generis due to Moses's direct line to God. All other prophets connected to God through the Active Intellect, which Maimonides refers to as the degree of angels called *ishim,* from which the prophet receives an overflow. Prophecy does not entail an immediate encounter with God but a conjunction with the lowest of the Separate Intellects, from which the prophet receives the prophetic emanation.

Nahmanides rejects Maimonides's prophetic theory: "one who apprehends the sight of an angel or its speech is not a prophet. It is not as the Master [Maimonides] decrees that every prophet aside from Moses received his prophecy via an angel."[16] Since Nahmanides does not consider speaking to an angel to be prophecy, Daniel cannot be properly termed a prophet, and neither can Hagar. Nahmanides must therefore propose another qualitative difference between the prophecy of Moses and all other prophets. In place of Maimonides's distinction between prophecy received from God and prophecy received from the Separate Intellects, the angels, Nahmanides distinguishes between prophecy received from different aspects of the Godhead itself: "Scripture distinguished the prophecy of our master Moses from the prophecy of the Patriarchs, as it says: 'I appeared to Abraham, Isaac, and Jacob through *El Shaddai*' (Exod 6:3), which is one of the Creator's holy names and not an angelic reference."[17] In Nahmanides's view, an encounter with beings that mediate between humans and the Godhead is no prophecy at all but a completely different phenomenon that he terms "opening of the eyes": "See how in all instances the Sages take it upon themselves to inform us that seeing an angel is not prophecy and that those who see angels and speak with them are not prophets, as I have mentioned regarding Daniel. Rather, it is a vision called 'opening of the eyes.' "[18] Once Nahmanides categorically excludes angelic revelation from prophecy, he must reinterpret those verses in the Torah where he agrees that genuine prophecy is occurring yet an angel features prominently. His interpretive move is to explain the biblical expression "the angel of the Lord" as a reference to an aspect of the Godhead, in this case Shekhinah, which is emanated from the Lord, from the Tetragrammaton. "The Angel of the Lord" expresses an ontologically close relationship between these two aspects, an internal expansion within the Godhead, in the same way that "the Hand of the Lord" signifies Shekhinah and its organic relationship to Tif'eret in Nahmanides's kabbalistic symbolism.[19] "The angel of the Lord" does not refer to some creation external to and sent by the Godhead, but a part of the very essence of the Godhead—"the Angel of the Lord."

Nahmanides makes this interpretive move even when it seems as if Scripture inserts an angelic figure to act as a go-between in disclosing God's revelation to a person. A clear example of this is the episode of the burning bush, which the verse describes as involving an angel: "The angel of the Lord appeared to him [Moses] in a flame of fire out of the midst of the bush" (Exod 3:2). In his commentary on the verse, Nahmanides begins by laying out Ibn Ezra's view, which he subsequently rejects:

> Scripture first says "The angel of the Lord appeared" (Exod 3:2) and later "The Lord saw that he had turned aside to look, and *elohim* called to him" (Exod 3:4); therefore, R. Abraham said that *elohim* here is the aforementioned angel, as in: "for I saw *elohim* face to face" (Gen 32:31). The reason for "I am the God (*Elohei*) of your father" (Exod 3:6) is because the agent [the angel] speaks as if he is the Principal [God].[20]

Nahmanides takes a quite different approach and understands the variation of divine names here to carry kabbalistic significance:

By way of truth, this "angel" is the Redeeming Angel, about which it says, "for My Name is in it" (Exod 23:21), and it is that which said to Jacob, "I am the God (*El*) which is the House of God" (Gen 31:13), and it is the subject in the clause, "And God (*Elohim*) called to him" (Exod 3:4). But this Attribute is called "Angel" with respect to governance of the world.[21]

The "angel of the Lord" in this verse is, in fact, a divine "Attribute," the sefirah of Shekhinah. Nahmanides lists a few other places in which Shekhinah is called the "Angel of the Lord," one of which refers to the guiding "Angel," about which God says, "for My Name is in it" (Exod 23:21). In his comment on that verse, Nahmanides develops his kabbalistic symbolism that identifies the Redeeming Angel with Shekhinah:

> But by way of truth, this angel that they have been promised here is the "Redeeming Angel" (Gen 48:16) in which is the Great Name: "because in *Yah* is the Lord, the Eternal Rock" (Isa 26:4), and it is that which said, "I am the God which is the House of God" (Gen 31:13), because it is the manner of the King to reside in His House. Scripture calls it "Angel" because the entire governance of this world is through that Attribute. Our Rabbis said that it is Metatron.[22]

This "Angel" is Shekhinah, that is, the Attribute that governs the entire world. The expression "My Name is in it" signifies the presence of Tif'eret in Shekhinah, or, as Nahmanides puts it, "it is the manner of the King to reside in His House," the House being none other than Shekhinah.[23]

The centrality of Shekhinah in Nahmanides's theory of prophecy is underscored by the exclusion of any encounter with angels from his definition of prophecy, and the consequent reinterpretation of certain appearances of the phrase "the angel of the Lord" to mean "the Angel of the Lord," that is, Shekhinah. This is reiterated in a long and fascinating piece in his Commentary on the Torah in which he attacks Maimonides's understanding of the precise function of the intermediate, created powers according to Targum Onkelos. In a few chapters of *The Guide of the Perplexed,* Maimonides recruits the Targum to fight on his side in his comprehensive war on anthropomorphism. He demonstrates how Onkelos's translation deflects anthropomorphic language away from God by transferring it onto other lesser powers. In such contexts, Onkelos adds a noun to God's name and generates a genitive construction: "the Glory of the Lord," "the Word of the Lord," and occasionally "before the

Lord." In Maimonides's reading of Onkelos, God created a Glory to intermediate between him and humans for purposes of revelation, and this essence
absorbs all anthropomorphic language that seems to describe God. The idea
of a Created Glory that is identical with the rabbinic Shekhinah developed
during the Middle Ages into a very powerful theological idea and hermeneutical tool that freed God from anthropomorphism, yet this created mediating
being removed God from being directly revealed. Nahmanides rejects this
position, which originated with R. Saadia Gaon and made its way even to the
German Pietists: "God forbid that that which is called Shekhinah is a Created
Glory distinct from the Glorious Name."[24] Shekhinah is part of the Godhead
itself. Later on in the piece, Nahmanides brings proof from Targum Yonatan
b. Uzziel on Ezek 3:12:

> Yonatan b. Uzziel said, "blessed is the Glory of the Lord from the place
> of the House of His *Shekhinah*." If the Glory intended by the verse is
> the true essence of the Creator, as in "please show me Your Glory"
> (Exod 33:18), which the Master [Maimonides] interprets this way, no-
> tice that it mentions "place," "house," and "*Shekhinah*," and if you
> say it is a Created Glory, which is Maimonides' opinion concerning
> "the Glory of the Lord filled the Tabernacle" (Exod 40:35) and other
> verses, how could they proclaim it "blessed"—one who blesses and
> prays to a Created Glory is like engaging in idolatry!? In the words of
> our Rabbis, there are many indications that the noun *Shekhinah* refers
> to God.[25]

Nahmanides points out the following problem. If, according to Maimonides,
"the Glory" sometimes refers to God himself, then how can Targum Yonatan
gloss Ezek 3:12 with words that seem to confine God to a particular space? If
one takes the alternative view that the Glory in that verse is a created being,
then how can anyone pray to it or bless it? Nahmanides solves this problem
by arguing that the Shekhinah mentioned in the verse is in fact God; otherwise, as an intermediary being it would reduce God's presence in the world
and attract its own religious devotion, which would border on idolatry.

From Nahmanides's point of view, the targumic phrases "Glory of the
Lord" and "Word of the Lord" have nothing to do with mitigating anthropomorphism. As he demonstrates, Onkelos employs these expressions even
when there is no problem of anthropomorphism. For example, in the verse
"Your complaints are not against us but against the Lord" (Exod 16:8), Onkelos renders it "against the Word of the Lord." Going in the other direction,

for some anthropomorphic phrases Onkelos does not place any noun next to the Tetragrammaton, as when he leaves "the finger of God" (Exod 31:18) as is. What, then, is the principle that guides Onkelos? Nahmanides finds the answer in kabbalah. When "Glory," "Word," or "before" precede the Tetragrammaton, they signify Shekhinah. When no such word is added, the original Hebrew signifies Tif'eret: "Indeed, these matters were known to Onkelos and Yonatan b. Uzziel through tradition, and those who know its secret are gratified. Concerning the Sinaitic theophany, Onkelos translates every mention of the word 'God' (*elohim*) in the pericope as 'Glory [of the Lord]' or 'Word of the Lord,' but does not do so for the Tetragrammaton. He did this deliberately and wisely."[26] Nahmanides's reading of the Tetragrammaton in a genitive construction as a reference to Shekhinah is widespread in his Torah commentary. He reads "angel of the Lord," "hand of the Lord," and "finger of God" as Angel of the Lord, Hand of the Lord, and Finger of God, all cognomens for Shekhinah. He takes the same position concerning all the relevant translations of Onkelos.[27] This interpretation, which assimilates the "angel of the Lord" and "glory of the Lord" into the Godhead itself by identifying them with Shekhinah, underscores that the first locus of prophetic revelation is Shekhinah. It should not surprise us, then, that one of the characteristic symbols of Shekhinah is "the Mouth of the Lord," as Shekhinah is the source of the defined and differentiated voice of God that reaches the prophet and the world.[28] By eliminating prophetic intermediaries, Nahmanides has to pay the price of anthropomorphism, yet he does so with no hesitation and perplexity, maintaining as he does that Shekhinah can move earthward or heavenward, and, as we shall soon see, can even be seen.

II

What set Moses apart from the rest of the prophets? Maimonides claimed that Moses spoke to God, while the rest spoke to angels. In Nahmanides's view, all communicated with God; the difference is through which aspect of God. Different levels of prophecy, according to Nahmanides, are determined by the directness of the prophet's connection to the Godhead, and especially to Tif'eret and Shekhinah. Nahmanides conceives of a four-tiered system of prophecy, which from top to bottom is as follows: Mosaic prophecy, the prophecy of all other prophets, the prophecy of prophets-in-training, and finally the prophecy of the Sages. As noted above, Tif'eret and Shekhinah play the major roles in Nahmanides's theory of prophecy, and it is worthwhile to begin by explaining the difference between the top two tiers, namely, Mosaic prophecy and prophecy of all other prophets.

Every prophet had a revelation of Shekhinah, the Weak Attribute of Judgment. Any relationship they may have had with Tif'eret, the potency of Lovingkindness and Mercy, was mediated through Shekhinah. Unique to Moses was a direct line to Tif'eret, granting him access to the overflowing power and superabundant Lovingkindness of the Godhead in the form of the Attribute of Mercy known as Tif'eret. The rest of the prophets came into contact with the Weak Attribute of Judgment, through which their perception of the Godhead was mediated. This essential difference is expressed in Scripture in the shift from God's revelation through El Shaddai to his revelation through the Tetragrammaton. As discussed in the previous chapter, this marks the historic, dramatic shift from the mediated presence of the Godhead in hidden miracles during the Patriarchal era to the immediate and observable presence of the Godhead in the manifest miracles wrought by Moses during the exodus and giving of the Torah.[29] Nahmanides understands Exod 6:3, "I appeared to Abraham, Isaac, and Jacob through El Shaddai, but I did not make Myself known to them through My name Y-HWH," to be the hermeneutic cipher for decoding the different names used in divine revelation:

> The way of truth follows the plain sense and meaning of the verse, saying: "I, the Lord [i.e., *Tif'eret*], have appeared to them through the Speculum of *El Shaddai* [i.e., *Shekhinah*]"—as in the meaning of [the verse], "I make Myself known to him through the Appearance (*mar'eh*)"[30] (Num 12:6)—"but I as the Lord did not make Myself known to them, for they did not see through the Speculum That Shines such that they would know Me"—as in the meaning of [the verse], "The Lord spoke to Moses Countenance to Countenance" (Exod 33:11). The Patriarchs knew the Unique Name but not through prophecy, so when Abraham converses with God he mentions either the Unique Name together with *aleph dalet* or *aleph dalet* alone. The Patriarchs received a revelation of *Shekhinah* and divine speech through the Weak Attribute of Judgment, and He governed them through it. He made Himself known to Moses and governed him through the Attribute of Mercy, which is through His Great Name, as in the meaning of [the verse], "Who made His Arm of Splendor [i.e., *Tif'eret*] march at the right hand of Moses" (Isa 63:12), and it is written, "Thus did you lead your people, to make for yourself a Name of Splendor

[i.e., *Tif'eret*]" (Isa 63:14). That is why hereafter Moses does not mention the name *El Shaddai*.[31]

Divine Lovingkindness and Mercy were revealed to the Patriarchs and other prophets solely by way of the Weak Attribute of Judgment. They could catch sight of the Tetragrammaton or Great Name only as it was reflected through Shekhinah, which is why the Patriarchs combined the Tetragrammaton with the name Adonai.[32] Moses enjoyed a direct, unmediated connection to the Great Name, to the Godhead's potencies of Mercy and Lovingkindness.[33]

Nahmanides uses this essential difference between Mosaic and other prophecy as a means to understanding the pericope of the giving of the Torah, especially a certain duality in describing the revelation at Sinai. In Nahmanides's kabbalistic symbolism, the Written Torah relates to the sefirah of Tif'eret, the Great Name. The Written Torah was given through the potency of this sefirah, which is why Moses, being directly connected to this sefirah, was the one who gave it to the people. The connection between Moses, the Great Name, and the giving of the Torah is clarified in Nahmanides's comment on Moses's query "they will ask me, 'what is His Name?'—what should I tell them?" (Exod 3:13). Nahmanides explains that Moses was trying to ascertain which divine Attribute was assigning him this mission: "He was saying, 'They will ask me whether my mission is through the Attribute of *El Shaddai* [i.e., *Shekhinah*], which stood by the Patriarchs, or through the Attribute of Supernal Mercy [i.e., *Tif'eret*], through which You will introduce signs and wonders new to the universe.' "[34] Nahmanides then gives the reason for Moses's doubt as to whether Shekhinah or Tif'eret would guide and govern him:

> This was because He told him, "I am the God of your father, the God of Abraham" (Exod 3:6) but did not explicitly state any of His holy names at all. Moses heard Him promise the assembly at Mount Sinai and the giving of the Torah, yet he knew that the Torah would not be given through the name *El Shaddai* mentioned in connection with the Patriarchs but only through the Great Name through which the world came into being.[35]

The giving of the Torah depended upon Moses's connection to Tif'eret, the Great Name through which the Torah was given.

The unmediated link between Moses and the Great Name during the giving of the Torah explains the double descriptions of the Sinaitic revelation and the various names of God that appear in the pericope. Take, for example, the verse depicting Moses's ascent up the mountain, in which two divine names appear: "Moses ascended towards God and the Lord called to him from the mountain, saying . . ." (Exod 19:3). Nahmanides explains the switch as follows: "The meaning of '[he] ascended towards God and the Lord called to him' is that he ascended towards the Glory of the Lord that abode upon the mountain in order to relate the Ten Commandments to the Jewish people, but He spoke to Moses through the Great Name, like the meaning [of the verses], 'If there shall be a prophet etc.' " (Num 12:6–7).[36] In other words, Moses ascended toward the Glory of the Lord, Shekhinah, that rested upon the mountain, but God spoke to him through the Great Name, Tif'eret. The rest of the Jewish people, however, heard the revelation through Shekhinah's intermediation. This discrepancy is apparent in the different divine names used for the revelation to Moses and the revelation to the people:

> If you comprehend this pericope you will understand that His Great Name descended upon Mount Sinai and abode upon it in fire, and it speaks to Moses. The speech throughout this pericope is through the Unique Name. [Moses's] ascent and going forth was towards the place of the Glory, as I explained above. [. . .] All of Israel heard the Voice of the Lord from the midst of the fire [associated with *Shekhinah*], which is what it speaks of [in the verse], "God spoke all of these words" (Exod 20:1), as our Rabbis said: " 'God' (*Elohim*) means the Judge."[37]

Nahmanides points out the complexity of the Sinaitic theophany recorded in Exodus 19. In the chapter, divine communication with Moses always occurs through the Tetragrammaton, yet God speaks to the people through the name "God" (Elohim). This alternation reflects the prophetic gap between Moses and the rest of the Jewish people, the result of Moses's uniquely direct connection to the Tetragrammaton.

The difference between Mosaic and other prophecy can be better understood through the following analogy. Moses and the rest of the prophets hear the same things, but Moses hears them directly and clearly from the Great Name, from Tif'eret, whereas the other prophets hear them indirectly and muffled through the veil of Shekhinah. But since, in Nahmanides's interpretation, the Torah identifies the theonym with the actual essence of the Godhead, the difference is even more profound. Contact with different sefirot means access to different prophetic subject matter, because that matter is identical with the sefirah itself. Prophecy is not some voice generated by

God that certain people are privy to; the Voice is a symbol of the Godhead itself, and revelation is the Godhead's self-disclosure of its multifaceted essence, all in accord with the mystical aptitude of the prophet.[38]

Nahmanides applies this gradated understanding of revelation to the entirety of the biblical corpus in order to distinguish the different subject matter. The Book of Ecclesiastes contains only the name "God" (Elohim) and not the Tetragrammaton, so Nahmanides understands it to be a revelation of Shekhinah alone, which would also explain the absence of the governance of the manifest miracle from the book. Only one aspect of the Godhead is involved in this revelation:

> Know that in this book Solomon does not mention the Unique Name at all; instead, he always mentions the name "God" (*Elohim*) [. . .] The reason is because this book speaks about the natural course of the world under the Sun—how it was created and how all people are governed through the Attribute of Judgment. The righteous in this book who follow Solomon's guidance are like Abraham, Isaac, and Jacob, to whom [God] appeared through *El Shaddai* [. . .] and for whom hidden miracles were performed [. . .] That is why the Patriarchs and the righteous of this book are, on rare occasion, subject to accidents, as this book says: "As it happens to the fool, so will it also happen to me" (Eccl 2:15).[39]

Prophetic contact with Shekhinah on its own yields a picture of the world in which the hidden miracle is the limit; one cannot see the overflowing, creative power of the deity, that is, Tif'eret.[40] The theology of Ecclesiastes therefore includes the possibility of the accidental at the margins of the hidden miracle. The limited self-disclosure of the Godhead in the Book of Ecclesiastes is at the root of the mishnaic dispute about the statuses of Ecclesiastes and Song of Songs:

> "and if they argued it was only about Ecclesiastes," in other words, because it only speaks through the name "God" (*Elohim*), the Attribute of Judgment, which exists in this world as the natural course of the world. The righteous of the Torah, however, who worship out of love are not subject to the judgments of this book, in which case it is not holy. They [the Sages] said there: "Like the opinion of Ben Azzai: '[so] they argued and so they voted' " that even Ecclesiastes renders the hands ritually impure, for at the end he filled in what was missing.[41]

The stark difference between the vitality and longing in Song of Songs and the detached, cold realism in Ecclesiastes can be traced to the different divine aspects reflected in the books: "Song of Songs is entirely through Love, which is the Attribute of Mercy and Lovingkindness, as it says: 'Lovingkindness (*Hesed*) to Abraham' (Mic 7:20) whom He loves, as it says: 'Abraham, My Love' (Isa 41:8). But here he [Solomon] speaks only about the accidental in the world through the Attribute of Judgment."[42] The canonization of Ecclesiastes would have remained in dispute had the Attribute of Love not been mentioned at the end of the book, when it says, "The end of the matter, all having been heard: fear God, and keep His commandments" (Eccl 12:13). Nahmanides understands this ultimate expression of "keep His commandments" as the sole hint in the entire book to something beyond fear and judgment, to love: "Now that he has transcended accidents and hinted at the conclusion, so he says one should fear the Attribute of Judgment and keep His commandments, so that through them he will become one who worships out of love."[43]

Another place where one can see the variability of revelation due to the different sefirot involved is in Nahmanides's explanation of the discrepancies between the two versions of the fourth commandment in the Decalogue. In the first list of the Ten Commandments, the Torah says, "Remember the day of the Sabbath to sanctify it" (Exod 20:7), but in the second list it says, "Keep the day of the Sabbath to sanctify it" (Deut 5:11). Nahmanides explains that the two versions depend on the difference between Moses and everyone else who received the Torah, which ultimately boils down to Tif'eret versus Shekhinah. In Nahmanides's kabbalistic symbolism, "Remember" is connected to Tif'eret and "Keep" to Shekhinah:

In the *Midrash* of Rabbi Nehuniah [*Sefer Ha-Bahir*] he mentions another great secret concerning "Remember" and "Keep." Generally speaking, remembering belongs to the Day and keeping to the Night. This is [the meaning of] the Rabbinic dictum that we should say on Sabbath Eve, "Come, Bride; come Bride," "Let us go out to greet the Bride-Queen," and they call the blessing of the Day "the great sanctification," for it is the Great Sanctification—understand this. It is also true that the Attribute of Remember is in the positive commandment, which flows from the Attribute of Love and belongs to the Attribute of Mercy, because someone who fulfills the command of his Master is beloved to Him and His Master has mercy upon him. The Attribute of Keep is in the negative commandment, which belongs to the

Attribute of Judgment and flows from the Attribute of Fear, because one who is careful not to do what his Master deems wrong fears Him.[44]

In kabbalistic symbolism, "Keep" is the Attribute of the Night, the Bride, namely, Shekhinah. Keep is tied to Shekhinah in its role as the Weak Attribute of Judgment, because the negative commandment demands care and restraint that is primarily driven by fear. "Remember," on the other hand, is the positive commandment, the ultimate source of which is in the Attribute of Love and Mercy that is Tif'eret, and which represents the active and creative aspect of human activity, similar to the Great Name itself.[45] Nahmanides uses this pairing of "Remember" with Tif'eret and "Keep" with Shekhinah to explain the midrash which states that "remember and keep were said in a single utterance" (Shevu'ot 20b): "Similarly, by way of truth they were said in a single utterance, because the All was in 'Remember' and 'Keep,' because the Torah is a Covenant of the World set out and kept in the All. He [Moses] hears 'Remember,' and they [Israel] [hear] 'Keep.' The enlightened person knows this from what we alluded to there."[46] "Remember" and "Keep" are both original expressions from a single revelation. Moses, because of his link to Tif'eret, heard "Remember," while the Jewish people, receiving the revelation through Shekhinah, heard the very same revelation as "Keep." The disparity in degree of prophecy, then, is not only expressed in the different divine names that appear in the Torah but in particular revelatory content.[47] What emerges from the foregoing analysis is that Moses's unmediated connection to Tifer'et not only exemplified his mystical exceptionality, but also granted him access to the Written Torah and other divine subject matter inchoate in the innermost recesses of the Godhead.

Nahmanides expands this idea to encompass all of Deuteronomy, which he ties to the sefirah of Shekhinah:

> By way of truth it seems to me that here, and throughout all of Deuteronomy, Moses speaks as if from the Mouth of the Almighty, like when he says: "If you listen to My commandments that I command you today, to love the Lord your God, and worship Him with all of your heart and all of your soul [. . .] then I shall give rain upon your land in its season" (Deut 11:13–14). Moses is no rainmaker for the land nor does he provide the grass of the field; rather, the divine word in the Torah is through Remember and in Repetition of the Torah it is through Keep, which is why Moses says everywhere in the Repetition of the Torah "the Lord your God," but in the Torah he mentions the Unique Name alone.[48]

The difference between the two lists of the Ten Commandments, between "Remember" and "Keep," reflects a profound divide between Deuteronomy and the preceding four books of the Pentateuch. Nahmanides considers Deuteronomy to be, in effect, Moses's translation of the revelation for the Jewish people. Deuteronomy is called "the Repetition of the Torah" because it is the revelation as heard by the Jewish people, as mediated through Shekhinah. The gradated theory of prophecy and revelation explains the singular manner in which God discloses himself in Deuteronomy: whenever the Tetragrammaton addresses the Jewish people, it is accompanied by a divine name— "the Lord your God." In this book, Tif'eret reveals itself through Shekhinah, symbolized by a divine name of godship,[49] whereas in the rest of the Pentateuch Tif'eret reveals itself directly to Moses without Shekhinah's involvement, symbolized by the Tetragrammaton, "the Lord." This tiered conception of revelation resolves apparent contradictions in the biblical corpus by attributing discrepancies to prophetic encounters with different aspects of the Godhead, specifically Tif'eret and Shekhinah according to Nahmanides. The modern documentary hypothesis in biblical scholarship famously bases itself upon differences in the divine names from document to document and helps to clarify conflicting passages, too. Nahmanides offers us his own theory of strata to explain the same discrepancies in the divine names. He does not seek to harmonize these sources in the plain, exoteric sense of the text but views the multiple layers of Scripture as reflective of the multilayered Godhead.

Nahmanides's concept of the Torah and of revelation, which are not the literal, univocal expression of God's exclusive, clear-cut will but the self-disclosure of his multifaceted essence, also appears in his understanding of the distinction between a vow and an oath. The Talmud establishes that an oath taken to fulfill or not fulfill a commandment is invalid, because everyone is already sworn from Mount Sinai to fulfill the commandments, and an oath cannot take effect once a prior oath has been made. A vow is different, however, so if someone vows not to sit in the sukkah or have marital relations with his or her spouse, the vow is valid. The classic Talmudic distinction that explains this, which Nahmanides also affirms, is that the oath is a personal obligation, that is, a prohibition that oath-takers take upon themselves, whereas the vow confers a kind of sacred status upon the object of the vow vis-à-vis the vower. An oath concerning the commandments cannot be valid because people cannot obligate themselves to do something they already have an obligation to do or to refrain from doing. In contrast, a vow is effective because it generates a status around an object and does not directly involve the legal person who has these preexisting obligations.

Nahmanides undergirds this distinction with a kabbalistic interpretation grounded in the midrash:

> The Sages have already hinted at the reason behind the matter in *Sifrei* (sec. 153) [in which] they said: "What is the difference between vows and oaths? Vows are like vowing by the Life of the King; oaths are like swearing by the King Himself" [. . .] The secret is that "oath" (*shevu'ah*) comes from the language of "seven" (*shiv'ah*), "For she [i.e., *Hokhmah*] built her House, hewed seven Pillars" (Prov 9:1), but the vow is through *Tevunah* [i.e., *Binah*], "the Beginning of His path, First of His work of old" (Prov 8:22). So, vows rise above the Torah and therefore can take effect upon something pertaining to a commandment as if it were something optional.[50]

The source of a vow is in Tevunah, the sefirah of Binah, which Nahmanides understands the rabbis to be referring to as "the Life of the King," the inner essence and spirit of "the King," which is the sefirah of Tif'eret. The oath, by comparison, demonstrates by its very name that it has its source in the seven lower sefirot and is linked to the King, Tif'eret. The obligation created by a vow halakhically binds the one who made it because the Torah as we have it is a somewhat limited revelation of the essence of Tif'eret and Shekhinah. The vow can trump the Torah itself because of the vow's supernal source in Binah. As Nahmanides writes in one of the two rare kabbalistic comments in his Talmudic novellae:

> The difference between vows and oaths is confidential. / In the [sefirotic] Structure the vow is foundational, / whereas the oath is clearly through the *vav* and final *he* / because the six [the letter *vav*] has been taken away. / Thus vows rise above the Torah / and are effective to annul a mitzvah, / which is not the case with an oath / since the fruit is from Saplings shared by both. / I say that this is perchance / the reason why vows about no substance / and those of exaggeration and persuasion / do not take effect without investigation, / because that which lacks Understanding [i.e., *Binah*] / he vowed without realizing.[51]

In this piece, Nahmanides uses the Tetragrammaton as an additional symbol for the sefirot. The Torah as a sefirotic revelation is represented by the two last letters of the Tetragrammaton, the final *vav* and final *he* (WH), which respectively represent Tif'eret and Shekhinah. The revelation of God's essence in the Torah is therefore tied to the lower, more distinct aspects of the Godhead, which Nahmanides refers to as "the Structure." Because the source of an obligation through an oath is the same as that of the Torah—"since the fruit is from Saplings shared by both"—an oath cannot apply to a commandment. A vow can take effect upon an object governed by a commandment because it is connected to the first two letters of the Tetragrammaton, the *yod* and first *he* (YH), which constitute a revealed essence of the Godhead that is located above that of the Torah. The halakhic distinction between vows and oaths flows from their different connections to the Godhead and is anchored in the conception of the Torah and revelation as the self-disclosure of the multifaceted essence of God. This conception, as we have said, is also reflected in the way Nahmanides assigns apparently contradictory works of Scripture to different aspects within the Godhead.

III

The nature of prophecy, including its intensity and differentiation, can be better understood by paying careful attention to the visual verbs Nahmanides analyzes as part of his articulation of the phenomenon of prophecy. Following his terminology will help us comprehend fully his gradations of prophecy and their differences: the prophecy of Moses, the rest of the prophets, the trainee prophets, the Holy Spirit, and the lowest level that Nahmanides refers to as "prophecy of the Sages."

Nahmanides uses two visual criteria in grading any given prophecy. The first is whether the prophet beholds Shekhinah or a mere reflection of it. The second does not concern the object of the prophet's vision but the prophet's state of consciousness during the vision—is his mind alert or foggy? Nahmanides alludes to this in his comment on the verse "You, O Lord, are seen eye to eye" (Num 14:14). The traditional interpretation of the verse understands this as direct, immediate revelation to the Israelites, which Nahmanides quotes as follows: "As for the doubling of 'eye to eye' (*'ayin be-'ayin*), the commentators have said it is like people who look into each other's eyes when speaking to each other, similar to 'and face to face the Lord spoke to you' (Deut 5:4)."[52] Nahmanides then presents the kabbalistic interpretation of the verse, which exemplifies his conception of prophecy in brief:

> By way of truth, *'ayin* means "appearance" (*mar'eh*)—"its appearance is like the appearance of bdellium" (Num 11:7), "I saw something that

had the appearance of amber" (Ezek 1:27). He [Moses] is saying, "Your Great Name [i.e., *Tif'eret*] is seen as an Appearance within an Appearance," which is also the meaning of the verse in Ezekiel: "Like an appearance of the Appearance I had seen, like the Appearance I had seen when I came to destroy the city, and appearances like the Appearance that I had seen by the river Chebar" (Ezek 43:3).[53]

In kabbalistic interpretation, *'ayin* does not have the usual meaning of "eye" but means "appearance" or "reflection." Nahmanides brings proof to this meaning of *'ayin* from Num 11:7. *'Ayin be-'ayin* does not mean "eye to eye," then, but "an Appearance within an Appearance." God's Great Name, Tif'eret, is revealed through a reflection of a reflection. Moreover, these appearances are also Appearances, that is, the sefirot themselves.[54] Put differently, the Jewish people witnessed a reflection of Shekhinah and did not merit seeing it directly, and through this reflection they could glimpse a reflection of Tif'eret.

What separates actual prophets from prophetic trainees has to do with their prophecy's degree of reflection and clarity. Nahmanides elaborates on this in his comment on Balaam's prophecy, for the Torah describes him as one "who sees a vision of Shaddai" (Num 24:4):

> He [Balaam] said "who sees a vision of *Shaddai*" because he now saw either through the Speculum [That Does Not Shine], like the first prophets, about whom it is said, "I appeared to Abraham, Isaac, and Jacob through *El Shaddai*" (Exod 6:3), or through a degree below them, since "a vision of *Shaddai*" is not *Shaddai*—they would see (*yir'u*) through *El Shaddai* and he visualizes (*yehezeh*) through a vision of *Shaddai*, which puts him two degrees beneath them. He therefore called himself "open-eyed," for that is the degree of prophetic apprentices, as he [Elisha] said, "open the eyes of etc." (2 Kgs 6:20). It already said as much about Balaam himself upon his seeing the angel: "The Lord opened the eyes of Balaam" (Num 22:31).[55]

Balaam was at two removes from the Patriarchs who saw through El Shaddai, that is, Shekhinah, because he visualized only "a vision of Shaddai," a reflection of Shekhinah. Similarly, Nahmanides notes a qualitative difference between a sight and a vision. The vision is very dim and fuzzy, which is why the revelation to Balaam is two degrees beneath those beheld by the Patriarchs and can be characterized as only an "opening of the eyes."[56] Nahmanides characterizes the different levels of prophecy, in this case those of the prophets and their apprentices, according to the degree to which the visionary object is beheld directly or through one or more intermediate reflections, and the degree of its clarity.[57]

Parallel, in a certain sense, to this prophetic level of prophets-in-training is what Nahmanides calls "the Holy Spirit" (*ruah ha-kodesh*). He discusses this in his commentary on Num 12:6–8, which he reads as follows:

> If there shall be a prophet among you, [a prophet of] the Lord, I shall make Myself known to him through the Appearance [i.e., *Shekhinah*]; I speak with him in a dream. Not so with my servant Moses; he is faithful in All (*Be-Kol*), My House [i.e., *Shekhinah*]. I speak with him Mouth to Mouth, a sight without riddles—he beholds the Image of the Lord.

Nahmanides explains:

> The meaning of the verse is that even if your prophet shall be a prophet of the Lord, he prophesies not through My Great Name but only through an Appearance or riddles. He mentioned this because many prophets would not attain this but be prophets of the Holy Spirit, as in the meaning of the verse, "the Spirit of the Lord spoke through me" (2 Sam 23:2), and this is "the Hand of the Lord" mentioned in Ezekiel and clarified in the words of Zachariah (Zach 1–2).[58]

The Holy Spirit, going by the scriptural designation "the Hand of the Lord" or "the Spirit of the Lord," is the prophetic encounter with Shekhinah without the presence of Tif'eret within it at all. While Moses had unmediated contact with Tif'eret and other prophets had it mediated through Shekhinah, those who merited only the Holy Spirit encountered Shekhinah alone[59] and had no contact of any kind with the Great Name.[60]

The centrality of the sight for categorizing the prophetic state comes to the fore in Nahmanides's description of Moses's unmediated relationship with Tif'eret. Nahmanides presents this in opposition to Maimonides's theory of prophecy. As part of his all-out war on anthropomorphism, Maimonides rejected the possibility of seeing God, and so he dealt with verbs indicating some kind of ocular perception of God in two ways. The first was to translate those verbs into terms of mental-conceptual apprehension or understanding, shifting the action and object from the senses to the mind.[61] The second was to translate the verbs literally but place them within the framework of a prophetic dream. For example, according to Maimonides, Jacob's struggle with the angel took place in a dream, because angels have no body with which to tussle. Jacob therefore, according to Maimonides, didn't struggle with the angel; he merely dreamed of such struggle. The three anthropomorphic angels who visited Abraham in the heat of the day also were figures in a dream. To be precise, such prophetic dreams are not revelations of God to the prophet within a dream state, but are dreams of the prophet.[62]

Nahmanides strongly criticizes this Maimonidean idea of the prophetic dream in a long passage on the Torah portion of Va-Yera. One line about Maimonides's position says it all: "These things contradict Scripture—it is forbidden to hear them, let alone believe them."[63] On his view, construing a prophecy as a dream empties the event of substantive content. Taking the above example, if Jacob only dreamed that he struggled with an angel, then why did he wake up with a limp? Nahmanides's position is that the prophetic dream is not the dream of a prophet, generated by processes internal to his imagination, but the revelation of God to the prophet in a dream state. Nahmanides also rejects the Maimonidean enterprise of translating the visual as mental; he considers the prophet's gaze to be quite literal.

This yearning to see God stands at the center of Nahmanides's interpretation of Moses's request of God to "please show me Your Glory" (Exod 33:18):

> He sought to see the Glory of the Lord through an actual sight. "Your Glory" here is possibly the Great Glory, the Speculum That Shines. The Lord answered him: "I shall pass the Attribute of All (*Kol*), My Goodness, before you, so that you may apprehend and contemplate All, My Goodness, more than any other man, because as for the sight of the Countenance that you have requested, you cannot see it.[64]

Nahmanides says "an actual sight" to highlight the fact that Moses hoped to see it with his own two eyes. He wanted to behold Tif'eret, which Nahmanides refers to as "the Great Glory, the Speculum That Shines," in his field of vision.[65] God rejected this request for a sight of the Countenance itself and enabled Moses to see only Shekhinah, which Nahmanides refers to as "the Attribute of All, My Goodness." Later, he returns to this: "The meaning of 'but My Countenance will not be visible' is the Radiant Countenance [i.e., *Tif'eret*], as I explained. It is possible that the term 'My Back' is in the sense of 'Back and Front I formed them' (Ps 139:5) according to the explanation of our Rabbis."[66] The Sages explained the verse from Psalms to mean that Adam was created *du partzufin,* double-faced, that is, male and female, which corresponds to the original harmony of Tif'eret and Shekhinah. By referencing this midrash, Nahmanides implies that "My Back" refers to She-khinah. Moses merited seeing Shekhinah directly, although Tif'eret could not be revealed through the visual medium. In his commentary on Mosaic proph-ecy in his novellae on Yevamot, Nahmanides makes this quite clear: "But Moses looked intellectually through the Speculum That Shines, which is the Splendor [i.e., *Tif'eret*] of Israel, but a sight of the Countenance was withheld from him."[67] This brief sentence is quite informative, as it tells us that cogni-tive understanding, "looking intellectually," is inferior to physical sight. Un-like other prophets, Moses did not relate to Tif'eret through the Weak Attribute of Judgment but through direct intellectual apprehension, albeit not actual sight.[68]

Moses stood in direct connection with Tif'eret, God's Attribute of Mercy and Abundance. He crossed over, one could say, the diminution caused by the Weak Attribute of Judgment, Shekhinah. He was able to accomplish this, however, only through intellectual sight, a lower level than physical sight. Still, he beheld Shekhinah directly and clearly, as Nahmanides writes about the expression "he beholds the Image of the Lord" (Num 12:8): "in it he be-holds the Image, he does not see it in a dream." Moses was superior to other prophets who saw "an Appearance within an Appearance," that is to say, who encountered Tif'eret as reflected by way of Shekhinah and beheld Shekhinah itself only through a prophetic dream or vision. Moses enjoyed a direct con-nection to Tif'eret during prophecy, but that was not his only unique pro-phetic attainment. He also had a continuously direct connection to Shekhinah. Nahmanides uses these unique qualities to explain that some statements of Moses, which appear to be his alone, actually originated in Shekhinah. He claims that they are not explicitly marked as prophetic because such labels appear only when Moses was excited from his regular, persistent state of con-nection with Shekhinah to communicate with Tif'eret. Even when Moses seemed to give his own orders, he was, in fact, engaged in what we would call prophecy. A prominent example is Moses's command to the sons of Korah and his assembly to take shovels and place incense upon them:

> My own opinion concerning this [command] and what he said to Aaron, "Take the fire-pan and place incense" (Num 17:11), is that the Hand of the Lord [i.e., *Shekhinah*] was upon him for them. This is called "the Holy Spirit," as in the books of David and Solomon which were [composed] through the Holy Spirit, and as he [David] said, "the Spirit of the Lord spoke through me, and its word was upon my

tongue" (2 Sam 23:2). [These are presented as Moses's words] because our master Moses was faithful in All, His House, in the manner which I have explained the term "the House" [Shekhinah] and I have mentioned many times. Since it is not the manner of Moses' prophecy, the word of the Lord is not mentioned in them.[69]

Moses's constant state of cleaving to Shekhinah—"he is faithful in All, My House"—is such that what would for other prophets be prophecy is not mentioned as the word of the Lord spoken to Moses.

The divine object beheld and its degree of clarity are thus what determine the gradations of prophecy. The superiority of contact with the Godhead through unmediated physical sight, rather than intellectual apprehension, is crucial for understanding Nahmanides's mystical conception of prophecy and is also what stands behind his vigorous opposition to Maimonides and some Geronese kabbalists that we will see below. Moses sought an "actual sight" of Tif'eret through the eye of the soul, once the fleshy, thick covering would be removed from it, but in the end he only merited "looking intellectually." Purified sight, the nature of which will be clarified below, is the highest level attainable by a prophet and is greater than apprehension. The difference in gradation between seeing and understanding appears in Nahmanides's comment on the following Talmudic dictum: "From the day the Temple was destroyed, prophecy was taken from the prophets but not from scholars" (Bava Batra 12a): "Rather, this is what it is saying: Although the prophecy of the prophets, which is through sight and vision, was taken away, the prophecy of the Sages, which is through wisdom, was not taken away, as they know the truth through the Holy Spirit in their midst."[70] Rabbinic prophecy lacks any visual foundation. It is not through a sight or vision; it is apprehended through wisdom alone by way of the Holy Spirit that abides in the midst of the Sages.[71] In Nahmanides's terminology of cleaving, one could say that while the soul of the Sage preserves its link to Shekhinah, which imbues the Sage's analyses with a prophetic quality, his body is unrefined and thus incapable of cleaving strongly enough to induce a sight or vision.

The nonmetaphorical reading of prophetic sight as physical sight in its various gradations, coupled with the prophet's relationship to different aspects of the Godhead itself, allows us to establish the following prophetic hierarchy for Nahmanides. At the summit is Mosaic prophecy, with Moses's direct connection to Tif'eret, although he was limited to "looking intellectually" because even for him, seeing Tif'eret was beyond reach. He could, however, see Shekhinah clearly and sharply. Next come the other prophets, who experienced the revelation of Tif'eret through the intermediation of Shekhinah and who beheld Shekhinah itself in the hazy reality of a dream. Below the prophets are the prophets-in-training, who did not see Shekhinah itself but a reflection of it. They also could not quite make out what they saw in this inferior visualization called "a vision of Shaddai." At the bottom are the Sages, who did not see anything at all, their prophetic attainment being limited to their wisdom.

The visual component in Nahmanides's prophetic theory, especially when viewed against Maimonides's systematic attempt to eradicate anthropomorphism, starkly begs the question of how Nahmanides deals with anthropomorphism, because "an actual sight" implies a spatially bounded form. To get a better grasp of the nature of prophetic experience and its relationship to mysticism and visual perception, which will shed light on this issue of anthropomorphism, we need to look at Nahmanides's description of Moses's state of consciousness. This description can be found in passages where Nahmanides describes the denizens of the World to Come as living forever in their bodies by cleaving to Shekhinah, which causes their bodies to become purified and rarefied. We discussed this phenomenon in Chapter 3, where we concluded that Nahmanides does not set up a sharp dichotomy between the material and the abstract but develops the idea of a gradual transition from subtlety to coarseness. This "subtlety" is a critical concept for understanding an essence that is immaterial yet is not completely abstract. This rarefied substance is similar to a body of energy or a being of light that cannot be perceived through the visual organs of the body. If the mystic achieves a high enough degree of cleaving and refinement, he can begin to see subtler beings by divesting himself of the physical eye and looking through the eye of the soul. This state of mystical amplification of the visual, which Nahmanides ties to prophecy, is described in Torat ha-Adam:

[This is] to convey that people of that world [the World to Come] can reach the level of Moses, whose soul transcended his body to the point where his bodily faculties were nullified, and who was enveloped at every moment in the Holy Spirit. [It was] as if his sight and hearing were through the eye of the soul alone—unlike the rest of the prophets whose physical eye mediates—by means of the nullification of the body and the soul shedding its [the body's] faculties so that the Holy Spirit could overflow onto it and thereby see through its own sight, as when Michael or Gabriel are seen. And this is the true sight and the proper hearing. For the philosophizers who negate the Torah at will have no ironclad argument against us that disproves this belief of ours that Gabriel can be seen or heard, and [which demonstrates that] the apprehension he [Daniel] acquired from Michael should be termed figurative.[72]

Moses was in a constant state of seeing with the eye of the soul without the mediation of the corporeal eye, what Nahmanides terms "true sight." Other prophets could attain such sight only on occasion, and even then their sight was dim. This refinement of the inner sense, as one can see from the passage above, also extends to hearing. One can make out certain sounds only with the inner, spiritual ear, which can receive the faintest frequencies, and Nahmanides calls this "proper hearing." Prophetic experience, then, includes a combination of seeing and hearing through inner spiritual senses that can pick up subtle things, provided the body is sufficiently purified and in a state of cleaving.

This passage is very important for Nahmanides's theory of prophecy, because it clearly connects mysticism with prophecy. Prophecy is not some voluntary experience initiated on God's end whenever he chooses to do so. Prophecy is a mystical state for which the prophet prepares himself through a long, complicated process until cleaving is achieved.[73] This link between cleaving and prophecy explains why Moses could have a prophecy at any time. Therefore, when the verse says "the Lord said suddenly to Moses, Aaron, and Miriam" (Num 12:4), the focus really must be on Aaron and Miriam, "because our master Moses was fit for prophecy at all times and his intellect was ready to cleave to the Glorious Name [i.e., *Shekhinah*] at every moment, as our Rabbis explained the reason for the separation from his wife."[74] In Nahmanides's understanding, cleaving does not entail leaving the body but does require that needs of the flesh be put out of the mystic's mind, which is why cleaving would necessitate conjugal abstinence. The degree of the prophet's cleaving and purification of the body, especially the physical eye, determines the depth of the divine revelation.[75] Prophetic mysticism is, in effect, an extended act of polishing the ethereal eye's lenses by removing the dense film of the corporeal eyes, and success in this constitutes a return to the primordial cleaving of Adam, since humanity's densification was an outcome of the fall.

That which the prophet beholds during prophecy cannot be perceived through one's normal visual sense, but that does not make the sight seen a metaphor for something cognized. In between visual perception and "looking intellectually" lies an intermediate state of seeing through the eye of the soul, which can perceive subtle matter.[76] This idea of prophetic sight is predicated upon the fact that for Nahmanides cleaving is not an ecstatic, out-of-body event experienced by the soul but a change in the state of the mystic's body, which becomes purified and refined from the dross of its densification, from the individualizing will, and from the drives of the body. The resultant body, which Nahmanides describes as a kind of luminous body, retains its sense perception—it still sees and hears—but during cleaving the senses are greatly amplified to detect stimuli beyond the threshold of the physical eye or ear.

The nonmetaphorical reading of prophetic sight as "actual sight" has far-reaching consequences for understanding Nahmanides's general approach and attests to his disagreement with other Geronese kabbalists about translating kabbalah into philosophical terminology. In his explanation of Moses's request to see the Godhead, R. Jacob b. Sheshet expresses his kabbalistic ideas philosophically, unlike Nahmanides:

> It was the innerness of this Speculum that Moses sought in saying "please show me Your Glory" (Exod 33:18). The meaning of "show me" is like "help me understand," as if to say, "that I can attain knowledge of the inner essence of this Glory and how it differs from all creations below it." He [the Lord] responded: "You cannot see My Countenance" (Exod 33:20), as if to say, "in order to contemplate it until you apprehend the essence of its innerness, but 'you can see My Back' (Exod 33:23)." All of this is apprehension of the heart through the sight of the intellect, as in, "my heart has seen much wisdom and knowledge" (Eccl 1:16).[77]

In contrast to R. Jacob b. Sheshet's translation of seeing as apprehension, the preservation of the sensory, noncognitive character of the prophetic experience is critical for Nahmanides, even though such perception refers to a purified sight of the most subtle of things.

The distinction between Nahmanides's understanding of the visual verbs, and that of the Geronese kabbalists, who take them to be a metaphor in those contexts, results in another divergence between their respective theories of prophecy. Based on the foregoing, Nahmanides limits Mosaic prophecy to cleaving to Shekhinah and "looking intellectually" at Tif'eret. The Geronese kabbalists, however, ratchet up prophecy more generally, and

Mosaic prophecy in particular, to higher aspects of the Godhead than Tif'eret.[78] R. Azriel's descriptions of cleaving and then of prophecy establish a different connection between mysticism and prophecy. His analogy for cleaving is the law governing communicating vessels: "But thought becomes disembodied and rises until the place of its source, and when it reaches there it stops and cannot rise further. I think a good parable for this is a spring of water that flows from the source—if you dig a hole below it so that water does not spread in all directions, the water will rise to the place of its source and not more. Likewise, thought does not rise above its source."[79] Thought's ascent is limited to its source in the sefirah of Hokhmah, in the same way that the waterline is limited by the height of its water source. R. Azriel depicts the cleaving of thought to its source in Hokhmah in terms of *unio mystica*: "Say to Wisdom [i.e., Hokhmah], 'You are my Sister' (Prov 7:4); in other words, cleave one's thought to Hokhmah in order that both become one thing."[80] This possibility of absolute cleaving is what gives the supplicant the capacity to draw down the divine efflux to the entire sefirotic configuration. In order to clarify the mystical technique of kabbalistic intention during prayer, R. Azriel returns to his metaphor about the source of a pool of water:

> Therefore, the pious ones (*hasidim*) of old would uplift their thought until the place of its source and have in mind the commandments and the Words [i.e., the *Sefirot*], and from the concentration and exceptionally cleaving thought the Words would be blessed, expand, and receive [the efflux] from the Privation of Thought. [This is] like someone who makes an opening in a pool of water and it spreads this way and that, because the cleaving thought is the Source, the Pool, and the Spring that does not cease.[81]

The one who cleaves is like someone who makes an opening in a pool of water and releases the efflux, which flows from Hokhmah down to the rest of the sefirot. In the continuation of the piece, R. Azriel moves from describing the relationship between cleaving and prayer to describing the relationship between cleaving and prophecy:

> The prophetic emanation was like this, for the prophet would seclude himself, concentrate his mind (lit. heart), and make his thought cleave above, and in accord with the cleaving of the prophecy the prophet could foresee the future. The prophets differed in their level [of prophecy], knowledge, and cleaving, and they would utter words as if they

were receiving them from on high, and as if they were possessed by [divine] speech like a fish caught on a fishing line.[82]

The prophetic technique included contemplation, according to R. Azriel, so he saw its similarity to the mystical intentions of prayer, which relied upon detaching human thought from the body and returning it to its source in the divine Thought, the sefirah of Hokhmah. The levels of prophecy correspond to the degree of cleaving achieved by the prophet, who was seized by the divine word like a fish on a line.[83]

Nahmanides, too, believes that the soul is emanated from Binah, which contains Tif'eret and Shekhinah. Yet, he does not consider prophecy to be the soul returning to its source in Binah, because the physical, sensate body plays a role in prophecy; it receives sustenance from Shekhinah and cleaves to it, thereby becoming an extension of Shekhinah itself. Since the soul does not leave the body to return to its divine source but instead radiates the emanation onto the body through the cleaving to Shekhinah, there is an upper limit to how high it can reach within the Godhead. The aspiration of all prophetic experience to "an actual sight" is also what sets the boundaries for prophetic cleaving. The philosophical understanding of prophetic sight posited by R. Azriel and R. Jacob b. Sheshet, by comparison, is couched in terms of mental apprehension and therefore allows the cleaving mystic to scale the supernal heights to more elevated aspects of the Godhead.

Nahmanides's prophetic theory does admit of cases in which revelation does not occur through a change in the body or its illumination but through abandonment of the body, which is in a state of shock. The Torah says that "God happened upon Balaam" (Num 23:4), which Nahmanides classifies as the lowest level in the hierarchy of revelation. The expression "happened upon" is not a verb that indicates prophecy: "This language is used concerning this man because he did not attain the level of prophecy."[84] This is followed by a rare, though quite detailed, description of mortal fear: "The meaning of 'God happened upon . . . he said to Him,' is that what happened to Balaam is like what happened to men of the Holy Spirit in their seclusion: a spirit whooshed past him, causing his hair to stand on end, fear and trembling came over him and all his limbs quaked, his comeliness was drained, and he fell on his face earthward."[85] This poetic description of the terror that seized the body during revelation is said about the "men of the Holy Spirit," who, the reader will recall, were not quite prophets, when they were engaged in their practice of isolation. We therefore can infer that the lower the prophetic level, the less the body participates organically in the prophetic process, because its involvement depends upon mystical preparation that exceeds the capabilities of the "men of the Holy Spirit."

The visual nature of prophecy emerges from Nahmanides's description of the revelation to Job "out of the whirlwind" (Job 38:1). This revelation, according to Nahmanides, was somewhat crude and not a fully mature prophecy:

> The meaning of "out of the whirlwind" is that the heavens were not opened for him so that he might see clearly visions of God, such as the Lord sitting on His Throne or an Angel speaking through him; instead, he heard a great whirlwind, apprehending what the prophets apprehend first at the beginning of a vision. As it says first of Ezekiel, "And I saw and behold! a storm wind was coming from the north" (Ezek 1:4), and likewise with Elijah it first says there, "Behold, the Lord passed by. There was a great and mighty wind, splitting mountains and shattering boulders ... After the wind, an earthquake ... After the earthquake, fire" (1 Kgs 19:11–12)—after which they apprehended the prophecy. [There is also decisive proof to this idea] in Ezekiel, too, after the wind was "a massive plume," which is the earthquake, and after that "a conjoined fire" (Ezek 1:4). Job apprehended the beginning of the vision, from which a voice went out to him responding to these retorts with strength, might, and a great storm, as is the practice in prophecies, like it says, "like the sound of mighty waters, like the voice of *Shaddai*, a tumult like the din of a host" (Ezek 1:24). Job apprehended this through hearing the whirlwind and the voice [issuing] from it, and from their nature he knew that it was the voice of God answering him with His words.[86]

Nahmanides describes the unfolding of prophecy here. It begins with a mighty wind, continues with an earthquake and visible fire, and reaches its pinnacle with a clear sight of God. Job merited apprehending only the first stage of this process, that is, the great storm from which he heard the divine voice speaking to him.[87] The voice, therefore, is the first step of a revelation that gradually passes from hearing to seeing and climaxes with the opening of Heaven and seeing an appearance of God.

When Nahmanides refers the prophetic aspiration to "an actual sight," which was expressed in Moses's yearning to see Tif'eret, he also determines the character of human existence in the eschatological era. As we learned above, Nahmanides conceives of the limits of direct mystical contact through the eye of the soul as dictated by human limitations. But the limits of what is humanly possible depend, in turn, on the state of the Godhead itself. The descent of Shekhinah due to the primordial crisis within the emanatory process and its potential, but not actual, unity with the rest of the Godhead makes it a kind of intervening barrier between the prophet-mystic and the rest of the configuration of the Godhead. The return of Shekhinah to its primeval state during the eschaton will affect the degree to which the mystic can apprehend the Godhead. As Nahmanides says about the World to Come:

> He [R. Berechiah] explained that this "World to Come" is Light, the Light that arose in Thought and was created before this world, to convey that this is the ultimate apprehension that man attains and by which he is elevated. Similarly, they say in *Beresheit Rabbah* that through this Light Adam saw from one end of the world to the other. This is the matter of Gazing at the Chariot, and through it one apprehends the truth of the creations in their totality.[88]

CHAPTER 6

Nahmanides's Conception of History

I

Nahmanides's conception of history reflects a profound departure from the linear model in favor of a cyclical one, and this shift was part of a greater trend in the main circles of medieval Jewish thinkers. At the heart of this cyclical model of time is the doctrine of cosmic cycles (*torat ha-shemittot*), according to which the seventh millennium, the World to Come, will be followed by a new cosmic cycle. Seven such cycles—fifty thousand years—culminate in a "jubilee year," at which point the divine efflux retreats back into its source in Absolute Privation, and the whole process restarts.

Under the linear model, the End of Days represents a stable period of the ultimate redemption, and the World to Come marks the end of the twists and turns of history. Under the cyclical model, the End of Days morphs into the beginning, and the World to Come signals the end of a divine movement that is reborn with the obliteration of the World to Come. Nahmanides is not blind to the unbridgeable gap between these two models, which comes to the fore in his discussion of the World to Come and humanity's eternal life within it: "[Adam] should have existed and lived forever if only he had not sinned that sin, and even though we believe in the destruction of the universe in the sabbatical year."[1] Nahmanides himself points out the impossibility of squaring the traditional account of the resurrected living eternally in the

World to Come with the destruction of the world at the end of the "sabbatical year."

Although he subscribed to this cyclical model, Nahmanides did not initiate this shift in the basic temporal paradigm of Jewish tradition. The cyclical paradigm entered mainstream medieval Judaism before his time, appearing earlier in key circles of medieval Jewish thinkers like R. Abraham b. Hiyya.[2] The cyclical paradigm of history in R. Abraham b. Hiyya's thought was a reasonable corollary of his astrological worldview, because if celestial bodies and their movements generate human history, then the march of history will seem to follow, more or less, the ecliptic circle of the zodiac.

Although these currents clearly influenced the thinking of Nahmanides and other contemporary kabbalists, it was the kabbalists who placed their own unique spin on it, since it touched upon the very core of their kabbalistic worldview.[3] At the heart of kabbalistic theosophy lies the intradivine tension between the divine organism's desire to retreat into the deepest recesses of Ein-Sof, and its autonomic drive to gush out and be emanated outward. If the efflux does not emerge, nothing exists beyond Ayin itself; if it does not return to Ayin, the emanation is liable to lose the source of its being. The connection between the doctrine of cosmic cycles as a historical paradigm and kabbalistic theosophy is rooted in the fact that the dialectic of the Godhead does not resolve into a stable synthesis but continues to pendulate outward and inward, to and from Ayin. The doctrine of cosmic cycles may have first appeared in kabbalistic theosophy as a foreign transplant from astrology, but it quickly took root and struck the very bedrock of kabbalah, because the circularity of historical time reflects the necessarily dynamic nature of the Godhead.

The cyclical character of divine movement is clearly evident in Nahmanides's commentary on the first chapter of Sefer Yetzirah. In his initial gloss on the composition, Nahmanides explains the meaning of the phrase "thirty-two [numerologically *lev*] paths of wisdom," which includes the twenty-two letters of the Hebrew alphabet and the ten sefirot:

> This number is meant [to allude] to Heart (*Lev*), and Heart is Will, like in the meaning of the verse, "is your will (*lev*) aligned with mine, the same way mine is with yours?" (2 Kgs 10:15). Because every thing exists so long as the Will is in it, and it becomes Naught (*Bal*) when the Will reverses itself to return all things to the way they were (*la-havayatan*, lit. "to their being"), as if drawing in its breath. And so the

Torah begins with the *bet* of *be-reshit* and ends with the *lamed* of *yisra'el* [*BaL*], as if to say that the essence will revert "to that which has possession of the Earth (*ha-Aretz*)" (Lev 27:24), which is *Ha-Afisah ha-Muhletet* (Absolute Privation). "*Muhletet*": the Aramaic translation of *la-tzemitut* ("forever") is *la-halutin*, "absolutely." It [Absolute Privation] is therefore hinted at, because the intellect cannot apprehend it.[4]

The initial and final letters of the Torah, which form the word *bal*, reflect the impermanence of the emanated universe. The universe's end at the cosmic "jubilee" is embedded in the Torah itself, in which the Heart (Lev)—the Will that sustains the universe—becomes Naught (Bal). Nahmanides wonderfully compares the tucking of the Godhead into itself and the reversal of Lev into Bal to the image of a person inhaling—"as if drawing in its breath." This would make the outward emanation from Ayin divine exhalation.[5]

This apocatastasis corresponds, as Nahmanides alludes, to the commandment of the jubilee year—"as if to say that the essence will revert 'to that which has possession of the Earth.'" In his Commentary on the Torah, Nahmanides weaves together the return of patrimonies to their original owners with the return of the Land, Shekhinah, to its source in the sefirah of Binah:

> That is [the meaning of] the verse, "and the Land shall observe a Sabbath" (Lev 25:2), "and you shall proclaim *deror* throughout the Land" (Lev 25:10), because it is the Land of Life (*ha-Aretz*) [i.e., *Shekhinah*] alluded to in the first verse [of the Torah], about which it is said, "and I shall Remember the Land" (Lev 26:42). I have already mentioned this many times. Perhaps our Rabbis alluded to this when they said, "Fifty gates of understanding were created in the world, and all were given to Moses save one" (*Rosh ha-Shanah* 21b), because every sabbatical cycle is the gate of one House, and they granted him knowledge of all of existence from beginning to end, aside from the Jubilee—the Holy.[6]

In Nahmanides's kabbalistic symbolism, the days of creation parallel the process of sefirotic emanation, and each day therefore represents one of the seven lower sefirot. These sefirot are referred to as "Days," because unlike the three higher sefirot, they are differentiated and measurable, in some sense. In keeping with this symbolism of Nahmanides, cycles of seven—days of the week, years in a sabbatical cycle, sabbatical cycles preceding the jubilee—parallel one another. Each of the seven sefirot can be represented as a Day, Year, or

Sabbatical Cycle. The forty-nine gates within Moses's apprehension are there-fore the seven apprehensible sefirot, whereas the fiftieth, Binah, is holy and cannot be apprehended. Shekhinah, which Nahmanides frequently refers to as "the Land" in his symbolism, returns to its source in Binah, which is re-ferred to as "Holy" and "the Jubilee."

Shekhinah's return during the cosmic jubilee also parallels the return of the human soul to its source within the divine emanation, as Nahmanides writes about the word *deror,* which is usually translated as "liberty": "By way of truth, *deror* is from the language of 'One generation (*dor*) goes and another generation (*dor*) comes' (Eccl 1:4). Similarly, 'jubilee' means that it returns to the Jubilee where its roots are, and it shall be for you."[7] According to this symbolism, the manumission of slaves during the jubilee returns them to their original free state, which in turn symbolizes the return of the totality of the configuration of the Godhead to its source: " 'and he shall serve him for-ever (*le-'olam*)' (Exod 21:6) [. . .] But the enlightened will comprehend that *le-'olam* is literal, that one who works until the jubilee has worked all the Days of the World (*'olam*)."[8] According to Nahmanides's unique interpretation, the slave working until the jubilee symbolizes the cosmic jubilee, the culmination of "all the Days of the World," which is to say a complete cycle of history and existence of the universe.[9]

Human history, Nahmanides maintains, is tightly connected to this sev-enfold divine cycle. History is a manifestation of the emanation of the sefirot and their return to their source, a protracted cycle of divine respiration, of the divine organism inhaling and exhaling. This is no linear history in which the World to Come exists forever; instead, the divine movement heads back to its source that preceded the creation of the universe, and the sefirot and cosmos are sucked back into Ayin. This divine breathing follows a predetermined count—the large cycle of smaller sabbatical cycles followed by the jubilee—and this tempo undermines the conception of a personal God who exercises his own free will. In writing about this apocatastasis, Nahmanides invokes God's Will: "every thing exists so long as the Will is in it, and it becomes Naught (Bal) when the Will reverses itself to return all things to the way they were."[10] From context, however, one can infer that Nahmanides does not in-tend the sovereign will exercised by a personal God, because the cosmic jubi-lee cycle is presented as an internal, essential mechanism that locks the divine movement into a preset rhythm and order. The meaning of "the Will" here, as in other contexts we have already seen, is the efflux that emerges from the Cause of causes that cleaves to a particular object or activity.

The doctrine of cosmic cycles and the secret of the jubilee are predicated upon this cyclicality of the divine movement. Moreover, Nahmanides seems to hold the view that at the end of fifty thousand years the cycle begins anew—why assume that God has only one respiratory cycle?[11] While Nahmanides does not state this outright, R. Abraham b. Hiyya had raised this possibility.[12] If this is true, it would put in a new light the question of creation within time. As discussed in Chapter 4, the Geronese kabbalists and Nahmanides radically changed the meaning of the belief in *creatio ex nihilo*.[13] According to Nahmanides, existence was not created from naught, from nonexistence, but from the divine Naught, Ayin. Ayin, or, to use another Nahmanidean expression, "Absolute Privation," is that which cannot be defined or delimited, not because it does not exist, but because of its infinite plenitude.[14] In the same manner that Nahmanides, following his predecessors, replaced the accepted and simple meaning of *creatio ex nihilo* with a radically new one, so the doctrine of cosmic cycles and the secret of the jubilee upend the usual understanding of the universe's creation within time. If we posit that the divine respiration is continuous and never-ending, then the world is not created within time but is re-created over and over ad infinitum.[15] Humans are caught in this current, although they possess the ability to affect its character and directionality.

The greatest medieval antagonist to the notion of the apocalyptic obliteration of existence was Maimonides. He dedicated three chapters of *The Guide of the Perplexed* to polemicizing against this notion,[16] and in his view the future eternality of the world is unassailable even if one believes that it was created de novo at a particular point in time.[17] His rejection of the apocalyptic vision of the universe's end connects to his view of Nature as the main medium of expression for God's wisdom and perfection; anything that threatens the causal structure of existence implies a deficiency in that wisdom and perfection. In keeping with his hermeneutics, Maimonides attempts to explain prophetic pronouncements about the end of the natural order as figurative expressions representing the dawn of a new eschatological age.

Nahmanides devotes a lengthy portion of his Discourse on Ecclesiastes to a polemic against Maimonides's view of Nature's eternality. Among other things, he tackles a few exegetical questions raised by Maimonides about the Apocalypse. One such question concerns the rabbinic saying that serves as the basis for the cyclical model: "The world exists for six millennia, and is destroyed for one" (Rosh ha-Shanah 31a). The simple reading is that the world will return to primordial chaos, and not to the divine Naught, for the Talmud refers to "those thousand years for which [the Holy One] shall return the world to tohu va-bohu" (Sanhedrin 92a). The dictum also does not deviate from the linear model, because after the destruction of the world, the redeemed world will exist without end. This source seemingly supports the Maimonidean view. Nahmanides reinterprets it, using the rabbinic dictum as a prooftext for his doctrine of cosmic cycles:

> It seems that in saying "tohu va-bohu" they mean Absolute Privation, and we should not be so exacting here with their language, for it is common to call something that ceases to exist "tohu va-bohu," both in Biblical and Rabbinic Hebrew. Since this is the case, the very same Sages who possess a tradition from the prophets [and] believe in *creatio de novo* and its existence are the ones who say that it shall cease to exist.[18]

On the face of it, the Talmudic statement speaks of annihilation, not "a return of all things to the way they were." This also seems to precede the End of Days and does not mark any particular stage of an ongoing cycle. Nahmanides, true to form, gives a new interpretation of the "tohu va-bohu" by reading it as a reference to Absolute Privation, which in his writings is a cognomen for Ayin or Ein-Sof, the undefined, undifferentiated divine being that preexists emanation. The paucity of biblical or Talmudic sources to support this contention does not, in Nahmanides's opinion, undermine its credibility, because its authority comes from an oral, esoteric tradition attributed to Moses at Sinai: "But one cannot grasp the truth of these and similar matters on one's own, only through tradition. This matter is clear in the Torah to anyone who has heard the reason for the commandments through tradition in the proper manner, that is, tradent from the mouth of tradent all the way to Moses from the mouth of the Almighty."[19] Although Nahmanides, in his polemic with Maimonides, claims that the cyclical paradigm of history comes from an esoteric tradition that one cannot dispute or slide under the microscope of reason, one can discern that this tradition in its kabbalistic garb interlocks perfectly with Nahmanides's basic theosophical position on the inner tension within the Godhead itself.

This deep shift from the linear to the cyclical model of time came out of the search for a causal mechanism that could account for not only the historical paradigm of kabbalah but also its theosophy and conception of ritual. The historical narrative found in the Bible and rabbinic literature is set within the framework of an interpersonal, covenantal relationship between God and

Israel. The changing fortunes of the Jewish people throughout history mirror the ups and downs of this relationship, and redemption is the great promise that this unconditional bond will turn rock solid at the End of Days. The cyclical paradigm of history, by contrast, belongs essentially to a universe in which gods and humans are subject to a preordained fate that fixes them in a repetitive process, and therein lies its deep connection to astrology.[20] In Nahmanides's version, to what extent does God have control over this cyclicality? Let us consider the image he uses: respiration. On one hand, we are not forced to breathe; on the other, we do not consciously decide to breathe by exercising our will. The cyclicality of divine life, imagined as God's breath, then, is not the result of a voluntary decision. At the same time, this movement is not forced upon the Godhead by some external factor, just as no external force compels us to breathe. Our breathing is neither forced nor deliberate; it is the direct manifestation of our being alive. In the same way, the cyclicality of the divine emanation is a clear expression of the divine essence— a living, breathing God, so to speak. Nahmanides's historical paradigm, therefore, does not necessarily imply the existence of something outside the Godhead that can impose its will upon it. Yet, the application of this necessary expression of the Godhead's essence to history in the form of the cyclical account resulted from discomfort with the interpersonal account of history. The religious thought of Nahmanides and other kabbalists was dominated by causal models that ultimately gave rise to this historical paradigm, which has a fixed structure that predetermines and foreknows the divine movement. The doctrine of cosmic cycles entails a mechanization of time that reverses the previous biblical rabbinic picture of time and history as a reflection and embodiment of an interpersonal covenant.

The broad cyclicality posited by the doctrine of cosmic cycles, as powerful and revolutionary as it may be, does not, on its own, supply more than historiosophy or meta-history. Nahmanides does not say a word, quite naturally, about what will happen to the world in the six following cosmic cycles. He also does not even hint at what the Torah will look like in those cycles, or what the state of humankind and the Jewish people will be in the forty-two thousand years after the World to Come. Nahmanides knows only the detailed human history of one cosmic sabbatical cycle that he refers to as "the Era of the Torah," the cycle in which he views himself situated and whose history he tries to interpret.[21] The Era of the Torah is the period in which the Torah is as we have it; it is the period between Original Sin and the World to Come. The Era of the Torah began with the intradivine fracture within the

Godhead and its reverberation on the human plane in the Original Sin, and it will end with the restoration of intradivine unity. In the meantime, humans possess free will and can choose to quicken or slow down the divine current that carries them. With respect to this in-between period, Nahmanides develops a complicated and sophisticated approach to history—that is, to the particular concrete story of one of the "Days of the World"—thereby shifting from meta-history to history itself.

Nahmanides's conception of history coalesces out of the following: biblical and rabbinic narratives, Sefer Yosippon (a tenth-century Hebrew work based on the Latin translations of Josephus and widely known in medieval Ashkenaz), information from his contemporary Christian world, and the Franco-German Jewish view of history. Nahmanides, as we have said, is not satisfied with the rather mechanistic meta-history provided by the doctrine of cosmic cycles. His interpretive sensitivity and familiarity with and keen insight into institutional and political realities enriched his historical perspective, giving it a feel of realism and rich complexity. His particular reading of history is embedded within the broad, circular structure of the "Days of the World" and at its base reflects a profoundly existential and metaphysical longing.

II

The key to understanding Nahmanides's conception of history can be found in his creative use of the midrashic maxim "everything that happened to the Forefathers is a sign for the progeny" (henceforth: the Forefathers-progeny principle). This maxim, which did not mature into a coherent interpretive approach in the midrash, became a cornerstone of Nahmanides's hermeneutics:

> I shall tell you a principle that you will discern in all of the coming Torah portions regarding Abraham, Isaac, and Jacob. It is something of great significance that our Rabbis mentioned in brief, saying, "everything that happened to the Forefathers is a sign for the progeny." Therefore, the verses dilate upon the travels, well-digging, and other occurrences (*mikrim*). One might think them superfluous matters of no value, but they all come to teach about the future.[22]

The narratives about the Patriarchs' journeys and other prosaic aspects of their lives do not in and of themselves justify the kind of detailed narration they receive in Genesis. Their importance lies in their implications for Jewish history, as Nahmanides writes at the end of his commentary on Genesis: "And so the Book of Genesis, which tells the story of the Forefathers' affairs, comes to its conclusion, / having related events of old and new ones that no one could yet envision."[23]

Using this concept, Nahmanides explains Abraham's entry into the land of Israel as a detailed parallel to the future entry of the Jewish people into the land in the days of Joshua:

> I would add that He had Abraham take possession of this place [the environs of Shechem] first, before He gave him the land. This hinted to him that his progeny would conquer that place first before they merited it, before the iniquity of the land's inhabitants was complete so that they could be exiled from there. Therefore it says, "and the Canaanites were then in the land" (Gen 12:6). When God gave him the land through a declaration, he then traveled from there and pitched his tent between Bethel and Ai, for that was the place that Joshua conquered first.[24]

Abraham's descent to Egypt and grand exit with riches likewise prefigures the Egyptian exile and exodus:

> Abraham, on account of a famine, descended to Egypt to sojourn there, to sustain himself during days of scarcity. The Egyptians oppressed him without cause by taking his wife. The Holy One avenged them with great afflictions, and brought him out of there with livestock, silver, and gold. Pharaoh even ordered men to send them off. It was hinted to him that his descendants would descend to Egypt on account of famine in order to sojourn there, the Egyptians would mistreat them and take their women . . ., the Holy One would avenge them with great afflictions until He would bring them out with silver, gold, and "very much livestock, both flocks and herds" (Exod 12:38), and they [the Egyptians] would press upon them in order to send them out of the land. Not one whit of what befell the Forefather failed to occur to his progeny.[25]

Nahmanides invested the various occurrences of the Patriarchs with typological significance for the future of the Jewish people,[26] although the main typology centers on the correspondence—in chronological order—between the Patriarchal figures and the future exiles. The movements of each Patriarch prefigures one of the three exiles. Abraham's exilic sojourn in Egypt signifies the first exile in Egypt, as we have seen, and in the same way Isaac's wandering in Gerar represents the second exile to Babylon:

> To my mind, this matter also includes a hint about the future. Abraham's exile to Egypt on account of the famine was a hint that his progeny would be exiled there, whereas his going to Abimelech was not an exile since he settled there willingly. Isaac's descent there [to Abimelech in Gerar] on account of the famine, however, does hint at exile, because he was exiled from his residence against his will and went to another land. Notice that he was exiled from his residence to the land of the Philistines, which was the land of his father's sojourn. This alludes to the exile to Babylonia, which was the place of their [the Jewish people's] Forefathers who lived in Ur Kasdim. And know that the aforementioned exile would be similar to Isaac's experience: they did not take his wife and all he had there was exile and fear. At the outset he [Abimelech] said, "Whoever touches this man or his wife shall surely die" (Gen 26:11), but after some time he changed his mind and said, "Leave us" (Gen 26:16). Subsequently, they restored relations with him through a covenant. And so it was with the Babylonian exile: they were exiled there because of the scorching famine, and once there they did not work them nor oppress them; in fact, the great ones became royal ministers. Later, they said: "Whoever among you are from His people, let his God be with him and ascend [to Jerusalem]" (Ezra 1:3), and warned the lords of Transjordan and the satraps about them. They subsequently put a stop to the building [of the Temple], which was at a standstill for a season and a time, after which they gave permission to build again, exhorting "that they may offer pleasing sacrifices to the God of Heaven and pray for the life of the king and his sons" (Ezra 6:10).[27]

Nahmanides does not settle for general structural parallelism; he sees the character and nature of the exile in the smallest detail of the prefigurative gesture. Isaac's peregrinations in Gerar did not constitute going to a foreign land, and, in the same way, the future Babylonian exile would be a descent to the land of the Jewish ancestors. The relative mildness of this exile, compared with slavery in Egypt, is signified by the difference between Abraham's treatment at the hands of the Egyptians and Isaac's treatment by Abimelech.[28]

Jacob's tormented life, including his encounters with Esau and the descent of his clan to Egypt, represents the third exile—the terrible exile of Edom.

Nahmanides understands Jacob's travel to his brother Esau in Seir as sinful, which alludes to the treaty Agrippa made with the Romans at the end of the Second Temple era: "In my opinion, this too hints that we instigated our downfall at the hands of Edom, because the kings of the Second Temple [era] made a treaty with the Romans, and some of them went to Rome, which was the reason for their downfall at their hands. This is mentioned in the words of our Rabbis and is published in books."[29] Jacob's emergence unscathed from his tussle with the angel hints, according to Nahmanides, that the Jews will overcome the religious and other kinds of persecution they have suffered at the hands of Christianity:

> The idea [of the *midrash*] is that the entire episode is a hint for the future, that Esau will lord it over a generation of Jacob's progeny until he nearly wipes them out. This was one generation in the period of the Mishnaic Sages, the generation of R. Yehudah b. Bava and his colleagues [. . .] There have been other generations where they treated us like this or even worse, but we have suffered it all and it has passed, as it hinted, "And Jacob arrived sound" (Gen 33:18).[30]

At the end of Jacob's life, he took his family to Egypt, and Nahmanides understands the details of this narrative as prefiguring the Roman exile:

> I have already mentioned that Jacob's descent to Egypt alludes to the third exile, which is our present exile under the dominion of the fourth beast, i.e., evil Edom. Jacob's sons themselves caused their own descent there by selling their brother Joseph, and Jacob descended there on account of the famine, thinking that he could be saved with his son in the house of his admirer, because Pharaoh loved Joseph like a son. They thought they would ascend from there when the famine ended in the Land of Canaan, as they said: " 'We have come to sojourn in this land for there is no pasture for your servants' flocks, the famine being severe in the Land of Canaan' " (Gen 47:4). But they did not ascend; instead, his [Jacob's] exile stretched on and he died there. His bones did ascend—Pharaoh's advisors and ministers brought them up and mourned solemnly for him. And so it is with us under Rome and Edom: our brothers caused us to come under their dominion by making a treaty with the Romans, and Agrippa, the last king of the Second Temple [era], fled to them for help. On account of the famine the inhabitants of Jerusalem were captured. Our exile has stretched on for so

long, and unlike the other exiles we know not its end. In it [i.e., exile] we are like the dead who say, "our bones have dried out . . . we are doomed" (Ezek 37:11). But they will elevate us from among all peoples as "an offering to the Lord" (Isa 66:20), they will mourn solemnly upon seeing our glory, and we will witness the vengeance of the Lord. May it be His will that we live long enough to see it.[31]

Beyond the typological correspondence between the travels of the three Patriarchs and the three exiles, there is also a profound link between their sins and the exiles. The Egyptian exile resulted from Abraham's conscious, voluntary, and sinful decision to descend to Egypt. The Edomite exile is tied to the sin of Jacob's conduct with Esau and his descent to Egypt, the same submissive behavior that was reenacted in Agrippa's appeal to the Romans for protection and a defense treaty.[32] Thus, Nahmanides applies the Forefathers-progeny principle in various contexts and with close attention to detail, although it mainly revolves around the travels and tribulations of the Patriarchs, taking them as prefigurations of the Israelites' entry into the land of Israel and their exiles from it.

A robust picture of Nahmanides's view of history also emerges from those sections of the Bible that he finds indicative of the Babylonian and Roman exiles. Nahmanides makes an important hermeneutic distinction between the blessings and curses that are mentioned in Leviticus and those that are mentioned in Deuteronomy, which he believes correspond to the Babylonian and Edomite-Roman exiles, respectively.[33] In his comments on these verses of the Torah, Nahmanides elaborates in exceptional detail how the verses spell out the character and order of exilic events. In Sefer ha-Ge'ulah (The Book of Redemption), which will be discussed at the end of the chapter, he gives a similarly comprehensive explication of Daniel's vision of the four beasts, which he treats as a historical and eschatological cipher. We should distinguish, though, his systematic use of the Forefathers-progeny principle, which bridges the past and future through typology, from his interpretation of various prophecies as bearing import for the future. The interpretation of various biblical prophecies as oriented toward the deep future is standard exegesis in Jewish interpretation of Scripture and has a long history. Amos Funkenstein showed that Nahmanides was the first Jewish exegete, however, to use a typological principle like "the occurrences of the Forefathers are a sign for the progeny," and he also noted that Nahmanides was adopting a hermeneutic widely used by Christian exegetes.[34] The Christological typology views biblical personae, things, and events as significations of the life, death, and resurrection of Jesus. The intent and meaning of scriptural verses thus could not be known until the events signified by Scripture eventually came to pass. The unfolding of history becomes a means of interpreting Scripture itself, which is supposed to reflect and correspond with it. Nahmanides may have borrowed this hermeneutical schema, but he also engaged in a polemic with its Christological function by replacing the anti-type of Jesus with the Jewish people.

Moreover, a dissection of the connections between signifier—the occurrences of the Patriarchs—and signified—the history of their descendants—reveals that Nahmanides integrates this hermeneutical principle into his kabbalistic thought and meta-historical worldview. The borrowing of this hermeneutic from the Christian world pertains only to the surface of Nahmanides's thought. To clarify his use of this Christian typology, we must present three senses in which signifier and signified correlate in typological interpretation. The first and narrowest sense is that God implanted events in history that symbolically represent the future. The uniqueness of these symbols is that they are not objects like icons nor are they linguistic expressions like metaphors; they are events that signify future occurrences. The second and broader sense maintains that typology operates in a fixed historical structure of parallelism. History, to borrow an idea from modern physics, is a kind of fractal structure. A fractal is something for which any given part of it has the same properties and form of the whole; one can say that it has self-similarity at every scale. For example, if one were to take any given coastline in Africa, which will have seemingly unique irregularities, zooming in on part of that coastline will reveal roughly the same pattern. The Forefathers-progeny principle is a kind of fractal image of history writ large, in which the character of smaller cycles of local events has the form of wider cycles and so on, until one zooms out to the entire sweep of history. The third and tightest sense of connection between signifier and signified is causal. According to this, beyond the fractal structure of events, the original, smallest, localized event causally sets in motion the future existence of what it signifies.

A careful reading of Nahmanides's Commentary on the Torah demonstrates that he uses the Forefathers-progeny principle to mean a causal connection that is broader than the symbolic-figurative one. This can be seen in the very first appearance of this hermeneutical principle in his commentary:

> I will tell you a principle that you will discern in all of the coming
> Torah portions regarding Abraham, Isaac, and Jacob. It is something

of great significance that our Rabbis mentioned in brief, saying, "everything that happened to the Forefathers is a sign for the progeny." [. . .] Because when something befalls one of the three Patriarchal prophets, he can deduce from it what is fated to happen to his offspring. Know that when any decree of the Activators goes from being a decree *in potentia* to a similitude *in actu* it will occur no matter what. That is why the prophets perform an action in their prophecies, as when Jeremiah ordered Baruch: "And when you finish reading the words of this scroll, tie a stone to it and hurl it into the Euphrates, and say, 'Thus shall Babylon sink etc.' " (Jer 51:63–64). This is also what Elisha was doing when he placed his arm upon the bow: "And Elisha said, 'Shoot' and he shot, and Elisha said, 'An arrow of victory for the Lord! An arrow of victory over Aram!' " (2 Kgs 13:17), and it says there: "The man of God was angry with him and said to him, 'If only you had struck five or six times! Then you would have annihilated Aram; now you shall defeat Aram [only] three times'" (2 Kgs 13:19). Therefore the Holy One had Abraham take possession of the Land and made similitudes for him regarding all that would come to happen to his offspring. Understand this.[35]

Nahmanides links the Forefathers-progeny principle to a magical technique that is not unique to the Patriarchs and can be identified in diverse prophetic gestures. A prophetic decree comes true when the prophet prefigures it with a gesture that represents the future event, thereby causing it to happen. This causative structure rests upon a talismanic notion that Nahmanides employs in various contexts. The talisman is an isomorphic, iconic structure whose similitude to the broader system of potencies in the universe attracts those potencies, enabling its user to effectuate something through their power. That is how Nahmanides explains, for example, Aaron's creation of the golden calf:

Aaron contemplated the potency of the Ox [i.e., of the divine Chariot in Ezekiel] and made them [the Israelites] a body in this form capable of receiving this potency through the zodiacal signs and hours, so that it could show them the way through the wilderness and guide their travels. Once they saw the ox [the golden calf] they said that it had been guiding them from the beginning, as it is written: "And the Lord (*va-Y-HWH*) [i.e., *Shekhinah*] went before them by day [in a pillar of cloud]" (Exod 13:21), and it is written: "And the Angel, God [*Shekhinah*], traveled [. . .] and came between the camp of Egypt [. . .] And there was the cloud and the darkness" (Exod 14:19–20). I have already explained that the "darkness" is the elemental Fire which is blackness, and the potency of this Fire, which is the Attribute of Judgment, receives a supernal power from the *Hayyah* called "Ox," which is from the Left [i.e., the side of the Chariot/Godhead]. Immediately after they saw that an ox had been made for them, they rejoiced, saying that this would be an excellent guide for them, the potency of which had raised them [out of Egypt] and assisted them until now.[36]

The calf's ability to draw down the divine potencies inheres in its isomorphism with the left side of the divine Chariot. In Nahmanides's typological history, this isomorphic talisman works not only with things but with events, too. The prophetic gesture that Nahmanides refers to as a "similitude in actu" creates a talisman that forms a channel within the fabric of reality for some future action, into which the active forces must of necessity flow.[37] Whereas most of the time this talismanic technique involves the creation of an isomorphic object, like the golden calf, with the occurrences of the Patriarchs and gestures of the prophets the talisman is the occurrence or gesture itself that produces the future event.

Nevertheless, there is a difference of utmost importance between the talismanic technique of the prophets and the occurrences of the Patriarchs. The prophets, as Nahmanides explains, make a gesture that partly simulates some future event in order to ensure the realization of the prophetic promise. The prophet creates a talisman because he knows the prophecy and wants to ensure its realization. With the Patriarchs, however, it is God who generates the talisman, as Nahmanides writes at the end of his introduction to the talismanic principle: "Therefore, the Holy One had Abraham take possession of the land and made similitudes for him regarding all that would come to happen to his offspring. Understand this."[38] As Abraham moves about from place to place, he does not know what will happen to his progeny. Unlike the later prophets, he does not make simulations of the future to ensure the future realization of God's will. It is God who leads Abraham to the plain of Moreh in order to secure Jewish entry into the land at that very location.[39] In this way, this talismanic principle about the Forefathers and their progeny reflects the causal structure created by the Godhead itself. The Godhead sets up such a structure in order to establish a trajectory within which it must act in the future. Nahmanides hinted at this esoteric aspect of the principle when he ended his introduction to it with the curt exhortation "Understand this," which he typically reserves for esoteric matters. In this case, he means the structure within which God is found, or, put differently, in which God has confined himself.

The causal conception of typology, the third sense listed above, makes further appearances in Nahmanides's oeuvre. In Torat Ha-Shem Temimah, which is a kind of refined summary of his ideas, he discusses the value of the detailed Patriarchal narratives. After elaborating upon the religious-ethical import of God's providential governance of the Patriarchs and their reward, Nahmanides introduces the typological hermeneutic: "In *Bereshit Rabbah* I found an idea that resolves all of this. They said: 'everything that happened to the Forefathers is a sign for the progeny,' and so it was. The Holy One wanted to inform His prophets of what would happen to them and their offspring, and He would bring the matter from the potential to the actual so that it would be signed and sealed."[40] The occurrence that befalls a Patriarch betokens the occurrence of a future event and moves it from the realm of promise to action. This causal-talismanic approach also generates inner coherence between the account of creation and the Patriarchal narratives, as Nahmanides himself says in summing up the book of Genesis: "Scripture has finished the book of Genesis, which is the book of Creation: the world's creation *ex nihilo,* the creation of all things, and all the occurrences of the Forefathers which are a kind of creation for their offspring, because all of their occurrences are figures of events that hint and foretell all that will happen to them in the future."[41] The Book of Genesis is the Book of Creation, including the creation of the universe and the creation of history. The book begins with the account of creation, which is the formation of Nature, and continues with the Patriarchal journeys and occurrences, which are the creation of history.

Another productive, and perhaps the most elaborate, use of this third, causal sense of typology is Nahmanides's understanding of the six days of creation, which he calls "the Days of the World." Nahmanides introduces his typology to explain the clause "which God created to do" (Gen 2:3):

> Know that the word "to do" (*la'asot*) also includes [the fact] that the six days of Creation are all the Days of the World, that it will exist for six thousand years. That is why they [the Sages] said, "a day for the Holy One is a thousand years." For the first two days the world was entirely water and nothing was completed, and they are an allusion to the first two millennia in which no one publicized the name of the Lord, as

they said: "two thousand [years] of *tohu*." [. . .] On the second [day He said] "let there be a firmament and let it separate" (Gen 1:6), for in it [the second millennium] the innocent, Noah and his sons, were separated from the guilty, who were punished through water.[42]

In the same passage, Nahmanides continues his detailed typological reading of the days of creation as millennia, eventually reaching the sixth day on which humanity was created, which corresponds to the sixth millennium: "This is the sixth millennium, because at its onset the carnivores, the kingdoms 'that did not know the Lord' (Judg 2:10), rule. But after a tenth of it, corresponding to the time it takes the sun to rise, the redeemer will come, about whom it is written, 'his throne is like the sun before Me' (Ps 89:37)—the son of David, who is made in the divine image."[43] According to Nahmanides, the word "to do" at the end of Gen 2:3 indicates that during the days of creation the entire tapestry of history—"all the Days of the World"—was created. The source of this creation lies in the symbolic, and therefore causal, connection between Nature and history.

The relationship between signifier and signified in typological interpretation therefore goes beyond symbolic representation. It also operates causally, although it is beyond the reach of magical activities that try to influence supernal powers for humans' betterment. This causality is part and parcel of the structure of divine activity, which ensures that its will will be done through the creation of a prefigurative simulation. This same causal principle of divine activity is expressed in the much broader framework of the circular-cyclical paradigm of the full sweep of history. Seven days, seven years, seven sabbatical cycles—these all fit together like proportional gears in a horological wheel train, and this causal works is based upon the inner structure of the Godhead itself. The point of similarity between Nahmanidean and Christian typology is therefore limited. In Christian typological interpretation, a representational relation between signifier and signified exists, and there is, in a sense, a kind of fractal structure in which the future is embedded in events of the past and can be uncovered through types, which are a kind of figure of the future. In Christian typology, however, the causal-talismanic structure is absent, not to mention the structure as the manner in which divine activity operates. Perhaps Christian typological interpretation influenced Nahmanides's hermeneutics to some degree, but after seeing the "Understand this" marker and following it into the theological depths of his hermeneutic, we have seen its uniqueness and how it links up with his meta-history.

III

In Nahmanides's interpretation, the occurrences of the Patriarchs mostly prefigure exile from and (re)entry into the land of Israel. Abraham's entry into the land represents the entry of the Israelites under Joshua's leadership, and his famine-induced sojourn in Egypt prefigures the Israelite exile in Egypt. Isaac's descent to Gerar signifies the Babylonian exile. Jacob's dealings with Esau and his descent to Egypt, in the wake of his sons, prefigure the Roman-Edomite exile. Not every movement of the Patriarchs and little detail of their lives realize God's will, prefiguring God's activities through occurrences that he orchestrates, because some of those that serve as portents of things to come are the result of the Patriarchs' unwitting sins that are against God's will. These sins are linked to those movements of the Patriarchs that signify exile.

At the end of the comment in which Nahmanides presents a detailed parallelism between Abraham's descent to Egypt and the descent of the Children of Israel there, he argues that this relocation, which determined the future fate of the Jewish people, had its source in sin:

> You should know that our Forefather Abraham unwittingly committed a great sin by bringing his saintly wife into the snare of iniquity due to his fear that they [the court of Pharaoh] might kill him. He should have trusted in his God to rescue him, his wife, and all that was his, because God has the power to succor and save. His [Abraham's] departure from the Land, about which he was commanded originally [to go there], on account of the famine was an iniquitous sin, because God would have redeemed him from death by famine. For this act, exile was decreed upon his offspring in the land of Egypt under Pharaoh's fist. Where there is judgment, there is sin.[44]

A similar correspondence exists between Jacob's sojourns and the fate of the Jewish people in the third, Roman-Edomite exile. In order to set up an elaborate typology, Nahmanides uses a story he knows from Sefer Yosippon and rabbinic literature, both of which maintain that Roman rule over the land of Israel began with the initiative of King Agrippa, who made a defense treaty with the Romans and involved them in the internecine battle he was waging in Jerusalem. Nahmanides views this invitation as a sin that led to exile— "because at the end of the Second Temple [era] King Agrippa went to Rome, and on account of his going there the Temple was destroyed"[45]—and sets up a parallel with two episodes in Jacob's life. The first is the descent of his family to Egypt during the famine to procure food. They hoped to be saved by the Egyptians and return to Canaan, yet their sojourn there ended in protracted exile and servitude. This parallels what happened with Agrippa, who put his faith in Roman assistance and got more than he bargained for: Roman domination.[46] The second episode that Nahmanides sees as typologically prefiguring Agrippa's act is when Jacob sent gift-laden emissaries to Seir in order to appease Esau. Nahmanides deems his searching out Esau to appease him as a sin akin to the one perpetrated by Agrippa:

> "to his brother Esau, toward the Land of Seir" (Gen 32:4). Because the south of the land of Israel borders Edom, and his father [Isaac] was living on southern land, he [Jacob] had to cross by way of Edom or near it; he therefore feared that Esau might hear [about his presence] and acted preemptively by sending emissaries to him in his land. The Sages already criticized him for this, saying in *Bereshit Rabbah:* " 'One who grabs a dog's ears [is a passerby who meddles in a fight that isn't his]' (Prov 26:17)—God said to him, 'He was going his way; did you have to send him [a message] saying, "So says your servant Jacob"?'" In my opinion, this too hints that we instigated our downfall at the hands of Edom, because the kings of the Second Temple [era] made a treaty with the Romans, and some of them went to Rome, which was the reason for their downfall at their hands. This is mentioned in the words of our Rabbis and is published in books.[47]

The correspondence between Patriarchal biography and the history of the Patriarchs' progeny constitutes the central axis around which Nahmanides's view of history turns—exile from the land and (re)entry into it. All of these Patriarchal sins have a shared dimension: failure to trust in God's promise. This is evident in Abraham's descent to Egypt to avoid starvation and Jacob's groveling posture toward Esau to avoid his deadly wrath. Devotion to God's will and placing trust in him is the essence of cleaving to God, and their reliance upon other measures for self-preservation reflects a rupture in their cleaving to the Godhead. The lack of this kind of trust leads to eventual exile, because living in the land is a form of cleaving. As we have learned in previous chapters, in the land of Israel Shekhinah's presence is unmediated, which is why it is governed by the hidden miracle. In the land, humanity's fate lies directly under the aegis of Shekhinah. Exile entails severance from cleaving to the Godhead, banishment to a place where humanity's link to the divine is routed through the signs of the zodiac.[48]

Exilic dislocation as disjunction from the divine has much older roots in the expulsion from Eden, when Adam was removed from the immediate presence of Shekhinah and his cleaving to it came to an end. This expulsion resulted from the Original Sin, which, together with the emergence of human autonomy, ruined the primordial harmony shared by humanity and the Godhead.[49] The parallelism between the expulsion from the Garden and exile from the land appears in the very first comment of Nahmanides's Commentary on the Bible, which opens with the well-known midrashic question of R. Yitzhak cited by Rashi: Why does the Torah begin with the creation of the universe instead of the first commandment in the Torah, "This month shall be for you" (Exod 12:2)? The question presupposes the marginal value of the nonhalakhic components of tradition and assigns primacy to the Torah's commandments. Nahmanides rejects this simple understanding of the question: "One can ask about it [this Aggadah] that there is great need to begin the Torah with 'In the beginning, God created Heaven and Earth' (Gen 1:1), because it is the root of faith . . .!"[50] From his point of view, what justifies the question is not the demotion of theology and history in favor of the law; quite the contrary, the creation of the universe is an esoteric subject of utmost importance, which is why it should not be put in writing at all: "the Account of Creation is a profound secret that cannot be understood from the verses, nor can it be truly known except by way of the tradition [stretching back] to our master Moses from the mouth of the Almighty, and those who know it are obligated to conceal it."[51] Rashi took R. Yitzhak to be saying that the Torah begins with the creation narrative in order to establish God's title to the universe, which justifies his eviction of the Canaanites from Canaan and his granting it to the Israelites. Nahmanides presents an alternative reading of R. Yitzhak's statement, which draws upon his understanding of geographical location and his broad historiosophical view:

> But R. Yitzhak gave a reason for this. Because the Torah began with "In the beginning, God created" (Gen 1:1) and the narrative of the entire creation until the creation of man, and that He put him in charge over His handiwork and placed everything beneath his feet, and the Garden of Eden, which is the choicest place created in this world, was made his residence, until his sin expelled him from there; the diluvial generation were expelled from the entire world due to their sin, only the innocent man among them and his sons surviving; and the sin of their offspring led to their dispersal in various places and

their scattering throughout the lands, and they seized the lands they came across for the clans of their people—since this is so, it is fitting for a people to lose its territory when it continues to sin and for another nation to inherit its land, for such has always been God's judgment on the earth. This is all the more true given that Scripture relates that Canaan is cursed and sold as an everlasting slave, and is not fit to inherit the choicest place in the ecumene; instead, the servants of the Lord, the offspring of His beloved, will inherit it, as in the import of the verse: "He gave them the lands of peoples and they inherit the toil of nations, so that they keep His laws and observe His instructions" (Ps 105:44–45). In other words, He expelled those who rebelled against Him and settled his servants there, so that they would know that they would possess it by serving Him, [but] if they would sin against Him the land would spew them out, as it had spewed out the people before them.[52]

Nahmanides does not read R. Yitzhak's response as a demonstration of God's sovereignty over the world as its Creator, but as setting up a paradigm of exile throughout the narrative cycles of Genesis: Adam is exiled from Eden, the diluvial generation is expunged from the entire world, the generation of the dispersion is scattered in every direction. The Garden of Eden and land of Israel are the "choicest places," which means that the privilege of inhabiting them is both temporary and conditional. Elsewhere, Nahmanides sets up a parallel between the Garden of Eden and the land of Israel.[53] This emerges from his climatic and kabbalistic theories, which consider these locations to be the center of the ecumene, meaning that they are places where Shekhinah is directly present, and the symbolic transparency of the space facilitates prophecy and contemplation.

This entry, exit, and return to the chosen land, which dictates not only the biography of the Patriarchs but Jewish history in general, is in effect an iteration of the basic tension revealed in the fate of Adam, who was disconnected from his primordial cleaving and expelled from "the choicest place." This fall had an existentially deeper source in the divine drama: Adam fell from his state of cleaving to Shekhinah and became an individualized being at precisely the same time as the great intradivine crisis occurred in which Shekhinah fell from its state of harmony with Tif'eret.[54] Jewish history similarly reflects this rupture: the detachment of the Jews from the Godhead, and from Shekhinah in particular, parallels the detachment of Shekhinah from the

Godhead, and from Tif'eret in particular. Human estrangement from the immediate divine presence is also estrangement of the Godhead from itself. Nahmanides thus has an entire set of correspondences that solidifies the link between the divine plane in which God is estranged from himself, the human plane in which Adam falls from his original state of cleaving, and the historical drama of expulsion from the best place on earth.

IV

The weakest link in the divine structure, which has from the dawn of time been in peril of becoming distanced and estranged from the rest of the Godhead, is Shekhinah. Nahmanides characterizes its fragile relationship with the other sefirot as unification "in potentia but not in actu."[55] Shekhinah first experienced "exile" when it fell from its primeval harmony with Tif'eret, which occurred simultaneously with Adam's disjunction from the Godhead. Shekhinah went deeper and farther into "exile" when the Jewish people were exiled from the land of Israel. Nahmanides explains the verse "For I raise My Hand [i.e., Shekhinah] to Heaven [i.e., Tif'eret]" (Deut 32:40), in which God expresses his oath to redeem the Jewish people, as referring to the divine drama between two sefirot:

> But by way of truth, since at the time of exile "the Splendor (*Tif'eret*) of Israel cast Earth [i.e., *Shekhinah*] from Heaven [i.e., *Tif'eret*]" (Eccl 2:1), He says that now, at a propitious time, He will raise it, the Great Hand that fights for Israel, to the Supernal Heaven. This is the meaning of [the latter half of the verse] "and I say, 'I Live forever' " (Deut 32:40), because I sustain my Strong Hand by whetting the flashing Blade and support it to lay hold on the Justice of Israel and take revenge upon My enemies, for then the Name will be complete and the Throne complete. The enlightened will understand.[56]

The "Great Hand" signifies Shekhinah,[57] which is lifted to the Supernal Heaven, to Tif'eret, after being cast down during the period of Jewish exile. Shekhinah's plummet from and eventual rise back to Tif'eret is the divine parallel to the trough of exile and crest of redemption in Jewish history.[58]

The pendulum of history swings from hardship to salvation and back in tandem with the complex movement between Shekhinah and Tif'eret. What distinguishes the redemption from Egypt from the future redemption is the extent and quality of Shekhinah's connection to Tif'eret:

"And the Lord (*va-Y-HWH*) went before them by day" (Exod 13:21).
They [the Sages] have already said that wherever it says "and the Lord
(*va-Y-HWH*)" [it means] He and His Court [i.e., *Shekhinah*], in which
case the verse means that the Lord abides in the cloud and goes before
them during the day in the pillar of cloud, and at night His Court
abides in the pillar of fire to illuminate [the way] for them. [. . .] I have
seen in *Shemot Rabbah:* " 'For you will not go out in haste . . . because
the Lord goes before you' (Isa 52:12)—in the past [it was] I and My
Court, as it says, 'And the Lord went before them by day,' I and My
Court; but in the future [it will be] I alone, as it says, 'because the Lord
goes before you etc.' (ibid.)." The secret of this *midrash* is as I have
mentioned, namely, that during the first redemption the Holy One
was with them during the day and His Court was with them at night,
but in the future His Attribute of Judgment will ascend to [the Attribute of] Mercy, and the Unique Name will go before them, because
the God of Jacob will gather them with it, "and night will be as bright
as day, darkness will be like light" (Ps 139:12), because the All (*Ha-Kol*)
will be unified with the Attribute of Mercy.[59]

According to Nahmanides, "the Court of the Lord" represents the Attribute
of Judgment, which is Shekhinah.[60] During the Egyptian exodus, Shekhinah
was still disjoined from Tif'eret, so Tif'eret led the way during the day and
Shekhinah did so at night. In the future redemption, the Attribute of
Judgment will ascend to the Attribute of Mercy, that is, Shekhinah will rise
up into Tif'eret, the Unique Name. This explains why the verse about the
future redemption has no conjunctive *vav* prefixed to the Tetragrammaton:
"because the Lord (Y-HWH) goes before you and the God of Israel will gather
you" (Isa 52:12). Tif'eret gathers them together with Shekhinah now that
Shekhinah has ascended to it. The overflowing power and superabundant
Lovingkindness of the Godhead appears in this redemption without any intermediation, in contrast to the redemption from Egypt, when Tif'eret had a
significant presence yet the divine harmony remained incomplete.[61] The future redemption will see Shekhinah's reassumption of its original, harmonious
position at the same level as Tif'eret, which signifies the return of the Jewish
people to "the choicest place," and the return of humanity to its primordial
state of cleaving.

In line with this correspondence between history and the intradivine
dynamic, Nahmanides distinguishes the First Temple from the Second. The

repatriation from Babylon was partial, as it included a small fraction of exiled Jews, and even those returnees did not enjoy true independence. According to rabbinic sources, the Second Temple itself lacked the miraculous signs of divine presence that had been present in the First Temple. Nahmanides formulates the difference between the First, Second, and future Third Temples in terms of Shekhinah's presence and its relationship to Tif'eret. He maps these onto his kabbalistic reading of the blessing Moses gave to the tribe of Benjamin: "Of Benjamin he said, 'The Beloved of the Lord shall abide securely upon him; it hovers over him all day long; and abides in his midst' " (Deut 33:12). In Nahmanides's kabbalistic lexicon of symbols, the "Beloved" is Shekhinah, and "the Lord" is Tif'eret, so he sees in this verse three states of Shekhinah's presence in the territory of Benjamin, in whose inheritance fell the Temple grounds:

> It is correct that these three [degrees of] abiding allude to the Temples. Concerning the First Temple it says, "shall abide securely upon him," as in the import of the verse, "and the Glory of the Lord filled the house of the Lord" (cf. 2 Chr 7:1 and 1 Kgs 8:10). About the Second Temple it says, "hovers over him all day long," since *Shekhinah* did not abide upon it but only covered and protected it, or literally hovered [. . .] [The clause] "and abides in his midst" is for the Days of the Messiah, for on that day "they will call Jerusalem 'the Throne of the Lord' " (Jer 3:17).[62]

The different degrees of closeness depicted in this verse between "the Beloved of the Lord," that is, Shekhinah, and Benjamin allude to historical realities. In the First Temple era, Shekhinah rested upon the Temple; in the Second Temple era, it only hovered over it.[63] In the messianic era, it will rest in the midst of the Third Temple and Jerusalem will be called "the Throne of the Lord," because it will house Shekhinah, which is the Throne of Tif'eret.[64]

Humans' fate as a reflection of the drama between Tif'eret and Shekhinah is expressed not only in the broad historiosophy of exile and redemption, but also in less monumental instances of divine retribution. Sodom and Gomorrah is one such example:

> The Lord said, "The outrage of Sodom and Gomorrah is so great, and their sin so grave! I will go down to see whether they have acted altogether according to the Cry [i.e., *Shekhinah*] that has reached Me [i.e., *Tif'eret*]; if not, I will know" (Gen 18:20–21).

Nahmanides explains this as referring to different aspects of the Godhead:

> I shall allude to you the opinion of those recipients of the truth. Our Rabbis expounded on the verse, "For behold the Lord leaves His place to descend and tread upon the high places of the Land" (Mic 1:3)—He shifts back and forth from Attribute to Attribute; He goes from the Attribute of Mercy and enters the Attribute of Judgment. This is the case here too: "The Lord said" to His Heart, "the outrage of Sodom and Gomorrah is great, I shall descend in the Attribute of Mercy to the Attribute of Judgment and look through Mercy: if they acted according to the Cry that has reached me through the Attribute of Judgment—obliteration; and if not, I shall know and have Mercy," as in, "and God knew" (Exod 2:25).[65]

According to Nahmanides's interpretation, Tif'eret, signified by the Name of Being, descends down to the Attribute of Judgment, to Shekhinah, to investigate the outcry.[66] The internal dialogue of the Godhead—"The Lord said to His Heart"—is explained as Tif'eret, "the Lord," addressing Shekhinah, "His Heart."[67] Abraham, unaware of the divine drama unfolding within the Godhead, believes that the people of Sodom are liable to be judged solely through the Attribute of Judgment, which is why he is concerned that it might act independently of the Attribute of Mercy and indiscriminately obliterate the guilty and the innocent: "The Anger (ha-Af) of the Holy One is His Attribute of Judgment, and Abraham thought that it would sweep away the innocent with the guilty, because he did not know that the Lord was considering them with His Mercy, as I explained. He therefore said that it would be good and right if He could forgive the entire place on account of the fifty innocents."[68] Abraham's entreaty demonstrates his not being privy to God's inner workings. In fact, he even has a mistaken conception of what would happen if the Attribute of Judgment were to punish alone:

> Even through the Attribute of Judgment, however, it would be impossible to kill the innocent with the guilty, because then the innocent would be like the guilty, and people would say, "serving God is worthless" (Mal 3:14). This is all the more true for the Attribute of Mercy, which is the Judge of All (Kol), the Earth, and metes out Justice, as in the import [of the verse], "And the Lord of Hosts is elevated in Justice" (Isa 5:16), and when we say [in the silent devotion] "the King, the Justice." This is also the meaning of the repetition of "Far be it

from You" (Gen 18:25). The Holy One agreed to forgive the entire place because he would govern them through the Attribute of Mercy. The fact that when God speaks it is written with "the Lord," *yod he* [the Tetragrammaton], but Abraham consistently mentions *aleph dalet* [*Elohim*], should tell you everything you need to know about this matter. This is clear.[69]

God does not, in fact, collectively punish the innocent along with the guilty, meaning that the charge of injustice—"Will the Anger sweep away the innocent with the guilty?"—has no legs to stand on. Additionally, Tif'eret, the Attribute of Mercy, takes part in judgment and actually tilts the scales of justice in favor of the guilty on account of the innocent. So, the connection between Tif'eret and the activity of Shekhinah determines humans' fate as one of strict judgment or mercy.

This passage is of great significance for the question of the source of evil and the degree of dualism in Nahmanides's kabbalistic conception of Judgment and Mercy. The independent activity of the Attribute of Judgment does not create a state of evil. Judgment working on its own acts as it ought to and does not kill the innocent along with the guilty. Tif'eret's involvement tilts Judgment toward Lovingkindness and does not set right any apparent injustice perpetrated by Shekhinah's independent activity. The shift between "God" when Abraham is speaking and "the Lord" when God is speaking signifies a shift from Judgment to Mercy. Divine providence comes in many forms, each of which depends on the degree of closeness between Tif'eret and Shekhinah.[70]

In other places, Nahmanides refers back to this kabbalistic interpretation of Gen 18:20–21, in which Shekhinah cries out to Tif'eret and the latter descends to Shekhinah to participate in judgment. On the verse "the Cry of the Children of Israel has reached Me" (Exod 3:9), Nahmanides writes: "By way of truth, the Cry of the Children of Israel is the Congregation of Israel [i.e., *Shekhinah*] which came crying out to Him, in the manner of [the verse] 'the Cry that has reached Me' (Gen 18:21), which I alluded to there."[71] The cry of the Israelites, which in the context of the verse simply means the cry of the oppressed Israelites under Egyptian oppression, is explained as Shekhinah itself coming and crying to Tif'eret. The speaker in this verse is "the Lord," the sefirah of Tif'eret, which is aroused to redemptive action by Shekhinah.[72]

Tif'eret's estrangement from Shekhinah because of the sins of humans abandons them to the sole dominion of the Attribute of Judgment, which brings punishment untempered by Lovingkindness and Mercy. Nahmanides explains the verse "The Lord was angry at His Heart" (Gen 6:6) as relating to two levels of the Godhead—"the Lord" and "His Heart"—and expresses the self-alienation of God from himself, that is, the distancing of Shekhinah from Tif'eret: "In *Bereshit Rabbah* they said an important idea about this through the parable[s] of the architect and the broker. It is a great secret that cannot be written down, and whoever knows it comprehends why it says the Unique Name here, whereas throughout the entire pericope and the flood [it has] the name 'God' (*Elohim*)."[73] The Unique Name, Tif'eret, is angry at "His Heart," Shekhinah.[74] The decoupling of Tif'eret and Shekhinah leaves the punishment of humans in the hands of Shekhinah alone, Judgment undiluted and unsoftened by Lovingkindness and Mercy. This explains the presence of the name of godship, Elohim, indicative of Shekhinah, in the flood narrative. When God is said to "Remember," usually as a result of a human petition for mercy from the Holy One, Nahmanides imagines this as God overcoming his self-estrangement. God, one could say, remembers his own "flesh and blood," or, more technically, Tif'eret returns to Shekhinah. This is how Nahmanides explains the appearance of the rainbow in the cloud, and the covenant God made with Noah that there would not be another flood:

> If you merit understanding their [the Sages'] words, then you know that the explanation of the verse is as follows: "My Bow," which is the [Weak] Attribute of Judgment placed in the cloud at a time of judgment, shall be [together with] the Sign of the Covenant, "And it shall be when I becloud the Earth with a cloud" (Gen 9:14), such that the Lord does not radiate His Countenance [i.e., *Tif'eret*] upon it [the Earth, i.e., *Shekhinah*] due to the sins of its inhabitants, the Attribute of Judgment "will appear" in the cloud, and I shall remember the Covenant through the Remembrance of Mercy, and I shall take pity upon the children that are on the earth.[75]

In Nahmanides's kabbalistic symbolism, divine "Remembrance" is an act of self-unification, it represents aspects of the Godhead interacting with one another and coming together. In a way, this idea of memory anticipated philosophical ideas of how a coherent sense of self is constructed. Memory strings together discrete events occurring at different times into a continuous flow tied to a particular self. It calls the diverse aspects of the self, some spurned or repressed, to the attention of one's consciousness. This understanding of memory appears in Nahmanides's comment on the verse "I shall remember

My covenant Jacob, and even My covenant Isaac, and even My covenant Abraham I shall Remember, and I shall Remember the Land" (Lev 26:42). R. Abraham Ibn Ezra already noted the grammatical difficulty presented by the phrase "My covenant Jacob," implying as it does that the covenant is Jacob, and so interprets it to mean that God will recall an event from the past—God shall remember "My covenant, the covenant of Jacob," and so with Isaac and Abraham. Nahmanides offers a kabbalistic interpretation of the verse that does not require these interpolations: "It is possible that by way of truth it is saying, 'I shall Remember Jacob, Isaac, and Abraham which are Covenantors,' for all of the Attributes are so called by being in the Covenant, 'and the Land,' which comprises them, 'I shall Remember' through the All (*Ba-Kol*)."[76] This kabbalistic interpretation fits the syntax perfectly, because it reads: "I shall Remember My Covenant, Jacob," that is, not the covenant with Jacob but the Covenant, the Attribute referred to as Jacob. Thus, "Jacob," "Isaac," and "Abraham" are understood as cognomens for the sefirot of Tif'eret, Gevurah, and Hesed, respectively. "Covenant" is a general term for a sefirah, and when God remembers the sefirot, including "the Land," Shekhinah, it brings redemption. Recall is first and foremost God looking at his complete self by unifying its estranged, alienated aspects, which initiates the process of return.

V

Beyond the theosophy and meta-history, Nahmanides's historical worldview draws upon the Franco-German one, to which he adds his own experiences, exquisite literary sensitivity, and attention to linguistic nuance. As we have seen above, Nahmanides uses the "Days of the World" typology to demonstrate correspondences between the Levitical covenant and the Babylonian exile, and between the Deuteronomic covenant and the Roman exile. He continues this work by drawing on his own historical experiences to serve as a kind of *pesher* (key) of certain pericopes in his Commentary on the Torah, whose meaning he believed to have become clear only after their historical realization.

The core of the historical worldview shaped in Franco-Germany consisted of Jewish suffering under the yoke of Christianity and the messianic expectation of the final act in the drama in Jewish history, in which the tables would be turned and the day would come when God would redeem Israel from its Christian oppressors. Nahmanides internalized this Franco-German tradition, which constituted its historical experience as the realization of the Jacob-Esau typology, and identified Christianity as the successor of the Roman Empire and Rome with Edom, and thus with Esau.[77] The clash between Judaism and Christianity was viewed as a reincarnation of the rivalry and hatred between Esau and Jacob. Nahmanides writes:

> Know that we rely upon the opinion of our Rabbis and so believe that today we are in the exile of Edom and that we will not rise out of it until the Messiah comes. As our elderly Patriarch said, "and it shall be when you are distraught" (Gen 27:40). We similarly expound "I shall fill the desolate one" (Ezek 26:2), and we have a complete verse [attesting to this]: "And saviors shall ascend Mount Zion to judge the Mountain of Esau, and the Kingdom shall be the Lord's" (Obad 1:21).[78]

The typological identification of Christianity with Edom and Esau establishes a pattern of relationships that generates an inverted mirror image of Christian theology.[79] Christians argue that the humiliation and subjugation of the Jewish people are a fundamental demonstration of the correctness of Christianity. Nahmanides, adopting the Franco-German typology, pins the redemption of the Jewish people to the downfall of Christianity; its collapse is at the forefront of messianic hopes and will establish the Lord's "Throne" in this world. Nahmanides has good cause to reference the rabbinic homily (Megillah 6a) on Ezek 26:2 in the passage above: "If someone tells you they are both destroyed, do not believe [it]; both inhabited, do not believe [it]; Caesarea desolate and Jerusalem inhabited, [or] Jerusalem desolate and Caesarea inhabited, believe [it], as it says 'I shall fill the desolate one' (Ezek 26:2)—if this one is full that one is desolate, if that one is full this one is desolate." In accordance with Franco-German typology, Nahmanides transposes this grim picture of the relationship between the Jewish people and Rome onto Judaism and Christianity. The two religions live out a historical drama that is a zero-sum game, in which, as if on a seesaw, the fall of one means the other must rise. This typology reappears in sharp form in Nahmanides's comment on the Israelite war against Amalek:

> Perhaps Moses feared that it [Amalek] might be victorious through its sword, because it was a nation who inherited the sword from the blessing of the old man [i.e., Isaac], who said to it, "You shall live by your sword" (Gen 27:40). War with this clan is the first and last for Israel, because Amalek is Esau's offspring, and he gave us battle as the leading

nation, and from Esau's progeny came our last exile and destruction [of the Temple], as our Rabbis say that today we are in the exile of Edom. And when he is vanquished and weakened, he and the many nations with him, we will be forever saved, as it said, "And saviors shall ascend Mount Zion to judge the Mountain of Esau, and the Kingdom shall be the Lord's" (Obad 1:21). Everything Moses and Joshua did with them in the first [encounter] will be done by Elijah and Messiah son of Joseph with their [Amalek's] descendants, which is why Moses exerted himself in the matter.[80]

The line in Sefer ha-Ge'ulah appears here as well—"our Rabbis say that today we are in the exile of Edom"—as does the Esau-Jacob typology, but Nahmanides adds an additional component. The first battle fought by Moses and Joshua against Amalek prefigures the ultimate battle fought by Elijah and Messiah ben Joseph against the kingdom of Edom—Christianity.[81] As explained earlier in the chapter, Nahmanides believes that typological prefigurations work causally, which explains Moses's conscious attempt to forge the necessary talismanic structure that would mold the future, ultimate confrontation in the Jews' favor.[82]

Placing the antagonism between Judaism and Christianity at the center of Jewish history and messianic hopes is characteristic of the Franco-German historical consciousness. Jews of the Islamicate painted an utterly different portrait of Jewish history. Ibn Ezra and Maimonides identified the fourth beast in Daniel's vision with Islam, which had tremendous ramifications for their view of history.[83] Since Jewish tradition reads Daniel's vision as a code for apocalyptic events, the identification of the final, fourth beast that would be defeated by the messiah is not some triviality. In the Middle Ages, the Jewish people found themselves in two different exiles, one Christian and one Muslim, and a question of great significance was which Jewry would be at the center of events as the final drama played out, and which would be a side story in that great, historic narrative. It should be of no surprise to learn that a particular author's geopolitical location and his conception of eschatological history usually were congruent.

Nahmanides's Franco-German predecessors who developed the typology identifying Esau with Christianity did not have a rich, direct discourse with Jews of the Islamicate. Nahmanides, as we saw in Chapter 2, had a uniquely synoptic view of twelfth-century Jewish cultures and their literary output, which influenced him greatly in his halakhic writing, religious philosophy, and scriptural exegesis. Here, too, he consolidated his account of history by comparing it with the historical narrative that flourished among Jews under Islamic rule. From his vantage point, he could see that someone's particular historical experience would affect their identification of the center of the religious drama. Like the Torah scholars of Franco-Germany, he identified Daniel's fourth beast with Rome: "the fourth beast that Daniel saw was Rome, which has exiled us and will be destroyed by the Messiah."[84] Further in the same piece, when Nahmanides tries to solidify this apocalyptic identification by sorting out the details, he makes the following comment about Ibn Ezra's identification of the fourth beast with the kingdom of Ishmael, namely, Islam:

> But Rabbi Abraham got this wrong and introduced the kingdom of Ishmael into them [i.e., the count of beasts] because it terrified him, so he argued: "How could such a great and mighty kingdom not be counted?" He made this claim out of ignorance—the four kingdoms Daniel saw rose in succession [. . .] It is known that Rome exiled us in the days of Vespasian and Titus, and not the Ishmaelites; therefore, wherever we may be, in Ishmael [the Islamicate] or even anywhere from India to Ethiopia, we are in the Roman exile, until its memory is obliterated and we are redeemed from it. Who knows, perhaps the kingdom of Ishmael will yet be destroyed before the Messiah! Rather, the fourth beast is the one which exiled us.[85]

Nahmanides considers the identification of Daniel's fourth beast with Islamic rule as an incorrect interpretation of Daniel's vision, a delusion of the despairing souls suffering under its grip. Had he been asked, Ibn Ezra probably would have made a similar diagnosis about the Franco-German typology. He did at least provide reasonable support for his opinion by claiming that since Greeks and Romans come from the same ethnic stock, the Kittim, they together make up one kingdom symbolized by the third beast. Nahmanides, however, does not subject his own historical outlook to the same criticism, and in his long polemic with Ibn Ezra's commentary on the identity of the fourth beast he argues that the kingdom of Ishmael is mentioned in Daniel's great apocalyptic drama as a kind of side point: "there is no trace of the kingdom of the Ishmaelites and their land in the words of Daniel aside from his reference to the southern king who is king of Egypt."[86] Beside the differences separating the Jewish communities of Christendom from those of the Islamicate with respect to halakhah and philosophy, Nahmanides's lengthy polemic against Ibn Ezra on the identity of the fourth beast highlights a profound historiosophical disagreement. To the array of existing cultural conflicts, we can now add their debate over which of the two Jewish diasporas would play the leading role in the eschatological drama. Each side amplified the threat of its own polity and muted the other's. Nahmanides and Ibn Ezra saw the unique history of their own exilic communities in Daniel's vision and positioned their own experiences at the center of the Jewish eschatological drama.

Nahmanides was aware of the significant historical problems with the Franco-German typology. After all is said and done, the Romans did not descend directly from Edom, and Christianity did not arise from Edom or from the pagan Roman Empire that destroyed the Temple and exiled the Jewish people. The Christians themselves leveled these difficulties at the Jewish typological identification of Rome with Edom, and they are what led to the reimagining of Roman history in Sefer Yosippon. By way of a convoluted narrative, the author injects Edomite blood into the beginning of the Roman genealogical line, in order to literally flesh out the typological identification of Edom with Rome.[87] In this version of history, which was well known in Franco-Germany, the midrashic typology of Edom-Rome followed a real bloodline. The Christianization of the Roman Empire during Constantine's reign extended the Edom-Rome typology by creating the Rome-Christianity connection, and by the associative principle Christianity became the successor of Edom.

Nahmanides dealt with this problem of the apparent ethnic discontinuity between Edom and Christianity in another way. He preserved the original Roman descent from the Kittim and forged the direct ethnic link between the Edomites and Christianity:

> The main intention in this is that the Edomites were the first to stray after the man who claimed he was the messiah, and they claimed divinity for him. They came to the land of Edom, and their error spread to nearby Rome. It became established there in the days of King Constantine by the Edomite-Roman who established for them the stratagems for the dominion of the bishop of Rome and their faith in him [the papacy]. The cause and root are the essence of everything; therefore Rome and Edom are considered one kingdom even though they are different nations. Due to all of this, they are kin and all have become one people with one land, owing to the fact they are of one mind.[88]

According to this story of Nahmanides's making, Christianity first spread among the Edomites. Moreover, the Edomites introduced Christology into Christianity by claiming godhood for the messiah. Unlike Sefer Yosippon's author, who linked the Edomites and Romans, in this passage Nahmanides makes the connection between the Edomites and the earliest Christians. Once the Roman Empire became Christian after Constantine's conversion at the hands of the bishop of Rome, the Edom-Rome-Christian circle was closed. Nahmanides did not use the traditional order of the midrashic typology for good reason. In his time, the Roman Empire was no longer the nemesis it had been in rabbinic literature, and the chief antagonist of the Jewish people was now Christianity, making the Edom-Christianity connection much more important than the Edom-Rome one. By placing Edomites at the forefront of nascent Christianity, Nahmanides transforms the Jewish-Christian rivalry into a direct ethnic continuation of the fraternal struggle between Jacob and Esau.[89] The allegorical typology that constituted the historical connection between Christianity and Judaism was solidified by a direct bloodline, in Nahmanides's telling of it.[90]

In his Commentary on the Torah, Nahmanides integrates into these lachrymose typologies quite a bit of the complex reality of the Jewish experience under the shadow of Christianity. According to him, Jacob's division of his party into two camps, in the hope that one would survive, prefigured the Jewish experience under medieval Christian rule: "This also hints that Esau's progeny will not decree the obliteration of our name but will commit terrible acts against some of us in some of their lands—one of their kings makes a decree in his land concerning our money or persons, while another king is merciful in his domain and saves the remnant."[91] Nahmanides does not ignore the Augustinian witness doctrine, which was intended to ensure the physical survival of the Jews and therefore prohibited killing them.[92] This condition serves as a springboard for a typological explanation of Jacob's behavior in advance of Esau's approach. In another context, Nahmanides even describes the temporary prosperity of the Jews in Christian Spain:

> But since we are exiles in the lands of our enemies our handiwork has not been cursed, nor the calving of our herd or the lambing of our flock, nor our vineyards, olive groves, or our plantings in the field; in fact, in the [diasporic] lands we are like the rest of the inhabitants or better off than they, for His mercy is upon us. [This is] because our stay in exile comes with the promise He said to us: "Yet, even then,

when they are in the land of their enemies, I will not reject them or spurn them so as to destroy them, annulling My Covenant [i.e., *Shekhinah*] with them: for I the Lord am their God" (Lev 26:44). In the Torah portion of *Im Be-Hukkotai,* I already explained the secret of this covenant, and how it applies to the period of our present exile under the dominion of the fourth beast. Afterwards, He promises redemption from it.[93]

The presence of Shekhinah, the "secret of this Covenant" to which Nahmanides refers, in the midst of the Jewish exile explains their seemingly inexplicable, even if only relative, prosperity in hostile lands. Nahmanides believed the days of this unstable condition were numbered, and in Sefer ha-Ge'ulah he thought he foresaw the dawn of redemption coming a few decades after the sun would set on his life.

VI

In Sefer ha-Ge'ulah, Nahmanides's broad meta-historical vision meets his own historical experience. He wrote this work of messianic calculation around the beginning of the sixth millennium, which according to the Jewish calendar begins in the year 1240, which saw heightened messianic expectation. Some of this grew out of the structural parallelism between the days of creation and the millennia counted since creation. If humans were created at the beginning of the sixth day, the redeemer would come at the beginning of the sixth millennium.[94] In 1240, Nahmanides was forty-six years old, at the height of his powers and productivity, and recognized as the leader of his generation. The beginning of the sixth millennium disappointed all those who had hung their hopes upon it, and Nahmanides wrote Sefer ha-Ge'ulah sometime after the rumored messiah failed to materialize. Despite the disillusionment, Nahmanides was a product of his time, and his calculations remain anchored to the beginning of the sixth millennium. Like quite a few contemporaries whose calculations served as precedents, he was convinced that he lived during the beginning of the End, as the terrible fourth beast, the empire of Christian Edom, breathed its last. His sense of the impending End was his justification for revealing its date:

Before we open our mouth to speak about the End, we must extricate ourselves from what the Sages said: "May those who calculate the End of Days be cursed." I say that the intent in this is what we have said, that some of them knew that the End would come a long time after them, like they said to R. Akiva: "Grass will grow in your jawbones and still the son of David will not have come," and they did not want the matter to be revealed to the masses lest it dash already frail hopes. But these arguments do not apply to us now because we are in the End of Days, and because other coreligionists have already written books about this. Therefore, it is not detrimental to the people when we also speak our mind about this matter.[95]

The ancient curse on those who calculate the End is not because the correct date is unknown and any calculation can only lead to deflated hopes; on the contrary, it is because those who know the End should not reveal it until it is imminent. The Sages prohibited revealing the End not because hopes will be dashed if an incorrect date is given, but in order to preserve false hope when the correct date is nowhere near the horizon.

This circular argument that one may reveal the End because it is nigh must have come from a high degree of confidence that it was fast approaching. This confidence, in turn, rested upon another tier of circular reasoning, namely, that in the end of times the signs of its arrival become clearer. God conceals the true date of the End from those who seek it when it is far off: better for speculators to crunch numbers and come up with an erroneous date in the near future than to be told the crushing, bitter truth that it is still centuries, if not millennia, away. The greatest Jewish leaders failed in their calculations because the End of Days was yet in the distant future, but as it nears one can discern its aura:

> since we must be closer than they [the Sages] to the End, and perhaps even really close given the long duration of the exile that has already passed, perhaps the decree decreed upon him [Daniel] to conceal it has lapsed, because the underlying reason for it is null, namely, that "it pertains to far-off days" (Dan 8:26). Because he said "many will wander (*yeshotetu*) and knowledge will increase" (Dan 12:4), it is hinted to us from here that we may contemplate (*le-shotet*) the End in this book and increase the opinions about it. When he says, "but the enlightened will understand" (Dan 12:10), we learn that when the End approaches, the enlightened will understand these hints.[96]

Nahmanides singled out the 118th year of the sixth millennium, 1358, as the year in which Messiah son of Joseph would appear, heralding the beginning of the End of Days. Forty-five years later, in 1403, Messiah son of David would come. Nahmanides arrived at these dates by combining allusions from Daniel's vision. He understood the verse "From the time the regular offering is abolished" (Dan 12:1) as indicating the coming of Messiah son of Joseph. Since the Second Temple was destroyed in 68 CE and the "days" in this verse indicate years, "1,290 days" yields 1358. A different verse produces a different number: "Happy is the one who waits and reaches 1,335 days" (Dan 12:12). This alludes to the additional forty-five years that would elapse between the advents of Messiah son of Joseph and Messiah son of David.[97] Not only does this year fit these and other allusions in Daniel, but it has an internal justification that makes it even more compelling. The arrival of the messiah in this year would make the number of years endured in exile equal to the number of years lived in the land of Israel—1,289 years.[98] This makes the punishment of the Jewish people condign; for every year enjoyed in the land, they must suffer a corresponding year in exile. The forty-five years between the appearance of each messiah parallel the forty years in the wilderness, and since these were preparatory years, they count neither toward the years in the land nor to the years in exile. The five-year discrepancy corresponds to the five years it took the Israelites to purify the land and apportion it to the tribes under the leadership of Joshua.[99]

The particular circumstances that led to the writing of Sefer ha-Ge'ulah and its intended audience remain unknown. Since long sections of it appear to be stitched together from pieces lifted verbatim from Nahmanides's Commentary on the Torah, which is also the case in his expository discourses, one can reasonably assume he wrote it after the first edition of that commentary. Perhaps he wrote it for a restricted audience, and, indeed, only a few manuscripts of the work survive (although it is easy to understand why it would not have been copied after 1358). Whatever the case may be, Nahmanides clearly felt the impending End in his bones, because he did not hold back from revealing its date in his Torah commentary, the only one of his works that we can confidently assume was intended for a very broad readership. In the comment where he reveals the date of the End, one can see a profound parallel between his consciousness of the immediacy of the End of Days, which would begin a few decades after his demise, and his larger historiosophical worldview. The enumeration of the final date, at the year 5118 from creation, appears at the end of his excursus on the typology of the "Days of the World," which connects Nature, the sefirot, and history. Nahmanides understands the fifth Day of the World to signify the domination of the nations and exile:

On the fifth day, "the waters brought forth swarms of living creatures, and birds that fly above the earth" (Gen 1:20). This is an allusion to the fifth millennium that begins 172 years after the destruction [of the Second Temple], because for its duration the nations shall rule. Mankind becomes "like the fish of the sea, like creeping things that have no ruler. He has fished them all up with a line, pulled them up in his trawl, and gathered them in his net" (Hab 1:14–15), but no one seeks the Lord.

On the morning of the sixth day, "Let the earth bring forth every kind of living creature: herbivores and carnivores of every kind" (Gen 1:24), and their creation preceded the sunrise, like it is written, "When the sun rises, they slink away and couch in their dens" (Ps 104:22). Then, man was created in the image of God, and this is the time of his dominion, as it says: "Man goes out to his work and to his labor until the evening" (Ps 104:23). This is the sixth millennium, because at its onset the carnivores, the kingdoms "that did not know the Lord" (Judg 2:10), rule. But after a tenth of it, corresponding to the time it takes the sun to rise, the redeemer will come, about whom it is written, "his throne is like the sun before Me" (Ps 89:37)—the son of David, who is made in the divine image, as it is written: "Someone like a human being came with clouds of heaven; he reached the Ancient of Days and was presented to Him. Dominion, glory, and kingship were given to him" (Dan 7:13–14). This will occur 118 years after five millennia, fulfilling the word of the Lord from the mouth of Daniel: "From the time the regular offering is abolished until the abomination is devastated will be 1290 years" (Dan 12:1).

The shift between the days, from the aquatic swarms and birds to the terrestrial animals, demonstrates that at the beginning of the sixth millennium there will arise a new empire, a dominant, powerful, and exceedingly terrifying nation, which will be closer to the truth than the preceding ones were.

The seventh day, the Sabbath, is an allusion to the World to Come, which is entirely a Sabbath and repose of eternal life.[100]

On the basis of the doctrine of cosmic cycles and his millenarian outlook, Nahmanides continues the typological connection between Adam and Messiah son of David made in the image of God and identifies the beginning of the sixth millennium as the End of Days. Based on the typology that sees the carnivorous beasts as the dominion of the kingdoms and the creation of humans as the messiah's advent, this piece explains why the redemption did not come immediately at the beginning of the sixth millennium in 1240, as a number of Nahmanides's predecessors had calculated it would. According to Nahmanides, the beasts were created at daybreak, whereas Adam was created later at sunrise.[101] Using the calculation found in tractate Pesahim 94a, the time between daybreak and sunrise is a tenth of the day; therefore, humans were created one hundred years after the sixth millennium, and perhaps it took a bit of time for them to find their feet. This explains why the redeemer tarries a little more than a hundred years after 1240. By paying close attention to the typological millenarian structure, Nahmanides is able to delay the date of the End long enough for the sun to rise. In summary, he joins his eschatological calculations based on Daniel to the typology that emerges from the doctrine of cosmic cycles, such that the prediction is for Messiah son of Joseph to be revealed 118 years after the beginning of the sixth millennium.

The End of Days comprises three stages: the Jewish people return to their land, humans return to their prelapsarian state of cleaving to the Godhead, and the Godhead returns to a state of unity in actu. All of these, however, Nahmanides believes are but the echo of the glacially paced divine inhalation. Our analysis of the esoteric component of his historical thinking has revealed a disconnect between viewing the unfolding of history as a reflection of the interpersonal, covenantal relationship between humans and God and imagining it as a kind of predetermined, necessary manifestation of the beating pulse of the Godhead. As Nahmanides conceives it, historical time is ultimately measured by the pendulum of the Jewish people swinging from exile to return and back, which reflects the cyclicality of the emanation and ingathering of the Godhead. In this model, the divine will is not some instrument used by a sovereign God to modify his relationship with humans, but an expression of the necessary, essential movement of the Godhead. This movement results in overextension and an ensuing fracture, which can be healed only by reuniting the partially separated aspects of the Godhead. This process may be foreordained, but, as Nahmanides explains in giving reasons for the commandments, humans can exercise their free will by choosing to facilitate this reunification of the Godhead, which they alone have the unique ability to do by performing the commandments during the period between sin and redemption.

CHAPTER 7

The Reasons for the Commandments

In the history of Jewish thought, a signal indicator of the originality, profundity, and influence of a particular mode of thinking is the manner in
which it recasts the meaning of halakhah and religious praxis. This is all the
more true when it is the brainchild of a halakhic titan like Nahmanides. Nahmanides's insights into the realm of the Godhead and into the process of
emanation from within Absolute Privation, his ideas about humanity's place
in the cosmos, his theories of prophecy and the miraculous—all of these
would have remained intellectual food for thought had they not endowed the
religious act with meaning. Nahmanides invested much energy into supplying reasons for the commandments, because in so doing he could translate his
metaphysical and anthropological ideas into a meaningful framework for the
performance of the commandments.

True to form, here too Nahmanides fashioned his particular approach
to the commandments by accepting and rejecting components central to the
positions of Rashi, R. Abraham Ibn Ezra, and Maimonides. Consequently,
his commentary exhibits multicolored and multitextured explanations of the
commandments, incorporating ethical, social, historical, medical, and magical strands; his lively and at times heated conversation with the various
rabbinic and medieval traditions produces this magnificent interweave. Nahmanides sets his rare interpretive genius to work on this near embarrassment
of riches, and with his keen analytical eye he is able to peer into the depths of

the social and psychological reality that underlies halakhah. On top of all this, or rather underneath it, he continues the kabbalistic tradition of proposing theurgic reasons for the commandments, which can be found, of course, in his brief explanations introduced with the formulaic phrase "by way of truth." An analysis of the meaning of theurgy and its general implications for what a commandment is should provide a good entry into Nahmanides's thought.

I

Yehezkel Kaufmann saw in the distinction between magic and ritual an essential component of the biblical notion of the commandment. Magic is the attempt to control, causally, natural or supernatural agents to humans' advantage. Ritual, by way of contrast, is not supposed to operate causally, inasmuch as it draws its power from the fulfillment of God's commandments and the implementation of his will. Magic is founded upon a scientific understanding of the world, which determines that specific actions must have, of necessity, particular effects. Ritual addresses itself not to Nature but to a personal god, and it does not seek to coerce but to appease. What sets apart the Bible from the myth of pagan ritual, according to Kaufmann, is its severance of the connection between law and Nature.[1] Myth supplies information about the natural limitations and regulations that apply to the gods, on which pagan ritual draws in order to causally manipulate the gods for humanity's betterment. The magic-averse Bible depicts a sovereign God who is not causally subject to any natural processes and who grants law standing by dint of the revelation of his will.

Gershom Scholem accepted Kaufmann's idea for biblical law and Talmudic halakhah but not for kabbalah, which he viewed as the resurgence of long-repressed myth and its return to the heart of Jewish tradition. Among the mythic elements of kabbalah that Scholem pointed to was the kabbalistic understanding of ritual as producing an intended effect.[2] This differs from magic in two ways: first, it does not affect the natural order but the innermost aspects of the Godhead itself, and second, it is not meant to improve humanity's condition but God's. This idea of ritual as a divine need, and of humans possessing the necessary power to maintain the divine configuration and restore its harmony through ritual, is called theurgy. According to Scholem, kabbalah's success in integrating itself into tradition was partly a result of its ability to invest the tiniest details of halakhah with cosmic significance. Scholem claims that myth, by way of kabbalah, quite paradoxically and surprisingly played a role in injecting profound meaning into a religious praxis that was originally intended to eliminate myth.

Kaufmann's sharp distinction between magic and ritual, as well as the assertion that the entire antique Jewish literature conceived of halakhah as severing ritual from Nature, has been criticized by contemporary scholars of note in the fields of biblical studies and kabbalah. According to them, in the Middle Ages kabbalah came to the surface from streams that ran deep—and mostly silent—in the Judaism of antiquity, and it continued to develop the earlier theurgical aspects of Scripture and rabbinic literature.[3] Although it is beyond the purview of this chapter to decide which opinion is correct, there does appear to be a tendency within rabbinic literature to root out magical-causal aspects of halakhic ritual, even if other trends do coexist with it.[4]

A classic example of the antimagical stance appears in the well-known mishnah in tractate Rosh ha-Shanah (3.8) that speaks about Moses's hand-raising during the battle against the Amalekites. An analysis of this episode and Nahmanides's interpretation of it will help us understand how he conceives of ritual's relationship to magic and theurgy. The verses depicting the battle seemingly attribute its outcome to the direct, magical effect of Moses's hand-raising: "Whenever Moses held up his hand, Israel prevailed; but whenever he let down his hand, Amalek prevailed. But Moses' hands grew heavy, so they took a stone and put it under him and he sat on it, while Aaron and Hur, one on each side, supported his hands; thus his hands remained steady until the sun set (Exod 17:11–12)." The mishnah rejects this straightforwardly magical account and raises a rhetorical objection: " 'Whenever Moses held up his hand etc.' Do the hands of Moses make or break the battle? Rather, it tells you that whenever Israel would look upward and make their hearts subservient to their Father in Heaven, they would prevail, and if not, they would fall (Rosh ha-Shanah, 3.8)." The mishnah rejects the magical reading and interprets the raising of Moses's hands to be a symbol of the Israelites' turning to God. In the mishnah, the prayer and entreaty of the Israelites turn the tide of the battle, not Moses's wizardry.

In his own interpretation of the battle against the Amalekites, Nahmanides takes a position that is practically the inverse of the mishnah's. Not only does he not minimize the causal basis of Moses's act, but he amplifies the effect of the hand-raising so that it reaches the very sefirot: "By way of truth, he raised ten fingers to the Height of Heaven to allude to the ten *sefirot,* in order to make it cleave to the Faith that fights for Israel. This explains the matter of the uplifted palms during the priestly blessing and its secret."[5] The raising of

Moses's hands brings about the cleaving of the sefirot to "Faith," which is none other than Shekhinah, whose cognomens include "Faith."[6] Since the human body is an icon of the sefirotic configuration, in which the ten fingers represent the ten sefirot, Moses successfully effects the unification of the sefirot. Because he makes the sefirot cleave to Shekhinah, which fights on behalf of the Israelites, its potency can flow onto them.[7]

Nahmanides claims that Moses's act provides the key to understanding the uplifting of the palms during the priestly blessing, a similar theurgic act performed through gestures of the body. In his brief exposition of the blessing's text, Nahmanides articulates the basic movement that is most meaningful for understanding the theurgic nature of the ritual act:

> By way of truth, the meaning of "Bless you and Keep you" [is] that the Blessing is from above, and it is the Keeper [i.e., *Shekhinah*] which keeps it [the Blessing], as in the meaning of "Remember" and "Keep."
>
> Furthermore, "May the Great Name [i.e., *Tif'eret*] illuminate His Countenance [i.e., *Shekhinah*]" that gazes at you, and so they [the Sages] said in *Sifrei* (*Be-Midbar,* sec. 41): "R. Natan says: This is the Radiance of the *Shekhinah*," "and may He favor you," so that you raise Favor in His eyes, like the import of the [rabbinic] statement: "My world, my world, would that you would raise Favor to my Countenance at all times."
>
> Furthermore, "May the Lord lift His Countenance" [i.e., *Tif'eret*] to the Supernal Heaven [i.e., *Binah*] above, "and make for you Peace" of the All (*Ha-Kol*) in your House [i.e., *Shekhinah*]. And so they said in *Sifrei* (*Be-Midbar,* sec. 42): "R. Natan says: This is the Peace of the Kingship of the House of David."
>
> "And they shall place My Great Name upon the Children of Israel and I shall bless them," because I (*Ani,* i.e., *Shekhinah*), the Speaker, am present with Peace.[8]

Nahmanides's exposition of the text of the blessing contains the two basic movements of the sefirot: top-down and bottom-up. The divine "Blessing" descends from above from the Cause of Causes all the way down to "the Keeper"—Shekhinah[9]—the divine reservoir that passes the blessing to the universe. Subsequently, Nahmanides briefly mentions how, as part of that same movement, "the Great Name," Tif'eret, which is represented by the Tetragrammaton, illuminates "the Countenance," a symbol for Shekhinah, that gazes at

Israel.[10] The other directionality, from below to above, is expressed in the verse "May the Lord lift His Countenance," which Nahmanides interprets as the raising of the Countenance, seemingly Tif'eret, to "the Supernal Heaven," Binah. This ascent joins all the sefirot—"the Peace of the All"—with Shekhinah, the "I" that blesses Israel.[11] Although the particulars of the blessing's symbolism are open to other interpretations,[12] on the whole it characterizes the basic structure of the theurgic act as a unificatory gesture that assures the continuation of the bidirectional flux.

For Nahmanides, the theurgic perspective is indispensable for understanding the commandments, and it shapes his view of humans' role in the world and humans' relationship to the Godhead. This comes across very clearly in his explanation of the category of commandments known as *hukkim* (decrees). Some medieval thinkers, taking up the rabbinic distinction between *mishpatim* (laws) and hukkim,[13] believed that hukkim are commandments that lack any reason, and mishpatim are those that have one or more reasons.[14] The extreme version of this maintains that the meaning of the hukkim lies in the very observance of them. These commandments are deliberately devoid of any reason, and, as such, observing them demonstrates a person's absolute obedience to God's fiat, because there cannot be any other reason for observing them. According to this, these hukkim, termed "decrees of the King," constitute the perfect test for distinguishing those prepared to serve God only as long as there is a reason to do so, from those who do not make their service contingent upon any reason whatsoever. Rashi was a prominent proponent of this position,[15] and Nahmanides takes him to task for it. According to Nahmanides, hukkim do not lack any reason whatsoever; they simply lack an overt reason, their true reason being hidden from the masses and known only to select individuals. So he writes about the reason for the prohibited sexual relationships in the Torah: "The illicit sexual relationships are in the category of *hukkim,* matters that are the decree of the King. A decree is that which arises in the wisdom of the king, who is wisest about the governance of his kingdom and understands the necessity and efficacy of what he commands throughout it, but he does not tell it to the people, only to the wisest of his counsellors."[16] In another context, Nahmanides makes the connection between hukkim and esotericism explicit:

> The intent in them is not that the royal decree of the King of kings can ever be reasonless, "for every utterance of God is pure" (Prov 30:5); rather, the *hukkim* are royal edicts that the king legislates for his

kingdom without revealing their purpose to the people. The people do not see the benefit in them, they wonder about them in their hearts but accept them out of fear of the regime. Likewise, the *hukkim* of the Holy One are His secrets in the Torah that people do not think are beneficial like the *mishpatim,* but all have a proper reason and perfect purpose.[17]

The assertion that hukkim possess an esoteric, theurgic purpose known to the Sages fundamentally alters the nature and understanding of the relationship between humans and God. For Rashi, humans' observance of the hukkim expresses their unconditional dependence upon God's will; for Nahmanides, the same observance expresses God's dependence upon humans' will.

In denying the arbitrariness of the hukkim, Nahmanides follows Maimonides's lead. As he says, "The Master's [Maimonides's] decree that the commandments have a reason is an extremely clear approach, for all of them have a reason, a purpose, and a corrective for man aside from their reward from the blessed One Who commands them."[18] Maimonides considered the Torah to be an expression of God's wisdom and not arbitrary will, which is why he stridently rejected the claim of the Kalām and its Jewish adherents that there can be a group of reasonless and purposeless commandments.[19] Maimonides did concede, however, that a minority of opinions in the midrashic and Talmudic literature does seem to maintain that some commandments have no reason. The idea of the commandment as fiat is expressed, according to Maimonides, in the Talmudic opinion that a prayer leader is dismissed who utters the supplication "may Your mercies reach bird nests," because "he makes the attributes of the Holy One merciful, but they are nothing but decrees" (Berakhot 33b).[20] Nahmanides affirms that every commandment has a reason even more unequivocally than did Maimonides. Nahmanides does not countenance the possibility that such a minority position can even exist, and he expends significant effort reinterpreting the above and other sources so that they fit his belief that all commandments have reasons.[21]

Despite the basic similarity of the positions of Maimonides and Nahmanides, they disagreed deeply about how to conceptualize the reasons for the commandments. Maimonides utterly discounted the possibility that the fulfillment of a commandment can have some mysterious effect upon the Godhead or the natural order. In a few chapters of *The Guide of the Perplexed* and *Mishneh Torah,* he vilified the use of God's name or sacred objects to magical ends. Were he to have known about the theurgic power the kabbalists attributed to the commandments, he would have denigrated it as idolatrous.[22] According to Maimonides, the meaning of a commandment derives from the manner in which it directs human activity and consciousness, and nothing more.

The structural similarity between the opinions of Maimonides and Nahmanides should not cause us to paper over the deep divide separating the two. Similarly, Nahmanides's unqualified belief that every commandment has a reason and purpose is not the result of Maimonidean influence, even if it may appear to the casual observer that he is merely restating Maimonides's position with a few minor adjustments. When Nahmanides invests the hukkim with esoteric-theurgic meaning, he reveals that his approach has ancient roots in early kabbalah. The divide between philosophers and kabbalists is tremendous, as we have remarked, yet their shared rejection of the "*hok* as fiat" idea held by Rashi and others reflects something akin to the rationalization of halakhah. This rationalization provides a teleological framework for the philosophers and a causal one for the kabbalists, supplying the meaning of ritual and its effects. The anthropomorphic image of a czar issuing ukases to test the loyalty and absolute obedience of his subjects is replaced by a complex set of causal networks through which humans can affect the Godhead itself. Maimonides wants to purify Nature and revelation of any arbitrariness, so he posits that there is divine reasoning behind the commandments, which results in a tension between God's will and God's wisdom. Nahmanides also wants to dispel any seeming arbitrariness of the hukkim, but his solution could not be more radical: he turns upside down the relations of dependence that the hukkim supposedly reflect. The existence of the hok does not reflect the subservience of the human subject to the arbitrary decree of the King but expresses humans' ability to have an effect upon the Godhead itself for the betterment of the Godhead. This conception, which lies at the base of the theurgic worldview, generates a great tension between obligation and sin, between hubris and self-effacement, which we will return to below.

In Nahmanides's view, the theurgic effect of performing the commandments reverses the drift of Shekhinah away from Tif'eret. Nahmanides defines the relationship between the two as a potential but not actual unity, and the purpose of a not insignificant number of the commandments is to bring about their unity in actu.[23] As such, he explains that the Hebrew word for the most meaningful and fundamental ritual, the sacrifice, is *korban*, because it derives from the Hebrew root (*k-r-b*) that indicates closeness: "Every sacrifice (*korban*) is from the language of closeness (*kereivah*) and unity."[24] Maimonides explained the telos of the sacrificial service as the eradication of idolatrous ritual by channeling it to one location and one deity, and Nahmanides lambastes this explanation. His criticism does not stem from a principled opposition to historicizing the commandments,[25] but from the fact that this particular historical explanation reduces one of the most important theurgic acts to a simple means of overcoming idolatrous impulses: "Heaven forfend that there is no purpose or desire in them aside from removing idol worship from the minds of the foolish."[26]

Nahmanides believes that the theurgic nature of the sacrifice is encapsulated by a biblical phrase that recurs in connection with the sacrifices, which is usually translated as "a fire-offering (*isheh*), a pleasing aroma (*reiah nihoah*) for the Lord (*la-Y-HWH*)." He reads this kabbalistically as referring to the conjunction of Shekhinah with Tif'eret. To understand this, let us begin with the Tetragrammaton at the end of this phrase, which indicates that the sacrifice is directed to Tif'eret:

> By way of truth, there is an esoteric secret in the sacrifices, which you can access via the statement of the Sages in the *Sifrei* (*Be-Midbar*, sec. 143) and at the end of [tractate] *Menahot* (110a): "R. Shimon b. 'Azzai said: 'Come see what is written in the pericope of the sacrifices, for there is no mention of *El, Elohekha, Elohim, Shaddai,* or *Tzeva'ot,* only *yod he,* the Unique Name . . .' " [. . .] They therefore said that it does not mention *El* or *Elohim* in the commands pertaining to the sacrifices but only "*isheh reiah nihoah la-Y-HWH*" for the intent is to the Lord alone; the offerer should neither intend nor have in mind anything save the Unique Name.[27]

By performing the sacrificial ritual, which is directed toward the Tetragrammaton, the offerer brings Shekhinah closer to Tif'eret. Nahmanides understands *isheh* not as an adjective like Ibn Ezra, but as a noun that refers to Shekhinah: "*Isheh* is a noun, like fire (*esh*) [. . .] But it does not say *esh* but *isheh,* which is as it sounds [*ishah,* 'Woman'], as He showed you on the mountain during the giving of the Torah. The sacrifice is thus through the Attribute of Judgment [i.e., *Shekhinah*]."[28] The unification of Shekhinah (*ishah*) with Tif'eret (*la-Y-HWH*) is represented by the adjective *nihoah,* a deverbal from the root *n-w-h* that Nahmanides understands as the cleaving referred to as "resting" with respect to the Holy Spirit: "*Nihoah* is from [the language of]

'The Spirit of Elijah rested (*nahah*) upon Elisha' (2 Kgs 2:15), 'And the Spirit rested (*tanah*) upon them' (Num 11:26). Every sacrifice is from the language of closeness and unity."[29] The focus of theurgic activity upon strengthening the relationship between Shekhinah and Tif'eret is better understood against the background of the primordial fracture within the sefirotic configuration, in which Shekhinah's unity with the other sefirot was broken. This divine need, however, actually predated Shekhinah's descent and Adam's sin, because ritual had always been a necessary lubricant for the divine works. This emerges from Nahmanides's understanding of the charge given to Adam in the Garden of Eden: "to work it and preserve it" (Gen 2:15). Nahmanides finds this baffling, because he believes that the trees of the Garden were eternal and did not need caring for:

> He [God] decreed that the trees of the Garden of Eden should ramify and bear fruit forever; their root would never wither in the earth nor would their trunk die in the dirt. They did not require work or pruning. Had they needed work, who would have worked them after Adam was banished from there? This is also the meaning of [the clause] "And the Lord God planted," because the plantings were His handiwork and perennial, as in the meaning of the verse, "Their leaves will not wither nor will their fruit fail [. . .] for their water comes from the Temple" (Ezek 47:12).[30]

The trees in the Garden were perennials in the literal sense, owing to their direct connection to the configuration of the sefirot and its efflux. The Garden's symbolic reflection of the sefirotic configuration flows not only from its creation as an extremely accurate replica of the sefirot on a lower plane of existence, but from its ontological proximity to the divine plane of existence.[31] One can see the divine plane through the Garden because it is a direct extension of it, and its conjunction with the divine renders its obliteration impossible. Adam's charge to work and preserve the Garden must perforce mean something entirely different from the cultivation of the Edenic orchard:

> Our Rabbis were aware of this. They said in *Bereshit Rabbah:* " 'to work it and preserve it'—these are the sacrifices" [. . .] By this they intend that the flora and all fauna require the Primal Potencies (*ha-kohot ha-rishonot*) which make their growth possible. Through sacrifices the Blessing is drawn to the Supernal Ones, and thenceforth to the flora in the Garden of Eden, and thenceforth they will exist and

live forever through rains of Favor and Blessing through which they grow. As they said: " 'The trees of the Lord have their fill, the cedars of Lebanon that He planted' (Ps 104:16)—R. Hanina said: Their lives are full, their waters are full, their cultivators are full." "Their lives" are the Supernal Foundations; "their waters" are "the bounteous Store" (Deut 28:12) that brings rain; "their cultivators" are their heavenly potencies, as they said: "There is not a single grass below that has no sign in the firmament that strikes it and says to it 'Grow!' As it says, 'Do you know the laws of heaven, do you enforce its dominion (*mishtaro*) upon the earth?' (Job 38:34)—an enforcer (*shoter*)."[32]

The sacrifices thus draw down the efflux that sustains the chain of being. First the sacrificial rite causes "the Blessing" to be "drawn to the Supernal Ones"; that is, it extracts the efflux from the Cause of Causes to the entire sefirotic configuration, referred to here as "the Supernal Ones." From there, it flows to the Garden's flora, which are nourished from and live off it, after which it is carried by the waters of the quadrifurcate river to the flora and fauna of the entire world.[33] Rain as we know it in its material and differentiated form is none other than the divine efflux that has undergone transformative densification during its descent from the supernal realm to ours, culminating in its form as rains of the divine Blessing. Rain's true source is the ethereal, undifferentiated Light radiated onto the Supernal Ones, and this Light gradually takes on the form of rains that sustain the entire world. The Garden of Eden, which is nourished from the Waters of the Temple, carries this efflux to the land of Israel in its rivers, whence all other lands are nourished.[34]

Besides the importance of this passage for tracing the divine efflux as it shapeshifts through the entire chain of being, it is also crucial for comprehending the theurgic act. Adam brought sacrifices when the Godhead was yet in its primordial, equilibrial state, before the diminution of "the Moon," that is, Shekhinah. The sacrificial rite cannot simply be a means of restoring the break precipitated by the Original Sin, because the theurgic effect of the rite was already drawing down the efflux when celestial harmony still prevailed. At the time, prior to his individuation into a mortal being possessing its own will, Adam also existed in a state of perfect cleaving to Shekhinah, thereby enjoying life everlasting.[35] We can infer from this that the theurgic act of offering a sacrifice was being performed by the Godhead itself, or, more precisely, by humans as undifferentiated extensions of the Godhead. Theurgy,

then, is a reflexive, divine act that ensures the perpetual and regular circula-
tion of the divine Blessing.[36] Ritual functions as a kind of internal mechanism
that allows the Godhead to conduct its own maintenance, and the mission of
humans as extensions of the Godhead is to perform the ritual that stabilizes
the Godhead. Theurgic activity constitutes *imitatio dei* insofar as humans
observe the commandments for the very same reason that God does. Drawing down the Blessing is not a human need but a divine one—it is the realization of God's desire, that drive of the divine Being to burst forth and seed the
universe with its efflux.

This archetypal ritual performed in the Garden of Eden requires us to
reopen the investigation into the reasons for the commandments. The traditional approach assumes that each commandment is a manifestation of God's
will, and so the discovery of reasons behind a specific commandment gives us
insight into why God's will is expressed in this particular way. In contradis-
tinction, the theurgic approach does not view each commandment as a willed
expression of the divine Sovereign, but as an intradivine measure that facilitates the divine movement, and as an act that God himself performs. The
giving of the Torah at Sinai did not, therefore, establish the power and validity of ritual; rather, it revealed the causal structure by which the Godhead had
configured itself since the beginning of time.

II

Ritual as an expression of God's essence, and not only as a manifestation
of God's sovereign will, is also evident in the uniqueness of the land of Israel
and in the privileging of space over time in Nahmanides's thought. In a few
places in his Commentary on the Torah and his discourses, Nahmanides repeats the assertion that the principal observance of the commandments applies only in the land of Israel.[37] This dependence upon the land encompasses
even those commandments that involve one's person and ostensibly have zero
connection to one's geographical location, such as laying phylacteries on one's
arm and head or affixing a mezuzah to a doorpost. Nahmanides completely
blurs the traditional distinction between those commandments dependent
upon the land and those not dependent upon it:

> Concerning this they [the Sages] said in *Sifrei* (*Devarim,* sec. 43):
> " 'you will perish quickly [. . . Therefore place these words of Mine
> etc.]' (Deut 11:17–18)—although I am exiling you from the land to

outside the land, distinguish yourselves through [observance of] the commandments, so that when you return they shall not be new for you. This can be compared parabolically to a king who was angry at his wife and cast her out to her father's house. He said to her: 'Wear your jewelry so that it will not be new for you when you return.' Similarly, Jeremiah said, 'Erect markers for yourself' (Jer 31:20)—these are the commandments through which the Jewish people distinguish themselves." When Scripture said, "you will perish quickly [. . .] Therefore place these words of Mine etc." it only obligates commandments pertaining to one's person, such as the phylacteries and mezuzahs, in exile, and they explained that it is so that they will not be new for us when we return to the land, because the essence (*ikkar*) of all the commandments is for those residing in the land of the Lord.[38]

The commandments as a whole have an essential, metaphysical, geographical prerequisite, such that even those commandments that have no visible connection to the land are observed outside the land only as a kind of training or rehearsal for the return to the land, when they will be observed in their fullness.

It may be true that Nahmanides relies upon the rabbinic homily in the Sifre, but there is no question that his conception of the primacy of the land of Israel goes way beyond the kind of centrality of the land posited by other medieval philosophers such as R. Judah Halevi.[39] The claim that prophecy can happen only in the land of Israel because of its inherent spiritual quality preceded Nahmanides, as did the assessment that those living outside the land observe the commandments incompletely. As for the latter, the classic explanation was that one cannot fulfill the full complement of commandments outside the land because of the inability to observe the land-dependent commandments. However, Nahmanides makes a much more radical claim when he empties the diasporic observance of all commandments of its essential value, a kind of keeping in shape as one awaits the ultimate return to the land.[40]

The commandments must be performed in the land not because God explicitly commands it, but because of the unique character of the land and its unmediated interface with Shekhinah. In the same passage, Nahmanides explains the ontological background of his conception of the land's centrality. Whereas other lands fall under the dominion of celestial ministers and zodiacal signs, the land of Israel is "the Lord's domain": "The Glorious Name is the supreme Power and highest Lord for the entire world, but the land of Israel—the center of the ecumene—is the Lord's domain, unique to His Name; He did not appoint over it an angelic sovereign, lord, or ruler."[41] Nahmanides forges a link between the climatic theory that defines the special character of the land based upon its location within the central clime,[42] and his own kabbalistic understanding of the special connection between the land of Israel and the sefirah of Shekhinah: "but if you merit understanding the first instance of 'the Earth' (ha-Aretz) mentioned in the verse [beginning with the word] be-reshit and mentioned in the Torah reading of Im Be-Hukkotai, you will know an exalted and esoteric secret."[43] The secret of "the first instance of 'the Earth' (ha-Aretz)" is explained in his lengthy commentary on the very first verse of the Torah. There, Nahmanides understands the word to refer to two entities standing in a symbolic relationship, the first more abstract and subtle than the second. The first "Earth" is Shekhinah, which is referred to as "the Earth" in kabbalistic symbolism, as opposed to Tif'eret, which is referred to as "Heaven."[44] The second "Earth" was created ex nihilo and according to Nahmanides is the Primal Matter, the hyle, the formless matter that had the capacity to receive all of the forms and thus served as the substrate for all of material existence as we know it.[45] A deep, causal link connects Shekhinah to this first hyle, because Shekhinah, too, has no essence of its own, and it receives all the divine Forms, the sefirot, in such a way that all existence can expand outward beneath it. Nahmanides makes a symbolic connection between the two more abstract referents of ha-Aretz—Shekhinah and the hyle—and the much more concrete aretz—the land of Israel. Like Shekhinah and the hyle, which are the ground for other existents, the land of Israel has at its center the Foundation Stone, from which the rest of the world was fashioned, and the land continues to sustain the existence of the world by serving as the focal point for the unmediated divine efflux and radiating it outward. Nahmanides alludes to this correspondence on the verse "the Land which the Lord your God seeks" (Deut 11:12): "There is a profound secret in it, because this Land is sought through the All, which is everything, and all lands are nourished from it in truth."[46]

The idea of the Torah and its commandments as "the law of the God of the land" (2 Kgs 17:26) is built upon a very specific understanding of the nature of the relationship between Shekhinah and the land of Israel. Their direct relationship makes the clearly bounded space of the land highly sensitive to sin, such that tremors of iniquity cause the land to convulse and expel its residents:

Know that the judgment of Sodom was due to the stature of the land of Israel, for it is part of "the Lord's domain" (2 Sam 20:19) and does not tolerate the depraved. Since it spews out the entire nation due to its depravity, it first spewed out this people who were the wickedest of them all, both to heaven and to people. [. . .] there are exceedingly evil and sinful nations to which He has not done this; rather, it was all due to the stature of this land, for the Temple of the Lord is there.[47]

This is so far as transgression of the commandments is concerned, but the same cause and effect holds true of their observance as well: performing them in the land of Israel promotes the presence of Shekhinah and its unification with the rest of the sefirot. This, in turn, creates a delimited field under the governance of the hidden miracle, which is identical to the prelapsarian state of the Garden of Eden: "when the commandments are observed, the land of Israel shall be like the world was at its beginning, prior to Adam's sin—no beast or creeping animal shall kill man [. . .] [This is] because the predaceousness of vicious beasts is only due to Adam's sin."[48] The status of the land of Israel within the cosmos and its unmediated relationship to Shekhinah place it outside the dominion of the zodiacal signs and ministers. In this space, the lines from sin to punishment and from observance to reward are directly connected and easily detected.[49]

With respect to the constructive, beneficial effect of the commandments upon the individual and society, being on one side of the border of the land of Israel or the other does not make one whit of difference. But from a kabbalistic point of view, the performance of a commandment has a theurgic effect due to the symbolic-isomorphic structure of the act, and the location where it is performed, Nahmanides claims, also has a decisive impact upon its theurgic efficacy.[50] This is what he means when he says that the principal performance of the commandments is in the land of Israel; outside the land, it would be like causal action at a distance, which, if it can work at all, is going to be very weak. From the kabbalistic perspective, observing the commandments outside the land is similar to practice or training for the ultimate return to the land, where the full significance of the commandments will be realized once more. Nahmanides reinforces his claim that the essential observance of the commandments is anchored to a particular location with a quotation from Ibn Ezra: "R. A[braham] wrote on the Torah portion of *Va-Yelekh* (Deut 31:16): 'We know that God is one and that variability comes from the recipients. God does not vary His actions, as they are all through wisdom. Service of God includes preserving the capacity of reception in accordance with the location. It is therefore written, "the law of the God of the land" (2 Kgs 17:26).' "[51] The causal link between the commandments and the land of Israel explains why the Patriarchs observed the commandments prior to the giving of the Torah at Sinai:

> It seems to me that our Rabbis believe that our forefather Abraham learned the entire Torah through the Holy Spirit, studying it deeply, including the reasons for its commandments and its secrets. He observed it in its entirety as one who is not commanded [to do so] yet does, but he only observed it in the land. Jacob married sisters only outside the land, as did Amram [who married his aunt]. For the commandments are "the law of the God of the land" (2 Kgs 17:26), even though we are enjoined [to observe] the commandments pertaining to our person wherever we may be. Our Rabbis already alluded to this secret, and I shall clue you in to it with God's help.[52]

For the Patriarchs, to live in the land meant compliance with the full complement of commandments. Crossing the border into the land could have fateful consequences, as evidenced tragically by Rachel's death upon the return of Jacob and his family to the land:

> This is [the meaning of] our forefather Jacob's command to his household and companions upon entering the land: "remove the foreign gods in your midst and be purified" (Gen 35:2). But the Lord has His ways, for Rachel died on the road when they first entered the land—in her merit she did not die outside the land; in his merit he did not live in the land with two sisters, and she was the spouse who married in violation of the prohibition against sororal polygyny. She apparently became pregnant with Benjamin before they entered Shechem, so he did not touch her at all in the land for the aforementioned reason.[53]

Once they entered the jurisdiction of the commandments, Jacob was no longer permitted to be married to two sisters. He therefore separated from Rachel upon entering the land. The Patriarchs observed the Torah as those who are not commanded to do so but do so anyway, because they comprehended its reasons and its secrets. In other words, they fathomed the causal reverberations of performing or transgressing a commandment. Their pre-Sinaitic observance of the commandments in the land of Israel reflects the precedence of space over time in observance of the commandments. Even before the giving of the Torah at Sinai, the Patriarchs were privy to under-standing its wisdom and so perceived the theurgic power of the command-ments. Their obligation did not derive from God revealing his will, which had yet to occur, but from peering into the essence of reality itself and ap-prehending its structure. Nahmanides does not need to broach the question of whether Jacob was commanded explicitly about the prohibition against illicit sexual relationships, because he observed the commandment in the land not on account of divine law but from his grasp of theurgy.[54]

Two ideas guide Nahmanides's original and radical version of the com-mandments' dependence upon the land. The first is the ontological, concrete connection between the primordial "Earth," Shekhinah, and the land of Israel in the great chain of being. The second is the centrality of theurgy to Nah-manides's understanding of the commandments. As we have said, from the perspective of the commandments' positive influence on the consciousness of individuals and on the structure of society, nothing should distinguish the land of Israel from the Diaspora. It is only with respect to satisfying the divine need, as measured by theurgic impact, that location plays a critical role. When Nahmanides claims that observing the commandments outside the land is only a kind of ongoing dress rehearsal for the real performance in the land, he shows us that the theurgic component of the commandments is the central one. In summary, these two ideas form the basis of the most extreme formula-tion of a geographically conditioned halakhah to be made in the Middle Ages.

III

If the theurgic activity of offering a sacrifice concentrates on the unifica-tion of the sefirot, then the paradigmatic sin is driving them apart and wreak-ing havoc within the great chain of being. The theurgic power of observing the commandments balances out the theurgic repercussion of their transgres-sion. Sin's effect upon the chain of being is made clearer in Nahmanides's approach to idolatry, because he constructs his conception of the prohibition by relating to the various rungs of existence:

Here I will mention that the verses demonstrate that there were three kinds of idolaters:

(1) The first ones began to worship the angels, which are the Sepa-rate Intellects, because they knew that some of them ruled over the nations, as it is written, "the minister of the kingdom of Greece"

(cf. Dan 10:20), "the minister of the kingdom of Persia" (Dan 10:13), and they believed that they had the power to be beneficent or maleficent. [. . .] In the Torah and throughout all of Scripture these are called "other *elohim*," "*elohim* of the nations" (Deut 6:14, etc.), because the angels are called *elohim*, as it says: "He is the God (*Elohei*) of *elohim*" (Deut 10:17) [. . .]

(2) The second type are idolaters who later worshipped the visible heavenly host, some worshipping the Sun or Moon, others some zodiacal sign or another, because every one of the nations knew the power of the zodiacal sign over it according to its dominion over their land, and they thought that by worshipping it the sign could be strengthened and be beneficent to them [. . .]

All of these groups had false prophets who would tell them some future events and inform them about some of what would happen to them by using the art of magic and soothsaying, for the zodiacal signs also have ministers residing in the air like the angels in heaven who know the future. As part of this type of worship, some of them would worship people, because upon seeing someone in possession of great dominion and a rising star, like Nebuchadnezzar, his countrymen would think that by worshipping him and aligning themselves with him their star would rise with his. And he, too, would think that because their thoughts cleaved to him his success would increase through the power of their souls channeled towards him. This was the thinking of Pharaoh, as our Rabbis said; of Sennacherib, for Scripture tells us that he thought, "I will ascend above the heights of clouds, I will be like the Most High" (Isa 14:14); and of Hiram and his fellows who made themselves gods—they were wicked, not downright foolish.

(3) The third type of idolaters subsequently worshipped the demons—the spirits—as I will, God-willing, explain, for some of them, too, were appointed over the nations to be masters of a particular land, to harm their beleaguered and feeble, as is well known about them from the science of necromancy and the words of our Rabbis. About this the verse said, "They make sacrifices to demons, not an angel (*eloah*), which they did not know as powerful; new arrivals from nearby that did not frighten your forebears" (Deut 32:17).[55]

Nahmanides distinguishes three types of idolaters. The first type worships the Separate Intellects, the angels called *elohim*. The second type worships the

Sun, Moon, and zodiacal signs. The third type worships the demons. Nahmanides believes that idolatry has substance—the angels do exercise some degree of dominion over the nations, the zodiacal signs do determine the fate of individuals and peoples. The worship of these powers, and even the near-deification of great emperors, is not superstitious rubbish or madness: "they were wicked, not downright foolish"; in fact, quite the contrary, their devotion can impact reality. To worship beings other than God is not a preposterous act based on a miscomprehension of the world, but an act of evil based on an accurate understanding of it. Likewise, pagan prophets can prophesy accurately about the future,[56] and demon worshippers can induce a malefic effect upon the fate of their enemies.[57] From Nahmanides's point of view, their effectiveness is a scientific fact: "as is well known about them from the science of necromancy."[58] By isolating one power from the rest of the chain of being, the idolater can alter the divinely willed order and the course of Nature. Idolatry attempts to impose human will upon the natural order by singling out one actor within the chain of being for manipulation, and, as such, its faithful are not guilty of a blunder but of rebellion.

These three types of idolatry that Nahmanides describes line up with various rungs of the natural world below the configuration of the sefirot in descending order: the Separate Intellects, the zodiacal signs, and the demons. In his Discourse on Ecclesiastes, Nahmanides neatly delineates this graded structure in a parallel account:

> The idea is that the Glorious Name created everything and put the power over the lower beings into supernal ones, placing over each and every nation in its own land a particular planet or zodiacal sign, as is known in astrology. This is [the meaning of] the verse, "that the Lord your God allotted" (Deut 4:19), mentioning the sun, moon, and planets, which are the astrological signs. It also mentioned the entire heavenly host, which are the angels on high, as in: "I saw the Lord sitting on His throne and the entire heavenly host standing by Him on His right and on His left" (1 Kgs 22:19). About all of them the verse says, "that the Lord your God allotted to all of the nations" (Deut 4:19), because they are all astrological signs in heaven, and the angels on high are higher than they are in order to rule over them, as it says, "the minister of the kingdom of Persia rises opposite me" (Dan 10:13), and it is written, "Behold, the minister of the kingdom of Greece comes" (Dan 10:20), and they are called "kings."[59]

Idolatry is the isolation of one force among many within the chain of being that the worshipper exploits through ritual.

This notion of polytheism links the prohibition against magic to idolatry. Nahmanides returns to the chain of being in his explanation of the prohibition against performing magic:

> When the blessed Creator created everything *ex nihilo,* he made the higher beings governors of the lower ones beneath them, and he placed the power of the earth and its inhabitants in the planets and zodiacal signs, in accordance with their governance and how they face them, as the science of astrology bears out. He further placed angels and ministers as governors over the planets and signs, which are their souls. Their governance, from their coming into being until forever, is a decree established for them by the Most High; however, one of His most astonishing wonders is that within the power of the upper governors He placed methods of reversal (*temurot*) and powers to oppose the governance of those below them, such that if the planetary aspect in its decan facing the earth is benefic or malefic for a land, nation, or person, the superior decans oppose it and reverse it through its own aspect, along the lines of what they said: "the opposite of *'oneg* (pleasure) is *nega'* (affliction)." [. . .] Therefore the author of *Sefer ha-Levanah,* the sage of necromancy, said that when the Moon—referred to as the World Sphere—is in the head of Aries, for example, and its face is opposite such-and-such, you should make a figure for such-and-such a thing and engrave upon it the name of the hour and the name of the angel appointed over it from the names mentioned in that book, and then make such-and-such a suffumigation in such-and-such a manner, and its aspect will become malefic to uproot and pull down, to destroy and overthrow; and when the moon is in such-and-such a sign and with such-and-such an aspect, make a figure and suffumigate in such a way so that all will be benefic, to build and plant. This too is the governance of the Moon through the power of its governors. However, the simple governance that is in its [the Moon's] course is the desire of the exalted Creator that He placed in them [its governors] since the beginning, and this is the opposite. This is the secret and power of magic about which they [the Sages] said that "it contradicts the heavenly household" (*Hullin* 7b); that is to say, it is the opposite of the simple powers and contradicts the heavenly household in some way or

another. Therefore, it is proper for the Torah to forbid them, so that the world can remain on its course and in its simple nature, which is the desire of its Creator. [. . .] Many are overly pious about augury, saying that there is no truth in it whatsoever, for how would a crow or crane know the future? But we cannot contradict what has been clearly observed by eyewitnesses, and the Rabbis also concede [their veracity].[60]

In diametric opposition to Maimonides, whom Nahmanides includes in a vague reference, Nahmanides believes that the effectiveness of magic is the very reason for its prohibition. The magician acts against the "heavenly house-hold" because he or she causes a deviation from the desire of the Creator, which refers here not to a specific act of willing but to the general order of things as it emerges from the Godhead's inner being.[61]

Nahmanides upholds the effectiveness of magical practices, but he does not present magic as some mysterious force—it is part and parcel of the elemental structure of Nature. The magician creates a talisman, a "figure," which replicates the manner in which the ministers, the angels, govern the constellations as a part of the chain of causality. In his defense of magic's effectiveness, Nahmanides presents a comprehensive scientific worldview that rivals the one Maimonides provided based on Aristotelian science. Nah-manides does not replace Aristotelian science with leaps of faith and by leav-ing reason at the door; quite the contrary, he repeats a number of times that the success of magic is an incontrovertible fact proved from experience, and he demonstrates how it is undergirded by an elaborate scientific theory. Clearly, Nahmanides was conversant in contemporary magical-hermetical science.[62]

The difference between Maimonides and Nahmanides cannot be cap-tured by the question of which one of the two worldviews is correct, because in the eyes of both men, each one's worldview best aligns with and serves to explain the Jewish tradition, so this takes on immense significance. In other words, each one takes his blueprint of how the world functions and overlays it on top of Jewish tradition, using it to explain and (re)interpret that tradi-tion. Maimonides claimed in *The Guide of the Perplexed* that to believe in the effectiveness of magic is to attribute real power to the planets and zodiacal signs, and he further claimed that ancient pagan ritual is embedded in magi-cal practices.[63] Halakhah condemns magic because it considers it to be based on a false, delusional belief, and banning it contributes to the broader halakhic enterprise of extirpating polytheism. In the same vein, Maimonides interprets the prohibitions against augury, soothsaying, and the like quite broadly, contending that they are chiefly intended to stamp out astrological belief and popular religion.[64] Moreover, according to him, the Torah has a blanket prohibition on all activities built upon a misapprehension of how the world operates, because they ultimately lead to the belief in the power of magic and, in turn, to the worship of celestial bodies.

Nahmanides, on the other hand, maintains that belief in magic serves a purpose in the Jewish world, and it was only the Greek philosophers who perverted this belief and corrupted it into heresy. This positive assessment of how the magical worldview correlates with Jewish belief, and his diatribe against Greek science, appears in his Torat Ha-Shem Temimah:

> From here you see the cruelty and obstinacy of the arch-philosopher, may his name be erased, for he rejects a number of phenomena seen by many that we know are true and that have been publicized through-out the world. In those early days, during Moses' lifetime for example, everyone knew about them, because the sciences in those days were spiritual, concerning demons, magic, and suffumigation to the heav-enly works. Not a single person would deny *creatio ex nihilo* or rebel against God, due to their closeness to the creation of the world and the Flood [. . .] But when the Greeks, a new people who had not inherited wisdom, arose, as the author of *Sefer ha-Kuzari* [R. Judah Halevi] ex-plained, that notorious man decided to believe in only what is percep-tible. He sought sciences of the perceptible and rejected everything spiritual, saying that the whole matter of demons and magic is naught, that everything in this world operates according to Nature.[65]

The scientific worldview upon which magic is predicated is populated by spiritual actors and so aligns more closely with the Torah, and Nahmanides lends it credibility through his brief history of science. Belief in magic and demons originated in the ancient Near East, yet its criticism in Aristotelian science stems from the Greeks, whom Nahmanides characterizes as whipper-snappers with no tradition to speak of. This could not be more at odds with Maimonides's account of scientific history, in which hermetic science is at-tributed to the pagan Sabaeans[66] and for whom Aristotle is something of a hero. The privileging of the empirical by Aristotelian science, Nahmanides argues, poses a real threat to the structure of belief and, in the end, leads to atheism. For Maimonides, Aristotelian science, which is founded on causal rationalism, liberates people from fantasies of the imagination and from the thrall of idolatry.

For Nahmanides, the relationship between the prohibition against magical practices, on one hand, and the obligation to perform theurgic acts, on the other, makes for a complex understanding of human initiative. The outlawing of magic is intended to tamp down humans' hubris and restrict their ability to harness natural, causal processes. The obligation to perform the theurgic commandments, however, turns humans into megalomaniacs, affecting as they do the Godhead itself. One would think that the hubris inherent to the theurgic act that brings the sefirot together is many times more amplified than that of the magician's conjuring. If we think about it further, however, that is not the case—in the theurgic act, humans cooperate with the inner divine desire in trying to stabilize the divine configuration and preserve the system's unity; in the magical ritual, humans attempt to isolate specific elements within the chain of being, thereby sundering their unity, and contravene the divine will.

The complete opposite of the theurgic act, and far more destructive than sorcery, is the esoteric side of idolatry, what is known as "cutting down the saplings." Nahmanides alludes to this in discussing the prohibition of idolatry: "By way of truth, you can understand the secret of the Countenance from what we have written, because the verse mentions about this assembly, 'Countenance within Countenance the Lord spoke to you' (Deut 5:4), and you will know the secret of the word 'other' (*aherim*), and the entire verse will be understood in its literal sense."[67] In his explanation of the sin of the golden calf, Nahmanides reveals a bit more of the esoteric aspect of idolatry and its connection to the rabbinic idea of "cutting down the saplings":

> "For your people has destroyed" (Exod 32:7)—the Lord said to Moses that they committed two terrible acts. First, "your people has destroyed (*shihet*)," and "destruction" means tearing down a structure, as in the verse: "and each man had an implement of destruction (*mishhato*) in his hand" (Ezek 9:1), "I am against you, O destroying mountain (*ha-mashhit*)" (Jer 51:25)—Babylon which tears down every wall and tower. The "destruction" in this instance is that which our Rabbis called "cutting down the saplings."[68]

In making the golden calf, the Israelites were ruining the structure of the sefirot and "cutting down the saplings."

Nahmanides lays bare the ritual logic of the golden calf and its connection to "cutting down the saplings" in a different comment:

> Aaron's intention [in making the golden calf] was because the Israelites were in a desolate wasteland, and destruction and desolation of the world come from the north, as it is written, " 'Out of the North calamity shall break forth upon all the inhabitants of the earth' " (Jer 1:14). This does not only refer to the king of Babylon, as the verse indicates exoterically, but to the Attribute of Judgment that enters the world from the Left to requite the evil of the earth's inhabitants, and note that in the Account of the Chariot, "the Countenance of the Ox is on the Left for the four of them" (Ezek 1:10). So, Aaron thought that the Destroyer would guide them through the wasteland, for that is where its great power lies.[69]

Aaron chose the calf because it symbolizes the Left side of the sefirotic configuration—the Attribute of Judgment. Since Judgment rules over areas of wilderness and wasteland, the sin of the golden calf was the attempt to affect the state of the Jewish people by worshipping the aspect of Judgment within the Godhead.[70] Singling out Judgment—most likely Shekhinah—from the rest of the sefirot, and trying to use it to some end, constitutes "cutting down the saplings." Nahmanides formulates his opinion against that of Ibn Ezra, who viewed the sin through an astrological lens as an effort to draw down power from the zodiacal signs. Nahmanides explains the sin as involving a much higher plane of existence, the sefirotic plane: "Rabbi Abraham said that here *elohim* is the Glory resting in the form of a body, and if you pay close attention to the first journey you will understand this. This does not seem correct to me, because the calf was not made through the astrological arts so that the Glory or Word could abide in its form, but rather they made this form to concentrate upon its essence during worship."[71] The esoteric dimension of idolatry, it turns out, structurally parallels the exoteric one. Both consist of an unwelcome human intrusion into higher rungs of the chain of being during which one link is isolated and exploited. Whereas the more exoteric idolatry stays within the bounds of the natural world below the divine realm, the more esoteric act of "cutting down the saplings" scales the heavens up to the innermost rungs of the Godhead itself to set one aspect of the Godhead apart from the rest of the sefirotic configuration. As the sin cuts that much more deeply, it becomes commensurately more egregious.[72]

A more detailed account of what "cutting down the saplings" signifies appears in Nahmanides's explanation of the sin committed by Nadav and Avihu:

> You can understand the sin of Nadav and Avihu from the fact that it said "they offered a foreign fire to the Countenance of the Lord" (Lev 10:1) and did not say "they offered incense to the Countenance of the Lord that He did not command," even though they placed incense for ('al) the Fire, as in the verse: "they shall place incense for Your Fury (Appekha)" (Deut 33:10), but "they set their hearts only upon This" (ibid., Lev 10:2), and it was not an isheh reiah nihoah [it did not reach Tif'eret].[73] This is the meaning of [the clause] "they placed incense for it ('aleha) [i.e., Shekhinah]"—it does not say "they placed for them ('aleihen) [i.e., Shekhinah and Tif'eret]" like it says concerning the congregation of Korah, "and put fire in them and place incense upon them" (Num 17:6), and further there, "and you shall place incense for them ('aleihen)" (Num 17:17). Here, in fact, it says "for it," to hint that they placed incense for the Fire alone, "and a fire came forth from the Countenance of the Lord and consumed them." Perhaps the fact that Scripture says "do not raise strange incense for it ('alav)" (Exod 30:9) alludes to this, that they should not make it [Shekhinah] "strange" [i.e., estranged from the other sefirot]. This is [the meaning of] that which it says, "in their drawing close to the Countenance of the Lord and they died" (Lev 16:1), because in offering to His Countenance they died.[74]

Nahmanides focuses the "cutting of the saplings" on the relationship between Shekhinah and Tif'eret, and he depicts it as an act that is the opposite of the desirable kind of sacrifice. Nadav and Avihu raised the incense on the fire, which symbolizes Shekhinah in Nahmanides's kabbalah, setting their hearts only on "This," a common cognomen for Shekhinah.[75] Similarly, the Torah describes them as offering incense "for it," Shekhinah, instead of "for them," Shekhinah and Tif'eret, and this change marks, in Nahmanides's view, their single-minded devotion to Shekhinah alone. Their incense-raising was not a reiah nihoah unifying Shekhinah with Tif'eret and was likely to estrange Shekhinah from the rest of the Godhead. As Nahmanides puts it: "they should not make it 'strange.' " This incense not only failed to achieve the desirable theurgic result, but in fact it engendered the opposite, harming Shekhinah and its relationship to the other sefirot, because Shekhinah is already the most vulnerable link in the entire divine structure and is prone to detachment.[76]

In Torat Ha-Shem Temimah, Nahmanides repeats his opinion on the sin of the golden calf, and he distinguishes clearly between Aaron and the rest of the Israelites. Aaron intended to create a talisman to guide the Jewish people through the wilderness as long as Moses was not around:

> Aaron contemplated the potency of the Ox [i.e., of the divine Chariot in Ezekiel] and made them a body in this form capable of receiving this potency through the zodiacal signs and hours, so that it could show them the way through the wilderness and guide their travels. Once they saw the ox [the golden calf] they said that it had been guiding them from the beginning, as it is written: "And the Lord (va-Y-HWH) [i.e., Shekhinah] went before them by day [in a pillar of cloud]" (Exod 13:21), and it is written: "And the Angel, God [i.e., Shekhinah], traveled [. . .] and came between the camp of Egypt [. . .] And there was the cloud and the darkness" (Exod 14:19–20). I have already explained that the "darkness" is the elemental Fire which is blackness, and the potency of this Fire, which is the Attribute of Judgment, receives a supernal power from the Hayyah called "Ox," which is from the Left [side of the Chariot/Godhead].[77]

Aaron committed no sin. In constructing the altar he did not intend to offer a sacrifice to the calf, which symbolizes Shekhinah, but to the Tetragrammaton: "He did not refrain from making an altar in front of it. 'He called out saying, "A festival for the Lord tomorrow" ' (Exod 32:5), but he did not say 'for the calf' or 'for elohim,' which comprises powers and idolatry, but for the Unique Name."[78] In his Commentary on the Torah, Nahmanides claims that had that sacrifice been directed to the Tetragrammaton, to Tif'eret, it would have empowered the talisman and drawn down power to it:

> Aaron thought . . . that if God were worshipped there a Spirit on high would be aroused, as it had been emanated upon Moses. This is why he said, "A festival for the Lord tomorrow" (Exod 32:5), so that the service and sacrifice would be for the Unique Name and to draw out the Will from it to the body with the form, for by it being in front of them they would concentrate upon its essence.[79]

Nahmanides does not consider it a sin to construct a talisman that can attract the power of Shekhinah through Tif'eret. The sin is in having improper intention, as reflected in the Israelites' worship of the calf as a representation of the Attribute of Judgment: "On the first day they said, 'This is your God, O Israel' (Exod 32:4), because with the right intention, 'This is your God, O Israel, which raised you out of the land of Egypt' is not idolatry, but after they prostrate themselves and offer sacrifices to it, it becomes a great evil."[80]

The very real, frightening power of idolatry is borne out by the striking similarity the scapegoat ritual in Yom Kippur bears to the worship of the golden calf. Nahmanides writes as follows about the he-goat designated for Azazel that is sent into the wilderness on the Day of Atonement:

> Now, the Torah completely forbade accepting their godship or worshipping them in any way, yet the Holy One commanded us to send a he-goat through the wilderness on the Day of Atonement to the minister who rules over areas of desolation, and it befits him because he is its master and desolation and ruin come through the emanation of his power, for he is the cause of the planets of ruin, bloodshed, wars, quarrels, wounds, blows, disunity, and destruction.[81]

The he-goat is sent to placate the Attribute ruling over desolate regions like the wilderness, whose symbol is the goat. While the sin of the golden calf was "cutting down the saplings," the he-goat is sent at God's bidding and so does not open a rift within the sefirotic structure. If sending the he-goat to Azazel were not at God's behest, it would be prohibited as an act of idolatry. Still, addressing this power in this way lacks the component that brings about divine closeness, which is why the he-goat is neither called a sacrifice nor brought on the altar—it falls to its death. This ritual addressed to one power teaches us that there is efficacy to idolatry and that it has the power to affect reality.

The scapegoat sent to Azazel, which bears a structural resemblance to idolatry, is part of a secondary category of hukkim. This category includes those practices that gentiles and idolaters considered idolatrous, the implication being that Jewish worshippers of God are hypocrites:

> This is why our Rabbis said "be-hukkotai" (Lev 26:3)—matters about which the evil inclination makes accusations and the nations of the world use as a refutation: wearing wool and linen, the red heifer, and the scapegoat. The nations of the world could not use sacrifices as a refutation because they are "for the ishim of the Lord," but they use

the scapegoat as a refutation because they think that we do as they do. The same is true of the red heifer, because it is done outside the camp, and it is similar to the scapegoat in that it is supposed to remove an impure spirit, as it is said about the future: "I will also make the idols and spirit of impurity vanish from the land" (Zach 13:2). From this you can understand why the one who sends the he-goat to Azazel and the one who burns the heifer must clean their clothing.[82]

In addition to the scapegoat intended for Azazel, we can add the red heifer (used for purification from the defilement due to contact with the dead), the heifer whose neck is broken (to provide absolution for an unsolved murder), the bird used in purification of the leper (*metzora‘*), and other, similar rituals performed outside the camp. The scapegoat and other rituals form a second category of hukkim that become grist for the polemical mill of idol worshippers, as they appear similar to "cutting down the saplings" since they appear to be directed to potencies that are not the Tetragrammaton. However, God himself gives permission to perform such rituals, and they are not considered sacrifices. To any observer, these acts appear to be bona fide pagan rituals, and the theurgic ritual does come within a hair of the terrible act of "cutting down the saplings." Whether the extremely fine line dividing them has been crossed depends on the intention accompanying the act. Nahmanides underscores this hairsbreadth in his commentary on the red heifer: "and it is given to Eleazar to be carried out in his presence even by a non-priest, but the adjutant observes the act so that it be done according to his intention, so that they not think an evil thought about it like the nations or Satan."[83] The commandment as theurgically unifying and joining and the sin as sundering and disjoining both hinge on the idea of humans as unique causal actors within the chain of being. Their pivotal role creates a profound tension within human ritual and humans' role in the cosmos, a tension between initiative and withdrawal.

Nahmanides, in opposition to Maimonides, does not ground the fight against idolatry and magic in an endeavor to extirpate false ideas and beliefs; instead, he contends that their prohibition flows from their very real power and is intended to limit the hubris of humans, molding them into passive creatures who go with the flow of divine will as it is, without tearing the fabric of existence.[84] From this perspective, the universe is like a massive ecosystem in which all elements form an organic unity, and if humans abuse one element and isolate it from the rest, they place the entire structure in jeopardy and are guilty of ruinous rebellion. At the same time, humans know that the commandments are not only about creating a relationship with God and shaping their personality and consciousness; they are aware of their theurgic effect upon the Godhead. Humans understand that the fate of the universe hangs in the balance and that fulfilling the commandments causally affects the outcome. What separates the forbidden act of rebellion from this obligatory undertaking, then, is to whom or what the act is intended and the inner intention of its performer. At its best, the fulfillment of a commandment is an act of humans, as extensions of the Godhead, upon the Godhead, in which human will and divine desire are attuned to each other, resulting in the fundamental divine movement of unity and the descent of the efflux.

IV

One can characterize the esoteric aspect of the commandments and their theurgic effects within Nahmanides's thought according to two foci, each of which has distinct causal principles: unity and attraction. While the two are linked, each one is directed toward a different goal and works through its own causal logic.

As an act of unification, a commandment tries to tighten the connection between the various aspects of the divine structure and keep them fastened to one another, because the dynamic nature of the structure itself threatens to pull it apart. This inner, dynamic tendency appears to have precipitated the intradivine crisis and Shekhinah's plunge at the time of the Original Sin, and the full complement of commandments is designed to restore Shekhinah's status from potential unity to actual unity.

As an act of attraction, a commandment draws down the divine efflux to the sefirotic configuration, from which the Godhead is drawn into the increasingly differentiated, concrete dimensions of being. Humans' task is to facilitate the outspreading of the Godhead and to draw its immediate presence into the universe, thereby realizing the intradivine movement, which the divine desires.

The effectiveness of the theurgic act in achieving sefirotic affinity or unity turns on the causal principle which dictates that an act performed upon a symbolic signifier can affect the signified. This principle of action at a distance by way of signifiers was the starting point of all medieval hermetic-magical science, and the kabbalists—Nahmanides among them—elevated this magical principle into a theurgic one. In presenting the commandments and their details, the Torah supplies the symbolic apparatus for carrying out theurgic activity, and Nahmanides employed this wide array of symbols in his kabbalistic interpretation of the commandments.

The first such symbol is the human body, which as the "image of God" functions as an iconic symbol of the sefirotic configuration, mainly the seven lower sefirot.[85] The gestures of the human body act at a distance through the body's signification of the sefirotic configuration. Among those commandments centered around the iconicity of the human body are circumcision,[86] the priestly blessing,[87] the laying of phylacteries,[88] the washing of the priests' hands and feet,[89] and the prohibition to leave a body unburied.[90]

Likewise, the veritable thesaurus of symbols that Nahmanides draws on to decode the kabbalistic reasons behind the commandments includes colors. For example, the redness of the red heifer is associated with the Attribute of Judgment,[91] and the blueness of the blue thread that is wrapped with the white tzitzith threads represents Shekhinah intertwined with the other sefirot.[92] This lexicon also includes various objects, such as the citron, palm frond, and other species, which respectively represent Shekhinah, Tif'eret, and the rest of the sefirot, such that taking them all together is an act of theurgic unification.[93] The musical qualities of sound also symbolize the sefirot, and the order of tekiah-teruah-tekiah (in the blowing of the shofar) symbolizes the unity of Shekhinah, symbolized by the teruah, with Tif'eret, symbolized by the tekiah.[94] At times, a relationship can represent the sefirot without each element having a one-on-one correspondence to a particular sefirah. The commandment to shoo away the mother bird is an interesting example, because the mother bird symbolizes Binah and the eggs or chicks symbolize the lower sefirot. The requirement to take the offspring without their mother signifies that human activity is limited to the seven lower sefirot.[95] The clearest and theurgically most important symbols are the names of God. Pronouncing them in the correct sequence and with the proper intention is the key to the secret of the blessings and the reading of the Shema', which among other things promote the unification of the sefirot with one another.[96] We see, then, that from the unificatory perspective, the commandments serve as a kind of sacred lexicon of significations and activities that tap into those significations, through which they achieve the desired theurgic effects.

The second focus of the reasons of the commandments is not supernal unification but attracting and drawing down the supernal into the lower realms. The commandments are intended to draw down the divine efflux and make it manifest in the concrete and differentiated dimensions of reality. The causal basis of this activity is talismanic and isomorphic. Based upon the principle of talismanic action, the particulars of the commandments are precise instructions for creating an isomorphic structure that is a kind of microcosm of the sefirotic system, which attracts the presence of the Godhead to the structure. This principle of creating a structure that resembles the supernal Chariot in order to attract the Godhead and draw its presence into it is described by Nahmanides when he talks about the seventy elders selected to judge the Jewish people:

> and He commanded this number of judges of Israel, because this number includes all opinions since it comprises all the powers, and nothing is beyond them. Likewise, at the giving of the Torah [it says], "and seventy elders of Israel" (Exod 24:1), because with this complete number it was fitting for the glory of *Shekhinah* to rest upon them, as it is in the supernal camp, for the Israelites are the hosts of the Lord on earth. Similarly, the Ark, cover, and Tabernacle were made in the figure of the ministers on high, and the tribes were organized in the likeness of the Chariot beheld by Ezekiel, in order to draw *Shekhinah* upon them on earth in the same way *Shekhinah* is in the heavens.[97]

The highest court, the Sanhedrin of seventy plus its president, and the configuration of the Israelite encampment are viewed as a kind of microcosm that allows the Godhead to manifest itself.[98] The Tabernacle and Temple mentioned in this piece are the paradigm for this kind of isomorphic talisman that draws down Shekhinah.[99] Concerning the cherubs, Nahmanides depicts a chain of isomorphic structures: the cherubs in the Temple have the figure of the cherubs on the Chariot seen by Ezekiel, which themselves represent the sefirotic "Cherubs," namely Shekhinah and Tif'eret: "This is the meaning of 'the figure of the Chariot' (1 Chr 28:18), because the cherubs that Ezekiel saw bearing the Glory were a figure of the Cherubs that are Glory (*Kavod*) and splendor, and the cherubs in the Tabernacle and Temple were a figure of them, because 'one high official is kept by a higher one, and both of them by still higher ones' (Eccl 5:7)."[100] It bears noting that this isomorphic activity that attracts and causes inhabitation actually replicates the way the Godhead itself operates. In a few places in Nahmanides's writings, it is manifestly obvious that the Godhead acts by projecting a figure that establishes a course of action it must take in the future. This modus operandi can be seen in diverse contexts, from the creation of humans to events that prefigure the course of history.[101] Drawing down the divine presence can be conceptualized, then, as the realization of the divine desire to well up and be emanated outward into the concrete existence that it creates.

These two theurgic foci of unification and attraction complement each other. Attraction and inhabitation without unification is liable to degrade into an act of "cutting down the saplings"; unification alone is liable to result in the Godhead retreating into itself unto Absolute Nothingness. A single ritual may thus feature both theurgic goals simultaneously, as seen above in the analysis of the priestly blessing.[102]

The existence of the entire universe and the particular historical condition of the Jewish people both depend upon the immediate presence of Shekhinah and Tif'eret in the lower, more concrete dimensions of reality. Nahmanides, however, underscores the fact that this is theocentric rather than anthropocentric. He formulates the inner divine impulse to gush out and be emanated outward, to dwell in the earthly plane, in connection with the function and purpose of the Tabernacle: "I shall dwell in the midst of the Children of Israel and be their God; and they will know that I am the Lord their God Who took them out of the land of Egypt in order to dwell in their midst" (Exod 22:45–46). Nahmanides begins by citing Ibn Ezra, who considered God's dwelling in the Tabernacle to be the ultimate goal of the exodus:

> But Rabbi Abraham said, "I only took them out of the land of Egypt in order to dwell in their midst," which is [the verse], "you shall worship God on this mountain" (Exod 3:12). This is a fine interpretation, and as such there is a great secret in this matter, because according to the simple reading the [presence of] *Shekhinah* among Israel serves a human need, rather than divine need. But it is actually like what the verse said, "Through Israel I [i.e., *Shekhinah*] become Splendorous (*etpa'ar*) [i.e., *Tif'eret*]" (Isa 49:3); and Joshua said, "what will You do for Your Great Name" (Josh 7:9); and there are many more verses like this: "He desired it (lit. her, i.e., *Shekhinah*) as His Seat" (Ps 132:13); "I will dwell here because I desire it (lit. her, i.e., *Shekhinah*)" (Ps 132:14); and it is written: "and I shall Remember the Land" (Lev 26:42).[103]

While theurgic activity of the unificatory variety looks like a divine need, the attractive variety that ensures the continued existence of humanity and the universe appears—on the face of it—to be a human need. What Nahmanides highlights here is that the presence of the Godhead is also a divine need, and through the theurgic-talismanic activity of building the Tabernacle, humans realize the divine aim not only of unification but also of spreading far and wide.

This aim and inclination to be emanated into the more concrete, material levels of existence are defined by Nahmanides as humans' purpose and the goal of the commandments. This purpose creates a fundamental link between Nahmanides's exoteric set of reasons for the commandments and his esoteric one. In the exoteric, he formulates the purpose of the commandments as testimony about, gratitude for, and the publicizing of God's existence and greatness:

> All of the commandments are intended to make us believe in our God and acknowledge Him for having created us. This is the intention of creation, for there was no other purpose to the original creation; the Most High has no desire in the lower beings except for man to know and acknowledge his God for having created him. The purpose of raising one's voice during prayers and the purpose of [having] synagogues and the merit of praying with the community are precisely this, so that people have a place to congregate and acknowledge God for having created them and having brought them into existence, and to publicly declare this and say before Him, "We are your creations."[104]

Nahmanides also defines the historical mission of the Jewish people as in line with this same goal of bringing the Name of God into the world. God's standing in the world depends upon the Jewish people, and the prophets called upon God to save the Jewish people for the sake of his Name:

> God created man in the lower realms so that he would recognize his Creator and acknowledge His Name, and he gave him free will (*reshut*) to do good or evil. When they all sinned willfully and denied His existence, He had only this people to His name, and through them He proclaimed, by means of signs and wonders, that He is the supreme Power and highest Lord, and thus became known to all nations. Now, if the memory of them is lost, the nations will forget His signs and deeds and no one will recount them.[105]

This passage presents the well-known motif of the Jewish people's mission to remind the world of God's Name and power in this world, but there is no mention of the causal activity involved in bringing God's presence into the world. Later on in the piece, Nahmanides links the historical task of publicizing God's Name and works with the theurgic act of drawing the Godhead into the universe:

Therefore, it is necessary, based on the Will involved in the creation of the world, that it be the Will of His Countenance to establish them as His people for all time, because of all the nations they are closest to Him and know Him best. [. . .] I have already alluded to a lofty and esoteric secret about the creation of man, according to which it is necessary for us to be His people and for Him to be our God, as in the idea of the verse, "Whoever is called by My Name and I have created for My Glory etc." (Isa 43:7).[106]

The mission of the Jewish people to publicize God's Name in the world has a theurgic dimension, which is the "lofty and esoteric secret" of humanity's creation. As beings created in the divine image, humans are a kind of talisman for drawing down Shekhinah into the world, and through their actions as signifiers of the Godhead they cause it to be emanated into the lower realms. If God created the universe out of a yearning to flow outside of himself, then we can say that he created humans as tools to make that happen.[107]

V

The theurgical aspect of the commandments does not express the full meaning of and reason behind the commandments. Nahmanides offers wide-ranging and profound exoteric reasons for the commandments, which explain them as beneficial to the individual and society. To take one example among many, he uses his medical expertise to explain the forbidden foods as detrimental to a person's physical and spiritual health.[108] For instance, he explains the prohibition against eating fruit from trees during the first three years of growth as follows: "The truth of the matter also is that the fruit at the beginning of a tree's planting contains a lot of contagious moisture that harms the body and is not good to eat, like a fish without scales and the [other] foods forbidden by the Torah, which are also injurious to the body."[109] Elsewhere, he points out that forbidden foods affect the purity of the soul. This kind of spiritual injury is indicated by the word "abomination": "It [the Torah] intends to further explain the forbidden foods and therefore said, 'Do not eat any abominable thing' (Deut 14:3), to convey that everything forbidden is abominable to the pure soul [. . .] The forbidden foods are coarse and they beget coarseness and solidification of the soul."[110] In his wider view of how the diverse commandments are categorized, Nahmanides distinguishes hukkim that lack any stated reason, in which the theurgic effect is crucial, from two other categories of commandments that have additional exoteric reasons, known as 'edot and mishpatim:

> The reason [the Torah states], "When your son asks you . . . what are the 'edot" (Deut 6:20) is that first he will ask what these commandments called 'edot (lit. testimonies) attest to, for they are a remembrance of His wonders and a testimony about them, such as the matzah, the sukkah, Passover, Sabbath, the phylacteries, and the mezuzah; [then he will ask] "what are the hukkim," because their reason is concealed in the Torah; [and finally] he will ask "what are the mishpatim" we mete out concerning these commandments, such that we stone someone who does labor on the Sabbath, burn whoever has relations with a woman and her mother, and give someone who plants a forbidden admixture forty lashes, because the mishpatim for maintaining a civilized society (yishuv ha-medinot) found in the laws about the ox, pit, and bailees and other such laws of the Torah are just and good, as is evident to any observer.[111]

The mishpatim that confound the inquisitive son concern the punishment of transgressors, because those involved in maintaining the social and moral order are transparently "just and good," as anyone can see. This broader category of mishpatim expresses the ethical aspect of Nahmanides's reasons for the commandments.

Nahmanides's alert and sharp moral consciousness is showcased in his Commentary on the Torah. He does not refrain from passing judgment on biblical heroes for their moral failings,[112] and his exposition of the reasons for the commandments reflects his moral sensitivity. Nahmanides's complex position on the relationship between halakhah and ethics can be better delineated by examining his positions on three issues: (1) the status of a moral obligation derived from reason rather than revelation, (2) the status of a moral norm and its obligatory force in an area that lies outside halakhic positive law, and (3) the reasons for interpersonal commandments.

Nahmanides rejects the argument that an obligation can be grounded in only revelation and God's explicit instruction. Human reason does possess the power to create moral norms that have significance even in God's eyes. Nahmanides writes about the punishment of the diluvian generation: " 'Injustice' (hamas) is theft and oppression. He gave Noah the reason [for the flood] as injustice and not degeneracy because injustice was a well-known, public sin, and our Rabbis said that on account of it their fate was sealed. The reason is that it is a rational commandment, so there was no need for a prophet to warn them about it."[113] The generation of the flood was punished for their thieving ways long before the seven Noahide laws were given, because not taking what belongs to someone else is a dictate of reason that applies even in the absence of explicit revelation. There exist, therefore, moral obligations that do not require divine revelation as they can be deduced from reason, and these obligations have religious standing such that God punishes those who do not observe them. Nahmanides thus opposes the claim that revelation has a monopoly on generating obligations and that Judaism precludes from the get-go the possibility of reason generating its own norms.[114]

In Torat Ha-Shem Temimah, Nahmanides contrasts his own position with the rabbinic midrash that pushes back the divine command to observe the seven Noahide laws, including theft, to the days of Adam. This midrash views the Noahide laws as embedded in the phraseology of God's command not to eat from the Tree of Knowledge:

> It was necessary, too, to convey that they [the generation of the flood] were punished on account of illicit sexual relationships and their degeneracy, as it is written, "And the sons of the judges observed people's daughters" (Gen 6:2), and it is written, "for all flesh has become degenerate" (Gen 6:12); and on account of theft, as it is written, "because the land was filled with injustice" (Gen 6:13). According to our Rabbis, they had already been commanded about these and the rest of the seven Noahide commandments since Adam, and they derived these from the allusion in the verse, "And the Lord God commanded Adam saying" (Gen 2:16), but [the verse] did not elaborate upon them because we are commanded to observe them from Sinai. But by way of *peshat,* these are rational commandments, and any creature that can recognize his Creator must be careful about them, like it was said about Abraham, "and they will keep the path of the Lord etc." (Gen 18:19), even though he was not given a commandment about it.[115]

Nahmanides is familiar with the midrash that explains the punishment of the diluvian generation as a consequence of not following the "explicit command" given to Adam. This midrash does not see any need to posit extrarevelatory moral obligations, because the generation of the flood had already been commanded about their transgressions.[116] Nahmanides rejects this possibility and instead presents his literary-contextual, peshat, reading, in which an obligation deduced from reason replaces this supposedly ancient divine command. At the end of the passage, he extends the power of reason to Abraham, who commanded his offspring to do what is just and right despite the lack of any relevant revelation.

Moral considerations appear as a binding force in another place in Nahmanides's writings, where he comments on the verse that relates to the giving of laws to the Israelites in the desert before the revelation at Sinai, "there He set for them a hok and mishpat, and there He tested them" (Exod 15:25). Rashi, following the midrash, interprets this as an episode of divine lawgiving, as signaled by the ostensibly legal terms hok and mishpat: "At Marah, He gave them some of the sections of the Torah so that they could delve into them: the Sabbath, the red heifer, and *dinin* [civil and criminal law]." Based on this list, hok and mishpat are distinct: the red heifer falls under the former, and dinin fall under the latter. Nahmanides prefers a different interpretation to that of the midrash:

> By way of *peshat,* when they began to enter the great, terrible wilderness, with an unquenchable thirst, he [Moses] appointed rules to govern their provisions and needs until their entry into a settled land, because a rule is called a *hok,* as in the import of [the verses] "provide me my regular (*hukki*) bread" (Prov 30:8), "the rules (*hukkot*) of heaven and earth" (Jer 33:25). It is also called a *mishpat* because it was justly calculated [. . .] and He placed *mishpatim* for them to live by: loving one's fellow, heeding the advice of elders, comporting oneself modestly in one's tent with respect to women and children, acting peaceably with those who come into the camp to peddle their wares, rebuking people so that the camps do not harbor those who shamelessly indulge in every abomination [. . .] Similarly, concerning Joshua it says, "Joshua made a covenant with the people on that day and set for them a *hok* and *mishpat* in Shechem" (Josh 24:25)—these are not the *hukkim* and *mishpatim* of the Torah but the mores of civilized society (*hanhagot ve-yishuv ha-medinot*), such as Joshua's stipulations mentioned by the Sages (*Bava Kamma,* 80b–81a) and the like.[117]

Against Rashi and the midrash, Nahmanides understands hok and mishpat as describing an entire field of binding legislation, unrelated to the divine biblical commandments, that maintains order in the camp, regulates its behavior, and sets forth mores and practices for a civilized society.[118] To the prohibition on theft derived from reason that we have already seen, Nahmanides now adds an entire set of laws whose validity derives from moral and pragmatic considerations. These ordinances preceded the giving of the Torah to Moses at Sinai and were not supplanted by it, as they were broadened in Joshua's time. According to Nahmanides, they constitute the category of "mores of civilized society," which his disciples Rashba and, much later, R. Nissim Gerondi (Ran) would invoke as the source of validity for medieval communal ordinances that were not part of the positive law of halakhah and at times even deviated from it. Following Nahmanides's use of this category, these great halakhists recognized this broad field of extrahalakhic legislation as an integral part of the Jewish tradition, with roots stretching back to Moses's governance before the giving of the Torah.[119]

The second issue that helps us elucidate Nahmanides's stance on the relationship between halakhah and morality concerns morality as a complement to a fully developed halakhah. The question of whether an independent moral obligation can exist is not at issue here; rather, the issue is how moral norms coexist with the revealed law and even reach beyond it into the supererogatory (*lifnim mi-shurat ha-din, middat hassidut,* etc.). This moral element complements the basic halakhic norms in two types of situations. In the first, the positivistic halakhic norms demand a threshold obligation that, morally speaking, falls short; a more appropriate act, though, would be "beyond the letter of the law," strictly speaking. In the second, the norms leave gaps because they do not cover the full scope of possible human activity, and general moral principles are used to fill in these lacunae. Nahmanides's approach to this area in which law and morality intersect is crucial to his conception of halakhah, which he formulates in his comment on the verse "Do what is right and good in the eyes of the Lord" (Deut 6:18):

> By way of *peshat* it is saying to observe God's commandments, *'edot,* and *hukkim,* and in so doing to have the intention to do what is good and right in His eyes alone. "so that it will be good for you" (Deut 6:18) is a promise, meaning that when you do what is good in His eyes it will be good for you, because the Lord is beneficent to those who are good and upright in their hearts. Our Rabbis have a fine *midrash* about this. They said that this refers to compromise and [going] beyond the letter of the law, by which they mean: first it said, "observe the commandments, *'edot,* and *hukkim* that He commanded you" (cf. Deut 6:17), and now it is saying, "pay mind to do what is good and right in His eyes even in those things about which He did not command you, because He loves what is good and right." This is a great

matter, because it is impossible for the Torah to mention all of man's
conduct with his neighbors and fellows, all of his business dealings,
and all of the conventions of civilized society (*tikkunei ha-yishuv ve-
ha-medinot*). So, after mentioning many of them, such as: "Do not be
a talebearer" (Lev 19:16), "Do not take revenge or bear a grudge" (Lev
19:18), "Do not stand idly by the blood of your neighbor" (Lev 19:16),
"Do not curse the deaf" (Lev 19:14), "Rise for the elderly" (Lev 19:32),
and so forth, it then stated a general principle that one should do what
is good, right, and equitable in everything, even if it entails compromise or going beyond the letter of the law. This is along the lines of
what they [the Sages] mentioned concerning the law of an abutting
field, or even "his youth is becoming," and "he speaks pleasantly
with people"—until he can be called wholehearted and upright in all
respects.[120]

On the basis of the literal-contextual approach, one could have said that the
directive to "do what is right and good" does not offer any new normative
content but is merely a general exhortation to perform what is "right and
good," namely, all the various kinds of commandments in the Torah. Instead,
Nahmanides develops a different interpretation that fits with the simple
meaning of the words and the context: the "right and good" is the spirit of the
law and demarcates an entire sphere of activity. This charge, then, does add
normative content of its own that pertains to a field otherwise unregulated by
halakhah.

This principle that Nahmanides articulates represents a strong criticism of
halakhic formalism, which sees law as inhering in and exhausted by the positive, written word. It considers human judgment irrelevant in the creation of
law. If the written law does not explicitly prohibit something, it is fully permissible. Not only does Nahmanides reject this view of the law, he offers a
compelling alternative. He posits that any rule-based system, however suc-
cessful, cannot possibly account for the entire gamut of potential human in-
teractions and moral contexts in which people must make decisions: "it is
impossible for the Torah to mention all of man's conduct with his neighbors
and fellows, all of his business dealings, and all of the conventions of civilized
society." Piling on additional details and distinctions to the existing set of
rules would not solve this problem; in fact, it would exacerbate it, because
more pieces means more interstices. This limitation of the written law can
be overcome only by way of a general directive that appeals to humans'

judgment and establishes the need to do what is good and right: "pay mind to do what is good and right in His eyes even in those things about which He did not command you, because He loves what is good and right."

This commandment of doing what is good and right therefore carries normative content, obligating humans to exercise their moral judgment in situations not covered by positive law. In such cases, one should be attuned to the spirit of the law and guided by the ultimate aim of doing what is right and good. As we can see from the passage above, Nahmanides attacks legal formalism from two angles. The first, as we have seen, concerns those cases for which no positive law was created. The second pertains to those instances in which a positive norm is on the books but does not meet the higher bar set by morality. This kind of action is referred to as "going beyond the letter of the law," that is, supplementing the existing norm with a more suitable norm. Nahmanides cites the Talmudic law concerning the sale of a field, under which the owner of a neighboring field has a right of first refusal. Strictly speaking, the halakhic right of ownership allows the field's owners to transfer the title of their property to whomever they so choose. The principle to do what is good and right complements this existing norm and obligates the field's owners to allow their neighbor to purchase the field first. The normative content of this all-encompassing principle of doing what is good and right therefore addresses both of these shortcomings: it fills in gaps left by the one-size-fits-all positive law, and it requires compliance with a higher standard of behavior than the one demanded formally by the existing law.

Criticism of the formalist position, and the use of general directives as an internal halakhic maneuver to plug the holes it leaves unfilled, constitutes a hermeneutic for Nahmanides in diverse contexts. So, besides the general guiding principle to do what is good and right, he considers two other guiding principles as crucial to his conceptualization of halakhah. The first of these principles is "You shall be holy" (Lev 19:2). Here, too, Nahmanides begins by citing the reading, in this instance espoused by Rashi, that this command is merely an exhortation to keep one's distance from forbidden relations and adds no normative content to the existing corpus of norms. Nahmanides rejects this interpretation and applies his hermeneutical-halakhic approach, which grants normative value to this overarching principle of "You shall be holy," like "Do what is right and good":

In my opinion, this separation (*perishut*) is not staying away from forbidden relations, as the master [Rashi] says, but it is the asceticism (*perishut*) mentioned throughout the Talmud, whose practitioners were called "ascetics" (*perushim*). The idea is that the Torah forbade illicit relationships and forbidden foods yet permitted a man to have relations with his wife and to eat meat and wine, in which case a sensualist can wallow in his lust with his wife or many wives and be a drunkard or glutton, cussing like the worst of them, because the Torah mentions no prohibition against it. Such a person would be a degenerate with the Torah's consent. Therefore, this verse follows what is absolutely prohibited and commands generally that we should abstain from overindulgence. One should limit sexual activity, in the same way that they [the Sages] said that Torah scholars should not be with their wives like roosters, and not engage in it except to the extent necessary for fulfilling the pertinent commandment. One should sanctify oneself by limiting one's wine intake, for Scripture refers to the Nazirite as "holy" (Num 6:5). [. . .] One should also watch one's mouth so that it does not become repugnant through gluttony and filthy talk . . . and sanctify oneself in this way until one attains asceticism (*perishut*), like their report about Rabbi Hiyya that he never had an idle conversation in his life. This general commandment, which comes after the enumeration of all of the absolute prohibitions, encompasses these and similar matters.[121]

Complete observance of the Torah's positive laws does not ensure the realization of its intent, which is why someone could be a law-abiding renegade. The instruction "You shall be holy," like "Do what is right and good," is a response to this inherent limitation of formalism, which gives expression to the spirit of the law in every area that is not explicitly forbidden. But whereas "Do what is right and good" is directed at the moral realm of interpersonal behavior, "You shall be holy" concerns asceticism and self-flagellation. Holiness, according to Nahmanides, arises from denying oneself the pleasures of the glutton or gastronome, drunkard or oenophile, lecher or philogynist, and it realizes the spirit of the Torah by placing a ceiling on the satisfaction of all desires and urges.

Nahmanides understands the explicit prohibitions in the Torah to be guided by an ascetic tendency that aims to inculcate the value of abstaining from even those things permitted for the satisfaction of one's urges. He rejects two other possible conceptions of the Torah's prohibitions on eating and sexuality. The first, which Maimonides sets forth in Shemonah Perakim (Eight

Chapters), introduction to tractate Avot, maintains that the prohibitions of the Torah sufficiently rein in humans' biological drives. To add to these prohibitions is to go down the misguided path of asceticism. Maimonides supports his position from the Talmudic criticism of Nazirism: "Is what the Torah prohibited not enough for you that you seek to prohibit other things for yourself?"[122] The second alternative Nahmanides rejects claims that the Torah's prohibitions target specific improper actions and do not intend to limit the biological instinct per se. Nahmanides himself conceives of the restrictions on eating and sexual intercourse as fundamental norms intended to lead the observant individual to curbing even permissible consumption. His ascetic tendency also finds expression in his praise for the Nazirite's act of self-sanctification in denying what is usually permitted, which as we saw above runs against some opinions in rabbinic literature.[123] For Nahmanides, the obligation of "You shall be holy" in relation to the realm of asceticism plays the same role here that the obligation of "Do what is right and good" does in the moral realm.

In his commentary on the commandments of "Do what is right and good" and "You shall be holy," Nahmanides combines his antiformalistic philosophy of halakhah with his hermeneutical assumption that these general directives are normative. In the continuation of his comment on "You shall be holy," Nahmanides turns his approach into a broad hermeneutical principle:

> Thus is the manner of the Torah to enumerate and then generalize. After the exhortation about the particulars of the laws governing all business interactions between individuals—"do not steal" (Deut 5:16), "do not rob" (Lev 19:13), "do not price gouge" (Lev 25:14), and the rest of the negative commandments—it stated generally: "Do what is good and right" (Deut 6:18), so that this positive commandment includes honesty, fairness, and further supererogatory conduct in favor of his fellows, as I intend to explain when I get there, God-willing. The same is true of the Sabbath: it prohibited the labors with a negative commandment and the exertions with a general positive commandment, as it says "rest" (Exod 23:12).[124]

Beyond the moral and ascetic, here Nahmanides brings his combination of legal philosophy and hermeneutics to bear on the work prohibited on the Sabbath and festivals. In his commentary on the positive commandment of "it should be a day of rest for you" (Lev 23:24), he gives a realistic, perceptive account of how one could turn these holy days into just another day without violating even a single biblically forbidden kind of labor. He then points to the general principle of rest intended to eliminate this potential profanation of these days, which could be accomplished even amidst rigorous and formal adherence to the prohibitions against work:

> It appears to me that this *midrash* intends to convey that we are biblically enjoined to rest on a Festival even from those things that do not constitute labor. One should not exert oneself all day counting grain, weighing fruit or metals, filling up wine barrels, moving utensils or stones from one house to another or one place to another. And if a city is surrounded by a wall whose gates are closed at night, people would lade the donkeys and bring wine, grapes, figs, and all other goods [to market] on the Festival; the marketplace would be bustling with commerce, stores open, storeowners extending credit, moneychangers at their tables with coin. Day laborers would rise early and hire themselves out like a regular weekday for these and other tasks. The holidays and even the Sabbath would become a free-for-all, because there is no [halakhically defined] labor in all this activity. The Torah therefore said "a day of rest," that it should be a day of cessation [of work] and rest, not a day of exertion and toil. This is a very fine explanation.[125]

The obligation that it be "a day of rest," which calls for rest and repose, fills the cracks that inevitably form from formal adherence to those positivistically prohibited labors of the Torah.[126]

In summary, in three areas of halakhah—morality, personal sanctity, and the Sabbath and festivals—Nahmanides innovates an antiformalist position that he also uses as a hermeneutic principle for understanding the general commands of the Torah itself. Alongside halakhah, there is a moral metaprinciple that covers the diverse sorts of gaps generated by the halakhic positive law and that installs an aspirational moral bar above the letter of the law.

VI

So far, we have examined two intersections between halakhah and morality: the standing of rational, moral obligations derived independent of revelation, and the existence of moral norms that complement the positive law of halakhah. Nahmanides also deals with a third encounter between halakhah and morality: morality as a paradigm for explaining the reasons behind commandments.

A paradigmatic example of Nahmanides's social acuity and its role in developing reasons for the commandments can be seen in his explanation for the gap between the punishment given to a rapist and to a seducer. The seducer is supposed to marry the seduced maiden, but should her father refuse, he instead pays a sum that reflects the cost of engagement gifts customarily sent by a groom to his virgin bride. The rapist, however, must marry the daughter and pay fifty shekels of silver. Nahmanides accounts for the difference as follows:

> The reason [for the difference] is that it is the way of the world for handsome young men to seduce older, beautiful girls, and it is not fitting for a sinner to profit; therefore, the Torah explained that he may not marry her against their will [hers and that of her father] and must pay them. Since she, too, sinned in the matter, he is not punished by being forced to marry her, and his payment of the fine suffices. After he marries her with her and her father's consent, she is like any other woman and the Torah does not grant her a *ketubbah*. It is also the practice of well-born sons to rape the daughters of men of lesser stature who have no power to stand up to them. It therefore said that in the case of rape "she will be a wife for him" (Deut 22:29)—against his will. According to our Rabbis, in this case as well she or her father can resist, because it is not appropriate for him to marry her against their will and perpetrate two wrongs against her. Sometimes, she will be of more dignified background than he and it is unconscionable that she should be debased by his sin. Justice dictates that the [choice of] marriage should be in their hands and not his; he must marry her against his will so that Jewish daughters not be victims of the powerful.[127]

Nahmanides explains the discrepancy between the two punishments of the rapist and seducer as a product of "the way of the world," namely, the structure of society and social stratification in a patriarchal world. His explanation reveals the sexual mores of the Middle Ages and his sober outlook on its society. The seduction of a maiden very often occurs, he tells us, at the hands of "handsome young men" of a lower class who seduce young women of a higher class. We should not allow marriage in such an instance because it would punish this well-bred young lady. In the case of rape it is the reverse, as the rapist tends to come from a higher social stratum and so is practically untouchable, leading him to treat lower-class women as sexual objects for gratifying his needs.[128] This man of means and power is punished by having to marry his victim and treat her with the legal and monetary standing granted to a woman married in the usual manner.[129]

Another instance where Nahmanides combines penetrating insight with social reality, psychology, and moral sensitivity is his understanding of the obligation to "keep yourself from every evil thing" (Deut 23:10) when the Israelite camp goes to war:

> The correct [interpretation] of the idea behind this commandment is that the verse warns about a time when sin is rampant. It is known that the practice of camps going to war is to eat everything disgusting, to steal, to perpetrate injustices, and to commit adultery and every disgraceful thing without shame. The most naturally upright people turn brutal and go berserk as the troop sallies forth to meet the enemy. Therefore, the verse warns about this: "keep yourself from every evil thing."[130]

Nahmanides observes that going into battle deeply alters the mentality of even the most upright person. A military camp on its way to fight the enemy can easily turn into a kind of moral no-man's-land, where warriors let their base desires run amok and they practice terrible cruelty, because they are about to do the most terrible thing of all—kill other human beings. It is impossible to suppress this until the time is right and then unleash it upon the enemy. Part of a soldier's emotional repertoire is heartlessness, because soldiers must dull their sensitivities if they are to withstand the trials of war. This vivid depiction of how leaving for battle affects the behavior and mentality of soldiers and of what goes on in camps of war serves as background for grasping what the Torah means by the general commandment to the Israelite military camp to "keep yourself from every evil thing."

VII

More than in any other area of his thought, Nahmanides's approach to the reasons for the commandments illustrates the complexity and duality of his world. The kabbalists of Provence and Gerona who preceded him also placed kabbalistic explanations of the commandments at the center of their focus. Not only did these kabbalists not disturb the surface of the halakhic act, they even understood the minutiae of its performance as having cosmic, theurgic significance. This does not mean that kabbalists limited themselves to giving theurgic meaning retroactively to the existing system of halakhah. They worked beneath the surface and transformed the inner character of halakhah, because they believed that kabbalah constitutes its spiritual dimension. By redefining the requisite intentionality of the ritual act, the Provençal and Geronese kabbalists effected a decisive change in the nature of the observance of the Torah and its commandments without so much as leaving an observable smudge. When two people observe the same commandment, one having in mind that it is a decree of the King that expresses absolute subservience to him, and the other intending to perform a theurgic act to fulfill a divine need, we cannot say they are performing the same act but interpreting it differently. This would fail to capture what kabbalah has wrought, which is, that the mental-spiritual component of fulfilling the halakhah reaches into the very heart of the act and remolds it. While we could describe someone training for a marathon and someone fleeing a mugger as performing the same outward motions and exercising the same muscle groups, we would be wrong to say that they are engaged in the same activity. Nahmanides possesses specific traditions about the kabbalistic significance of various commandments that differ from those of the Geronese kabbalists, but he was a partner to this broad, dramatic development that they initiated;[131] and he even cites—against his usual tendency—R. Ezra of Gerona's reason, recorded in his composition on the 613 commandments, for the proscription of certain admixtures.[132]

Where Nahmanides parts with the slightly older kabbalists is in providing an additional exoteric set of reasons for the commandments that is at once rich and profound. These exoteric reasons, which include social-moral ones that showcase Nahmanides's rare quality of piercing insight into and judgment of diverse social situations, stand in a complicated relationship and tension with his esoteric, kabbalistic ones. The exoteric reasons can stand alone, independent of the esoteric ones, and since the writing of his Commentary on the Torah until today, the former have edified its many readers, who have no understanding whatsoever of Nahmanides's cryptic kabbalistic allusions. One could argue that the presentation of the exoteric and esoteric side by side does not create tension or pose a problem but is in fact a testament to his multifaceted personality and talent as a kabbalist, exegete, and halakhist. One could even point to a nonnegligible degree of continuity between his exoteric and esoteric explanations of the commandments. We saw this above regarding idolatry, where the exoteric meaning is the worship of planets and zodiacal signs and the esoteric meaning is "cutting down the saplings," and according to both the prohibition is intended to forestall the isolation and manipulation of one entity within the chain of being. Nevertheless, while these two aspects of the exoteric and esoteric may create a complementary structure, it is subject to great inner tension. This arises from their irreconcilable differences on what the essence of a commandment is and how to view humans and their relationship to the Godhead. In the exoteric stratum, commandments are orders given by the King that have good reasons; in the esoteric one, commandments are expressions of the inner workings of all reality, through which humans can have an effect upon the Godhead without needing explicit instructions.

As we have seen in other areas of Nahmanides's thought, his integration of kabbalah minimizes the personal, anthropomorphic image of God. In the midrash, God is anthropomorphic, appearing in the image of humans; in kabbalah, the anthropos is an icon of the configuration of divine aspects. From the theurgic perspective, God is not a sovereign lawgiver but a being with multiple aspects that humans can bring together and draw down into the lower realms of reality. The theurgic power of the commandments existed in the land of Israel long before the giving of the Torah. The conception of God underlying the exoteric reasons and the conception of God underlying the esoteric reasons could not be more different. In the exoteric reasons, God intends to shape human consciousness and behavior; in the esoteric reasons, humans affect the state of the Godhead. This tension between the two is the source of an internal contradiction, to all appearances intentional, within Nahmanides's reasons for the commandments. Exoterically, he avows that the commandments were all given for the benefit of humans alone: "benefit of the commandments is not for the Holy One Himself but for man himself, to keep him from harm, a wrong belief, or a repugnant character trait, or to remind him of the miracles and wonders of the Creator, to know the Lord."[133] When Nahmanides writes about the Tabernacle as a talisman that draws down the divine efflux, he describes the commandments as a "divine need."

Perhaps the observance of a commandment can have a dual function, benefiting both humans and God simultaneously. But the difference between the exoteric and esoteric conceptions of the commandments does not lie only in the goal; it inheres in the frame of mind that each demands of the commanded, and the gap between the two is unbridgeable. One can see this readily in the exoteric and esoteric reasons for the sacrifice. In the exoteric explanation, Nahmanides describes the sacrifice as a substitute that atones for a man not sacrificing himself:

because man's activities are executed in thought, speech, and action, the Lord commanded him to bring a sacrifice when he sins. He lays his hands upon it, in correspondence to action; he confesses with his mouth, in correspondence to speech; he burns the entrails and kidneys, for they are the organs of thought and desire, and the legs, in correspondence to man's hands and feet that do all the work; he sprinkles the blood upon the altar, in correspondence to the blood commingled with his soul—in order for man to contemplate, as he performs all of this, that he sinned to his God in body and soul and his own blood ought to be spilled and his body burnt, were it not for the kindness of the Creator who accepts this sacrifice as a substitute and atonement, so that its blood replaces his blood.[134]

In contrast to this description of the sinner's self-nullification, the theurgic explanation of the sacrifice maximizes humans' role, for it is they who have the ability to mend the ancient tear they made within the Godhead. The tension between these two conceptions of humans' role reflects a tension within the theurgic perspective itself, in which the commandment profoundly expresses humans' cosmic power and the sin of their hubris.

CHAPTER 8

Esotericism and Tradition

1

The idea that Jewish tradition includes an esoteric body of teachings reached its height in the Middle Ages. Every great school of Jewish thought during this period—the philosophical, kabbalistic, astrological, and magical—presented its own teachings as the authentic secret tradition of Judaism. The most important medieval compositions were dedicated to explaining this esoteric layer of Jewish tradition, and so the compositions themselves were written esoterically, the author, authors, or circles taking care to conceal as they revealed. This rise of esotericism in the twelfth century also was not confined to one school of Jewish thought, appearing as a prominent feature in writings as diverse as Ibn Ezra's commentaries on the Torah and Maimonides's philosophical treatise *The Guide of the Perplexed.* This trend continued into the thirteenth century, during which Nahmanides was one of its most important, avowed proponents.

The preponderance of evidence from the previous chapters of this book makes it quite clear that the esoteric side of Nahmanides's oeuvre resembles the ones found in the works of Ibn Ezra and Maimonides. The esoteric is not some additional level tacked on to the preexisting, fully formed structure of the exoteric; rather, it constitutes its very foundation and thereby fundamentally alters the meaning of religious life, in terms of both its foundational concepts and beliefs and the structuring of the religious praxis and its mean-ing.[1] While previous chapters were devoted to elucidating Nahmanides's eso-teric positions on a wide range of issues, this chapter focuses on clarifying how he understands the esoteric medium itself, a medium that wrought pro-found changes to the meaning of Judaism in the Middle Ages.

Nahmanides distributed approximately 260 brief, enigmatic, and challeng-ing kabbalistic allusions throughout his Commentary on the Torah, many of which he introduced with the formula "By way of truth." The inclusion of such allusions in a work as widely published as this commentary, which he intended for a broad audience, was an original and paradoxical literary deci-sion. By placing the esoteric layer within the body of the commentary, Nah-manides created a two-tiered work aimed simultaneously at two readerships, such that each of its two parts is a self-contained literary unit. The exoteric component of the commentary is certainly an independent, self-sufficient unit, and its rare qualities edified—and still continue to edify—many readers who had no business with the esoteric. The esoteric component, which con-cerns biblical secrets and so is written in esoteric code, also merited indepen-dent treatment. R. Shem Tov Ibn Gaon and R. Meir b. Solomon Abusahulah, both grand-disciples of Nahmanides, excerpted the kabbalistic comments and wrote supercommentaries devoted to their elucidation. In writing a work that brought both the exoteric and esoteric under one roof and addressed two audi-ences at once, Nahmanides was continuing Ibn Ezra's literary tradition, but in the history of kabbalah this was a first. Nahmanides rejected two other pos-sible writing strategies that clearly distinguish the two different layers, both of which were employed by contemporaries and disciples. Someone unversed in esoteric wisdom who tries to understand the esoteric commentaries on the Aggadah by Rabbis Ezra and Azriel of Gerona will come up empty-handed. If the same person peruses the exoteric commentary on the Aggadah written by Nahmanides's most prominent disciple, R. Solomon b. Abraham Ibn Adret (Rashba), he or she might never guess that this great halakhist and Talmudist was also a kabbalist of note. This leads us to ask: What led Nahmanides to this unique literary decision? What was his view of esotericism?

These questions grow in strength when one considers the profound para-dox of allusive writing. At the end of the day, the very declaration that a secret exists is the first step toward its full disclosure. If something is top secret, the only people who know about it are those who need to; not only does no one else know the content of the secret, they do not even know that a secret exists. The inclusion of allusions in one's writing, even if they are scattered and accompanied by strong warnings against explaining or trying to decipher them, unavoidably invites their intensive analysis. It should not surprise us to learn that in the same way other medieval esoteric corpuses, such as Ibn Ezra's Torah commentary and Maimonides's *Guide,* attained canonical status, so too Nahmanides's Commentary on the Torah merited having a number of works dedicated to laying bare its secrets. The long line of such commentaries in both print and manuscript attests to the collapse of esotericism in the thirteenth and fourteenth centuries, partly due to the problematics inherent to the allusive medium itself.

Nahmanides, as we will soon see, was among the strictest in handling esoteric matters. His allusive writing is so sparing that were it not for the oral traditions written down by Rashba's students, it is doubtful whether we would be able to crack his allusions at all. In the introduction to his Torah commentary, he declares that one should not speculate about matters of kabbalah, because they depend entirely upon traditions confided by master to disciple. Yet the allusiveness intended to weed out the uninitiated in fact seems to have broadcast a siren song, compelling readers to use speculation in order to fill in what was left unsaid. In which case, one may ask, why write anything down at all? How did Nahmanides conceive of kabbalistic knowledge and the appropriate channels for its transmission, and how did that conception fit into his own method of writing? To answer these questions we must take in a broader view of how the prominent Geronese kabbalists—Rabbis Ezra, Azriel, and Jacob b. Sheshet—transmitted kabbalistic material, and then zoom in on Nahmanides, who formed his own unique and complex position against theirs.

A document from the beginning of kabbalah's historical record reveals that Nahmanides was at the center of a storm concerning kabbalistic esotericism. R. Isaac the Blind, the great mentor of the Geronese kabbalists, sent an epistle to Nahmanides and R. Jonah Gerondi, Nahmanides's first cousin, about the appropriate methods of transmitting kabbalistic lore and about the alarming breakdown of esoteric discipline that had begun at the beginning of the thirteenth century. This letter, first published and analyzed by Gershom Scholem, clearly brings to the fore the tensions among the earliest known kabbalists concerning esotericism. The opening line reads: "Wise as old men and vigorous as young, my teachers and colleagues whom I cherish, the enlightened scholars R. Jonah and R. Moses, God-fearing men of truth who act righteously [and will receive] a true reward."[2] This salutation demonstrates that Nahmanides was no disciple of R. Isaac, although the latter was an authority and source of kabbalistic traditions in whom Nahmanides displayed great interest. In the epistle, R. Isaac describes grave changes in kabbalistic esotericism that occurred during the first decades of the thirteenth century. He fulminates against the dissemination of kabbalah, which was antithetical to the policy and practice of his ancestors:

> I have not been defiant or disloyal—I have not spoken until now due to my great fear and alarm upon seeing sages, scholars, and pious men engage in long discourses and presume to write down great and sublime matters in their books and letters. But what is written cannot be contained by a cabinet, because often it is lost or its owner dies, and the books fall into the hands of fools and scoffers, and the name of Heaven is thus desecrated. And this is in fact what happened to them. As long as I was still with them, in this life, I warned them many times about them, but after my separation from them they have been the cause of much harm. I am of an entirely different habit, since my fathers were prominent men in the land and taught Torah to the public, yet not a word escaped their lips and they conducted themselves with them as with those unversed in [esoteric] wisdom, and I observed them and learned my lesson. I have also heard from the lands around you and from inhabitants of Burgos that they openly hold forth on these matters, in the marketplaces and in the streets, in confused and hasty discourses, and from their words it is clearly perceptible that their heart has turned from the Most High and they "cut down the saplings," whereas these Things [the *sefirot*] are united as the flame is bound to the coal, for the Ruler is singular and has no second.[3]

R. Isaac refers to the earliest kabbalists known to us from the second half of the twelfth century, R. Abraham b. Isaac (Ravi Abad), who authored Sefer ha-Eshkol, and his son-in-law R. Abraham b. David (Ra'avad), as conservative, silent kabbalists. Not only did they refrain from writing down hints of any kind, but they even carried themselves as if they knew nothing about any Jewish esoteric tradition. But esoteric practice was violated by his disciples Rabbis Ezra and Azriel, against whom, Scholem surmised, part of R. Isaac's criticism was leveled.[4] R. Isaac briefly notes the circumstances in which they disseminated their doctrines: "but after my separation from them they have been the cause of much harm." The breakdown in the organic chain of transmission controlled by the tradent, and the urge felt by his disciples to set up their own independent center, generated the circumstances for breaking the silence. The reason R. Isaac gives for not writing down the Torah's secrets is that the written word is bound to end up in the hands of those who do not understand it properly or those who would deride it, resulting in the desecration of God's name. Scholem raised the possibility that R. Isaac the Blind penned this letter in light of a polemical letter written by R. Meir b. Simeon ha-Me'ili, in which he decried kabbalah as a heresy that infringes upon God's unity. Aside from R. Meir's scathing criticism of kabbalah, the letter describes the destruction of kabbalistic works with the approval of R. Meshullam b. Moses, R. Meir's uncle and the author of Sefer ha-Hashlamah. According to Scholem, R. Isaac blames his students for their carelessness that led to this desecration of God's name.

While R. Isaac thinks highly of the Geronese kabbalists, referring to them as "sages, scholars, and pious men" even if they ended up being "the cause of much harm," his attitude to the Burgalese kabbalists is completely hostile. He does not give them the benefit of the doubt to assume they blundered in spreading kabbalistic ideas. The kabbalists of Burgos, in his eyes, publicly infect others with heresy as they deconstruct the Godhead and misapprehend the sefirotic relationships, "cutting down the saplings": "They openly hold forth on these matters, in the marketplaces and in the streets, in confused and hasty discourses, and from their words it is clearly perceptible that their heart has turned from the Most High and they 'cut down the saplings,' whereas these Things are united as the flame is bound to the coal." Regardless of the particular circumstances that gave rise to the letter, we can conclude from it that the kabbalists policed their own silence, because the doctrine of the sefirot entails a theology that walks an extremely fine and dangerous line between theological unity and multiplicity. The disclosure of such a nuanced position was liable to influence the simpleminded to believe in divine multiplicity out of blind trust in what they thought to be the esoteric tradition; at the very least, it would give kabbalah's antagonists ammunition for charging kabbalists with heresy. The teachings of kabbalah border on heresy and so had to be restricted to spiritual adepts alone. Those worthy of being initiated into the mysteries had to be capable of negotiating the difficult theological terrain without slipping into the abyss of multiplicity, of distinguishing belief from misbelief by a hair.

We do not have the original letter sent by Nahmanides and R. Jonah to which R. Isaac was responding. Scholem interpreted R. Isaac's response as offering guidance to younger kabbalists who might not have been his direct disciples but still respected him as a sagacious authority. In Scholem's opinion, R. Isaac was cautioning Nahmanides and R. Jonah not to repeat the errors of the Geronese and Burgalese kabbalists and to observe strict silence concerning kabbalistic lore. Moshe Idel argues for a very different and quite plausible reading: Nahmanides and R. Jonah had lodged a complaint about the breaches made by Rabbis Ezra and Azriel, who had studied under R. Isaac in Gerona, so the latter was apologizing for their conduct.[5] This letter, together with other sources, proves that R. Jonah was a member of kabbalistic circles, despite the fact that he did not leave even a hint to his knowledge of kabbalistic mysteries.[6] The fact that we come by this information only from external sources demonstrates that although R. Jonah was well versed in kabbalah, he followed the lead of earlier, tight-lipped kabbalists like Ra'avad, as would his own student Rashba. All of these kabbalists concealed their knowledge of esoteric matters from any and all who were not part of the inner circle of kabbalists. R. Isaac the Blind's letter appears to have been written in the middle of the 1230s, by which time R. Jonah already would have been recognized as one of the greatest halakhists and ethicists of his generation. This makes it difficult to support Scholem's reading that R. Isaac was imploring R. Jonah not to divulge the Torah's secrets. Nahmanides also would have been at the height of his powers as a halakhist and had not yet composed his Commentary on the Torah, which contains kabbalistic allusions (although there were two allusions in his Talmudic novellae), so his strict esotericism also poses a challenge for this reading.[7] This gives more credence to the reading proposed by Idel, namely, that this letter exposes the gap between Nahmanides and R. Jonah, on one hand, and the Geronese kabbalists, on the other, concerning esoteric discipline. The former requested that R. Isaac make the latter toe the line, to which he responded that he himself hailed from a long line of strict esotericists and had already reprimanded them a number of times when they were under his control—to no avail. This letter, then, reflects a serious controversy between R. Jonah, Nahmanides, and the Geronese kabbalists about the requirements of secrecy, and below we uncover its roots by examining the views expressed by various kabbalists about esotericism.

As mentioned above, the writings of the Geronese kabbalists—Rabbis Ezra, Azriel, and, later, Jacob b. Sheshet—changed the way kabbalistic knowledge was transmitted. Close reading of what they say and how they say it reveals the engine of change to have been their differing notions about the nature of such knowledge. In R. Azriel's case, he revealed the kabbalistic teachings by translating them into Neoplatonic terminology, thereby lending the kabbalistic corpus a rarely encountered clarity. R. Jacob viewed the kabbalistic corpus as a fundamentally open body of knowledge, which is subject to the same innovation and controversy that is part and parcel of Talmudic dialectics. In their articulation of kabbalistic allusion and doctrines, R. Azriel transposed the doctrine of the sefirot into a Neoplatonic key, and R. Jacob inserted kabbalistic knowledge into the framework of the rest of the Oral Torah, ridding this open knowledge of its hermetical seals.[8] Idel has recognized that Nahmanides crafted his own position on the nature of kabbalistic knowledge and the manner of its transmission in opposition to this exoteric tendency of R. Azriel and R. Jacob.[9] A careful analysis of Nahmanides's position in comparison to that of the Geronese kabbalists aids us in teasing out his thoughts on esotericism and the practices of his school for transmitting kabbalah.

II

In the introduction to his Commentary on the Torah, Nahmanides defines his position on the question of the kabbalah's esoteric nature:

> I hereby bring into a faithful covenant / which does present / proper admonishment / to anyone who peruses this book: do not apply reason / or come up with ideas about any of the allusions that I write about the Torah's secret doctrine. / I tell him in earnest / that through the application of logic and insight my words cannot be comprehended or grasped in the slightest, / except from the mouth of a scholarly tradent to the ear of a scholarly recipient. Speculation about them is foolish, / contemplation is useless, / deleterious and to no purpose. / Let him [the reader] not trust the one who has strayed, not trust in what is useless / for only misfortune will come from its speculations, / because about the Lord they will express perversion / that has no expiation / [. . .] and let them pay heed to what our holy Rabbis said: Do not expound what is greater than you, do not investigate what is more powerful than you, do not contemplate what is beyond you, do not inquire into what is concealed from you—contemplate what you have been permitted, for you have no business with concealed matters.[10]

In diametric opposition to R. Jacob b. Sheshet's conception of kabbalah, Nahmanides depicts it as a field of closed knowledge. Whereas R. Jacob encouraged his reader to make extrapolations for the greater glory of the Torah, Nahmanides cautions against making any deductions or interpretations based on speculation. The nature of kabbalah is just as it sounds—kabbalah, what is received and transmitted from one generation to the next, nothing less and certainly nothing more, especially not speculation produced by the human mind. Kabbalistic creativity outside the guardianship of tradition carries the danger of irremediable heresy. The esoteric tradition transmits secrets of the Torah that no mere mortal could arrive at by way of the intellect. At the same time, it establishes the conceptual Rubicon separating faith from heresy. Earlier in the same introduction, Nahmanides emphasizes the nature of kabbalah as a closed tradition. The mysteries of the Torah were transmitted to Moses at Sinai: "He [God] first informed him [Moses] of the creation of heaven and earth and all their hosts, that is, the creation of everything up above and down below. If so, everything said through prophecy about the Account of the Chariot and Account of Creation and about which the Sages have a tradition [. . .] were all said to our master Moses."[11] Later, when Nahmanides describes the possibility of reading the Torah another way by dividing up the sequence of letters in a different manner, which yields an extremely lengthy sequence of divine names, he states that this kind of reading was transmitted to Moses: "it was given to our master Moses according to the division [that yields] the reading of the commandments, and the reading of the names was orally transmitted to him."[12]

Nahmanides considers kabbalah to be an esoteric tradition transmitted from generation to generation, but this stands in considerable tension with another central theme in the introduction to his Torah commentary. He conceives of the biblical text as all-encompassing, comprising everything, such that its surface layer constitutes only one possible reading, the tip of the iceberg that stretches down into its depths. He writes briefly, "everything was written in the Torah, either explicitly or allusively," and then expands upon it further: "everything was written in the Torah explicitly or allusively, via words, numerologies, letterforms—those written properly or those with odd forms, such as the bent and crooked ones—or in the tittles of the letters and their crownlets."[13] This idea of the total semantic fullness of the Torah seems to suggest the possibility of discovering its secrets by way of the appropriate exegetical technique—no tradition necessary. Nahmanides closes off this possibility of infinite exegesis by asserting that not only are the actual secrets transmitted viva voce from one generation to the next, but even the interpretive allusions are under the lock and key of tradition: "these allusions cannot be understood except through [the tradition transmitted] orally all the way back to Moses at Sinai."[14]

In contrast to R. Jacob b. Sheshet, Nahmanides considers the tight lid kept on the Torah's secrets to be deeply linked to the closed nature of this field of knowledge.[15] His stark distinction between tradition on one hand and reason on the other is dictated by his fundamental stance that considers reason powerless in matters of theosophy, which is completely antithetical to R. Azriel's outlook. One can know the theosophical mysteries only through tradition, and any attempt at theosophical speculation will end in heresy and an improper understanding of the sefirot. For this reason, Nahmanides upholds the traditional understanding of the rabbinic calls for esotericism, with which he ends his introduction. They do not concern the inexpressibility of the ineffable aspects of the Godhead, as the Geronese kabbalists would have it, but the freewheeling treatment of the privately and guardedly transmitted tradition. Readers should not try to uncover the meaning of Nahmanides's allusions, not for themselves and certainly not for others, unless they possess a tradition passed from one initiated scholar to another—this is what the Sages meant.

Nahmanides himself uses this concept of kabbalah as a pristine tradition that delegitimates all innovation in two types of situations: first, whenever he strongly opposes rival kabbalistic interpretations that contradict his own tradition; and second, wherever he observes a self-imposed silence due to the absence of any tradition from his teachers that might illuminate a given text.[16] Modern scholars of Nahmanides have debated the extent to which tradition cemented his kabbalistic positions, and the degree of exegetical license he allowed himself.[17] An analysis of his own statements about the nature of kabbalah and a study of his hermeneutics, combined with evidence from the writings of his disciples and school, all inform us that he operated within a very restrictive framework of tradition. Nahmanides more generally emphasizes the nature of kabbalah as a tradition, and he refers to a number of kabbalistic doctrines such as the secret of impregnation and the doctrine of cosmic cycles as teachings handed down from one person to another since Moses received them from the Almighty at Sinai. About the doctrine of cosmic cycles he says the following: "But one cannot grasp the truth of these and similar matters on one's own, only through tradition. This matter is clear in the Torah to anyone who has heard the reason for the commandments through tradition in the proper manner, that is, tradent from the mouth of tradent all the way to Moses from the mouth of the Almighty. This applies to the import of the sabbatical years and jubilees."[18] Of course, one can make the argument that appeals to tradition sometimes mask intense creativity and originality, but these declarations of conservatism match Nahmanides's inter-pretive tone. In contrast to R. Jacob b. Sheshet and most definitely the Zohar, Nahmanides's kabbalistic exegesis has a stable, systematic quality to it; there is no discussion or proposal of legitimate alternatives to weigh against one another. The tentativeness and inquisitiveness that so characterize interpre-tive creativity, and certainly the delight that comes from expanding the fron-tiers of Torah, cannot be found in Nahmanides's kabbalistic writing.

From his writings and the compositions of his students we can identify quite clearly those components of kabbalistic doctrine that Nahmanides pos-sessed as part of a fixed, immutable tradition. The first component is his theosophical account of the nature of the sefirot, their order of emanation, and their interrelationships. The one pure, unadulterated piece of theosophi-cal writing by Nahmanides is his commentary on Sefer Yetzirah, although he ends it rather abruptly not too far in because he says his exegetical tradition runs out at that point. His reluctance to continue the commentary is telling, for he certainly was not wanting for ideas and did not lack exegetical prowess. The second component consists of the mystical practices he possessed, such as the secret of the blessings and the kabbalistic intentions in prayer. Nah-manides himself does not reveal anything related to this aspect of his kabba-listic tradition; he only notes the existence of secret traditions about these matters. It is his students who reveal to us that he possessed traditions about various kinds of theurgic activities that differed from those of R. Isaac the Blind and his disciples.[19] The third component is his kabbalistic lexicon, in which scriptural theonyms and expressions are understood as symbols or cog-nomens of particular sefirot or kabbalistic concepts. Nahmanides is excep-tionally systematic in his understanding and use of terms, which reflects the fact that his lexicon is rigidly fixed. Words like "This" (*Zot*) and "House" (*Bayit*) are cognomens for Shekhinah and nothing else. In this way, Nahman-ides stands apart from later kabbalists in Castile who occasionally would interpret the same symbols in different ways to fit the context and their par-ticular views. The enormous importance of this lexicon within Nahmanides's kabbalah is evident in the debate that erupted in his kabbalistic school over the correct referent of "Zion." R. Shem Tov Ibn Gaon reports that Rashba had a Nahmanidean tradition that understood it as a referent to the sefirah of Yesod, whereas R. Isaac b. Todros found evidence in Nahmanides's Commen-tary on the Torah that it refers to the sefirah of Shekhinah.[20] This degree of precision shows that this was no trivial matter—the symbolic lexicon was of utmost importance. Now, the fact that Nahmanides's kabbalah has inflexible components that he treated as a tradition set in stone does not mean that every kabbalistic interpretation he offered is merely a partial copy of the original, oral tradition he received. One reasonably can raise the possibility that Nahmanides used this fixed lexicon creatively, even if he undoubtedly received it together with a list of contexts in which it was to be applied.

Nahmanides's conception of the kabbalistic corpus as one of closed knowledge shapes his allusions. He makes it truly difficult to extract anything from them; he does not leave any loose threads that one can tug at and thereby unravel the whole mystery. It is difficult to give any explanation, even an incorrect one, of his terse, enigmatic formulations. His consistent esotericism, which is based on his conception of kabbalah and breaks from the practice of his Geronese predecessors, begs the following question: If someone can know and comprehend kabbalistic secrets only via the personal, private instruction of a teacher versed in the oral tradition, and one also should not try to learn anything from allusions, then what purpose does writing them serve? Why does Nahmanides lace his commentary with a sizable number of enigmatic allusions to the secrets of the Torah? Put differently, why does he not adopt the stricter esotericism of Ra'avad before him or of his contemporary and cousin R. Jonah and never let on that he knows such things? After all, despite Nahmanides's warning not to try to decipher his allusions, and perhaps even because of it, a nonnegligible number of works were written with the express purpose of elucidating and elaborating upon those allusions. If a thinker announces the existence of a secret and even hints at its contents, then notwithstanding the enigmatic nature of the hint and repeated warnings against trying to figure it out, he or she is testing the limits of esotericism. Nahmanides wants to divulge the secrets without actually spelling them out, staking out his esoteric position against the straightforward disclosures of other kabbalists. How did this great esotericist of the thirteenth century test the boundaries of his esotericism?

In his Commentary on the Torah, Nahmanides discusses the famous question of R. Yitzhak, who asked why the Torah begins with the creation narrative and not the first commandment concerning the new moon. He takes it as a foregone conclusion that R. Yitzhak could not have been suggesting that creation should not be recorded at all, because absent that foundation the very idea of revelation would be undermined entirely. Nahmanides therefore maintains that he was asking why the expansive narrative of creation was necessary:

The Account of Creation is a profound secret that cannot be understood from the verses, nor can it be truly known except by way of the
tradition [stretching back] to our master Moses from the mouth of the
Almighty, and those who know it are obligated to conceal it. Therefore, Rabbi Yitzhak said that the Torah need not begin with "Through
the Beginning (*Reshit*) He created" nor the narrative about what was
created *ex nihilo* (*nivra*) on the first day, nor what was fashioned *ex
materia* (*na'asah*) on the second day and the remaining days, nor the
extended section about the formation of Adam and Eve, their sin and
punishment, the story of the Garden of Eden and Adam's expulsion
from it, because none of this can be fully understood from Scripture.[21]

Nahmanides reiterates here his conception of kabbalah as closed knowledge,
which leads him to argue that this should stay the author's hand from writing
anything relating to the Torah's secrets, even allusively. R. Yitzhak's question
could be asked even more strongly about Nahmanides's own kabbalistic
allusions.

Nahmanides himself gives one answer to this question when he deviates
from the esoteric boundaries that he sets for himself. In such instances, he is
pressured to disclose his kabbalistic traditions because of a polemic with esoteric traditions of Maimonides and, chiefly, Ibn Ezra. Ibn Ezra was the first
medieval Bible commentator to interlace a widely available commentary with
esoteric matters. His goal was twofold: to establish that the secrets of the Torah are hermetic-astrological, and to define those who know them as the truly
enlightened. This compelled Nahmanides to use the medium of his own Bible commentary to publish hints about an alternative esoteric body of knowledge, thereby challenging Ibn Ezra on both counts. Throughout the length of
his own commentary, Nahmanides engages in a complex and ambivalent dialogue with Ibn Ezra, because beyond the many standard exegetical disputes
one commentator has with another, Nahmanides also battles Ibn Ezra for
control of the Torah's inner sanctum and the definition of the religious elite.
This rivalry is expressed in many ways, one of which is Nahmanides's slightly
ironic use of Ibn Ezra's signature line, "the enlightened will understand."
Nahmanides's "enlightened" are not those au courant of the hermetic-astrological disciplines but those with a clear grasp of the kabbalistic traditions
Nahmanides transmits from his teachers.

This disclosure due to the struggle over the Torah's secrets stands out
in two statements he makes about the attitude of the enlightened toward

rabbinic literature. Ibn Ezra mockingly criticized Rashi's inclusion of midrashim in his Torah commentary, particularly when a given midrash, according to him, was never meant to be exegetical but homiletic and didactic: "This
is the path of our wise men / in lands Greek and Roman: / they pay no attention to grammatical form / but rely upon the methodology of *derash* like *Lekah
Tov* and *Or 'Einayim*. / But since the *midrashim* can be found in the books of
our predecessors, / to what end do they weary us by writing them again, these
successors?"[22] Ibn Ezra uses the midrashim Rashi cites about the word *be-reshit*
to exemplify this, because they say *reshit* refers to a variety of things: the Torah,
fear of God, the first fruits, and so on. After citing Rashi, Nahmanides shows
his strikingly different attitude to this cluster of midrashim:

> Rashi wrote: "This verse begs to be interpreted homiletically, as our
> Rabbis expounded it: 'For the Torah which is called "the beginning
> (*reshit*) of His path" (Prov 8:22), and for Israel who are called "the first
> (*reshit*) of His harvest" (Jer 2:3).' This Rabbinic *midrash* is impenetra-
> bly sealed, because they found many things that are called *reshit* and
> have *midrashim* about all of them, and those of little faith speak of
> their great quantity."[23]

His polemic with Ibn Ezra, whom Nahmanides refers to as one of those
with "little faith," leads him to clarify the esoteric dimension behind the midrashim on the word *be-reshit:* "They [the Sages] intend by this that the word
be-Reshit [through *Reshit*] hints that the world was created through the ten
sefirot and is an allusion to the *sefirah* called *Hokhmah,* in which is the foundation of All (*Kol*)."[24] In a relatively long passage on kabbalistic matters, Nahmanides continues to explain the symbolic meaning of these midrashim,
some of which refer to the sefirah of Hokhmah and some to the sefirah of
Shekhinah, each of which is a *reshit,* a beginning: Hokhmah is the initial
singularity of the sefirotic world, and the universe emerges from Shekhinah.
At the end of the piece, Nahmanides concludes: "It is impossible to discuss
this matter at length in writing and the allusion can cause much harm, because people will make all sorts of untrue speculations about it. I have mentioned this to shut up those of little faith and meager wisdom, who mock the
words of our Rabbis."[25] By his own testimony, Nahmanides is forced to explain the Torah's secrets because he needs to discredit Ibn Ezra's ideas.[26] The
disclosure, or even intimation, of a purported esoteric doctrine requires a response even from strict esotericists, which entails revealing more than they
would like.

Nahmanides's apology for breaking the seal of secrecy for polemical purposes sharpens his problematic position as keeper of secrets. Nahmanides,
who firmly believes that the secrets of the Torah can only be acquired through
tradition and not deduced by reason, recognizes that allusive writing is an
utterly invalid mode of transmission, as in the previous citation: "the allusion
can cause much harm, because people will make all sorts of untrue speculations about it." The essential function of the allusion is to invite insightful
readers to make deductions by the force of their reason in the confidence that
they can do so. This leaves the closed-knowledge esotericist with two options:
reveal the secret entirely and without allusion (in writing available to everyone, which is certainly prohibited) or observe pin-drop silence. Oral instruction that is allusive and indirect is also a possibility, because the teacher can
oversee the process and monitor the kinds of inferences the disciple makes.
Writing down the allusion, however, is problematic—period. If Nahmanides
were to agree with R. Jacob b. Sheshet that students should be invited to use
their own minds to fill in the blanks and broaden the corpus, then the allusive
method would be appropriate, but he doesn't. According to Nahmanides,
written allusions are superfluous for the reader who has received the Torah's
secrets from one of its tradents, and for the one who has not, they are not
merely unhelpful but harmful, because the human mind is primed to fill in
missing pieces via inference and extrapolation.

In "Sha'ar ha-Gemul," Nahmanides states that the answer to the problem
of evil is connected to the secret of impregnation, "one of the secrets of the
Torah which were hidden except from those who merited them through the
tradition. Explaining them in writing is forbidden, and hinting has no benefit."[27] Since allusion is an invalid medium for transmitting secrets, Nahmanides goes on to present two alternative possibilities for the reader:

> the thinking individual should attribute the tribulations of the person
> who knows himself to be righteous and the tranquility of the wicked
> to the aforementioned secret included under the name "the secret of
> impregnation" (sod ha-'ibbur). That is, if God sees fit that one should
> grasp it based on the true tradition by protecting him greatly from
> misconception and error, for not many are wise; if one has not heard
> it, he should leave the matter to those who know it.[28]

The reader has two options: either hear the secret via a reliable oral tradition,
or rely upon those who know it. Allusion is categorically rejected as an intermediate category. After all is said and done, Nahmanides did resort to using

allusions, meaning that he was forced not only to bring to light what he would have rather kept under wraps, but to use methods of communication that he deemed problematic.

Nahmanides does not deny that the technique of allusion presumes that the enlightened can fill in the blanks on their own. He directs his enlightened readers to various conclusions by way of recurring formulations, such as, "But if you merit understanding the secret of the word *be-reshit,* and why it does not place ['God'] first to say 'God created *be-reshit,*' [then] you will know that by way of truth Scripture speaks of lower things and alludes to supernal ones."[29] Elsewhere, Nahmanides writes:

> The truth is that the blessing on the Sabbath day is the Fount of Bless-
> ings, which is the Everlasting Foundation, "and He sanctified it" (Gen
> 2:3), because it draws from the Holy [i.e., *Binah*]. And if you under-
> stand what I speak of you will grasp what they said in *Bereshit Rabbah*
> that it has no consort, and their further statement, "The Congregation
> of Israel shall be your consort," and you will comprehend that on the
> Sabbath there is truly an additional soul.[30]

When he explains the significance of the sabbatical and jubilee years, he writes: "Take note, for they [the Sages] have alerted us here to one of the Torah's great secrets [. . .] So, incline your ear to hear what I am permitted to impart to you about it in the language I choose to use, and if you are worthy you will comprehend it."[31] Instructions such as these, which direct the kabbalah maven to deduce additional aspects of the secret, appear in many passages where Nahmanides mentions secrets of the Torah.[32] Thus Nahmanides, who was pressured into his allusive writing, encourages enlightened readers to introduce their own reason into the very realm where it is ineffective and even dangerous. He minimizes this inherent problem by modifying the allusive medium. He does intend for his allusions to convey additional information to the enlightened, but he encodes it so well that readers would need to have significant erudition in order to decipher it. By making this prerequisite knowledge a necessary condition for drawing any inferences, Nahmanides can rest assured that readers will make the proper ones. Any readers without this background will find the allusion unintelligible and intractable, such that they cannot wring even mistaken ideas from it. Indeed, without the super-commentaries of Rashba's students, who made use of oral traditions passed from Nahmanides to his disciples, we would be at a loss in deciphering them. Nahmanides calibrates the hint to such a degree that it allows the transfer of knowledge only if readers have the necessary erudition, which ensures that any inferences drawn are correct. In sum, aside from the usual use of allusion as a filter, in Nahmanides's deft hands it also acts uniquely to channel the readers' deductions along a predetermined path.

To better understand this, let us distinguish between two kinds of allusion: the vertical and the horizontal. The vertical allusion gestures toward esoteric matters pertaining to the configuration of the sefirot. In this type of allusion, the secret understanding of the verse is a reflection of the divine drama: the relationship between the sefirot, the order of their emanation, the complex and complicated balance between them that must be sustained. The horizontal allusion, by comparison, points to the network of symbols. Its purpose is to thicken the symbolic meaning of a particular signifier, to join dissimilar or similar expressions in seemingly different contexts into one unified framework.

Nahmanides's allusions mostly fall under the second category of the horizontal parallel, which builds up a complete network of expressions and symbols and gives them kabbalistic meaning. A characteristic example of such an allusion can be found in his comment on the clause "the Lord blessed Abraham through the All (*ba-Kol*)" (Gen 24:1). Nahmanides explains the relationship between Shekhinah and the All and then says: "If you comprehend what I have written, you will understand the accursed women's statement that 'Ever since we stopped raising incense to the Queen of Heaven, we have lacked All (*Kol*)' (Jer 44:18), and why the word is written without an *aleph* [i.e., *malkat* as opposed to *mele'khet*], and you will apprehend obscure matters in the Pentateuch and the rest of Scripture."[33] Nahmanides directs the attention of enlightened readers to another usage of the word *kol* elsewhere in Scripture and suggests that it be interpreted in the same symbolic manner as here, thereby connecting the two seemingly irrelevant verses. The allusion introduces readers to "obscure matters in the Pentateuch and the rest of Scripture." One could say that within his overall exegetical enterprise the role of the sefirotic structure is to explain webs of scriptural meaning. The allusion orients the enlightened so that they can plumb the depths of scriptural verses and relevant rabbinic midrashim, enabling them to put it all together. The horizontal nature of the majority of Nahmanides's allusions demonstrates that his use of allusion leans strongly toward interpretation instead of theosophy.

Nahmanides is of course familiar with the vertical aspect of the kabbalistic secret. A clear example appears in his depiction of the Garden of Eden and the Tabernacle. He perceives existence more generally and humans

specifically as possessing an isomorphic form that reflects the sefirotic configuration and the mystery of the Godhead. The Garden of Eden and the
Tabernacle are spaces in which their isomorphic-symbolic nature is clearest
and most reflective, and, as such, contemplating them enables one to behold
sharply and clearly the configuration of the Godhead itself:

> The Garden of Eden, its four rivers, the Tree of Life, the Tree of Will
> that God planted therein [. . .]—all are literal and just as they sound,
> that is the absolute truth of the matter. And it is a wondrous mystery,
> for they are like blueprints for understanding the secret of a profound
> matter. [. . .] Similarly, the holy work of the Tabernacle [. . .] every-
> thing in every single place—implements, forms of the cherubs—were
> all to understand the secrets of the activity of the supernal, intermedi-
> ate, and lowly worlds, with allusions there to the existence of the entire
> Chariot.[34]

But Nahmanides himself does not use the allusion vertically: "their secret is
profound and possessed by recipients of the faith."[35] He is not even willing to
sketch a rudimentary map for comprehending the configuration of the sefirot
and the isomorphic structure of reality, as R. Jacob b. Sheshet had done in his
Sha'ar ha-Shamayim. Nahmanides maintains that such secrets should be
transmitted orally.

The horizontal-exegetical allusion in Nahmanides's commentary lowers
the cost of a mistake, because in the worst case scenario enlightened readers
incorrectly use their reason to assign an unwarranted kabbalistic interpretation to a difficult verse. For example, they might interpret a particular instance of the word kol as referring to Kol, a kabbalistic cognomen of Shekhinah,
when in truth it merely means "everything" and has no esoteric resonance.
One pays a much steeper price for a mistaken inference drawn from a vertical-
theosophical allusion about the sefirotic system, because it constitutes a flaw
in one's conception of God that has the makings of heresy. Nahmanides the
esotericist, who views kabbalah as closed knowledge, therefore uses the en-
coded, horizontal type of allusion as a way of dealing with the problematics of
allusion.[36]

Nahmanides developed his view on esotericism and his specific method of
transmitting esoteric traditions in his writings as part of a two-front war. The
first front was against the Geronese exotericists who attempted to redefine the
restrictions of esotericism. Nahmanides stood in this breach by utterly rejecting the idea of kabbalah as open knowledge and by substituting it with the

conception of kabbalah as closed knowledge. He tried to repair the damage done by validating only one medium for kabbalistic instruction—oral transmission from a master of kabbalah to an initiated disciple. The second front was against Ibn Ezra, who claimed that the esoteric stratum of the Torah could be found in his commentary and that the enlightened were those versed in the hermetic-astrological tradition. In his Commentary on the Torah, Nahmanides was in constant dialogue with Ibn Ezra's commentary, so he considered it an excellent medium in which to reveal a systematic alternative to Ibn Ezra's esoteric worldview. He broke Ibn Ezra's monopoly on determining the innermost meaning of the Torah and the identity of its elite, intimating that they are quite different from what Ibn Ezra would have his readers believe. Ibn Ezra's allusions forced Nahmanides to reveal, even if only through his own allusions, more than he would have wanted to expose. In the battle between these two opposing forces, the unique Nahmanidean allusion was born.

One can see that Nahmanides's unique position on kabbalistic secrecy did not take shape within a vacuum. In the Middle Ages, the idea of a secret body of teachings grew to be a very influential category in exegesis and general culture. As we saw earlier, Nahmanides's position on disclosure was a clear response to Ibn Ezra and the Geronese kabbalists. But as with everything Nahmanidean, there is a deeper dimension here to be explored: Nahmanides was grappling with the paradoxical nature of the esoteric itself. We can better understand this by taking a step back and making a few points about how the idea of the esoteric realm was a very powerful tool for integrating and incorporating non-Jewish cosmological and theological ideas into the very heart of Jewish tradition during the twelfth and thirteenth centuries.

During the Middle Ages, astrological, hermetic, Aristotelian, Neoplatonic, Gnostic, and a host of other ideas made their way to the heart of Judaism in the guise of the Torah's esoteric doctrine. In the screened space of the esoteric, particularistic Jewish traditions and non-Jewish ones mingled, and external ideas could be incorporated as an integral part of the Jewish tradition through the esoteric medium. This phenomenon was in full force during the Middle Ages and was made possible by two structural elements of the esoteric realm. The first, and simplest, is the interpretive space that the esoteric lends to Scripture. The addition of an esoteric dimension to the words of the canonical text allows for a nearly unlimited expansion of the text's "semantic capacity." Once the words are treated like a code, the text becomes so elastic that it can be stretched to include things that are increasingly more diverse and radical. The very idea of an esoteric level of meaning creates a new and powerful tool: foreign ideas can be absorbed from the outside world and incorporated into the core of tradition. Ibn Ezra was the first Bible commentator to make systematic use of the category of the esoteric interpretively, and it enabled him to claim that the astrological worldview, which seems so distant from the surface of the text, constitutes its inner meaning. Ibn Ezra obviously was not the only one to take this interpretive potential, afforded by the idea of the esoteric layer, to the extreme, although he did break new ground in developing it into a tool that could systematically import the scientific worldview of the surrounding culture into the Torah.

The second element of the esoteric secret is more complicated but also more significant, and it concerns the paradoxical nature of the secret. The justification for esotericism is the desire to keep the precious secret from being pawed and sullied by those unworthy of handling it. But the very nature of the esoteric means that very few outsiders can ever access it. In the future, someone could claim that some new body of knowledge is in fact the esoteric Jewish tradition of yore. Some might come out against it and argue that they have never heard of such ideas being part of tradition, to which he or she could reply: this information has been kept completely secret, so it is no surprise that you have not detected any traces of it in the tradition familiar to you. The restricted area, it turns out, is most open ended and diverse. One can pass off a radical idea as the secret teaching of Jewish tradition because there is nothing observable to measure it against. Critics of Ibn Ezra's magical-astrological secrets cannot go on the offensive armed merely with the argument that such ideas are absent from Jewish tradition, because he can easily deflect it with the counterclaim that the superstructure of tradition cannot prove anything about the concealed substructure. No wonder, then, that diverse medieval thinkers could argue in favor of radically different and even contradictory traditions as the concealed truth of the Torah. In the entire twelfth and thirteenth centuries, could there have been anything more different and incompatible than Nahmanides's Commentary on the Torah, with its "way of truth," and Maimonides's *Guide,* two canonical works that viewed and presented themselves as disclosing, to some degree, the true esoteric Jewish tradition? Esotericism served as a powerful medium through which a variety of systems of thought were integrated into the heart of the Jewish tradition. This phenomenon makes apparent the paradox of esotericism discussed above in its most radical form. The declaration of this field of knowledge as a restricted area, in order to protect, supervise, and maintain it in its pure, fixed, traditional state, became its own undoing, allowing in squatters of all stripes.

It is important to point out that the internalization of these diverse doctrines into mainstream Jewish tradition by way of the esoteric did not only legitimate them, it granted them pride of place. Once these worldviews became accepted as the esoteric secrets of the Torah, they were fittingly haloed and hallowed as the profoundest teachings of Judaism, comprising part of its deep meaning. Through the medium of the esoteric, medieval Judaism developed an unusually flexible and capacious intellectual tradition that could digest the worldviews of the surrounding, non-Jewish majority with all of their baggage and transmute them into the innermost, profoundest meaning of Judaism.

Within Nahmanides's approach one can discern his attempt to deal with the paradoxical instability of the esoteric, which was supposed to have been the most guarded element of Jewish tradition. Already in his lifetime there were signs that the barriers were gone and the field open. This field of secrecy was extremely fertile ground for the development of radical and even contradictory doctrines that altered the character of Jewish tradition while remaining out of sight. Nahmanides participated in this scramble for esoterica when he included a stratum of enigmatic allusions in his Commentary on the Torah, and when he openly stood his ground in the contest for control over the esoteric realm. The wide dissemination of his Torah commentary, coupled with his authority as a master halakhist, contributed greatly to the canonization of kabbalah as the Jewish esoteric corpus. Nevertheless, he tried to stabilize the field of the esoteric and reestablish its boundaries: he employed strict and exacting methods of initiation and transmission, and he claimed that the secret tradition of kabbalah had been orally transmitted for untold generations and thus was not open to logical speculation.

In the third part of the *Guide*, Maimonides briefly alluded to what he considered to be the esoteric sanctum sanctorum of the Account of the Chariot, and in the preceding introduction he claimed that he had no tradition regarding the esoteric body of Torah. He believed that the innermost meaning of Judaism had been lost over time because the organic lines of transmission had become corrupted; the secret had been kept quite well until it was utterly lost from the world. Maimonides freely admitted that he reconstructed the secrets of the Torah using his own reasoning, and out of fear that the profoundest meaning of Judaism would vanish upon his demise, he allowed himself to reveal more than is usually permissible and to at least put the chapter headings on paper. Nahmanides provided a completely different account of the source of the Torah's secrets in his possession—he received them via an uncorrupted oral tradition, and one cannot employ reason whatsoever concerning them. With this, Nahmanides completely restricted the widespread, liberal use of the esoteric. But aside from his attempt to constrain the explosive nature of the esoteric realm as such, it might be safe to speculate that Nahmanides's anchoring of his own esoteric teachings as a received tradition enabled him to come to grips with the gap that his own writings generated between the revealed and the concealed.

Conclusion

NAHMANIDES BETWEEN ASHKENAZ AND ANDALUSIA

In the 1230s, a raging controversy broke out in Provence over the writings of Maimonides. One central party to this conflict was a first cousin of Nahmanides, R. Jonah Gerondi, who together with his teacher R. Solomon of Montpellier and his colleague R. David b. Saul formed the so-called anti-Maimunist camp in Montpellier. After R. Solomon launched his campaign against Maimonides, Maimonideans in Provence, the "Maimunists," rallied and vigorously counterattacked. Under siege from all quarters, R. Solomon sent R. Jonah northward to recruit reinforcements from the Torah scholars of northern France, apparently in the hopes that bringing them into the fray would level the playing field. R. Jonah, who had studied under Tosafists in Évreux, naturally was considered the best candidate for this mission. The northern French scholars did not fully grasp the cultural milieu in which Maimonides had been active, nor did they appreciate his monumental contributions, so they did not accord him the kind of respect that even his opponents in Provence, Aragon, and Castile had shown him. They answered R. Solomon's plea for assistance with perhaps even greater fervor than he had expected. After investigating the matter, they placed *The Guide of the Perplexed* and the first book of the Mishneh Torah, the philosophy-laden Sefer ha-Madda', under a ban, apparently even ordering that copies of these works be burned or buried. What particularly fueled their rage were the allegorical readings and naturalistic tendencies of the *Guide,* as well as Maimonides's assertion in his "Laws of Repentance" that people who ascribed corporeality to God are heretics and they have no place in the World to Come.

Sefer ha-Madda' includes far more extreme philosophical positions than the ruling that excludes from the Jewish collective those who conceive of God as having some kind of body and denies them entry into the World to Come. For the anti-Maimunists, however, this ruling was more than enough. Maimonides's position was a personal affront to the world of pious individuals who took pains to observe every jot and tittle of the law yet did not spend time contemplating metaphysical issues of this nature. In fact, had someone thought to ask, they probably would have responded to questions about God with a variety of anthropomorphic notions. This ideal type of unquestioning faith and boundless self-sacrifice was the hallmark of Ashkenazic religiosity, and Maimonides's harsh condemnation was interpreted as seeking to rid the world of it. One can also certainly posit, as Gershom Scholem did, that beyond coming to the defense of the simple Jew's way of life, the anti-Maimunists were trying to uphold the fundamentally anthropomorphic conceptions held by some elite Ashkenazic Jews and the mystical anthropomorphism of the kabbalists.[1] Had Maimonides's theological positions and intolerance been expressed only in works of religious thought or philosophy, perhaps the anti-Maimunists would have passed them over in silence, but their inclusion in such a widely available and well-thumbed halakhic code was correctly perceived as a power grab by Maimonides, who was installing himself as the final authority on matters of theology and turning his considered opinion into incontestable, binding doctrine.

Maimunists responded in kind with an excommunication of their own, singling out R. Solomon and his disciples, and they sent one of the most distinguished representatives of Provençal Maimonidean culture, R. David Kimhi (Radak), to obtain the backing of Spanish communities, which were seen as natural allies in the fight for Maimonides's Andalusian culture. The Maimunists hoped that the endorsement of those communities would counterbalance the opposition from Provence and northern France, but they were disappointed. Radak met only partial success in Spain, because the culture of central and northeastern Iberia had undergone a profound change at the beginning of the thirteenth century. In Toledo, R. Meir Abulafia and R. Judah Alfakar openly refused to support the excommunication of the anti-Maimunists.

This controversy, whose chronology has been carefully chronicled by various historians, quickly escalated from an ideological debate to a fierce conflict that left deep scars in the memory of its participants and witnesses.[2] In the conflict, open season was declared on one individual, against whom any means of attack was on the table—R. Jonah. His Maimunist adversaries tried to remove him from the picture through character assassination. They revived an old claim that one of his ancestors had a halakhically invalid marriage, making him a bastard. Since Nahmanides was his first cousin, this genealogical stain spread to him as well, and some of the most rancorous letters that he sent to Provence addressed the Torah leaders there, demanding that they retract the blot smeared on his family and remove those responsible for it from their midst.[3] From a passage in one of the letters, which he wrote to the central rabbinic figure in Provence, R. Meshullam b. Moses, author of Sefer ha-Hashlamah, it sounds as if he too was a candidate for excommunication because of his kabbalistic opinions. One can perhaps find direct evidence of this in one of the letters sent by Maimunists in Béziers, in which they explicitly attacked R. Jonah and mentioned the illicit relationship in his bloodline. In the very same letter, the Maimunists roundly condemned the kabbalistic tendencies of R. Jonah's unnamed associate: "One is called a man of faith but is an unbeliever, / of God he has no fear. / Each day he seeks out Sandalfon, Dalfon, Hasadon, / and Beelzebub, god of Ekron. / He compounds his guilt and transgression / by offering to Nergal, Ashimah, Adrammelech and Anammelech supplication / with fear and trepidation."[4] This scathing equation of kabbalists with idolaters might have been directed at Nahmanides.[5] In Nahmanides's letter to R. Meshullam b. Moses, which might have been a response to the letter sent from Béziers or some other letter, Nahmanides summoned his Provençal adversaries to court, where he would be vindicated for his kabbalistic theology:

> Let us figure out, between us, what is good, and whether we adhere to the faith of our forefathers. / And whoever lifts his eyes to the azure / and perhaps does not become lost in deep contemplation / of the Wheel, Sphere, and Chariots through intellection, / maybe he turns his thought / to the paths hewn by the flame of God, / before the land [of Israel], other lands, and heaven were wrought / —will you sell them to the slaughter for your rash, / to suck out the marrow and consume the flesh, / until your words bring them to their knees, / stretched out for correction on your pillory?[6]

Nahmanides made sure not to aim his barbs directly at the leading Torah scholars of Provence, because he did not want to make new enemies. He called for them to rein in those rogue elements whom he refers to as "juveniles," who controlled the tone, pace, and direction of the polemic. Yet, in the continuation he also lodged a complaint against the Provençal leadership as abetting, even if only indirectly, his persecutors: "But you lend a hand to those who transgress through heresy and denigration, / such that whoever expounds any haggadah is delivered into their hand for obliteration."[7] The persecution of those who "expound any haggadah" seems to refer to thinkers like the Geronese kabbalists, who produced aggadic commentaries that interpreted Aggadah as the symbolic key for kabbalistic notions.[8] R. Meshullam's response to Nahmanides is not extant, but it seems that in the wake of the Maimonidean controversy he supported his nephew R. Meir b. Simeon ha-Me'ili, who banned and burned kabbalistic writings. It would be fascinating to know how he responded to Nahmanides, who had turned to him, among others, to defend him against his anti-kabbalist persecutors.

Nahmanides was sucked into this whirlpool of personal attacks against his will, but his greatest contribution came from his deliberate intervention. For the duration of the controversy, he was only in his thirties, but still he played a unique, influential role in its development. Two of his letters illustrate his heavyweight status despite his relatively young age. These letters were addressed to the leading lights of the Jewish world: one was sent to the communities of Aragon, Navarre, and Castile, and the other to the Torah scholars of northern France. The two letters were addressed to utterly different Jewish communities, to the external forces that each of the two Provençal factions were trying to win over to their own side—the French on one hand and the Spaniards on the other. Nahmanides employed the same strategy in both letters, which reflects his attempt to prevent a local conflict from engulfing and polarizing the entire Jewish world and rending it apart from within. In his letter to Spanish communities, he urged them to refuse to support the ban on the anti-Maimunists; in his letter to the French rabbis, he worked to repeal their ban on Maimonides's writings. From a Maimunist letter sent from Lunel, one can sense the weight Nahmanides's letter had in the ultimate decision by the rabbis to retract their ban: "And when they [the rabbis of northern France] saw our correspondence, / the letters of most of our populace, / and the letter of the great, pious sage who is faithful to the Holy One, / R. Moses b. Nahman, / they were ashamed of their actions / and regretted their excommunications."[9] Nahmanides exerted comparable influence, with opposite consequences, in thwarting Radak's mission to the Spanish communities, from which Radak had hoped to extract a ban on the anti-Maimunists in Provence.[10]

As the polemic grew more extreme, each side dug in and doubled down. Nahmanides stood out as the only figure who tried to offer a way out—a solution that would reduce the inflammation surrounding the controversy and shrink it back down to a legitimate, internal debate, thereby preventing it from blowing up into a violent, worldwide conflict with Jewish authorities issuing excommunications across geographical and cultural boundaries. Of the key personalities in the controversy, Nahmanides also was the only one who held considerable sway in both camps. All of this is a testament to his political savvy and outstanding leadership, which were already in evidence at his young age. Moreover, his unique approach and his ability to maintain an impressive level of discourse with both sides afford us insight into his cultural worldview, which was formed along the seam dividing Andalusia from Ashkenaz.

Nahmanides's letter to the Spanish communities is relatively brief and does not reveal his fundamental positions. He calls on these communities not to trust the delegates from Provence, whom he describes in condemnatory terms: "For already I have seen / concerning this matter people leading others into sin. / They are coming our way with seductive writings in their hands, / winning hearts and prejudicing minds."[11] According to Nahmanides's account, which may be true, R. Solomon did not pursue a ban on Maimonides's writings but warned people about certain ideas contained in them. The blame for that ban fell squarely on the shoulders of the French rabbis: "And even if the rabbis of northern France, whose Talmudic waters we drink, said that the sun in its zenith / ought to be concealed in its sheath, / and ordered that the lustrous moon be occulted / and the stars beclouded, / the rabbi [R. Solomon] who makes his case before you is guilty of no sin, because he was having a civil disagreement with his fellow."[12] The addressees had no reason to excommunicate R. Solomon, and certainly not before giving him a fair hearing in person. He had legitimate grounds for his dispute: R. Solomon "was having a civil disagreement with his fellow; whereas the other party, who is given to exaggerating, / well the racket he makes is quite revealing."[13]

Nahmanides traced the rapid deterioration in civility, which culminated in bans and counterbans, to the harsh response of the French rabbis. He therefore devoted most of his attention to them, sending them a long epistle with the aim of procuring an annulment of the ban on the *Guide* and Sefer ha-Madda'. This letter included, among other things, high praise for Maimonides and his work, which is why it presents a real challenge for getting a good grasp of Nahmanides's attitude toward Maimonides and Andalusian culture in general. Scholars who have analyzed his attitude have split into two camps. The first camp reads the letter as a calculated political move intended to calm things down and let cooler heads prevail. It does not reflect the positions Nahmanides truly held, which these scholars believe were thoroughly anti-Maimonidean. The second camp views the letter as Nahmanides's true sentiments toward Maimonides and believes it is indicative of his generally positive appraisal of Andalusian Judaism. They see evidence of this in other areas of his thought, such as his attitude toward Aggadah in his Commentary on the Torah and his willingness to include the comments of R. Abraham Ibn Ezra and ideas of Maimonides in his own commentary.[14] Understanding this letter in light of Nahmanides's other writings is crucial for figuring out where to locate him culturally. These two readings of Nahmanides, in my opinion, do not capture his complexity or align with his self-perception. As such, we ought to carefully analyze his letter to northern France in order to appreciate properly his presentation of Maimonides, the significance of his proposal for resolving or at least reducing the conflict, and how both of these fit into the larger context of his thought and other writings.[15]

Nahmanides's first argument against the conduct of the French rabbis does not relate to the object of their criticism, Maimonides, but rather to the means. He asserts that any ban is futile because one cannot budge a venerated colossus, which is what Maimonides was in major realms of the Jewish world. Maimonides's admirers in those areas would never stand for such an affront and would reflexively react by producing their own decrees of excommunication— better not to open that Pandora's box at all, Nahmanides says. In his own words:

> When these communities hear this anathema pronounced, they will shrug off their fears / and show no respect for Torah leaders; / they will plot to defy the rabbis of France. / Each will come to his fellow's assistance / to gird loins and summon courage on behalf of the words of the great Master [Maimonides], encouraging those who learn his works, "Stay strong! / Flash [with insight] like lightning!" / in order to provide succor, so that they devote even more time to their contemplation / and carry on with great determination. / The Torah will become like two, / and all of Israel will bifurcate, too.[16]

Although Nahmanides had been speaking explicitly about the communities of Yemen immediately before this quotation, communities in which they held Maimonides in the highest esteem and even inserted his name into the kaddish prayer, this reaction was not limited by any means to those communities alone. If the ban were to be extended to the communities of Catalonia, they would meet resistance, even though these communities unreservedly supported R. Solomon. They too were in awe of Maimonides, even if they did not agree with everything he said or wrote: "Take note: in our communities we accord much respect to the great Master [Maimonides] and are greatly indignant on his behalf, for the honor of his Torah, piety, / dignity, and majesty— / not because we are of two minds / and have lost our way, straying from the path of our fine Rabbis / for the philosophical vanities of the gentiles."[17] Even if the Barcelonans might have thought about enforcing the ban on the *Guide,* they would never have done the same concerning Sefer ha-Madda': "Even if they might consider part of your decree, and as a result quarantine the *Guide of the Perplexed* / and seal the lips of those who would speak about what is in its text, / because their mind is like the needle's eye and they cannot follow his train of thought nor his ways can they fathom, / what would they say about *Sefer ha-Madda',* divinely inspired writing that they copy verbatim."[18] According to Nahmanides, the disconnect between the Jewish cultures of northern France and Spain led the French rabbis to underestimate the legend that Maimonides was outside of Franco-Germany. Unaware of this, they produced their hasty ban. But more than that, the cultural gap meant that they misperceived who Maimonides was and what he was all about. Nahmanides tried to address this by placing Maimonides's works back into their original cultural context:

> Even if you [the northern French rabbis] have been raised in the bosom of faith, / rooted in the courtyards of tradition, robust and full of youth, / how can you not look beyond your horizons? / For he fortified the hopeless and those enslaved by their passions! / He sated them with our faith and quenched their thirsty souls with our traditions, / instead of the Greek nonsense with which they had stuffed themselves, feeding their bellies terrible notions / [. . .] Did he trouble himself for you, Geonim of the Talmud? He was practically forced, against his will, / to construct a literary haven for those in Greek philosophy's thrall, / far away from Aristotle and Galen—have you heard what they had to say, / have their proofs led you astray?[19]

In this passage, Nahmanides justifies Maimonides's involvement in Aristotelian philosophy and other non-Jewish disciplines. They did not exert a profound influence on him, nor did he feel a deep affinity for them; he merely used whatever tools were necessary to address the religious crisis ushered in by philosophy. The French rabbis cannot possibly understand the crisis experienced by these individuals because they are out of reach of Greek-Arabic philosophy, and without seeing its corrosive effect, they cannot truly appreciate the cure that is Maimonides's work. In this account, Nahmanides reads Maimonides very moderately. Maimonides's great achievement was not the integration of Aristotelian philosophy into Judaism, but the defense of the latter from the former. As he puts it: "he is a shield from the arrowhead / of the Greeks who promulgate falsehood; / he hoists up those drowning in their [the Greeks'] flooded well, mired in their mud."[20] This partial reading of Maimonides's engagement with philosophy is not a Nahmanidean invention. Regarding the most crucial questions raised by Aristotelian philosophy, whether the world is eternal or de novo, Maimonides in his *Guide* did systematically defend the belief in God's creation of the world de novo. If this presentation means that Nahmanides viewed Maimonides as a kindred spirit, we should ask: Which Maimonides? Maimonides famously left himself and his writings open to a multitude of interpretations, and Nahmanides specifically chose the more conservative one, which his philosophical interpreters, such as Samuel Ibn Tibbon, undoubtedly would have rejected.

Nahmanides's moderate and conservative interpretation of Maimonides comes into much sharper relief elsewhere in the letter, when he tries to defuse the arguments of the French rabbis one by one. The French listed the notable absence of Gehenna from Maimonides's entire theory of divine retribution as one of the reasons for banning Sefer ha-Madda'. In "Laws of Repentance," Maimonides asserts that the ultimate punishment of the soul is being annihilated: "the ultimate form of retribution is that the soul is excised and obliterated."[21] Although he goes into great detail about the World to Come and its spirituality, the details of punishment in Gehenna are noticeably missing. In his letter, Nahmanides brings proof from rabbinic literature that the soul of the wicked is obliterated, in which case annihilation genuinely is the worst form of divine retribution. Maimonides does not even mention Gehenna, but Nahmanides brings proof that Maimonides believes in its existence from a single word: "they judge (*danin*) him according to his sins and he has a portion in the World to Come."[22] If we take Nahmanides's word for it, Maimonides did not mention Gehenna outright and certainly did not go into any detail about it, but he did leave detectable traces of his belief in its existence, since he mentions in one word that a person is judged after death. If the word *danin* can encompass the entire process of postmortem retribution, surely there is room to squeeze Gehenna into it too. The problem with this is not that it is farfetched, but that Maimonides had a deliberate reason for omitting Gehenna. He identified the immortality of the soul with the eternality of the knowledge one acquires during one's lifetime, so whoever fails to achieve intellectual perfection fades into nothingness. As a naturalistic philosopher, Maimonides had no use for Gehenna except as a metaphor for this total obliteration. Beside this more radical reading, Maimonides left open the possibility of being read more moderately and traditionally, but the opening in this case is about as big as the eye of a needle. This ambiguity works to Maimonides's benefit, as Nahmanides noticed the opening here, however small it may be, and used it to portray Maimonides as a moderate thinker who was faithful to tradition.

Whether Nahmanides truly believed what he wrote about Maimonides's intention is not all that important, although the fact that he presents a similar reading in his Torat ha-Adam, a work not intended to calm tensions and restore peace, seems to indicate that he did.[23] Whatever the case may be, Nahmanides defended and showed true admiration for a figure who entered the dangerous waters of philosophy to rescue the floundering. Because of Nahmanides's moderate view of him, Maimonides is sometimes a source of inspiration and at other times a worthy, legitimate opponent. For this reason, in his Torah commentary and discourses Nahmanides deflects his attacks on philosophy away from Maimonides and onto the gentile philosophers, even when he knows that Maimonides voiced the very same opinions. One example that stands out appears in his harsh attack on those who deny the existence of demons:

> This can be known about spirits through the science of necromancy, and it also can be known about the Intellects through the Torah's hints, for those who understand their secret—but I cannot explain. We need to muzzle the mouths of the natural philosophizers who are drawn after the Greek, who denied [the existence of] everything that he could not apprehend with his senses, and had the gall to suspect—he and his wicked students—anything that he could not apprehend with his reason of being untrue.[24]

Maimonides and Nahmanides also sharply disagreed about a number of fundamental issues, such as the nature of prophecy and the reasons for the commandments. In all of them, Nahmanides was careful to distinguish ad rem attacks on Maimonides's positions from ad hominem ones on the illustrious man himself, and did not engage in the latter. He saved his vitriol, delivered in a personal tone, for the philosophers.[25] In his letter, after he clarifies where Gehenna appears in Sefer ha-Madda‘, Nahmanides clearly evinces the direct link between his moderate reading of Maimonides and his admiration of him: "This is our clear opinion about the words in this book. / Therefore, we treat it preciously / and have committed it to memory; / unlike you, we have not rejected it utterly."[26] Those who read the letter as a calculated political act, and so as not representative of Nahmanides's real opinions, seem to me to be mistaken, especially when one reads it in light of his attitude toward Maimonides in the rest of his writings. The strategy he employed in the controversy by appealing to both sides to deescalate, in order to put a stop to the mutually assured excommunication and downgrade the feud from a regional conflict with sectarian potential to an internal debate, was not a local, tactical position he took to restore peaceful—or at least tolerant—relations and keep the divided house standing. This position is consistent with his general worldview and his broader methodology within his commentaries on the Talmud and the Torah. Part of what makes Nahmanides's Commentary on the Torah unique is his synoptic view of the Jewish world with all of its diversity, and the way he forms his own opinion by sifting and sorting through these riches. Nahmanides, as quite a few scholars have shown, drew a lot on Ibn Ezra and Maimonides, those exemplars of Andalusian culture, who served as a dependable font of inspiration for his commentary. At the same time, he engaged in constant conversation with Rashi's Torah commentary and the entire world it represents. He described Rashi's place in his commentary as follows: "To illuminate my way I will use the lights of the pure candelabrum, / the commentaries of our master Solomon—the magnificent garland and glorious diadem— / crowned with Scripture, Mishnah, and Talmud, / he gets the first word. / I ponder his every comment, / with which I am besotted."[27] Nahmanides's tangled relationship with Ashkenaz and Andalusia is also conspicuous in his halakhic writings. On one hand, his adherence to the Halakhot of R. Isaac Alfasi (Rif) makes his rulings characteristically Spanish, but on the other, his defenses of Rif often employ the analytical toolkit and study methods developed in northern and southern France.[28]

All that said, the attempt to situate Nahmanides and his worldview along the cultural interface between Ashkenaz and Andalusia is based only on the exoteric elements of his oeuvre and perforce cannot be the whole truth. In the esoteric layer of his Torah commentary, what he terms the "way of truth," Nahmanides speaks a language that would have equally baffled Ibn Ezra and

Maimonides, Rashi, and the Tosafists. The worldview glimpsed in Nahmanides's allusions has nothing in common with the secret doctrines of the other medieval esotericists such as Ibn Ezra and Maimonides. In addition, the vibrant pluralism of the exoteric layer shifts into a flat monotone in the esoteric. The kabbalistic pieces in his commentary that are supposed to reveal some of the "way of truth" also differ in their manner of writing. Unlike in his exoteric writings, here Nahmanides does not relate to the positions of any other kabbalists, such as R. Isaac the Blind or his Geronese disciples. In these pieces, Nahmanides doffs his thinking cap and does not engage in debate or discussion; he acts as a pure conduit for kabbalistic traditions, even if he transmits them only through allusion. There is an immense gap between what he writes openly and what he alludes to secretly, which is one of the reasons he uses the esoteric medium. When we peel back the exoteric and peer into his esoteric world, which is where the roots of his thought lie, we find that the categories of Ashkenaz and Andalusia fall miserably short, because this kind of thought is neither here nor there—it demands wholly new categories.

Nahmanides's letter to the rabbis of northern France exposes this divergence between the revealed and the concealed in his thought. Recall that Maimonides was attacked for his forceful rejection of any notion of God that smacks of anthropomorphism, and Nahmanides gave a long, detailed defense of his position. Unlike his approach to the issue of Gehenna, here Nahmanides did not try to read Maimonides differently; instead, he laid out the long tradition of antianthropomorphic positions taken by the luminaries of the Jewish people, including R. Eleazar b. R. Judah, a respected figure in the Ashkenazic world. We know of some French halakhists, such as R. Moses Taku of the early thirteenth century, who wrote blistering attacks on the philosophically oriented Jewish thinkers. In his work Ktav Tamim, R. Moses Taku supported reading Aggadah literally and assessed Maimonides's rejection of anthropomorphism as undermining the entire authority of Aggadah.[29] Nahmanides is interested in presenting this position as that held by an insignificant minority: "I have heard others say that you criticize Sefer ha-Madda' for saying that there is no form or figure on high. Why have our masters found fault with him for this matter, when every Gaon in his composition and every early scholar of Babylonia and Spain in his liturgical poetry / have considered anyone deviating from this guilty of idiocy?"[30] After he has demonstrated unequivocally that a long, unbroken chain of the greatest Torah sages has rejected anthropomorphism, Nahmanides alludes to the fact that on the esoteric level, there is an idea of the divine form:

the Cause of causes, / more blessed than all blessings and praises, / cannot be described through a body or figure or confined to spaces: / How can he be depicted in spatial dimensions, / when he cannot be encompassed by Heaven and the Heaven of Heavens? / Although [in] some of the homilies pure, / through rocks burst forth rivers (cf. Job 28:10), / which have boughs and offshoots, / producing fruit and fruit of fruits. / When their secret is analyzed, / those who know it are gratified.[31]

Nahmanides, as we know, conceived of the lower seven sefirot as configured in the form of the human body, and in prophetic revelation Shekhinah takes on human form as well.[32] He does not agree with the de-anthropomorphists that all anthropomorphism must be rejected, but he also does not accept the literality of all anthropomorphic aggadot. These few lines in the letter are written carefully and precisely, and in these lines Nahmanides distinguishes between the "Cause of causes," or Ein-Sof, which indeed has no shape or form, and other lower dimensions of God depicted in the aggadot: "through rocks burst forth rivers." Nahmanides's sophisticated theology does not result from taking all aggadot literally, as the French believed, but from interpreting them symbolically and joining them with sefirotic theosophy. He does not spell out, or even hint at, the nature of the concealed meaning of midrashic anthropomorphism. To let on any more would have been to sink his own attempt to create a consensus on the issue of anthropomorphism.

When Nahmanides faced the escalating crisis before him, he used the duality of the exoteric and esoteric to solve it. Exoterically, he tried to create as broad a consensus as possible, which would include tolerance for divergent opinions. He then plunged the disagreement deep down into the realm of the esoteric secret, thereby preserving coexistence within the community. As long as each party remains loyal to the codes of concealment articulated in the tradition regarding the secrets of Torah, a radical divergence is tolerable and a coexistence of secrecy is achievable. In the very same community, and even the very same synagogue, two people might be living and praying side by side while harboring completely antithetical, firmly held beliefs. This tolerance was facilitated by, among other things, the structure of the secret. One group can believe that what it knows is superior to what everyone else knows, and so they preserve it as a secret. Another group may deem that knowledge to be nonsense, or even heresy, which, if it cannot be eradicated, is best kept under wraps. In order to strike a delicate balance within the Jewish world, whose internal unity was collapsing and which was accelerating toward internecine war, Nahmanides tried to preserve pluralism on the surface and move the discord underground. The displacement of the esoteric stratum was not absolute, however, because Nahmanides mentioned the existence of an esoteric doctrine known only to a closed circle. He did this to preserve the primacy of kabbalah as the secret tradition of the Torah, but because it was not exposed to the public, it could not weaken the exoteric consensus. In this way, his approach to the conflict matches the two-tiered structure of his Commentary on the Torah. In the exoteric, Nahmanides has open discussions that draw upon the entire range of Jewish medieval interpretation and thought; in the esoteric, he presents a single approach that is worlds apart from the ideas and authorities he converses with in the exoteric discourse.

This idea of using esotericism to enable the coexistence of radically different and even contradictory opinions finds expression in one aspect of the compact Nahmanides tried to get the rabbis of northern France and their opponents to sign. He suggested that those who mock the aggadot be excommunicated and the ban on Maimonides's books be lifted. In addition, although the *Guide* did not need to be buried or forbidden from study, Nahmanides proposed that public study and instruction of it be banned:

> and as for those who learn the *Guide of the Perplexed* in groups, / place your fearsome hand to their lips, / because the great Master, its author, ordered: "Do you not explain it and do not publish it." He also said as much at the beginning of his book: "I abjure by God every reader of this book not to explicate even one word of it, and not to explain to someone else anything except what is clear and explicit in the words of famous Torah sages who have preceded me. But to teach that which none of our Geonim said—do not teach that to anyone else." This is a quote of the Master's words.[33]

The prohibition against group study of the *Guide* fits the esotericism Nahmanides used for his kabbalah, and he brings support for it from Maimonides's own esotericism. Nahmanides applied similar restrictions to his own esoteric tradition, incorporating into the introduction to his Commentary on the Torah an oath and prohibition governing any attempt to explicate and explain the kabbalistic hints that stud his commentary. He did not think it necessary to conceal the *Guide* because it contains the Torah's secrets, philosophy being the privileged secret doctrine of Judaism; we know that for Nahmanides the Torah's secrets are the kabbalistic "way of truth" and not philosophy. Rather, he wanted to remove it from the public forum, pushing it out of view and into the esoteric periphery. This solution would be better received than the heavy-handed ban on or destruction of Maimonides's works, because Maimonides, who himself viewed the *Guide* as an exposition of the Account of the Chariot and Account of Creation, wanted it kept secret, and Nahmanides himself imposed esoteric restrictions on his kabbalistic traditions.[34] The secret thus constitutes a duality: on one hand, it is the profoundest, preserved, and privileged aspect of tradition; on the other hand, its concealment pushes it into the shadows so as to reduce its effects on the external, revealed aspect of tradition. This duality lies at the base of Nahmanides's attempt to stop the raging cultural war.

Nahmanides perceived that one of the most significant factors leading to the outbreak of this culture war was a breakdown in esoteric discipline, particularly in the wake of the translation and explanation of the *Guide*. From R. Isaac the Blind's letter to Nahmanides and R. Jonah, we learned that a similar crisis ensued when R. Isaac's Geronese disciples, Rabbis Ezra and Azriel, spread kabbalistic ideas.[35] In southern France, kabbalistic works condemned as heretical were buried and burned, to the extent that kabbalah was driven out of the Midi entirely. Nahmanides tried to put out the flames by trying to restore the firm boundaries of concealment. Both philosophical and kabbalistic writings needed to be kept under lock and key, and not only to protect their writers from the fury of the establishment and society. Esotericism enables the maintenance of communal unity, even when community members possess mutually exclusive esoteric doctrines that their fellows would judge heretical.

In the exoteric layer of Nahmanides's religious thought, halakhah, and Torah commentary, one could characterize him as the first European Jew. His Commentary on the Torah is an all-inclusive discourse dictated by intimate familiarity with and basic tolerance for all forms of contemporary Jewish culture, from Andalusia to Ashkenaz. In his halakhic works, his methodology draws from R. Abraham b. David (Ra'avad) of southern France and R. Jacob b. Meir (Rabbeinu Tam) of northern France, yet his actual halakhic positions are characteristically Spanish. Still, his historical perspective is that of the Franco-German—he sees the central historical drama as unfolding between Christians and Jews.[36] His role in the Maimonidean controversy also displays this uniquely synoptic view of the Jewish world. He was the only participant who tried to build bridges between the Maimunists and the French Tosafists, and his exclusive cultural situation enabled him to simultaneously address both warring factions, and to great effect. His kabbalistic positions, on the other hand, do not admit variety and cannot be plotted on a graph where Ashkenaz and Andalusia are the only two variables. His kabbalistic thought, one could say, is equidistantly remote from both.

The gap between the revealed and the concealed in Nahmanides's oeuvre can be characterized by a recurring phenomenon we have encountered in the chapters dealing with the various elements of his thought. The more deeply we dig into the esoteric layer of his thought and expose the kabbalistic thinking underlying his positions, the more the personal dimensions of the Godhead grow fainter and dissolve, revealing a causal system with its own internal dynamic. Revelation does not occur—and so the Torah was not given—at the behest of the divine Sovereign; revelation is the manifestation of the multifaceted divine essence. Creation ex nihilo is a process of emanation from the divine Naught, which, under the influence of Neoplatonism, is depicted as a gradual transition of thickening and differentiation that ultimately returns back to its source, only to be repeated again because the process has no beginning or end. The divine will does not reflect a voluntary determination but the inner essence of the divine movement, of its respiration. One would have thought that the miraculous is where the sovereign will of God is most clearly at work, that a miracle involves God purposefully interceding and breaking the causal chain. In Nahmanides's kabbalistic doctrine, the manifest and hidden miracles mark different aspects within the divine being, each of which operates according to the rules of its own position. History is not a stage on which God reveals his sovereignty and interacts with humans as a personal God. The "Days of the World" are the fixed, cyclical movement in which the Godhead is trapped, at the heart of which is a great cosmic rift that stitches itself back together over eons of time. The Torah in its present form is but one revelation of this cyclical movement, which provides humans—who gained free will through the fall—the causal capacity to help bring the divine configuration back together, however partially. When the Godhead returns to actual, complete unity, human will as separate from divine will will cease, and so the Era of the Torah with its commandments and laws will come to an end. The anomic foundations underlying this conception stand in considerable tension with Nahmanides's standing as the greatest halakhist of the thirteenth century.

This large picture, which emerges from systematically exposing the components of Nahmanides's esoteric thought, requires a reevaluation of how Nahmanides conceived of kabbalah itself. Gershom Scholem described kabbalah in general as the return of the myth, long repressed by biblical and Talmudic tradition, to the heart of Judaism.[37] Other scholars, in disagreement with Scholem, accepted the definition of kabbalah as myth but discovered elements in medieval kabbalah that appear to develop earlier mythic components of Jewish tradition found in Scripture and the Talmud, which Scholem and other scholars had ignored. According to them, if we take a second, closer look at rabbinic literature, which previously had seemed naturally antimythic, we can make out the roots of kabbalistic myths.[38] The use of this category of myth to explain kabbalah raises a difficulty, because myth itself is an obscure category given an abundance of diverse and contradictory definitions. Under which sense of myth can Nahmanides's kabbalah be properly termed a revival of Jewish myth?

One notion of myth does not define it in terms of a particular worldview but in terms of the internal, spiritual impulse that gives rise to it. Myth, in this sense, springs from the primordial elements of the human soul; its source resides in the creative, unconstrained poetic imagination. Myth is alive and gushes forth; it is magnificent and intense. Philosophy as a reflective activity sterilizes and imprisons this imaginative, living power in a discursive cast. Myth is a creative force, a sacred story about gods that is concrete rather than abstract, a narrative rather than an argument and a structure.[39] When one overlays this description on the history of kabbalah it aligns nicely with the poetic outpourings of the Zohar, but it does not match Nahmanides's kabbalistic writings in the slightest. His carefully calibrated allusions are inserted into a very coherent and consistent framework that lacks any poetic creativity or narrativity.[40]

The second sense of myth, which Yehezkel Kaufmann espoused, does not describe it as a concrete story as opposed to abstract logic, but views it as reflecting a particular conception of the gods that opposes any monotheistic belief system. As such, myth subjects a god or gods to some primordial law, and so in mythological stories the gods endure processes of life and death. The monotheistic belief of Scripture, according to Kaufmann, liberates the deity from the shackles of these causal laws and establishes him as a personality with a will of his own—an absolute Sovereign. This distinction between myth and monotheism is also supposed to account for the difference between pagan ritual and the rites of Scripture. Pagan ritual is at base magical because it acts on those causal factors to which a god is subject. Scriptural ritual, by comparison, is established by the sovereign command of God, and the meaning of its fulfillment is obedience to God's will. Pagan prophecy is a technique of knowing the future and the fate that governs god and humans alike; biblical prophecy is a message from God revealing his will to humans. From Kaufmann's perspective, one can certainly characterize Nahmanides's kabbalah as mythic. In his theurgic conception of the commandments as fulfilling a divine need, his cyclical paradigm of history, and his conception of revelation as revealing God's essence, we watch as God the Sovereign and his voluntarism recede. But if one continues to follow Kaufmann, it turns out that philosophy, too, is mythic because it removes the sovereign will from God.[41] Kaufmann viewed Aristotelian and Neoplatonic ideas of the Godhead, especially Spinozistic ones, as the apex of myth, because these streams conceived of God as part of the natural system of laws and not as an actor distinct from this system.

Characterizing the difference between the exoteric and esoteric aspects of Nahmanides's thought on the basis of the presence or absence of myth does not do justice to his kabbalah. According to the first definition of myth as the primal expression of the religious imagination through concrete narrative, Nahmanides's kabbalah certainly does not fit. It is conservative, terse, and sparing in its mythological elements; at most one could say that it systematically crystallizes the living system of mythical symbols that preceded it.[42] If we take the second definition of myth as a worldview in which gods are subject to a particular system of rules, then Nahmanides's kabbalah is in fact mythical, but in this sense his kabbalistic myth would be indistinguishable from medieval Jewish philosophy.

Positioning myth and its place as the medium for organizing and defining the main developments and tensions in medieval Jewish thought becomes completely inadequate when we study carefully Nahmanides's kabbalah. The accepted dichotomy formulated by Scholem, for portraying the great divide between medieval Jewish philosophers and kabbalists as the tension between mythos and logos, and the struggle between intuitive, poetic mythmakers and discursive rationalists, is insufficient as a tool for a deep understanding of what is occurring in the medieval period at large and in the thought of Nahmanides in particular as one of the founding fathers of kabbalah. It seems worthwhile to posit an alternative perspective to shed light on the development of medieval Jewish thought and kabbalah that centers around a tension between two fundamentally contrasting ways of perceiving the totality of being.

The first way is the legacy of scriptural and midrashic Jewish tradition, in which all of existence, history, Nature, and revelation reflects a set of interpersonal relationships between humans and God. Humans read the signs of this personal God in their lives and fates. They understand their relationship with God in the context of the hierarchical, interpersonal relationships between subject and King, son and Father, wife and Husband, accused and Judge. The depth and complexity of the religious posture flows from, among other things, the concentration of multiple roles upon a single personality, from the transition from one role to another in different contexts, and sometimes from the overturning of the hierarchy. The second way is to view Nature and its causal structure as a fundamental category of explanation. While the interpersonal model provides motives and reasons as the main way of making sense of the world, the second offers causes and laws as its basic interpretive category. We should not look to myth's resurgence to explain the difference between Nahmanides's exoteric and esoteric thought, but to the search for a causal mechanism, to his replacement of the divine personality with a divine entity. Kabbalah and philosophy differ essentially in so many ways, but they both share a perspective of tremendous importance: the supremacy of "Nature" and causality as a primary category of perceiving the totality of being.

The religious act that arguably most embodies this significant shift is prayer. At root, prayer is an act of appeasement and persuasion that is wholly constructed on the interpersonal relationship between humans and God. Servants come to appease their Masters, children ingratiate themselves with their parents. In the Middle Ages, prayer as an expression of this relationship begins to fade and morphs into something new: for kabbalists it becomes a cosmic, causal act performed with specific intentions, and for philosophers it represents a time for philosophical contemplation and meditation.

Nahmanides does have a different view of what "Nature" is, and it is much more dynamic and organic than the concept of nature held by the philosophers, but both replace the anthropomorphic relational explanations with a causal system. Likewise, Nahmanides and other kabbalists conceive of humans and their place in the hierarchy of the universe in an utterly different manner from philosophers, but still humans who impact the divine world act through the basic categories of causality.

This "victory of causality" was shared by all esoteric Jewish traditions of the Middle Ages. Despite their vastly divergent and even incompatible esoteric doctrines, all felt ill at ease with the traditional worldview of Scripture and rabbinic literature. Astrology, philosophy, and kabbalah each confronted the anthropomorphism of Scripture and midrash. Ibn Ezra emphasized hermetical-astrological elements of a causal character; Maimonides shared the Aristotelian conception of Nature, creating a constant tension between wisdom and

will; Nahmanides presented an organic, multifaceted Godhead whose equilibrium depends causally on human theurgic activity. Each school of thought
conceived of the causal mechanism in its own way, but they all struggle with
the relational divine subject, positing a causal structure in the depth of the
esoteric layers of their thought. If the struggle between Athens and Jerusalem
can be expressed in terms of the struggle between wisdom and will, then the
influence of Athens penetrated deeply into kabbalah, because the kabbalists
internalized the natural worldview as the basic picture of the world.

In Nahmanides's causal view of the world, religious life is not intended to
rehabilitate and restore the religious interpersonal relationship from a place of
estrangement, rejection, or concealment to one of love and presence. Humans are caught in the cyclical rise and fall of the divine tide. But even before
the end of the world, at which time humans will be redeemed from death,
law, and blind causality, it is within humans' power, by nullifying their will
and cleaving to the divine, to rise above the inert chain of being to the very
breath of the Godhead itself. In this way humans shed their thickened, differentiated existence and become refined beings of light that are sustained by
Shekhinah itself, and through their spiritual sight they can peer into the inner
structure of all existence. During this period between sin and redemption
humans can do more than reach a mystical space of symbolic transparency;
they can observe the commandments and be partners in fulfilling the divine
desire, which is a need that arises necessarily from the Godhead's very essence.
Humans serve to instantiate the divine movement itself, which at the same
time yearns to retreat within and above and simultaneously to spread its presence throughout all reality.

The Geronese kabbalists of Nahmanides's time, Rabbis Ezra, Azriel, and
Jacob b. Sheshet, expended their energies on kabbalah alone. Nahmanides,
on the other hand, left a rich, brilliant legacy of work in the revealed aspects
of Jewish tradition. He was, without a doubt, both the greatest halakhist and
the greatest biblical exegete of the thirteenth century, and generations of Torah scholars and Bible commentators would draw from, rely on, and be inspired by his writings. For the Geronese kabbalists, the tension between the
revealed and the concealed meant that there was an irreconcilable discrepancy
between what they believed—and alluded to in writing—and the face they
showed the outside world. For Nahmanides, this tension did not create a wall
between him and those around him; it sundered his heart and soul into two.
The "way of truth" that he championed is not some profound addition to
the exoteric philological-contextual and homiletic modes of interpretation. It

often does not sit well or is visibly at odds with the revealed dimension of his world. The fact that he encompassed them all within his personality presumably put him under tremendous intellectual and religious tension. It seems that Nahmanides dealt with this tension by anchoring the esoteric aspect of his worldview in Sinai and treating it as a tradition beyond question—one could not add to or take anything away from it. If he had believed in kabbalah as open knowledge that is subject to speculation, innovation, and creativity, it is highly doubtful that he could have held together all the distinct areas of creativity. The multifaceted nature of his exoteric output, be it in his Torah commentary or Talmudic novellae, forms an impressively rich mosaic of erudition and creativity. When we add the esoteric layer to the mix, Nahmanides emerges not only as a man of prodigious creativity and breathtaking range, but also as a paradoxical personality, whose esoteric thought contributed greatly to a sweeping transformation that Jewish tradition underwent during the Middle Ages.

Abbreviations

DDK   *Derashah 'al Divrei Kohelet* (Discourse on Ecclesiastes)—references
             are to the edition in *KR,* vol. 1; manuscripts did not differ
             significantly from the printed version.

DRH   *Derashah le-Rosh ha-Shanah* (Discourse on the New Year)—
             references are to the edition in *KR,* vol. 1; manuscripts did not
             differ significantly from the printed version.

DTHT   *Derashat Torat Ha-Shem Temimah*—references are to *Derashat ha-
             Ramban: Torat Ha-Shem Temimah ha-Shelemah,* ed. Yehudah Meir
             Devir (Jerusalem, 2006), which incorporates the relevant
             manuscript readings, although I also provide the corresponding
             page numbers in *KR,* vol. 1.

Hassagot   *Sefer ha-Mitzvot le-ha-Rambam . . . 'im Hassagot ha-Ramban,* ed.
             Charles Ber Chavel (Jerusalem: Mossad Harav Kook, 1981).

KR   *Kitvei Ramban* (Collected Writings)—*Kitvei Rabbeinu Mosheh ben
             Nahman,* ed. Charles Ber Chavel, 2 vols. (Jerusalem: Mossad Harav
             Kook, c1963).

Novellae H/M Hershler edition Makhon ha-Talmud ha-Israeli ha-Shalem/
             Makhon Ma'arava edition.

PHT   *Peirush ha-Torah* (Commentary on the Torah)—I have mostly used
             the quite dependable, although understandably imperfect, edition
             published in *Mikra'ot Gedolot ha-Keter,* which is conveniently
             available on the internet at www.mgketer.org. Still, when referring

to a comment on a particular verse, I use the numbering in
Peirushei ha-Torah, ed. Charles Ber Chavel, 2 vols. (Jerusalem:
Mossad Harav Kook, c1965) out of convenience, rather than
ha-Keter's.

PSI   *Peirush le-Sefer Iyyov* (Commentary on Job)—references are to the
edition in *KR,* vol. 1; manuscripts did not differ significantly from
the printed version.

Responsa   *Teshuvot Rabbeinu Mosheh ben Nahman,* ed. Chaim Ber Chavel
(Jerusalem: Mossad Harav Kook, 1975).

SHG   *Sefer ha-Geʾulah* (Book of Redemption)—references are to the
edition in *KR,* vol. 1; manuscripts did not differ significantly from
the printed version.

THA   *Torat ha-Adam* (Instruction of Man)—references are to the edition
in *KR,* vol. 2, but I relied heavily on manuscripts, as *Torat ha-Adam*
is perhaps the most textually corrupt of all of Nahmanides's
writings.

Notes

INTRODUCTION

1. *She'elot u-Teshuvot le-R. Yitzhak bar Sheshet,* ed. David Metzger (Jerusalem: Machon Yerushalayim, 1993), no. 157, 1:166a.
2. For Keter Shem Tov, I used MS Vat. Barb. Or. 110, 91r–137v. Abusahulah's composition (although some scholars have attributed it to R. Joshua Ibn Shuʻeib, another of Rashba's disciples) has been printed as *Be'ur le-Perush ha-Ramban 'al ha-Torah,* ed. Jacob Shapira (Warsaw, 1875; repr. Jerusalem: Eshkol Press, 1977). On the transmission of Nahmanides's traditions among his students, see Daniel Abrams, "Orality in the Kabbalistic School of Nahmanides: Preserving and Interpreting Esoteric Traditions and Texts," *Jewish Studies Quarterly* 3 (1996): 85–102. Another valuable resource for deciphering Nahmanides's allusions is *Sefer Me'irat 'Einayim by R. Isaac of Acre,* ed. Amos Goldreich (Jerusalem: Hebrew University, 1981; Heb.). Additional scholarship concerning the commentaries on Nahmanides's esoteric doctrines can be found in Moshe Idel, "An Unknown Commentary on Nachmanides' Mystic Doctrines," *Daat* 2/3 (Summer-Winter 1978): 121–126 (Heb.), and Idel, "An Anonymous Commentary on the Pentateuch, from the Circle of R. Solomon Ibn Adret," *Michael* 11 (1989): 9–21. See also Haviva Pedaya, *Nahmanides: Cyclical Time and Holy Text* (Tel-Aviv: 'Am 'Oved, 2003), 102–106 (Heb.).
3. In recent studies Oded Israeli attempts to minimize the place of kabbalah in Nahmanides's religious outlook; see "Halakhah, Science and Secret: The Status of the Kabbalah in Nahmanides' Halakhic Work," *Dinei Israel* 32 (2015): 115–130 (Heb.). As will be apparent from the rest of this book, I think that kabbalah played a foundational role in Nahmanides's religious outlook and practice.

4. See Yitzhak Baer, *A History of the Jews in Christian Spain,* trans. Louis Schoffman (Philadelphia: Jewish Publication Society, 1978), 1:142–144; Bernard Septimus, "Communal Struggle in Barcelona during the Maimonidean Controversy," *Tarbiz* 42 (1973): 389–400 (Heb.); Septimus, "Piety and Power in Thirteenth-Century Catalonia," *Studies in Medieval Jewish History and Literature* (Cambridge, MA: Harvard University Press, 1979), 197–230; Yom Tov Assis, *The Golden Age of Aragonese Jewry: Community and Society in the Crown of Aragon, 1217–1327* (London: Littman Library of Jewish Civilization, 1997), 308–314. For a comprehensive account of the status of the Jews in the kingdom of Aragon and of King Jaime I's relationship with his Jewry, see Yom Tov Assis, "The Jews in the Crown of Aragon and Its Dominions," in *Moreshet Sepharad: The Sephardi Legacy,* ed. Haim Beinart (Jerusalem: Magnes, 1992), 44–102.

5. See the conclusion to this book.

6. The literature on Nahmanides's role in Jewish-Christian polemic is extensive; see David Berger, "The Barcelona Disputation," *AJS Review* 20 (1995): 379–388; Robert Chazan, *Barcelona and Beyond: The Disputation of 1263 and Its Aftermath* (Berkeley: University of California Press, 1992); and Nina Caputo, *Nahmanides in Medieval Catalonia: History, Community and Messianism* (Notre Dame: University of Notre Dame Press, 2007), 91–128.

7. This book-length attempt to provide a picture of sufficiently broad scope is the culmination of a long period of research into Nahmanides's halakhic writings and thought. Some of the chapters of this book have been published previously as independent articles in various scholarly fora: Ch. 2: "Nahmanides' Conception of the History of Halakhah and the Minhag," *Zion* 67 (2002): 25–56 (Heb.); ch. 3: "Nachmanides' Conception of Death, Sin, Law and Redemption," *Tarbiz* 71 (2002): 133–162 (Heb.); ch. 4: "Esoteric Doctrine of the Hidden Miracle—The Layers of Being in the Teaching of Nahmanides," *Kabbalah* 7 (2002): 257–280 (Heb.); and ch. 8: *Concealment and Revelation: Esotericism in Jewish Thought and Its Philosophical Implications,* trans. Jackie Feldman (Princeton: Princeton University Press, 2007), 83–92.

8. Chayim Henoch, *Nachmanides: Philosopher and Mystic* (Jerusalem: Harry Fischel Institute for Talmudic Research, 1978; Heb.), translated into English without footnotes as *Ramban: Philosopher and Kabbalist, on the Basis of His Exegesis to the Mitzvoth* (Northvale, NJ: Jason Aronson, 1998); and Pedaya, *Nahmanides.* See also David Novak, *The Theology of Nahmanides Systematically Presented* (Atlanta: Scholars Press, 1992), which is an interesting attempt to present Nahmanides, on the basis of his exoteric writings, as a systematic theologian working in the context of and against other medieval theologies. For short monographs on Nahmanides's life, see Izak Unna, *Rabbi Mosheh ben Nahman (ha-Ramban): Hayyav u-Fe'ulato,* exp. ed. (Jerusalem: Kiryat Sefer, 1954); and Charles Ber Chavel, *Rabbenu Mosheh ben Nahman: Toledot Hayyav, Zemano, ve-Hibburav* (Jerusalem: Mossad Harav Kook, 1967).

9. Many texts were erronousely ascribed to Nahmanides, given his stature and authority. One such text is the "Discourse for Wedding," which is alien to his vocabulary and thinking. In regard to the ascription of the "Discourse for Wedding," I take a

different position from that of Oded Israeli, who perceives the discourse as one of Nahmanides's earlier writings; see Oded Israeli, " 'Beginnings of Kabbalah' in Nahmanides's Discourse on Wedding," *Pe'amim* 153 (2017): 87–124 (Heb).

10. On the relationship between Nahmanides's sermon Torat Ha-Shem Temimah and his Commentary on the Torah, see Oded Israeli, "From the Sermon 'Toraht Ha-shem Temimah' to the Commentary on the Torah: Milestones in Nachmanides' Writings," *Tarbiz* 83 (2015): 163–195 (Heb.).

11. Nahmanides's extensive interest in gathering and engaging a wide spectrum of sources continued until the end of his creative life. In their monumental work on the additions that Nahmanides added to his Commentary on the Torah, Yosef Ofer and Jonathan Jacobs show that some of these additions were inspired by new sources that Nahmanides discovered and integrated. See *Nahmanides' Additions to the Commentary on the Torah That Were Written in the Land of Israel* (Jerusalem: Herzog, 2013), 45–54. See also Jonathan Jacobs, "New Books That Became Known to Nahmanides When He Arrived to the Land of Israel," *JSIJ—Jewish Studies, an Internet Journal* 11 (2012): 1–14 (Heb.).

12. On Nahmanides's teachers, see Shalem Yahalom, "R. Nathan b. R. Meir, Nachmanides' Teacher," *Pe'amim* 91 (2002): 5–25 (Heb.), and Yahalom, "R. Judah b. Yakar—His Biography and His Impact on the Work of Nachmanides," *Sidra* 17 (2001–2002): 79–107 (Heb.).

13. The Tosafists and Maimonides do not appear prominently in Nahmanides's early work Milhamot ha-Shem, as they would later in his novellae. On this development in Nahmanides's halakhic compositions, see Israel M. Ta-Shma, *Talmudic Commentary in Europe and North Africa: Literary History,* 2nd ed., vol. 2 (Jerusalem: Magnes, 2004), 43–44 (Heb.), and *Hiddushei ha-Ramban le-Massekhet Ketubbot,* ed. Ezra D. Chwat (Jerusalem, 1990), 33.

14. On this development, see Harold J. Berman, *Law and Revolution: The Formation of the Western Legal Tradition* (Cambridge, MA: Harvard University Press, 1983), 161–163, 298–299.

15. On this figure, see Gershom Scholem, *The Beginning of Kabbalah* (Jerusalem: Schocken Press, 1948), 240–243 (Heb.); *Ha-Kabbalah be-Girona,* ed. Yosef Ben-Shlomo (Jerusalem: Mif'al ha-Shikhpul, 1964), 79–80.

16. Gershom Scholem described Nahmanidean kabbalah as part of Geronese kabbalah, but Moshe Idel has pointed out the essential differences between these two traditions. See Moshe Idel, "Nahmanides: Kabbalah, Halakhah, and Spiritual Leadership," *Tarbiz* 64 (1995): 535–580 (Heb.).

17. On his close ties with King Jaime I of Aragon, see Baer, *History,* 1:105–106. Hananel Mack tries to show how this relationship influenced his interpretation of the biblical figure of Pharaoh in his Commentary on the Torah; Hananel Mack, "From the Eyes of Nahmanides: His Attitude to Pharaoh of Egypt and Jewish Status in the Kingdom of Aragon-Catalonia," *Sefunot* 7 (22) (1999): 33–47 (Heb.).

18. Nahmanides seems to have known Arabic and so was not beholden to the translations of Maimonides's work in order to know it firsthand. Occasionally, he made corrections to the translations in his citations of *The Guide of the Perplexed* and Maimonides's

commentary on the Mishnah. He also appears to have translated Sefer ha-Mitzvot without relying on existing translations. See Raphael Jospe, "Ramban (Nahmanides) and Arabic," *Tarbiz* 57 (1987): 67–93 (Heb.). In the medieval period there were two widespread translations of *The Guide of the Perplexed*, those by Al-Charizi and Ibn Tibon. Yosef Ofer and Jonathan Jacobs (*Nahmanides' Additions*, 49–50) showed that Nahmanides in the earlier layers of his Commentary on the Torah used Al-Charizi's translation, while later, in his additions to the commentary stemming from his last years in the land of Israel, he relied more on Ibn Tibon's translation, which might have been known to him only during that period.

CHAPTER 1. NAHMANIDES'S PHILOSOPHY OF HALAKHAH

1. Nahmanides expressed doubt about the entire enterprise of enumerating the commandments and about the number 613 put forth by R. Simlai in the Talmud (Makkot 23b). It would appear that such a task had no place in his schedule. Regarding the number 613, Nahmanides says: "I, in my poverty, [and] despite all of this [the foregoing], harbor a doubt in my heart about this dictum: do all agree to it or is there controversy? Another doubt: is it a Mosaic law from Sinai [. . .] or merely an *asmakhta* [an artificial retrojection onto the biblical text] based on this numerology?" (*Hassagot*, 1). On Nahmanides's loyalty to the Earlier Authorities and its implication for his halakhic creativity, as well as the meaning of "Earlier Authorities," see ch. 2, esp. sec. II.

2. For the exposition of Maimonides's approach and the Geonim, see Moshe Halbertal, *Maimonides: Life and Thought* (Princeton: Princeton University Press, 2014), ch. 2, and Moshe Halbertal, *People of the Book: Canon, Meaning, and Authority* (Cambridge, MA: Harvard University Press, 1997), 54–72. The explanation of the respective hermeneutical theories of Maimonides and Nahmanides is an extension of my treatment of the issue in Halbertal, "Maimonides' *Book of Commandments:* The Architecture of Halakhah and Its Theory of Interpretation," *Tarbiz* 59 (1990): 457–480 (Heb.).

3. Abraham Ibn Daud, *A Critical Edition with a Translation and Notes of* The Book of Tradition *(Sefer Ha-Qabbalah)*, ed. Gerson D. Cohen (Philadelphia: Jewish Publication Society of America, 1967), 3–4, with slight adjustments.

4. Most Geonim viewed the Oral Torah as a tradition received at Sinai; see David Sklare, *Samuel ben Hofni Gaon and His Cultural World* (Leiden: Brill, 1996), 158–165. R. Nissim b. Jacob Gaon wrote: "We have no need to bring proofs that would establish the truth of the Sages' tradition and the accuracy of their transmission, because the earlier authorities have already established it. But I will clarify the time in which the Mishnah, and also the Talmud, were written. I say that the tradition has not changed in transmission and that the tradition has been preserved by our nation [. . .] and the nation has not deviated from this practice since the days of Moses and until 150 years after the destruction of the Second Temple" (*Mafteah le Man'ulei ha-Talmud*, ed. Jacob Goldenthal [Vienna, 1847; repr. Jerusalem: Makor, 1971], 2b). This does not mean, however, that every Geonic opinion was cut from the same cloth. R. Saadia Gaon, for example, took the rather extreme position that the Mishnah was transmitted to Moses at Sinai exactly as we have it today. R. Sherira Gaon, by

comparison, believed that the halakhic details were transmitted via tradition but Sages organized and formulated them in different ways. The unique formulation of the Mishnah and its particular organization of laws can be sourced, according to R. Sherira, to R. Akiva and his students. See Benjamin Manasseh Lewin, *Iggeret Rav Sherira Ga'on* (Jerusalem: Makor, 1972), 4–6 (Heb.). For a further exposition of R. Saadia's conception, see *Saadya's Commentary on Genesis*, ed. and trans. Moshe Zucker (New York: Jewish Theological Seminary of America, 1984), 185–187 (Heb.), and *Rabbi Saadiah Gaon's Commentary on the Book of Creation*, ed. and trans. Michael Linetsky (Northvale, NJ: Jason Aronson, 2002), 24–26. R. Samuel b. Hofni Gaon was also exceptional; see Sklare, *Samuel ben Hofni*, 218–221.

5. On the anti-Karaite background of Sefer ha-Kabbalah, see the introduction by Gerson Cohen in Ibn Daud, *Book of Tradition*, xliii–lxii.

6. Most Geonim refused, *ab initio*, to grant interpretation the power to clarify halakhah. See Moshe Zucker, "Fragments from Rav Saadya Gaon's Commentary to the Pentateuch from Mss.," *Sura* 2 (1955–1956): 323–331 (Heb.); Zucker, "Fragments of the *Kitāb Taḥsīl Al-Sharā'i' Al-Samā'iyah*," *Tarbiz* 41 (1972): 373–410 (Heb.); José Faur, *Studies in the Mishne Torah* (Jerusalem: Mossad Harav Kook, 1978), 74–98 (Heb.). On the tension within Geonic tradition on this issue, see Sklare, *Samuel ben Hofni*.

7. *Hakdamot ha-Rambam la-Mishnah*, ed. and trans. Yitzhak Shailat (Jerusalem: Ma'aliyot, 1992), 40.

8. On this term, see below, sec. VI.

9. *Hakdamot*, 40.

10. On this term, see below, sec. VI.

11. Mordechai Z. Cohen, *Opening the Gates of Interpretation: Maimonides' Biblical Hermeneutics in Light of His Geonic-Andalusian Heritage and Muslim Milieu* (Leiden: Brill, 2011), 264, with minor adjustments. The original Hebrew and Judeo-Arabic can be found respectively in *Hakdamot*, 28–29 and 328.

12. This novel position of Maimonides, against that of the majority of the Geonim, which believes in human activity as an ingredient of halakhah, was formulated by Chaim Tchernowitz, *Toledot ha-Halakhah*, vol. 1 (New York: Va'ad ha-Yovel, 1945), 88. For a comparison between the positions of Maimonides and Ibn Daud, see David Hartman, *Maimonides: Torah and Philosophic Quest* (Philadelphia: Jewish Publication Society of America, 1976): 112–116; Gerald Blidstein, "Traditional and Institutional Authority—On Oral Law in Maimonides," *Da'at* 16 (1986): 14–15 (Heb.) (repr. Blidstein, *Studies in Halakhic and Aggadic Thought* [Be'er Sheva: Ben-Gurion University Press, 2004], 138–139 [Heb.]).

13. On this term, see below, sec. VI.

14. *Hakdamot*, 40–41.

15. *She'elot u-Teshuvot Havvot Ya'ir* (Ramat-Gan: Mekhon 'Eked Sefarim, 1997), 2:552 (no. 192).

16. For Maimonides's conception of controversy and its source, see the continuation, esp. sec. VIII.

17. In his treatise on logic, Maimonides terms such legal inferences "dialectic syllogisms"; see Israel Efros, "Maimonides' Treatise on Logic (*Makālah fi-Sinā'at Al-Mantik*): The

Original Arabic and Three Hebrew Translations," *Proceedings of the American Academy for Jewish Research* 8 (1937–1938): 48. This terminological choice connects to the fact that premises in practical legal deductions are neither true nor false but pertain to what he terms "conventions." His use of a coherence theory of truth dovetails with this, for if the premises were true or false in terms of correspondence, then one should have been able to make the same claim about their conclusions.

18. Consistent with this view that chronology plays no role in the structure of halakhic authority, Maimonides states in the introduction to the Mishneh Torah that the authority of the Talmud does not derive from its antecedence vis-à-vis subsequent authorities, but from its dissemination throughout the Jewish world and adoption as an authoritative work by Torah scholars.

19. "When I directed my thoughts to this goal, I searched my heart on the manner in which to divide this composition and what its arrangement ought to be. [. . .] It became clear to me that the optimal division would be to make groupings of laws in lieu of the tractates of the Mishnah [. . .] In service of this goal I deemed it necessary first to enumerate, in the book's preface, all the positive and negative commandments so that the division of the book will include them all, such that there will be no commandment whose full complement of laws will not be discussed [. . .] All of this is to ensure that nothing will elude me such that I shall not discuss it; by including them in the enumeration of the commandments I will be secured against this" (*Sefer ha-Mitzvot: Makor ve-Targum,* ed. and trans. Yosef Kafih [Jerusalem: Mossad Harav Kook, 1971], 3–4).

20. Although the various enumerators adopted a variety of approaches to the method and purpose of enumeration, the conception of the commandment as an organizational category—which appears in Principle Seven of Sefer ha-Mitzvot—is Maimonides's innovation. See Halbertal, "*Book of Commandments,*" 460n7.

21. *Sefer ha-Mitzvot,* 4.

22. Ibid., 21. This explains why, for example, the biblical commands that require a betrothed maiden who fornicated be stoned, or burned if she is the daughter of a priest, are not counted as commandments independent of the commandment pertaining to the adulterous wife. These commands simply fill in the details about the punishment adulterous women receive. Maimonides continues the same tack in Principle Nine, where he refuses to count the prohibitions against gleaning one's vineyard (Lev 19:10) and one's olive grove (Deut 24:20) as separate ones, despite their independent presentation in the Torah, "because these are not two prohibitions but a single injunction regarding one matter, which is that one may not take grain or fruit that one forgot when harvesting them" (ibid., 37). On this conception of the commandment in Maimonides's writings, see Yaakov Levinger, *Maimonides' Techniques of Codification: A Study in the Method of Mishneh Torah* (Jerusalem: Magnes, 1965), 78–87 (Heb.).

23. "After reflecting on this, and recognizing that this enumeration has spread amongst the people, I realized that when I mention the true and appropriate enumeration in an apodictic manner without any proof, the first reader who reads it will consider it mistaken, and proof of the mistake, to his mind, will be that it is the opposite of what so-and-so wrote" (*Sefer ha-Mitzvot,* 5–6).

24. For this group of Principles and their significance, see below, sec. X.
25. *Sefer ha-Mitzvot,* 9.
26. Ibid.
27. In this chapter, the capitalized terms "Rabbinic" and "Biblical" are used exclusively to refer to the halakhic categories referred to as *de-rabbanan* and *de-oraita,* respectively, in Hebrew.
28. The attempt to include all of halakhah, with all its detail, in the revelation at Sinai is a motif frequently encountered in rabbinic literature; see Sifra, "Be-Hukkotai," 8.13; Yerushalmi, Pe'ah, 2.6 (17a), Megillah 4.1 (74d), Hagigah 1.8 (76d); Tanhuma, ed. Buber, "Ki Tissa," 17; Va-Yikra Rabbah 22.1.
29. *Sefer ha-Mitzvot,* 10.
30. Ibid., 11.
31. For an analysis of this kind of idea, see Yochanan Silman, *The Voice Heard at Sinai: Once or Ongoing?* (Jerusalem: Magnes, 1999), ch. 6 (Heb.).
32. "But if a prophet should claim that God told him that the ruling regarding a particular commandment is such-and-such, and that the *qiyās* of so-and-so is correct, that prophet should be killed because he is a false prophet, as we have established, because there is no Torah after the first messenger [Moses], nor is there addition or removal—'it is not in Heaven' (Deut 30:12)" (*Hakdamot,* 36).
33. "We do not believe any prophet who arises after our master Moses on account of a sign alone [. . .] but because Moses commanded it in the Torah [. . .] Therefore, if a prophet arose and performed great signs and wonders and sought to contradict the Torah of our master Moses, we do not listen to him [. . .] and since we only believe the wonder because Moses commanded it, how can we accept this sign which comes to contradict the prophecy of Moses which we saw and heard?" (Mishneh Torah, "Laws of the Foundations of the Torah," 8:2–3). On prophetic authority in Maimonides's thought, see Halbertal, *Maimonides,* 126–127.
34. *Sefer ha-Mitzvot,* 10–11.
35. On this overarching tendency of Nahmanides, see ch. 2.
36. In the rest of the chapter, all instances of "the Master" in Nahmanides's glosses are references to Maimonides unless otherwise noted.
37. *Hassagot,* 28.
38. See ibid., 23–24.
39. See ibid., 28.
40. Ibid., 8.
41. Ibid., 8–9.
42. It runs for more than ten pages—ibid., 10–19.
43. Ibid., 19.
44. *Sefer ha-Mitzvot,* 9.
45. See *PHT,* Num 8:2, where Nahmanides shows the Torah's lengthy allusion to Hanukkah.
46. *Hassagot,* 47–48.
47. This debate has major halakhic implications; see ibid., 50–51.
48. Ibid., 12.

49. Ibid.

50. One can solve this difficulty for Maimonides by arguing that although the obligation to obey the words of the rabbis is a second-order one, the actual content of their enactments does not have the same status as the obligation to obey them. On this, see Chavel's sources in ibid., 14, s.v. *ve-lo shel 'ikkar*.

51. Ibid., 16–17.

52. Ibid., 15.

53. Ibid., 19.

54. Ibid., 17.

55. Ibid., 18.

56. Ibid., 17.

57. For other attempts to resolve the contradiction between the obligation to obey and the Mishnah in Horayot, see R. Issachar Baer Eylenburg, *Sefer Be'er Sheva'* (ed. prin. Venice, 1614), 7; R. Baruch Halevi Epstein, *Torah Temimah* (ed. prin. Vilna: The Widow and Brothers and Romm, 1902), Deut 17:10; and the lengthy treatment in Gerald J. Blidstein, "Even If He Tells You Right Is Left," in *Studies in Halakha and Jewish Thought Presented to Emmanuel Rackman*, ed. Moshe Beer (Ramat Gan: Bar Ilan University Press, 1994), 221–241 (Heb.). For an analysis of the court's authority, see Avi Sagi, "Models of Authority and the Duty of Obedience in Halakhic Literature," *AJS Review* 20 (1995): 1–24, and Halbertal, *People of the Book*, 81–89.

58. For various medieval interpretations of Nahmanides's constitutive approach, see below, secs. XI–XII.

59. *Sefer ha-Mitzvot*, 12.

60. Many of Maimonides's commentators have argued that derivations made via the thirteen middot are in fact halakhically Biblical; they simply are not included in the enumeration of the 613 commandments. As such, many commentators have explained that the expression "from the words of the Sages (*mi-divrei soferim*)" does not entail a Rabbinic law but rather a Biblical one derived by the Sages. For examples, see Maggid Mishneh and Kesef Mishneh to the Mishneh Torah, "Laws of Marriage," 1:2. For a broad survey of interpretations of "the words of the Sages," see Jacob Neubauer, *Ha-Rambam 'al Divrei Soferim: Shittato ve-Shittat Mefareshav* (Jerusalem: Mossad Harav Kook, 1956/1957). The endeavor to square Maimonides's positions with Talmudic sources, and sometimes with his very own rulings based on those sources, need not change our reading of Principle Two. In the Judeo-Arabic original, Maimonides says that if rabbinic tradents do not make it clear that a law derived from the middot is Biblical, then it is Rabbinic—he explicitly uses the Aramaic term for Rabbinic, *de-rabbanan* (see *Sefer ha-Mitzvot*, 13). The matter is also clear in a responsum of his—see *Teshuvot ha-Rambam*, ed. Abraham Hayyim Freimann (Jerusalem: Mekize Nirdamim, 1934), no. 166; *Teshuvot ha-Rambam*, ed. Joshua Blau, rev. ed. (Jerusalem: Reuven Mas; Kiryat Ono: Machon Mishnat ha-Rambam, 2014), no. 355. See further Levinger, *Maimonides' Techniques*, 46–50.

61. *Guf Torah*, see the Mishnah in Hagigah, 1.8.

62. Cohen, *Opening the Gates*, 288–289, with minor adjustments. The original Hebrew and Judeo-Arabic can be found in *Sefer ha-Mitzvot*, 13.

63. See above, sec. I.

64. One of many possible examples from the Babylonian Talmud: "Half a measure: R. Yohanan said the Torah prohibits it, and Reish Lakish said the Torah permits it. R. Yohanan challenged Reish Lakish: I only know that anything that has a [Biblical] punishment has a [Biblical] prohibition, [but] the *koy* and half a measure do not have a [Biblical] punishment, so perhaps they do not have a [Biblical] prohibition? The verse states, 'any fat' (Lev 7:23). [Reish Lakish responds:] It is Rabbinic and merely an *asmakhta*" (Yoma 74a). This sugya exemplifies a common Talmudic phenomenon. Rabbi Yohanan opines that a half measure of something prohibited by the Torah is Biblically prohibited, so he proves from the verse that one should not eat "any fat" (Lev 7:23), a half measure. Reish Lakish, who thinks a half measure is only a Rabbinic prohibition, retorts that this interpretation is only an *asmakhta*. This sugya is an example of debate about whether a specific prohibition is Biblical or not, debate that should be impossible according to Maimonides because only what is received can be Biblical, and anything received cannot be the subject of debate. Moreover, the yard-stick used by the Talmud to assess whether a given law is Biblical is not whether the law was received or not, but whether its scriptural derivation is genuine or an *asmakhta*.

65. Regarding the procedure concerning a betrothed maiden accused of fornication, which Maimonides considers a received law, R. Eliezer expresses disagreement in Sifrei Devarim, sec. 237, and Ketubbot 46a. Much ink has been spilled over controversy concerning received matters. See, in particular, R. Yair Bacharach, *Havvot Ya'ir*, no. 192.

66. *Hassagot*, 51.

67. Ibid., 32.

68. Ibid., 33. Also: "for they consider derivations (*midrashim*) through *gezerah shavah* (verbal congruity) and analogy (*heqqesh*) to be principles of the Torah [. . .] the fundamental basis of the Talmud is that everything expounded in the Talmud through one of the thirteen *middot* is fully Biblical and constitutes an interpretation of the Torah said to Moses at Sinai" (ibid., 36–37).

69. Ibid., 34.

70. Ibid., 31.

71. *Sefer ha-Mitzvot*, 15. In note 60 above, I noted the approach which maintains that Maimonides considered derivations arrived at through the thirteen middot to be Biblical, and I rejected it through an analysis of the language used in Principle Two. A different approach could claim that Maimonides understands the laws to be Rabbinic since all derivations via the thirteen middot are considered an *asmakhta*. The conceptual question Nahmanides raises rejects both approaches. Maimonides does not think the thirteen middot are just vehicles for creating *asmakhta'ot*, yet he also considers their halakhic products to be Rabbinic. Kafih understood Maimonides to mean that they are all *asmakhta'ot*; see Yosef Kafih, "From the Words of the Sages," in *Iyyunim be-Sifrut Hazal, ba-Miqra, u-ve-Toledot Yisra'el* (Ramat-Gan: Bar-Ilan University, 1982), 248–255 (Heb.). I do not believe this approach has any basis in Maimonides's words, since he says explicitly that they are not *asmakhta'ot*.

72. *Sefer ha-Mitzvot,* 15.

73. Ibid., 333 (negative commandment no. 336).

74. On this, see ibid., 333–334 (no. 336), 242–243 (no. 135), and 276 (no. 194).

75. *Hakdamot,* 40.

76. Ibid., 39.

77. *Istikhrāj,* whose precise translation is "to extrapolate through *qiyās,*" recurs quite frequently in the introduction to his Mishnah commentary: "and concerning that which he [Joshua] did not hear from the prophet [Moses], concerning the branches he extrapolated (*istakhraja*) the law through *qiyās,* through the thirteen rules given to him at Sinai" (ibid., 28); "Know that prophecy is ineffective in reasoning the interpretation of the Torah and extrapolating (*istikhrāj*) the branches through the thirteen *middot*" (ibid., 29). In Hebrew, Kafih preferred to translate this Arabic verb with the *qal* construction of *l-m-d,* meaning "learn" or "infer," even though he is conscious that it would be more literally rendered by the *hif'il* construction of *y-tz-',* meaning "extract" or "extrapolate" (see *Sefer ha-Mitzvot,* 12n89). Shailat in his *Hakdamot* translated this verb more literally "to extrapolate (*le-hotzi*) via *heqqesh* [*qiyās*]," which makes eminent sense, seeing as Maimonides himself used that Hebrew verb in connection with the thirteen *middot* in his "Laws of Torah Study" in the Mishneh Torah (see immediately below).

78. "The people in every generation would make the words of their predecessors the root (*'asl*), from which they would extrapolate and make inferences. There is no dispute about the received roots (*al-'usūl*)" (*Hakdamot,* 37). Maimonides described those who erroneously maintained that received laws are the subject of dispute as follows: "they found that the interpretation is received from Moses, which as we have established is correct, but they did not distinguish between received roots (*al-'usūl*) and extrapolated inferences" (ibid., 41). He then says that, in theory, "two people who have equal insight, analytical ability, and knowledge of the roots from which inferences can be made will not come to disagree at all in what they extrapolate through *qiyās*" (ibid.).

79. Mishneh Torah, "Laws of Torah Study," 1:11.

80. Cohen, *Opening the Gates,* 264, with minor adjustments. The original Hebrew and Judeo-Arabic can be found respectively in *Hakdamot,* 28–29 and 328.

81. In his *Treatise on Logic,* Maimonides defines the technical term *qiyās* in the following manner: "A little reflection will make it evident that from any two distinct propositions nothing else will ever result, as when we say, 'Every man is an animal,' and 'Every fire is hot,' and 'Every snow is cold.' Even if the number of the distinct propositions is indefinitely increased, nothing will result from their combination. But if they are connected in some form, so that another proposition follows from them, then the combination of these two propositions is called a syllogism" (Efros, "Maimonides' Treatise on Logic," 40).

82. The use of middot as rules of inference, defined technically as *al-maqāyīs al-jadaliyya,* is quite similar to the way *qiyās* is understood within the larger scheme of interpretation in Islamic jurisprudence. *Qiyās* has the very specific meaning of an analogy used to derive conclusions from undisputed material about a matter that has no precedent.

See Noel J. Coulson, *A History of Islamic Law* (Edinburgh: University Press, 1964), 60; and Joseph Schacht, *The Origins of Muhammadan Jurisprudence* (Oxford: Clarendon, 1959), 99.

83. In modern hermeneutic theories, we find formulations that attempt to subvert the idea of "the text alone," the text by itself. In such theories there is no such thing, because meaning is not some hidden thing beyond the text that the reader must uncover and expose. Meaning is created when an interpreter responds to a text. Hans Georg Gadamer puts forth this theory of interpretation when he claims that interpretation does not discover the meaning of the text. Understanding a text is not like knowing the object in front of you; it depends on the mind of the reader and that reader's ideas. According to Gadamer, there is no neutral vantage point from which to expose the meaning of a text because the human condition is essentially historical. Even if a neutral vantage point of this sort were to exist, it would not even be clear that the text would have meaning of any kind when viewed from it. The same claim is made in more psychological terms in reader-response theory. These approaches do not see any gap between text and interpretation, because there is no text-by-itself separate from the interpretation. See Hans Georg Gadamer, *Truth and Method* (London: Continuum, 1979), 129–214; Jane Tompkins, ed., *Reader-Response Criticism: From Formalism to Post-Structuralism* (Baltimore: Johns Hopkins University Press, 1980).

84. According to this, the kernel's meaning is clear from a simple reading or through tradition and does not require interpretation. It is worth noting that Maimonides does not refrain from using midrash to clarify terms in the text when he thinks that it reflects their simple meaning. Wherever he does not think that a midrash is the literal-contextual interpretation (peshat), he either claims that it is a received midrash and tries to find an explicit attestation to its Biblical status in the Talmud, or he rejects the midrashic reading as definitional on the Biblical level. For examples of his use of midrash to clarify Scripture and of his rejection of midrashim that he does not believe clarify Scripture, see *Sefer ha-Mitzvot*, positive commandments, nos. 5–6, 8, 94–95; negative commandments, nos. 4, 45–46, 153, 179, 199, 287, 290, 299, 322. On Maimonides's concept of peshat, see Cohen, *Opening the Gates*, chs. 5–6.

85. This conception of interpretation is premised upon the text having a meaning before any interpretation. This meaning is immediately grasped and enables the very act of interpretation. Disagreement between interpreters is made possible by their agreement on some kernel of meaning.

86. *Hassagot*, 17.

87. *Sefer ha-Mitzvot*, 13–14.

88. *Hassagot*, 44.

89. Nahmanides uses the peshat rule in an original manner within a halakhic context when he invents the death penalty for someone who violates a decree of excommunication: "I say perhaps, if you will forgive me, that this is the peshat of what is written in the Torah: 'No human being who has been proscribed can be ransomed; he shall surely be put to death' (Lev 27:29). As if to say, when all have reached a consensus about him and he has been proscribed [excommunicated] by them, whoever violates

it cannot be ransomed through money but is liable for death. Do not silence us about this because our Rabbis expounded the verse about something else [. . .] for even so, the verse does not leave the realm of its [Scripture's] *peshat,* as it is written: 'God spoke one thing, [but] I have heard two' (Ps 62:12)—the written text serves both this and that" (*Mishpat ha-Herem,* in *Novellae, Shev'uot-Niddah,* H296–297). See also Ra'avad's gloss to Mishneh Torah, "Laws of Theft," 9:7. A parallel to Nahmanides's conception can be found in R. Jacob b. Sheshet, *Sefer Emunah u-Vittahon, KR,* 2:379.

90. *Hassagot,* 45.
91. Ibid.
92. For this approach, see E. D. Hirsch, *The Aims of Interpretation* (Chicago: University of Chicago Press, 1976); Hirsch, *Validity in Interpretation* (New Haven: Yale University Press, 1967).
93. Sec. VI.
94. In a case of controversy over interpretation through the thirteen middot, Maimonides implies that there is a correct answer: "two people who have equal insight, analytical ability, and knowledge of the roots from which inferences can be made will not come to disagree at all in what they extrapolate through *qiyās,* and if they disagree it will be minimal. For example, we find that Shammai and Hillel only had disputes about individual laws, because the *qiyās* of the two, in everything they extrapolated through *qiyās,* was quite similar, and the principles which one had received were like those received by the other. But when their students' pursuit slackened, and their *qiyās* weakened in relation to that of their teachers Shammai and Hillel, controversy arose when they investigated many matters, owing to the fact that the *qiyās* of each of them was according to the power of his intellect and what he possessed of the principles" (*Hakdamot,* 41). There is only one correct answer, and controversy exists due to the students' weakened powers of reasoning and their inadequate drive and pursuit of wisdom. Controversy is proportionate to the quality of learning and reasoning possessed by given interpreters, and if they are of high enough caliber, debate will be nearly nonexistent, as with Shammai and Hillel. On the issue of whether there is one correct answer to questions of legal interpretation, see Ronald Dworkin, *Taking Rights Seriously* (Cambridge, MA: Harvard University Press, 1977), in which he argues that there is a correct answer. For an alternative view, see Aharon Barak, *Judicial Discretion,* trans. Yadin Kaufmann (New Haven: Yale University Press, 1989).
95. The interpretive model that I put forward here to explain Maimonides's position, in which new rules are derived from premises through flexible rules of inference, directly links existing law to situations in which a judge must decide the law in an unprecedented case. When interpreters make new laws, they are not doing so on the basis of considerations independent of existing law, but neither are they merely interpreting the existing law. They are attempting to intuit what the existing law would rule in a case that is not explicitly covered by the law. This kind of deliberation is similar to Dworkin's account of judicial interpretation, which in new cases also does not operate independently of existing law and precedent. See Ronald Dworkin, *Law's Empire* (Cambridge, MA: Harvard University Press, 1986), 176–225.

96. "If the high court expounded through one of the *middot* what they saw fit to be the law and gave a ruling, and afterwards another court arose that considered a different reason correct which would contravene that ruling, then it should contravene that ruling and rule as it sees fit, for it says: 'to the judge that will be in those days' (Deut 17:9)—you are only obligated to follow the court of your generation" (*Mishneh Torah,* "Laws of Rebels," 2:1).

97. *The Guide of the Perplexed,* translated with introduction and notes by Shlomo Pines (Chicago: University of Chicago Press, 1963), III:41, 563, with minor adjustments.

98. *Hakdamot,* 40–41.

99. In the Mishneh Torah, Maimonides broadly construes the prohibition against adding or taking away from the Torah, which fits nicely with what he writes in the *Guide.* He rules that any court which claims Biblical status for one of its enactments violates this prohibition. See "Laws of Rebels," 2:9, and for a narrower understanding of the prohibition, see Ra'avad ad loc. See also at length in Gerald J. Blidstein, *Authority and Controversy in Maimonidean Law* (Tel-Aviv: Kibbutz ha-Me'uhad, 2002), 153–167 (Heb.).

100. An analysis of the category of "a Mosaic law from Sinai" leaves a lot of room to posit that Maimonides considers it Rabbinic. Nahmanides disagrees with Maimonides on this question in his *Hassagot.* For Maimonides's opinion, see David Henshke, "The Basis of Maimonides' Concept of Halacha," *Shenaton ha-Mishpat ha-'Ivri* 20 (1995–1997): 103–149 (Heb.). He argues that because he considers it Rabbinic, the weight of Maimonides's conception does not rest on the stature of Moses but on what is written in the Torah. This claim, however, assumes that Maimonides understands the category literally; namely, there is a tradition that a given law was orally transmitted to Moses at Sinai and then transmitted through tradition. Talmudic sugyot do not bear this out, however, because time and again when no scriptural source can be found for a particular law, the Talmud places it into this category, labeling it an early halakhic tradition that is incontestable. A number of medieval halakhists thought that such laws were Rabbinic because of the way the Talmud uses this category in the structure of these sugyot. In this way, the category differs from received interpretations that the Talmud explicitly states are Biblical.

101. *Hassagot,* 44.

102. On earlier sources for Nahmanides's conception of the Torah and its connection to divine names, see Moshe Idel, "The Concept of the Torah in Heikhalot Literature and Its Metamorphoses in Kabbalah," *Jerusalem Studies in Jewish Thought* 1 (1981): 27–30 (Heb.).

103. *PHT,* introduction (ed. Chavel, 1:6–7).

104. See Gershom Scholem, "The Meaning of the Torah in Jewish Mysticism," ch. 2 in *On the Kabbalah and Its Symbolism,* trans. Ralph Manheim (New York: Schocken, 1965), 32–86. For Nahmanides's concept of the Torah, see Haviva Pedaya, *Nahmanides: Cyclical Time and Holy Text* (Tel-Aviv: 'Am 'Oved, 2003), chs. 5–6 (Heb.).

105. On sefirot as "voices," see *PHT,* Exod 19:20 and Deut 5:19. See also R. Ezra of Gerona's commentary on Song of Songs, in *KR,* 2:487–488.

106. See Nahmanides's comments on the Torah scroll that the king is obligated to possess his whole life: "By way of truth, 'it shall be with him' (Deut 17:19) [means] the Torah itself shall be with Him, in the manner of [the verse] 'and the Lord gave *Hokhmah* to Solomon' (1 Kgs 5:26), and it says, 'And Solomon sat on the Throne of the Lord as King' (1 Chr 29:23)" (*PHT,* Deut 17:19).

107. Nahmanides's concept of the Torah also ties into his approach to the Hebrew language. In his Torah commentary, he criticizes Maimonides's approach to the holiness of Hebrew, and their disagreement forms an important backdrop for understanding their contrasting attitudes toward revelation. Maimonides views the holiness of the "holy tongue" in its lack of specific terms for genitalia and sexual relations (*Guide,* III:8). Nahmanides rejects this functional approach and considers it holy because it is the language of God, through which God created the world and in which his names are uttered. The "holy tongue," as an expression of God's essence, possesses creative and generative power. See *PHT,* Exod 30:13.

108. *PHT,* introduction (ed. Chavel, 1:5).

109. Ibid. (ed. Chavel, 1:7).

110. *Sefer ha-Mitzvot,* 19.

111. Ibid., 26.

112. Ibid., 27–28.

113. Ibid., 29.

114. Ibid., 18.

115. Ibid., 32.

116. *Hassagot,* 67.

117. Ibid., 68.

118. Ibid., 86–87.

119. On the difference between these schools and their hermeneutics, see Jacob Nahum Epstein, *Introduction to Tannaitic Literature,* ed. Ezra Zion Melamed (Jerusalem: Magnes, c1957), 521–536 (Heb.).

120. Maimonides and Nahmanides have a similar disagreement in Principle Nine about repeated prohibitions. As cited above, Maimonides says they should not be enumerated because the repetition does not entail a new prohibition or additional lashes but is a rhetorical device intended to reinforce the original prohibition: "sometimes prohibition after prohibition is said about the same matter for reinforcement" (*Sefer ha-Mitzvot,* 33). Nahmanides, on the other hand, detects additional levels of normativity with each repetition, each of which either constitutes a prohibition with different content or obligates another set of lashes: "They have explained that many times multiple prohibitions require lashes in accord with the number of prohibitions. But one condition applies, namely, that the prohibitions must be redundant and not needed for some *midrash* about the commandment, only to repeat the proscription" (*Hassagot,* 99). Multiple prohibitions against the same act not only serve to reinforce the original prohibition and add caution, but they add either lashes or normative content of some kind.

121. *Sefer ha-Mitzvot,* 6.

122. *Hassagot,* 139–140.

123. *PHT,* Deut 17:11.

124. *Hassagot,* 17 and 18.

125. The question turns on how to read "even if they err." If the clause continues to describe the subjective view of the scholar who disagrees with the court, it aligns with the stronger reading, as they are only mistaken from his perspective; if it is stated as an objective fact, then the court can err, which reflects the weaker reading.

126. On this ambivalence within the sugya itself, see Halbertal, *People of the Book,* 86–89.

127. *Sefer ha-Hinnukh,* no. 496, and see also no. 78.

128. *Hiddushei ha-Ritva, Massekhet 'Eiruvin,* ed. R. Moses Goldstein (Jerusalem: Mossad Harav Kook, 1983), 107 (13b, s.v. *ellu ve-ellu*).

129. Ran read Nahmanides a third way in the third and seventh discourses of his Derashot. Against the author of Sefer ha-Hinnukh, he writes that revelation included future disputes of the Sages: "this teaches that the Holy One showed Moses the details of the Torah, the fine points of the Sages, and what the Sages would innovate in the future [. . .] 'fine points of the Sages' refers to those disputes and disagreements between the Sages of Israel, all of which Moses learned from the mouth of the Almighty, and the decision between them follows the consensus of the Sages of the generation" (*Derashot ha-Ran ha-Shalem—Menukkad,* ed. Leon A. Feldman and Mordechai Leib Katzenellenbogen [Jerusalem: Mossad Harav Kook, 2016], 46–47). Unlike Ritva, however, the fact that all sides of the disputed issue were revealed at Sinai does not endow them with equal value: "even the opinion of someone who did not apprehend the truth was said to Moses at Sinai" (ibid., 46). From God's perspective, among the diverse opinions God revealed at Sinai, one is more truthful than the rest, and the Sages are to decide the law without knowing which one God considers more truthful. The constitutive ability of the Sages is weaker here than in Ritva's account, because they do not constitute the truth but the norm that must be followed. Paradoxically, however, their position is also stronger here, because even when the Sages are informed by way of a heavenly voice of God's opinion about the truth (as occurred in the narrative about the oven of Akhnai), they are forbidden to follow it and must follow their own reasoning: "They all saw that R. Eliezer was closer to the truth than they were, that all of his signs were true and correct and Heaven had decided in favor of his opinion, yet they still acted according to their consensus, since their intellect inclined towards rendering impure. Even though they knew that their consensus was the opposite of the truth, they refused to render pure, and they would have been in violation of the Torah had they rendered pure since their intellect inclined towards rendering impure, for the decision is entrusted to the Sages of each generation" (ibid., 47). On Ran's position, see Avi Sagi, *"Elu va-Elu": A Study on the Meaning of Halakhic Discourse* (Tel-Aviv: Ha-Kibbutz ha-Me'uhad, 1996), 80–82 (Heb.).

130. Commentary to 'Edduyot 1.5. For an additional medieval source from the Provençal-French world presenting such a position, see R. Jacob of Marvège, *She'elot u-Teshuvot min ha-Shamayim* (Jerusalem: Mossad Harav Kook, 1957), 3.

131. Perhaps Ritva refers to the kabbalistic tradition about all-inclusive revelation found in the writings of the Geronese kabbalists. R. Ezra of Gerona writes in his

commentary on Song of Songs: "it emerged from the inner Voice, and that Voice split into seventy branches, corresponding to the seventy aspects of the Torah, the aspects change and reverse from every side to impure and pure, forbidden and permitted, invalid and valid, each alongside the other, by which the impurity and purity of the creeping thing were understood. At that time, the prophets of every generation received their prophecy, and the eminent Sages of the future [received] their major rulings and debates" (*KR*, 2:478). See also R. Azriel of Gerona, *Commentary on Talmudic Aggadoth*, ed. Isaiah Tishby, 2nd ed. (Jerusalem: Magnes, 1982), 74–75 (Heb.). For a broad analysis of the notion of controversy in halakhah and its various implications for the multifaceted character of halakhah, see Sagi, "*Elu va-Elu*." See also Sagi's discussion of Nahmanides's conception of interpretation in Sagi, "Canonic Scripture and the Hermeneutical Challenge: A Critical Review in Light of Nahmanides," *Da'at* 50–52 (2003): 121–141 (Heb.). See Blidstein, *Authority and Controversy*, 275–285.

132. *PHT,* Deut 17:11.
133. *PHT,* Num 11:16.
134. Also relevant is the prayer over the ruins of Jerusalem attributed to Nahmanides, in which he describes the Sanhedrin that used to convene in the Temple: "And there you [i.e., Jerusalem] chose a place, / the hewn-stone office, / crowned by its seventy elders and its Sanhedrin, / the ministers of the Holy and ministers of God lending it splendor and distinction, / arranged according to the configuration of the ministers in heaven, / the president presiding in unification / corresponding to the 'one nation' " (*KR*, 1:425). Chavel's edition has *shirei*, "songs," which does not make sense in the context. A manuscript copied in 1286 (MS New York—JTS 8124 [IMHM 11315], 1r), only a decade after Nahmanides's death, as well as some later manuscripts, reads *sarei* ("ministers") instead. It also has an additional *sarei* in the following line, which has been included, since it fits with the piece above from Nahmanides's Torah commentary.
135. For the presence of God during adjudication, see *PHT,* Exod 21:6, where he disagrees with R. Abraham Ibn Ezra.
136. *Novellae, Bava Batra* 12a, s.v. *ha de-amerinan mi-yom*, M15.
137. For all of the ideas that follow, see at length ch. 5, esp. sec. III.
138. *THA, KR,* 2:308.
139. For Nahmanides's treatment of cleaving to the divine, see ch. 4.

CHAPTER 2. CUSTOM AND THE HISTORY OF HALAKHAH

1. These developments have been described and analyzed at length in Ephraim Urbach, *The Tosafists,* 4th ed., 2 vols. (Jerusalem: Mosad Bialik, 1980) (Heb.); Haym Soloveitchik, "Three Themes in Sefer Hasidim," *AJS Review* 1 (1976): 311–361; and Israel M. Ta-Shma, *Talmudic Commentary in Europe and North Africa: Literary History,* 2nd ed., vol. 1 (Jerusalem: Magnes, 2000), 32–117 (Heb.).
2. Haym Soloveitchik analyzes Ra'avad's manner of carving out his own path in his Talmudic commentary and the independence of Ra'avad's output from Geonic traditions. See Haym Soloveitchik, "Rabad of Posquières: A Programmatic Essay," in

Studies in the History of Jewish Society in the Middle Ages and in the Modern Period: Presented to Professor Jacob Katz on his Seventy-Fifth Birthday by His Students and Friends, ed. Emmanuel Etkes and Yosef Salmon (Jerusalem: Magnes, 1980), 11–14. See also Yaacov Sussman, "Ra'avad on *Shekalim?* A Bibliographical and Historical Riddle," in *Me'ah She'arim: Studies in Medieval Jewish Spiritual Life in Memory of Isadore Twersky,* ed. Ezra Fleischer et al. (Jerusalem: Magnes, 2001), 159n106 (Heb.).

3. *Sefer ha-Mitzvot: Makor ve-Targum,* ed. and trans. Yosef Kafih (Jerusalem: Mossad Harav Kook, 1971), 11. Maimonides does not spare the rod of criticism in the other Principles of Sefer ha-Mitzvot either: "He has made such a mess of this Principle that there is no need to respond. In fact, it would not prove easy to respond on account of the utter chaos of things that he has wrought" (ibid., 52). In the continuation: "God knows and is witness that all of this, in my opinion, is a complete hodgepodge, and there is nowise need to speak about it, for one can clearly see in it its own refutation" (ibid., 53).

4. Ibid., 6.

5. Tosafist influence upon Nahmanides's methods of study has been discussed already in various contexts. See Shraga Abramson, *The Rules of the Talmud in Nahmanides' Words* (Jerusalem: Mossad Harav Kook, 1971), 8–9 (Heb.); Ta-Shma, *Talmudic Commentary,* vol. 2 (Jerusalem: Magnes, 2004), 38–45 (Heb.).

6. Nahmanides's relationship with the halakhic teachings and positions of the Geonim and Rif has been treated by Bernard Septimus, who put his finger on the Sephardic orientation in Nahmanides's halakhic writings. See his "Open Rebuke and Concealed Love: Nahmanides and the Andalusian Tradition," in *Rabbi Moses Nahmanides and His Literary Virtuosity,* ed. Isadore Twersky (Cambridge, MA: Harvard University Press, 1983), 30–34. See also Ta-Shma, *Talmudic Commentary,* vol. 2, 34 (Heb.); Tsvi Groner, "Legal Decisions of *Rishonim,* and Their Attitudes towards Their Predecessors," in *Me'ah She'arim,* 267–278 (Heb.).

7. The terminology employed here by Nahmanides of "Earlier Authorities" and "Later Authorities," or Rishonim and Aharonim, is discussed below in sec. II.

8. Introduction to *Hassagot,* 25.

9. Ibid., 25–26.

10. Ibid., 26.

11. Ibid., 25.

12. Nahmanides systematically rejects Talmudic readings proposed by Rashi to resolve some difficulty in a sugya, preferring instead the textual versions of the Geonim, R. Hananel b. Hushiel (Rabbeinu Hananel), or those found in Iberian copies of the Talmud. In this way he remains loyal to Spanish tradition, in which the editing of texts did not gain the traction it did in northern France and Germany. On this, see Ta-Shma, *Talmudic Commentary,* vol. 2, 41–42 (Heb.). Nahmanides also quite frequently rejects Rashi's interpretations in favor of Geonic traditions. For example, we find in his novellae to Bava Metzi'a: "I found that Rabbeinu Hayya [Gaon], in his *Sefer ha-Mekah,* permitted [the futures contract even when the seller did not own the produce] when he [the buyer] acquired it with money, which is like the other version

that I have written [above] and not like the opinion of Rashi. The tradition of the Geonim is decisive" (Bava Metzi'a 62b, s.v. *amar Rabbah*, M89/H370). Two parallel examples of his preference for Geonic positions over those of Rabbeinu Tam can be found in his novellae: "Our masters [the Geonim] explained that the letter *lamed* stands for a side post (*lehi*) that stands by itself [. . .] Rabbeinu Tam used to say [it stands for] childbirth (*leidah*) [. . .] but we rely on the tradition" (*Novellae*, Kiddushin 52b, s.v. *Ya'aL QeGaM*, M53/H246); and the parallel: "against the words of R. Jacob [Tam], who explained the *lamed* [as standing for the law concerning] childbirth (*leidah*) here, and in accord with the tradition of the Geonim" (*Novellae*, Niddah 37a, s.v. *ve-ha de-tanya*, M35/H152). In another context, Nahmanides repeats his emphasis of Geonic superiority over Rabbeinu Tam: "Rather, the Geonic consensus is primary, and we accept the tradition" (*Novellae*, Bava Metzi'a 114a, s.v. *ve-ha de-iba'ei lehu*, M147/H648–649). Elsewhere Nahmanides rejects one of Rabbeinu Tam's radical innovations about how to write a bill of divorce: "R[abbeinu] Tam explains '[write] husband so-and-so and every one of his names' to mean that he must write explicitly 'husband so-and-so who is called such-and-such,' but it [the explanation] is not accurate [. . .] I have already told you that the Earlier Authorities (*Rishonim*) [i.e., Geonim] wrote to write it without specifying" (*Novellae*, Gittin 34b, s.v. *matnitin ba-rishonah*, M51/H202). In yet another place, after Nahmanides cites the positions of Rabbeinu Tam and Ra'avad, he brings an opposing position that accords with that of the Geonim and asserts that one should not disagree with them: "We have seen our masters the Geonim, Rabbeinu Hayya and Rabbeinu Hananel explain it in this way, and it is inappropriate to disagree with the Geonim" (*Novellae*, Bava Metzi'a 47b, s.v. *bi-shelama le-Reish Lakish*, M77/H314). An additional instance in which Nahmanides places a Geonic position in opposition to Ra'avad and the Tosafists appears in a gloss in Nahmanides's Sefer ha-Zekhut: "It is true that our northern French masters instructed us so [i.e., like Ra'avad's opinion] [. . .] But what can we do about the Geonim, who all explained . . ." (*Sefer ha-Zekhut*, Ketubbot 56b).

13. Introduction to *Hassagot*, 27. In a few places Nahmanides emphasizes that Rif is not perfect and should not be followed blindly: "For there is no perfection save that of God Himself" (*Milhamot ha-Shem*, Yevamot 9a); "Although the dread of his wisdom is upon us, there is no favoritism in judgment" (*Responsa*, no. 25, 45).

14. Nahmanides exaggerates a few times about Rif. In his novellae to Gittin he asserts, "We rely on him in every matter" (*Novellae*, Gittin 36a, s.v. *ha de-tanya Rabbi*, M57/H226). The designations "Fathers of the World" and "Pillars of the World" refer to R. Hayya Ga'on and Rif: "Moreover, nobody may budge from the words of the Pillars of the World" (*Novellae*, Bava Batra 131b, s.v. *ha de-amar Rav Yehudah*, M146). In a poetic fragment of Milhamot ha-Shem to Ketubbot, Nahmanides implies that Rif was a sui generis phenomenon in the annals of halakhah, privy to quasi-revelation: "May God save us from overweening speech and remove from our path any impediment, / for in the footsteps of his messenger whom before us He has sent / we go forth to instruct, / relying upon that which he has apportioned to us of his intellect, / and trusting in the Scriptural verse: 'God's secret is for those who fear Him; He informs them of His covenant' (Ps 25:14)" (*Milhamot ha-Shem*, Ketubbot 50a).

15. In his introduction to Milhamot ha-Shem, Nahmanides typologically trifurcates Rif's writings: (1) In most cases, Rif is the champion of subsequent disagreements with him. (2) In cases where Rif and his opponents seem equally matched, the law should rule in accordance with Rif's opinion "without tending to the right or left of what he says. As the Sages taught, there were two [scholars], one who rendered impure and the other pure, one prohibited and the other permitted. But if one was greater than his colleague in wisdom or number, follow him." (3) In a minority of cases Rif's position appears mistaken, so one cannot be lenient in accord with his opinion—one should therefore decide stringently out of doubt: "There are cases in which we provide justification for the words of *Rabbeinu*, even if they are far from the simple sense of the *sugya* or *sugyot*. Our intention in this is to reveal to students the merit therein, and we do not shy away from telling anyone who looks in our book that doubt remains. This is permitted us because we have come to vindicate *Rabbeinu ha-Gadol* and the words of the Earlier Authorities (*Rishonim*) [i.e., the Geonim]. Our obligation is to him, as the Sages of Israel have instructed their disciples: 'If a legal ruling of mine comes before you after [my] death, do not tear it up but do not learn from it. Do not tear it up—perhaps if I were alive I would have my reasons. Do not learn from it—for a judge has nothing save what his eyes see.' The result is that we must be concerned about the words of *Rabbeinu* for purposes of stringency, not leniency. But this is in the minority of instances." Nahmanides follows the Talmud (Sanhedrin 6b) in his use of the rule that "a judge has nothing save what his eyes see," in order to provide himself the freedom to rule against Rif when Rif seems wrong. Nevertheless, he restricts this freedom to cases where Rif is lenient! In fact, in most of his novellae Nahmanides adheres to this limited principle, ruling stringently only whenever he disagrees with Rif. (Obviously he adopts this self-imposed restriction with respect to only Rif and not to any of his successors, with whom Nahmanides disagrees by taking a more stringent or lenient position.) See, for example, his novellae to Gittin: "I still have my doubts about this and so am stringent" (*Novellae*, Gittin 63b, s.v. *havah 'uvdah*, M82/H341); "If I were worthy enough to disagree I would validate it [. . .] Still I aver that it is dubious and we take a stringent tack on this" (ibid., 66b, s.v. *ve-amar Rav Hisda*, M89/H372); "But *Rabbeinu ha-Gadol* and the Geonim did not find it of [enough] concern to write about it. A scrupulous, self-disciplined person (*ba'al nefesh*) should be concerned for himself" (*Novellae*, Niddah 42a, s.v. *ha di-be'a mineih*, M40/H174).

16. In the words of Nahmanides, "*Rabbeinu Ha-Gaon* is Rav Hayya Gaon" (*Milhamot ha-Shem*, Bava Kamma 33b). In one case where Nahmanides rules with the Geonim against Rif, he mentions R. Sherira Gaon with exalted language: "When we follow the words of the Earlier Authorities (*Rishonim*) we have none but those of the Gaon, Father of Israel (*Avihem shel Yisra'el*)—Rav Sherira Gaon" (*Milhamot ha-Shem*, Pesahim 24b). Nahmanides also refers to R. Hayya Gaon as "Father of Israel" (see *Milhamot ha-Shem*, Hullin 12a), holding him in very high regard: "What Rabbeinu Sherira and his son Rabbeinu Hayya, who is equivalent to a majority of the *Sanhedrin*, wrote accords with the words of *Rabbeinu ha-Gadol*" (*Milhamot ha-Shem*, Ketubbot 21a).

17. See, respectively, in his novellae: Yevamot 24b, s.v. *ve-akshinan i hakhei*, M22/H73; Yevamot 30b, s.v. *u-le-Rava ha-niha*, M31/H101; Yevamot 109b, s.v. *ta'ama de-Rabban Gamali'el*, M107/H362; Ketubbot 85b, s.v. *ha-mokher shetar hov*, M92/H452/Ch233; 'Avodah Zarah 41a, s.v. *ha de-amar Shemu'el*, M29/H140.

18. Nahmanides does not share Maimonides's admiration for Ri Migash; see, for example, "Here both Rabbi Halevi and his disciple Rabbi Moses made a serious error" (*Novellae*, Shevu'ot 25a, s.v. *ha de-amar Rava*, M32/H114). Elsewhere, he writes about Ri Migash: "I do not know what he is talking about" (*Novellae*, Ketubbot 18b, s.v. *piresh Rashi z"l*, M28/Ch107; s.v. *ve-okiman ela i itmar*, H115). The other leading Torah scholars of North Africa and Andalusia—Rabbeinu Ephraim and R. Isaac Ghiyyat—also receive businesslike treatment, devoid of the respect or awe accorded to Rif. Nahmanides disagrees with them as equals, and sometimes he dismisses their opinions as erroneous.

19. In one example from his novellae, he calls an idea of Rabbeinu Tam "incorrect" (*Novellae*, Bava Batra 2a, s.v. *matnitin makom she-nahagu*, M1). Sometimes he indulges in wordplay: "*Sefer ha-Yashar* contains an interpretation that is not straight (*yashar*)" ('Avodah Zarah 73b, s.v. *mezagan ve-'eirevan*, M70/H374).

20. He refers to Ra'avad with the rare adjective *kadosh*, "holy," both in his introduction to Sefer ha-Zekhut and in his preface to Hilkhot Niddah: "I have been preceded by someone holy, / who expounds and of whom exposition is worthy, / and he has composed about them [the laws concerning menstruation] a respectable work for those who possess chastity" (*Hilkhot Niddah*, M3/H259). In all that pertains to halakhah, however, Ra'avad and his positions do not possess authoritative standing for Nahmanides, even with the profound impact Ra'avad had on Nahmanides's methods of thinking and creativity. For example: "I then saw the responsum of the aforementioned R. Abraham, who went to lengths to have his words stand up, but they neither stand up nor withstand scrutiny" (*Novellae*, Bava Metzi'a 98b, s.v. *ha di-tenan zeh omer*, M135/H590). See also his novella on tractate Niddah, where after quoting and discussing an interpretation of Ra'avad, he concludes, "This interpretation is unthinkable, for it perverts the manner of the Talmud" (*Novellae*, Niddah 67a, s.v. *ha de-amerinan ve-leit hilkheta*, M66/H251). One does not find these sorts of expressions aimed at Rif in Nahmanides's writings; see what Nahmanides writes about Ra'avad in *Responsa*, no. 89, 134 with note 21, and see Chavel's comment in 45n11.

21. Nahmanides mentions Tosafist influence upon him in his introduction to Kuntres Dina de-Garmi: "The northern French sages have mostly passed from this world, / they are the instructors, the teachers, the ones who reveal to us all that is concealed" (*Kuntres Dina de-Garmi*, M181/H106). In his novellae to Hullin he says about the Tosafists that "our Torah is theirs" (*Novellae*, Hullin 94a, s.v. *kullah shema'ata*, M106/H519). However, he does not consider their opinions as particularly authoritative, and he certainly will not lie down before them. In quite a few cases, especially when dealing with unattributed Tosafist comments, Nahmanides expresses reservations about their line of thinking, their forced answers, and their hairsplitting reading of the text, which lacks sensitivity to its structure and meaning: "Because of this

[question] the Tosafists are forced to come up with ideas, which are baseless" (*Novellae*, Gittin 66b, s.v. *ve-amar Rav Hisda*, M88/H368). In his novellae to Ketubbot we find an expression he occasionally uses about the Tosafist method: "they parse the passage to pieces but it comes to nothing" (*Novellae*, Ketubbot 26b, s.v. *matnitin ha-ishah*, M41/H189/Ch135). Elsewhere, he concludes a discussion of the Tosafist approach by saying, "this interpretation is useless because it is forced, it is worthless" (*Novellae*, Yevamot 53a, s.v. *ha-niha le-Rabbi Yohanan*, M61/H303).

22. Nahmanides occasionally indulges in biting witticisms at Razah's expense. For example: "That Razah's interpretation of this passage started off a chick and ended up an egg" (*Milhamot ha-Shem*, Bava Batra 38b). The use of the distal demonstrative in "that Razah" is rife in Nahmanides's writings and suits the condescending, polemical tone that Nahmanides adopts against Razah. Even Razah's father does not escape Nahmanides's sharp tongue. Regarding the letter of consolation Razah's father penned to his son, Nahmanides writes, "With this his father consoled him with vacuous consolations" (*Milhamot ha-Shem*, Bava Metzi'a 65a). Cynical quips often trail Razah's grandiloquence. When Rif asserts that a congregation does not recite a voluntary silent 'amidah prayer because the public cannot offer a voluntary sacrifice, Razah says: " 'It is beyond my ken, so lofty that I cannot grasp' (Ps 139:6) why he saw fit to utter such a thing, when the entire Talmud is filled with [instances of] the public bringing voluntary burnt offerings" (*Ha-Ma'or ha-Katon*, Berakhot 13a). In the continuation Razah brings two examples that he believes demonstrate a voluntary offering being brought by the public. Nahmanides responds: "We have finished the thorough search, and the only ones found in the Talmud are those that he copied here from the words of Rabbeinu Ephraim" (*Milhamot ha-Shem*, ad loc.). Another instance of mockery concerns a different composition authored by Razah, Sefer Divrei ha-Rivot: "I have already seen what he said about this in *The Book of Strife*, and I ascribe to it the verse, 'It is honorable for a man to desist from strife (Prov 20:3)' " (*Milhamot ha-Shem*, Bava Metzi'a 58a). These expressions form part of his rhetorical endeavor to isolate Razah from the other halakhists, as if it were better for everyone had he never existed at all. In the handful of references to Razah in Nahmanides's novellae the tone is much the same. In one example from tractate Shabbat, he refers to Razah with "others said," which is followed by "this too is nonsense" (*Novellae*, Shabbat 139b, s.v. *ha de-amerinan met*, M123/H456).

23. "I have already completed my composition on the first part [of Razah's writings] in a different manner, for my younger days fired me / and my youth made me fiery. / I was zealous for *Rabbeinu ha-Gadol* R. Isaac Alfasi / [. . .] But after revisiting [it] I relented, / after contemplating [it] I reoriented, / lest I be as if making a name for myself through this labor, which does not do honor to the master [i.e., Rif]. [. . .] I have therefore refrained throughout this Order, which is the Order of *Mo'ed*, from responding to the aforementioned master, except to requite the victim, by which I mean to vindicate the words of *Rabbeinu ha-Gadol* and elucidate it [*sic*]" (Introduction to *Milhamot ha-Shem*). My impression is that this declaration notwithstanding, there is no discernible change in tone or in the harshness of his glosses on Razah's *Ha-Ma'or ha-Katon* in Milhamot ha-Shem on the Order of Mo'ed.

24. Nahmanides displays a unique blend of awe and respect toward Rabbi Meir ha-Levi Abulafia (Ramah) the handful of times he mentions him in his novellae: "I asked Rabbi Meir, prince of the Levite (*ha-Levi*) princes [. . .] Thus responded the great prince, 'may lips kiss he who responded correctly' (Prov 24:26)" (*Novellae*, Bava Batra 34a, s.v. *ve-ha de-amar leih Rabbi Abba*, M49). See also his address to Ramah, whom he regarded as a reliable authority on early Spanish customs, on the question of saying *el melekh ne'eman* (*Novellae*, Berakhot 2a, s.v. *kevar hayah*, H3/Berakhot 11b, s.v. *mi-she-kara keri'at shema'*, M3); R. Menahem b. Solomon ha-Meiri, *Magen Avot*, ed. Isaac Last (London, 1909), sec. 1, 14–21.

25. The Talmud (Rosh ha-Shanah 35a) limits Rabban Gamaliel's position by saying that "Rabban Gamaliel only exempted the people in the fields." According to Rashi, only those in the fields have their obligations discharged by the prayer of the prayer leader, because they are incapable of doing so themselves. Those present in the synagogue, who are quite capable, cannot discharge their obligation by way of the prayer leader. This makes the Geonic custom particularly difficult for Rashi. Nahmanides, following Rabbeinu Hananel and his version of the Talmudic text, rejects Rashi's opinion and believes that those in the field discharge their obligation even if they cannot hear the prayer leader. Those in the synagogue, however, discharge it only if they hear the prayer leader, but they still do not need to recite the silent 'amidah in order to fulfill their obligation. See *Novellae*, Rosh ha-Shanah 35a, s.v. *lo patar*, M32/H90–91.

26. The additions of malkhuyot appear within the third blessing of the 'amidah, so the additions recited by the prayer leader result in nine, not ten, total blessings.

27. The sources for this Geonic custom are cited in *Otzar ha-Geonim, Rosh ha-Shanah*, ed. Benjamin Manasseh Lewin (Jerusalem: Hebrew University, 1933), 68–70.

28. *DRH, KR*, 1:181.

29. *Ha-Ma'or ha-Katon*, Rosh ha-Shanah 11a. For the practice in northern France, see the responsum of R. Joseph Bonfils cited in *Mahzor Vitry*, ed. Aryeh Goldschmidt, vol. 3 (Jerusalem: Makhon Otzar Ha-Poskim, 2009), 699–701 (= *Machsor Vitry* [Nürnberg, 1923], 352).

30. *DRH, KR*, 1:181–182.

31. Ibid., 182.

32. On the uses of the Jerusalem Talmud within Nahmanides's methodology, see Yaacov Sussman, "Chapters of the Yerushalmi," in *Talmudic Studies*, vol. 2, ed. Moshe Bar-Asher and David Rosenthal (Jerusalem: Magnes, 1993), 281 (Heb.); and see at length Shalem Yahalom, "Nachmanides and the Palestinian Talmud," *Shenaton ha-Mishpat ha-'Ivri* 23 (2005): 25–71 (Heb.). A comprehensive account of Nahmanides's interpretations of the Jerusalem Talmud appear in the extremely valuable volumes edited by Yoel Florsheim: *Peirushei ha-Rambam li-Yerushalmi: Seder Zera'im* (Jerusalem: Mossad Harav Kook, 2003); *Peirushei ha-Rambam li-Yerushalmi: Seder Mo'ed* (Jerusalem: Mossad Harav Kook, 2004); *Peirushei ha-Rambam li-Yerushalmi: Seder Nashim*, vol. 1 (Jerusalem: Mossad Harav Kook, 2005); *Peirushei ha-Rambam li-Yerushalmi: Seder Nashim*, vol. 2 (Jerusalem: Mossad Harav Kook, 2006); *Peirushei ha-Rambam li-Yerushalmi: Seder Nezikin* (Jerusalem: Mossad Harav Kook, 2009); and *Peirushei ha-Rambam li-Yerushalmi: Mavo u-Firkei Siyyum* (Jerusalem: Mossad Harav Kook, 2013).

33. On the importance of the distinction between Rishonim and Aharonim, see Israel Jacob Yuval, "*Rishonim* and *Aharonim, Antiqui et Moderni* (Periodization and Self-Awareness in Ashkenaz)," *Zion* 57 (1992): 369–394 (Heb.), and see the literature cited there in note 2. On the consequences of this distinction and its general relationship to "the law follows later authorities," as well as its significance for the conception of time within halakhah, see Israel M. Ta-Shma, *Ritual, Custom, and Reality in Franco-Germany, 1000–1350* (Jerusalem: Magnes, 1996), 57–78 (Heb.); Yuval, "Rishonim and Aharonim," 376–386 (Heb.); Shai Wosner, "*Hilcheta ke-Batray*—A New Perspective," *Shenaton ha-Mishpat ha-'Ivri* 20 (1995–1997): 151–167 (Heb.). On the idea of periodization and closure in halakhah, see Shlomo Zalman Havlin, "On Literary Closure as the Basis for Periodization in Halakhah," in *Researches in Talmudic Literature: A Study Conference in Honour of the Eightieth Birthday of Shaul Lieberman*, ed. Samuel Re'em (Jerusalem: Israel Academy of Sciences and Humanities, 1983), 148–192 (Heb.).

34. *Milhamot ha-Shem*, Pesahim 19a. Also: "We have seen *Rishonim*, such as the authors of *Halakhot Gedolot* [i.e., Kayyara] and *Halakhot Pesukot* [i.e., R. Yehudai Gaon, attributed], write things similar to *Rabbeinu*. This is an ancient dispute which the *Rishonim* have already covered" (*Milhamot Ha-Shem*, Pesahim 19b); "The *Rishonim* and *Rabbeinu* ruled" (*Novellae*, Yevamot 27a, s.v. *u-maskana Rav Ashi amar*, M26/H84); "We have seen that *Rabbeinu* and the *Rishonim* wrote it in their codes" (*Novellae*, Yevamot 65b, s.v. *hu omer hippilah*, H243; s.v. *ve-ha de-amerinan hippilah*, M72).

35. *Milhamot ha-Shem*, Pesahim 26b.

36. *Milhamot ha-Shem*, Rosh ha-Shanah 8b.

37. *THA, KR*, 2:226. Many instances of the same appear in his novellae and Milhamot ha-Shem: "But we find it mystifying that the greatest of the Geonim did not rely on the Jerusalem Talmud in deciding the law. Likewise, I have seen that the authors of [*Sefer*] *Metivot* wrote this in their [compendium of] laws. Perhaps it was a tradition the *Rishonim* possessed" (*Milhamot ha-Shem*, Mo'ed Katan 16a); "The perplexity is considerable, because some of the Geonim wrote that moist peppercorns require the blessing 'Who creates the fruit of the earth,' based on the [Talmud's] question from 'tree for food—this is the pepper tree.' This is also the opinion of Rav Hayya Gaon. But it should be the contrary, because it makes sense to recite the blessing 'Who creates the fruit of the tree'! Perhaps the *Rishonim* believed [. . .] We will accept the Geonic tradition" (*Novellae*, Berakhot 36b, s.v. *u-le-'inyan pilpelin*, M12/H15); "The Geonim and *Rishonim* extrapolated thus [. . .] We will accept the tradition" (*Novellae*, 'Avodah Zarah 30a, s.v. *yayin mevushal*, M14/H57).

38. *Ha-Ma'or ha-Gadol*, Bava Batra 70a.

39. *Milhamot ha-Shem*, Bava Batra 70a.

40. *Novellae*, Bava Batra 40b, s.v. *u-mefarekinan modeh Rava*, M57.

41. *Novellae*, Shabbat 74b, s.v. *ha de-amerinan tolesh*, M66–67/H262. And so in another piece: "The matter is obvious and well-known, but I have been forced to write it because one of the great Later codifiers . . ." (*Novellae*, Kiddushin 78a, s.v. *ha de-amerinan u-modeh Abayyei*, M82/H360). I translate the noun *Sefarad* and the adjective *Sefaradi* in primary sources as "Andalusia" and "Andalusian" because that more

clearly captures the intended halakhic and spiritual culture rather than "Spain" and "Spanish."

42. *Novellae*, Shabbat 22b, s.v. *le-man de-amar hanakhah*, M21/H82. Also: "Ra'avad wrote [. . .] but I looked into the words of the *Rishonim* and found Rav Aha Gaon of Shabha who wrote in the *She'ilta* [. . .] which is reasonable" (*Novellae*, Hullin 15b, s.v. *muttar la-bari*, M26–27/H123–124).

43. *Novellae*, Kiddushin 65a, s.v. *ha de-amerinan ve-im natan get*, M68/H305. Other examples: "So ruled the *Rishonim*, such as Rav Aha Gaon of Shabha, and even Rabbeinu Hananel, and all Later rabbis of Andalusia" (*Milhamot ha-Shem*, Hullin 29a); "R. Joseph Halevi Ibn Migash has an interpretation of this passage, as do some of the Earlier Geonim" (*Novellae*, Shabbat 84b, s.v. *ha di-tenan she-zore'in*, M77/H298); "Such is the opinion of *Rabbeinu ha-Gadol* Rif, and the opinion of R. Samuel [Ha-Nagid] and Later rabbis of Andalusia" (*Novellae*, Kiddushin 25b, s.v. *matnitin be-hemah*, M30; s.v. *va-hakhamim omerim bi-meshikhah*, H140); "We have received such a tradition from the Geonim and the Later rabbis of Andalusia" (*Novellae*, Bava Batra 59a, s.v. *ha di-tenan be-matnitin*, M81).

44. *Novellae*, Makkot 5a, s.v. *matnitin ba'u aherim*, M7/H30.

45. Ibid., M7/H31.

46. Characteristic of Nahmanides, conservatism does not mean blind trust. In his novellae to Bava Metzi'a he argues that a particular reading of a Talmudic passage is not in fact part of the original Talmudic text but is an explanation added to the text from a work by R. Yehudai Gaon. He rejects the interpretation of the Gaon, saying: "Although the *Rishonim* were angels, we are men, and the truth will show us its path" (*Novellae*, Bava Metzi'a 98a, s.v. *u-le-Rami bar Hama*, M133/H584). The superiority of the Rishonim does not negate the need for truth, for although the Aharonim might not be angels, they are still men.

47. *Novellae*, Makkot 5a, s.v. *matnitin ba'u aherim*, M7/H33.

48. *Milhamot ha-Shem*, Bava Metzi'a 36a. In his introduction to Milhamot ha-Shem, Nahmanides establishes that in a debate where the opinions are equally weighted, one should follow Rif because he possessed greater wisdom. He then adds: "And all the more so because he is antecedent, which should shut down any prospective dissenter, for he should say 'the elder has already ruled.'" Rif's antecedence disallows arguing with him—his rulings are binding. Nahmanides does not, however, view the anteriority of every medieval scholar as reason enough to prevent disagreement with them.

49. *Ha-Ma'or ha-Katon*, Pesahim 17a.

50. *Hassagot ha-Ra'avad*, Pesahim 16b.

51. Ta-Shma analyzed at length the conception of Franco-German custom and its complicated relationship with the written law of the Talmud in his *Early Franco-German Ritual and Custom*, 3rd rev. ed. (Jerusalem: Magnes, 1999), 13–105 (Heb.).

52. *Ha-Ma'or ha-Katon*, Pesahim 16b.

53. See Israel Ta-Shma, "The Nature and Characteristics of 'Sefer ha-Maor' by R. Zerahya ha-Levi," *Shenaton ha-Mishpat ha-'Ivri* 5 (1978): 395–404 (Heb.); Ta-Shma, *Rabbi Zerahiah ha-Levi Ba'al ha-Ma'or u-Venei Hugo* (Jerusalem: Mossad Harav Kook, 1992), 86–91 (Heb.).

54. *Ha-Ma'or ha-Katon,* Pesahim 16b–17a.

55. Limiting the baraita and accompanying sugya to a custom erroneously thought to be the law creates an additional important difference between Razah and Nahmanides. The latter believes that Torah scholars make mistakes, and it is incumbent upon the scholarly new arrival to disabuse them of their erroneous custom by permitting it in their presence. This is an intense and interesting position on the question of halakhic error, and Meiri decries it: "Moreover, let us consider what we are saying. He [Nahmanides] says, 'That which is permitted but others have the custom to prohibit, one may not permit in their presence,' and it [the Talmud] qualifies it [saying] '[in the presence of] Samaritans'; in other words, the same is true for all who are not Torah scholars, but it would be permitted [in the presence of] Torah scholars [. . .] Do we suspect Torah scholars of making mistakes about ritual matters?" (*Magen Avot,* 93). Nahmanides's position explains the behavior of his students as presented by Meiri. Nahmanides's disciples who immigrated to Perpignan systematically criticized many of the local customs and did not follow them. Meiri, who was forced to defend each and every local custom, apparently viewed the position adopted by Nahmanides's disciples as fundamentally flawed. Meiri mentions this flaw in his criticism of Nahmanides's theory of custom and his opinion that one can attribute error to Torah scholars, which allowed Nahmanides's disciples to undermine the traditions of the renowned Provence. If so, beyond the local disputes between Nahmanides's disciples and Meiri about this or that custom, something more essential and profound was at issue, namely, whether a Torah scholar can accuse other reputable Torah scholars of being mistaken and go on to permit in their presence what has been customarily forbidden.

56. Underlying Razah's basic distinction is the aforementioned ruling in the Jerusalem Talmud, which does seem to imply, as Razah believes it does, that a prohibited practice mistakenly thought to be the law may be permitted even in the presence of ignoramuses. Nahmanides explains the Jerusalem Talmud to be speaking of a case in which a man came to consult a scholar, and because that man's observance of the practice can be presumed to be already weak, permitting the prohibited practice would not cause the man who consulted the scholar to permit real prohibitions on his own.

57. Questions on Nahmanides's theory, and on every other theory of custom known to Meiri, were raised in Meiri's *Magen Avot.* For the questions on Nahmanides's theory in particular, see *Magen Avot,* 93–94.

58. According to the sugya at hand, rabbinic scholars are not commonly found among city residents (*benei medinah*).

59. *Milhamot ha-Shem,* Pesahim 17a.

60. Ibid.

61. Haym Soloveitchik, *Pawnbroking: A Study in the Inter-Relationship between Halakhah, Economic Activity, and Communal Self-Image* (Jerusalem: Magnes, 1985), 111–112 (Heb.).

62. "Whence do we know that we are commanded to blow the shofar on this day [the New Year], and whence do we know that the written Torah is the Mosaic Torah

written from the mouth of the Almighty? Only by the mouth of the People of Israel, and if they attest to this, then they also attest that through this practice do we discharge our obligation" (*Otzar ha-Ge'onim*, Rosh ha-Shanah, 62).

63. *Milhamot ha-Shem*, Pesahim 17a.
64. A broad discussion of the halakhic issue of wearing adornments in Ashkenaz can be found in Ta-Shma, *Ritual, Custom, and Reality*, 130–148 (Heb.).
65. *Sefer Ra'avan*, ed. David Deblitzky, vol. 2 (Bnei Brak, 2008), no. 349, 342–343.
66. *Novellae*, Shabbat 57a, s.v. *matnitin lo be-hutei tzemer*, M49/H191.
67. See *Sefer ha-Yashar: Helek ha-Hiddushim*, ed. Simon Solomon Schlesinger (Jerusalem: Kiryat Sefer, 1959), no. 245(b), 150–151. While Rabbeinu Tam grounds his position upon a novel reading of the passage in Bekhorot, in *Mahzor Vitry* and other Franco-German sources another permissive reason appears: "Nowadays we are not concerned that the rainwater will outnumber the flowing [water], and we immerse in all the rivers of the world, be it Nisan or Tishri, because it is uncommon" (*Machsor Vitry*, 612). See *Sefer Ra'avan*, no. 326; *Sefer Ha-Oreh*, ed. Salomon Buber (Lviv, 1905; repr. Jerusalem: Makhon Yerushalaim, 1966/1967), 175; *Or Zaru'a ha-Shalem*, vol. 2, pt. 1 (Jerusalem: Makhon Torani Yeshivat Or Etzion, 2013), no. 363:15, 126–129 (= ed. Zhitomir, 1862, vol. 1, 99–100).
68. *Novellae*, Shabbat 65b, s.v. *shema yirbu*, M55/H217.
69. Ibid., M55/H218.
70. Rabbeinu Tam's opinion is cited in *Mahzor Vitry*, 727–731 (*Machsor Vitry*, 362–365); *Shibbolei ha-Leket ha-Shalem*, ed. Samuel Kalman Mirsky (New York: Makhon Sura, 1967), 209–218 (sec. 28). For the earlier background of the dispute over the place of liturgical poetry within prayer, see Avraham Grossman, *The Early Sages of France*, 3rd ed. (Jerusalem: Magnes, 2001), 91–92 with notes 29–30 (Heb.).
71. *Novellae*, Berakhot 49a, s.v. *kasheh li*, M16/H33. Nahmanides's rejection of Franco-German liturgical customs is also evident in his endeavor to stop the saying of *el melekeh ne'eman*, after Razah had instituted its recitation in Catalonia in the train of Franco-German custom. See *Novellae*, Berakhot 2a, s.v. *kevar hayah*, H1–5/Berakhot 11b, s.v. *mi-she-kara keri'at shema'*, M3–4; and so Meiri, *Magen Avot*, no. 1. On this episode see Ta-Shma, *Early Franco-German Ritual and Custom*, 285–298 (Heb.). Ta-Shma notes that R. Jonah Gerondi, Nahmanides's cousin and a student of Tosafists and German Pietists, was the one who introduced Franco-German customs into northern Iberia (see *[Talmidei] Rabbeinu Yonah* on the Rif, Berakhot 5b). On the Franco-German stratum in R. Jonah's writings, see Israel Ta-Shma, "Ashkenazi Hasidism in Spain: R. Jonah Gerondi—The Man and His Work," in *Exile and Diaspora: Studies in the History of the Jewish People*, ed. Aaron Mirsky et al. (Jerusalem: Ben-Zvi Institute, 1988), 165–194 (Heb.). Nahmanides himself, however, rejects Franco-German customs one by one. Another characteristic and important example of his rejection of Franco-German customs and rulings can be seen in what he writes on the question of the precedence of levirate marriage over *halitzah* (the waiver of such marriage): "From here, too, the words of the Geonim find support, for they rule that levirate marriage takes precedence, like the conclusion of the passage and like Rava's explanation of our *mishnah*. There is no cause for concern, even though the

Franco-Germans are concerned about it" (*Novellae*, Yevamot 39b, s.v. *ve-amar Rav ve-ein kofin*, M42/H137). On the precedence of levirate marriage over *halitzah* in Spain versus Franco-Germany, see Jacob Katz, "Levirate Marriage and *Halitzah* in the Post-Talmudic Period," *Halakhah and Kabbalah* (Jerusalem: Magnes, 1984), 127–174 (Heb.).

72. *Responsa*, no. 42, 71.

73. *THA, KR*, 2:260. This is based on a saying in the Jerusalem Talmud; see, Pe'ah 7.5 (20c).

74. *Novellae*, Bava Batra 144b, s.v. *ha de-amerinan makom she-nahagu*, M159.

75. Nahmanides, following the Tosafists, does approve of communal practices that facilitate economic dealings with Christians, even though they should be prohibited under the guidelines that limit commerce with idolaters. See *Novellae*, 'Avodah Zarah, 18–20, 41, 200–202. In these instances, Nahmanides finds a reason internal to the sugya to justify the communal practice, but he also appends the remark that "a scrupulous, self-disciplined person (*ba'al nefesh*) should act stringently." By comparison, on a different economic question, that is, the cancellation of debts at the end of the sabbatical year, Nahmanides understands it to apply outside the land of Israel, rejecting Ra'avad's idea that this custom is solely the province of supererogatory custom: "Since the people refrain from cancelling [debts] and transgress what is written in the Torah, some scholars have had second thoughts and they entertain doubts about these matters to be lenient, because the people will heed them in this but will not heed them to act stringently" (*Novellae*, Gittin 36a, s.v. *ha de-tanya Rabbi omer*, M57/H226–227).

76. *Novellae*, Megillah 21b, s.v. *be'a mineih Ulla*, H27; Megillah 22a, s.v. *likrei terei pesukei*, M27.

77. Ibid., H27/M30.

78. For an additional instance in which Nahmanides accepts Geonic tradition over his own reasoning, see above, note 37.

79. *Novellae*, Ta'anit 15a, s.v. *mah she-shaninu*, M10/H11.

80. On this, see the responsum of R. Sherira Gaon in *Otzar ha-Ge'onim, Massekhet Ta'anit*, ed. Benjamin Manasseh Lewin (Jerusalem: Hebrew University, 1933), 24.

81. *DRH, KR*, 1:140–141. See what he writes in his novellae to tractate Ta'anit: "For them [the Geonim] it is as it is written there [in the responsum of R. Sherira Gaon]—a definite custom observed since the days of their forefathers (*avot rishonim*) and up until now. Since we have clarified the matter through Talmudic proofs, and Geonic practice serves as precedent for us, no cause for concern or room for doubt remains and the practice ought to be adopted" (*Novellae*, Ta'anit 15a, s.v. *mah she-shaninu*, M11/H14).

82. *Milhamot ha-Shem*, Rosh ha-Shanah 12b.

83. *Novellae*, Hullin 46a, s.v. *ha de-amar Rava*, M58/H288.

84. On the source of the expression and its use in Franco-Germany, see Ta-Shma, *Ritual, Custom, and Reality*, 28n33 (Heb.). In his novellae to tractate Ketubbot, Nahmanides uses a similar expression to defend the widespread local custom of reciting the seven nuptial blessings (*sheva' berakhot*) on the Sabbath after the bridegroom exited the synagogue and the bride went to meet him with an entourage, which was not in

proximity to the Sabbath meal and its Grace after Meals: "Some contemporary scholars have protested that the people should not say them, but this is improper because this custom of theirs is Torah. And so it should be, for we find in tractate *Soferim* as follows: 'Our rabbis had the practice in the morning to recite the nuptial blessing over a cup in the company of ten [men] and [with] new faces [present] all seven days, and so in the evening before the meal.' We see, therefore, that we recite it before the meal" (*Novellae*, Ketubbot 8a, s.v. *u-feirush panim hadashot*, M12/H43–44/Ch73). It is worth noting that Nahmanides does not adopt the generic language of "the custom of Israel is Torah," but rather "this custom of theirs is Torah," and he then follows up with a proof for the local custom from tractate Soferim and the Jerusalem Talmud. Regarding this and other Catalonian customs in Nahmanides's consuetudinary theory, see Ezra Chwat, "The Status of Custom in the Writings of the Ramban and His Catalonian School," *Shenaton ha-Mishpat ha-'Ivri* 18–19 (1992–1994): 439–453 (Heb.). In this article, Chwat discusses another Catalonian custom over which Nahmanides disputed the Geonic tradition—whether one recites a *birkat ha-mitzvah* (blessing over a ritual act) over the recitation of Hallel on the first night of Passover (see *Novellae*, Pesahim 117b, s.v. *ve-omer 'alav birkat ha-shir*, M16). Although some Geonim disagreed with the custom, Nahmanides demonstrates that his own opinion can be found in Kayyara's Halakhot Gedolot, and he goes to lengths to demonstrate that aside from proof for the custom in tractate Soferim, one can explain the Babylonian Talmud in tractate 'Eiruvin to accord with the custom.

85. I will take the same approach regarding another statement of Nahmanides that lent weight to custom when set against law: "Even if Elijah were to come and permit [it], we would not listen to him, for the people have already become accustomed." Nahmanides cites this in the context of his argument with Razah and Rabbeinu Tam about inspecting a blistered lung that is closest to the chest cavity wall. Razah cites a responsum of Rabbeinu Tam that permits inspecting such a lung, which follows the opinion of R. Nehemiah b. R. Yosef at Hullin 48a. Nahmanides, who disallows this leniency, says: "If you say, has not R. Jacob ruled that the law follows Rabbi Nehemiah [. . .] That is not so, for we follow the more stringent opinion for biblical prohibitions [. . .] There is no need to go on about this for the prohibition has already spread throughout Israel, and it is a tradition from the Geonim and sages of each generation. Even were Elijah to come and permit [it], we would not listen to him, for the people have already become accustomed, as they said in tractate *Yevamot*" (*Milhamot ha-Shem*, Hullin 12a). Nahmanides adds Geonic tradition to this prevalent practice, which is why Elijah has no sway.

86. For a discussion of this enactment, the consequent dissent, and its import for women's status, see Avraham Grossman, *Pious and Rebellious: Jewish Women in Medieval Europe*, trans. Jonathan Chipman (Waltham, MA: Brandeis University Press, 2004), 240–252.

87. *Sefer ha-Yashar: Helek ha-She'elot ve-ha-Teshuvot* (Berlin, 1898), no. 24, 40.

88. *Mishneh Torah*, "Laws of Marriage," 14:14.

89. *Novellae*, Ketubbot 63b, s.v. *u-mashhinan lah*, Ch198; s.v. *ve-hanei millei*, M74/H365–366.

90. Ibid., Ch198–199/M74/H366.

91. In his Milhamot ha-Shem, Nahmanides's opposition to the Geonic enactment is more moderate. He writes it as a response to Razah, who claimed that the enactment was an ad hoc emergency measure (*hora'at sha'ah*) that did not bind future generations. Nahmanides writes: "Regarding Razah's claim that the enactment of the [Geonic] academy was an emergency measure, *Rabbeinu ha-Gadol* had better familiarity with this enactment than any of us, and we see from his words that it was [also] enacted for posterity. Razah's words here are nothing but beguiling, for he intends to dispute them [the Geonim] by saying that we judge her [the rebellious wife] by Talmudic law—he is simply being polite. The truth is that they enacted it for posterity, and they practiced it until the days of *Rabbeinu*; for 500 years this enactment did not budge. [. . .] But one who wishes to be stringent and not coerce, following the Talmudic law, has not lost out, and let him be blessed" (*Milhamot ha-Shem*, Ketubbot 27a). Nahmanides is satisfied here as well to make a statement that expresses doubts about the Geonic enactment, even stating that one who acts stringently in line with the Talmudic law should be blessed.

92. The conception of Geonic custom as reflective of a tradition received from the Talmud enables us to better distinguish between Nahmanides's attitude toward the Geonim and toward Rif. The Geonim outrank the Aharonim not because of their wisdom, but because of their chronological anteriority and geographical location in the Torah centers of Babylonia, which afforded them living contact with the Talmudic tradition. He therefore considers them a group, a link in the chain of tradition, with which one cannot disagree, especially when they present a uniform position. Rif is better tied to Geonic tradition than the Aharonim, according to Nahmanides, but Rif's superiority lies in his wisdom. The different respective sources Nahmanides gives for the superiority of the Geonim and Rif are exemplified by his discussion of the permissibility of placing white linen tzitzith upon a linen garment. Rif permits it, even if no blue woolen tzitzith will be attached, but Razah and Rabbeinu Tam both disagree and prohibit it. At the beginning of his gloss on Rif, Razah claims: "One should know that all of the Geonim who ever lived unanimously prohibited putting linen tzitzith upon a tallit, and no one dissented, until along came Rif and permitted it to himself and instructed others to do so" (*Ha-Ma'or ha-Katon*, Shabbat 11b). At the end of the piece, Razah complains that the prevalent custom follows Rif: "The custom of our predecessors who came after Rif was to rely on him in the way a man seeks God's word, and our current practice spread from him" (ibid., Shabbat 12a). Nahmanides responds to the claim that Rif went against the Geonic tradition: "If the words of the Earlier Geonim were thus, and we had received a tradition, we would accept it. But since the reason of the *Rishonim* is only because they said 'you would think to say it is like Rava['s statement],' and it is well known that it is not as they [the Geonim] thought but like what *Rabbeinu ha-Gadol* wrote, it is proper to rely on him" (*Milhamot ha-Shem*, Shabbat 11b). When it comes to tradition, the Geonim have the upper hand, but in matters of reasoning Rif's opinion wins out, and Nahmanides says we should rely on his opinion. At the same time, Nahmanides rejects Rif's custom—as attested by Rif's students and the elders of Iberia—to have the shofar blown on the

Sabbath in his presence. Rif's reasoning in this matter is unknown, and Nahmanides asserts, "Nevertheless, the people have not relied on this, and there is no place in the world in which they blow the shofar on the Sabbath" (*DRH, KR,* 1:175).

93. According to Ta-Shma, the very use of the title "novellae" to describe expository writing on the Talmud was a product of Nahmanides's study hall. See Ta-Shma, *Ha-Nigle She-Banistar: The Halachic Residue in the Zohar, A Contribution to the Study of the Zohar* (Tel-Aviv: Ha-Kibbutz ha-Me'uhad, 2001), 54–56 (Heb.).

94. On the conservative nature of Nahmanides's Kabbalah, see Moshe Idel, "Nahmanides: Kabbalah, Halakhah, and Spiritual Leadership," *Tarbiz* 64 (1995): 535–580 (Heb.).

95. See below, ch. 8. See also Moshe Halbertal, *Concealment and Revelation: Esotericism in Jewish Thought and Its Philosophical Implications,* trans. Jackie Feldman (Princeton: Princeton University Press, 2007), 69–92.

96. On the creativity of the Zohar, see Daniel C. Matt, "*Matnita Dilan:* A Technique of Innovation in the Zohar," in *The Age of the Zohar,* ed. Joseph Dan (= *Jerusalem Studies in Jewish Thought* 8) (1989): 123–145 (Heb.); Yehuda Liebes, "Zohar and Eros," *Alpayim* 9 (1994): 57–119 (Heb.).

97. *Milhamot ha-Shem,* Hullin 3b. For the same expression, see *Milhamot ha-Shem,* Shabbat 48a; *Novellae,* Hullin 3b, s.v. *bodek sakkin,* M8/H26; *Novellae,* Bava Metzi'a 42a, s.v. *kesafim ein lahem shemirah,* M67/H267.

98. *KR,* 1:366.

99. On this development in Nahmanides's halakhic writings, see Ta-Shma, *Talmudic Commentary,* vol. 2, 43–44 (Heb.); and *Hiddushei ha-Ramban le-Massekhet Ketubbot,* ed. Ezra D. Chwat (Jerusalem, 1990), 33.

100. On this development, see Harold J. Berman, *Law and Revolution: The Formation of the Western Legal Tradition* (Cambridge, MA: Harvard University Press, 1983), 161–163, 298–299.

CHAPTER 3. DEATH, SIN, LAW, AND REDEMPTION

1. On his esoteric approach, see my *Concealment and Revelation: Esotericism in Jewish Thought and Its Philosophical Implications,* trans. Jackie Feldman (Princeton: Princeton University Press, 2007), 83–92. See also below, ch. 8.

2. On vows and oaths, see *Novellae,* Shevu'ot 29a, s.v. *ha di-tenan shevu'at shav,* M35/ s.v. *ve-okimna le-matni[tin],* H131, and see Israel Ta-Shma, *Talmudic Commentary in Europe and North Africa: Literary History,* 2nd ed., vol. 2 (Jerusalem: Magnes, 2004), 52–53 with note 74 (Heb.). See further below, ch. 5, sec. II.

3. *Novellae,* Yevamot 49b, s.v. *kol ha-nevi'im,* M55–56/H186. See ch. 5, note 54.

4. See below, note 15.

5. For the meaning of this phrase and its import in Nahmanides's thought, see below, sec. II.

6. On philosophy as a way of life, see Pierre Hadot, *Philosophy as a Way of Life: Spiritual Exercises from Socrates to Foucault,* trans. Michael Chase (Oxford: Blackwell, 1995); Martha Nussbaum, *The Therapy of Desire: Theory and Practice in Hellenistic Ethics* (Princeton: Princeton University Press, 1996).

7. *Metza'er 'atzmo 'al minhago shel 'olam,* according to the manuscript witnesses mentioned in Yitzhak Shailat, *Rambam Meduyyak,* vol. 14: *Sefer Shofetim* (Jerusalem: Ma'aliyot, 2006), "Laws of Mourning," 13:11, 357n4. The standard printed edition, which reads *metza'er 'atzmo yoter 'al minhago shel 'olam,* leaves itself open to being parsed as follows: "And one who pains himself more than is the way of the world is a fool." In the manuscripts, *minhago shel 'olam* means "nature's course"; in the printed edition, it could be taken to mean "common practice."

8. On this term, see below, note 25.

9. *THA, KR,* 2:12.

10. Ibid., 2:14.

11. Ibid.

12. Ibid.

13. Ibid.

14. Ibid.

15. This issue has been explored by scholars of Nahmanides. See Bezalel Safran, "R. Azriel and Nahmanides: Two Views of the Fall of Man," in *Rabbi Moses Nahmanides (Ramban): Explorations in His Religious and Literary Virtuosity,* ed. Isadore Twersky (Cambridge, MA: Harvard University Press, 1983), 75–106; Haviva Pedaya, *Name and Sanctuary in the Teaching of R. Isaac the Blind* (Jerusalem: Magnes, 2001), 244–284 (Heb.); Haviva Pedaya, *Nahmanides: Cyclical Time and Holy Text* (Tel-Aviv: 'Am 'Oved, 2003), 314–332 (Heb.); Yair Lorberbaum, "The Image of God in Nahmanides' Kabbalah," *Kabbalah* 5 (2000): 287–326 (Heb.). The approaches of these scholars share the claim that Nahmanides's insistence upon preservation of the body connects to the war he waged as a halakhist against the antinomian and spiritualizing tendencies within medieval mysticism and philosophy. I intend to present a different approach to this issue, in which I emphasize, inter alia, the anomian character of Nahmanides's own position.

16. *PHT,* Gen 2:17.

17. *THA, KR,* 2:304.

18. See *Mishneh Torah,* "Laws of Repentance," 8:2–7.

19. See Safran, "R. Azriel," 75–82.

20. *PHT,* Gen 2:9.

21. On this see R. Bahya b. Asher Ibn Halawa, *Rabbeinu Bahya 'al Ha-Torah,* ed. Charles Chavel, vol. 1 (Jerusalem: Mossad Harav Kook, 1966), 78; *Midrash Rabbeinu Bachya: Torah Commentary by Rabbi Bachya ben Asher,* trans. Eliyahu Munk, vol. 1 (Jerusalem: Lambda, 2003), 112–113.

22. *PHT,* Deut 30:6.

23. Safran and other scholars have argued that Nahmanides developed some of his ideas, such as the body's preservation at the time of resurrection, in response to spiritualizing tendencies within medieval Jewish thought that had antinomian implications, or as part of a polemic against—to trot out all the usual medieval suspects—Christian dogma. See Safran, "R. Azriel," 106; Pedaya, *Name and Sanctuary,* 283; Lorberbaum, "Image of God," 324n139. But we see here that Nahmanides took distinctively anomian positions himself.

24. Despite the profound differences dividing R. Azriel and Nahmanides on humanity's prelapsarian nature, the argument that the very existence of a separate will is the source of sin can be found in the writings of R. Azriel, who may in fact be the earlier source for this position. See Isaiah Tishby, *The Wisdom of the Zohar: An Anthology of Texts*, trans. David Goldstein, vol. 3 (Oxford: Oxford University Press, 1989), 984–985.

25. Shlomo Pines, "Nahmanides on Adam in the Garden of Eden in the Context of Other Interpretations of Genesis, Chapters 2 and 3," in *Exile and Diaspora: Studies in the History of the Jewish People Presented to Professor Haim Beinart on the Occasion of His Seventieth Birthday*, ed. Aharon Mirsky, Avraham Grossman, and Yosef Kaplan (Jerusalem: Ben-Zvi Institute, 1988), 159–164 (Heb.). For an additional connection between Nahmanides and Christian hermeneutics, see Amos Funkenstein, "Nachmanides' Typological Reading of History," *Zion* 45 (1980): 35–59 (Heb.). As far as I am aware, Nahmanides was the first Jewish commentator to use the expression *ha-het ha-kadmoni*, meaning the original or primordial sin, which appears to stem from Christian sources. It does not appear in rabbinic literature or medieval Jewish literature before Nahmanides's time, and he uses it twice in Torat ha-Adam (*KR*, 2:12 and 2:306).

26. *PHT*, Deut 11:22.

27. Ibid., Lev 18:4.

28. For Nahmanides's independent stance on these matters, including his attitude toward the Neoplatonism of Azriel of Gerona, see Moshe Idel, "Nahmanides: Kabbalah, Halakhah, and Spiritual Leadership," *Tarbiz* 64 (1995): 533–542 (Heb.); Haviva Pedaya, "The Spiritual vs. the Concrete Land of Israel in the Geronese School of Kabbalah," in *The Land of Israel in Medieval Jewish Thought*, ed. Moshe Hallamish and Aviezer Ravitzky (Jerusalem: Ben-Zvi Institute, 1991), 233–289 (Heb.).

29. *THA, KR*, 2:304.

30. Ibid., 2:305–306.

31. Ibid., 2:308.

32. For more on Nahmanides's understanding of cleaving to the divine, see Chayim Henoch, *Nachmanides: Philosopher and Mystic* (Jerusalem: Harry Fischel Institute for Talmudic Research, 1978), 243–261 (Heb.); trans. without footnotes in Henoch, *Ramban: Philosopher and Kabbalist, on the Basis of His Exegesis to the Mitzvoth* (Northvale, NJ: Jason Aronson, 1998), 187–196. For a subtle and incisive analysis of cleaving in Nahmanides's thought, see Adam Afterman, *Devequt: Mystical Intimacy in Medieval Jewish Thought* (Los Angeles: Cherub, 2011), ch. 12 (Heb.).

33. *THA, KR*, 2:304.

34. Ibid., 2:306.

35. On the question of the relationship between causation and immortality, see ch. 4, esp. sec. IV.

36. On the transformation of the cleaving body into a luminous body, see Moshe Idel, "Some Remarks on Ritual and Mysticism in Geronese Kabbalah," *Journal of Jewish Thought and Philosophy* 3 (1993): 111–130.

37. On early Jewish and Christian traditions about the decline in the state of Adam's body, see Gary A. Anderson, *The Genesis of Perfection: Adam and Eve in Jewish and Christian Imagination* (Louisville: Westminster John Knox, 2001), 121–132.

38. *PHT,* Gen 2:17. On the pericope of the manna in Exodus, Nahmanides discusses at length the relationship between the manna and Shekhinah's radiance and between manna consumption and cleaving: "For the soul in its thought cleaves to the supernal, finds the Repose of Life, and elicits its wish from it. [. . .] And those in the World to Come will be sustained through the delight they enjoy from the radiance of *Shekhinah* when they cleave to it through the 'coronet' upon their heads. The 'Coronet' (*'Atarah*) is the [divine] Attribute referred to by that name [i.e., *Shekhinah*], about which the verse says: 'the Lord of Hosts shall be a Coronet of beauty' (Isa 28:5), and about which it says, 'the Coronet with which his mother coronated him' (Songs 3:11). They [the Sages] hinted at the subsistence of those in the World to Come and hinted at the source of the manna" (ibid., Exod 16:6).

39. *THA, KR,* 2:306.

40. See above, note 23.

41. *THA, KR,* 2:307.

42. Ibid., 2:299.

43. On the idea of the eye of the soul, see Elliot Wolfson, *Through a Speculum That Shines* (Princeton: Princeton University Press, 1994), 294–306.

44. On mysticism as a heightening experience, see Jess Byron Hollenback, *Mysticism: Experience, Response, and Empowerment* (University Park: Pennsylvania State University Press, 1996).

45. *THA, KR,* 2:307.

46. Ibid., 2:303.

47. See *THA, KR,* 2:290–291; and so *PHT,* Gen 2:3. See further ch. 6, sec. I.

48. On the preservation of halakhah in Maimonidean messianism, see Gershom Scholem, "Toward an Understanding of the Messianic Idea in Judaism," in *The Messianic Idea in Judaism and Other Essays in Jewish Spirituality* (New York: Schocken, 1971), 24–33; David Hartman, "Maimonides' Approach to Messianism and Its Contemporary Implications," *Daat* 2–3 (1978–1979): 5–33; Dov Schwartz, *Messianism in Medieval Jewish Thought,* trans. Batya Stein (Brighton, MA: Academic Studies Press, 2017), 56–76.

49. The canonical corpus of midrashic and aggadic literature in Nahmanides's writings is broad. Beyond the classic midrashim, it includes Pirkei de-Rabbi Eliezer, the Heikhalot literature, Sefer ha-Bahir, and other late midrashim.

50. See *Mishneh Torah,* "Laws of Repentance," 8:5.

51. *The Guide of the Perplexed,* translated with introduction and notes by Shlomo Pines (Chicago: University of Chicago Press, 1963), I:2. For an extended treatment, see Sara Klein-Braslavy, *Maimonides' Interpretations of the Adam Stories in Genesis: A Study in Maimonides' Anthropology* (Jerusalem: R. Mas, 1987), 80–168 (Heb.), which is partially translated in Sara Klein-Braslavy, *Maimonides as Biblical Interpreter* (Boston: Academic Studies Press, 2011), 51–69.

52. See *Mishneh Torah,* "Laws of Repentance," 8:5.

53. *THA, KR,* 2:285.

54. Ibid., 2:298.

55. "Given this statement there is no doubt that they [the Sages] wish to elevate that fire and make it as ethereal as possible, to the point that they attributed its creation to the

second day [. . .] because the creations of the first [day] were more rarefied and proximate to the first cause and to the primordial element than those created on the second day, and so [those on] the second [day] than those on the third" (ibid., 2:286).

56. Ibid.

57. Ibid., 2:287–288. He also writes: "The Holy One created the souls of the righteous, which are without a doubt a pure and rarefied spirit—it is not a body, it cannot be delimited, it cannot be defined spatially, and it cannot be captured in wineskins like other spirits. Rather, it is of the caste of angels and exceptionally transcendent. This is not the place to explain all that is apprehended from it. Scripture attests to this, as it says, 'And He blew into his nostrils the breath of Life' (Gen 2:7), [that is] to say that it was given from God's breath, and not from the concatenation of causes" (ibid., 2:285). For more on the source of humanity's soul, see ch. 4, note 59.

58. Ibid., 2:288–289.

59. Ibid., 2:289.

60. Ibid., 2:296.

61. On Nahmanides's conception of the Garden of Eden and its meaning within his general interpretive perspective, see Pedaya, *Name and Sanctuary*, 270–271; Elliot R. Wolfson, "By Way of Truth: Aspects of Nahmanides' Kabbalistic Hermeneutic," *AJS Review* 14 (Autumn, 1989): 112–116.

62. On the theme of the dual Garden of Eden in Nahmanides's thought, see Avishai Bar Asher, *The Journeys of the Soul: Garden of Eden in the Thought and Imagination of Medieval Kabbalistic Literature* (Jerusalem: Magnes, 2019), 111–134 (Heb.).

63. *THA, KR*, 2:298.

64. Ibid., 2:305.

65. The allusions in Nahmanides's writings were spelled out in the writings of his grand-disciples. Thus, for instance, R. Shem Tov Ibn Gaon wrote: "*Bohu*—as if to say it is within it (*bo hu*), it being the [sefirotic] structure that comprises the six directions, which takes on the human form above" (Keter Shem Tov, 96r[a]). See Lorberbaum, "Image of God."

66. On the iconicity of the body, see further below, ch. 7, secs. I and IV.

67. On the connection between the World to Come and the Garden of Eden with respect to freedom from inert causality, see ch. 4, esp. sec. VI. In Nahmanides's view, the return of the sefirot to their original limits divests the zodiacal entities of their sovereignty, which was induced by the divine emanation overstepping its bounds, and the suboptimal state that will be rectified. As Nahmanides comments: "He is the supreme Power Who rules over everything, and in the end He will call to account the lofty host on high in order to remove the dominion of the supernal beings and to lay waste to the configuration of the planets" (*PHT*, Lev 18:25). See Pedaya, *Name and Sanctuary*, 250–251.

68. *THA, KR*, 2:305.

69. Perhaps in every sabbatical cycle the body undergoes further rarefaction.

70. For a discussion of Nahmanides's conception of history and the doctrine of cosmic cycles, see ch. 6, esp. sec. I.

71. An exceptionally anomian approach to the doctrine of cosmic cycles is developed in Sefer ha-Temunah; see Gershom Scholem, *Ha-Kabbalah shel Sefer ha-Temunah ve-Shel Avraham Abulafia*, ed. Yosef Ben-Shlomo (Jerusalem: Akademon, 1969), 19–84 (Heb.). See as well Gershom Scholem, *Origins of the Kabbalah*, ed. R. J. Zwi Werblowsky, trans. Allan Arkush (Philadelphia: Jewish Publication Society, 1987), 460–474.

72. Nahmanides comments about the Generation of Dispersion that "they were cutting down the saplings, and their sin was similar to their father's [i.e., Adam's]" (*PHT,* Gen 11:2).

73. See the extensive treatment below, ch. 4, sec. I.

74. On the crisis within the process of divine emanation as Nahmanides understands it, see Pedaya, *Name and Sanctuary,* 257; Pedaya, *Nahmanides,* 359–379. See also Moshe Idel, "Leviathan and Its Consort: From Talmudic to Kabbalistic Myth," in *Myth in Judaism,* ed. Moshe Idel and Ithamar Gruenwald (Jerusalem: Zalman Shazar Center, 2004), 164–170 (Heb.).

75. On the sources of the myth about the diminution of the Moon in midrashic literature and its development in kabbalistic literature, see Yehuda Liebes, "*De Natura Dei:* On the Development of the Jewish Myth," in *Studies in Jewish Myth and Messianism,* trans. Batya Stein (Albany: State University of New York Press, 1993), 47–54.

76. *PHT,* Gen 1:12.

77. Keter Shem Tov, 92r(b)–92v(c).

78. In Pesikta de-Rav Kahana, ed. Mandelbaum, 23.1, 334, Adam's sin is said to have taken place in the tenth hour of Sabbath Eve.

79. Keter Shem Tov, 97r(a–b).

80. Ibid., 98r(b)–98v(c).

81. *Sefer Me'irat 'Einayim by R. Isaac of Acre,* ed. Amos Goldreich (Jerusalem: Hebrew University, 1981), 8 (Heb.).

82. See *PHT,* Gen 3:16. For another source regarding the originally equivalent statures of the Sun and Moon and their eventual return thereto, see ibid., Gen 38:29, together with Keter Shem Tov, 102r(b)–102v(c). The ancient catastrophe of Shekhinah's fall from its original state of harmony with Tif'eret and its new position as the lowliest sefirah turned Shekhinah into the weakest link of the divine structure; see below, the beginning of ch. 5. For a discussion of this among Nahmanides's disciples, see Moshe Idel, *R. Menahem Recanati the Kabbalist* (Jerusalem: Schocken, 1998), 215–219 (Heb.).

83. Concerning the isomorphic, analogous nature of the three planes—the sefirotic fracture, the lunar diminution, and Adam's sin—R. Isaac of Acre says: "It is all one matter, except that this one is the Spirit of God, holy and sanctified, blessed and praised, while the others are physical creatures. Eve's intent concerning her husband Adam in eating the fruit was to eat it with designs of rising above him and ruling over him, so that he would be in need of her potency. But when she saw that the consumption harmed her, that she was punished through it, she said: 'I will feed my husband as well so that he too will be punished, and his stature will not be greater than mine.' She was punished for this intention. But the opposite happened—she became in need of her husband's potency, she desired him all day long to receive his efflux and

stature. Similarly, when the Coronet brought suit because two Kings should not use one Crown, seeking [it] for herself, her light was diminished and she became a Speculum That Does Not Shine, because *Teshuvah* [*Binah*], which is the Holy One, said to Her: 'Go and reduce Yourself' " (*Me'irat 'Einayim*, ed. Goldreich, 8).

84. Keter Shem Tov, 98r(b).

CHAPTER 4. MIRACLES AND THE CHAIN OF BEING

1. See above, ch. 3, secs. VI–VII.
2. *PHT*, Gen 1:1.
3. *DTHT*, 65 (= *KR*, 1:156). In the continuation of his comment to Gen 1:1, he likewise writes, "Behold this creation is like a fine, subtle point that has no substance."
4. On the meanings of *tohu* and *bohu*, see *PHT*, Gen 1:1.
5. Ibid.
6. Ibid.
7. R. Shem Tov Ibn Gaon wrote: "*Tohu* is what we call 'Green Line,' which is *Teshuvah* [*Binah*]. *Bohu*—as if to say it is within it (*bo hu*), 'it' being the [sefirotic] structure that comprises the six directions, which takes on the human form above" (Keter Shem Tov, 96r[a]).
8. See Nahmanides's commentary on Sefer Yetzirah: "the essence will revert 'to that which has possession of the Earth (*ha-Aretz*)' (Lev 27:24) which is Absolute Privation" (Gershom Scholem, "*Peirusho ha-Amitti shel ha-Ramban le-Sefer Yetzirah ve-Divrei Kabbalah Aherim ha-Mityahasim Elav,*" in *Studies in Kabbalah [1]*, ed. Yosef Ben-Shlomo and Moshe Idel [Tel-Aviv: 'Am 'Oved, 1998], 88 [Heb.], with Scholem's footnote 8).
9. *PHT*, Gen 1:1. On this transformation in the understanding of *creatio ex nihilo*, see Gershom Scholem, *Origins of the Kabbalah*, ed. R. J. Zwi Werblowsky and trans. Allan Arkush (Philadelphia: Jewish Publication Society; Princeton: Princeton University Press, 1987), 422–427.
10. *PHT*, Gen 1:8.
11. See Nahmanides's words: "It seems to me that this point, through putting on [lit. wearing] the form and becoming *bohu*, is what the Sages called the Foundation Stone, from which the world was established" (*PHT*, Gen 1:1). In Nahmanides's oeuvre, "the Foundation Stone" is a cognomen of Shekhinah.
12. See Moshe Idel, "On *Zimzum* in Kabbalah and in Scholarship," in *Lurianic Kabbalah*, ed. Rachel Elior and Yehuda Liebes (Jerusalem: 'Daf-Noy' Press), 1992, 59–68 (Heb.).
13. Scholem, "*Peirusho ha-Amitti*," 88–89.
14. Scholem explains that the "darkness" is Ayin, from which the paths of Hokhmah emanated, but this interpretation is difficult to sustain. Nahmanides writes: "Each path inscribes upon the darkness the letters in their forms," from which one can see that the darkness is the created substrate upon which the Light engraves. See ibid., 106n20. On this see Idel, "On *Zimzum*," 63–64.
15. Scholem, "*Peirusho ha-Amitti*," 88.
16. Ibid., 96.
17. *THA, KR*, 2:286.

18. See below, ch. 6, sec. I.

19. Gershom Scholem, *Ha-Kabbalah be-Girona,* ed. Yosef Ben-Shlomo (Jerusalem: Mif'al ha-Shikhpul, 1964), 306 (Heb.).

20. *PHT,* Exod 13:16. Similar statements that are dismissive of the whole category of Nature can be found in *DTHT,* 58–59 (= *KR,* 1:153), and *DDK, KR,* 1:192. Beyond the principle of eliminating Nature, one can also infer from the introduction to Nahmanides's Commentary on Job that no fundamental distinction exists between hidden and revealed miracles: "Logically, there is no difference whether we say that such-and-such righteous man shall live out his days of eighty years in peace and quiet, and so-and-so who ate the priestly tithe [while impure] will die [. . .] and the splitting of the Red Sea and the manna falling for forty years" (*PSI, KR,* 1:18).

21. David Berger, "Miracles and the Natural Order in Nahmanides," in *Rabbi Moses Nahmanides (Ramban): Explorations in His Religious and Literary Virtuosity,* ed. Isadore Twersky (Cambridge, MA: Harvard University Press, 1983), 107–128.

22. *PSI, KR,* 1:108–109. The translation follows Berger, "Miracles," 119–120, with a few substantive changes based on manuscript readings and style.

23. See *PHT,* Lev 26:12 and Gen 18:19. In ibid., Gen 19:8, he wrote: "God dealt with both of them through *keri* (cf. Lev 26:24) and left them to accidents (*mikrim*)."

24. His responsum on astrology and divination reflects this position. After bringing a number of proofs to the credibility of astrological predictions, Nahmanides makes the following argument: "one can infer from this that he [R. Akiva] believed in them [. . .] Sometimes, however, the Holy One performs a miracle for those who fear Him by nullifying the decree of the stars for them, and these are among the hidden miracles which occur in the ordinary manner of the world and upon which the entire Torah depends. Consequently, one should not consult astrologers but should rather go about life with simple faith, as it says, 'Be wholehearted with the Lord your God' (Deut 18:13) [. . .] But if someone sees in his horoscope that a particular day is inauspicious for his work, he should avoid it and not rely upon a miracle. It is my view that it is prohibited to go counter to the zodiacal signs [by relying] upon a miracle" (*KR,* 1:379; trans. Berger, "Miracles," 123, with minor stylistic modifications).

25. See *The Guide of the Perplexed,* translated with introduction and notes by Shlomo Pines (Chicago: University of Chicago Press, 1963), III:18.

26. Another difference between Maimonides and Nahmanides that Berger emphasizes concerns punishment of the wicked. Nahmanides writes that God also breaks the rules of Nature for the thoroughly wicked when he punishes them in a miraculous manner. Only those in the middle group, according to Nahmanides, are left to accidents; the pious and the wicked both experience miracles. This is not the view of Maimonides. See Berger, "Miracles," 120–121.

27. To this one can add the divine providence over the Jewish people more generally, and the specific type that operates through the hidden miracle when they are situated in the land of Israel. On the pious individual as well as the collective in the land, see below, secs. IV–V.

28. An exception can be found in Bezalel Safran's short discussion of the kabbalistic angle to this issue in his article "R. Azriel and Nahmanides: Two Views of the Fall of Man,"

in *Rabbi Moses Nahmanides (Ramban): Explorations in His Religious and Literary Virtuosity,* ed. Isadore Twersky (Cambridge, MA: Harvard University Press, 1983), 102n101. See also Moshe Idel, *Kabbalah: New Perspectives* (New Haven: Yale University Press, 1988), 46 with 292n57.

29. *PHT,* Gen 17:1.

30. Among Nahmanides's disciples, "the Lower Attribute of Judgment" and "the Weak Attribute of Judgment" are used quite regularly as cognomens for Shekhinah, which is contrasted with the sefirah of Din, known as "the Upper Attribute of Judgment" or "the Harsh Attribute of Judgment." R. Shem Tov Ibn Gaon describes the tenth sefirah as follows: "The tenth *sefirah* is called the Congregation of Israel, Justice, the Lower Attribute of Judgment, the Weak Attribute of Judgment" (Keter Shem Tov, 94v[c]). See R. Isaac of Acre, *Sefer Me'irat 'Einayim by R. Isaac of Acre,* ed. Amos Goldreich (Jerusalem: Hebrew University, 1981), 4 (Heb.).

31. *PHT,* Gen 17:1.

32. For this identification, see below, ch. 6, note 57.

33. *PHT,* Exod 6:2.

34. Ibid., Exod 3:13.

35. *DDK, KR,* 1:192.

36. *DTHT,* 54–55 (= *KR,* 1:152).

37. Nahmanides consistently distinguishes between "the Unique Name" or "the Great Name" and "the Glorious Name." The former two always refer to the sefirah of Tif'eret, whereas the latter refers to the sefirah of Shekhinah. One can see this readily in the quotation above from his Discourse on Ecclesiastes: "Through the Unique Name overt signs and wonders are newly created in the world." Similarly: "wonders that publicly changed Nature and were performed through the Unique Name that He told him" (*PHT,* Gen 17:1). The Tetragrammaton that represents Tif'eret is also called the Great Name: "Or they will say the Great Name has not appeared to you through the Attribute of Mercy to perform signs and wonders for us, as you have said, because you are no greater than the Patriarchs" (ibid., Exod 4:1). "The Glorious Name" in Nahmanides's kabbalah is the cognomen of Shekhinah, signifying divinity and sovereignty. R. Shem Tov Ibn Gaon notes Nahmanides's consistent usage of the terms: "Know a rule regarding the Master's words: he calls *Tif'eret* 'the Great Name' and *Malkhut* [*Shekhinah*] 'the Glorious Name' " (Keter Shem Tov, 104v[d]).

38. *PHT,* Lev 26:11. See also ibid., Exod 13:16.

39. On this term, see ch. 5, sec. III with note 54.

40. *PHT,* Exod 6:2.

41. In his kabbalah, Nahmanides extensively uses the cognomen "the Speculum That Does not Shine" for Shekhinah and "the Speculum That Shines" for Tif'eret. See, for example, R. Shem Tov Ibn Gaon: " 'The Speculum That Shines' is *Tif'eret,* and 'the Speculum That Does not Shine' is *'Atarah* [*Shekhinah*]" (Keter Shem Tov, 99v[c–d]).

42. On the secret of the Countenance, see *PHT,* Exod 33:14, and below, ch. 5, notes 8–9.

43. Ibid., Gen 17:1.

44. *DDK, KR,* 1:191–192. Nahmanides believes that the Book of Ecclesiastes was written through the Attribute of Judgment, which explains why the Sages debated whether the

book renders one's hands ritually impure: " 'and if they argued it was only about Ecclesiastes,' in other words, because it only speaks through the name 'God' (*Elohim*), the Attribute of Judgment, which exists in the world as the natural course of the world" (ibid., 1:195). Nahmanides places Ecclesiastes in opposition to Song of Songs and Proverbs, which do mention the Tetragrammaton; see ibid., 191 and 195. In his Commentary on Job, Nahmanides repeats this astonishing idea that certain books of Scripture were composed as a revelation of the sefirah of Shekhinah alone, which is why they reflect a theology that seems to contradict the rest of the biblical corpus: "I have explained to you Job's complaint throughout this entire work, together with the other arguments that appear in the verses, as I will, God willing, explain. Now I have perused this book and the Awesome Name (*shem ha-nora*) appears neither in Job's arguments nor in the statements of his friends; they mention only the names of godship and *Shaddai*, which was the name they had received from the Patriarchs, as it is written: 'I appeared to Abraham, Isaac, and Jacob through *El Shaddai*' (Exod 6:3). [. . .] it does not mention the Glorious Name, which is the Essential Name, perhaps because Job was not privy to its secret—[how] it governs the lowly realms and introduces new signs and wonders into the world—because this matter was revealed to our master Moses. The rule is that he who understands the verse 'I appeared to Abraham, Isaac etc.' knows this" (*PSI, KR,* 1:33–34). The absence of the Tetragrammaton from the speeches of Job and his friends reflects, in Nahmanides's view, the limits of their apprehension. Nahmanides attributes this limitation to the fact that Job received his tradition from the Patriarchs and, as such, was unaware of the Unique Name known only to Moses. Nahmanides fleshes out the connection between the personae in the Book of Job and Abraham in his preface to the book, where he identifies Job and his companions as part of Abraham's extended family, who, among other things, received Abraham's kabbalistic tradition; see ibid., 1:27–28. Nahmanides's idea that the divine names within a scriptural book and the kinds of miracles it records both reflect the theological nature of that book is ultimately derived from R. Abraham Ibn Ezra, from whom he also borrowed the distinction between the hidden miracle and manifest miracle: "For this reason Moses mentioned to Pharaoh only 'the Lord,' which is the 'God of the Hebrews,' by which the recipient of its power can perform new wonders. Therefore, you will not find this name in the Book of Ecclesiastes, because it speaks about theology and the power that the All receives, not an individual like Moses" (*Yesod Mora ve-Sod Torah,* ed. Joseph Cohen and Uriel Simon [Ramat-Gan: Bar-Ilan University, 2008], 198). On the broader connection between the various books of Scripture and the sefirot, see ch. 5, sec. II.

45. It is worth pointing out that in this passage Nahmanides offers an explanation for Solomon's claim of arbitrariness—"As it happens to the fool, so will it also happen to me" (Eccl 2:15). According to Nahmanides, the righteous who cleave to El Shaddai are not subject to accidents except on rare occasions when the closeness of Shekhinah to Nature results in the limited and unusual dominion of accidents over even those cleaving to Shekhinah. He asserts that those cleaving to the Unique Name, to Tif'eret, are completely free of accidents. The transition from Tif'eret to Shekhinah does not entail only the gradual loss of the Godhead's creative power, but also the loss of complete freedom from accidents.

46. *PSI, KR,* 1:108.

47. For more on the difference between the prophecy of Moses and that of other prophets, see below, ch. 5, esp. sec. II.

48. On the connection between prophecy and cleaving, see *PHT,* Deut 13:2.

49. Ibid., Exod 4:1. Elsewhere, Nahmanides explains the midrash that understands Exod 6:3 ("I appeared to Abraham, Isaac, and Jacob through El Shaddai, but I did not make Myself known to them through My name *Y-HWH*") as a rebuke to Moses as follows: "They therefore expound that it was a rebuke to Moses, saying to him: Look, the Patriarchs whose level of prophecy did not reach yours, since they saw only through *El Shaddai,* believed in Me [. . .] So you, who have known Me through the Great Name by which I have made a promise to you, should trust in my Mercy and promise Israel in My name that I will perform signs and wonders for them" (ibid., Exod 6:2).

50. Ibid., Lev 18:4. In "Sha'ar ha-Gemul," Nahmanides describes Moses's stature: "[This is] to convey that people of that world can reach the level of Moses, whose soul transcended his body to the point where his bodily faculties were nullified, and who was enveloped at every moment in the Holy Spirit. [It was] as if his sight and hearing were through the eye of the soul alone" (*THA, KR,* 2:299).

51. *THA, KR,* 2:305.

52. Ibid., 2:308.

53. The connection between cleaving and the hidden miracle, and the definition of cleaving as abandonment of human interest, both stand at the foundation of Nahmanides's perspective on the permissibility of practicing medicine. People who seek the services of a physician submit themselves to the dominion of Nature's causality by their very patienthood, which consequentially allows physicians to heal them: "This is [the import] of their [the Sages'] dictum that 'people do not require medical treatment, but they have become accustomed' (*Berakhot* 60a). If people do not require medical treatment, a person would fall ill in accord with the punishment for their sin and be healed by God's will, but they have become accustomed to medical treatment, so God has left them to the accidents of Nature. This was their intent in saying, 'and shall cause him to be thoroughly healed' (Exod 21:19)—from here we derive that 'permission is granted to a doctor to heal' (*Bava Kamma* 85a). They did not say 'permission is granted to the sick to be healed,' because once the patient is ill and presents himself for healing—since he is accustomed to medical treatment and does not belong to the congregation of the Lord whose 'lot is with Life' (cf. Ps 17:14)—the physician need not refrain from healing him" (*PHT,* Lev 26:11).

54. *Hiddushei ha-Rashba: Peirush ha-Haggadot,* ed. Aryeh Leib Feldman (Jerusalem: Mossad Harav Kook, 1991), 124–125.

55. *THA, KR,* 2:304.

56. Nahmanides employs the same terms to describe Originary Adam's subsistence upon the radiance of the Shekhinah that he uses for the radiance of the body that occurs with the nullification of the bodily faculties through cleaving to Shekhinah: "We likewise believe in, and all hold to be true, the visibility of the spiritual faculty upon the gloomy body as it cleaves to the Supernal Intellect, as with Moses's facial radiance being like the surface of the Sun and that of Joshua like the surface of the Moon. Our

Rabbis spoke similarly of Adam and anyone cleaving to his Creator and clothing himself in the Holy Spirit" (ibid., 2:305).

57. The shift from God's will as volitional action to the will as a type of potency or essence was already made by Solomon Ibn Gabirol within Neoplatonic philosophy. Obviously such a shift utterly blunts the significance of the question of the world's eternality or creation. Regarding will as an essence that cleaves to something, Nahmanides writes: "The idea is to convey that they exist in His desire, and should the desire become detached from them momentarily they would revert to nothing" (*PHT,* Gen 1:4). For identification of the will with the sefirah of Keter in Nahmanides's commentary on Sefer Yetzirah, see the text in Scholem, "*Peirusho ha-Amitti,*" 94, with Scholem's footnote 33.

58. *PHT,* Gen 2:17.

59. Nahmanides believes that sefirah of Binah is the source of the human soul and that God transfers part of his essence to humans: "because one who blows in the nostrils of someone else gives him his breath. This is [the meaning of] the verse, 'the breath of *Shaddai* gives them *Binah* (*tevinem*)' (Job 32:8), for it is from the foundation of *Binah* by way of Truth [*Tif'eret*] and Faith [*Shekhinah*]" (*PHT,* Gen 2:7). On Nahmanides's concept of the divine source of the soul, see Scholem, *Ha-Kabbalah be-Girona,* 399–407; Moshe Hallamish, "On the Origin of a Dictum in the Kabbalistic Literature: 'Whoever Blows, Does So from His Inner Essence,'" *Bar-Ilan Annual* 13 (1976): 211–223 (Heb.); and see the comprehensive study by Moshe Idel, "*Nishmat Eloha:* On the Divinity of the Soul in Nahmanides and His Schools," in *Life as a Midrash, Perspectives in Jewish Psychology,* ed. Shahar Arzy et al. (Tel-Aviv: Yedi'ot Aharonot, 2004), 338–380 (Heb.).

60. For more on the question of will and desire, see the introduction to Nahmanides's Commentary on Job, where he writes about angels as possessors of will and desire: "From the plain sense of the verses and from their [the Sages'] opinion it would seem that he [Satan] and the other angels act out of their own desire and will, for they yearn to bring about those effects for which they are the cause" (*PSI, KR,* 1:25). Desire is an internal inclination to do something, but it need not imply freedom of choice or autonomy. For a discussion of the question of the divine will and the doctrine of cosmic cycles, see ch. 6, sec. I. See also Haviva Pedaya, *Nahmanides: Cyclical Time and Holy Text* (Tel-Aviv: 'Am 'Oved, 2003), 274–293 (Heb.).

61. *PHT,* Exod 6:2.

62. *Peirushei ha-Torah le-Rabbeinu Avraham Ibn 'Ezra,* ed. Asher Weiser (Jerusalem: Mossad Harav Kook, 1976), 2:34–35 (Exod 3:15). In Ibn Ezra's usage, "the glorious Name" is a reference to the Tetragrammaton, whereas Nahmanides uses "the Glorious Name" to refer to Shekhinah.

63. Ibid.

64. Ibid., 2:47 (Exod 6:3).

65. Ibid.

66. Ibid., 3:171 (Num 20:8).

67. Ibid., 1:19 (Gen 1:26). The meaning of the term "the All" (*Ha-Kol*) in Ibn Ezra's thought is subject to debate by its expositors. Elliot Wolfson understands it as the

first hypostasis of God, which is also defined as the demiurge; see Elliot Wolfson, "God, the Demiurge, and the Intellect: On the Usage of the Word *Kol* in Abraham Ibn Ezra," *Revue des Études Juives* 149 (1990): 77–111. Howard Kreisel, on the other hand, supports the interpretation of "the All" as a reference to God; see Howard Kreisel, "On the Term *Kol* in Abraham Ibn Ezra: A Reappraisal," *Revue des Études Juives* 153 (1994): 29–66.

68. Ibn Ezra writes about Balaam: "because a created being cannot change the work of the Creator or His decree. The secret is that the individual cannot change the individual, only the decree of the All (*Ha-Kol*) can change the decree of the individual. But I cannot disclose this secret for it is profound" (Ibn Ezra, *Peirushei ha-Torah*, 3:181 [Num 22:28]). On the talismanic context of the miracle, see his short commentary to Exod 3:13: "because a triune has the power to receive and does not need a biune; therefore, Moses is able to produce through the power of the Name signs and wonders the likes of which were not created on the whole earth. [. . .] The power of the Name produces signs and creates bodies in accord with the receiver. Whoever understands this secret of the Name knows the prophecy of 'And the Lord appeared to him' (Gen 18:1), 'a man struggled with him' (Gen 32:25), and the wonder of the [burning] bush" (ibid., 2:246 [Exod 3:13]).

69. Dov Schwartz has described at length a similarly parallel shift from an astrological-magical conception to a theurgic one in Nahmanides's doctrine; see Dov Schwartz, *Studies on Astral Magic in Medieval Jewish Thought*, trans. David Louvish and Batya Stein (Leiden: Brill, 2005), 55–66, and Schwartz, "From Theurgy to Magic: The Evolution of the Magical-Talismanic Justification of Sacrifice in the Circle of Nahmanides and His Interpreters," *Aleph* 1 (2001): 165–213. For the relation of Nahmanides to Ibn Ezra's esoteric doctrine, see Miriam Skalertz, *Zer Rimonim: Studies in Bible and Its Commentary Dedicated to Prof. Rimon Kasher*, ed. Michael Avioz, Eli Asis, and Yael Shemesh (Atlanta: Society of Biblical Literature, 2013) 503–523 (Heb.).

70. *PHT*, Lev 26:11. On the direct connection between the Jewish collective and Shekhinah, see ibid., Exod 19:5.

71. Ibid., Lev 18:25.

72. Ibid.

73. Ibid., Exod 19:5.

74. Ibid., Deut 11:10. On the connection between Shekhinah and the All, see ibid., Gen 24:1.

75. See ibid., Gen 26:5 and 29:21. On this issue, see the lengthy discussion in ch. 6, secs. II–III.

76. *PHT*, Lev 18:25.

77. Ibid., Deut 30:6.

78. *PHT*, Lev 26:6.

79. On the parallelism between the Garden of Eden and the land of Israel, see Haviva Pedaya, "The Spiritual vs. the Concrete Land of Israel in the Geronese School of Kabbalah," in *The Land of Israel in Medieval Jewish Thought*, ed. Moshe Hallamish and Aviezer Ravitzky (Jerusalem: Ben-Zvi Institute, 1991), 278–280 (Heb.).

80. *DTHT,* 62 (= *KR,* 1:155).
81. *PHT,* Lev 26:6.
82. Ibid., Lev 26:12.
83. Ibid., Lev 18:25.
84. In a few sentences, Ephraim Gottlieb captured this tension by comparing Nahmanides's position with occasionalism: "Nahmanides, in contrast, recognized the laws of Nature but to these laws he added an additional causal factor, namely, the observance of the commandments. Divine providence over the Jewish people depends upon their observance of the commandments, which is the only means by which the laws of Nature can be altered." Ephraim Gottlieb, *Studies in the Kabbalah Literature,* ed. Joseph Hacker (Tel-Aviv: Chaim Rosenberg School of Jewish Studies, Tel-Aviv University, 1976), 266 (Heb.). See further ibid., 36–37. Gottlieb cites R. Meir Ibn Gabbai (ibid., 36n28) who maintained that the hidden miracle is simply another level of causality, which Gottlieb understands to be Nahmanides's opinion too: "According to this, Nahmanides does not intend to say that the promise is a hidden miracle because the promised reward lacks a causal connection to the commandments. Nahmanides intends to distinguish between a causal connection manifest through the visible laws of Nature and the hidden causal link which is invisible" (ibid., 37). For an additional discussion of the tension between the theory of the miracle and the causal assumptions that form part of the kabbalistic conception of the commandment, see Chayim Henoch, *Nachmanides: Philosopher and Mystic* (Jerusalem: Harry Fischel Institute for Talmudic Research, 1978), 56n171 (Heb.).

CHAPTER 5. REVELATION AND PROPHECY

1. *PHT,* Lev 23:36.
2. Ibid.
3. This symbolic reading of the citron and palm frond has implications for the way they are taken in discharging the obligation. See Israel M. Ta-Shma, *Nigle she-ba-Nistar: Halachic Residue in the Zohar,* rev. ed. (Tel-Aviv: Ha-Kibbutz ha-Me'uhad, 2001), 46 (Heb.); and Moshe Idel, *R. Menahem Recanati the Kabbalist* (Jerusalem: Schocken, 1998), 221 with notes 46–47 (Heb.).
4. *PHT,* Lev 23:40.
5. The identification of Shekhinah with "Atzeret" and Shekhinah's dual nature are also present in Nahmanides's explanation of why the seventh day of Passover is also referred to as 'Atzeret: "By way of truth, 'Atzeret is the Congregation of Israel, and it comes to teach us the secret of the day. But it is not the same as 'Atzeret of the Eighth [Day], because the Eighth is a Festival unto itself, and the sacrifice is for the Congregation of Israel, unlike the sacrifices of the [preceding] seven days [of *Sukkot*]. The Seventh Day of Passover, by contrast, is part of the Festival. It is called 'Atzeret because sometimes it is counted as Eighth and sometimes it is in the All. It is like the Sabbath, which has both 'Keep' and 'Remember,' 'Glory of the Day' and 'Glory of the Night' " (ibid., Deut 16:4). 'Atzeret, which is the Congregation of Israel, i.e., Shekhinah, can be like both the seventh day of Passover and the eighth of Shemini 'Atzeret because of its ambiguity. The Seventh Day sometimes comprises not only

Tif'eret but also Shekhinah. This is similar to the Sabbath, which, Nahmanides explains, has this dual nature expressed through the two commands of "Remember" and "Keep." In Nahmanides's kabbalistic symbolism, "Remember" refers to Tif'eret and "Keep" to Shekhinah. These two, in turn, correspond to the "Glory of the Day" and "Glory of the Night," which are also Tif'eret and Shekhinah, respectively. On these symbols, see ibid., Exod 20:8 and Deut 5:5.

6. On the absence in Nahmanides's kabbalah of Keter, Hokhmah, and Binah as sefirot that can serve as the object of human contemplation and comprehension, or as sefirot upon which human theurgic activity can have an effect, see the in-depth treatment in Haviva Pedaya, *Nahmanides: Cyclical Time and Holy Text* (Tel-Aviv: 'Am 'Oved, 2003), 392–402 (Heb.).

7. On Shekhinah as "the Back," see *PHT*, Exod 33:23.

8. On Shekhinah as "the Countenance," Nahmanides writes as follows: "By way of truth, 'you should seek *shikhno*' (Deut 12:5) [means] you should seek His Glory, 'and you should go there' to see the Countenance of the Master, the Lord, God of Israel. Thence [i.e., from *shikhno*] the Sages say '*Shekhinah*' " (ibid., Deut 12:5). See also ibid., Num 15:25 and Num 6:24. See further below, sec. III.

9. In Nahmanidean kabbalistic parlance, both Tif'eret and Shekhinah share "the Countenance" as a cognomen. "Countenance within Countenance" thus characterizes the connection between Tif'eret and Shekhinah. See *PHT*, Exod 18:20 ("this is the meaning of Countenance within Countenance"), Gen 46:1 (end), and Exod 20:16. Only Tif'eret, however, has the specific cognomen of "the Radiant Countenance." The dual referentiality of "the Countenance" is the kabbalistic key to understanding a seemingly confusing debate between Moses and God in Exod 33:14–15, where God says, "My Countenance shall go with you and grant you safety," to which Moses responds, "If your Countenance does not go, do not take us out of this." According to Nahmanides's comment ad loc., God promises the presence of the Countenance, i.e., Shekhinah, in the midst of the Jewish people, whereas Moses seeks the Radiant Countenance, i.e., Tif'eret. See also ibid., Gen 48:22: "the Light of the Countenance is Jacob's."

10. See Ibn Ezra's introduction to his commentary on the Pentateuch, *Peirushei ha-Torah le-Rabbeinu Avraham Ibn 'Ezra*, ed. Asher Weiser (Jerusalem: Mossad Harav Kook, 1976), 1:7–8.

11. For Nahmanides's allusive disclosure of kabbalistic secrets as a response to Ibn Ezra, see ch. 8, sec. II.

12. *PHT*, Gen 1:1.

13. See above, ch. 4, sec. I. This parallel is repeated in many places in Nahmanides's oeuvre, but it is exemplified, inter alia, by Shekhinah's cognomen Hokhmat Shelomoh, "the Wisdom of Solomon," while Hokhmah is referred to as a Hokhmat Elohim, "the Wisdom of God." The deep connection between these two sefirot appears in the kabbalistic interpretation that Nahmanides offers for the two divine names of the Tetragrammaton and of *Ehyeh:* "He [God] explained to him [Moses] that *Ehyeh* Who commanded him to tell them is this Great Name, for they are equivalent in their language and letters. The last two letters [*YH*] of the first name [*'HYH*] are the first

ones of the second name [*Y-HWH*] because in the first they symbolize *Hokhmat Shelomoh*, as it is written, 'And the Lord gave *Hokhmah* to Solomon' (1 Kgs 5:26), and in this one [*Y-HWH*] they symbolize *Hokhmat Elohim*. The letter *aleph* in the first ['HYH] symbolizes primordiality and unity and the *yod* in the second [*Y-HWH*] [symbolizes] the ten ineffable *sefirot*" (ibid., Exod 3:13 [end]). Nahmanides believes that these two names symbolize the entirety of the divine emanation: the *aleph* at the beginning of *Ehyeh* symbolizes the unity and primordiality of the sefirot that have their source in Absolute Privation; the *yod* in the Tetragrammaton symbolizes the ten sefirot. The letters *yod* and *he* at the beginning of the Tetragrammaton represent the sefirah of Hokhmah, which is called Hokhmat Elohim, and the ones at the end of *Ehyeh* represent Shekhinah, which is called Hokhmat Shelomoh.

14. Shekhinah serves as the focal point for the direct relationship between the Godhead and the world, which is reflected by the different symbols for Shekhinah in Nahmanides's Torah commentary. Shekhinah can be referred to ostensively and directly defined, which explains why Shekhinah is often referred to by the masculine or feminine forms of the proximate demonstrative "this" (*zeh/zot*)—see *PHT,* end of Gen 2:20 ("from Man This was taken") and Deut 33:1 ("This is the Blessing"). An additional instance in which Nahmanides construes a demonstrative as a reference to Shekhinah is in his interpretation of the clause "and This is for Judah": "But by way of truth, he [Moses] singled out this Attribute for [the tribe of] Judah, because war is their province, and Kingship (*Malkhut* = *Shekhinah*) is theirs forever. This is what helps him defeat his enemies. It is the secret of the verse, 'and [David] said to teach the Judeans [the] Bow; behold it is written in the Book of Yashar' (2 Sam 1:18), because it is the Bow which appeared in the cloud, about which it is said, 'This is the Sign of the Covenant' (Gen 9:12)" (ibid., Deut 33:7). In his remarks on the verse "With This shall Aaron enter the Holy," Nahmanides provides a list of the various contexts in which a demonstrative can be understood as a symbol for Shekhinah (ibid., Lev 16:2). See also his interpretation of the sin of Nadav and Avihu: "they set their hearts only upon This" (ibid., Lev 10:2). For the masculine demonstrative as symbolizing Shekhinah, see Nahmanides's comment on the verse "and This shall be for you the Sign" (ibid., Exod 3:12—for another possible meaning of this symbol, see ibid., Exod 15:2). According to Nahmanides, the possibility of direct human contact with Shekhinah, as opposed to the other sefirot, explains the shift from the second person to the third person in the fixed text of every blessing that contains the divine name. The one reciting the blessing begins with an address in the second person— "Blessed are You"—but continues in the third person—"Who has sanctified us through His commandments" or "Who has chosen us" and so on (see ibid., Exod 16:26). Shekhinah is also referred to by the first-person pronoun "I" (*ani*), the Self; see the parallel set up by Nahmanides between "This" and "I" in ibid., Lev 26:16.

15. Ibid., Deut 33:23. For "the House" as a symbol for Shekhinah, see Nahmanides's interpretation of "Bethel" (*beit el*) in ibid., Gen 31:13. Regarding Shekhinah as "the Bride" that comprises the All, see ibid., Gen 24:1, where Nahmanides refers to Shekhinah as the Attribute "through which He governs all." While Nahmanides understands the Bride in Song of Songs to be Shekhinah, he makes sparing use of sexual

imagery to describe the symbolic relationship between Tif'eret and Shekhinah. Nevertheless, he does still emphasize its femininity—see ibid., Num 11:15, where he understands grammatically feminine references to God as pertaining to Shekhinah.

16. Ibid., Gen 18:1. See also *DTHT*, 44 (= *KR*, 1:148).

17. *PHT*, Gen 18:1.

18. Nahmanides writes about Balaam: " 'God happened upon Balaam' (Num 23:4). This language is used concerning this man because he did not attain the level of prophecy [. . .] It therefore says concerning him, 'God came to Balaam' (Num 22:20), because such language is not used for prophets but for those who have not reached that level. Likewise, 'God came to Abimelech' (Gen 20:3), and 'God came to Laban' (Gen 31:24). Perhaps this means the arrival of the Will through speech from the Supernal One to the Intellects that cause dreams, because Balaam also was lying down (Num 24:4) during the day, a deep sleep coming over him, yet he was open-eyed" (*PHT*, Num 23:4). Oneiric revelation by way of the Intellects, the angels, is not prophecy, so the terminology of speaking (*d-b-r/ '-m-r*) does not appear.

19. On the identification of "the Great Hand" and "the Hand of the Lord" with Shekhinah, see below, ch. 6, note 57.

20. Ibid., Exod 3:2.

21. Ibid.

22. Ibid., Exod 23:20. Nahmanides identifies Metatron with Shekhinah; see ibid., Exod 12:12. For extended discussion of Metatron, see ibid., Exod 24:1 (end). The identification of "the Angel of the Lord" with Shekhinah and Metatron also appears in the writings of R. Ezra of Gerona. See R. Azriel of Gerona, *Commentary on Talmudic Aggadoth*, ed. Isaiah Tishby, 2nd ed. (Jerusalem: Magnes, Hebrew University, 1982), 10–11 (Heb.).

23. For further disagreements between Ibn Ezra and Nahmanides about the meaning of "angel," see *PHT*, Gen 46:1 and 48:15, and concerning the kabbalistic rendering of "I am the God which is the House of God" (Gen 31:13), see his commentary ad loc.

24. Ibid., Gen 46:1.

25. Ibid.

26. Ibid.

27. See also what Nahmanides says about Targum Onkelos in ibid., Exod 20:16.

28. On Shekhinah as "the Mouth of the Lord," see ibid., Num 20:1 (end) and Num 10:6.

29. See above, ch. 4, secs. III–IV.

30. On this term, see below, sec. III with note 54.

31. *PHT*, Exod 6:2.

32. See as well ibid., Gen 17:1, Exod 3:13, Deut 4:12, and Deut 5:19.

33. Nahmanides also uses this distinction to explain the difference between God speaking from Heaven—Tif'eret—and God descending onto Mount Sinai in fire—Shekhinah. See ibid., Exod 20:19. The same revelatory pattern is present in the tabernacle, which Nahmanides views as a parallel to Mount Sinai; see ibid., Lev 1:1.

34. Ibid., Exod 3:13.

35. Ibid.

36. Ibid., Exod 19:3.

37. Ibid., Exod 19:20.

38. For an analysis of Nahmanides's conception of the Torah as a sequence of divine names that discloses the Godhead's essence, see above, ch. 1, sec. IX.

39. *DDK, KR,* 1:191–192.

40. In Commentary on Job, Nahmanides notes that in the first chapter there is variability in the divine names, whereas in the rest of the book "God" (Elohim) is used exclusively in the conversations between Job and his companions. He views this as the key to understanding Job's view of the world and the reason behind his grievances: "Now I have perused this book and the Awesome Name (*shem ha-nora*) appears neither in Job's arguments nor in the statements of his friends; they mention only the names of godship and *Shaddai,* which was the name they had received from the Patriarchs, as it is written: 'I appeared to Abraham, Isaac, and Jacob through El Shaddai' (Exod 6:3). [. . .] it does not mention the Glorious Name, which is the Essential Name, perhaps because Job was not privy to its secret, [how] it governs the lowly realms and introduces new signs and wonders into the world, because this matter was revealed to our master Moses. The rule is that he who understands the verse 'I appeared to Abraham, Isaac etc.' knows this" (*PSI,* 1:33–34). Job, who according to Nahmanides received his tradition from the Patriarchs, did not know the Unique Name of Tif'eret, and so his understanding of divine providence in the world was perforce limited.

41. *DDK, KR,* 1:195.

42. Ibid., 1:199.

43. Ibid. Nowhere in Ecclesiastes does Nahmanides see an example of "suffering out of love," that is, suffering with no sin to justify it, because the source of the book is Shekhinah, the Attribute of Judgment, and in Nahmanides's kabbalah suffering out of love is linked to the "secret of impregnation" (*sod ha-'ibbur*), according to which the sinning soul returns to a body to rectify its past sins. The source of the secret of impregnation is in the Attribute of Mercy, since this second chance granted the soul is an undeserved kindness. According to Nahmanides, Solomon alludes to the secret in a mere few words: "One generation goes and another generation comes" (Eccl 1:4). As Nahmanides writes: "The principle is that one ought to believe that there is no death without sin and no suffering without iniquity. One should not view oneself favorably but examine one's deeds [. . .] Do not challenge me from what they [the Sages] said about suffering out of love. Nevertheless, there is a great secret in it that one cannot know at all except through the tradition, an exceedingly clear explanation that leaves no doubts in anyone's mind. It is the answer spoken by Elihu; it is mentioned in a psalm of Asaph; it is alluded to by Solomon but he does not expand upon it, cutting it short for the reason that I have mentioned, viz. the Book of Ecclesiastes is based upon the Attribute of Judgment which exists in the world through the name 'God' (*Elohim*)" (ibid., 1:199).

44. *PHT,* Exod 20:8.

45. Nahmanides mostly maps the Attribute of Judgment onto Shekhinah and the Attribute of Mercy onto Tif'eret, rather than onto the higher sefirot of Din or Hesed. See ch. 6, note 66.

46. *PHT,* Deut 5:5.

47. Another interesting source concerning the revelatory divide between Tif'eret and Shekhinah pertains to the Oral Torah and Shekhinah. It is well known that in kabbalistic symbolism the Oral Torah is linked to Shekhinah and the Written Torah to Tif'eret. Through the rich interpretations of the Oral Torah, the Written Torah undergoes a further degree of delineation and differentiation. While Nahmanides is aware of this identification, in a few places he redefines the concept of the Oral Torah. He does not view it as that which adds to the Written Torah, because even some elements of the Written Torah are called "Oral Torah" and attributed to Shekhinah in his writings. The first five of the Ten Commandments, according to Nahmanides, are intended for the Glory of the Creator, whereas the last five are for the betterment of humanity. He then says: "From this it should be clear to you why there were two [tablets], because until 'Honor your father' it corresponds to the Written Torah, and thereafter it corresponds to the Oral Torah. This would appear to be what our Rabbis were hinting at when they said: ' "Two tablets"—corresponding to Heaven and Earth, and corresponding to the Groom and Bride, and corresponding to two Men of Honor, and corresponding to two Worlds'—all of this is one allusion, and the enlightened will understand [the secret]" (ibid., Exod 20:13). Those aspects of the Torah intended for humanity's benefit represent Shekhinah and the Oral Torah, even if they are part and parcel of the Written Torah. Nahmanides makes a similar point, albeit in a different context, on the verse "This is the *hok* of the Torah" (Num 19:2): "Therefore the verse said, 'This is the *Hok* of the Torah,' as if to say that which is hewn (*ha-nehkeket*) from the Torah: the Oral Torah. Therefore it is a heifer and it is red from the Attribute of Judgment" (ibid., Num 19:2). "The *Hok* of the Torah" that is hewn from the Torah, namely, emanated from Tif'eret, is Shekhinah, which is referred to in Nahmanides's kabbalistic symbolism as "This." The heifer is red because it represents the activity of Shekhinah, the Attribute of Judgment, which Nahmanides refers to as "the Oral Torah."
48. Ibid., Deut 5:5.
49. On the difference between the covenant in Leviticus (in the portion of Be-Hukkotai) said in the language of "I" (*ani*), as opposed to the covenant in Deuteronomy (in the portion of Ki Tavo) said in the language of "the Lord your God," see ibid., Lev 26:16.
50. Ibid., Num 30:3.
51. *Novellae*, Shevu'ot 29a, s.v. *ha di-tenan*, M36/s.v. *ve-okimna*, H131.
52. *PHT*, Num 14:14.
53. Ibid.
54. This interpretation of *'ayin be-'ayin* appears in the second of the two kabbalistic passages in Nahmanides's Talmudic novellae (the first, about oaths and vows, was discussed above in sec. II). The Talmud distinguishes between Moses, who looked through the Speculum That Shines, and the rest of the prophets, who looked through the Speculum That Does Not Shine. Nahmanides remarks about this: "The true interpretation is that all of the prophets perceived through the eye and beheld, as in the meaning of [the verse], 'and the appearance of the Glory of the Lord was like a consuming fire' (Exod 24:17), and this is what the verse said, 'and through the Hand of the prophets I am imagined' (Hos 12:11). Based on my limited understanding, this is

what the verse said, 'You, O Lord, Who (*asher*) are seen *'ayin be-'ayin*,' for the term *'ayin* in many scriptural verses is like 'appearance,' and *asher* means 'because.' The explanation of this verse is that our master Moses said to the Holy One: 'Is not your Great Name in the midst of this people? Because [*asher*] the Appearance within the Appearance [*'ayin be-'ayin*], which is seen, is your Great Name, may it be elevated and blessed, and You cleave to the Congregation of Israel, so it is impossible to annihilate them, like the meaning of the verse, 'for My Name is in it' (Exod 23:21)" (*Novellae*, Yevamot 49b, s.v. *kol ha-nevi'im*, H186/M55–56). In this passage *'ayin be-'ayin* does not describe the manner of revelation but the status of the sefirot of Tif'eret and Shekhinah. The "Appearance" is not only the sefirotic reflection to the prophet but also a cognomen of the sefirah itself, because the sefirot themselves reflect one another. "The Appearance within the Appearance" indicates the presence of Tif'eret within Shekhinah: "Because [*asher*] the Appearance within the Appearance [*'ayin be-'ayin*], which is seen, is your Great Name, may it be elevated and blessed, and You cleave to the Congregation of Israel [i.e., *Shekhinah*], so it is impossible to annihilate them, like the meaning of the verse, 'for My Name [*Tif'eret*] is in it [the Redeeming Angel, i.e., *Shekhinah*]' (Exod 23:21)." Tif'eret's conjunction with Shekhinah saved the Jewish people from annihilation, because the separation of Shekhinah from Tif'eret would have granted the Attribute of Judgment free rein. *'Ayin be-'ayin* therefore signifies the cleaving of the two sefirot. The imagery of reflection is an interesting way of depicting the relationship between unity and multiplicity, because a reflected image cannot be removed from a mirror yet it is not the thing itself. The sefirot themselves are reflections in essence, not only in their manner of revelatory disclosure to prophets.

55. *PHT,* Num 24:1.
56. We can see from here that "opening of the eyes" is a low-level prophetic state that parallels the "vision of *Shaddai*." In other places in his Commentary on the Torah, however, Nahmanides seems to equate this with seeing an angel, which he does not consider prophecy at all and is even lower than the "vision of *Shaddai*." Nahmanides writes about the Lord opening Balaam's eyes: "From this verse we learn that Balaam was not a prophet, for if he were a prophet how could he have needed an 'opening of the eyes' to see the angel, which is how Scripture speaks concerning those who have not attained prophecy [. . .] subsequently he merited an opening of the eyes to see the angel and he spoke to it, and at the end he reached the level of the 'vision of *Shaddai*' " (ibid., Num 22:31). See what Nahmanides writes about "opening of the eyes" in ibid., Gen 18:1, where this level also appears to be beneath prophecy.
57. Beside the distinction between the prophecy of Moses and the Israelites at the giving of the Torah, Nahmanides makes an additional distinction between the elders who beheld Shekhinah and the rest of the nation: "through this sight the elders apprehended more than the rest of the people to whom He showed of his Earth [i.e., *Shekhinah*] its great fire (cf. Deut 4:36), for the people [saw] through the partition of cloud and darkness" (ibid., Exod 24:10). On illicit glimpses of Shekhinah, see ibid., Gen 19:17.
58. Ibid., Num 12:6.

59. Nahmanides repeats this later in the same passage: "the Great Name is within the Appearance and through it, not through the Great Name, it makes itself known to the prophet, as He said, 'but I did not make Myself known to them through My name Y-HWH' (Exod 6:3)" (ibid.).

60. Nahmanides uses "the Holy Spirit" in different senses in his writings; see below, note 71.

61. See, for example, *The Guide of the Perplexed,* translated with introduction and notes by Shlomo Pines (Chicago: University of Chicago Press, 1963), I:44 and I:54.

62. Ibid., II:42.

63. *PHT,* Gen 18:1.

64. Ibid., Exod 33:18.

65. Nahmanides must face a challenge generated by his own kabbalistic symbolism, in which "the Glory" usually refers to the sefirah of Shekhinah, which would mean that Moses was requesting to see Shekhinah. He therefore posits, with some hesitation, that it speaks here not of "the Glory" but "the Great Glory," which is Tif'eret. On the relationship between the Glory and Shekhinah, see Nahmanides's long comment about Onkelos in ibid., Gen 46:1.

66. Ibid., Exod 33:23. As noted at the beginning of the chapter, sometimes "the Countenance" refers to Tif'eret and at other times to Shekhinah, but "the Radiant Countenance" is always Tif'eret; see note 9 above. Other Geronese kabbalists also used this cognomen; see R. Azriel, *Commentary,* 4, l. 10.

67. *Novellae,* Yevamot 49b, s.v. *kol ha-nevi'im,* H186/M56.

68. In his explanation of the verse that distinguishes Mosaic prophecy from other kinds, Nahmanides employs the two criteria mentioned above to grade the various levels of prophecy: " 'I shall make Myself known to him through the Appearance [i.e., *Shekhinah*]' (Num 12:6). The verse does not say 'I shall appear to him through the Appearance' but 'I shall make Myself known to him.' This verse is like 'I appeared to Abraham, Isaac, and Jacob through *El Shaddai*' (Exod 6:3), namely, that the Great Name is within the Appearance and through it, not through the Great Name, it makes itself known to the prophet, as He said, 'but I did not make Myself known to them through My name Y-HWH' (Exod 6:3). He said that speech would be in a dream, but 'Not so with my servant Moses' because 'in All, My House' [i.e., *Shekhinah*], through which the prophets see dreams, he is faithful and knows of his own accord all of the Attributes. Speech from Me comes to him Mouth to Mouth and in it he beholds the Image, he does not see it in a dream. [In] the language of the *Sifrei:* ' "he beholds the Image of the Lord" (Num 12:8)—this is the vision of the Back' " (*PHT,* Num 12:6).

69. Ibid., Num 16:5.

70. *Novellae,* Bava Batra 12a, s.v. *ha de-amerinan mi-yom,* M15.

71. Sometimes Nahmanides classifies "the Holy Spirit" as a level beneath prophecy, but at other times he identifies it with prophecy. Seeing an angel, as we have noted, is not considered prophecy under Nahmanides's prophetic theory, so Daniel is not considered a prophet. Instead, Daniel belongs to the group of "men of the Holy Spirit" who are beneath the prophets: "and when they [the angels, i.e., the Separate Intellects]

appear to prophets or men of the Holy Spirit like Daniel they apprehend them through visions of the intellective soul when it reaches the levels of prophecy or the level beneath it" (*PHT,* Num 22:23). The expression "men of the Holy Spirit" appears later in his commentary on the same pericope in ibid., Num 23:4. In other places, however, he describes the revelation of Shekhinah to a prophet in terms of "the Holy Spirit," as in the previously cited passage from ibid., Num 16:5, and also in ibid., Num 12:6. See also what Nahmanides writes about the revelation to Abraham: "because until now the Lord had not appeared to him or made Himself known to him neither in a sight or vision; rather, 'Leave your land' (Gen 12:1) was said to him in a nocturnal dream or through the Holy Spirit" (ibid., Gen 12:6). In these short lines Nahmanides lays out the many gradations of revelation, and the list includes the Holy Spirit: sight, vision, dream, and the Holy Spirit. About foreknowledge through the Urim and Thummim he writes: "This level is that of the Holy Spirit, which is beneath prophecy but above the heavenly voice used in the Second Temple after prophecy and the Urim and Thummim had ceased" (ibid., Exod 28:30).

In his commentary on Sefer Yetzirah, Nahmanides interprets "the Holy Spirit" as the symbol for the first sefirah of Keter. The sefirah of Hokhmah is referred to as "the Holy," and Keter is "the Spirit" within "the Holy"—the Holy Spirit. " 'Sound, Spirit, and Speech which is the Holy Spirit.' That is, there is no spirit that does not include these three things: sound, spirit, and speech. A sound, like the sound heard by the agitation of the air, and there is a spirit within it that agitates and reaches the ear of the listener, and the word gives it form. In similar fashion, these three things are present in the most rarefied form possible in the first *sefirah,* which is the Holy Spirit. That is, like the spirit in man, which is the breath inside the body, so is the Spirit in the Holy, the Holy being *Hokhmah.* On account of the emanation of things prophecy is called the Holy Spirit, even though prophecy does not reach there [i.e., *Hokhmah*]" (Gershom Scholem, "*Peirusho ha-Amitti shel ha-Ramban le-Sefer Yetzirah ve-Divrei Kabbalah Aherim ha-Mityahasim Elav,*" in Scholem, *Studies in Kabbalah [1],* ed. Yosef Ben-Shlomo and Moshe Idel [Tel-Aviv: 'Am 'Oved, 1998], 95 [Heb.]).

72. *THA, KR,* 2:299.

73. Concerning the connection between prophecy and cleaving, Nahmanides writes about the clause "who heard the Voice of the Living God speaking out of the midst of the fire" (Deut 5:23): "Perhaps one can explain that it mentions this ['Living'] to convey that upon hearing the Voice of God, which is the Source of Life, a person's soul will cleave to its source and no longer live a life of the flesh" (*PHT,* Deut 5:23).

74. Ibid., Num 12:4.

75. As we saw in the previous two chapters, Nahmanides describes the state of cleaving as one of *unio mystica*—"their becoming one entity"—in Torat ha-Adam. If we combine this with his conception of prophecy as cleaving and of the uniqueness of Mosaic prophecy, something fascinating emerges. By virtue of Moses's prophetic state, he was able to serve as the conduit for the prophecy of the seventy elders: "I will come down and speak with you there, and I will hold back (*ve-atzalti*) [. . .] the idea here is to convey that the elders who are said to have prophesied did not hear speech from the

Lord, nor did He reveal Himself to them in a sight or dream; rather, the Lord speaks with Moses and from the reserve (*atzilut*) of the Spirit of Moses they know the prophecy" (ibid., Num 11:17). Nahmanides explains the use of '-*tz-l* here to mean something held in reserve so that it is with (*etzel*) the giver, and thus the Lord held back some of the Spirit from which the elders received the prophecy. According to this, Moses was not only God's messenger who delivered his word to the elders, but the elders themselves prophesied through the Spirit placed upon Moses because of his identity with Shekhinah.

76. There are three kinds of sight: one, through the physical eyes; two, through the eye of the soul, which enables one to see subtle matter; and three, through the intellect, which is not really seeing but a metaphor for intellectual apprehension. Nahmanides relates to all three in his discussion of biblical personalities beholding angels. On one hand, an angel cannot be seen with the physical eyes, but on the other hand, through the Holy Spirit one can see it through the eye of the soul. Seeing an angel is not a metaphor for intellectual apprehension, according to Nahmanides: " 'And the she-ass saw the angel of the Lord' (Num 22:23)—angels of God, the Separate Intellects, cannot be seen by the visual sense, because they are not a body perceptible through sight. When they appear to prophets or men of the Holy Spirit, like Daniel, they apprehend them through visions of the intellective soul when it reaches the level of prophecy or the level beneath it. But it is utterly impossible for them to be apprehended by the eyes of an animal; therefore, you can explain 'the she-ass saw' [to mean that] it sensed something frightening it from passing, which was the angel which placed itself as an adversary. This is like the meaning of 'my heart has seen much wisdom and knowledge' (Eccl 1:16), which is speaking about apprehension and not sight" (ibid., Num 22:23). Concerning these rarefied yet still corporeal beings, which are imperceptible to the human or animal senses in their natural state, see Nahmanides's statement about demons: "their creation was similarly from two elements, from Fire and Air, which gave them a body imperceptible and inapprehensible to any of the senses, just as the animal soul cannot be apprehended by the senses due to its subtlety. This body is spiritual [and] can fly due to its subtlety and lightness like fire and wind" (ibid., Lev 17:7).

77. *Meshiv Devarim Nekhohim,* ed. Georges Vajda and Ephraim Gottlieb (Jerusalem: Israel Academy of Science and Humanities, 1968), 128 (Heb.).

78. See the aggadic commentary of R. Ezra of Gerona: "In truth, our master Moses, master of all the prophets, only apprehended the last five *sefirot,* and he sought to apprehend the five as they are articulated, but He responded to him: 'You cannot see My Countenance' " (R. Azriel, *Commentary,* 7–8).

79. Ibid., 39.

80. Ibid., 20.

81. Ibid., 40.

82. Ibid., 40–41.

83. For an in-depth analysis of this image and the theory of cleaving and prophecy it embodies, see Haviva Pedaya, " 'Possessed by Speech': Towards an Understanding of the Prophetic-Ecstatic Pattern among Early Kabbalists," *Tarbiz* 65 (1996): 565–636 (Heb.).

84. *PHT*, Num 23:4.
85. Ibid.
86. *PSI, KR*, 1:115.
87. See further *PHT*, Gen 3:8. On the possibility of seeing Shekhinah, see ibid., Num 4:20.
88. *THA, KR*, 2:307. Furthermore: "In this world the Sages apprehend through the Holy Spirit seven *sefirot* [. . .] In the Days of the Messiah the eighth *sefirah* will be apprehended, and they [the Sages] hint to it. In the World to Come the apprehension will be complete with all ten *sefirot*, and they allude to them" (ibid., 2:303).

CHAPTER 6. NAHMANIDES'S CONCEPTION OF HISTORY

1. *THA, KR*, 2:305.
2. Concerning the doctrine of cosmic cycles in medieval Jewish thought, see Shalom Rosenberg, "The Return to the Garden of Eden: Reflections on the History of the Idea of Restorative Redemption in Medieval Jewish Philosophy," in *The Messianic Idea in Jewish Thought: A Study Conference in Honour of the Eightieth Birthday of Gershom Scholem* (Jerusalem: Israel Academy of Science, 1990), 37–86 (Heb.).
3. See Gershom Scholem, *Ha-Kabbalah shel Sefer ha-Temunah ve-Shel Avraham Abulafia*, ed. Yosef Ben-Shlomo (Jerusalem: Akademon, 1969), 19–84 (Heb.); Scholem, *Origins of the Kabbalah*, ed. R. J. Zwi Werblowsky and trans. Allan Arkush (Philadelphia: Jewish Publication Society; Princeton: Princeton University Press, 1987), 460–475. For general and historical background about the cyclical concept of time in antique and medieval Islam and Christianity, see Rosenberg, "Return to the Garden," notes 9–13; Haviva Pedaya, *Nahmanides: Cyclical Time and Holy Text* (Tel-Aviv: 'Am 'Oved, 2003), 4–11 (Heb.). I am not convinced that there is evidence of the cyclical paradigm in Talmudic literature or midrash before the Middle Ages. Some rabbinic formulations do seem to imply the existence of a single cycle, but I have yet to find evidence of an iterative cycle.
4. Gershom Scholem, *"Peirusho ha-Amitti shel ha-Ramban le-Sefer Yetzirah ve-Divrei Kabbalah Aherim ha-Mityahasim Elav,"* in Scholem, *Studies in Kabbalah (1)*, ed. Yosef Ben-Shlomo and Moshe Idel (Tel-Aviv: 'Am 'Oved, 1998), 87–88 (Heb.).
5. See above, ch. 4, note 59.
6. *PHT*, Lev 25:2. For another reference to "the Land of Life," see ibid., Gen 1:26. Regarding "I shall Remember the Land" (Lev 26:42), see below, the end of sec. IV.
7. Ibid., Lev 25:10. In the context of the secret of impregnation (*sod ha-'ibbur*), i.e., transmigration, Nahmanides explains the word "generation" (*dor*) as related to the Hebrew word for "sphere," which according to him is *dur. Dor*, as he understands it, is that which comes and goes, like the rotation of a sphere: "It seems that the meaning of *dor* is from the language of [the verse] 'He shall violently turn and toss you like a sphere (*ka-dur*) to a land of broad expanse' (Isa 22:18), because the *kaf* is not part of the root, and it is so called because the generations rotate—one generation comes, another generation goes" (*DDK, KR*, 1:186).

8. *PHT,* Exod 21:6. Nahmanides does not interpret *le-'olam* as a specific period of time but as the cosmic "Days of the World," that is, the period that parallels the existence of the universe. This contradicts R. Abraham Ibn Ezra, who explains that *'olam* denotes a period of time. Here is Nahmanides again: "R. A[braham] forgot what he perceived correctly and wrote down elsewhere."

9. For more on the meaning of *le-'olam* in the context of the permanence or impermanence of the universe, and the meaning of the jubilee, see *DDK, KR,* 1:188–190. See also R. Ezra of Gerona on the connection between the return of patrimonies to their original owners and the return of the sefirot to their original source in Yakov M. Travis, "Kabbalistic Foundations of Jewish Spiritual Practice: Rabbi Ezra of Gerona— On the Kabbalistic Meaning of the Mizvot," PhD diss., Brandeis University, 2002, 259–261 in Eng., 42–43 in Heb. (in *KR,* 2:539).

10. Scholem, "*Peirusho ha-Amitti,*" 87.

11. R. Jacob b. Sheshet explicitly supported such a position: "Therefore, one cannot say that the Earth will exist forever, indefinitely and endlessly, because in truth it returns to its Foundation and is recreated by the Will of the Creator, and blessed is the one who knows what will be at the end, since one may not speculate about it, but there is no doubt that after it [the Earth] returns to its Foundation it will be recreated" (*Meshiv Devarim Nekhohim,* ed. Georges Vajda and Ephraim Gottlieb [Jerusalem: Israel Academy of Science and Humanities, 1968], 94, ll. 67–70 [Heb.]). On this issue, see Rosenberg, "Return to the Garden," note 33.

12. *Sefer Megillat ha-Megalleh,* ed. Ze'ev Poznanski (Berlin, 1924), 10–11.

13. See ch. 4, sec. I.

14. On this transformation of the concept of *creatio ex nihilo,* see Scholem, *Origins of the Kabbalah,* 422–427.

15. On the ceaseless oscillatory motion of the divine will, Nahmanides writes in his commentary on Sefer Yetzirah: " 'They [the ten sefirot] are boundless,' as we explained, and 'His Word is in them dashing to and fro.' This is the Will that goes forth to *Ein-Sof* (*me-Ein Sof*), and their end is in dashing to and fro" (Scholem, "*Peirusho ha-Amitti,*" 94). In his critical apparatus, Scholem notes an alternative reading in MS Leiden: "that goes forth endlessly (*me-ein ketz*) and ceaselessly by dashing to and fro." As Scholem notes in endnote 36, on the basis of this reading and the commentary of R. Meir b. Solomon Abusahulah on Sefer Yetzirah, Nahmanides is speaking of the never-ending movement of the will outward and inward and not about Ein-Sof. Scholem's reading is supported by the fact that Nahmanides never uses "Ein-Sof" as a noun referring to God in his writings. See Moshe Idel, "On *Zimzum* in Kabbalah and in Scholarship," in *Lurianic Kabbalah,* ed. Rachel Elior and Yehuda Liebes (Jerusalem: 'Daf-Noy,' 1992), 62 (Heb.).

16. *The Guide of the Perplexed,* translated with introduction and notes by Shlomo Pines (Chicago: University of Chicago Press, 1963), II:27–29.

17. It is worth noting that in R. Abraham b. Hiyya's discussion of time's terminability, the argument that time has a beginning is what leads him to the argument that it must needs have an end, too. See *Megillat ha-Megalleh,* 10, ll. 13–15.

18. *DDK, KR,* 1:188.

19. Ibid., 1:190.

20. The link between cyclical time and myth has received scholarly treatment in Mircea Eliade, *The Myth of the Eternal Return: Or, Cosmos and History*, trans. Willard Trask (Princeton: Princeton University Press, 1971).

21. Regarding the Era of the Torah, Nahmanides writes: "From the time of Creation, man could do as he pleased, [he could be] righteous or wicked. And so it has been for the entire Era of the Torah" (*PHT*, Deut 31:6). See above, ch. 3, esp. sec. II.

22. Ibid., Gen 12:6.

23. Ibid., end of Gen.

24. Ibid., Gen 12:6.

25. Ibid., Gen 12:10.

26. Nahmanides believes that the defeat of the four kings at Abraham's hands signifies the ultimate victory of the Jewish people over the four kingdoms that would rule the world: "This occurrence befell Abraham to convey that four kingdoms would arise to dominate the world, and that at the end his progeny would overcome them and they would all fall by their hand" (ibid., Gen 14:1).

27. Ibid., Gen 26:1.

28. In line with the symbolism that identifies a well with the Temple, the three wells that Isaac dug allude to and signify the three Temples—the first, the second, and the third yet to come. See ibid., Gen 27:20 and 29:2.

29. Ibid., Gen 32:4. Jacob's division of his camp to prevent Esau from annihilating his family alludes to the exilic conditions in which Nahmanides found himself: "This also hints that Esau's progeny will not decree the obliteration of our name but will commit terrible acts against some of us in some of their lands—one of their kings makes a decree in his land concerning our money or persons, while another king is merciful in his domain and saves the remnant" (ibid., Gen 32:9). A few verses later, Nahmanides writes about Jacob leaving space between each gift to Esau: "[it] is a hint that the tributes and taxes collected from his progeny by Esau's descendants would have some respite and break between them" (ibid., Gen 32:17).

30. Ibid., Gen 32:26. See what Nahmanides writes about the general connection between Jacob's encounter with Esau and the Roman exile in ibid., Gen 34:15.

31. Ibid., Gen 47:28. See also ibid., Gen 43:14.

32. "That is the exile in which we were exiled to Rome because King Agrippa went there" (ibid., Deut 28:42).

33. See ibid., Lev 26:16 and Deut 28:42. See also *SHG, KR*, 1:267–268.

34. Amos Funkenstein, "Nachmanides' Typological Reading of History," *Zion* 45 (1980): 35–59 (Heb.).

35. *PHT*, Gen 12:6.

36. *DTHT*, 103 (= *KR*, 1:172).

37. He reiterates his notion of typological interpretation in his comment on Jacob's blessing to Joseph, in which he mentions Joseph's inheritance: "I have given you one portion more than your brothers, which I have taken out of the hand of the Amorite with my sword and my bow" (Gen 48:22). In dealing with the question of when Jacob used a bow or sword, Nahmanides says: "I also find it very likely that Jacob did what

prophets do—he outstretched his arm with a sword toward the land of the Amorite and shot arrows there so that it could be conquered by his progeny, similar to what Elisha did: 'and he placed his hands upon the king's hands [. . .] And Elisha said, "Shoot" and he shot' (2 Kgs 13:16–17). Even though Scripture does not relate this, it alludes to it in this verse. This could be the reason it says 'I have taken,' because from that time the land was taken for his progeny" (*PHT,* Gen 48:22).

38. Ibid., Gen 12:6.

39. See also what Nahmanides writes about Jacob's entry into Shechem; ibid., Gen 34:18.

40. *DTHT,* 114 (= *KR,* 1:174).

41. *PHT,* preface to Exodus.

42. Ibid., Gen 2:3.

43. Ibid.

44. Ibid., Gen 12:10.

45. Ibid., Lev 26:16.

46. See above, sec. II.

47. *PHT,* Gen 32:4.

48. See esp. ch. 4, secs. IV–V.

49. See above, ch. 3.

50. Ibid., Gen 1:1.

51. Ibid.

52. Ibid.

53. See, for example, ibid., Lev 26:6: "when the commandments are observed, the land of Israel shall be like the world was at its beginning, prior to Adam's sin."

54. See above, ch. 3, sec. VII.

55. *PHT,* Lev 23:40. On the standing of Shekhinah within the Godhead, see the beginning of ch. 5.

56. Ibid., Deut 32:40.

57. According to Nahmanides, "the Hand of the Lord" is a cognomen of Shekhinah: "and as it says, 'And Israel saw the Great Hand' (Exod 14:31), because the Hand alludes to the Attribute of Judgment which is the Great, Avenging Hand [. . .] He [David] likewise explained, 'Why, O sea, do you flee?' (Ps 114:5)—'From the presence of the God of Jacob' (114:7). They similarly said in the *Mekhilta:* 'When they went down to the sea, the *Shekhinah* was with them, as it says, "And the Angel, God, traveled" (Exod 14:19).' And in *Shemot Rabbah:* 'His Might is none other than Judgment, as it says, "the Might of the King loves Judgment" (Ps 94:4)' " (ibid., Exod 15:2).

58. Nahmanides repeats this interpretation of divine hand-raising as symbolizing the return of Shekhinah to Tif'eret: "But by way of truth, 'I raised My Hand' (Exod 6:8) [means] that I lifted the Arm of My Might [*Shekhinah*] to Me [*Tif'eret*] so that the Land [*Shekhinah*] be given to them [the *sefirot* symbolized by Abraham, Isaac, and Jacob]. Likewise: 'For I raise My Hand to Heaven' (Deut 32:40) [means] that I will raise the Great Arm to Heaven so that Life [*Tif'eret*] will be in it forever. But [the verse] 'He raised his Right Hand and Left Hand to Heaven' (Dan 12:7) does not have this meaning, for it is said about the angel wearing linen who swears 'by the Life of the World' (Dan 12:7)" (ibid., Exod 6:8). The last verse seems to refer to the

conjunction of Din and Hesed with Binah, which is called both "Life of the World" and "Heaven," because "Heaven," that is, Tif'eret, has its own "Heaven," Binah.

59. Ibid., Exod 13:21.

60. Additionally, Nahmanides writes concerning the symbolism of the Lord's Court and Shekhinah: "[the Holy One has] another Attribute called 'Daughter' which is emanated from it [*Ha-Kol*, the All], and through it He governs all, and this is the Court of the Holy One alluded to in every occurrence of the word 'and the Lord' (*va-Y-HWH*). It is this that is called 'the Bride' (*Kallah*) in Song of Songs, because it comprises the All, and which the Sages refer to as 'the Congregation (*Keneset*) of Israel' in many places, because it is the encompassing (*kenisat*) of the All" (ibid., Gen 24:1).

61. Relevant here is what Nahmanides writes about Jacob's blessing to his children, "and *El Shaddai* should grant you Mercy" (Gen 43:14), before their return to Egypt with Benjamin: "The intent [in *Bereshit Rabbah*] is that Jacob's descent alludes to our exile under the dominion of Edom, as I will explain, and the prophet [Jacob] foresaw it and prayed in a general manner for the moment and for generations [to come]. According to their exposition this verse contains a great secret, because he [Jacob] said: 'and *El Shaddai*,' through the Attribute of Judgment, 'should grant you Mercy' of His Countenance, it should raise you from the Attribute of Judgment to the Attribute of Mercy. The enlightened will understand" (ibid., Gen 43:14).

62. Ibid., Deut 33:12.

63. Similarly, in Sefer ha-Ge'ulah he writes: "*Shekhinah* did not dwell with them during the Second Temple [era], as it [the era] also had no prophecy except at the beginning of the construction—Haggai, Zachariah, and Malachi" (*SHG, KR,* 1:265). As mentioned earlier in the chapter, Nahmanides distinguishes the curses and blessings recorded in Leviticus from those in Deuteronomy, attributing the former to the exile after the destruction of the First Temple and the latter to the exile following the destruction of the Second Temple. One textual difference between the pericopes concerns the speaker: in Leviticus it is the Lord, whereas in Deuteronomy it is Moses. Nahmanides raises this point as follows: "The first covenant, which is in this Torah portion [*Be-Hukkotai*], was made by the Holy One, because his Great Name was with us in the First Temple. But the second covenant, which is in the Torah portion of *Ve-Hayah Ki Tavo*, was from the mouth of Moses, to remove His *Shekhinah* completely, because the Second Temple only had the Glory (*Kavod*) of His Name, as it says, 'I will look on it with favor and be Glorified (*ekkaved/ah*)' (Hag 1:8); the additional *he* [of the longer, cohortative form *ekkavedah*] is a hint to the second [letter *he*] of the Great Name. The Rabbis have expounded another *midrash* about this, too: 'It [the missing *he*] is a hint to the five things absent from the Second Temple etc.' " (ibid., Lev 26:16). Nahmanides appears to be relating to the form *ekkaved* preserved in the written text (*ketiv*) of the verse in Haggai, which has no final *he*, as opposed to the form *ekkavedah* preserved in the reading tradition (*kerei*), which does have a final *he*. Nahmanides ties the missing *he* of this word to the second *he* of the Tetragrammaton, as this last letter symbolizes Shekhinah. See also what Nahmanides writes about the connection between the Fourth Day, on which the luminaries were created, and the fourth millennium, in which the First and Second Temples were built: "On this Day all of the

Children of Israel had Light, 'for the Glory of the Lord filled the house of the Lord'
(1 Kgs 8:11), and the Light of Israel was a fire upon the altar, crouching there like a
lion, consuming the sacrifices. But afterwards He diminished their Light and they
were exiled, like it [the Light] disappears during the new Moon. It then shone for
them during the entire Second Temple era, when the fire on the altar crouched like a
dog. The two Luminaries set at twilight of the day, and the Temple was destroyed"
(ibid., Gen 2:1).

64. On the symbolism of sefirot as Thrones for one another, Nahmanides writes: "the
word 'Heaven' and the word 'Throne' contain a lofty and esoteric secret, for Heaven
has its own Heaven and the Throne has its own Throne" (ibid., Gen 1:8).

65. Ibid., Gen 18:20.

66. The centrality of the Tif'eret-Shekhinah axis in Nahmanides's thought becomes abun-
dantly clear in his consistent translation of the Attributes of Judgment and Mercy into
the sefirot of Tif'eret and Shekhinah. For example: "By way of truth, [it says YH instead of Y-HWH] because the salvation at the sea was entirely through the Angel of
God, about which it is written, 'for My Name is in it' (Exod 23:21), and as it says, 'And
Israel saw the Great Hand' (Exod 14:31), because the Hand alludes to the Attribute
of Judgment [. . .] They similarly said in the *Mekhilta:* 'When they went down to the
sea, the *Shekhinah* was with them, as it says, "And the Angel of God traveled" (Exod
14:19).' And in *Shemot Rabbah:* 'His Might is none other than Judgment, as it says,
"the Might of the King loves Justice" (Ps 94:4)' " (ibid., Exod 15:2). Nahmanides received a kind of kabbalistic thesaurus that includes the many cognomens of Shekhinah,
which he applies to the Attribute of Judgment. Shekhinah is "the Angel of God"—or,
as Nahmanides suggests, it might be read "the Angel, God"—which bears the Name
of the Lord, and here he identifies it explicitly with the Attribute of Judgment. In the
continuation, he relates to Tif'eret as the Attribute of Mercy.

67. See also Nahmanides's interpretation of "His Heart" in ibid., Gen 6:6, cited below in
the continuation.

68. Ibid., Gen 18:23.

69. Ibid.

70. A similar interaction can be found in the debate between Moses and God: "Then the
Holy One responded to him [Moses]: 'My Countenance shall go' (Exod 23:14)—the
Angel of the Covenant that you desire, in which My Countenance will be visible, and
about which it is said at a propitious time 'for My Name is in it' (Exod 23:21). 'I will
rest (*va-hanihoti*) it for you' (Exod 23:14) so that it will not act with you through the
Strong Attribute of Judgment, but through the Attribute that comprises the Attribute
of Mercy. [This is] from the usage [of the verse] 'It will be that when the Lord your
God gives you rest (*be-haniah*) from all of your enemies' (Deut 25:19), and like the
import of the verse, 'My anger shall be spent and I shall rest (*va-hanihoti*) my fury
through them and be consoled' (Ezek 5:13). Then Moses responded: 'If your
Countenance does not go, with your Essence and Glory, do not take us out of this,
for we want you to be with us Countenance within Countenance.' Because those
were the terms from the Torah portion of *Va-Era,* and thus he mentioned above,
'through Great Power and a Strong Hand' (Exod 32:11). See how he seeks that He

should ascend with them to the land with Great Power and a Strong Hand, just as He took them out of Egypt" (ibid., Exod 33:14). God had said earlier that he would send an Angel, Shekhinah, to lead them: "and Moses said to Him, 'You have not informed me who this angel is that you will send with me, if it is the first Angel which has Your Name in it'" (ibid., Exod 33:12). Shekhinah is the Attribute of Judgment that comprises the Attribute of Mercy, which is why it is not the Strong but Weak Attribute of Judgment. Moses, however, seeks God's presence "Countenance within Countenance," the conjunction of Tif'eret with Shekhinah.

71. Ibid., Exod 3:9.

72. In the same context, Nahmanides says: " 'I am descending to save it [the nation]' (Exod 3:8), for I have revealed Myself upon this mountain in the fire, as in the meaning of [the verse] 'And the Lord descended upon Mount Sinai' (Exod 19:20), because 'the Lord descended upon it in the fire' (Exod 19:18). Alternatively, it is like [the verse] 'I will go down to see whether they have acted altogether according to the Cry that has reached Me' (Gen 18:21), the secret of which I have explained already" (ibid., Exod 3:8). See also Nahmanides's commentary on Exod 2:25, where he cites Sefer Ha-Bahir (Daniel Abrams, ed., *Book Bahir: An Edition Based on the Earliest Manuscripts* [Los Angeles: Cherub, 1994], sec. 51, 147 [Heb.]). According to Nahmanides, Exod 2:23–25 appears to be talking about Tif'eret "remembering" Shekhinah, and "God knew" (*y-d-'*) indicates the intimate connection between man and wife, as in the usage of that root at the beginning of Genesis.

73. *PHT,* Gen 6:6.

74. On the verse "behold I am devastating them with (*et*) the Earth" (Gen 6:9), Nahmanides comments: "By way of truth it is like '*et* Heaven and *et* Earth' (Gen 1:1), because the Earth will be devastated, and through the distancing of the Earth they will be devastated, making them devastated for the World to Come, in the manner of [the verse] '[the Lord] was angry at His Heart' (Gen 6:6). This is what they [the Sages] alluded to in *Bereshit Rabbah:* '[Like] a prince who had a wet nurse, whenever he would do something offensive his wet nurse would be chastised etc.' " (ibid., Gen 6:9). The "Earth," Shekhinah, is devastated on account of humanity's sins because they cause Tif'eret to pull away from it, which leads to the destruction of humankind.

75. Ibid., Gen 9:12.

76. Ibid., Lev 26:42.

77. On the history of this typology, see Gerson D. Cohen, "Esau as Symbol in Early Medieval Thought," in Cohen, *Studies in the Variety of Rabbinic Cultures* (Philadelphia: Jewish Publication Society, 1991), 243–269.

78. *SHG, KR,* 1:284.

79. See Israel Jacob Yuval, *Two Nations in Your Womb: Perceptions of Jews and Christians in Late Antiquity and the Middle Ages,* trans. Barbara Harshav and Jonathan Chipman (Berkeley: University of California Press, 2006), 1–30.

80. *PHT,* Exod 17:9. The connections between Moses and Elijah and between Joshua and Messiah son of Joseph are not coincidental because Joshua was a descendant of Joseph.

81. On Balaam's prophecy, "Edom becomes a possession, Yea, Seir a possession of its enemies, but Israel is triumphant" (Num 24:18), Nahmanides writes: "The downfall of
Edom will be by the hand of the Messiah, because our current exile under the dominion of Rome is considered to be Edom's [. . .] That is why Balaam mentioned Edom,
because it is he who contests our sovereignty, and concerning him it is said, 'one people
shall be mightier than the other' (Gen 25:23). He prophesies that Edom's collapse will
not be complete until the eschaton at the hand of the rising star" (ibid., Num 24:18).

82. The equation of Esau, Edom, Rome, and Christianity enables Nahmanides to better
understand the number and character of the princes of Edom mentioned at the end
of Va-Yishlah: "Their [the Sages'] intent in this [midrash in Pirkei de-Rabbi Eli'ezer] is
what I have told you a number of times, that the occurrences of the primogenitors are
a hint to their descendants. These last princes number ten plus Magdiel, an allusion
to the ten kings of Edom who would rule as the fourth kingdom, ruling over the
Land of Edom, and the tenth would rule over Rome, whence their kingdom would
spread subsequently to the entire world" (ibid., Gen 36:43). Another parallel between
the history of Rome and that of Esau's progeny can be found on Nahmanides's comment on "Therein they buried Isaac," ibid., Gen 49:31.

83. See R. Saadia Gaon, Dani'el 'im Targum u-Ferush Rabbenu Sa'adya, trans. and ed.
Yosef Kafih (Jerusalem: Ha-Va'ad le-Hotza'at Sifrei Rasag, 1980), Ar. original 268–
270, Heb. trans. 552–553. On the identification of the fourth beast with Ishmael, see
Ibn Ezra to Dan 7:11, and see also Maimonides, "Iggeret Teiman," in Iggerot ha-Rambam, ed. Yitzhak Shailat, vol. 1 (Ma'aleh Adumim: Shailat Press, 1995), 123–124, and
in English translation, "Epistle to Yemen," in A Maimonides Reader, ed. Isadore
Twersky (New York: Behrman House, 1972), 443–444.

84. PHT, Num 24:20.

85. Ibid.

86. SHG, KR, 1:287.

87. On the attempt to create such a genealogy in Sefer Yosippon, see Cohen, "Esau."

88. SHG, KR, 1:284–285.

89. This may also be connected to the metaphysical origin of Esau; see Nahmanides's
commentary on the he-goat sent to Azazel discussed below, ch. 7, sec. III.

90. From our discussion here, one can see the full complexity of Nahmanides's relationship to rabbinic literature and the Aggadah. Rabbinic sources created the Edom-
Rome typology, and the shortest route to extend it to Christianity is through the
Christianization of the Roman Empire. Nahmanides is dissatisfied with this because
the Edom-Rome link is weak—they were, in fact, two different nations. Instead, he
weaves Edom into the origins of Christianity and completes the Roman connection
via the Christianization of the Roman Empire.

91. PHT, Gen 32:9.

92. In his commentary on the struggle between Jacob and the angel and the resulting
wound, which the midrash understands as an allusion to a period of religious persecution, Nahmanides hints to the Crusaders: "There have been other generations
where they treated us like this or even worse, but we have suffered it all and it has
passed, as it hinted, 'And Jacob arrived sound' (Gen 33:18)" (ibid., Gen 32:26).

93. Ibid., Deut 28:42.

94. For discussion of messianic calculations tied to the millennium, see Yuval, *Two Nations*, 257–295.

95. *SHG, KR*, 1:290.

96. Ibid.

97. "He said, from the time the regular offering is abolished through the destruction of the Temple, until the complete annihilation of the abomination that abolished it, will be 1290 years. At that time, Messiah son of Ephraim, about whom we have a tradition, will be revealed and lay waste to the abomination. The tradition about him in *Pirkei Heikhalot* relates that for forty years he will gather in some of the far-flung, wage wars, and die in the war of Gog, after which Messiah son of David will be revealed and defeat them, and he will gather us all in and purify us" (ibid., 1:291).

98. See ibid., 1:294. One arrives at the number of years the Jewish people inhabited the land of Israel as follows: 440 years before the building of the First Temple, 410 for which the First Temple stood, 19 years between the return authorized by Cyrus until the building of the Second Temple, and 420 years for which the Second Temple stood.

99. See ibid.

100. *PHT*, Gen 2:3.

101. In this piece, Nahmanides also relates to the distinction between the creatures of the sea and the birds created on the fifth day, and the animals created on the sixth day. The animals represent a more highly developed stage of the nations, which Nahmanides seems to attribute to Islam: "there will arise a new empire, a dominant, powerful, and exceedingly terrifying nation." This language is used to describe Daniel's fourth beast (Dan 7:7), and unless Nahmanides is merely borrowing a biblical expression here, he is deviating from his usual identification of Daniel's fourth beast with Christianity. This also seems difficult because of the fact that the rise of Ishmael-Islam occurred centuries before the beginning of the sixth millennium. Yuval speculates that perhaps Nahmanides refers to the conquest of Jerusalem by the Mamluks at the beginning of the millennium; see Yuval, *Two Nations*, 299–300.

CHAPTER 7. THE REASONS FOR THE COMMANDMENTS

1. See Yehezkel Kaufmann, *Toledot ha-Emunah ha-Yisre'elit mi-Yemei Kedem 'Ad Sof Bayit Sheni* (Tel-Aviv: Mosad Bialik 'al yedei Devir, 1947), 2:532–588.

2. On Scholem's basic agreement with Kaufmann in describing Talmudic ritual, see Gershom Scholem, *On the Kabbalah and Its Symbolism*, trans. Ralph Manheim (New York: Schocken, 1965), 120–122. See further below, Conclusion.

3. For an attempt to uncover the midrashic and Talmudic sources that kabbalah draws on and develops, see Moshe Idel, *Kabbalah: New Perspectives* (New Haven: Yale University Press, 1988), 156–199. See at length in Yehuda Liebes, "*De Natura Dei:* On the Development of the Jewish Myth," in *Studies in Jewish Myth and Messianism*, trans. Batya Stein (Albany: State University of New York Press, 1993), 1–64. See also Yair Lorberbaum, *Image of God* (Jerusalem: Schocken, 2004), 156–169 (Heb.), and esp. 166–169 for more on the concept of theurgy and a summary of the various scholarly positions.

4. See, for example, Ephraim E. Urbach, *The Sages, Their Concepts and Beliefs*, trans. Israel Abrahams (Jerusalem: Magnes, 1975), 98–101.

5. *PHT*, Exod 17:12.

6. Like the Geronese kabbalists, Nahmanides interprets "Truth" as a symbol for Tif'eret and "Faith" as a symbol for Shekhinah. See what Nahmanides writes about the sefirotic source of the soul through "Truth and Faith" in ibid., Gen 2:7.

7. On the iconicity of the human body and its capacity for theurgic activity, see below, sec. IV. A parallel to this can be found in the writings of R. Ezra of Gerona; see Yakov M. Travis, "Kabbalistic Foundations of Jewish Spiritual Practice: Rabbi Ezra of Gerona—On the Kabbalistic Meaning of the Mizvot," PhD diss., Brandeis University, 2002, 229–231 in Eng., 23–24 in Heb. (= *KR*, 2:530).

8. *PHT*, Num 6:24.

9. Nahmanides hints here that "the Keeper" is Shekhinah. For more on the secret of "Remember" and "Keep," see above, ch. 5, sec. II.

10. On the secret of the Countenance, see ch. 5, notes 8–9.

11. On the "I" as a cognomen of Shekhinah, see ch. 5, end of note 14. In Nahmanides's writings, "Peace" symbolizes the unification of Shekhinah with Yesod or Tif'eret. On the absence of a sin offering as one of the additional offerings on the Sabbath, Nahmanides writes: "unlike the rest of the additional sacrifices [on holidays], there is no sin-offering among the additional sacrifices on the Sabbath because the Congregation of Israel [i.e., *Shekhinah*] is its consort and the All (*Ha-Kol*) is Peace—the enlightened will understand" (*PHT*, Num 28:2). In his comment on the verse "I shall bring Peace into the Land" (Lev 26:6), Nahmanides treats "Peace" as referring both to a particular sefirah and to a state of unification: "By way of truth, He will bring Peace into conjunction with the Land, and this is the Peace of the All (*Ha-Kol*), which is equivalent to the All (*Ha-Kol*)" (*PHT*, Lev 26:6).

12. See R. Shem Tov Ibn Gaon, *Keter Shem Tov*, 127v(d)–128r(b), and R. Meir b. Solomon Abusahulah, *Be'ur le-Feirush ha-Ramban 'al ha-Torah*, ed. Jacob Shapira (Warsaw, 1875), 29a.

13. See Urbach, *The Sages*, 376–383, with 850–851n40.

14. On the history of the distinction between *hukkim* and *mishpatim* and its significance in rabbinic sources and medieval thought, see Yitzhak Heinemann, *Ta'amei ha-Mitzvot be-Sifrut Yisra'el*, 5th ed., vol. 1 (Jerusalem: ha-Mador ha-dati ba-Mahlakah le-'inyenei ha-no'ar ve-he-halutz shel ha-Histadrut ha-Tziyyonit, 1966).

15. Rashi on Lev 19:19.

16. *PHT*, Lev 18:6.

17. Ibid., Lev 19:19. An additional formulation of this position emerges from Nahmanides's lengthy discourse on the reasons for the commandments, which appears in his comment on the commandment to shoo away the mother bird before taking the eggs: "They [the Sages] have explained that the only obstacle to [grasping] the Torah's reasons is the blindness of our intellect, and that the reason for the most inscrutable of them [the commandments] was revealed to the Sages of Israel. They have made many similar statements, and there are many indications of this in the Pentateuch and the rest of Scripture" (ibid., Deut 22:6). Concerning the question of the wise son,

"and what are the *hukkim*," Nahmanides writes: "because their reason is concealed in the Torah" (ibid., Deut 6:20), and elsewhere: "because of the concealment of the reason for the *hukkim*" (ibid., Deut 5:4). Nahmanides believes that the etymology of *hok* has zero connection to a fiat. Thus, while Rashi followed the midrash in explaining the clause "There He set for them a *hok* and *mishpat*" (Exod 15:25) to mean laws with reasons and those without, Nahmanides gives a different explanation: "a rule is called a *hok*, as in: 'provide me my regular (*hukki*) bread' (Prov 30:8), 'the rules (*hukkot*) of heaven and earth' (Jer 33:25)" (ibid., Exod 15:25). Nahmanides understands *hok* to imply regularity and order.

18. Ibid., Deut 22:6.

19. On Nahmanides's indebtedness to and divergence from Maimonides on the issue of the reasons for the commandments, see at length Josef Stern, *Problems and Parables of Law: Maimonides and Nahmanides on Reasons for the Commandments* (Albany: SUNY Press, 1998), chs. 4 and 6.

20. *The Guide of the Perplexed*, translated with introduction and notes by Shlomo Pines (Chicago: University of Chicago Press, 1963), III:48.

21. Nahmanides works hard to give a detailed explanation of those rabbinic turns of phrase that imply the commandments' arbitrariness. He argues that the phrase *gezerat melekh*, which is typically understood to mean divine fiat, does not necessarily mean the decree is baseless. He also interprets the dictum which states that the commandments were not given except "to refine people" as referring to actual refinement of character and not a mere test of character. On this, see *PHT*, Deut 22:6. For a discussion of Nahmanides's position in this piece, where he explains the commandments as being for humans' benefit alone, and his position to be discussed below, namely, that the commandments fulfill a divine need, see Stern, *Problems and Parables*, 81–85.

22. Maimonides uses very harsh language when inveighing against the magical understanding of the commandments and ritual objects. See Mishneh Torah, "Laws of Idolatry," 1:2; "Laws of the Phylacteries and the Mezuzah," 5:4 and 6:13. See also *Mishnah 'im Perush Rabbenu Moshe ben Maimon: Maqor ve-Targum*, ed. Yosef Kafih, vol. 3: *Seder Nashim* (Jerusalem: Mossad Harav Kook, 1964), Sotah 7.4. See also *Guide*, I:63, concerning the holy names of God. On this issue, see the long discussion in Aviezer Ravitzky, "Maimonides and His Disciples on Linguistic Magic and 'the Madness of the Writers of Amulets,' " in *Jewish Culture in the Eye of the Storm: A Jubilee Book in Honor of Yosef Ahituv*, ed. Abraham Sagi and Nahem Ilan (Tel-Aviv: ha-Kibbutz ha-Me'uhad, 2002), 431–458 (Heb.).

23. See above, the beginning of ch. 5.

24. *PHT*, Lev 1:9.

25. Maimonides believes that the key to understanding the hukkim lies in the ancient pagan context in which the Torah set forth its commandments. On his view, the Torah neutralizes idolatry through two kinds of commandments: one kind requires the performance of activities that are quite similar to pagan rituals in order to channel them in the right direction and limit their impact, and another kind demands actions that are essentially opposed to pagan practices. Some of Maimonides's critics argued that his historicization of the commandments would undermine the authority of

halakhah, for once the reasons behind the commandments no longer apply, presumably their meaning goes with them. Nahmanides explains most hukkim theurgically, but he does not eschew historical explanations within the philological-contextual, or peshat, level of interpretation. For example, he explains the prohibition against planting an *asherah* tree as follows: "It prohibited it because it is the practice of idolaters to plant trees at the entrance of their temples" (ibid., Deut 16:21). He also cites Maimonides's explanation of the prohibition against offering leaven or honey upon the altar as perfectly plausible: "The reason for [prohibiting] leaven and honey may be what the Master [Maimonides] wrote in *The Guide of the Perplexed.* He said that he found in their books that idolaters had a practice to offer all of their bread-offerings with leaven and to baste all of their sacrifices with honey; therefore, it prohibited them to the Most High" (ibid., Lev 2:11). In his comment about the prohibition on mixing wool and linen, Nahmanides also quotes Maimonides's historical explanation without any real objection (ibid., Lev 19:19). See also what Nahmanides writes about the prohibition on eating blood and its complex relationship with Maimonides's historical explanation in ibid., Deut 12:22. In certain places, Nahmanides disagrees with Maimonides's historical explanation, but he does not see the historical interpretation as an inherently invalid approach. On occasion, Nahmanides even proposes an alternative historical explanation, such as his reason for the prohibition against using iron in the construction of the altar in ibid., Deut 20:23. On Nahmanides's historical-contextual interpretation of the commandments and the Maimonidean connection, see Stern, *Problems and Parables,* 134–136.

26. *PHT,* Lev 1:9.

27. Ibid.

28. Ibid.

29. Ibid. This secret of the sacrifice appears elsewhere in Nahmanides's writings as well; see ibid., Gen 7:1 and 12:6, Num 15:25 and 28:2. He also writes about how Jethro did not comprehend it in ibid., Exod 18:13. Although Nahmanides understands sacrifices to be intended for the Tetragrammaton, he still maintains that there can be nuances and differences of emphasis in the various sacrifices; see what he says about the incense offering in ibid., Exod 30:1. See, as well, his commentary on the sin-offering of the *nasi* in ibid., Lev 4:2. This can affect whether a sacrifice should be male or female; see ibid., Lev 3:1 and 5:15. On the difference between a fire-offering and peace-offering, see ibid., Gen 46:1.

30. Ibid., Gen 2:8.

31. For Nahmanides's notion of the Garden of Eden, see above, ch. 3, sec. V, and ch. 4, sec. VI.

32. *PHT,* Gen 2:8.

33. In another place Nahmanides writes in a similar vein: "And in *Bereshit Rabbah:* 'Another explanation: "to work (*le-'ovdah*) it and preserve (*u-le-shomrah*) it"— these are the sacrifices, for it says "you shall serve (*ta'avdun*) God on this mountain" (Exod 3:12), which is what is written, "you shall make sure (*tishmeru*) to offer to Me at its appointed time" (Num 28:2).' They hinted that the sacrifices cause growth and development of the Tree of Life, the Tree of Will, and the other trees of the

Garden of Eden, and they [the sacrifices] are their work and preservation" (*PHT,* Gen 3:22).

34. For more on the land of Israel, see below, sec. II.

35. See above, ch. 3.

36. For various conceptions of theurgy and the distinction between restorative theurgy and theurgy of the status quo, see Charles Mopsik, *Les grands textes de la Cabale: Les rites qui font Dieu* (Lagrasse: Verdier, 1993).

37. "Or it alludes that the essence (*ikkar*) of all the commandments is in the land, as I hinted to in the secret of the land" (*PHT,* Deut 4:5).

38. *PHT,* Lev 18:25. See also ibid., Deut 11:18, and *DDK, KR,* 1:200–202.

39. On Halevi's approach to the land of Israel, see Yochanan Silman, "The Earthliness of Eretz Israel," in *The Land of Israel in Medieval Jewish Thought,* ed. Moshe Hallamish and Aviezer Ravitzky (Jerusalem: Ben-Zvi Institute, 1991), 79–89 (Heb.).

40. On the uniqueness of Nahmanides's position on this, see Aviezer Ravitzky, " 'Waymarks to Zion': The History of an Idea," in *The Land of Israel,* ed. Hallamish and Ravitzky, 8–13 (Heb.).

41. *PHT,* Lev 18:25.

42. See also *DTHT,* 30 (= *KR,* 1:143). For the climatic theories about the land of Israel in the Middle Ages, see Abraham Melamed, "The Land of Israel and Climate Theory in Medieval Jewish Thought," and Dov Schwartz, "Land, Place, Star: The Status of the Land of Israel in Neoplatonic Thought of the Fourteenth Century," in *The Land of Israel,* ed. Hallamish and Ravitzky, 52–78 and 138–150 (Heb.).

43. *PHT,* Lev 18:25.

44. On the kabbalistic symbolism of the land of Israel in Nahmanides's thought, see Haviva Pedaya,"The Spiritual vs. the Concrete Land of Israel in the Geronese School of Kabbalah," in *The Land of Israel,* ed. Hallamish and Ravitzky, 264–270 (Heb.). Pedaya raises the possibility that "the Earth" is a cognomen of Hokhmah in Nahmanides's kabbalistic symbolism; however, in Nahmanides's kabbalistic interpretation of Deut 32:1, he writes: "By way of truth, they are the primordial Heaven and Earth mentioned in *be-reshit,* for it is they that enter the covenant with Israel. Therefore, he [Moses] said that they should listen and hear the conditions and how it will be made through them. And he said, 'Let My Takeaway fall like rain' (Deut 32:2), because what he took from Heaven and his Utterance from Earth will fall upon Israel and flow upon them. 'For when I call the Name of the Lord' (Deut 32:3), through Heaven, 'render greatness to our God,' through the Earth—and he is speaking to Israel. Joshua's 'stone' also alludes to this Earth, because 'from there it shepherds the Stone of Israel' (Gen 49:24), which I have already explained. Likewise, 'The Stone which the Builders rejected became the Keystone; This is from the Lord' (Ps 118:22–23). Joshua therefore said, 'The Stone, This, shall be a witness for us' (Josh 24:27). Also: 'For behold the Stone which I placed before Joshua, on the one Stone are seven Appearances etc.' (Zach 3:9). The enlightened will understand" (*PHT,* Deut 32:1–3). Nahmanides identifies "the Earth," Shekhinah, which served as a witness to the covenant with the Israelites, with the symbolic stone erected by Joshua as a testimony. He then brings a series of verses that include "the Stone" as a symbol for

Shekhinah, some that also mention "This," another cognomen for Shekhinah—"the Stone of Israel," "the Keystone," etc. On "the Stone" as a cognomen for Shekhinah, see Nahmanides's comment on Gen 49:24, which he alluded to in the quotation above: " 'From there'—from the Hands of the Mighty One of Jacob, it shepherds the Stone of Israel, this is the 'plumb Stone' (Zach 4:7), which was the Keystone from the Lord (Ps 118:22–23). It is called 'the Stone of Israel,' like the Sages said, 'the Congregation of Israel.' The meaning behind 'Stone' is that in the Structure it completes the All (*Ha-Kol*)." Nahmanides, then, explicitly considers the primordial "Earth" to be a reference to Shekhinah.

45. On the earthly hyle and the chain of being, see ch. 4, sec. I.

46. *PHT,* Deut 11:10.

47. Ibid., Gen 19:5. He writes further, elsewhere: " 'the God of Heaven and the God of the Earth (*ha-Aretz*)': the Holy One is called the God of the land (*eretz*) of Israel, as it is written, 'they did not know the law of the God of the land (*ha-aretz*)' (2 Kgs 17:26), and it is written, 'They spoke about the God of Jerusalem as [they spoke] about the gods of the nations of the earth' (2 Chr 32:19). There is a secret in this that I shall yet write, with God's help" (ibid., Gen 24:3).

48. Ibid., Lev 26:6.

49. See above, ch. 4, sec. V.

50. Perhaps Nahmanides's belief that the kabbalistic significance of observing the commandments is limited to the land of Israel drove his relocation to the Kingdom of Acre. One hears an echo of this in his *Discourse on Rosh ha-Shanah* delivered in Acre. At one point, he explains the presence of Shekhinah in the land of Israel and says that the land's spiritual stature brought him there: "This is what brought me out of my land and displaced me from my residence. I have left my home, I have abandoned my heritage; I have become like a crow to my sons, cruel to my daughters, because I want the wandering of my soul to be in my mother's bosom." Although the final clause here is corrupt (this translation follows Chavel's emendation in *DRH, KR,* 1:151), the gist of it remains the same. Concerning the motives for Nahmanides's move to the land of Israel, see Moshe Idel, "On the Land of Israel in Medieval Jewish Mysticism," in *The Land of Israel,* ed. Hallamish and Ravitzky, 205–206 (Heb.). For a different explanation for Nahmanides's move, which is tied to his understanding of the land of Israel as a gate and ladder, see Pedaya, "Spiritual vs. Concrete," 285–286.

51. *PHT,* Lev 18:25. For more effects of this causal connection between Shekhinah and the land, see Nahmanides's commentary on the sartorial and domiciliary *tzara'at* that occurred only in the land of Israel, in ibid., Lev 13:47.

52. Ibid., Gen 26:5.

53. Ibid., Lev 18:25.

54. In a variety of other instances, Nahmanides similarly explains that pre-Sinaitic personalities in the Bible observed commandments not out of obligation but out of their knowledge of the underlying causal mechanism. About the levirate marriage that Er and Onan refused to perform with Tamar, he writes: "In fact, this matter is one of the Torah's greatest secrets about the nature of man, which can be seen by the perceptive, to whom the Lord has given eyes to see and ears to hear. The wise ancients who lived

before [the giving of] the Torah knew that there was a great benefit in levirate marriage, such that the brother should be first and afterwards other relatives, for any close
kin from his family who inherits provides [this] benefit. Customarily, the brother or
father or a close relative married the widow of the deceased, but we do not know if
this custom predated Judah. In *Bereshit Rabbah* they [the Sages] said that Judah was
first to observe the commandment of levirate marriage, because having received the
secret from his ancestors he was eager to fulfill it. When the Torah later forbade
the wife of some relatives, the Holy One wished to lift the prohibition concerning the
wife of one's brother for levirate marriage, but not the prohibition concerning the
wife of a paternal uncle, son, or others, because it was more common with the brother
and its benefit surer than with them, as I have mentioned. [. . .] The ancient sages of
Israel, in their knowledge of this lofty matter, established the ancient practice to perform this act with all heirs so long as there was no prohibition of consanguinity, and
they called it 'redemption,' which is the matter of Boaz and the meaning of [the
words of] Naomi and her neighbors. The enlightened will understand" (ibid., Gen
38:8). In addition, see Nahmanides's discussion of the prohibition on sexual relations
with a menstruant in ibid., Gen 31:35 (and for more about the menstruant, see ibid.,
Lev 12:4 and 18:19). It is worth noting that this causal basis of the law is much broader
than the law itself. In the earlier stage, any relative could perform the levirate marriage, but later, after the giving of the Torah, only the brother may do so. This pattern
recurs with the treatment of the menstruant, as many of the strictures found in the
Baraita de-Niddah are not accepted in halakhah even by Nahmanides, who fails to
mention many of them in his Hilkhot Niddah.

55. *PHT,* Exod 20:3.
56. Nahmanides also writes about the ability to prophesy through teraphim: "The word
[*terafim*] is derived from 'weak-handed (*refeh yadayim*)' (2 Sam 17:2), 'you are weak
(*nirpim*)' (Exod 5:17). They are called 'weak' (*rafim*) so that their name alludes to the
fact that their oracle is like a weak prophecy, which mostly comes true but disap-
points on rare occasion, as it says, 'for the teraphim have spoken delusion' (Zach
10:2). See how those of little faith would make them into their gods" (ibid., Gen
31:19). In the same vein, see his discussion of how false prophets mostly have prophecies of real substance in ibid., Deut 13:2.
57. See *DTHT,* 45–50 (= *KR,* 1:149–150).
58. Elsewhere Nahmanides writes: "The matter is clear without it if you contemplate what
Separate Intellects and spirits have to do with a sacrifice. This can be known about
spirits through the science of necromancy, and it also can be known about the Intellects
through the Torah's hints, for those who understand their secret—but I cannot explain. We need to muzzle the mouths of the natural philosophizers who are drawn
after the Greek, who denied [the existence of] everything that he could not apprehend
with his senses, and had the gall to suspect—he and his wicked students—anything
that he could not apprehend with his reason of being untrue" (*PHT,* Lev 16:8). For
Nahmanides, demons are a part of the natural world. Acknowledging their existence
does not require a leap of faith because it is empirically supported. Nahmanides presents an alternative account that rivals that of the philosophers; see ibid., Lev 17:7.

59. *DDK, KR,* 1:200. See also *PHT,* Lev 18:25.

60. *PHT,* Deut 18:9.

61. On the notion of the divine "desire," see above, ch. 4, sec. IV.

62. For Nahmanides's scientific worldview, see Y. Tzvi Langermann, "Acceptance and Devaluation: Nahmanides' Attitude towards Science," *Journal of Jewish Thought and Philosophy* 1 (1992): 223–245.

63. See *Guide,* III:37.

64. On Maimonides's attitude toward magic, see Isadore Twersky, "Halakha and Science: Perspectives on the Epistemology of Maimonides," *Shenaton ha-Mishpat ha-'Ivri* 14–15 (1988–1989): 136–147 (Heb.); Twersky, *Introduction to the Code of Maimonides* (Mishneh Torah) (New Haven: Yale University Press, 1980), 479–484; and Dov Schwartz, "Magic, Experimental Science, and Scientific Method in Maimonides' Teachings," in *Joseph Baruch Sermoneta Memorial Volume,* ed. Aviezer Ravitzky (Jerusalem: Hebrew University, 1998), 25–45 (Heb.). On the debate between Maimonides and Nahmanides about the status of magic, see Stern, *Problems and Parables,* ch. 4.

65. *DTHT,* 40–41 (= *KR,* 1:147).

66. *Guide,* III:37.

67. *PHT,* Exod 20:3.

68. Ibid., Exod 32:7.

69. Ibid., Exod 32:1.

70. Nahmanides writes: "The meaning of 'bulls for the Lord' is that the whole time Israel was in the wilderness they feared the Attribute of Judgment, and this was their error in making the [golden] calf" (ibid., Exod 24:5).

71. Ibid., Exod 32:1. On the connection between the astrological and kabbalistic in Nahmanides's commentary and his attitude toward Ibn Ezra, see Dov Schwartz, *Studies on Astral Magic in Medieval Jewish Thought,* trans. David Louvish and Batya Stein (Leiden: Brill, 2005), 55–66.

72. For more on Nahmanides's understanding of idolatry, see Moshe Halbertal and Avishai Margalit, *Idolatry,* trans. Naomi Goldblum (Cambridge, MA: Harvard University Press, 1992), ch. 7.

73. See above, sec. I.

74. *PHT,* Lev 10:2.

75. For the explanation of the symbol "This," see ch. 5, note 14.

76. On the sin of Adam and "the cutting of the saplings," see above, ch. 3, secs. VI–VII. In other contexts within Nahmanides's oeuvre, this "cutting" is quite clearly the separation of Shekhinah from the rest of the sefirotic configuration. A good example is his explanation of the four species. He understands the taking of the citron, symbolizing Shekhinah, together with the palm bundle, symbolizing Tif'eret and other sefirot, as a unification intended to undo the disunity that resulted from Adam taking the Fruit, symbolized by the citron, from the Tree, symbolized by the palm (see *PHT,* Lev 23:40). For additional material on the "cutting" directed at Shekhinah, see his commentary on the verse "Whoever slaughters to *elohim* will be proscribed, except to the Lord alone" (Exod 22:19): "Along these lines there is also something very profound

here, from which the secret of the sacrifices can be understood, and the enlightened can figure it out from what we have written elsewhere" (ibid., Exod 22:19). The exoteric reading of *elohim* is the "angels on high," but esoterically it is Shekhinah, to the exclusion of Tif'eret. Nahmanides's conception of "cutting down the saplings" also emerges in his discussion of the order of the shofar blowing. According to his opinion, a teruah alludes to the Attribute of Judgment, to Shekhinah: "the teruah alludes to the Attribute of Judgment [. . .] therefore Moses said, 'your enemies will scatter and your foes will flee before Your Countenance' (Num 10:31), and I have already explained the secret of the Countenance in [my commentary on] the Ten Commandments" (ibid., Num 10:6). The tekiah alludes to the Attribute of Mercy: "the extended blast (*peshutah*) alludes to the Attribute of Mercy, for His Right is extended (*peshutah*) to receive penitents" (ibid.). See also *DRH, KR,* 1:220–221. The sequence of tekiah-teruah-tekiah symbolizes the unity of the sefirotic configuration: "The Rabbis transmitted [the tradition]: an extended blast before it and an extended blast after it, and a teruah in the middle, so that one does not cut down the saplings on the New Year or Day of Atonement, and over the sacrifice, but the intent is that this is for the Tekiah [i.e., *Tif'eret*] and that is for the Teruah [i.e., *Shekhinah*]. The enlightened will understand" (*PHT,* Num 10:6). In another place Nahmanides writes: "By way of truth it says, 'Take great care . . . lest you destroy (*tashhitun*)' (Deut 4:15–16), because the Lord grew angry with me out of concern about this: 'Lest you forget the Covenant of the Lord your God through the consuming fire atop the mountain, and make for yourselves an image of All (*Kol*)'" (ibid., Deut 4:21). The "destruction" here of "cutting down the saplings" is through worshipping "the image of All," which is Shekhinah, referred to as "All." The Israelites are liable to "cut down the saplings" because Shekhinah appeared to them in the fire on top of the mountain, so they are forbidden from forgetting "the Covenant of the Lord your God," namely, the presence of Tif'eret within Shekhinah. On the Sinaitic revelation as an event that could lead to "cutting down the saplings," Nahmanides writes: " 'Take great care' (Deut 4:15)—he [Moses] is warning them lest they be led astray by the voice they heard and cause destruction by cutting down the saplings" (ibid., Deut 4:15). R. Azriel's commentary on the Aggadah contains a different perspective on "cutting down the saplings," according to which the cutters concentrate on Din and Hesed in their divine service and leave out Tif'eret and Shekhinah. See R. Azriel of Gerona, *Commentary on Talmudic Aggadoth,* ed. Isaiah Tishby, 2nd ed. (Jerusalem: Magnes, 1982), 16–18 (Heb.).

77. *DTHT,* 103 (= *KR,* 1:172).
78. Ibid., 104 (= *KR,* 1:172).
79. *PHT,* Exod 32:1.
80. *DTHT,* 105 (= *KR,* 1:173). This idea has important halakhic implications regarding magic, because by limiting the kinds of prohibited magical activity, Nahmanides creates an overlap between idolatry and magic, practically speaking. This explains why he permitted the creation of a talisman in the form of a lion for medical purposes, as his main disciple R. Solomon Ibn Adret (Rashba) attested: "I heard from my master R. Moses b. Nahman that he would make it in the form of a lion, like you are saying,

and he had no reservations" (*She'elot u-Teshuvot ha-Rashba* [Jerusalem: Makhon Yerushalayim, 1997], 1:825). Similarly, in one of his own responsa, Nahmanides limits the prohibitions against augury and soothsaying in a polemic against Maimonides's opinion. According to him, people should not consult their horoscope ab initio, but they may coordinate their activity on the basis of astrological considerations, assuming they are general astrological principles known to the public or more specific ones known to the individual through prior halakhic violation. Not only that, but unless one is exceptionally pious, one must act on the basis of astrological considerations because one may not rely upon a miracle. On this, see *KR*, 1:378–381. Concerning Nahmanides's understanding of power and influence, see Jonathan Garb, *Manifestations of Power in Jewish Mysticism* (Jerusalem: Magnes, 2004/2005), 105–112 (Heb.).

81. *PHT*, Lev 16:8.

82. Ibid. In an additional piece, Nahmanides describes a subcategory within hukkim that receives the scorn of idolaters; see ibid., Lev 19:19. Nahmanides repeats this in his commentary on the performance of the red heifer ritual outside the Temple (ibid., Lev 19:20), on the heifer whose neck is broken (ibid., Deut 21:4), and on the purification of the *metzora'* and its connection to the secret of the scapegoat (ibid., Lev 21:4, end). See also ibid., Exod 29:14.

83. Ibid., Num 19:2.

84. Nahmanides explains the prohibition against certain kinds of admixtures along these lines, too: "one who grafts two species alters and challenges the order of Creation, as if he considers that the Holy One did not sufficiently perfect the world, and he wishes to lend a hand in creating the world by adding creations to it" (ibid., Lev 19:19). In the same piece, Nahmanides adds a kabbalistic interpretation that he ascribes to a "colleague": "One of our fellows (*me-havereinu*) adds another reason for forbidden mixtures, so that one does not confuse the potencies that grow the flora such that one suckles from the other. [. . .] I have already written on the portion of *Be-Reshit* (Gen 1:11) that the Foundations of all plants are in the Supernal Ones, whence the Lord commands the Blessing, Life to the World. Thus, whoever mixes forbidden mixtures contradicts and confounds the order of Creation" (ibid.). Nahmanides appears to be quoting R. Ezra of Gerona's explanation for the prohibition of forbidden mixtures, which appears in his composition on the 613 commandments; see Travis, "Kabbalistic Foundations," 273–274 in Eng., 54 in Heb. (= *KR*, 2:544). See R. Isaac of Acre, *Sefer Me'irat 'Einayim by R. Isaac of Acre*, ed. Amos Goldreich (Jerusalem: Hebrew University, 1981), 8 (Heb.), and *PHT*, Gen 1:11.

85. On Nahmanides's understanding of humans as "the image of God," see above, ch. 3, note 64.

86. For the reason underlying circumcision, see *PHT*, Gen 17:9.

87. See above, sec. I.

88. "Since the All (*Ha-Kol*) within the All (*Ba-Kol*) is the Sign on the Hand, our ancestors transmitted from the mouth of the Almighty that it should be a single house, as in the import of the verse, 'My Sister (*Ahoti*) the Bride (*Kallah*) is My Sister' (Songs 5:1), because it [*Shekhinah*] is unified (*mit'ahedet*) and comprises (*kelulah*) the thirty-two

paths [of wisdom], and it is written: 'His Left is beneath My Head' (Songs 2:5). And it says, 'as a remembrance between your eyes' (Exod 13:9), that they [the four houses] must be placed in the place of remembrance, between the eyes where the brain begins, and this is the Beginning of Remembrance, holding the Forms after they leave its presence, and they surround the entire head with their straps, and the knot is at the Back of the brain which Keeps the Remembrance" (*PHT,* Exod 13:16). The left arm on which the phylactery is placed symbolizes Shekhinah as it comprises the All, which is why its multiple passages must be housed in a single unit. The phylactery on the head, however, is placed between the eyes, that is, the part of the head where memory is said to reside, and this apparently symbolizes Binah, in which the divine "Forms," the sefirot, are still distinct from one another. As such, the four pieces of parchment in this phylactery are housed separately. The human body functions here as an iconic structure symbolizing the continuity and unity of the entire sefirotic configuration.

89. Nahmanides writes: "By way of truth, [it is] because man's beginning and end are in the hands and feet, for the hands reach higher than the entire body when raised and the feet are below, and in the human form they are an allusion to the ten *sefirot,* such that the entire body is between them. As they said in *Sefer Yetzirah:* 'He made a covenant with him [Abraham] between the ten fingers of his hands and between the ten toes of his feet through the word of the tongue and the circumcision of the phallus.' Therefore, the servants of the Most High were commanded to wash their hands and feet. This washing is for holiness" (ibid., Exod 30:19).

90. See ibid., Deut 21:22.

91. Ibid., Num 19:2.

92. "Rather, the Remembrance is through the blue (*tekhelet*) thread which alludes to the Attribute that comprises the All (*Ha-Kol*), which is in the All and is the Aim (*Takhlit*) of the All. It therefore said, 'and you shall Remember All (*Kol*),' which is 'the commandment of the Lord' (Num 15:39). This is [the import of] what they said: 'for the blue is similar to the Sea, and the Sea is similar to the Firmament, and the Firmament is similar to the Throne of Glory, etc.' The similarity is in name, and also the color is the boundary (*takhlit*) of visual perception, because from afar all appear in that color, which is why it is called *Tekhelet.* It also said, 'do not stray after your heart' to caution them not to make an error about it, which is what our Rabbis expounded: ' "after your heart" (Num 15:39)—this is heresy; "that you stray" (ibid.)— this is idolatry,' so that from the Blue they should not come to think about heresy or idolatry; instead, the All should be Tzitzith [intertwined], 'and you shall see it and Remember' (ibid.)" (ibid., Num 15:31). Not only does the blue color represent Shekhinah, but the concern about "straying" after one's heart and eyes here appears to be referring to "cutting down the saplings." See the broad color symbolism in ibid., Num 2:7.

93. In his explanation of the reason for taking the citron and palm bundle, Nahmanides makes a connection to Adam's sin: "By way of truth, the 'fruit of the desirable tree' is the Fruit which is most desired and through which Primordial Adam sinned [. . .] Note the sin was through it alone, yet we appease His Countenance together with the

other species. The frond of 'Palms' is the Head, the Median Line is doubled and higher than them all. The 'Branch of a Chain Tree' [the myrtle] alludes to the three *sefirot* on one Branch, as in the import of the verse, 'from the Hands of the Mighty One of Jacob' (Gen 49:24). [. . .] From here you understand and comprehend that the Citron is not included in the [Palm] Bundle yet is a sine qua non for it, for it corresponds to [*Shemini*] *Atzeret*, which is a Festival unto itself and redress of the First. Thus they are one *in potentia* but not *in actu*" (ibid., Lev 23:40).

94. The scriptural emphasis on the tekiah in some contexts and the teruah in others is used by Nahmanides as indicating the symbolic expression of the Attributes of Judgment or Mercy in some particular activity. See, for example, his comment on Num 10:6, cited above in note 76. See the relatively long excursus about the teruah on the New Year and Day of Atonement, and the relationship of the sefirah of Binah, also known by the cognomen "Repentance," to the Attributes of Judgment and Mercy: "Since it comprises Mercy it is preceded and succeeded by a tekiah. It therefore said that 'those who know the Teruah' are 'elevated' through Righteousness, 'because You are the Splendor (*Tif'eret*) of their Might' (Ps 89:16–18). Clearly the All depends upon Repentance, but on the New Year it is unified with the Attribute of Judgment and governs its world, and on the Day of Atonement [it is unified] with the Attribute of Mercy. This is the [meaning of the] Rabbinic saying: 'The King sits on the Throne of Judgment etc.' The New Year is a day of Judgment through Mercy and the Day of Atonement is a day of Mercy through Judgment" (ibid., Lev 23:24). This symbolism of the shofar's sounds also appears in R. Ezra of Gerona's composition on the commandments; see Travis, "Kabbalistic Foundations," 261–263 in Eng., 44 in Heb. (= *KR*, 2:539–540).

95. See *PHT*, Deut 22:6.

96. On the secret of the reading of the Shema', see ibid., Deut 6:4. Nahmanides mentions a separate corpus, a secret that he does not spell out, which he calls "the secret of the blessings"; see ibid., Exod 16:8, with the supercommentary of R. Shem Tov Ibn Gaon in his Keter Shem Tov. See also Nahmanides's comments on "the Blessing," which is none other than the efflux emanated from Binah, in ibid., Exod 15:26. On the intentions during prayer, and the difference between the traditions from the study hall of R. Isaac the Blind and those of Nahmanides, see Moshe Idel, "On R. Isaac Sagi Nahor's Mystical Intention of the Eighteen Benedictions," in *Massu'ot: Studies in Kabbalistic Literature and Jewish Philosophy*, ed. Michal Oron and Amos Goldreich (Tel-Aviv: Bialik Institute, 1994), 42–47 (Heb.).

97. *PHT*, Num 11:16.

98. For a comprehensive talismanic description of how the Israelite camp changed location, see ibid., Num 2:2.

99. Nahmanides sets up a parallelism between the presence of Tif'eret within Shekhinah on Mount Sinai and the indwelling of the Godhead in the Tabernacle and Temple; see *PHT*, Exod 25:25, the introduction to Numbers, and Exod 31:2.

100. *PHT*, Exod 25:21. The priestly vestments also functioned as a talisman; see *PHT*, Exod 28:2 and 28:35.

101. On this, see above, ch. 6, sec. II.

102. See above, sec. I.

103. *PHT,* Exod 29:46.

104. Ibid., Exod 13:16. In Torat Ha-Shem Temimah he writes: "Internalize the fact that the Holy One created all lowly things to benefit and serve man, for beside this we have no other reason for the creation of the lowly flora and fauna that do not recognize their Creator, and He created man so that he would recognize his blessed Creator. But if man does not know the One Who created him at all, and certainly if he does not know that his Creator deems one act chosen and desirable and another repulsive and abominable, then man is like a beast and the purpose of his creation is null" (*DTHT,* 28 [= *KR,* 1:142–143]).

105. *PHT,* Deut 32:26.

106. Ibid.

107. The decisive role humans play in enabling Shekhinah to spread out and down through the various rungs of existence also appears in Nahmanides's interpretation of the sin of Moloch: "They [the Sages] already alluded to this in their *midrash,* when they said: 'Whoever benefits from this world without [making] a blessing is considered to be stealing from the Holy One and the Congregation of Israel, as it says, "Whoever steals from his Father and Mother and says it is no iniquity is a friend to the destroyer (*mashhit*)" (Prov 28:24)—"his Father" is none other than the Holy One [*Tif'eret*], and "his Mother" is none other than the Congregation of Israel [*Shekhinah*]' [. . .] Because the desire (*hefetz*) in creation was that they should bless His Great Name for it, from which the world will be sustained; and if [they do] not, it will be elevated through His Great Name and *Shekhinah* will rise away from Israel. This is all the more true when he brings the fruit to Moloch, for he detests the Pride of Jacob [i.e., *Tif'eret*] and His Tabernacle (*Mishkeno,* i.e., *Shekhinah*)" (ibid., Lev 20:3).

108. For this kind of medical discussion in which he mentions the scientific position of Greek philosophers in a positive light, see ibid., Lev 12:2.

109. Ibid., Lev 19:23. As for why the Torah prohibits consuming fish that lack fins or scales, Nahmanides writes: "The reason for the fins and scales is that those possessing them always live in the upper, clear water and they grow from the air that enters there; therefore, they contain some warmth that keeps out the abundant moisture, in the same way that wool, hair, and nails do so for people and animals. Whatever does not have fins or scales always dwells in the murky sea bottom, and on account of the abundant moisture and absence of heat they keep nothing out, therefore possessing a contagious cold humor, which is nearly lethal, and in some swampy fetid water it is lethal" (ibid., Lev 11:9). See also his comment on the connection between the ritual impurity of the male emission and illness (ibid., Lev 16:11), the connection he makes between optical theory and medicine concerning the *tzara'at* affliction (ibid., Lev 13:3), and the prohibition on having relations with a menstruant and the ensuing harm (ibid., Lev 12:4 and 18:19).

110. Ibid., Deut 14:3. "The reason for the prohibition on the birds is their cruel nature, and perhaps it is true of the animals as well, because none of the ruminants with parted hooves predate, while all the rest are predatory. There is a difference in their

constitution, as the Sages mentioned: the milk of the pure animals curdles, but the milk of the impure does not congeal and can never become cheese—you see that they are different. Perhaps because of this they are harmful to the reproductive organs, so that the seed produced from their humor is cold and moist and cannot produce a child at all or cannot do so properly. [This is] aside from the fact that the permitted animals have a medically sound benefit. I have seen in a few books of medical observations that if a suckling is fed sow's milk then that child will become a leper, and this indicates that all of them have very bad qualities" (ibid., Lev 11:13). About the prohibition against consuming blood he writes in a similar vein: "It is also well known that the ingested food becomes part of the consumer's body and they become one. But if someone consumes the 'soul of the flesh,' it combines with his blood to become one in his heart, thickening and coarsening man's soul and drawing it to the nature of the animal soul contained in the food, because the blood does not need to be digested like other foods which are broken down through digestion, and man's soul becomes dependent upon the blood of the animal" (ibid., Lev 17:11).

111. Ibid., Deut 6:20.

112. Nahmanides's moral conviction leads him to criticize biblical heroes even when Scripture fails to do so outright and the verses do not necessitate taking a critical stance. For example, he says about Sarah's oppression of Hagar, "Our Foremother sinned in this oppression, as did Abraham by letting it happen" (ibid., Gen 16:6). On Abraham handing Sarah over to Pharaoh, Nahmanides has this to say: "You should know that our Forefather Abraham unwittingly committed a great sin by bringing his saintly wife into the snare of iniquity due to his fear that they might kill him" (ibid., Gen 12:10). On a similar matter, see ibid., Gen 21:12. Later in his commentary on Genesis, Nahmanides explains Jacob's criticism of Simeon and Levi as follows: "Perhaps Jacob was angry and cursed their rage for the killing of the townspeople who had not wronged him, when it would have been fitting for them to kill Shechem alone" (ibid., Gen 34:13). He repeats this: "I have already explained that Jacob was furious with Simeon and Levi for killing the townspeople because they [Simeon and Levi] perpetrated an injustice, for they [the Shechemites] had not wronged them at all, they had entered the covenant and been circumcised" (ibid., Gen 49:5). In addition, see Nahmanides's criticism of Jephthah's vow and his attitude toward his daughter; ibid., Lev 27:29.

113. Ibid., Gen 6:13. See also ibid., Gen 6:2.

114. For more on the relationship between law and morality in Nahmanides's thought, and particularly as it relates to this broader issue, see Moshe Halbertal, *Interpretive Revolutions in the Making: Values as Interpretive Considerations in Midrashei Halakhah* (Jerusalem: Magnes, 1997), 22–33 (Heb.); Abraham Sagi, *Judaism: Between Religion and Morality* (Tel-Aviv: ha-Kibbutz ha-Me'uhad, c1998), 86–91 (Heb.). See also David Novak, *The Theology of Nahmanides Systematically Presented* (Atlanta: Scholars Press, 1992), 118–122.

115. *DTHT,* 106 (= *KR,* 1:173).

116. For a similar discussion of the question, see R. Joseph Albo, Sefer ha-'Ikkarim, 3.7.

117. *PHT,* Exod 15:25.

118. "The mores of civilized society" is a recurring phrase in Nahmanides's commentary by which he explains his conception of *dinin;* see ibid., Lev 18:4 and Deut 6:20.

119. On the connection between Nahmanides's idea and how communal authority is conceptualized in the writings of Rashba and Ran, see Menachem Lorberbaum, *Politics and the Limits of Law: Secularizing the Political in Medieval Jewish Thought* (Stanford, CA: Stanford University Press, 2001), 106–123.

120. *PHT,* Deut 6:18.

121. Ibid., Lev 19:2.

122. For this position of Maimonides, see Shemonah Perakim, ch. 4.

123. Concerning the sin-offering that the Nazirite must bring, Nahmanides writes: "he should have been a Nazirite forever and remained a Nazirite, consecrated to the Lord his God all of his days [. . .] so he requires atonement for his reentry into the pollution of worldly desires" (*PHT,* Num 6:11). As for sexuality, Nahmanides writes on the prohibition against having relations with a menstruant: "Scripture prohibited the menstruant because of the reason that I mentioned, namely, that sexual intercourse is only permitted for preservation [of the species] from the seed" (ibid., Lev 18:19). Note his extreme formulation: "You should know that the Torah considers sexual intercourse repulsive and disgusting except for the preservation of the species, and that which does not produce a child is prohibited. Similarly, that which is not conducive to preservation [of the species] and will not flourish is prohibited by the Torah" (ibid., Lev 18:6).

124. Ibid., Lev 19:2.

125. *PHT,* Lev 23:24. See also *DRH, KR,* 1:218.

126. The Sages' prohibitions on different kinds of exertion (*shevut*) may be rabbinic only in their legal standing (*de-rabbanan*), but the principle that underlies them, requiring rest and avoidance of exertion even when no biblically prohibited labor is involved, is biblical (*de-oraita*). This raises another important halakhic distinction: the specific norms derived through this principle have only rabbinic status (*de-rabbanan*). For Nahmanides's understanding of the prohibition on labor during the intermediate days of the festival, see *PHT,* Lev 23:7.

127. Ibid., Exod 22:15.

128. Nahmanides takes a similar approach in his unique explanation of the commandment not to reduce the *she'er, kesut,* and *'onah* of one's Jewish maidservant. While Rashi and Ibn Ezra explain the three terms as referring to food, clothing, and sexual relations, respectively, Nahmanides explains all three as tied to sexual relations and a concern that the maidservant will be treated poorly: *she'er* refers to physical contact and closeness during sexual relations, which is associated with *kesut,* the bedding, and *'onah* is the obligation of conjugal relations: "The import of the verse is that if he takes another [wife], he may not reduce this one's intimacy, bedding, and period of love, for such is the practice concerning maidens. The reason is so that the other [the new] wife will not sit with him on a stately bed and thereon become one flesh, while he treats this one like a concubine, lying with her occasionally and on the floor, as one does with a prostitute. Perhaps he will say, 'I purchased her as a maidservant, so she will be a concubine in my house,' so the verse prevents him from

doing so. The Sages similarly said that *she'erah* is physical contact, so that he does not treat her in the manner of the Persians who have relations while clothed. This interpretation is correct, for Scripture consistently refers to intercourse euphemistically and briefly, which is why it alludes to it here by saying 'her *she'er, kesut,* and *'onah,'* the three things involved when a man and woman are together. This comports with the law, and providing the woman's food and clothing is a Rabbinic enactment" (ibid., Exod 21:9).

129. This combination of psychological realism, moral sensitivity, and exegetical precision is also evident in Nahmanides's comment on the command that is commonly translated as "love your fellow like yourself" (Lev 19:18): " 'Love your fellow like yourself' is hyperbole, because a human heart cannot accept loving one's friend as it loves oneself. Moreover, R. Akiva already taught: 'Your life precedes the life of your fellow.' Rather, the commandment of the Torah is to love one's fellow in everything in the same way one loves every good for oneself. Perhaps because it did not say 'love (*et*) your friend like yourself' and [instead] equated them with the word 'for (*le-*) your fellow,' and likewise in reference to the convert 'love for him (*lo*) like yourself' (Lev 19:34), it should be interpreted as follows: he should equate the love of both in his mind. Because sometimes a person loves his fellow in certain matters, and he wishes him wealth but not wisdom and so on, and even if he loves him totally, he may wish that his beloved fellow should merit wealth, property, honor, knowledge, and wisdom, but not that he should be equal to him—his heart's desire is always that he himself should have more of every good than him. The verse commands that one should not harbor this petty jealousy in his heart but love when his fellow has an abundance of good things, just as a person does for themselves and does not love halfheartedly" (ibid., Lev 19:17).

130. Ibid., Deut 23:10.

131. In some of Nahmanides's kabbalistic reasons for the commandments, he does not present the theurgic effect as emerging from the intention accompanying the act—as far as one can tell, the theurgic unification of taking the palm bundle with the citron, for example, is effected regardless of whether the taker understands their symbolism. Intention is crucial, however, in sacrifices and prayer. The sacrifice must be directed toward the Great Name, Tif'eret, and this intention is not represented or reflected by any of the external components of the sacrificial act.

132. See above, note 84.

133. *PHT,* Deut 22:6.

134. Ibid., Lev 1:9.

CHAPTER 8. ESOTERICISM AND TRADITION

1. This chapter on Nahmanides's conception of esotericism follows my discussion in Moshe Halbertal, *Concealment and Revelation: Esotericism in Jewish Thought and Its Philosophical Implications* (Princeton: Princeton University Press, 2007), 83–92.

2. Gershom Scholem, "A New Document Concerning the Early History of Kabbalah," in Scholem, *Studies in Kabbalah (I),* ed. Yosef Ben-Shlomo and Moshe Idel (Tel-Aviv: 'Am 'Oved, 1998), 9 (Heb.).

3. Translation, with changes, from Gershom Scholem, *Origins of the Kabbalah,* ed. R. J. Zwi Werblowsky and trans. Allan Arkush (Philadelphia: Jewish Publication Society; Princeton: Princeton University Press, 1987), 394–395. The Hebrew appears in Scholem, "New Document," 9–10.
4. Moshe Idel, in fact, reads the letter as R. Isaac's attempted self-defense against Nahmanides's criticism. Scholem reverses the relationship: it is R. Isaac's instructions that lead to Nahmanides's strict esotericism. See Idel, "Nahmanides: Kabbalah, Halakhah, and Spiritual Leadership," *Tarbiz* 64 (1995): 535–547 (Heb.).
5. See ibid.
6. See Scholem, "New Document," 11.
7. Cited in ch. 5, secs. II–III.
8. For a broad description of Azriel's and Bar Sheshet's conception of kabbalistic knowledge, see Halbertal, *Concealment and Revelation*, chs. 9–10. Of the Geronese kabbalists, R. Ezra did not give a substantial reason for disclosure. In the introduction to his commentary on Song of Songs, he justifies writing down the Torah's secrets in terms reminiscent of Maimonides's description of the crisis concerning the esoteric tradition. See *KR*, 2:479. One can also discern from his words that the philosophical exegesis of Song of Songs expedited the composition of his kabbalistic commentary on it; see *KR*, 2:480.
9. Idel, "Nahmanides," 550–559.
10. *PHT,* introduction (ed. Chavel, 1:7–8). Yosef Ofer and Yehonatan Jacobs pointed to the fact that this passage was among the additions that Nahmanides added to his commentary in his later revisions of the commentary when he was in the land of Israel; see *Nahmanides' Additions to the Commentary on the Torah That Were Written in the Land of Israel* (Jerusalem: Herzog, 2013), 93–96 (Heb.). The fact that this passage was added later by Nahmanides to his commentary was among the reasons that led Oded Israeli to introduce the claim that Nahmanides changed his views concerning esotericism and he became more conservative in his later years of life. See Oded Israeli, "Early and Late in the Transmission of the Secrets in Nahmanides' Commentary on the Torah," *Zion* 79 (2014): 477–506 (Heb.).
11. *PHT,* introduction (ed. Chavel, 1:3).
12. Ibid. Nahmanides saw the appropriate response to Job's complaint in the words of Elihu, which allude to the secret of impregnation. In relating to the inner stratum of the work, Nahmanides writes: "In truth, in this matter is one of the great secrets of the Torah that cannot be apprehended by contemplation; the one who is privy to them learns from a teacher all the way back to our master Moses from the mouth of the Almighty, and it is mentioned in the words of Elihu" (*PSI, KR,* 1:23; see also 1:115). This raises the question of how a kabbalistic secret transmitted from master to disciple for generations ended up in the mouth of Elihu, a figure who proves difficult to connect to the known chain of kabbalistic tradition. This question bothered Nahmanides too, and in his Discourse on Ecclesiastes he included Elihu in the chain of transmission: "the truth is that what Elihu said contains ideas received from men of the Torah; therefore, I say that 'from the family of Ram' (Job 32:2) is Abraham" (*DDK, KR,* 1:199). See also *PSI, KR,* 1:28. According to Nahmanides, kabbalah is an

internal Jewish tradition: "This is true, because the Torah contains the secrets of the Account of Creation mentioned by Onkelos, and the secret of the Account of the Chariot, and many other secrets said one-on-one, which are only transmitted to the pious of Israel" (*DTHT,* 63 [= *KR,* 1:155]).

13. *PHT,* introduction (ed. Chavel, 6–7).

14. Ibid. King Solomon poses an interesting case for Nahmanides, because elsewhere in the introduction he writes that Solomon acquired his wisdom from interpreting the Torah: "everything can be learned from the Torah. King Solomon, to whom God gave wisdom and understanding, acquired it all from the Torah, and he learned from it until he knew the secret of the entire natural world" (ibid. [ed. Chavel, 1:5]. By comparison, in discourse Torat Ha-Shem Temimah, Nahmanides writes, "and Solomon learned it from the tradition of the Torah" (*DTHT,* 79 [= *KR,* 1:162]).

15. Nahmanides's attitude toward the role of reason in evaluating kabbalistic interpretations can be seen in his lengthy citation from R. Ezra of Gerona's commentary on Song of Songs, in which R. Ezra interpreted a passage from the Book of Job as referring to secrets of the Torah. Nahmanides responds to that interpretation as follows: "This is their [the kabbalists'] approach to these verses. The ideas themselves deserve much praise, but we do not know if the context can support this interpretation. If it is a tradition, we will accept it" (*PSI, KR,* 1:90). Nahmanides doubts that the interpretation will withstand a reasoned analysis, but he is prepared to put aside his reasoning at the possibility that it is a tradition, in which case "we will accept it."

16. See at length Moshe Idel, "We Have No Kabbalistic Tradition on This," in *Rabbi Moses Nahmanides and His Literary Virtuosity,* ed. Isadore Twersky (Cambridge, MA: Harvard University Press, 1983), 51–73.

17. Elliot R. Wolfson, "By Way of Truth: Aspects of Nahmanides' Kabbalistic Hermeneutic," *AJS Review* 14 (Autumn, 1989): 103–178; and see also Haviva Pedaya, *Nahmanides: Cyclical Time and Holy Text* (Tel-Aviv: 'Am 'Oved, 2003), 191–193 (Heb.). For a challenge to the view that Nahmanides saw in Kabbalah a closed knowledge, see Yair Lorberbaum, "Is It the Case that Nahmanides' Kabbalah Is a 'Closed Knowledge'?" *Zion* 82 (2017): 309–354 (Heb.).

18. *DDK, KR,* 1:190.

19. See, for example, R. Shem Tov Ibn Gaon, *Keter Shem Tov,* 106v[d]–109r[a].

20. See ibid., 94r[b], and R. Meir b. Solomon Abusahulah, *Be'ur le-Feirush ha-Ramban 'al ha-Torah,* ed. Jacob Shapira (Warsaw, 1875), 34b. See, too, R. Isaac of Acre, *Sefer Me'irat 'Einayim by R. Isaac of Acre,* ed. Amos Goldreich (Jerusalem: Hebrew University, 1981), 246 (Heb.).

21. *PHT,* Gen 1:1.

22. *Peirushei ha-Torah le-Rabbeinu Avraham Ibn 'Ezra,* ed. Asher Weiser (Jerusalem: Mossad Harav Kook, 1976), 7.

23. *PHT,* Gen 1:1.

24. Ibid.

25. Ibid.

26. In another place, Nahmanides reveals secrets of the Torah as a polemic against Ibn Ezra's own esoteric doctrines. One midrash says that the verse which says "the Lord

blessed Abraham *ba-kol*" (Gen 24:1) means that Abraham had a daughter "whose name is *ba-kol*," which Nahmanides understands kabbalistically. Nahmanides writes at the end of a relatively long kabbalistic passage: "If the one who exalted himself on account of his secrets were to have known this, he would have been struck speechless and stopped being impertinent towards the words of our Rabbis; therefore, I have written this to close the mouths of those who speak insolently about the righteous" (ibid., Gen 24:1).

27. *THA, KR,* 2:279.
28. Ibid., 2:281.
29. *PHT,* Gen 1:1.
30. Ibid., Gen 2:3.
31. Ibid., Lev 25:2.
32. See further examples in ibid., Gen 1:14, 2:3, 7:6, 11:2, 17:17, 24:1; Exod 20:3, 22:19.
33. Ibid., Gen 24:1.
34. *THA, KR,* 2:296. On the exegetical and kabbalistic perspective reflected in this position, see Wolfson, "By Way of Truth," 103–178.
35. *THA, KR,* 2:297.
36. A conspicuous exception to Nahmanides's esotericism can be found in Sefer ha-Ge'ulah; see ch. 6, sec. VI.

CONCLUSION

1. See Gershom Scholem, *Origins of the Kabbalah,* ed. R. J. Zwi Werblowsky and trans. Allan Arkush (Philadelphia: Jewish Publication Society; Princeton: Princeton University Press, 1987), 403–410.
2. The most exhaustively detailed account of the polemic and its consequences can be found in Azriel Shohat, "Concerning the First Controversy on the Writings of Maimonides," *Zion* 36 (1971): 27–60 (Heb.). For a bibliography of earlier attempts to reconstruct and interpret the polemic, see ibid., 27nn2–3.
3. See the letters in *KR,* 1:353–364.
4. See Bernard Septimus, "Communal Struggle in Barcelona during the Maimonidean Controversy," *Tarbiz* 42 (1973): 392–393 (Heb.).
5. Ibid.
6. *KR,* 1:363.
7. Ibid.
8. See Scholem, *Origins,* 410n106.
9. Joseph Shatzmiller, "Towards a Picture of the First Maimonidean Controversy," *Zion* 34 (1969): 142 (Heb.).
10. See Shohat, "Concerning the First Controversy," 42.
11. *KR,* 1:332.
12. Ibid.
13. Ibid.
14. Various scholars have tried to figure out where to situate Nahmanides culturally with respect to Andalusia and Ashkenaz. Bernard Septimus has stressed Nahmanides's affinity to Andalusia; see, at length, his "Open Rebuke and Concealed Love: Nahmanides

and the Andalusian Tradition," in *Rabbi Moses Nahmanides and His Literary Virtuosity*, ed. Isadore Twersky (Cambridge, MA: Harvard University Press, 1983), 11–34. For an extensive bibliography of those who have considered Nahmanides to be a pure antirationalist, see ibid., 14n12, and David Berger, "How Did Nahmanides Propose to Resolve the Maimonidean Controversy?," in *Me'ah She'arim: Studies in Medieval Jewish Spiritual Life in Memory of Isadore Twersky*, ed. Ezra Fleischer et al. (Jerusalem: Magnes, 2001), 137n3 (Heb.). Other viewpoints emphasize the influence of the Andalusian philosophical tradition on Nahmanides; see Berger, ibid., 137n4. One important aspect of this debate concerns Nahmanides's attitude toward Aggadah. He famously proclaimed during the disputation in Barcelona that Talmudic Aggadah is not binding. Like our letter here, context raises the possibility that this was not his true opinion and that ulterior motives were at play. Scholars debated this extensively, some attributing it to the circumstances of the disputation and others to the Geonic-Andalusian tradition that did not consider Aggadah canonical. For a discussion of the issue, see Shalem Yahalom, "The Barcelona Disputation and the Status of Aggadah in Nahmanides' Teachings," *Zion* 69 (2004): 25–43 (Heb.), and see the extensive bibliography on the various positions in notes 5–9.

15. For an insightful discussion of Nahmanides's role in the Maimonidean controversy as a key to understanding his larger approach and to his leadership position, see Nina Caputo, *Nahmanides in Medieval Catalonia: History, Community, and Messianism* (Notre Dame, IN: University of Notre Dame Press, 2007), 19–51.

16. *KR*, 1:341.

17. Ibid., 1:343.

18. Ibid.

19. Ibid., 1:339.

20. Ibid., 1:340.

21. Mishneh Torah, "Laws of Repentance," 8:5.

22. Ibid., 3:5.

23. Nahmanides defends Maimonides's conception of Hell there, where it does not appear tied to any polemic. Moreover, the discussion there is not apologetic, given that he includes criticisms of Maimonides that are not mentioned in the epistle: "Although the Master [Maimonides] did not sufficiently explain that this annihilation takes place through punishment and suffering, there is proof in his words to judge him favorably. He wrote in one chapter of the aforementioned book: 'All of the wicked whose iniquities are greater [than their merits], they judge them according to their sins and they have a portion in the World to Come, for all Israel has a portion in the World to Come . . .' [. . .] If there is no place of punishment and suffering for the soul, then what is the judgment by which the wicked person is judged according to his wickedness and has a portion in the World to Come in the end?" (*THA, KR*, 2:291–292). In the continuation of the piece, Nahmanides has an additional discussion about Maimonides's treatment of Gehenna in his Commentary on the Mishnah, in the introduction to chapter Helek, which he leaves out of his letter.

24. *PHT,* Lev 16:8.

25. He writes in Torat Ha-Shem Temimah: "From here you see the cruelty and obstinacy of the arch-philosopher, may his name be erased" (*DTHT,* 40 [= *KR,* 1:147]), and in his Discourse on Ecclesiastes: "this heresy spread among the Greeks due to this question. They said that the Creator does not know particulars, and they make repulsive arguments—because intentions reflect a lack in the one having them and so constitute something additional, as is known from the book of the chief rebel, may his and his adherents' names be erased" (*DDK, KR,* 1:194). Since the moderate Maimonides cannot maintain such opinions, he cannot be attacked for them, which is not the case with denying demons' existence.

26. *KR,* 1:345.

27. *PHT,* introductory poem.

28. See above, ch. 2.

29. See Joseph Dan, introduction to *Ketav Tamim* (Jerusalem: Merkaz Dinur, 1984), 15–20 (Heb.).

30. *KR,* 1:345.

31. Ibid., 1:346.

32. In the letter, he upholds the de-anthropomorphist position using the doctrine of the Glory espoused by R. Saadia Gaon and the German Pietists, but in his Commentary on the Torah he rejects the theory entirely. In his theosophy, the Glory is a revelation of Shekhinah, which is part of the essence of the Godhead and not some intermediate entity.

33. Ibid., 1:349. Regarding the agreement Nahmanides strove to achieve, see Berger, "How Did Nahmanides?," 135–146.

34. R. Solomon Ibn Adret (Rashba), Nahmanides's disciple, took a similar approach in the controversy over the study of philosophy that erupted at the beginning of the fourteenth century. Rashba's approach was also linked to the duality of the esoteric medium, as I have tried to show elsewhere. See Moshe Halbertal, *Concealment and Revelation: Esotericism in Jewish Thought and Its Philosophical Implications,* trans. Jackie Feldman (Princeton: Princeton University Press, 2007), 120–134.

35. See ch. 8, sec. I.

36. See above, ch. 6, sec. V.

37. Gershom Scholem, *Major Trends in Jewish Mysticism,* rev. ed. (New York: Schocken Books, 1961), ch. 1.

38. See above, ch. 7, note 3.

39. This depiction of myth is widespread in the theoretical literature; see, for example, Paul Ricouer, *The Symbolism of Evil,* trans. Emerson Buchanan (New York: Harper & Row, 1967), 5. This definition of myth as a productive tool for analyzing the history of Jewish myth has been adopted by a number of scholars, including Moshe Idel and Yehudah Liebes. See Moshe Idel, "Leviathan and Its Consort: From Talmudic to Kabbalistic Myth," in *Myth in Judaism,* ed. Moshe Idel and Ithamar Gruenwald (Jerusalem: Zalman Shazar Center, 2004), 149–150 (Heb.); and Yehudah Liebes, "*De Natura Dei:* On the Development of the Jewish Myth," in *Studies in Jewish Myth and Messianism,* trans. Batya Stein (Albany: State University of New York Press, 1993), 2.

40. For example, in Nahmanides's kabbalah the midrashic story about the diminution of the Moon goes from being a tale of anthropomorphized celestial bodies to an intradivine dynamic involving various divine potencies, in which their hyperdifferentiation led to a change in the divine structure. See above, ch. 3, sec. VII.

41. Kaufmann defines his view of myth in Yehezkel Kaufmann, *Toledot ha-Emunah ha-Yisre'elit mi-Yemei Kedem 'Ad Sof Bayit Sheni* (Tel-Aviv: Mosad Bialik 'al yedei Devir, 1947), 2:221–254.

42. Yehudah Liebes, who considers mythos, in contrast to logos, as a "sacred story," points to the "crystallization of myth" in the writings of some kabbalists, which he attributes to the influence of philosophy, among other things; see Liebes, "*De Natura Dei*," 3–4.

General Index

Aaron, 160, 192, 195, 214, 241, 261, 263
Abimelech, 210
Abraham, 146, 153, 160, 176, 180, 183, 189, 208, 213, 228
R. Abraham b. David (Ra'avad), 6, 7, 10, 101, 102
   and custom, 81, 82, 87, 88–89, 355n75
   esoteric tradition, 289, 291, 296
   and the Geonim, 68
   and the goal of Talmud study, 11
   and Nahmanides, 71, 73–74, 79, 320
R. Abraham b. Hiyya, 138, 202, 205
R. Abraham b. Isaac Av Beit Din (Ravi Abad), 79, 289
R. Abraham Ibn Daud. See *Sefer ha-Kabbalah*
R. Abraham Ibn Ezra, 6, 312, 316
   commentaries on the Torah, 5, 138, 173–174, 176, 228, 246, 261, 304
   esotericism, 286, 287, 288, 297–298, 303, 324
   idea of God, 5
   and Jewish eschatological history, 230, 231–232, 269, 382n8

   reasons for the commandments, 239, 253
   theory of the miraculous and divine names, 147, 148, 159–161, 164
Adam, 107, 113, 114, 115–117, 126, 128–132, 157–159, 164–167, 195, 200, 201, 252, 297
   du partzufin, 133, 191
   and free will, 109–112, 134, 137
   and Messiah son of David, 237–238
   and the Noahide laws, 273
   and Shekhinah, 220–222, 247–248
Agrippa, 211 212, 218–219
R. Akiva, 53–54, 85
Amalek, 229–230, 241
'Amram, 253
Andalusia. *See* Sepharad
anthropomorphism, 5, 177, 308. *See also* Midrash: theology
Rav Ashi, 75, 85, 94–95, 96
Ashkenaz: Franco-German halakhists, 6, 7, 71
   and controversy, 59, 60
   and custom, 75, 88, 90–92, 94, 95, 96, 98

the World to Come and Sabbath, 237
See also *Sha'ar ha-Gemul*
Nahmanides's halakhic philosophy and
    analysis, 1, 6, 7, 9–12, 46, 55, 61, 68–
    69, 320
    antiformalism and morality/ethics,
        272–282
    the constitutive approach, 31–33, 46, 55,
        61–62, 65
    and the Decalogue, 182, 184, 186,
        376n47, 396n76
    geocultural horizons and political
        circumstances, 6, 7–8, 101–102
    and Geonim and Andalusian halakhah,
        77
    and kabbalah and esotericism, 8, 48–49,
        65–66, 98, 99–101, 104, 286–288
    and mourning, 104–105, 106
    and ritual, 242, 245–249
    and *Sefer ha-Mitzvot*, 11–12, 29, 65, 69–
        72, 73, 81
    and *Sefer ha-Mitzvot*, Principle I, 18,
        25–29
    and *Sefer ha-Mitzvot*, Principle II, 33,
        35–37, 48, 49
    and *Sefer ha-Mitzvot*, Principles III-
        XIV, 52–55
    and Talmud: Babylonian and Jerusalem,
        76–77
    Talmudic novellae, 1, 3, 6, 7, 9, 11, 68,
        71, 79, 100, 102, 326
    Talmudic novellae and custom, 90, 92,
        95, 97
    Talmudic novellae and kabbalistic
        tradition, 104, 187, 192, 291
    and theory of halakhah, 11–12, 25
    See also halakhah's fundamental
        concepts; Maimonidean controversy;
        Moses; Nahmanides and
        Maimonides; Nahmanides's reasons
        for the commandments; Talisman
Nahmanides's kabbalah: the sefirot, 49,
    119, 125, 156, 168, 189, 236, 241–242,
    295, 301–302, 318

Binah, 124, 128, 132, 139, 140, 142, 158,
    172, 187, 198, 203, 204, 267, 300
chain/emanation of Sefirot and return
    to their source, 137, 139–140, 142, 204
and the days of creation, 203
differentiation of, 131, 203, 266
dynamic structure/potencies of God,
    169, 266
equilibrium and disruption of
    configuration, 130–134, 143, 169, 248
Gevurah/the Primordial Snake, 132–133,
    134, 147
hierarchy: first three Sefirot, 109, 128,
    139
hierarchy: seven lower Sefirot, 127, 128,
    139, 187, 203–204, 267, 318
Hokhma, 139, 140, 141, 142, 172, 174,
    175, 187, 298
and the human body, 127, 242, 267–
    271, 318
Keter, 139, 141–142, 172
and Original/paradigmatic Sin, 128,
    130–134, 167, 172, 222, 247, 248, 254–
    255, 260–263, 265, 266, 283–284
and the Patriarchs, 228
prelapsarian state of Sefirot, 128–129
Shekhinah, 114–118, 124, 127, 135, 248,
    263, 268, 271, 295, 298, 301, 302, 325
Shekhinah: estranged/exiled from the
    sefirotic configuration, 136, 167, 168,
    171–172, 200, 222, 242, 247, 252, 261,
    262, 266
Shekhinah: Glorious Name/Elohim/
    Shaddai, 62–65, 112–113, 155, 161,
    180–181
Shekhinah as the Back/Beginning/the
    Countenance, 173–175, 191–192
Shekhinah as the congregation of Israel,
    171, 174, 300
Shekhinah as Covenant/Faith, 227–228,
    234, 241
Shekhinah and the land of Israel and
    Zion, 162–164, 166, 167–168, 250–
    254, 295

Index of Sources

Page numbers are in bold.